Learn T-SQL Querying

A guide to developing efficient and elegant T-SQL code

Pedro Lopes
Pam Lahoud

BIRMINGHAM - MUMBAI

Learn T-SQL Querying

Commissioning Editor: Sunith Shetty
Acquisition Editor: Yogesh Deokar
Content Development Editor: Nathanya Dias
Technical Editor: Vibhuti Gawde
Copy Editor: Safis Editing
Project Coordinator: Kirti Pisat
Proofreader: Safis Editing
Indexer: Priyanka Dhadke
Graphics: Jisha Chirayil
Production Coordinator: Arvindkumar Gupta

First published: May 2019

Production reference: 1020519

Published by Packt Publishing Ltd.
Livery Place
35 Livery Street
Birmingham
B3 2PB, UK.

ISBN 978-1-78934-881-1

www.packtpub.com

Foreword

We live in a world of ever-increasing amounts of data, and data management systems have become ever-more critical pieces of our daily lives. From banks to e-commerce websites, almost every one of these interactions stores data in a database under the hood. For software or data practitioners, it is almost essential to know how to use databases effectively to deliver compelling solutions in each of these interactions that customers see in their daily lives.

Unfortunately, databases can be daunting to learn for the uninitiated. While the core concepts of SQL are straightforward once you know the rules of the system, getting over that initial hurdle can be challenging if you are not comfortable with set theory from math classes. Often, developers are thrust into database programming when writing applications, and the programming environments can differ greatly. Most programming environments (Java, C#, C++, Python, and so on) use procedural or imperative models to write out methods and functions to control a program, while SQL is much more declarative and requires understanding a bit about the data schema to be able to write effective queries. These differences in approach often lead to coding patterns against a database that can perform poorly, causing frustration until a different approach is tried that leverages the power of the relational model.

In the years I've spent working with customers on architectural reviews and designing solutions to work at the highest scales on SQL Server and SQL Azure, it is critical to know how to use the right approaches to get results efficiently from the database layer. This requires an understanding of the system through the logical layer of designing tables and writing SQL queries to the indexes and other physical database aspects that ultimately govern the performance limits of your application. Knowing how to balance CPU, memory, I/O, and network throughput give you the power to understand algorithmically which kinds of solutions can scale to the limits of the hardware. When you add the broader industry transition from on-premises data centers to public cloud infrastructure, where you move from a buy to a rent model, getting optimal performance becomes a monthly opportunity to tune your application to save money as your business grows instead of just buying a giant machine and hoping the application still performs on it as your business grows year-on-year.

Pam and Pedro have years of experience of working with customers, and specifically working on the problems that get escalated to Microsoft from customer support to the product team. This experience is both challenging and extremely fun—you get paid to learn by drinking from a firehose of information all day, every day. This experience informs insights and wisdom about how customers commonly get stuck using SQL Server/SQL Azure and how to learn from those lessons. Their team has also built tooling to automate many of the common pain points they see in customer upgrades, so knowing how to use those saves time and headaches compared to doing it by yourself. Many of the tips, insights, and best-practice patterns also come from the hard work of making the most demanding customers succeed every day. This book is a great way for someone to get a jump start on writing great data-driven applications and solutions based on SQL.

Conor Cunningham

Partner Architect – SQL Server and Azure SQL – Microsoft

Contributors

About the authors

Pedro Lopes is a Program Manager in the Database Systems group, based in Redmond, WA, USA. He has over 19 years of industry experience and has been with Microsoft for 9 years. He is currently responsible for program management of Database Engine features for in-market and vNext versions of SQL Server, with a special focus on the Relational Engine. He has extensive experience with query performance troubleshooting and is a regular speaker at numerous conferences such as SQLBits, PASS Summit, SQLIntersection, Microsoft Ignite, and Microsoft Build. He blogs about SQL on the SQL Server Team blog. He has authored several tools in the Tiger toolbox on GitHub: AdaptiveIndexDefrag maintenance solution, BPCheck, and usp_WhatsUp.

> *I dedicate this book to my life partner Sandra for her support through working evenings and weekends; to Bob Ward and Guillaume Kieffer that inspired me to look deeper into SQL Server and awoke the performance troubleshooter in me almost 20 years ago, whom I have the privilege of calling friends today; and to all new and experienced SQL Server users that ever had to write or fix T-SQL queries and asked: why is SQL Server doing this?*

Pam Lahoud is a Program Manager in the Database Systems group, based in Redmond, WA, USA. She has been with Microsoft for 13 years and is currently responsible for program management of Database Engine features for in-market and vNext versions of SQL Server, with a special focus on the Storage Engine area. She is passionate about SQL Server performance and has focused on performance tuning and optimization, particularly from the developer's perspective, throughout her career. She is a SQL Server 2008 Microsoft Certified Master (MCM) with over 20 years of experience working with SQL Server.

> *To Andrew and Linus, for spending countless nights and weekends without me. To my computer illiterate friends Jodie, Liza, and Erin, who I know will proudly display this book on their shelves in spite of having no idea what any of this means. And to my mom, who bought me my first computer when I was 8 years old, and said "Sure!" when I decided adding computer science as a second major in my junior year of college seemed like a good idea.*

About the reviewers

Joel Redman is a Senior Software Engineer with over 20 years of experience in embedded, scientific, and database software programming. He is currently employed at Microsoft for the last 7 years, working on SQL Server, primarily in support of the Query Optimizer and other query processing engine features.

Bob Ward is a Principal Architect for the Microsoft Azure Data SQL Server team, which owns the development for all SQL Server versions. Bob has worked for Microsoft for 25+ years on every version of SQL Server shipped from OS/2 1.1 to SQL Server 2019 including Azure. Bob is a well-known speaker on SQL Server, often presenting talks on new releases, internals, and performance at events such as SQL PASS Summit, SQLBits, SQLIntersection, and Microsoft Inspire and Microsoft Ignite. Bob is the author of the new book *Pro SQL Server on Linux* available from Apress Media.

Tim Chapman is a Microsoft Certified Master (MCM) and Principal Premier Field Engineer at Microsoft, where he has worked for over 8 years. Tim's area of technical expertise focuses on performance tuning, high availability, T-SQL and PowerShell development, and customer training. Before coming to Microsoft, Tim was a contributor to the SQL MVP community for three years and has had the privilege of speaking at many SQL Server events such as SQLIntersection, the PASS Summit, SQL Connections, SQL Saturdays, SQL Rally, SQL Nexus, and SQL Server Days Belgium. Tim has over 17 years of database architecture, programming, and administration experience. Tim has contributed to the *SQL Server MVP Deep Dives 2* book as well as the *SQL Server 2012 Bible.*

Argenis Fernandez is a Principal Program Manager with the Microsoft SQL Server team based in Redmond, WA. Previously, Argenis worked as a Principal Architect for Pure Storage, and as a Lead Database Operations Engineer at SurveyMonkey. He is a founding member of the Security Virtual Chapter for PASS. Argenis is a SQL community enthusiast and speaks frequently at major SQL Server and Microsoft Data Platform conferences, including the PASS Summit, SQLBits, and Microsoft Ignite. He is also a Microsoft Certified Master (MCM) on SQL Server, former VMware vExpert, and former Microsoft Data Platform MVP.

Packt is searching for authors like you

If you're interested in becoming an author for Packt, please visit `authors.packtpub.com` and apply today. We have worked with thousands of developers and tech professionals, just like you, to help them share their insight with the global tech community. You can make a general application, apply for a specific hot topic that we are recruiting an author for, or submit your own idea.

Table of Contents

Section 2: Dos and Donts of T-SQL

Section 3: Assemble Your Query Troubleshooting Toolbox

Preface

Transact-SQL (T-SQL) is Microsoft's proprietary extension to the SQL language, which is used with Microsoft SQL Server and Azure SQL Database. This book is a useful guide to learning the art of writing efficient T-SQL code in modern SQL Server versions, as well as Azure SQL Database.

This book will get you started with query processing fundamentals to help you write powerful, performant T-SQL queries. You will then focus on query execution plans and understand how to leverage them for troubleshooting. In the later chapters, you will learn how to identify various T-SQL patterns and anti-patterns. This will help you analyze execution plans to gain insights into current performance, as well as to determine whether or not a query is scalable. You will also learn to build diagnostic queries using Dynamic Management Views (DMVs) and Dynamic Management Functions (DMFs) to address various challenges in T-SQL execution. Next, you will study how to leverage the built-in tools of SQL Server to shorten the time taken to address query performance and scalability issues. In the concluding chapters, the book will guide you through implementing various features such as Extended Events, Query Store, and Query Tuning Assistant using hands-on examples.

By the end of this book, you will have the skills to determine query performance bottlenecks, avoid pitfalls, and discover anti-patterns in use in your existing T-SQL code.

Who this book is for

This book is for database administrators, database developers, data analysts, data scientists, and T-SQL practitioners who want to get started with writing T-SQL code and troubleshooting query performance issues through the help of practical examples.

What this book covers

`Chapter 1`, *Anatomy of a Query*, shows you how to write solid, performant T-SQL. Users will become familiar with how SQL Server runs T-SQL syntax to deliver the intended result sets in a scalable fashion. In this chapter, we'll cover the basic building blocks that make up a T-SQL statement, as well as how SQL Server interprets those blocks to begin the process of executing our queries. The concepts introduced in this chapter will be used throughout the remaining sections of the book to explain most patterns and anti-patterns, as well as mitigation strategies.

`Chapter 2`, *Understanding Query Processing*, introduces the fact that the way a T-SQL query is written and submitted to the server influences how it is interpreted and executed by SQL Server. Even before a single T-SQL query is written, the choice of development style (for example, using stored procedures versus ad hoc statements) can have a direct impact on the performance of the application.

`Chapter 3`, *Mechanics of the Query Optimizer*, explores the internals of SQL Server query optimization and defines many important concepts that any database professional who writes T-SQL queries will keep coming back to, especially when troubleshooting query performance issues. The Cardinality Estimator (CE) is a fundamental part of SQL Server's Query Optimizer; knowing how it uses statistics, and the importance of keeping updated and relevant statistics for the overall query optimization process, empowers database professionals to write good queries—queries that both drive and leverage good database schema designs.

`Chapter 4`, *Exploring Query Execution Plans*, will leave the reader with a good understanding of the various elements that make up a query execution plan in SQL Server. Nearly everything we need to understand and troubleshoot the performance of our T-SQL queries can be found somewhere in the plan, either in the visible part of the plan, or in the properties windows, which we can access by right-clicking the operators.

`Chapter 5`, *Writing Elegant T-SQL Queries*, will leave the reader with a better understanding of some of the aspects that database professionals need to keep in mind to write good queries, and how to identify some of the inefficiencies that may surface if the predicates expressed in queries are not supported by a suitable index design. These are all but a part of the intricacies of writing good, scalable T-SQL code.

`Chapter 6`, *Easily-Identified T-SQL Anti-Patterns*, covers a few T-SQL anti-patterns, such as SELECT * syntax, OR logic, and functions in our predicates, that are relatively easy to find simply by looking at our T-SQL code and how it is written. The scenarios covered in this chapter are some of the most common examples of patterns that prevent our T-SQL queries from scaling well and maintaining the expected level of performance throughout the lifetime of applications. All are easy to detect, and most have simple workarounds. Therefore, when writing queries, try to avoid these anti-patterns by leveraging some of the techniques we outline here.

`Chapter 7`, *Discovering T-SQL Anti-Patterns in Depth*, covers some performance pitfalls that are not always obvious when writing T-SQL queries. Using the knowledge and tools covered in earlier chapters, together with the anti-patterns discussed in this chapter, we should now be able to dig deeper into our query execution plans and uncover issues that have the potential to impact performance and scalability before they reach production.

`Chapter 8`, *Building Diagnostic Queries Using DMVs and DMFs*, covers examples of how to use Dynamic Management Views (DMVs) and Dynamic Management Functions (DMFs), which can be a powerful troubleshooting tool when it comes to diagnosing query performance issues. They are lightweight, easy to use, and provide a breadth of information that is useful for zeroing in on performance issues.

`Chapter 9`, *Building XEvent Profiler Traces*, introduces the Extended Events (XEvents) engine in SQL Server and how you can leverage XEvent traces to gather detailed data about query execution and performance. While DMVs are great for point in time and cumulative analysis, there are some issues that can only be diagnosed by catching queries and related data in real time. This is where tracing with XEvents is useful. We'll also discuss the various free tools from Microsoft that can be used to quickly and easily configure, capture, and analyze XEvent traces. Together with DMVs, we now have several tools in our toolbelt that can be used to diagnose and troubleshoot the various issues covered in the book.

`Chapter 10`, *Comparative Analysis of Query Plans*, covers the rich UI features available in SQL Server Management Studio (SSMS) to make query plan analysis easier. First, Query Plan Comparison that allows us to quickly and easily compare query plans to determine what differences may help explain what changed between two plans. Next, Query Plan Analyzer which allows us to zero in on problem areas in the query plan such as inaccurate cardinality estimates with the click of a button.

`Chapter 11`, *Tracking Performance History with Query Store*, covers the important topic of storing query performance statistics in the flight recorder that is the Query Store, which allows us to access query plans and their runtime statistics, along with how they change over time. We can now more easily find resolutions for performance problems. We can easily identify plans that must be tuned, or for quick mitigation, just return to a good known plan that has been stored in Query Store. We'll cover how to use either system views or SSMS to uncover the highest resource-consuming queries executing in our databases and help us quickly find and fix query performance issues that are related to plan changes, which greatly simplifies query performance troubleshooting.

`Chapter 12`, *Troubleshooting Live Queries*, covers how Lightweight Profiling together with tools such as Live Query Statistics and Activity Monitor are invaluable tools for troubleshooting and solving query performance issues, namely those queries that take hours to complete, or never do.

`Chapter 13`, *Managing Optimizer Changes with the Query Tuning Assistant*, introduces a feature: the Query Tuning Assistant (QTA). QTA aims to address some of the most common causes of cardinality estimation related performance regressions that may affect our T-SQL queries after an upgrade from an older version of SQL Server to a newer version, namely SQL Server 2016 and above.

To get the most out of this book

Previous knowledge of T-SQL querying is not required to get started on this book.

Download the example code files

You can download the example code files for this book from your account at `www.packt.com`. If you purchased this book elsewhere, you can visit `www.packt.com/support` and register to have the files emailed directly to you.

You can download the code files by following these steps:

1. Log in or register at `www.packt.com`.
2. Select the **SUPPORT** tab.
3. Click on **Code Downloads & Errata**.
4. Enter the name of the book in the **Search** box and follow the onscreen instructions.

Once the file is downloaded, please make sure that you unzip or extract the folder using the latest version of:

- WinRAR/7-Zip for Windows
- Zipeg/iZip/UnRarX for Mac
- 7-Zip/PeaZip for Linux

The code bundle for the book is also hosted on GitHub at `https://github.com/PacktPublishing/Learn-T-SQL-Querying`. In case there's an update to the code, it will be updated on the existing GitHub repository.

The examples used throughout the book are designed for use on SQL Server 2017 and SQL Server 2019, but they should work on any version of SQL Server, 2012 or later. The Developer Edition of SQL Server is free for development environments and can be used to run all the code samples.

The sample databases AdventureWorks2016_EXT (referred to as AdventureWorks) and AdventureWorksDW2016_EXT (referred to as AdventureWorksDW) were both used for various scripts, and can be found on GitHub at `https://github.com/Microsoft/sql-server-samples/releases/tag/adventureworks`.

Some tools used in the book are not available with SQL Server. RML Utilities can be found at `https://www.microsoft.com/download/details.aspx?id=4511`, and Pssdiag/Sqldiag Manager can be found on GitHub at `https://github.com/Microsoft/DiagManager`.

We also have other code bundles from our rich catalog of books and videos available at `https://github.com/PacktPublishing/`. Check them out!

Download the color images

We also provide a PDF file that has color images of the screenshots/diagrams used in this book. You can download it here: `http://www.packtpub.com/sites/default/files/downloads/9781789348811_ColorImages.pdf`.

Conventions used

There are a number of text conventions used throughout this book.

`CodeInText`: Indicates code words in text, database table names, folder names, filenames, file extensions, path names, dummy URLs, user input, and Twitter handles. Here is an example: "For example, if our table contains 1,000,000 rows, the calculation is `SQRT(1000 * 1000000) = 31622`."

A block of code is set as follows:

```
SELECT NationalIDNumber, JobTitle, MaritalStatus
INTO HumanResources.Employee2
FROM HumanResources.Employee;
```

When we wish to draw your attention to a particular part of a code block, the relevant lines or items are set in bold:

```
[default]
exten => s,1,Dial(Zap/1|30)
exten => s,2,Voicemail(u100)
exten => s,102,Voicemail(b100)
exten => i,1,Voicemail(s0)
```

Bold: Indicates a new term, an important word, or words that you see onscreen. For example, words in menus or dialog boxes appear in the text like this. Here is an example: "For reference, the **QueryTimeStats** property for this query execution plan is in the following screenshot."

Warnings or important notes appear like this.

Tips and tricks appear like this.

Get in touch

Feedback from our readers is always welcome.

General feedback: If you have questions about any aspect of this book, mention the book title in the subject of your message and email us at `customercare@packtpub.com`.

Errata: Although we have taken every care to ensure the accuracy of our content, mistakes do happen. If you have found a mistake in this book, we would be grateful if you would report this to us. Please visit `www.packt.com/submit-errata`, selecting your book, clicking on the Errata Submission Form link, and entering the details.

Piracy: If you come across any illegal copies of our works in any form on the Internet, we would be grateful if you would provide us with the location address or website name. Please contact us at `copyright@packt.com` with a link to the material.

If you are interested in becoming an author: If there is a topic that you have expertise in and you are interested in either writing or contributing to a book, please visit `authors.packtpub.com`.

Reviews

Please leave a review. Once you have read and used this book, why not leave a review on the site that you purchased it from? Potential readers can then see and use your unbiased opinion to make purchase decisions, we at Packt can understand what you think about our products, and our authors can see your feedback on their book. Thank you!

For more information about Packt, please visit `packt.com`.

1
Section 1: Query Processing Fundamentals

To understand how to write solid, performant T-SQL, users should know how SQL Server runs T-SQL syntax to deliver the intended result sets in a scalable fashion. This section introduces the reader to concepts that are used throughout the remaining sections of this book to explain most patterns and anti-patterns, as well as mitigation strategies.

The following chapters are included in this section:

- `Chapter 1`, *Anatomy of a Query*
- `Chapter 2`, *Understanding Query Processing*
- `Chapter 3`, *Mechanics of the Query Optimizer*

1
Anatomy of a Query

Transact-SQL, or **T-SQL**, as it has come to be commonly known, is the language that is used to communicate with Microsoft SQL Server. Any actions a user wishes to perform in a server, such as retrieving or modifying data in a database, creating objects, changing server configurations, and so on, are all done via a T-SQL command.

In this chapter, we will be introduced to the typical components of a T-SQL statement, including the logical order with which SQL Server processes a statement. This is essential for introducing the reader to why certain query writing patterns work best and to provide a fundamental reference for better understanding the other chapters.

There are four main groups of T-SQL statements that we can have in a **R**elational **D**ata**b**ase **M**anagement **S**ystem (RDBMS) like SQL Server:

- **Data Control Language** statements, also known as **DCL**, are used to handle control access to a database or parts of the database. T-SQL commands such as **GRANT** and **REVOKE** are used to change permissions on objects (known as securables), or to add users to SQL Server.
- **Transactional Control Language** statements, also known as **TCL**, are used to control transactions in SQL Server with T-SQL commands such as `BEGIN TRANSACTION`, `COMMIT TRANSACTION`, or **ROLLBACK**.
- **Data Definition Language** statements, also known as **DDL**, are used to create, change, or delete the database and any objects contained within such as tables or indexes. Examples of DDL include **CREATE**, **ALTER**, `CREATE OR ALTER`, or **DROP** T-SQL commands.
- **Data Manipulation Language** statements, also known as **DML**, can be distilled into 3 logical operations on a database:
    - Retrieving data via the **SELECT** statement.
    - Updating and Inserting data, also known as **UPSERTs**, via the **UPDATE** and **INSERT** statements.

- Deleting data via the **DELETE** statement.
- There is also a **MERGE** statement. This is a conditional structure that combines **UPDATEs**, **INSERTs** and/or **DELETEs** into a single statement, which together with **SELECTs**, make up the fundamental DML operations available in SQL Server.

While all these types of statements must be parsed and validated by the Database Engine before execution, with very few exceptions only DML statements are optimized. This means that the way DML statements are constructed can have an impact on their resulting performance, so care must be taken to write them efficiently. For this reason, we will focus on DML statements throughout the course of this book.

In this chapter we will cover the following topics:

- Building blocks of a T-SQL statement
- Logical statement-processing flow

Building blocks of a T-SQL statement

When writing a T-SQL statement, the following three actions are required:

1. Express the intended operation, such as reading or changing data
2. Provide a target or source list of affected tables
3. Provide a condition that filters the affected records

The intended operation is determined by the presence of the following clauses:

- The **SELECT** clause lists columns or expressions that will be displayed in the result set
- The **DELETE**, **INSERT**, or **UPDATE** clauses state the target table or view for these logical operations

As for the affected tables and filters, they are determined by the following clauses:

- The **FROM** clause lists the source tables, views and/or sub-queries that contain the data to be queried
- The **WHERE** clause states one or more conditions that will serve to filter the result set to the desired rows

The preceding clauses determine which data will be manipulated. The formatting of the results can be further modified by adding any of the following parts:

- The **ORDER BY** clause defines the order in which the rows will be returned
- The **GROUP BY** clause aggregates rows together based on the criteria provided (typically combined with aggregate functions in the **SELECT** clause)
- The **HAVING** clause applies a predicate to the results (different than the **WHERE** clause, which applies a predicate to the source rows)

SELECT

The **SELECT** clause defines the columns and expressions that will be returned in the results and is the only element that is required to form a valid T-SQL data retrieval statement. Elements in the **SELECT** statement can be as simple as a single constant value, or as complex as a full T-SQL sub-query, but generally it is a comma-separated list of columns from tables and views in a database.

The following query will return a single row with a single column:

```
SELECT 1;
```

In the following screenshot we can see the result:

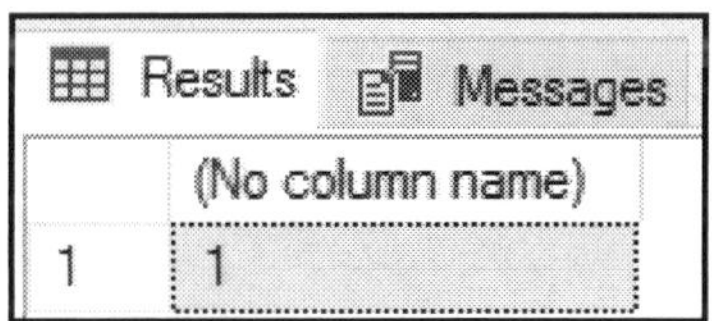

The **SELECT** clause can also be used to format the results by providing column aliases or using expressions to modify the data. Aliases are created with the optional keyword **AS**, followed by the intended column name to be displayed in the result set:

```
SELECT Name AS ProductName, LEFT(ProductNumber, 2) AS ProductCode,
ISNULL(color, 'No Color') AS Color [...]
```

Note that, in the results, any row that has a value for **Color** will display that value, whereas any row that has a null color will display **No Color** instead:

	ProductName	ProductCode	Color
1	Adjustable Race	AR	No Color
2	Bearing Ball	BA	No Color
3	BB Ball Bearing	BE	No Color
4	Headset Ball Bearings	BE	No Color
5	Blade	BL	No Color

DISTINCT

DISTINCT specifies that repeated rows in the result set are collapsed into a single row.

```
SELECT DISTINCT Name AS ProductName, LEFT(ProductNumber, 2) AS ProductCode,
ISNULL(color, 'No Color') AS Color [...]
```

TOP

The **TOP** clause specifies that from the applicable rows, the results set only produces a predetermined number of rows, set in percentage or absolute number.

```
SELECT TOP 25 Name AS ProductName, LEFT(ProductNumber, 2) AS ProductCode,
ISNULL(color, 'No Color') AS Color [...]
```

FROM

The **FROM** clause specifies the tables or views used in the **SELECT**, **DELETE**, and **UPDATE** statements. It is required unless a **SELECT** list contains only constants, variables or arithmetic expressions, or an **UPDATE** clause does not contain references to other tables other than the target (for example, a join is not needed).

It can be a single table, a derived table (a table created from a nested sub-query), a **Table-Valued Function** (**TVF**), or it can be several tables and/or views joined together.

If the desired result set contains data from more than one table or view, joins can be used to link rows from one table to another. There are essentially the following three types of logical joins that are expressed when writing a query:

- Inner joins
- Outer joins (left, right, and full)
- Cross joins

In specific scenarios, SQL Server may infer the intended type of logical join operation. However, it is best to always explicitly state the type of required logical join operation the reader intends to implement.

When specifying multiple tables and/or views in the **FROM** clause, it is helpful to create aliases for these objects, which can be used within the query, such as in the **SELECT** clause. This is particularly useful when different objects have columns with the same names. In this case, we must disambiguate the columns throughout the query, and an alias allows us to do this without having to specify the entire object name. So, as is the case for column aliases, a table, view, or function alias is created with the **AS** keyword.

INNER JOIN

Inner joins compare the rows from two tables based on conditions specified in the query. Typically, this type of join would be used to intersect rows that have the same value in a specific column or set of columns. The only rows that would be returned are the ones that have matching rows in both tables, as represented in black in the following diagram:

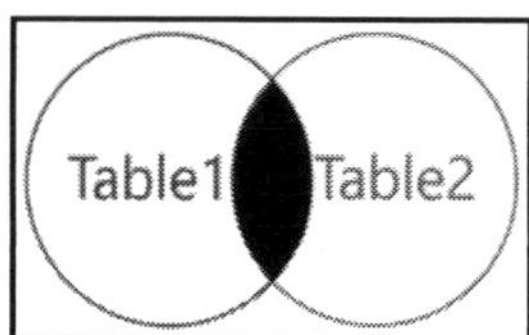

For example, the **AdventureWorks** sample database has a **Product** table that contains the **ProductID** and **Name** columns and a **ProductInventory** table that contains the **ProductID** and **Quantity** columns. To write a query that returns the product name and the quantity together, an inner join can be used to combine rows from the **Product** table with rows from the **ProductInventory** table based on matching values in the **ProductID** column. In this case, only products that have rows in both tables will be returned. The query would look like the following:

```
SELECT Name AS ProductName, Quantity
FROM Production.Product
INNER JOIN Production.ProductInventory ON Product.ProductID =
ProductInventory.ProductID;
```

OUTER JOIN

Outer joins are used to return all the data in one table, plus any matching rows in the other table. In the left outer join, the entire left table is returned along with any matching rows from the right table. If there is no matching row on the right, null values will be returned for these columns:

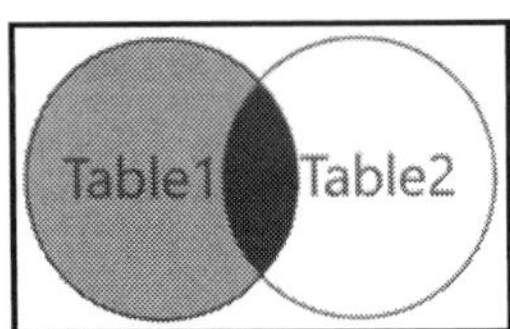

Building on the preceding example, there are some rows in the **Product** table that are not currently in inventory; therefore, there are no rows with these product IDs in the **ProductInventory** table. To return all the products, whether they have matching rows in the **ProductInventory** table or not, a left outer join can be used.

In this case, rows with no inventory will return **NULL** for the **Quantity** column:

```
SELECT Name AS ProductName, Quantity
FROM Production.Product
LEFT OUTER JOIN Production.ProductInventory ON Product.ProductID =
ProductInventory.ProductID;
```

So, following on from what was covered previously in the **SELECT** clause section, **NULL** can be replaced by zeros in the results, if desired, by using an expression:

```
SELECT Name AS ProductName, ISNULL(Quantity, 0) AS Quantity
FROM Production.Product
LEFT OUTER JOIN Production.ProductInventory ON Product.ProductID =
ProductInventory.ProductID;
```

In a right outer join, all the rows from the right table are returned along with any matching rows from the left table (and **NULL** for the left columns if no match exists):

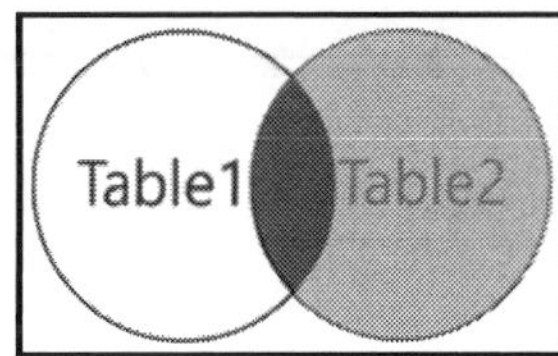

If there are products in the **ProductInventory** table that are not in the **Products** table for some reason, a right outer join would return all the quantities whether they have a corresponding name or not, and a **NULL** value for the **Name** column if no matching row exists in the **Products** table:

```
SELECT Name AS ProductName, Quantity
FROM Production.Product
RIGHT OUTER JOIN Production.ProductInventory ON Product.ProductID =
ProductInventory.ProductID;
```

In this case, it might be good to display the **ProductID** column if the **Name** column is null:

```
SELECT ISNULL(Name, ProductInventory.ProductID) AS ProductName, Quantity
FROM Production.Product
RIGHT OUTER JOIN Production.ProductInventory ON Product.ProductID =
ProductInventory.ProductID;
```

For full outer joins, all rows are returned from both tables; if rows are matched, they are combined into a single row in the results:

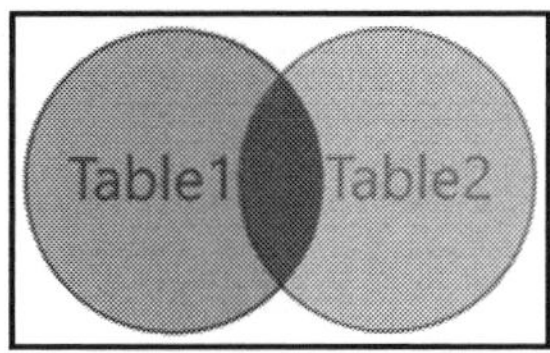

Using a full outer join, all the rows from both the **Product** and the **ProductInventory** tables will be returned. The **Name** column will be **NULL** for rows that appear only in the **ProductInventory** table, and the **Quantity** column will be **NULL** for rows that appear only in the **Product** table:

```
SELECT ISNULL(Name, ProductInventory.ProductID) AS ProductName,
ISNULL(Quantity, 0) AS Quantity
FROM Production.Product
FULL OUTER JOIN Production.ProductInventory ON Product.ProductID =
ProductInventory.ProductID;
```

In all the preceding examples, SQL Server can recognize the intended type of join is outer, even if the **OUTER** clause is not present. For example, writing **LEFT JOIN** instead of **LEFT OUTER JOIN**.

CROSS JOIN

Cross joins are also called **Cartesian products**. In a cross join, every row in the left table is returned, and each of these rows is combined with all the rows from the right table. If the left table has 10 rows and the right table 100 rows, then the cross join produces 1000 rows.

APPLY

APPLY is like a cross join in the type of result set that it produces, but usable only with functions. In a cross join, both inputs (left and right) are tables or views that already exist in the database, with a fixed definition. However, **APPLY** is used in scenarios where a join cannot be used. In **APPLY**, one of the inputs (the right) is not physically materialized in the database because its output is dependent on input parameters, such as in the case of a table-valued function (TVF).

For example, the **AdventureWorks** sample database has a **SalesPerson** table that contains the **BusinessEntityID** and **SalesYTD** columns, and a **ufnGetContactInformation** TVF that returns the **FirstName**, **LastName**, and **JobTitle** columns. The TVF creates a runtime abstraction for columns that exist in multiple underlying tables, like building a table on-the-fly. To write a query that returns the year-to-date (YTD) sales per sales person, together with their name and job title, a cross apply can be used to return all rows from the **SalesPerson** table, and each of those rows is combined with the rows coming from the **ufnGetContactInformation** TVF.

The query would look like the following code block:

```
SELECT SP.SalesYTD, P.FirstName, P.LastName, P.JobTitle
FROM Sales.SalesPerson AS SP
CROSS APPLY dbo.ufnGetContactInformation (SP.BusinessEntityID) AS P;
```

In the following screenshot, the results of the **ufnGetContactInformation** function are displayed alongside the **SalesYTD** column, just as if they came from another table using a simple inner or outer join:

	SalesYTD	FirstName	LastName	JobTitle
1	559697.5639	Stephen	Jiang	North American Sales Manager
2	3763178.1787	Michael	Blythe	Sales Representative
3	4251368.5497	Linda	Mitchell	Sales Representative
4	3189418.3662	Jillian	Carson	Sales Representative
5	1453719.4653	Garrett	Vargas	Sales Representative

However, the following query produces an error (ID 4104) because a join cannot be used directly with a TVF:

```
SELECT SP.SalesYTD, P.FirstName, P.LastName, P.JobTitle
FROM Sales.SalesPerson AS SP
CROSS JOIN dbo.ufnGetContactInformation (SP.BusinessEntityID) AS P;
```

WHERE

The **WHERE** clause specifies the search condition that determines whether a row should be returned in the result set. Rows will be returned only if the entire **WHERE** clause evaluates to **TRUE**. Each condition within the **WHERE** clause is referred to as a **predicate**. There is no limit to the number of predicates that can appear in a **WHERE** clause, and predicates are combined using the **AND**, **OR**, and **NOT** logical operators.

For example, the **AdventureWorks** sample database has a **Product** table that contains the **Name** and **ProductID** columns, a **ProductInventory** table that contains the **Quantity**, **LocationID**, and **ProductID** columns, and a **Location** table that contains the **LocationID** and **Name** columns. A query that returns the current product inventory per location, for the entire **Touring** line of products would look like the following code block:

```
SELECT P.Name AS ProductName, [PI].Quantity, L.Name AS LocationName
FROM Production.Product AS P
INNER JOIN Production.ProductInventory AS [PI] ON P.ProductID =
[PI].ProductID
INNER JOIN Production.Location AS L ON [PI].LocationID = L.LocationID
WHERE P.Name LIKE 'Touring%';
```

The following screenshot shows that all the **ProductName** values in the result set begin with the word **Touring**:

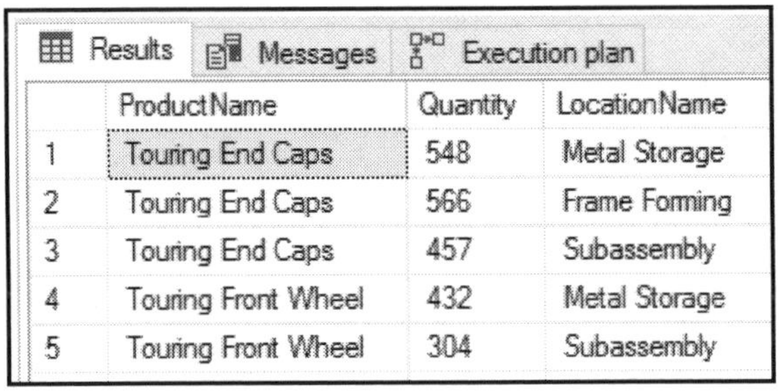

Results | Messages | Execution plan

	ProductName	Quantity	LocationName
1	Touring End Caps	548	Metal Storage
2	Touring End Caps	566	Frame Forming
3	Touring End Caps	457	Subassembly
4	Touring Front Wheel	432	Metal Storage
5	Touring Front Wheel	304	Subassembly

ORDER BY

The **ORDER BY** clause orders the results. The default order is ascending, meaning that the **ASC** keyword can be omitted. To produce the result set in descending order, **DESC** must be set explicitly. Building on the same example from the *WHERE* section, the following code block is used to explicitly present results in descending order of product name and location name:

```
SELECT P.Name AS ProductName, [PI].Quantity, L.Name AS LocationName
FROM Production.Product AS P
INNER JOIN Production.ProductInventory AS [PI] ON P.ProductID =
[PI].ProductID
INNER JOIN Production.Location AS L ON [PI].LocationID = L.LocationID
WHERE P.Name LIKE 'Touring%'
ORDER BY P.Name DESC, L.Name DESC;
```

The following screenshot shows the results in the specified order:

	ProductName	Quantity	LocationName
1	Touring End Caps	457	Subassembly
2	Touring End Caps	548	Metal Storage
3	Touring End Caps	566	Frame Forming
4	Touring Front Wheel	304	Subassembly
5	Touring Front Wheel	432	Metal Storage

GROUP BY

GROUP BY aggregates the results on the required column names or expressions. Building on the same example from the **ORDER BY** section, we want to know the overall product quantity per product name and location, from the following code snippet. The **Quantity** column is using the aggregate function `SUM`. Therefore, the remaining columns need to be contained in the aggregation `GROUP BY` clause:

```
SELECT P.Name AS ProductName, SUM([PI].Quantity) AS Total_Quantity, L.Name
AS LocationName
FROM Production.Product AS P
INNER JOIN Production.ProductInventory AS [PI] ON P.ProductID =
[PI].ProductID
INNER JOIN Production.Location AS L ON [PI].LocationID = L.LocationID
WHERE P.Name LIKE 'Touring%'
GROUP BY P.Name, L.Name
ORDER BY P.Name DESC, L.Name DESC;
```

The following screenshot shows the results with one row per set as defined by the **GROUP BY** clause:

	ProductName	Total_Quantity	LocationName
1	Touring-Panniers, Large	72	Finished Goods Storage
2	Touring-3000 Yellow, 62	91	Finished Goods Storage
3	Touring-3000 Yellow, 62	72	Final Assembly
4	Touring-3000 Yellow, 58	81	Finished Goods Storage
5	Touring-3000 Yellow, 58	116	Final Assembly

Aggregations can be further specified by using the following keywords:

- **ROLLUP**: Specifies the creation of subtotals and totals for the required column names or expressions.
- **CUBE**: Specifies the creation of subtotals and totals for all combinations of columns in the **GROUP BY** clause.
- **GROUPING SETS**: Allows the use of multiple **GROUP BY** clauses, such as using **ROLLUP** and **CUBE** together.

HAVING

HAVING further filters the result based on values in the results, rather than the actual data. A **HAVING** clause only applies to columns that are included in the **GROUP BY** clause or in an aggregate function. Building on the same example used in the *WHERE, ORDER BY,* and *GROUP BY* sections, here we want to additionally know which locations carry an inventory of over 100 items per product. For that, after the **GROUP BY** clause, the query has a **HAVING** clause over the aggregate function, where its result is greater than **100**:

```
SELECT P.Name AS ProductName, SUM([PI].Quantity) AS Total_Quantity, L.Name
AS LocationName
FROM Production.Product AS P
INNER JOIN Production.ProductInventory AS [PI] ON P.ProductID =
[PI].ProductID
INNER JOIN Production.Location AS L ON [PI].LocationID = L.LocationID
WHERE P.Name LIKE 'Touring%'
GROUP BY P.Name, L.Name
HAVING SUM([PI].Quantity) > 100
ORDER BY P.Name DESC, L.Name DESC;
```

The following screenshot shows the results as containing only rows with an aggregate **Total_Quantity** greater than 100:

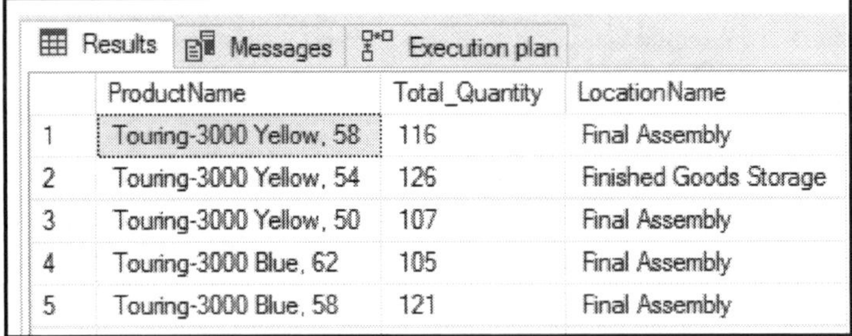

	ProductName	Total_Quantity	LocationName
1	Touring-3000 Yellow, 58	116	Final Assembly
2	Touring-3000 Yellow, 54	126	Finished Goods Storage
3	Touring-3000 Yellow, 50	107	Final Assembly
4	Touring-3000 Blue, 62	105	Final Assembly
5	Touring-3000 Blue, 58	121	Final Assembly

Logical statement processing flow

When writing T-SQL, it is important to be familiar with the order in which the SQL Server Database Engine interprets queries, to later create an execution plan. This helps anticipate possible performance issues from poorly written queries. However, it also helps to understand cases of unintended results. The following steps outline the process that the database engine follows to process a T-SQL statement:

1. Parse the query for correctness; in other words, validate the syntax.
2. Build a structure that represents the logic of the query as expressed by the developer—a **query tree**, also called a **sequence tree.**
3. Process all the source and target objects stated in the **FROM** clause (tables, views, TVFs), together with the intended logical operation (**JOIN**, **APPLY**) to perform on those objects.
4. Apply whatever pre-filters are defined in the **WHERE** clause that can reduce the number of incoming rows from those objects.
5. Apply any aggregation defined in **GROUP BY**, followed by any filters that can only be applied to the aggregations.
6. Keep only the required columns for the output, and account for any limits stated in a **TOP** or **DISTINCT** clause.
7. Order the resulting row set as specified by the **ORDER BY** clause, and make the result set available for the client.

Keep in mind that even though **TOP** is processed before the **ORDER BY** clause, during execution the entire result set is sorted before the **TOP** clause is applied.

It becomes clearer now that properly defining how tables are joined (the logical join type) is important to any scalable T-SQL query, namely by carefully planning on which columns the tables are joined. For example, in an inner join, these join arguments are the first level of data filtering that can be enforced, because only the rows that represent the intersection of two tables are eligible for subsequent operations.

Then, it also makes sense to filter out rows from the result set using a **WHERE** clause, before applying any post-filtering conditions that apply to sub-groupings using a **HAVING** clause. This is because SQL Server evaluates a **WHERE** clause before a **HAVING** clause, and it can limit the row count earlier in the execution phase, translating into reduced I/O and memory requirements, and also reduced CPU usage when applying the post-filter to the group.

The following diagram summarizes the logical statement processing flow for the building blocks discussed in this chapter:

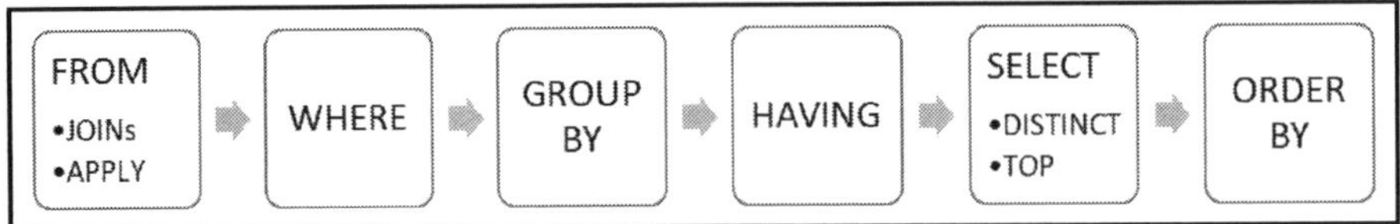

Summary

To understand how to write solid, performant T-SQL, users should become familiar with how SQL Server runs T-SQL syntax to deliver the intended result sets in a scalable fashion. In this chapter, we covered the basic building blocks that make up a T-SQL statement, as well as how SQL Server interprets those blocks to begin the process of executing the user's query. The concepts introduced in this chapter will be used throughout the remaining sections of the book to explain most patterns and anti-patterns, as well as mitigation strategies.

In the next chapter, we will build on our knowledge of how SQL Server processes T-SQL statements to understand how the Query Processor optimizes, caches, and ultimately executes the query.

2
Understanding Query Processing

Now that we have learned the basics of writing T-SQL queries and how SQL Server interprets them, the next logical step is to understand how SQL Server processes and ultimately executes the query. The Query Processor includes query compilation, query optimization, and query execution essentials; how does SQL Server compile an incoming T-SQL statement? How does SQL Server optimize and execute a T-SQL statement? How does SQL Server use parameters? Are parameters an advantage? Why does a SQL Server cache execution plans for certain T-SQL statements but not others? When is that an advantage and when is it a problem? This is information that any T-SQL practitioner needs to keep as reference for proactive T-SQL query writing, as well as reactive troubleshooting and optimization purposes. This chapter will be referenced throughout all chapters, as we bridge architectural topics to real-world usage. The main stages of query processing can be seen in the following overview diagram, which we will expand on throughout this chapter:

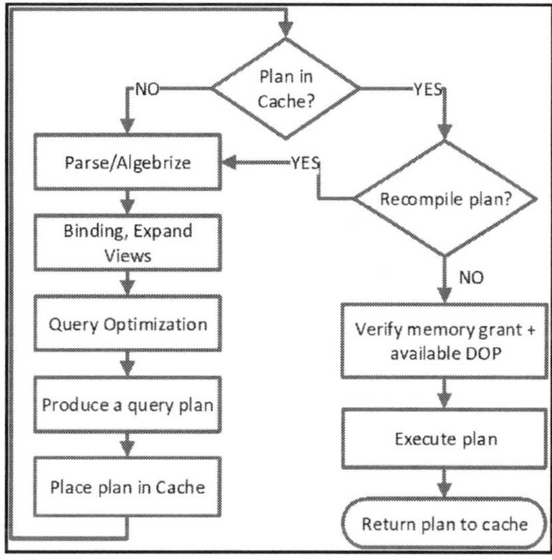

In this chapter we will cover the following topics:

- Query compilation essentials
- Query optimization essentials
- Query execution essentials
- Plan caching and reuse
- The importance of parameters

Query compilation essentials

The Query Processor is the component inside the SQL Server Database Engine that is responsible for compiling a query. In this section, we will focus on the highlighted sections of the following diagram, which handle query compilation:

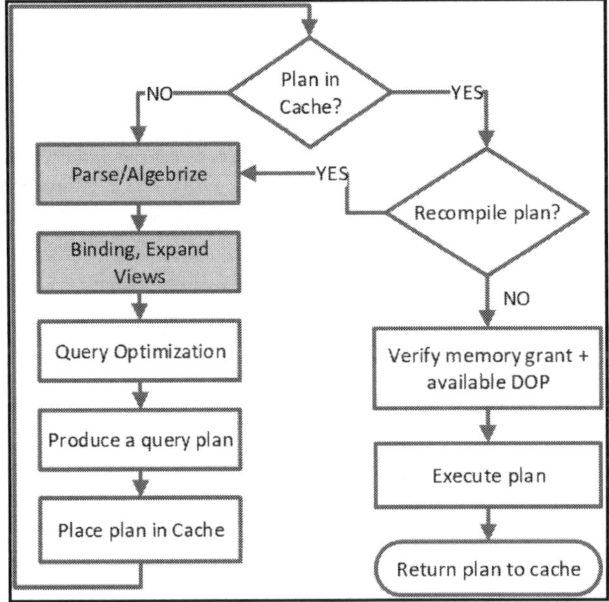

The first stage of query processing is generally known as query compilation and includes a series of tasks that will eventually lead to the creation of a query plan. When an incoming T-SQL statement is **parsed** to perform syntax validations and ensure that it is correct T-SQL, a query hash value representing that statement as it was written is generated. If that query hash is already mapped to a cached query plan, it can just attempt to reuse that plan. However, if a query plan for the incoming query is not already found in the cache, query compilation proceeds with the following tasks:

1. Perform **binding**, which is the process of verifying that the referenced tables and columns exist in the database schema.
2. References to a view are replaced with the definition of that view. (This is called **expanding the view**.)
3. **Load metadata** for the referenced tables and columns:
    1. The definition of tables, indexes, views, constraints, and so on that apply to the query
    2. Data distribution statistics on the applicable schema objects
4. Verify whgether **data conversions** are required for the query:

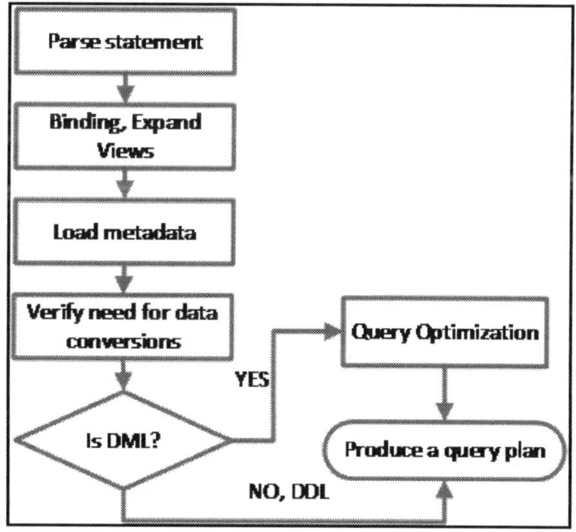

When the query-compilation process is complete, a structure that can be used by the Query Optimizer is produced, known as the algebrizer tree or query tree.

If the T-SQL statement is a **Data Definition Language** (**DDL**) statement, there's no possible optimization, and so a plan is produced and executed immediately. However, if the T-SQL statement is a **Data Manipulation Language** (**DML**) statement, SQL Server will move to an exploratory process known as query optimization.

Query optimization essentials

The Query Processor is also the component inside the SQL Server Database Engine that is responsible for query optimization. This is the second stage of query processing and its goal is to produce a query plan that can then be cached for all subsequent uses of the same query. In this section, we will focus on the highlighted sections of the following diagram, which handle query optimization:

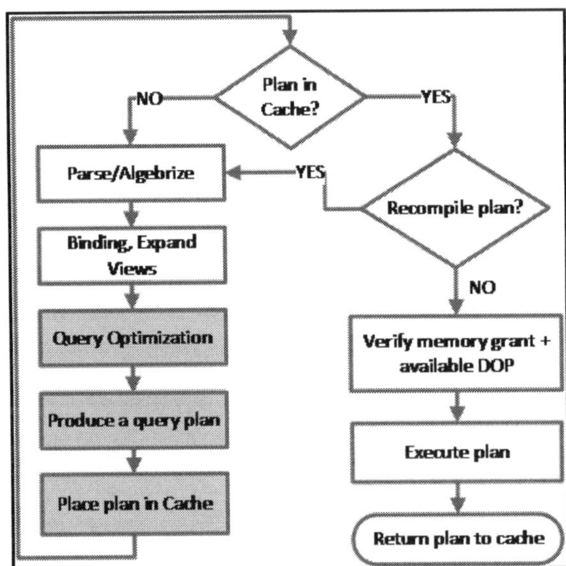

SQL Server uses cost-based optimization, which means that the Query Optimizer is driven mostly by estimations of the required cost to access and transform data (such as joins and aggregations) that will produce the intended result set. The purpose of the optimization process is to reasonably minimize the I/O, memory, and compute resources needed to execute a query in the fastest way possible. But it is also a time-bound process and can time out. This means that the Query Optimizer may not iterate through all the possible optimization permutations of a given T-SQL statement, but rather stops itself after finding an estimated good enough compromise between low resource usage and faster execution times.

For this, the Query Optimizer takes several inputs to later produce what is called a **query execution plan**. These inputs are as follows:

- The incoming T-SQL statement, including any input parameters
- The loaded metadata

We will further discuss the role of statistics in `Chapter 3`, *Mechanics of the Query Optimizer*, and dive deeper into execution plans in `Chapter 4`, *Exploring Query Execution Plans*.

As part of the optimization process, SQL Server also uses internal transformation rules and some heuristics to narrow the optimization space, that is, to narrow the number of transformation rules that can be applied to the incoming T-SQL statement.

SQL Server has over 400 transformation rules that are applicable depending on the incoming T-SQL statement. For reference, these rules are exposed in the undocumented Dynamic Management View (DMV), **sys.dm_exec_query_transformation_stats**. The **name** column in this DMV contains the internal name for the transformation rule. An example is **LOJNtoNL**, which is an implementation rule to transform a logical **LEFT OUTER JOIN** to a physical nested loops join operator.

And so, the SQL Server Query Optimizer may transform the T-SQL statement as written by a developer before it is allowed to execute. This is because T-SQL is a declarative language: a developer declares what is intended, but SQL Server determines how to carry out the declared intent.

The Query Optimizer will consider numerous strategies to search for an efficient execution plan:

- **Logical operator precedence**: When a complex expression has multiple operators, operator precedence determines the sequence in which the operations are performed. For example, in a query that uses comparison and arithmetic operators, the arithmetic operators are handled before the comparison operators.
- **Index selection**: Are there indexes to cover the whole or parts of the query? This is done based on which search and join predicates are used, and which columns are required for the query output.

- **Logical join reordering**: The order in which tables are actually joined may not be the same order as they are written in the T-SQL statement itself. SQL Server uses heuristics as well as statistics to narrow the number of possible join permutations to test, and then estimates which join order results in early filtering of rows and less resource usage. For example, depending on how a query that joins six tables is written, possible join reordering permutations range from roughly 700 to over 30,000.
- **Partitioning**: Is data partitioned? If so, and depending on the predicate, can SQL Server avoid accessing some partitions that are not relevant for the query?
- **Parallelism**: Is it estimated that execution will be more efficient if multiple CPUs are used?
- **Whether to expand views**: Is it better to use an indexed view, or to expand and inline the view definition to account for the base tables?
- **Join elimination**: Are two tables being joined in a way that the number of rows resulting from that join is zero based on existing constraints? If so, the join may not even be executed.
- Sub-query elimination: This follows the same principle as join elimination. Was it estimated that the correlated or non-correlated sub-query will produce zero rows? If so, the sub-query may not even be executed.
- **Constraint simplification**: Is there an active constraint that prevents any rows from being generated? For example, does a column have a non-nullable constraint, but the query predicate searches for null values in that column? If so, that part of the query may not even be executed.
- **Halloween protection**: Is this an update plan? If so, is there a need to add a blocking operator?

An update plan has two parts: a **read** part that identifies the rows to be updated and a **write** part that performs the updates, which must be executed in two separate steps. In other words, the actual update of rows must not affect the selection of which rows to update. This problem of ensuring that the write part of an update plan does not affect the read part is known as **Halloween protection** as it was discovered by IBM researchers more than 40 years ago, on Halloween.

For the Query Optimizer to do its job efficiently in the shortest amount of time possible, data professionals need to do their part, which can be distilled into the following three principles:

- **Design for performance**: Ensure that our tables were designed with purposeful use of the appropriate data types and lengths, that our most-used predicates are covered by indexes, and that the engine is allowed to identify and create the required statistical information.
- **Write simple T-SQL queries**: Be purposeful with the number of joined tables, with how the joins are expressed, with the number of columns needed for the result set, how parameters and variables are declared, and which data transformations are used. Complexity comes at a cost and it may be a wise strategy to break down long T-SQL statements into smaller parts that create intermediate result sets.
- **Maintain our database health**: From a performance standpoint alone, ensure that index maintenance and statistics updates are done regularly.

At this point, it starts to become clear that how we write a query is fundamental to achieving good performance. But it is equally important to make sure the Query Optimizer is given a chance to do its job to produce an efficient query plan. That job is dependent on having metadata available that accurately portrays data distribution in base tables and indexes. In the `Chapter 5`, *Writing Elegant T-SQL Queries*, we will further distill what data professionals need to know to write efficient T-SQL that performs well.

Also, in `Chapter 3`, *Mechanics of the Query Optimizer* we will cover the Query Optimizer and the estimation process in greater detail. Understanding how SQL Server optimizes a query and what the process looks like is a fundamental step toward troubleshooting query performance—a task that any data professional will do at some point in their career.

Query execution essentials

Query execution is driven by the relational engine in SQL Server. This means executing the plan that resulted from the optimization process. In this section, we will focus on the highlighted sections of the following diagram, which handle query execution:

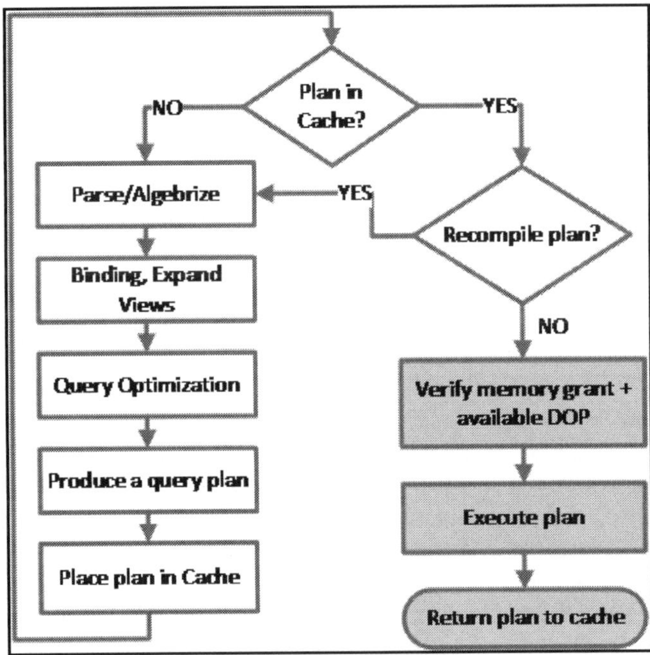

Before execution starts, the relational engine needs to initialize the estimated amount of memory necessary to run the query, known as a **memory grant**. Along with the actual execution, the relational engine schedules the worker threads (also known as **threads**, or **workers**) for the processes to run on and provides inter-thread communication. The number of worker threads spawned depends on the following two key aspects:

- Whether the plan was eligible for parallelism as determined by the Query Optimizer.
- The actual available **Degree of Parallelism (DOP)** in the system, based on current load. This may differ from estimated DOP, which is based on the server configuration's **Max Degree of Parallelism (MAXDOP)**. For example, the MAXDOP may be 8 but the available DOP at runtime can be only 2, which impacts query performance.

During execution, as the parts of the plan that require data from the base tables are processed, the relational engine requests that the storage engine provide data from the relevant rowsets. The data returned from the storage engine is processed into the format defined by the T-SQL statement, and returns the result set to the client.

The preceding key aspects do not change even on highly concurrent systems. However, as SQL Server needs to handle many requests with limited resources, this is achieved with waiting and queuing.

To understand waits and queues in SQL Server, it is important to introduce other query-execution-related concepts. From an execution standpoint, this is what happens when a client application needs to execute a query:

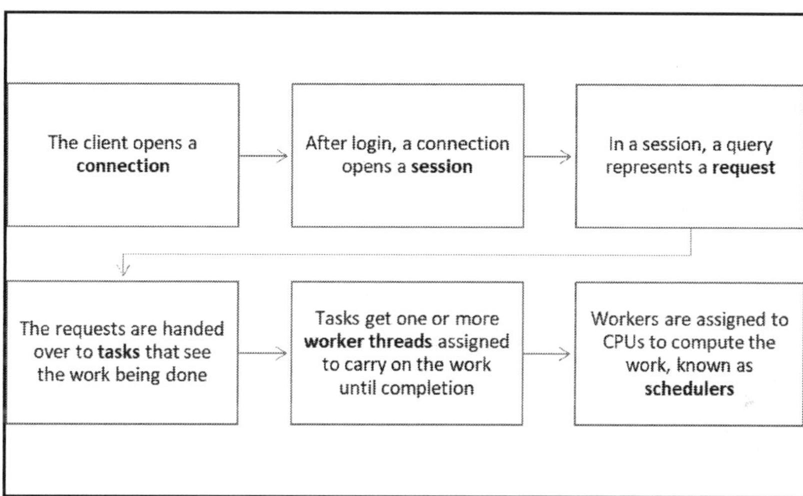

Tasks and workers can naturally accumulate waits until a request completes. We will see how to monitor these in `Chapter 8`, *Building Diagnostic Queries Using DMVs and DMFs*. These waits are surfaced in each request, which can exist with different statuses during its execution:

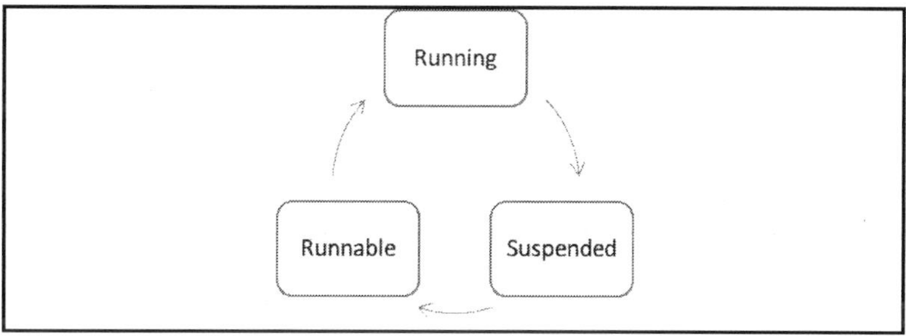

Let's explore the different statuses mentioned in the preceding diagram:

- **Running**: When a task is actively running within a scheduler.
- **Runnable**: When a task is waiting on a first-in first-out queue for scheduler time, and otherwise has access to required resources such as data pages.
- **Suspended**: When a task that is running in a scheduler finds out that a required resource is not available at the moment, such as a data page, it voluntarily yields its allotted processor time, so that another request can proceed instead of allowing for idle processor time. However, a task can be in this state before it even gets on a scheduler. For example, if there isn't enough memory to grant to a new incoming query, that query must wait for memory to become available before starting the actual execution.

All these concepts and terms play a fundamental role in understanding query execution and are also important to keep in mind when troubleshooting query performance. We will further explore how to detect some of these execution conditions in `Chapter 4`, *Exploring Query Execution Plans*.

Plan caching and reuse

As we have now established, the process of optimizing a query can consume a large quantity of resources and take a significant amount of time, so it makes sense to avoid that effort if possible whenever a query is executed. SQL Server caches nearly every plan that is created so that it can be reused when the same query is executed again. But not all execution plans are eligible for caching. For example, no **DDL** statements are cached, such as `CREATE TABLE`. As for **DML** statements, most simple forms that only have one possible execution plan are also not cached, such as `INSERT INTO ... VALUES`.

There are several different methods for plan caching. The method we will use is typically based on how the query is called from the client. The different methods of plan caching that will be covered in this section are the following:

- Stored procedures
- Ad hoc plan caching
- Parameterization (Simple and Forced)
- The **sp_executesql** procedure
- Prepared statements

Stored procedures

A stored procedure is a group of one or more T-SQL statements that is stored as an object in a SQL Server database. Stored procedures are like procedures in other programming languages in that they can accept input parameters and return output parameters, they can contain control-flow logic, such as conditional statements (`IF ... ELSE`), loops (`WHILE`), and error handling (`TRY ... CATCH`), and they can return a status value to the caller that indicates success or failure. They can even contain calls to other stored procedures. There are many benefits to using stored procedures, but in this section, we will focus mainly on their benefit of reducing the overhead of the compilation process through caching.

The first time a stored procedure is executed, SQL Server compiles and optimizes the T-SQL within the procedure, and the resulting execution plan is cached for future use. Every subsequent call to the procedure reuses the cached plan, until the plan is removed from the cache due to any of the following reasons:

- Memory pressure
- Server restart
- Plan invalidation, that is, when the underlying objects are changed in some way or a significant amount of data is changed

Stored procedures are the preferred method for plan caching as they provide the most effective mechanism of caching and reusing query plans in SQL Server.

Ad hoc plan caching

An ad hoc query is a T-SQL query that is sent to the server as a block of text with no parameter markers or other constructs. They are typically built on the fly, such as a query that is typed into a query window in **SQL Server Management Studio** (**SSMS**) and executed, or one that is sent to the server using the **EXECUTE** command as in the following code example which can be executed in the **AdventureWorks** sample database:

```
EXECUTE (N'SELECT LastName, FirstName, MiddleName FROM Person.Person WHERE
PersonType = N''EM'';')
```

The letter **N** preceding a string in a T-SQL script indicates that the string should be interpreted as Unicode with UTF-16 encoding. In order to avoid implicit data-type conversions, be sure to specify **N** for all Unicode string literals when writing T-SQL scripts that involve the **NCHAR** and **NVARCHAR** data types.

The process of parsing and optimizing an ad hoc query is like that of a stored procedure, and will be just as costly, so it is worth it for SQL Server to store the resulting plan in the cache in case the same query is ever executed again. The problem with ad hoc caching is that it is extremely difficult to ensure that the resulting plan is reused.

For SQL Server to reuse an ad hoc plan, the incoming query must match the cached query **exactly**. Every character must be the same, including spaces, line breaks, and capitalization. This even includes comments since they are part of the statement. This is because SQL Server uses a hash function across the entire string to match the T-SQL statement. If even one character is off, the hash values will not match, and SQL Server will again compile, optimize, and cache the incoming ad hoc statement. For this reason, ad hoc caching cannot be relied upon as an effective caching mechanism.

Even if the database is configured to use a case-insensitive collation, the ad hoc plan matching is still case-sensitive because of the algorithm being used to generate the hash value for the query string.

If there are many ad hoc queries being sent to a SQL Server, the plan cache can become bloated with single-use plans. This can cause performance issues on the system as the plan cache will be unnecessarily large, taking up memory that could be better used elsewhere in the system. In this case, turning on the optimize for ad hoc workloads server configuration option is recommended. When this option is turned on, SQL Server will cache a small plan stub object the first time an ad hoc query is executed. This object takes up much less space than a full plan object and will minimize the size of the ad hoc cache. If the query is ever executed a second time, the full plan will be cached.

See `Chapter 8`, *Building Diagnostic Queries Using DMVs and DMFs,* for a query that will help identify single-use plans in the cache.

Parameterization

Parameterization is the practice of replacing a literal value in a T-SQL statement with a parameter marker. Building on the example from the *Ad hoc plan caching* section, the following code block shows an example of a parameterized query executed in the **AdventureWorks** sample database:

```
DECLARE @PersonType AS nchar(2) = N'EM';
SELECT LastName, FirstName, MiddleName
FROM Person.Person
WHERE PersonType = @PersonType;
```

In this case, the literal value, **EM**, is moved from the T-SQL statement itself into a **DECLARE** statement, and the variable is used in the query instead. This allows the query plan to be reused for different **@PersonType** values, whereas sending different values directly in the query string would result in a separate cached ad hoc plan.

Simple parameterization

In order to minimize the impact of ad hoc queries, SQL Server will automatically parameterize some simple queries by default. This is called **Simple parameterization** and is the default setting of the parameterization database option. With parameterization set to Simple, SQL Server will automatically replace literal values in an ad hoc query with parameter markers in order to make the resulting query plan reusable. This works for some queries, but there is a very small class of queries that can be parameterized this way.

As an example, the query we introduced previously in the *Parameterization* section would not be automatically parameterized in simple mode because it is considered unsafe. This is because different **PersonType** values may yield a different number of rows, and thus require a different execution plan. However, the following query executed in the **AdventureWorks** sample database would qualify for simple automatic parameterization:

```
SELECT LastName, FirstName, MiddleName
FROM Person.Person
WHERE BusinessEntityID = 5;
```

This query would not be cached as is. SQL Server would convert the literal value of **5** to a parameter marker, and it would look something like this in the cache:

```
(@1 tinyint) SELECT LastName, FirstName, MiddleName
FROM Person.Person
WHERE BusinessEntityID = @1;
```

Forced parameterization

If an application tends to generate many ad hoc queries, and there is no way to modify the application to parameterize the queries, the **Parameterization** database option can be changed to Forced. When **Forced Parameterization** is turned on, SQL Server will replace **ALL** literal values in **ALL** ad hoc queries with parameter markers. Take the example of the following query executed in the **AdventureWorks** sample database:

```
SELECT LastName, FirstName, MiddleName
FROM Person.Person
WHERE PersonType = N'EM' AND BusinessEntityID IN (5, 7, 13, 17, 19);
```

This query would be automatically parameterized under Forced Parameterization, as follows:

```
(@1 nchar(2), @2 int, @3 int, @4 int, @5 int, @6 int)  SELECT LastName,
FirstName, MiddleName
FROM Person.Person
WHERE PersonType = @1 AND BusinessEntityID IN (@2, @3, @4, @5, @6);
```

This has the benefit of increasing the reusability of all ad hoc queries, but there are some risks to parameterizing all literal values in all queries, which will be discussed later in section *The importance of parameters*.

The sp_executesql procedure

The **sp_executesql** procedure is the recommended method for sending an ad hoc T-SQL statement to SQL Server. If stored procedures cannot be leveraged for some reason, such as when T-SQL statements must be constructed dynamically by the application, **sp_executesql** allows the user to send an ad hoc T-SQL statement as a parameterized query, which uses a similar caching mechanism to stored procedures. This ensures that the plan can be reused whenever the same query is executed again. Building on our example from the *Ad hoc plan caching* section, we can rewrite the query using **sp_executesql**, as in the following example which can be executed in the **AdventureWorks** sample database:

```
EXECUTE sp_executesql @stmt = N'SELECT LastName, FirstName, MiddleName
FROM Person.Person
WHERE PersonType = @PersonType;'
                     , @params = N'@PersonType nchar(2)'
                     , @PersonType = N'EM';
```

This ensures that any time the same query is sent with the same parameter markers, the plan will be reused, even if the statement is dynamically generated by the application.

Prepared statements

Another method for sending parameterized T-SQL statements to SQL Server is by using prepared statements. Leveraging prepared statements involves the following three different system procedures:

- **sp_prepare**: Defines the statement and parameters that are to be executed, creates an execution plan for the query, and sends a statement handle back to the caller, which can be used for subsequent executions
- **sp_execute**: Executes the statement defined by **sp_prepare** by sending the statement handle along with any parameters to SQL Server
- **sp_unprepare**: Discards the execution plan created by **sp_prepare** for the query specified by the statement handle

Steps *1* and *2* can optionally be combined into a single **sp_prepexec** statement to save a roundtrip to the server.

This method is not generally recommended for plan reuse as it is a legacy construct and may not take advantage of some of the benefits of parameterized statements that **sp_executesql** and stored procedures can leverage. It is worth mentioning, however, because it is used by some cross-platform database connectivity libraries, such as **Open Database Connectivity** (**ODBC**) or **Java Database Connectivity** (**JDBC**), as the default mechanism for sending queries to SQL Server.

How query processing impacts plan reuse

It's important to contextualize what happens in terms of query processing that can result in plan caching and reuse. In this section, we will focus on the highlighted sections of the following diagram, which determine whether a query plan can be reused from the cache or needs to be recompiled:

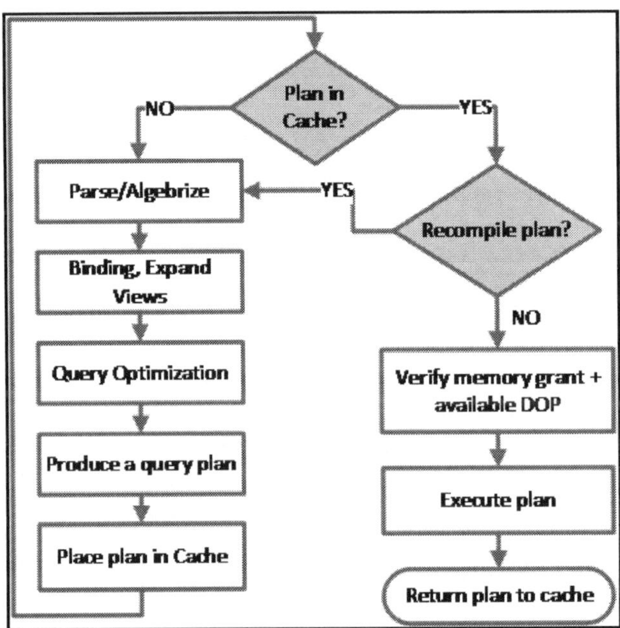

As mentioned, when an incoming T-SQL statement is parsed, a query hash value representing that statement as it was written is generated, and if that query hash is already mapped to a cached query plan, it can just attempt to reuse that plan unless special circumstances exist that don't even allow plan caching, such as when the **RECOMPILE** hint is present in the T-SQL statement.

Assuming no such pre-existing conditions exist, after matching the query hash with a plan hash, the currently-cached plan is tested for correctness, meaning that SQL Server will check whether anything has changed in the underlying referenced objects that would require the plan to be recompiled. For example, if a new index was created or if an existing index referenced in the plan was dropped, the plan must be recompiled.

If the cached plan is found to be correct, SQL Server also checks whether enough data has changed to warrant a new plan. This refers to the statistics objects associated with tables and indexes used in the T-SQL statement, and if any are deemed outdated—meaning its modification counter is high enough as it relates to the overall cardinality of the table to consider it stale.

We will further discuss the role of statistics in `Chapter 3`, *Mechanics of the Query Optimizer*.

If nothing has significantly changed, the query plan can be executed, as we discussed in the *Query execution essentials* section.

The following diagram depicts the high-level process for an already-cached plan that can be executed as is:

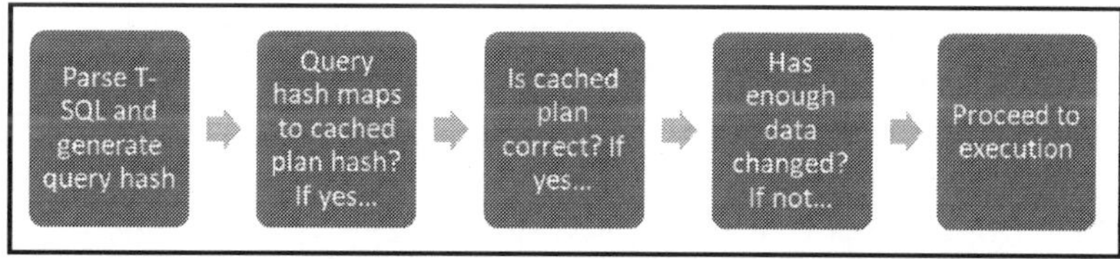

However, if any of the preceding checks fail, SQL Server invalidates the cached plan and a new query plan needs to be compiled, as the available optimization space may be different from the last time the plan was compiled and cached. In this case, the T-SQL statement needs to undergo recompilation and go through the optimization process driven by the Query Optimizer so that a new query execution plan is generated. (We will describe this process in greater detail in `Chapter 3`, *Mechanics of the Query Optimizer*.) If eligible, this newly-generated query plan is cached.

The same process is followed for new incoming queries where no query plan is yet cached.

The importance of parameters

As we discussed in the *How query processing impacts plan reuse* section on caching methods, the primary reason to parameterize queries is to ensure that query execution plans get reused. But why is this important and what other reasons might there be to use parameters?

Security

One reason to use parameterized queries is for security. Using a properly formatted parameterized query can protect against SQL injection attacks. A SQL injection attack is where a malicious user can execute database code (in this case, T-SQL) on a server by appending it to a data-entry field in the application. As an example, imagine we have an application that contains a form that asks the user to enter their name into a text box. If the application were to use an ad hoc statement to insert this data into the database, it would generally concatenate a T-SQL string with the user input, as in the following code:

```
DECLARE @sql nvarchar(MAX);
SET @sql = N'INSERT Users (Name) VALUES (''' + <user input> + ''');';
EXECUTE (@sql);
```

A malicious user might enter the `Bob'); DROP TABLE Users; --` value into the text box.

If this is the case, the actual code that gets sent to SQL Server would look like the following:

```
INSERT Users (Name) VALUES ('Bob'); DROP TABLE Users; --');
```

This is valid T-SQL syntax that would successfully execute. It would first insert a row into the **Users** table with the **Name** column set to **'Bob'**, then it would drop the **Users** table. This would of course break the application, and unless there was some sort of auditing in place, we would never know what happened.

Let's look at this example again using a parameterized query. The code might look like the following:

```
EXECUTE sp_executesql @stmt = N'INSERT Users (Name) VALUES (@name)',
@params = N'@name nvarchar(100)', @name = <user input>
```

This time, if the user were to send the same input, rather than executing the query that the user embedded in the string, the SQL Server will insert a row into the **Users** table, with the **Name** column set to `('Bob'); DROP TABLE Users; --'`. This would obviously look a bit strange, but it wouldn't break the application or breach security.

Performance

Another reason to leverage parameters is performance. In a busy SQL Server system, particularly one that has a primarily **Online Transaction Processing (OLTP)** workload, we may have hundreds or even thousands of queries executing per second.

Assume that each one of these queries took about 100 ms to compile and consumed about the same amount of CPU. This would mean that each second on the system, the server could be consuming hundreds of seconds of CPU time just compiling queries. That's a lot of resources to consume in just preparing the queries for execution, and it doesn't leave a lot of overhead for actually executing them.

Also recall that when plans are not reused, the procedure cache can become very large and consume memory that in turn won't be available for storing data and executing queries. In short, a system that spends too much time compiling queries may become CPU- and/or memory-bound and may perform poorly.

Parameter sniffing

Given that query plan reuse is so important, why wouldn't SQL Server parameterize every query that comes in by default? One of the reasons is to avoid query performance issues that may result from parameter sniffing. Parameter sniffing is something SQL Server does in order to optimize a parameterized query. The first time a stored procedure or other parameterized query executes, the input parameter values are used to drive the optimization process and produce the execution plan, as discussed in the *Query optimization essentials* section.

That execution plan will then be cached and reused by subsequent executions of the procedure or query. For most queries, this is a good thing because using a specific value will result in a more accurate cost estimation. In some situations, however, particularly where the data is skewed in some way, the parameters that are sent the first time the query is executed may not represent the typical use case of the query, and the plan that is generated may perform poorly when other parameter values are sent. This is a case where reusing a plan might not be a good thing.

Parameter sniffing is a very common cause of plan variability and performance issues in SQL Server. We will discuss this behavior in more detail in `Chapter 6`, *Easily Identified T-SQL Anti-Patterns*, and `Chapter 7`, *Discovering T-SQL Anti-Patterns in Depth*.

To cache or not to cache

In general, caching and reusing query plans is a good thing, and writing T-SQL code that encourages plan reuse is recommended.

In some cases, such as with a reporting or **Online Analytic Processing (OLAP)** workloads, caching queries might make less sense. These types of systems tend to have a heavy ad hoc workload. The queries that run are typically long-running and, while they may consume a large quantity of resources in a single execution, they typically run with less frequency than OLTP systems. Since these queries tend to be long-running, saving a few hundred milliseconds by reusing a cached plan doesn't make as much sense as creating a new plan that is designed specifically to execute that query. Spending that time compiling a new plan may even result in saving more time in the long run, since a fresh plan will likely perform better than a plan that was generated based on a different set of parameter values.

In summary, for most workloads in SQL Server, leveraging stored procedures and/or parameterized queries is recommended to encourage plan reuse. For workloads that have heavy ad hoc queries and/or long-running reporting-style queries, consider enabling the **Optimize for Ad hoc Workloads** server setting and leveraging the **RECOMPILE** hint to guarantee a new plan for each execution (provided that the queries are run with a low frequency). Also, be sure to review `Chapter 8`, *Building Diagnostic Queries Using DMVs and DMFs*, for techniques to identify single-use plans, monitor for excessive recompilation, and identify plan variability and potential parameter-sniffing issues.

Summary

At this point, it is beginning to become clear that the way a T-SQL query is written and submitted to the server influences how it is going to be interpreted and executed by SQL Server. Even before a single T-SQL query is written, the choice of development style (for example, using stored procedures versus ad hoc statements) can have a direct impact on the performance of the application.

As we continue our exploration of the internals of SQL Server query processing and optimization, we will find more and more opportunities to write T-SQL queries in a way that encourages optimal query performance.

3
Mechanics of the Query Optimizer

The next step in our journey toward writing efficient T-SQL queries is understanding how the SQL Server database engine optimizes a query; we will do so by exploring T-SQL query optimization internals and architecture, starting with the infamous **cardinality estimation** process and its building blocks. From there, we will understand how the Query Optimizer uses that information to produce a just-in-time, good-enough execution plan. This chapter will be referenced throughout this book, as we apply architectural topics to real-world uses.

Before we get started, it's important to have a common frame of reference about the following terms:

- **Cardinality**: Cardinality in a database is defined as the number of records, also called **tuples**, in each table or view.
- **Frequency**: This term represents the average number of occurrences of a given value in a column or column set. It's defined as the number of rows times the density.
- **Density**: This term represents the average number of duplicate values in each column or column set, in other words, the average distribution of unique values in the data. It's defined as 1 divided by the number of distinct values.
- **Selectivity**: This term represents the fraction of the row count that satisfies a given predicate, between zero and one. This is calculated as the predicate cardinality (*Pc*) divided by the table cardinality (*Tc*) multiplied by one hundred: $(Pc \div Tc) \times 100\%$. As the average number of duplicates decreases (the density), the selectivity of a value increases. For example, in a table that represents streets and cities in a country, many streets and cities have the same name, but each street and city combination has a unique zip code. An index on the zip code is more selective than an index on the street or city because the zip code has a much lower density than a street or city.

- **Statistics**: Statistics are the metadata objects that we referred to in `Chapter 2`, *Understanding Query Processing*. They maintain information on the distribution of data in a table or indexed view, over a specific column or column set. We will discuss the role of statistics in more detail in the *Introducing the Cardinality Estimator* section.
- **Histogram**: This is a bucketized representation of the distribution of data in a specific column that is kept in a statistic object. These histograms hold aggregate information on the number of rows (cardinality) and distinct values (density) for up to 200 ranges of data values, named histogram steps. For any statistics object, the histogram is always created for the first column only. For multi-column statistics, this means that the histogram does not contain information about any additional column.

In this chapter, we will cover the following topics:

- Introducing the Cardinality Estimator
- Understanding the query optimization workflow

Introducing the Cardinality Estimator

In `Chapter 2`, *Understanding Query Processing*, we discussed how the Query Optimizer is a fundamental piece of the overall query processor. In this chapter, we will dig deeper into the core component of cost-based query optimization: the **Cardinality Estimator** (**CE**).

As the name suggests, the role of the CE is to provide fundamental estimation input to the query optimization process. For example, the cardinality of a table that contains the name of every living human on Earth today is about 7,600,000,000. But if a predicate is applied on this table to find only inhabitants of the United States of America, the cardinality after the predicate is applied is only 327,000,000. Reading through 7,600,000,000 or 327,000,000 records may result in different data-access operations, such as a full scan or a range scan in this case. As such, early knowledge of the estimated number of rows is fundamental for creating an accurate query execution plan. It would be very inefficient if SQL Server had to incur the high cost of accessing actual data to make this estimation – that would be like executing the query in order to figure out how to execute the query. Instead, it uses metadata kept in statistics.

Statistics are the building blocks for the process of CE: if statistics don't accurately portray underlying data distributions, the Query Optimizer will work with inaccurate data and estimate cardinalities that don't adhere to the reality of the data.

To ensure statistics are kept updated, SQL Server keeps a modification counter on each table referenced by the statistic and, when enough changes have been made to the table or indexed view columns tracked by a statistic, an update to that statistic is needed. When a query is compiled or recompiled, SQL Server loads all required statistics based on which columns are being used and determines whether statistics need to be updated.

If the database option for automatic statistics update is enabled (which is the default), SQL Server will update the outdated statistic before proceeding with query execution of any execution plan that referenced that statistic – this is known as a synchronous update. If asynchronous automatic statistics update is enabled, SQL Server will proceed with query execution based on the existing statistic as-is and update the outdated statistic as a background process. Once any statistics object has been updated, the next time any cached query plan that references that statistic is loaded for use, it is recompiled.

Up to SQL Server 2014, unless trace flag 2371 is used, SQL Server uses a threshold based on the percentage of rows changed. This is regardless of the number of rows in the table. You can know more about the threshold, in the following link `https://docs.microsoft.com/en-us/sql/relational-databases/statistics/statistics?view=sql-server-2017`, under the topic *Statistics Options*, and sub heading *AUTO_UPDATE_STATISTICS Option*.

Starting with SQL Server 2016, and database compatibility level 130, SQL Server uses a effective threshold that had been introduced in earlier versions under the trace flag 2371, which keeps adjusting for the number of rows in the table or indexed view. This is the result of comparing the SQL Server 2014 threshold with the square root of the product of 1000 and the current table's cardinality. The smallest number resulting from this comparison is used. For example, if our table contains 1,000,000 rows, the calculation is `SQRT(1000 * 1000000) = 31622`. When the table grows to 2,000,000 rows, the threshold is only 44,721 rows, whereas the SQL Server 2014 threshold would be 400,500 rows. With this change, statistics on large tables are updated more often, which decreases the chances of producing an inefficient query execution plan and the likely consequence is poor query performance.

Database compatibility level is a setting that tells SQL Server to execute T-SQL statements in that database using the same functional and query optimization behaviors that were the default for a given database engine version. For example, SQL Server 2016 introduced database compatibility level 130 and a set of new default behaviors, but setting database compatibility level 120 forces functional and query optimization behaviors that were the default in SQL Server 2014, which maps to the version when database compatibility level 120 was introduced.

The CE operates with on mathematical models based on certain assumptions about the T-SQL statements that will be executed. These assumptions are considered during computations to find what should be reasonable predictions about how many rows are expected to flow through each plan operator, and these predictions are used in the query optimization process to estimate the cost of each query plan.

CE 70, as introduced back in SQL Server 7.0, used four basic assumptions about how users query their data:

- **Independence assumption**: Data distributions on different columns of the same table are assumed to be independent of each other, and predicates on different columns of the same table are therefore also independent of each other. This is known as the Independence assumption. For example, in a fictitious database for a large retail store chain where customer data is stored, a report shows which customers exist per store location using a query like the following example: `SELECT * FROM Customers WHERE FirstName = 'James' AND City = 'San Francisco'`. We can assume there are many Jameses in San Francisco, so these two columns are independent.
- **Uniformity assumption**: Distinct values are evenly distributed in a given histogram and all have the same frequency. This is known as the uniformity assumption.
- **Simple Containment**: Join predicates are assumed to be dependent on filter predicates. When users query data joining different tables and set a filter predicate on these tables, it's assumed that the filters apply to the joined data and are considered when estimating the number of rows returned by the join. This is called Simple Containment. For the example of a fictitious database for the same large retail store chain, different tables record items sold and items returned, and a report shows the number of returns per sold item type and date, using a query like the following example: `SELECT * FROM Sales INNER JOIN Returns ON Sales.ReceiptID = Returns.ReceiptID WHERE Sales.Type = 'Toys' AND Returns.Date = '2019-04-18'`. Throughout the year we have a fairly steady number of returns per items sold and the estimation shouldn't change for any given day. However, when the query predicate changes to `WHERE Sales.Type = 'Toys' AND Returns.Date = '2018-12-27'` then accounting for filters can greatly impact estimations, because in the days after Christmas it's expected that many toys are returned.
- **Inclusion assumption**: For filter predicates where a column equals a constant (for example, `WHERE col1 = 10`), it is assumed the constant always exists in that column. This is called the **Inclusion** assumption.

But application workloads don't always follow the model assumptions, which can result in inefficiently-optimized query execution plans.

We will discuss some out-of-model T-SQL constructs in more detail in `Chapter 6`, *Easily Identified T-SQL Anti-Patterns*, and `Chapter 7`, *Discovering T-SQL Anti-Patterns in Depth.*

Observation of, and experience with, query performance led to a major redesign of the CE, with the release of SQL Server 2014 and CE 120.

The main objectives of this new CE were as follows:

- To improve the quality of cardinality estimation for a broad range of queries and modern workloads, such as **Online Transaction Processing** (**OLTP**), **Data Warehousing** (**DW**), and **Decision Support Systems** (**DSS**)
- To generate more efficient and predictable query execution plans for most use cases, especially complex queries

With that new release, some model assumptions about how users queried their data were changed:

- **Independence** became partial **Correlation**, where a combination of the different column values is not necessarily independent, and it's assumed this resembles real-life data-querying patterns. For the example of a fictitious database for a large retail store chain where customer data is stored, a report lists the names of all customers using a query like the following example: `SELECT * FROM Customers WHERE FirstName = 'James' AND LastName = 'Kirk'`. We can assume a tight correlation between a customer first and last names, meaning that while there are many Jameses, there are not many James Kirks.
- **Simple Containment** became **Base Containment**, meaning that filter predicates and join predicates are independent. For the example of a fictitious database for the same large retail store chain where the HR department runs a report that shows the base salary for full-time employees, using a query like the following example: `SELECT * FROM Payroll INNER JOIN Employee ON Payroll.EmployeeID = Employee.EmployeeID WHERE Payroll.CompType = 'Base' AND Employee.Type = 'FTE'`. All employees have a base salary and the workforce has one-third FTEs, one-third part-time employees, and one-third contractors, so for any different employee type that is queried, whether the WHERE clause is there or not, the estimation wouldn't change and the default base containment works best.

It's common to see these CE models referred to as **legacy CE** and **new CE**. These are in fact side-by-side implementations and more accurately referred to as CE 70, and CE 120, or higher. Being side by side means that developers can opt in for either CE version, as newer changes and enhancements are filtered by the database compatibility level.

We will see examples of how these CE assumptions cannot cover all workloads in `Chapter 13`, *Managing Optimizer Changes with the Query Tuning Assistant.*

CE versions are tied to the database compatibility level setting of the SQL Server version when it was first introduced. The following table contains a mapping reference between database compatibility levels and CE versions:

Introduced in SQL Server version	Database compatibility level	CE version
2008 and 2008 R2	100	70
2012	110	70
2014	120	120
2016	120	130
2017	140	140
2019	150	150

This mapping between database compatibility levels and CE versions is especially useful when the topic is application certification. For example, if a given application were written and optimized for SQL Server 2012 (CE 70) and later upgraded as-is to SQL Server 2017 (CE 140), there's a chance that part of that application's workload may be susceptible to the model changes of a higher CE version, and as a result may perform worse than it did in SQL Server 2012. These types of performance regressions can be easily handled, and SQL Server includes several features designed to assist in overcoming a number of these regressions. We will further discuss these in `Chapters 8`, *Building Diagnostic Queries Using DMVs and DMFs*, through `Chapter 12`, *Troubleshooting Live Queries*, where we discuss how to assemble our query troubleshooting toolbox.

CE 120+ changes target mainly non-leaf-level operators that support logical operations, such as **JOIN**, **UNION**, **GROUP BY**, and **DISTINCT**. Other T-SQL constructs that only exist at runtime still behave the same, such as **multi-statement table-valued functions** (**MSTVFs**), table variables, local variables, and table-valued parameters. We will discuss these out-of-model constructs in `Chapter 7`, *Discovering T-SQL Anti-Patterns in Depth.*

The inverse is the more common case though, where without refactoring a query, CE 120+ can do a better job of optimizing a query plan than CE 70. For example, the **AdventureWorks** sample database has several tables with employee data. To write a query that returns the employee name and details such as contacts, address, and job title, a series of inner joins is used.

The query would look like the following example:

```
SELECT e.[BusinessEntityID], p.[Title], p.[FirstName], p.[MiddleName],
    p.[LastName], p.[Suffix], e.[JobTitle], pp.[PhoneNumber],
    pnt.[Name] AS [PhoneNumberType], ea.[EmailAddress],
    p.[EmailPromotion], a.[AddressLine1], a.[AddressLine2],
    a.[City], sp.[Name] AS [StateProvinceName], a.[PostalCode],
    cr.[Name] AS [CountryRegionName], p.[AdditionalContactInfo]
FROM [HumanResources].[Employee] AS e
INNER JOIN [Person].[Person] AS p
    ON RTRIM(LTRIM(p.[BusinessEntityID])) =
RTRIM(LTRIM(e.[BusinessEntityID]))
INNER JOIN [Person].[BusinessEntityAddress] AS bea
    ON RTRIM(LTRIM(bea.[BusinessEntityID])) =
RTRIM(LTRIM(e.[BusinessEntityID]))
INNER JOIN [Person].[Address] AS a
    ON RTRIM(LTRIM(a.[AddressID])) = RTRIM(LTRIM(bea.[AddressID]))
INNER JOIN [Person].[StateProvince] AS sp
    ON RTRIM(LTRIM(sp.[StateProvinceID])) =
RTRIM(LTRIM(a.[StateProvinceID]))
INNER JOIN [Person].[CountryRegion] AS cr
    ON RTRIM(LTRIM(cr.[CountryRegionCode])) =
RTRIM(LTRIM(sp.[CountryRegionCode]))
LEFT OUTER JOIN [Person].[PersonPhone] AS pp
    ON RTRIM(LTRIM(pp.BusinessEntityID)) =
RTRIM(LTRIM(p.[BusinessEntityID]))
LEFT OUTER JOIN [Person].[PhoneNumberType] AS pnt
    ON RTRIM(LTRIM(pp.[PhoneNumberTypeID])) =
RTRIM(LTRIM(pnt.[PhoneNumberTypeID]))
LEFT OUTER JOIN [Person].[EmailAddress] AS ea
    ON RTRIM(LTRIM(p.[BusinessEntityID])) =
RTRIM(LTRIM(ea.[BusinessEntityID]));
```

With CE 70, the elapsed execution time for this query is 101,975 ms. But with the exact same query on the exact same database on CE 140, the elapsed execution time is only 103 ms.

As seen in the following screenshot, the query execution plans are radically different in shape, and, given the observed execution times, better optimized using newer versions of the CE.

The query plan shape for CE 70 is as follows:

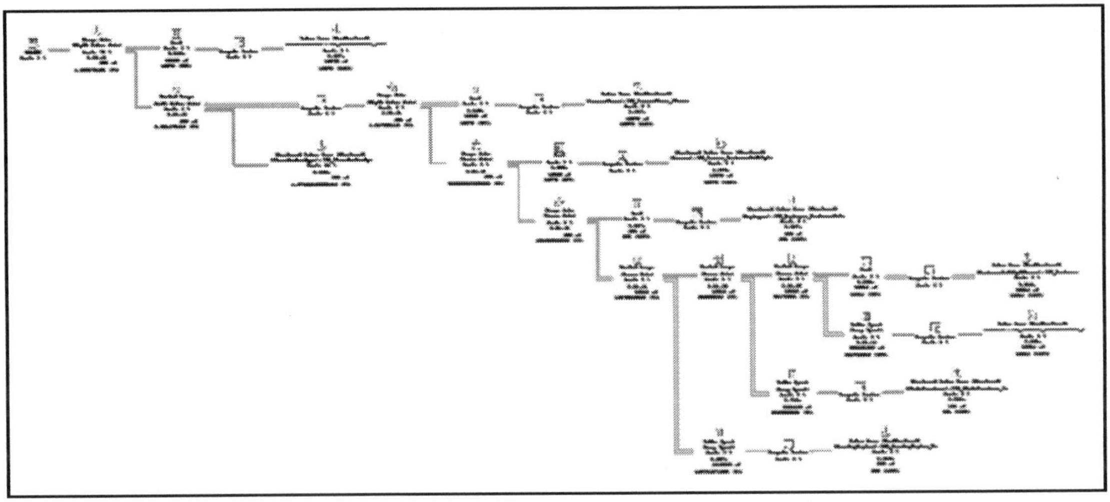

The query plan shape for CE 140 is as follows:

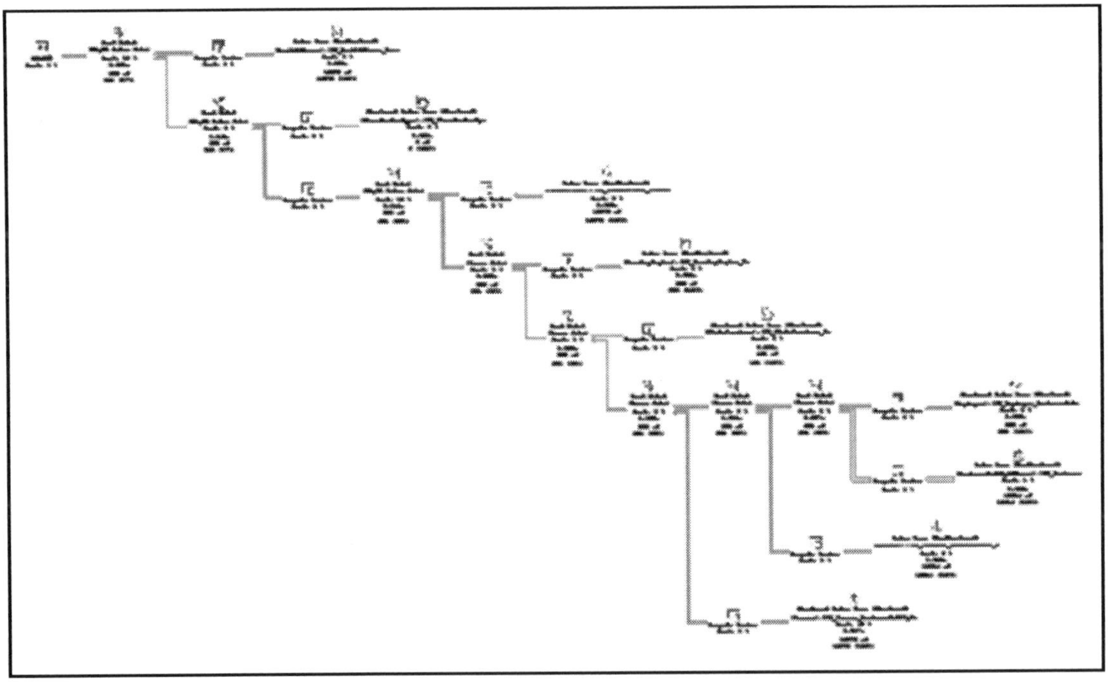

We will revisit the preceding query example in greater depth in `Chapter 4`, *Exploring Query Execution Plans*, and `Chapter 10`, *Troubleshooting Live Queries*.

Understanding the query optimization workflow

Now it's time to take a deeper look at how SQL Server creates optimized query execution plans. As mentioned in `Chapter 2`, *Understanding Query Processing*, this is the second phase of query processing, and for the most part only **Data Manipulation Language (DML)** statements undergo query optimization. The query optimization process is defined by the following cumulative stages:

- **Trivial Plan**
- **Exploration** which in turn, includes three phases in itself:
    - **Transaction processing**
    - **Quick plan**
    - **Full optimization**

In the Exploration stage, what differentiates between the several phases is the increasing sets of rules applicable to each one as the search for a good-enough query plan progresses. Users can learn about the optimization level of a given query execution plan by looking at the properties of that plan. The following sections include sample execution plans to illustrate the concepts covered here. Query execution plans will be discussed in more detail in `Chapter 4`, *Exploring Query Execution Plans*.

The Trivial Plan stage

As mentioned in the *Query optimization essentials* section of `Chapter 2`, *Understanding Query Processing*, SQL Server does cost-based optimization. But this has an expensive startup cost and so SQL Server will try to avoid this cost for simple queries that may only have one possible query execution plan.

The Trivial Plan stage generates plans for which there are no alternatives, and which require a cost-based decision. The following examples can be executed in the **AdventureWorks** sample database.

The following is a `SELECT ... INTO` or `INSERT INTO` statement over a single table with no conditions:

```
SELECT NationalIDNumber, JobTitle, MaritalStatus
INTO HumanResources.Employee2
FROM HumanResources.Employee;
```

The preceding query produces the following execution plan:

T-SQL
SELECT INTO
Cost: 0 %
Table Insert
[Employee2]
Cost: 74 %
0.029s
290 of
290 (100%)
Clustered Index Scan (Clustered)
[Employee].[PK_Employee_BusinessEnt...
Cost: 26 %
0.008s
290 of
290 (100%)

The following is an `INSERT INTO` statement over a single table with a simple condition covered by an index:

```
INSERT INTO HumanResources.Employee2
SELECT NationalIDNumber, JobTitle, MaritalStatus
FROM HumanResources.Employee
WHERE BusinessEntityID < 10;
```

The preceding query produces the following execution plan:

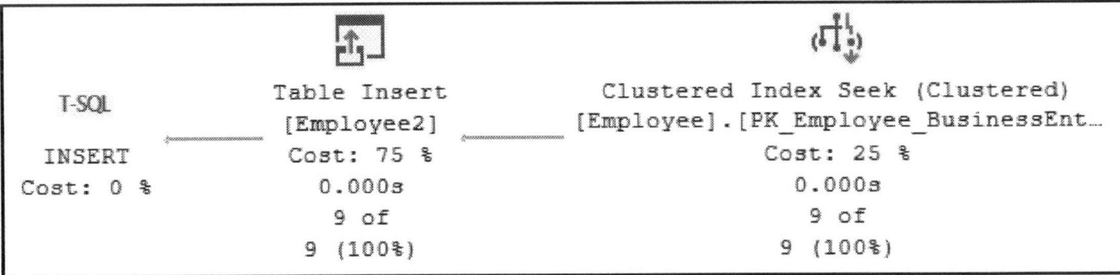

The following is an **INSERT** statement with a **VALUES** clause:

```
INSERT INTO HumanResources.Employee2
VALUES (87656896, 'CIO', 'M');
```

The preceding query produces the following execution plan:

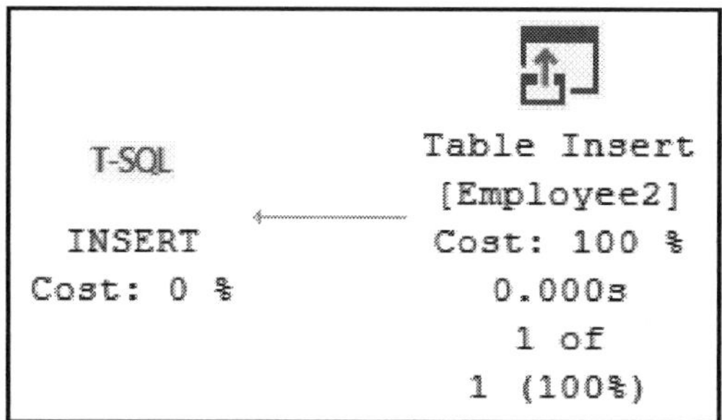

The information on the optimization level is stored in the execution plan under the **Optimization Level** property, with a value of **TRIVIAL**, as shown in the following screenshot:

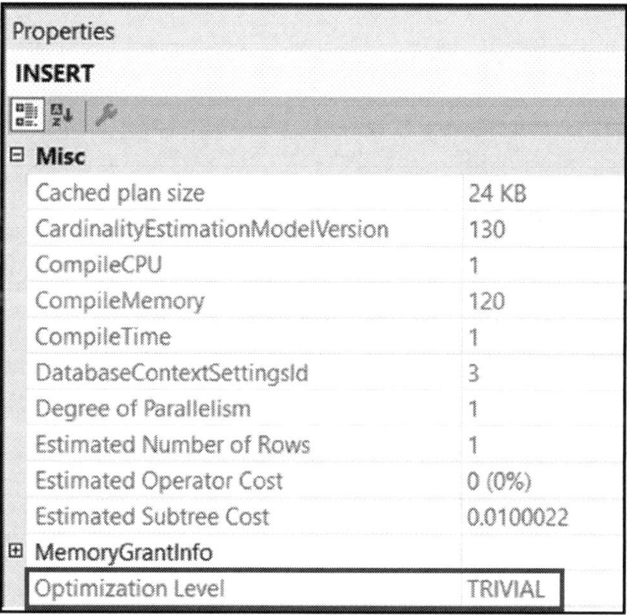

The Trivial Plan stage typically finds very inexpensive query plans that are not affected by cardinality estimations.

The Exploration stage

If the Trivial Plan stage doesn't find a suitable plan, it's time to enter the cost-based optimization stage, known as **Exploration**, whose goal is to find a good-enough query execution plan based on the minimum estimated cost to access and join data. If this stage is used, the information on the optimization level is still stored in the execution plan under the same **Optimization Level** property, with a value of **FULL**.

A good-enough plan refers to the search optimization space and how SQL Server may not actually iterate through all possible plan combinations, but rather may look for a plan that meets its internal thresholds for a good-enough balance between the estimated resource usage and execution times.

The Exploration stage is where the CE comes into play. SQL Server loads statistics and performs some tasks in preparation for cost-based optimization.

These tasks are as follows:

- **Simplification** transforms some sub-queries into semi-joins, and even detects whether parts of the query can skip execution, for example avoiding empty tables or searching a table column for a **NULL** predicate when that table column has a trusted `NOT NULL` constraint.
- **Normalization** uses the query's filter predicates and some heuristics to reorder join operations, and predicates are pushed-down to the algebrizer tree.

The cost-based optimization process itself is composed of three phases that we discuss in the next sections: Transaction Processing, Quick Plan, and Full Optimization.

Transaction Processing

This is phase zero, and suitable for OLTP-centric queries that are simple yet may have more than one possible query plan. When this phase completes, SQL Server compares the estimated cost of the plan that was found with an internal cost threshold. If the cost of the plan that was found is cheaper than this internal threshold, SQL Server will stop further optimizations and use the plan found by the transaction processing phase.

Quick plan

This is phase one and is used if the plan found by the transaction processing phase is still more expensive than the internal threshold. This phase expands the search for a good-enough plan to cover rule-based join reordering and spools that may benefit moderately complex queries. To determine whether a good-enough plan has been found, as the Query Optimizer generates each potential query plan, it compares the cost of the plan that was just evaluated with the estimated cost of continuing to search for better plan alternatives. This effectively establishes a timeout so that we don't spend more time optimizing the query than we would spend executing the current plan. If a plan has been found with a cost lower than the cost threshold for the quick plan and lower than the timeout, optimization is stopped, and that good-enough plan is used. This avoids incurring additional compilation costs.

This timeout is not a fixed number, but rather a non-linear value that is related to the complexity of the incoming T-SQL statement. Complexity is translated into cost, so the higher the cost of the query plan, the higher the threshold will be for that plan.

If the plan cost that the quick plan phase found is greater than the server configuration for the **Cost Threshold for Parallelism** and the server is a multiprocessor machine, then parallelism is considered. However, if the plan cost from the quick plan phase is less than the configured **Cost Threshold for Parallelism**, only serial plans are considered going forward.

Even if a parallel plan is produced, this doesn't mean the query plan will be executed on multiple processors. If existing processors are too busy to withstand running a query on multiple CPUs—technically meaning that there aren't enough available schedulers—then the plan will be executed on a single processor. If the MAXDOP server configuration is set to `1`, parallelism is not considered at all in the optimization process.

Full optimization

This is phase two and is used for complex queries, where the plan produced by phase one is still considered more expensive than the cost of searching for more alternative plans—the timeout defined previously. All internal transformation rules are available for use at this point but scoped to the search space defined in the preparation tasks, and parallelism is also considered.

The **full optimization** phase can go through a comprehensive set of optimization alternatives, which can make it time-consuming, especially if a query plan was not found in any preceding phase because phase two must produce a plan.

The timeout defined in the *Quick plan* section is the only condition that limits searching for a good-enough plan during full optimization. If a query plan was found before the timeout is hit, the execution plan will store information under the **Reason For Early Termination Of Statement Optimization** property about the outcome of the optimization stage, in this case showing the value **Good Enough Plan Found** value.

If the timeout is hit, the Query Optimizer will fall back on the lowest cost plan found so far. The execution plan will still store information under the **Reason For Early Termination Of Statement Optimization** property, in this case showing the value **Time Out**.

This property can be seen in the following example of a query executed in the **AdventureWorks** sample database :

```
SELECT pp.FirstName, pp.LastName, pa.AddressLine1,
    pa.City, pa.PostalCode
FROM Person.Address AS pa
INNER JOIN Person.BusinessEntityAddress AS pbea
    ON pa.AddressID = pbea.AddressID
INNER JOIN Person.Person AS pp
    ON pbea.BusinessEntityID = pp.BusinessEntityID
WHERE pa.AddressID = 100;
```

See the following screenshot with the **Reason For Early Termination Of Statement Optimization** property:

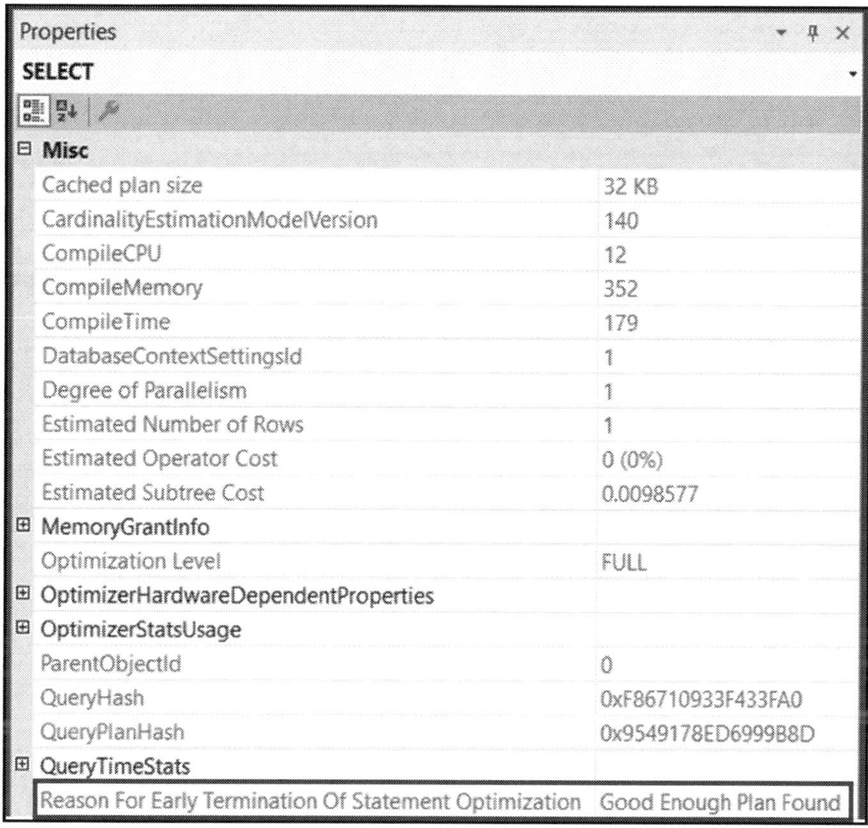

The following graphic represents the query optimization workflow as described in this chapter:

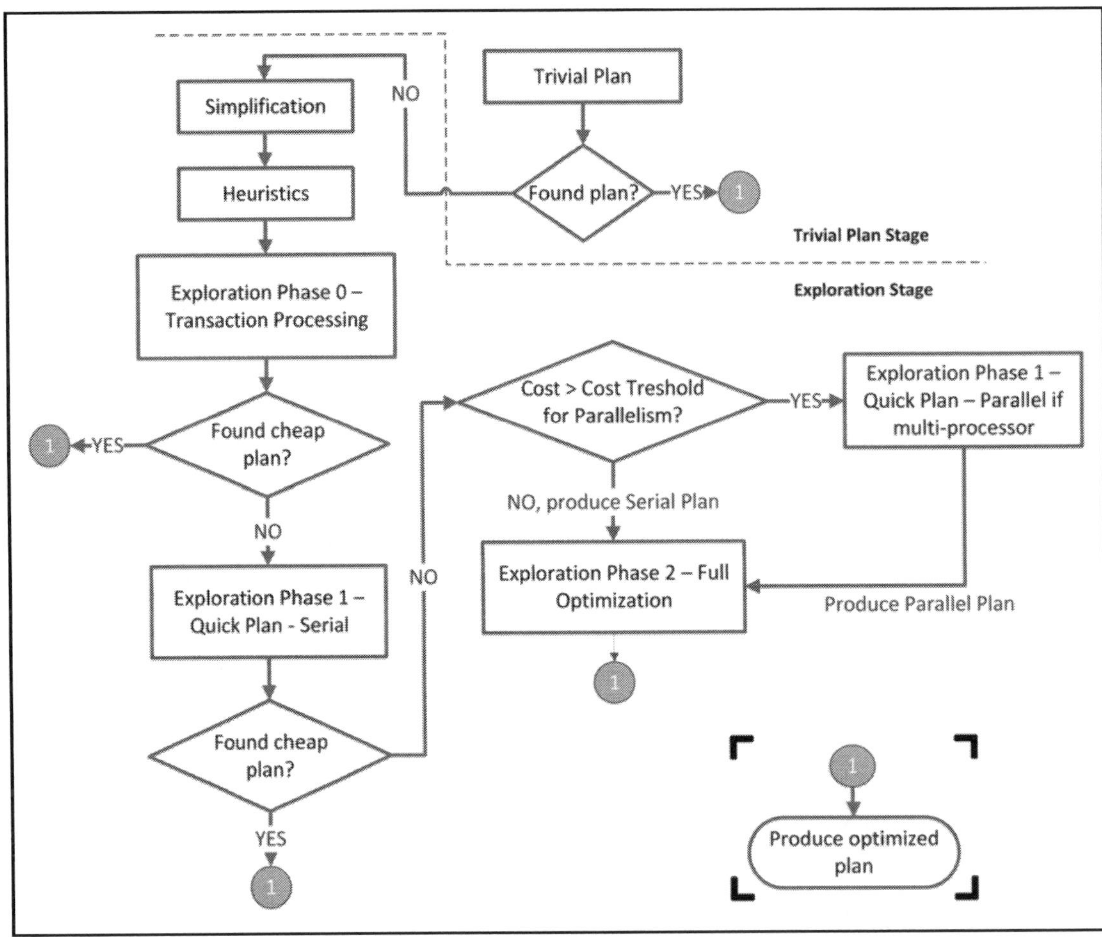

For reference, the undocumented dynamic management view **sys.dm_exec_query_optimizer_info** exposes some interesting statistics gathered by Query Optimizer such as the number of optimizations that have been evaluated, as well as the drill-down of optimizations per stage, or the number of optimization-affecting hints have been used.

Knobs for query optimization

As advanced as the query optimization process is, inefficient plans are still a possibility, which is why a database developer can use hints in the T-SQL statement and guide the Query Optimizer toward producing an intended plan. There are several classes of thoroughly-documented query hints that affect query optimization, and it is important to call out a few that can be useful when troubleshooting a query performance issue, some of which we will use in upcoming chapters.

Keep in mind that hints force certain behaviors with T-SQL statement optimization and execution. Microsoft recommends that hints are thoroughly tested and only used as a last resort. Hinted statements must be reviewed with every upgrade to a new major version to determine whether they are still needed, as new versions may change behavior, rendering the hint unnecessary or even harmful.

Let's look at some available hints for the Query Optimizer:

- **FORCE ORDER**: This is a hint that will prevent any join-reordering optimizations and has a tangible impact on the query optimization process. When joining tables or views, we discussed in the *Quick plan* section how join reordering is driven by the goal of reducing row count flowing through the operators in a query plan as early as possible. There are edge cases however, where join reordering may negatively affect the search for a good-enough plan, especially when estimations are based on skewed or outdated statistics. If the developer knows that the join order, such as it was written in the T-SQL statement, should be efficient enough, because the smaller tables are already used upfront to limit the row count for subsequent table joins, then testing the use of this hint may yield good results in such scenarios.
- **MAXDOP**: This hint overrides the system-wide **Max Degree of Parallelism (MAXDOP)**. Depending on its setting, this hint can affect parallel plan eligibility. For example, if a query has excessive waits on parallelism, using the **MAXDOP** hint to lower or remove parallelism may be a valid option.

- **NOEXPAND**: This hint directs the Query Optimizer to skip access to underlying tables when evaluating an indexed view as a possible substitute for part of a query. When the **NOEXPAND** hint is present, the Query Optimizer will use the view as if it were a table with a clustered index, including automatically creating statistics if needed. For example, if a query uses an indexed view that is being expanded by the Query Optimizer and this results in an inefficient query plan, the a developer can include the **NOEXPAND** hint to make the Query Optimizer forcibly evaluate the use of an index on a view. Note that Azure SQL Database, while sharing the exact same database engine code, doesn't require this hint to automatically use indexed views.
- **USE HINT**: This hint is not a single hint, like the other query hints, but rather a new class of hints introduced in SQL Server 2016. Its goal is to provide knobs to purposefully guide the Query Optimizer and query execution toward an intended outcome set by the developer. Every version of SQL Server since 2016 has introduced new **USE HINT** hints, and the list of supported hints can be accessed using the dynamic management view: **sys.dm_exec_valid_use_hints**. Hints included here can change some Query Optimizer model assumptions, disable certain default behaviors, or even force the entire Query Optimizer to behave as it would under a given database compatibility level. There are many uses for these hints, depending on the query performance troubleshooting scenario that database professionals may face, and we will look further into some of these in upcoming chapters. In `Chapter 13`, *Managing Optimizer Changes with the Query Tuning Assistant*, we will also cover a tool that can be used to discover such hints.

Summary

We explored the internals of SQL Server query optimization and defined many important concepts that any database professional who writes T-SQL queries will keep coming back to, especially when troubleshooting query performance issues. The CE is a fundamental part of SQL Server's Query Optimizer; knowing how it uses statistics, and the importance of keeping updated and relevant statistics for the overall query optimization process, empowers database professionals to write good queries—queries that both drive and leverage good database schema designs. But also, understanding the main estimation model assumptions allows us to account for these when writing queries and to avoid pitfalls that hurt query performance. We will see these pitfalls in much more detail in `Chapter 6`, *Easily-Identified T-SQL Anti-Patterns*, and `Chapter 7`, *Discovering T-SQL Anti-Patterns in Depth*.

If, at the end of the optimization process, we still have a plan that is perceived to be inefficient, some avenues of investigation can help us determine the potential reasons for this inefficiency:

- Is it a bad CE? Analyze the execution plan to find the ratio between estimated and actual rows in costly operators. Perhaps the statistics are stalled and need to be updated?
- Is it a parameter-sensitive plan? Is it a dynamic unparameterized T-SQL statement? Or perhaps parameter-sniffing has caused a skewed query plan? The importance of parameters was discussed in `Chapter 2`, *Understanding Query Processing*, in the *The importance of parameters* section.
- Is it an inadequate physical database design? Are there missing indexes? Are data types for keys inadequate, thus leading to unwarranted conversions that affect estimations? Is referential integrity enforced by triggers instead of indexed foreign keys?

These are some of the aspects we must investigate as a potential source of plan inefficiency. In the next chapter, we will learn how to identify these inefficiencies by investigating the various aspects of query execution plans.

2
Section 2: Dos and Donts of T-SQL

This section serves as an introduction to query execution plans and how to leverage them for query troubleshooting, basic guidelines for writing efficient queries, and common T-SQL query patterns and anti-patterns.

The following chapters are included in this section:

- `Chapter 4`, *Exploring Query Execution Plans*
- `Chapter 5`, *Writing Elegant T-SQL Query*
- `Chapter 6`, *Easily Identified T-SQL Anti-Patterns*
- `Chapter 7`, *Discovering T-SQL Anti-Patterns in Depth*

4
Exploring Query Execution Plans

In the previous chapters, we learned how to construct a T-SQL query, how SQL Server processes a query, and how the query is optimized, which results in an execution plan that can be cached and reused by subsequent query executions. Now that we understand the steps SQL Server follows to produce a plan and execute a query, we can investigate an execution plan to examine the results of this process and begin analyzing how we can improve the performance of our queries.

Query execution plans are often referred to as a **showplan**, which is a textual, XML, or graphical representation of the plan.

Think of a query execution plan as a map that provides information on the physical operators that implement the logical operations discussed in `Chapter 1`, *Anatomy of a Query*, as well as the execution context for that query, which provides information about the system on which the query was executed. Each physical operator is identified in the plan with a unique node ID.

So far, we've used the terms **query plan** and **query execution plan** interchangeably. However, in SQL Server, there is the notion of an **actual plan** and an **estimated plan**. These differ only in the fact the **actual plan** has runtime data collected during actual execution (hence query execution plan), whereas the **estimated plan** is the output of the Query Optimizer that is put in the plan cache (hence query plan, without the execution moniker).

Going forward, we will refer to plans in a more precise fashion, depending on whether they have runtime data.

The estimated plan, known simply as a query plan, includes the following:

- Methods used to retrieve data from a table or indexed view
- Sequence of data-retrieval operations
- Order with which tables or indexed views are joined; refer to `Chapter 3`, *Mechanics of the Query Optimizer*, where we discussed join reordering
- Use of temporary structures in TempDB (worktables and workfiles)
- Estimated row counts, iterations, and costs from each step
- How data is aggregated

Additionally, an actual plan, also known as a **query execution plan**, includes the following:

- Use of parallelism
- Actual row counts and iterations
- Query execution warnings
- Query execution metrics, such as elapsed time, CPU time, presence of trace flags, memory usage, version of the CE, and top waits

Whether all this information is available or just a subset depends on the version of SQL Server on which the query execution plan was captured.

So, analyzing a query execution plan is a skill that allows database professionals to identify the following:

- High-cost operations in a single query or batch
- Indexing needs, such as identifying when a scan is better than a seek or vice versa
- Outdated statistics that no longer accurately portray underlying data distributions
- Unexpected large row counts being passed from operator to operator
- Query or schema modification needs, for example when a query references multiple levels of nested views; that is, views that reference views that reference views that reference common tables at all levels

With these skills, developers and query writers in general can visually analyze how queries they write actually perform beyond simply looking at elapsed time. For **database administrators (DBAs)**, these skills allow them to identify heavy hitters running in SQL Server that perhaps weren't a problem during development time, to analyze the queries and provide mitigations based on query execution plan analysis.

In this chapter, the following topics will be covered:

- Accessing a query plan
- Navigating a query plan
- Query plan operators of interest
- Query plan properties of interest

Accessing a query plan

To access the estimated plans, which are the direct result of the optimization process, we can use either T-SQL commands or graphical tools. For the examples shown in this chapter, we use **SQL Server Management Studio (SSMS)**.

For most users, query plans in text format are harder to read and analyze; therefore, we will use graphical query plan examples throughout the book.

The **SHOWPLAN_TEXT**, **SHOWPLAN_ALL**, and **SHOWPLAN_XML** commands provide text-based information on query plans with different degrees of detail. Using any of these commands means SQL Server will not execute the T-SQL statements, but show the query plan as produced by the Query Optimizer.

Take an example of a query that can be executed in the scope of the **AdventureWorks** sample database:

```
SELECT pp.FirstName, pp.LastName, pa.AddressLine1, pa.City, pa.PostalCode
FROM Person.Address AS pa
INNER JOIN Person.BusinessEntityAddress AS pbea ON pa.AddressID =
pbea.AddressID
INNER JOIN Person.Person AS pp ON pbea.BusinessEntityID =
pp.BusinessEntityID
WHERE pa.AddressID = 100;
```

Let's see what each of the following options provides in terms of query plan view:

- **SHOWPLAN_TEXT**: This option shows all the steps involved in processing the query, including the type of join that was used, the order in which tables are accessed, and the indexes used for each table:

```
StmtText
  |--Nested Loops(Inner Join)
       |--Clustered Index Seek(OBJECT:([AdventureWorks2016_EXT].[Person].[Address].[PK_Address_AddressID] AS [pa]), SEEK:([pa].[AddressID]=(100)) ORDERED FORW...
       |--Nested Loops(Inner Join, OUTER REFERENCES:([pbea].[BusinessEntityID]))
            |--Index Seek(OBJECT:([AdventureWorks2016_EXT].[Person].[BusinessEntityAddress].[IX_BusinessEntityAddress_AddressID] AS [pbea]), SEEK:([pbea].[AddressID]=...
            |--Clustered Index Seek(OBJECT:([AdventureWorks2016_EXT].[Person].[Person].[PK_Person_BusinessEntityID] AS [pp]), SEEK:([pp].[BusinessEntityID]=[Adventure...
```

- **SHOWPLAN_ALL**: This option shows the same estimated plan as **SHOWPLAN_TEXT**. This option represents a text output tree, but adds details on each of the physical operations that would be executed, such as the estimated size of the result rows, the estimated CPU time, and the total cost estimations. Notice the amount of information produced:

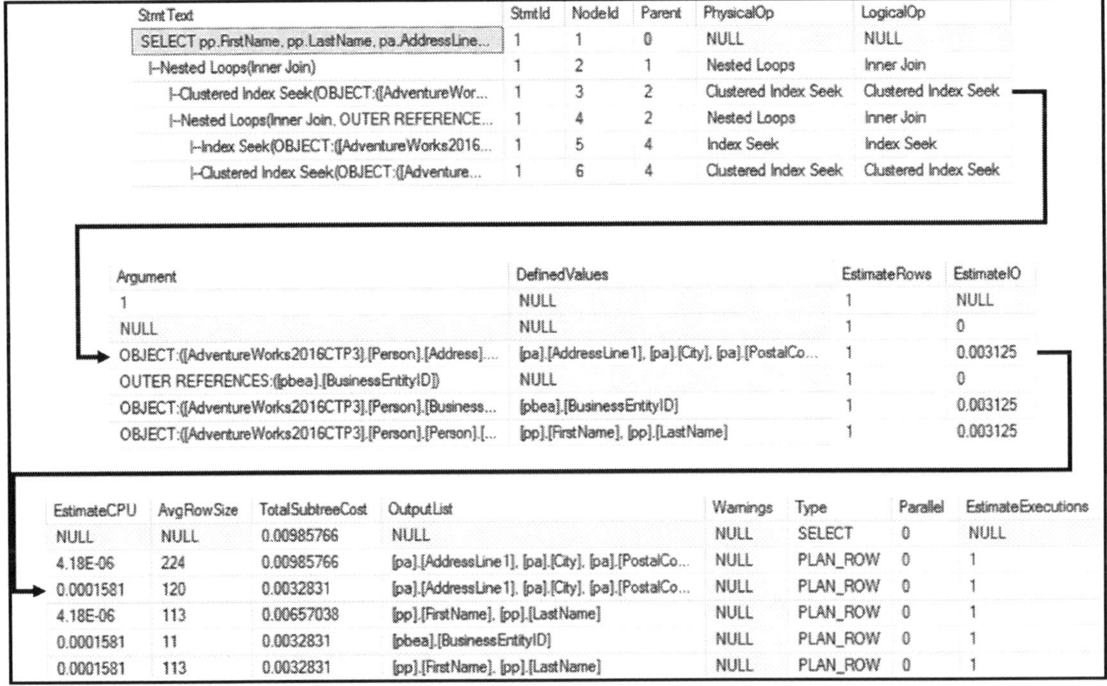

<table>
<tr><th>StmtText</th><th>StmtId</th><th>NodeId</th><th>Parent</th><th>PhysicalOp</th><th>LogicalOp</th></tr>
<tr><td>SELECT pp.FirstName, pp.LastName, pa.AddressLine...</td><td>1</td><td>1</td><td>0</td><td>NULL</td><td>NULL</td></tr>
<tr><td>|--Nested Loops(Inner Join)</td><td>1</td><td>2</td><td>1</td><td>Nested Loops</td><td>Inner Join</td></tr>
<tr><td>|--Clustered Index Seek(OBJECT:([AdventureWor...</td><td>1</td><td>3</td><td>2</td><td>Clustered Index Seek</td><td>Clustered Index Seek</td></tr>
<tr><td>|--Nested Loops(Inner Join, OUTER REFERENCE...</td><td>1</td><td>4</td><td>2</td><td>Nested Loops</td><td>Inner Join</td></tr>
<tr><td>|--Index Seek(OBJECT:([AdventureWorks2016...</td><td>1</td><td>5</td><td>4</td><td>Index Seek</td><td>Index Seek</td></tr>
<tr><td>|--Clustered Index Seek(OBJECT:([Adventure...</td><td>1</td><td>6</td><td>4</td><td>Clustered Index Seek</td><td>Clustered Index Seek</td></tr>
</table>

Argument	DefinedValues	EstimateRows	EstimateIO
1	NULL	1	NULL
NULL	NULL	1	0
OBJECT:([AdventureWorks2016CTP3].[Person].[Address]....	[pa].[AddressLine1], [pa].[City], [pa].[PostalCo...	1	0.003125
OUTER REFERENCES:([pbea].[BusinessEntityID])	NULL	1	0
OBJECT:([AdventureWorks2016CTP3].[Person].[Business...	[pbea].[BusinessEntityID]	1	0.003125
OBJECT:([AdventureWorks2016CTP3].[Person].[Person].[...	[pp].[FirstName], [pp].[LastName]	1	0.003125

EstimateCPU	AvgRowSize	TotalSubtreeCost	OutputList	Warnings	Type	Parallel	EstimateExecutions
NULL	NULL	0.00985766	NULL	NULL	SELECT	0	NULL
4.18E-06	224	0.00985766	[pa].[AddressLine1], [pa].[City], [pa].[PostalCo...	NULL	PLAN_ROW	0	1
0.0001581	120	0.0032831	[pa].[AddressLine1], [pa].[City], [pa].[PostalCo...	NULL	PLAN_ROW	0	1
4.18E-06	113	0.00657038	[pp].[FirstName], [pp].[LastName]	NULL	PLAN_ROW	0	1
0.0001581	11	0.0032831	[pbea].[BusinessEntityID]	NULL	PLAN_ROW	0	1
0.0001581	113	0.0032831	[pp].[FirstName], [pp].[LastName]	NULL	PLAN_ROW	0	1

- **SHOWPLAN_XML**: This option produces the same estimated plan but as an XML output tree:

Microsoft SQL Server 2005 XML Showplan
`<ShowPlanXML xmlns="http://schemas.microsoft.com/sqlserver/2004/07/showplan" Version="1.481" Build="14.0.3045.14"><BatchSequence><Batch><Statemen...`

Because it is generated as a link when used in SSMS, it can be interpreted by SSMS as a graphical estimated plan, and clicking the link will display this graphical plan:

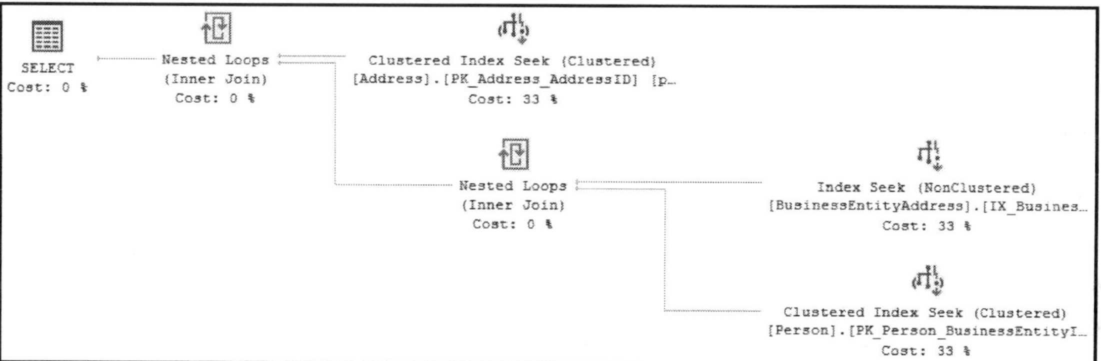

Notice that because it is an estimated plan, the arrows are all the same width. This is because there's no actual data movement between operators given that this plan was not executed. To access all the properties returned by **SHOWPLAN_ALL**, plus many more, right-click the **SELECT** operator and click on **Properties**. We will see these properties in greater detail in the *Query plan properties of interest* section.

SHOWPLAN_XML is the option is used by SSMS when the **Display Estimated Execution Plan (CTRL+L)** button is clicked:

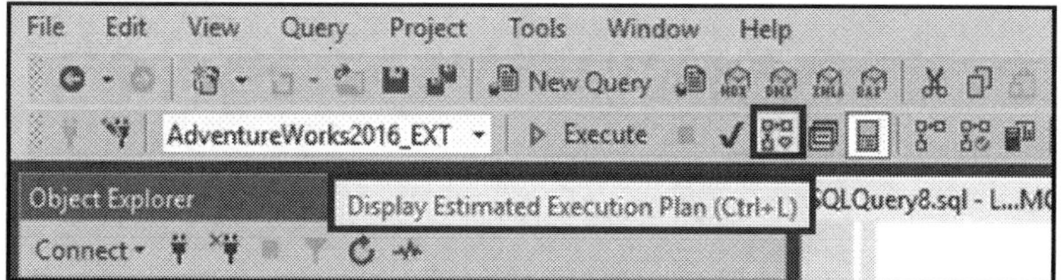

To access the actual plans, which are the optimized plans after being executed, we can again use either T-SQL commands or graphical tools. The **STATISTICS PROFILE** and **STATISTICS XML** commands provide text-based information on query plans with different degrees of detail. Using either of these commands means SQL Server will execute the T-SQL statements, and generate the actual plan, or query execution plan.

- **STATISTICS PROFILE**: This option shows the same plan as **SHOWPLAN_ALL**, incremented with the actual rows and executes to display an actual plan, or a query execution plan:

Rows	Executes	StmtText	StmtId	NodeId	Parent	PhysicalOp	LogicalOp
1	1	SELECT pp.FirstName, pp.LastName, pa.AddressLine...	1	1	0	NULL	NULL
1	1	|--Nested Loops(Inner Join)	1	2	1	Nested Loops	Inner Join
1	1	|--Clustered Index Seek(OBJECT:([AdventureWor...	1	3	2	Clustered Index Seek	Clustered Index Seek
1	1	|--Nested Loops(Inner Join, OUTER REFERENC...	1	4	2	Nested Loops	Inner Join
1	1	|--Index Seek(OBJECT:([AdventureWorks2016...	1	5	4	Index Seek	Index Seek
1	1	|--Clustered Index Seek(OBJECT:([Adventure...	1	6	4	Clustered Index Seek	Clustered Index Seek

Argument	DefinedValues	EstimateRows	EstimateIO
NULL	NULL	1	NULL
NULL	NULL	1	0
OBJECT:([AdventureWorks2016CTP3].[Person].[Addre...	[pa].[AddressLine1], [pa].[City], [pa].[PostalCo...	1	0.003125
OUTER REFERENCES:([pbea].[BusinessEntityID])	NULL	1	0
OBJECT:([AdventureWorks2016CTP3].[Person].[Busin...	[pbea].[BusinessEntityID]	1	0.003125
OBJECT:([AdventureWorks2016CTP3].[Person].[Perso...	[pp].[FirstName], [pp].[LastName]	1	0.003125

EstimateCPU	AvgRowSize	TotalSubtreeCost	OutputList	Warnings	Type	Parallel	EstimateExecutions
NULL	NULL	0.00985766	NULL	NULL	SELECT	0	NULL
4.18E-06	224	0.00985766	[pa].[AddressLine1], [pa].[City], [pa].[PostalCo...	NULL	PLAN_ROW	0	1
0.0001581	120	0.0032831	[pa].[AddressLine1], [pa].[City], [pa].[PostalCo...	NULL	PLAN_ROW	0	1
4.18E-06	113	0.00657038	[pp].[FirstName], [pp].[LastName]	NULL	PLAN_ROW	0	1
0.0001581	11	0.0032831	[pbea].[BusinessEntityID]	NULL	PLAN_ROW	0	1
0.0001581	113	0.0032831	[pp].[FirstName], [pp].[LastName]	NULL	PLAN_ROW	0	1

- **STATISTICS XML**: This option is the actual plan counterpart of **SHOWPLAN_XML**. In the following screenshot, we see what appears to be the same output as **SHOWPLAN_XML**:

Microsoft SQL Server 2005 XML Showplan
<ShowPlanXML xmlns="http://schemas.microsoft.com/sqlserver/2004/07/showplan" Version="1.481" Build="14.0.3045.14"><BatchSequence><Batch><Statemen...

However, expanding the XML (or if using SSMS, clicking on the link), we see we have the actual plan, or the query execution plan:

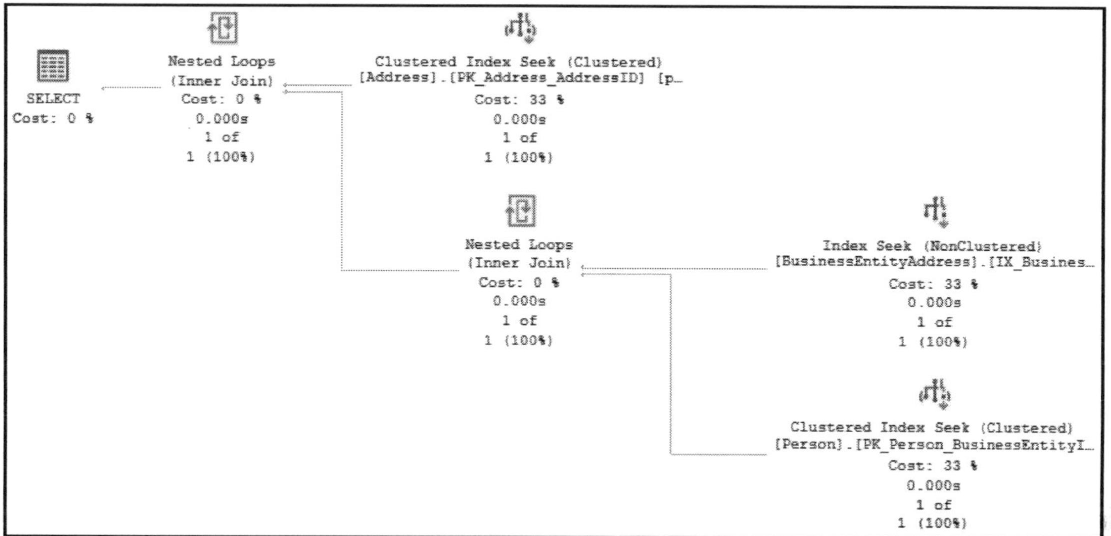

STATISTICS XML is the option used by SSMS when the **Display Actual Execution Plan (CTRL+M)** button is clicked:

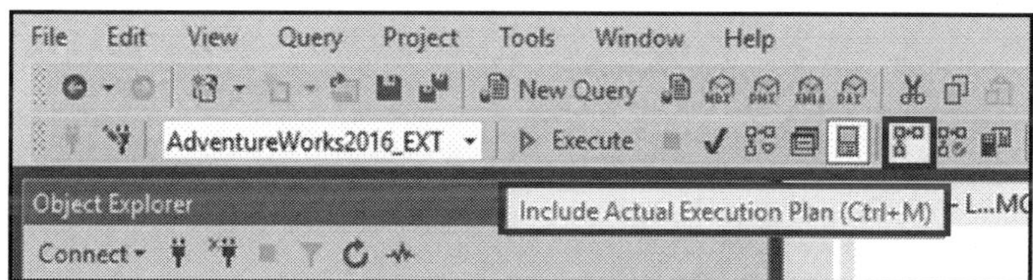

To access all the properties already seen with **SHOWPLAN_XML** incremented with runtime statistics and warnings (if any), right-click the **SELECT** operator and click on **Properties**. Again, we will see these properties in greater detail in the *Query plan properties of interest* section.

Navigating a query plan

So far, we have mentioned query execution plans, and have even shown some simple examples to illustrate some points in `Chapter 3`, *Mechanics of the Query Optimizer*. However, it is important for any database professional to understand how to read and analyze a query execution plan as a way to visually identify positive changes in a plan shape. The remaining chapters in this book will show query execution plans in more detail for different scenarios of T-SQL patterns and anti-patterns.

Query plans are like trees, where each join branch can represent an entirely separate query.

To understand how to navigate a showplan or query plan, let's use a practical example of a query executed in the **AdventureWorks** sample database:

```
SELECT p.Title +' '+ p.FirstName +' '+ p.LastName AS FullName,
       c.AccountNumber, s.Name AS StoreName
FROM Person.Person p
INNER JOIN Sales.Customer c ON c.PersonID = p.BusinessEntityID
INNER JOIN Sales.Store s ON s.BusinessEntityID = c.StoreID
WHERE p.LastName = 'Koski';
```

This query generates the execution plan seen in the following screenshot. For any graphical query execution plan, the flow of data is read from right to left and top to bottom:

1. Result sets 1 and 2 are joined using a **Nested Loops** join, creating result set 3.
2. Result sets 3 and 4 are joined using a **Hash Match** join, creating result set 5.
3. Result sets 5 and 6 are joined using a Nested Loops join, creating the result set for the **SELECT** clause:

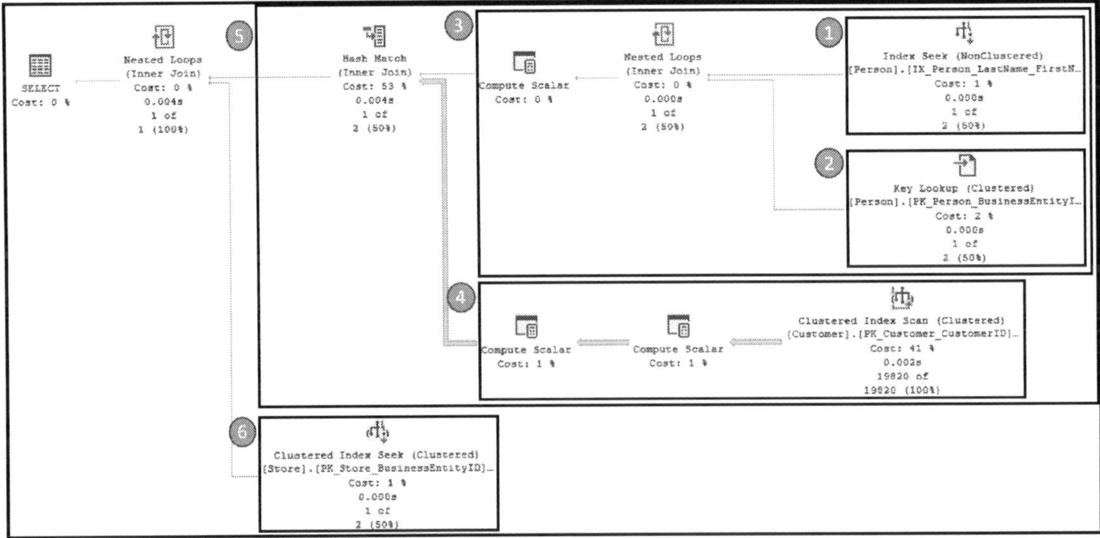

In an actual plan, the width of the arrows provides an indication of the number of rows flowing through each operator, such as the thicker arrow seen coming from **Clustered Index Scan** on table **Customer** (as seen in the following region of the preceding plan). This can often be a clue to high resource usage and a potential hot-spot in the plan:

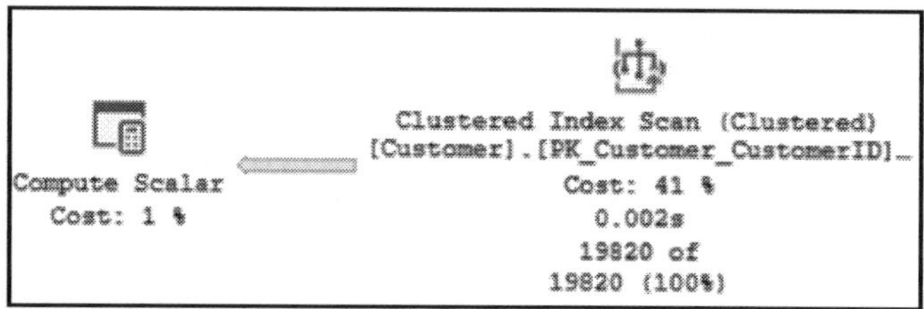

Also notice how in the latest versions of SQL Server it becomes easier to distinguish an actual plan from an estimated plan. In an actual plan, or query execution plan, each operator has information about the elapsed execution time and a comparison of estimated and actual number of rows flowing through the operator. In the previous **Clustered Index Scan**, we see this operator read 19,820 rows of 19,820 estimated rows, with a 100 percent match and a perfect estimation.

Recent versions of SSMS have greatly improved the navigation experience of a graphical query plan: click + hold your mouse button anywhere inside the **Execution Plan** tab, and then drag your mouse to quickly navigate to the query plan. Or use *Ctrl* + mouse wheel to zoom in and out easily.

For joins, how the showplan is read depends on the type of physical join; the top represents the outer table for **Nested Loops** and the build table for a hash; the bottom represents the inner table for the **Nested Loops** and the probe table for the **Hash Match**. Result sets are created from each join pair, which is then passed to the next join. We will discuss join types, seeks, lookups, and other operators in the *Query plan operators of interest* section.

The following screenshot shows a **Nested Loops** join with an **Index Seek** on the **Person** table as the outer table, and the **Key Lookup** on the **Person** table as the inner table:

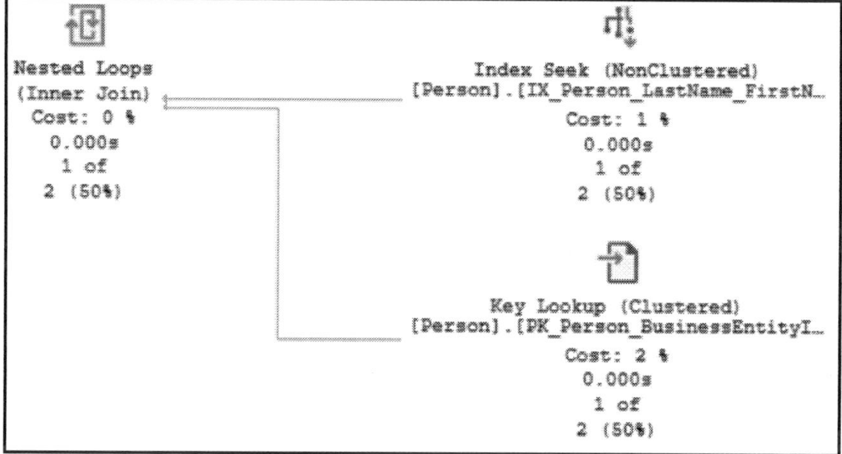

In the preceding screenshot, we see the **Index Seek** operator read 1 row of 2 estimated rows, with a 50% match and a skewed estimation.

If the order of magnitude between estimated rows and actual rows is large, this means the Query Optimizer may not have had good statistics on the table's data distribution during query optimization. Usually, the first reaction to such a scenario is to update the relevant statistics on the table and verify whether estimations improved to be a near 100% match.

For any plan captured as text (actual or estimated), note that these are read top to bottom, with the |-- characters indicating the nesting levels of the tree.

For the same query we used to generate the graphical plan, **STATISTICS PROFILE** shows the following query tree:

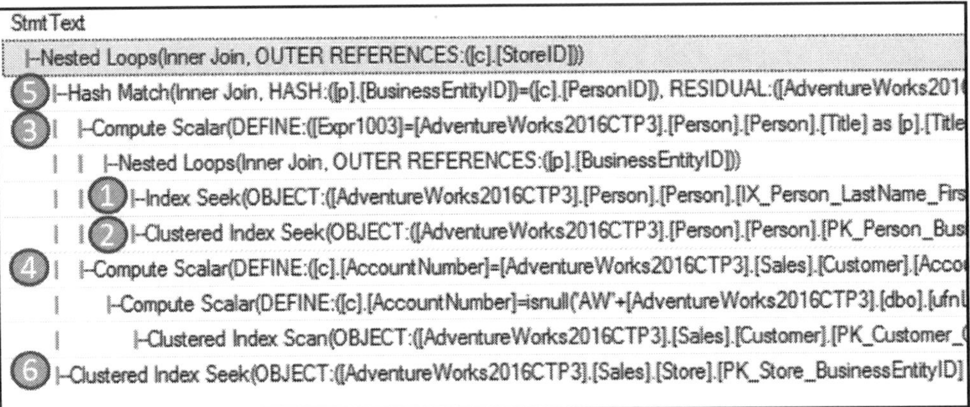

For this query's plan, we apply the same approach to read the plan:

1. Result sets 1 and 2 are joined using a **Nested Loops** join, creating result set 3.
2. Result sets 3 and 4 are joined using a **Hash Match** join, creating result set 5.
3. Result sets 5 and 6 are joined using a **Nested Loops** join.

Query plan operators of interest

The different icons that are visible in a query execution plan are called operators. **Logical** operators describe a relational operation, such as, **INNER JOIN**. **Physical** operators implement the logical operation with a specific algorithm. So, when we examine a query plan, we are looking at physical operators.

Each physical operator represents a task that needs to be performed to complete the query, such as accessing data with a seek or a scan, joining data with a **Hash Match** or a **Nested Loops**, and sorting data. Some operators are especially relevant to understand while writing T-SQL that scales well. We will look at these operators, understand what they do, how they implement the physical operation behind the logical operation in T-SQL statements, and become familiar with aspects that will be important in the upcoming chapters where we explore T-SQL patterns and anti-patterns.

Blocking versus non-blocking operators

We can think of an execution plan as a pipeline. Data from one operator flows to the next operator from right to left. A blocking operator is one where the entire input must be consumed, and the operation completed before the first row can be output to the next operator. An example of a blocking operator is a sort. When data is sorted, it is impossible to know what the first-row output by the operator should be until the entire sort is complete. A non-blocking operator is one where data may be output to the next operator in the plan before the operation is complete. When there are no blocking operators in a plan, data can flow through the plan uninterrupted, and results will be returned from the query before execution is complete. With a blocking operator, anything past that operator in the query cannot be processed until the blocking operator is complete, which typically means that no results will be returned to the client until the entire query is complete.

Data-access operators

Data-access operators are used to retrieve data from tables and indexes in SQL Server. Rowstore is the traditional storage mechanism for most **Relational Database Management Systems (RDBMS)**. In a rowstore index, each page of data contains all the columns for one or more rows of data in the table, and so the entire row is stored contiguously across all columns. There are two types of rowstore indexes in SQL Server: clustered and non-clustered. Both index types are stored as a **B+Tree** data structure, but clustered indexes contain the entire data row at the leaf level, while non-clustered indexes contain only the index columns and a pointer to the data row.

Instead of treating all nodes equal like a B-Tree, the B+Tree structure has two types of nodes. The lowest level nodes, also called leaf nodes, hold the actual data. All other nodes including the root node only hold the key values and pointers to the next nodes. B+Trees are self-balancing tree data structures that tend to be wide rather than tall, although the specific structure depends on the definition of the index. We will discuss index structures in more detail later in this section.

There are two different ways to access data in an index: a seek or a scan. A seek is used when a predicate present in the query matches the key(s) of an index. In this case, SQL Server can use the values of the predicate to limit the amount of data that must be searched by following the pointers within the index from the root to the leaf page to locate matching rows. If the predicate can't be used for some reason, then an index may be scanned. In this case, SQL Server starts at the root of the index and reads down to the leaf level, then reads all the leaf-level pages of the index, searching for the required rows to return.

The following diagram shows an example of an index structure in SQL Server with a **Seek** versus a **Scan** operation:

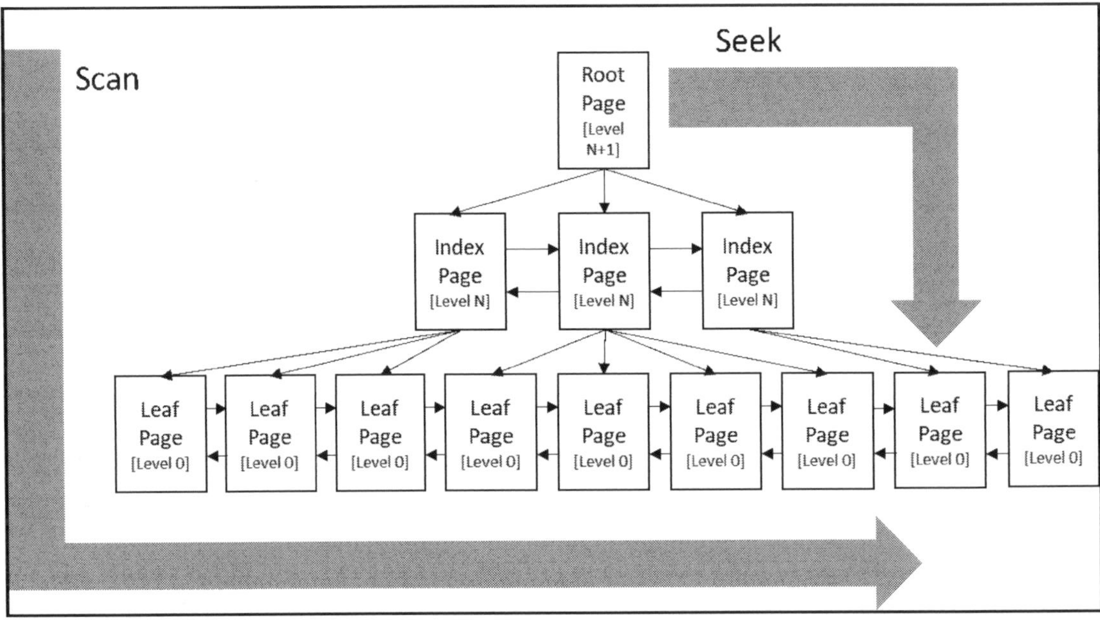

As mentioned, this applies to both clustered and non-clustered indexes, the only difference is with a clustered index, the leaf level contains the actual data pages, while the non-clustered index contains index pages with pointers to the data pages. We will discuss indexes in more detail in the *Basic index guidelines* section of `Chapter 5`, *Writing Elegant T-SQL Queries*.

If a table does not have a clustered index, it is stored as a heap data structure. Heaps do not have the organizational structure that a B+Tree has, they are essentially just a collection of pages. The only way to access a heap is by scanning it. Since there is no structure to the heap, the only way to find all the pages that belong to a heap is to scan special metadata pages called **Index Allocation Map (IAM)** pages. Each table or index in SQL Server has at least one IAM page that lists out all the pages that belong to that object. If the object is large enough, there may be more than one IAM page, in which case the first IAM page will contain a pointer to the next IAM page, and so on.

This following diagram shows an example of a scan operation on a heap:

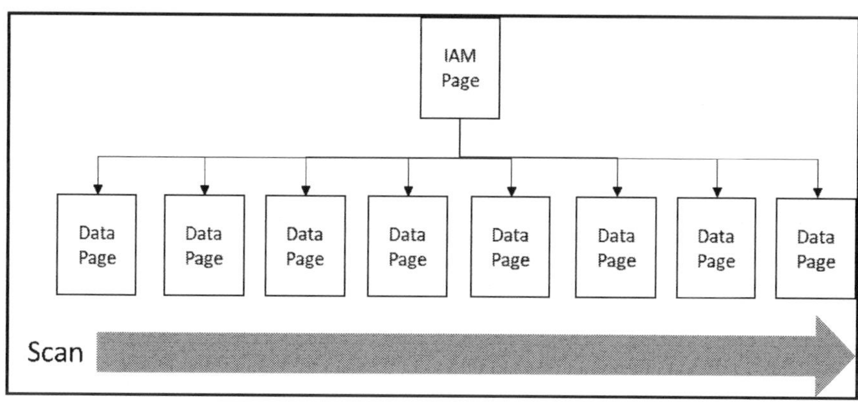

During optimization, SQL Server will decide how to access the data required to satisfy the query based on the columns referenced in the query, the available indexes, and the cost of the different operations using the estimated cardinality as a cost basis. On the surface, it may seem like a scan is more expensive than a seek, but depending on how many rows are returned, it may be more efficient to scan.

As we discussed in `Chapter 3`, *Mechanics of the Query Optimizer*, SQL Server uses statistics along with some basic assumptions to estimate cardinality. If the estimation is off by a large amount, SQL Server may choose an inefficient operator to access the data. If creating appropriate indexes and updating statistics does not correct the issue, it's possible that an incorrect assumption is causing the cardinality estimate to be off. In this case, employing a hint may be the easiest way to improve the query.

The following hints are helpful in influencing the query optimizer to choose a more efficient data-access operator:

- **INDEX (index_name)**: This hint forces SQL Server to use an index that we specify.
- **FORCESEEK (index_name (column_name))**: This hint forces SQL Server to perform a seek operation. Optionally, we can specify the index and columns to be used in the seek. It can also be combined with the **INDEX** hint in order to supply an index for the seek without specifying the columns.
- **FORCESCAN**: This hint forces SQL Server to perform a scan operation. It can also be combined with the **INDEX** hint to force a scan of a specific index.

Table Scan

The **Table Scan** operator represents a scan operation on a heap. A table scan is a non-blocking operator that reads every page of the object and scans them for the desired rows. As illustrated in the preceding screenshot, a heap does not have any order or structure, so the rows will be output in a random order.

Here is an example of a query executed in the **AdventureWorks** sample database with a **Table Scan** operator:

```
SELECT * FROM DatabaseLog;
```

The query generates the following execution plan:

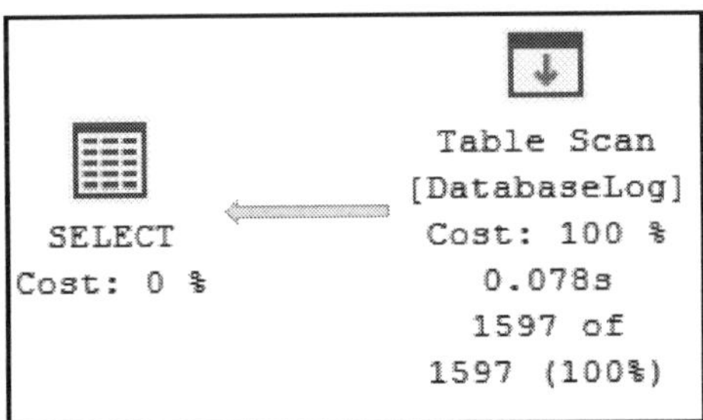

While a table scan may generate a large amount of I/O depending on the size of the table, the operator itself does not require a large amount of additional memory or CPU, the cost is generally based on the cost of the I/O.

Clustered Index Scan

The **Clustered Index Scan** operator is non-blocking and represents a scan operation on a clustered index. Remember that a clustered index contains the data pages of the table at the leaf level, so this is effectively a table scan. Because the clustered index is organized into a tree structure, the data is logically ordered by the keys of the index. This doesn't necessarily mean the data will be returned in order; if no **ORDER BY** clause is specified in the query, the data may be returned in random order. If there is an **ORDER BY** in the query that matches the clustered index key or there is some other benefit to outputting the data in order, SQL Server may choose to do an ordered scan of the clustered index. This is helpful because it may prevent SQL Server from having to sort the data later, which can be an expensive operation. As with a table scan, the cost of a clustered index scan is generally based on the cost of the I/O generated, there is no additional memory or CPU required.

Here is an example of a query executed in the **AdventureWorks** sample database with a **Clustered Index Scan** operator:

```
SELECT * FROM Person.Person;
```

The query generates the following execution plan:

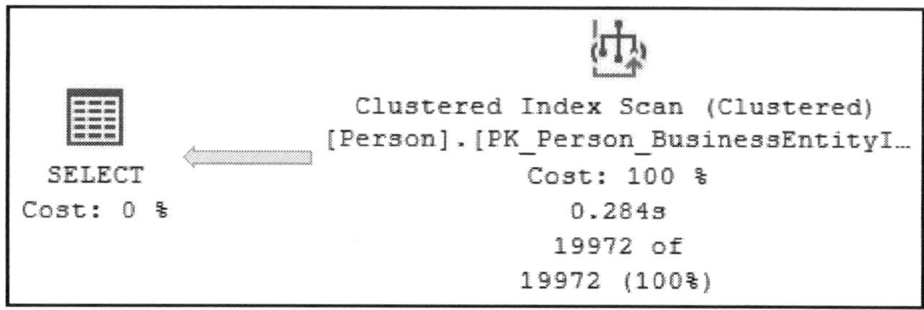

In this case, there was no **ORDER BY** clause in the query, so SQL Server performed an unordered scan. We can confirm this by looking at the properties of the operator, either by hovering over the icon with our mouse, or by right-clicking it and choosing **Properties** from the pop-up menu, as in the following screenshot:

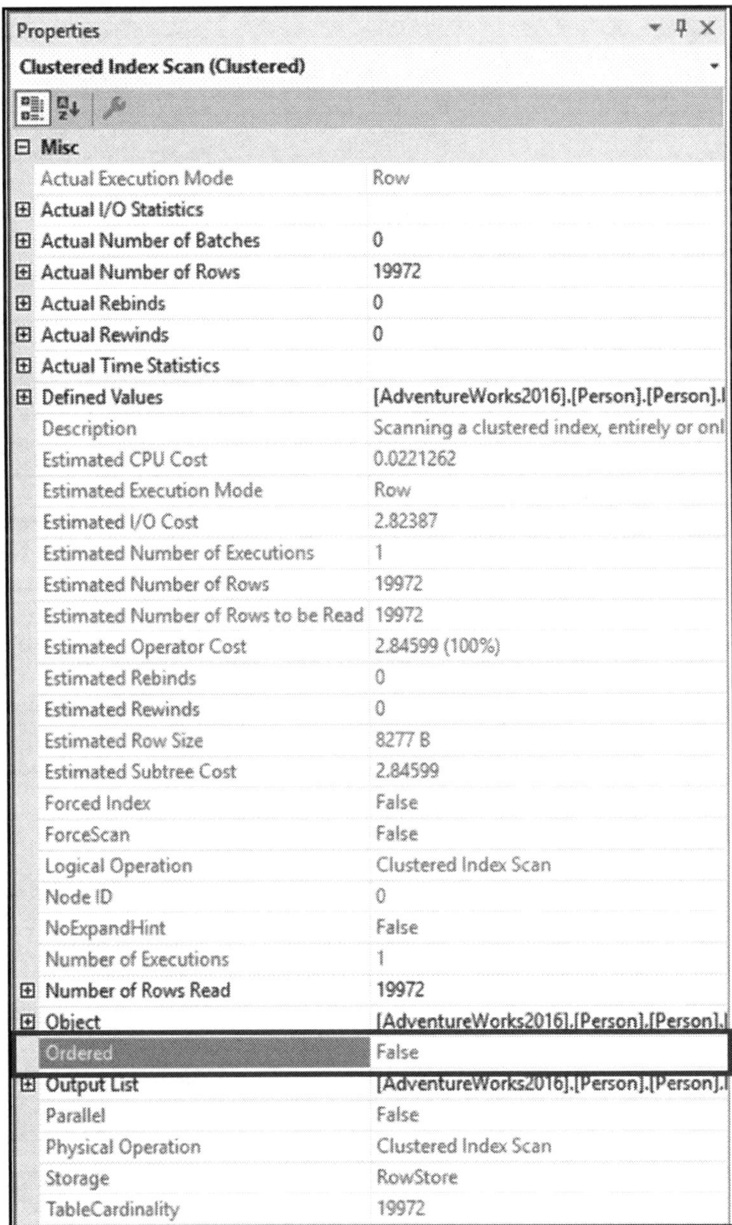

NonClustered Index Scan

A **NonClustered Index Scan** is effectively the same as a Clustered Index Scan. The difference is that the leaf level of a non-clustered index contains index pages rather than data pages, which means this is generally less I/O than a clustered index scan and is not analogous with a table scan.

The following is an example of a query executed in the **AdventureWorks** sample database with a NonClustered Index Scan:

```
SELECT LastName, FirstName
FROM Person.Person
WHERE FirstName = N'Andrew';
```

The query generates the following execution plan:

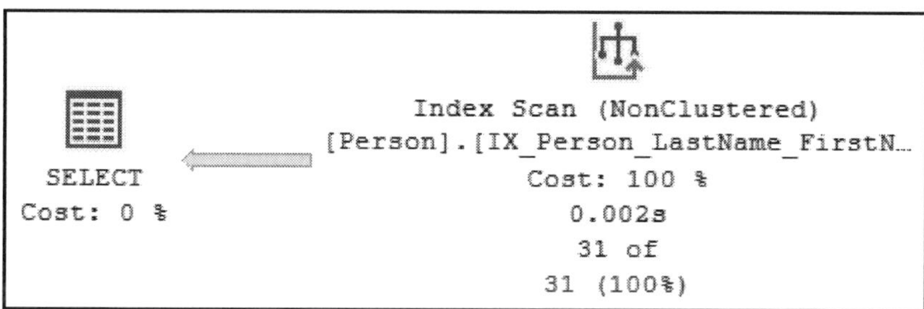

SQL Server will generally choose to do a non-clustered index scan when an index is present that contains all the columns in the query (also known as a covering index) but does not support the predicate. In this case, the index contains the **FirstName** column as a key column, but it is the second column in the index, so if we are searching for **FirstName** only, it cannot be used as a seek predicate in the index. This non-clustered index scan will be slightly cheaper than doing a clustered index scan because the non-clustered index is narrower (meaning it has less columns) and will take less I/O to scan.

You may have noticed that there is a *Missing Index Suggestion* in the execution plan in the previous example. This is generated when SQL Server would benefit from an index that is not present. Looking for missing index suggestions is one way to help optimize our queries. We'll be discussing more things to look for in execution plans in the *Query plan properties of interest* section of this chapter.

NonClustered Index Seek

A **NonClustered Index Seek** operator represents a seek operation against a non-clustered index. This is also a non-blocking operator, and again is based mainly on the cost of I/O, requiring no additional memory or CPU. An index seek is a quick way to locate rows that match a predicate in the **WHERE** clause of a query, if the keys of the index match the predicate.

The following example shows a query executed in the **AdventureWorks** sample database with a NonClustered Index Seek:

```
SELECT LastName, FirstName
FROM Person.Person
WHERE LastName = N'Maxwell';
```

The query generates the following execution plan:

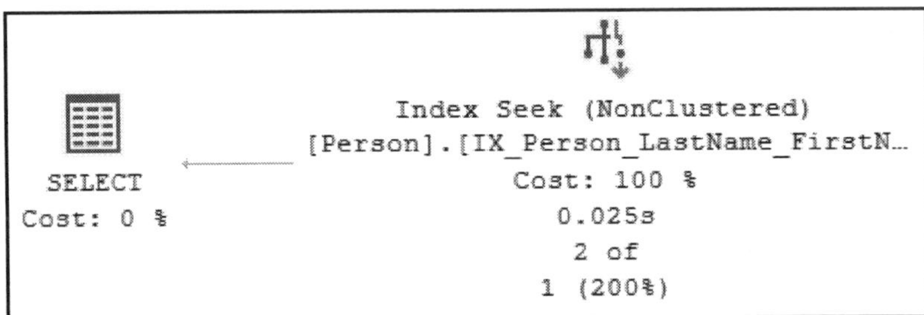

A NonClustered Index Seek operator may also be used to return a contiguous range of rows based on the keys of the index. This is referred to as a range scan. This is different from a non-clustered index scan in that not every row of the index is scanned, SQL Server uses the values in the predicate to search only the range of matching keys in the index. The only way to know whether an index seek is a singleton seek or a range scan is to look at the properties of the index, as seen in the following screenshot. If the seek predicate is a single value, it's a seek. If the seek predicate is a range of values, it's a range scan:

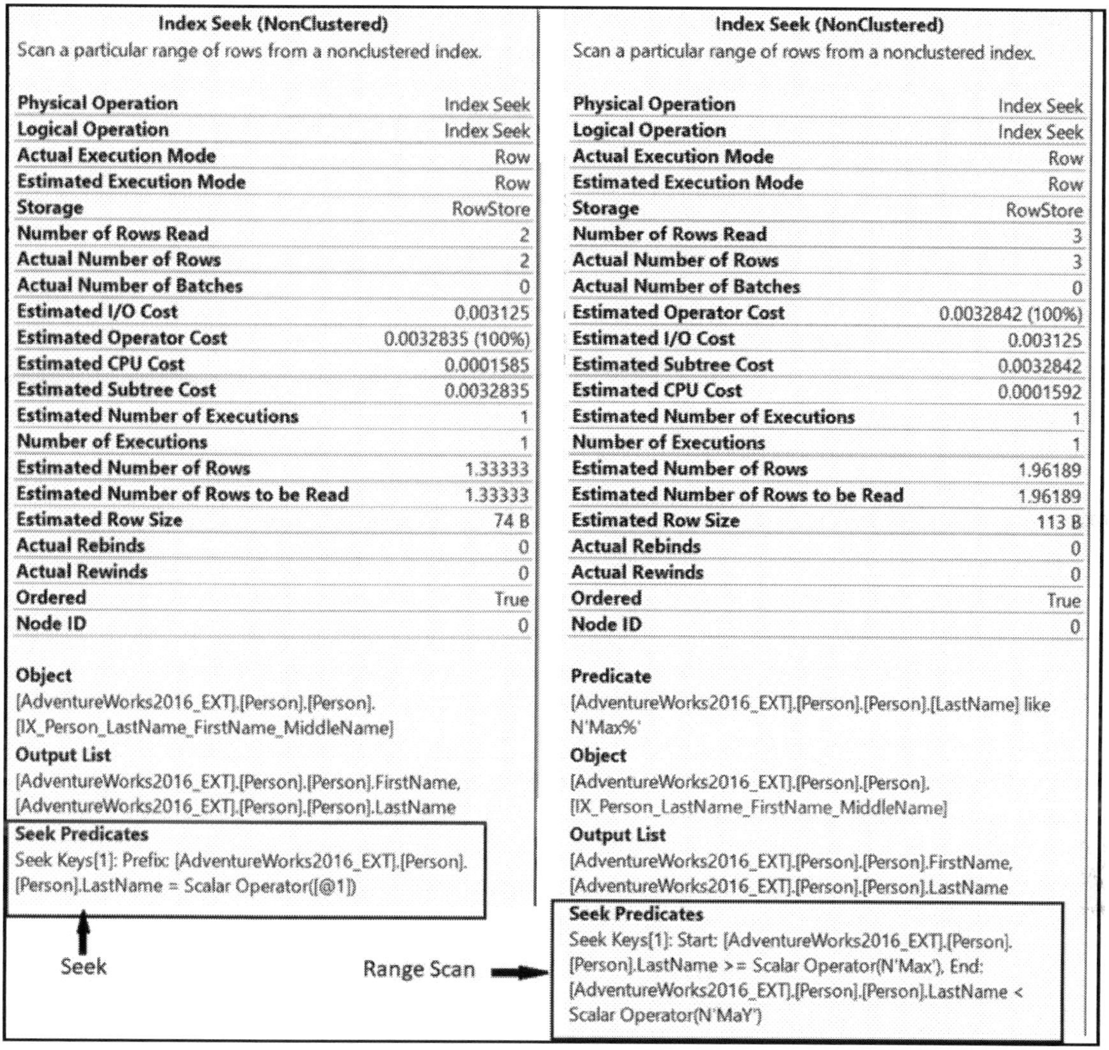

Index Seek (NonClustered)

Scan a particular range of rows from a nonclustered index.

Physical Operation	Index Seek
Logical Operation	Index Seek
Actual Execution Mode	Row
Estimated Execution Mode	Row
Storage	RowStore
Number of Rows Read	2
Actual Number of Rows	2
Actual Number of Batches	0
Estimated I/O Cost	0.003125
Estimated Operator Cost	0.0032835 (100%)
Estimated CPU Cost	0.0001585
Estimated Subtree Cost	0.0032835
Estimated Number of Executions	1
Number of Executions	1
Estimated Number of Rows	1.33333
Estimated Number of Rows to be Read	1.33333
Estimated Row Size	74 B
Actual Rebinds	0
Actual Rewinds	0
Ordered	True
Node ID	0

Object
[AdventureWorks2016_EXT].[Person].[Person].[IX_Person_LastName_FirstName_MiddleName]
Output List
[AdventureWorks2016_EXT].[Person].[Person].FirstName, [AdventureWorks2016_EXT].[Person].[Person].LastName
Seek Predicates
Seek Keys[1]: Prefix: [AdventureWorks2016_EXT].[Person].[Person].LastName = Scalar Operator([@1])

Seek

Index Seek (NonClustered)

Scan a particular range of rows from a nonclustered index.

Physical Operation	Index Seek
Logical Operation	Index Seek
Actual Execution Mode	Row
Estimated Execution Mode	Row
Storage	RowStore
Number of Rows Read	3
Actual Number of Rows	3
Actual Number of Batches	0
Estimated Operator Cost	0.0032842 (100%)
Estimated I/O Cost	0.003125
Estimated Subtree Cost	0.0032842
Estimated CPU Cost	0.0001592
Estimated Number of Executions	1
Number of Executions	1
Estimated Number of Rows	1.96189
Estimated Number of Rows to be Read	1.96189
Estimated Row Size	113 B
Actual Rebinds	0
Actual Rewinds	0
Ordered	True
Node ID	0

Predicate
[AdventureWorks2016_EXT].[Person].[Person].[LastName] like N'Max%'
Object
[AdventureWorks2016_EXT].[Person].[Person].[IX_Person_LastName_FirstName_MiddleName]
Output List
[AdventureWorks2016_EXT].[Person].[Person].FirstName, [AdventureWorks2016_EXT].[Person].[Person].LastName
Seek Predicates
Seek Keys[1]: Start: [AdventureWorks2016_EXT].[Person].[Person].LastName >= Scalar Operator(N'Max'), End: [AdventureWorks2016_EXT].[Person].[Person].LastName < Scalar Operator(N'MaY')

Range Scan

Clustered Index Seek

A **Clustered Index Seek** operator represents a seek operation against a clustered index. This is essentially the same as a NonClustered Index Seek operator, except that the leaf level contains data pages, so the entire row can be output in addition to the index columns.

The following example shows a query executed in the **AdventureWorks** sample database with a Clustered Index Seek operator:

```
SELECT LastName, FirstName
FROM Person.Person
WHERE BusinessEntityID = 5;
```

The query generates the following execution plan:

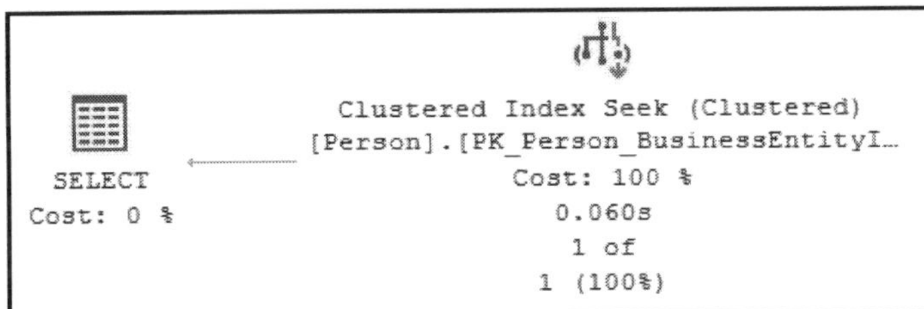

Lookups

When a non-clustered index is used to locate rows, only the index columns are present at the leaf level of the index. If there are additional columns required from the underlying data pages because they are referenced in the **SELECT** list or elsewhere in the query, an additional step is required to retrieve this data. The leaf level of the non-clustered index contains a pointer to the data row, which must be followed in order to retrieve the rest of the data in the row. This operation is called a lookup.

The format of the pointer in the non-clustered index depends on the underlying table storage. For heaps, we store a row ID, which is made up of the file ID, page ID, and slot ID (a slot is where the row is stored on the page) of the row. For clustered indexes, we can leverage the B+Tree structure of the index to find the row instead, so the key of the clustered index is stored in the non-clustered indexes. Because of this difference, there are two different types of lookup operations: key lookups and **row ID (RID)** lookups. If the underlying table is stored as a heap, an RID lookup is used. If the underlying table is stored as a clustered index, a key lookup is used (note that a key lookup is simply a clustered index seek under the covers).

If you've been working with SQL Server for a while, you may remember lookups being referred to as **bookmark lookups**. This is what they were called in SQL Server 2000. A bookmark lookup refers to lookups in general but doesn't distinguish between a key lookup and an RID lookup. This distinction wasn't made in the execution plan until SQL Server 2005.

The presence of a lookup operator in a query plan indicates that the query is not **covered**. A covered query means that all the columns required to satisfy the query are present in a single index. Similarly, a covering index is an index that contains all the columns necessary to satisfy the query without accessing the base table. We will talk more about covering indexes in `Chapter 5`, *Writing Elegant T-SQL Queries*.

RID Lookups

As mentioned, an **RID Lookup** operator represents a lookup from a non-clustered index into a heap.

The following example shows a query executed in the **AdventureWorks** sample database with an RID Lookup:

```
SELECT *
FROM DatabaseLog
WHERE DatabaseLogID = 5;
```

The query generates the following execution plan:

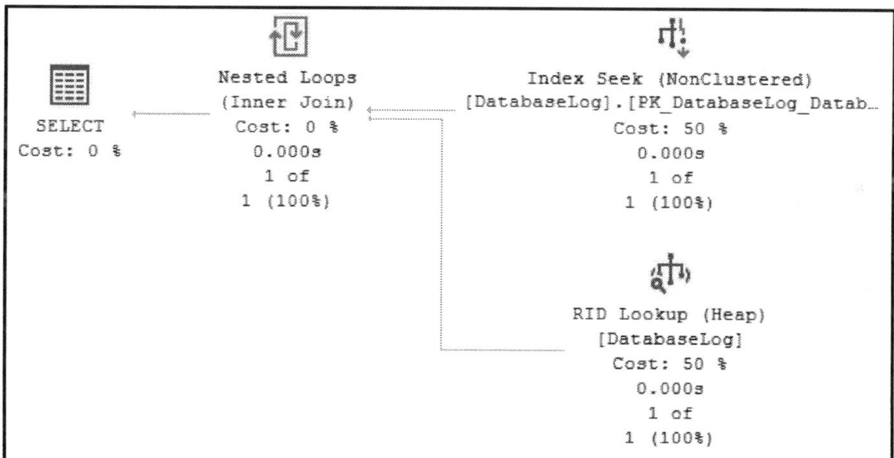

Notice that the results of the RID Lookup are being joined to the non-clustered index seek via a Nested Loops join operator (we will discuss join operators later in this section).

Key Lookups

A **Key Lookup** operator represents a lookup from a non-clustered index into a clustered index. It is effectively a clustered index seek.

The following example shows a query executed in the **AdventureWorks** sample database with a Key Lookup:

```
SELECT *
FROM Person.Person
WHERE LastName = N'Maxwell';
```

The query generates the following execution plan:

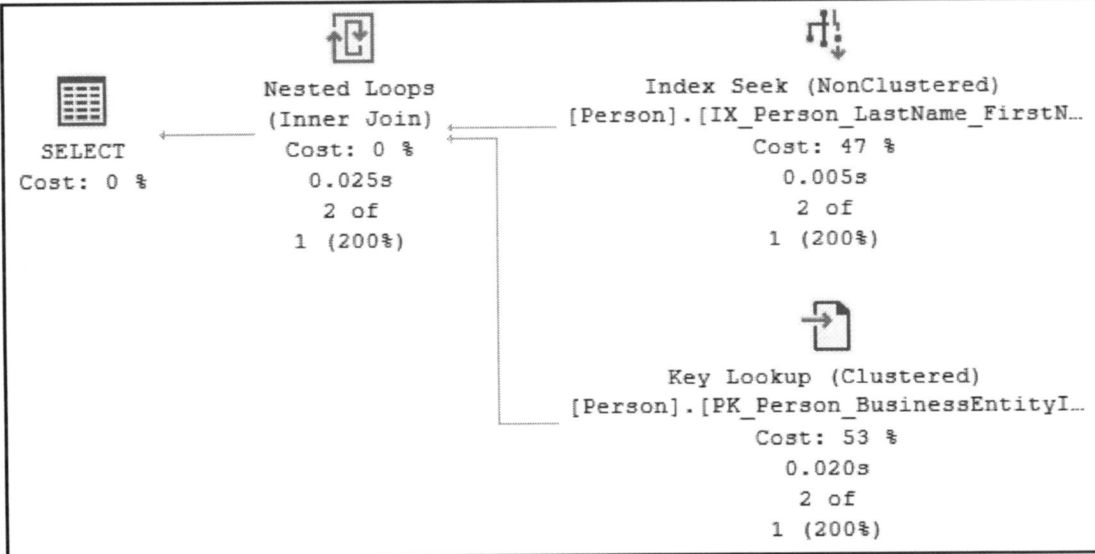

Notice how the key lookup is joined to the non-clustered index seek in the same manner a the RID Lookup.

Columnstore Index Scan

The indexes we've discussed so far are what are referred to as rowstore indexes. These perform well for **Online Transaction Processing (OLTP)** workloads, but **Data Warehouse (DW)** or **Online Analytical Processing (OLAP)** workloads often benefit from a different type of data storage called columnstore. In a columnstore index, a page of data contains a single column for one or more rows of data in the table. Columnstore indexes were introduced in SQL Server 2012 and provide a way to store large amounts of read-only or read-mostly data in a heavily-compressed format with specialized operators that can process large amounts of data quickly. The only way to access data in a columnstore index is with the **Columnstore Index Scan** operator.

The following example shows a query executed in the **AdventureWorksDW** sample database with a Columnstore Index Scan operator:

```
SELECT *
FROM FactResellerSalesXL_CCI
WHERE SalesAmount > 10000;
```

The query generates the following execution plan:

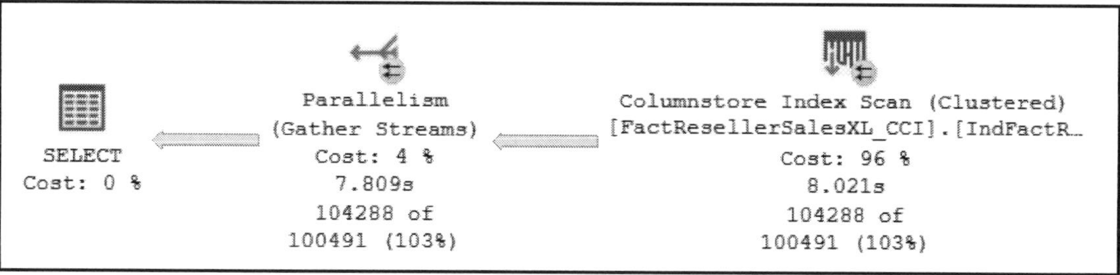

Joins

Join operators are used to join the results of two previous operators in the query plan. They may be joining entire tables or indexes, or they may be joining the results of previous operators in the plan. When we discussed joins in `Chapter 1`, *Anatomy of a Query*, we talked about **INNER**, **OUTER**, and **CROSS** joins. These are the logical joins that we would write in our T-SQL statement that tell SQL Server how to combine the rows of multiple tables and views. The join operators in a query plan define the algorithms that SQL Server will use to perform the join. The choice of which join algorithm to use is based on a cost estimate, not on the type of join being performed.

The physical join operators that SQL Server may choose from are Nested Loops, merges, and Hash joins. The choice of which operation to perform is generally based on how many rows will be joined and whether there are appropriate indexes to support the join. As with data-access operators, if SQL Server estimates this cost incorrectly, it may choose an inefficient join operation. If updating statistics and creating appropriate indexes does not solve the problem, hints can be used to force SQL Server to use the join operation that we specify.

The following join hints are available:

- **LOOP**: Specifies that SQL Server should perform a Nested Loops join
- **HASH**: Specifies that SQL Server should perform a Hash join
- **MERGE**: Specifies that SQL Server should perform a Merge Join
- **REMOTE**: Specifies that when joining with a table on a remote SQL Server instance via a linked Server connection, SQL Server should perform the join on the remote instance

There are two input to each join operator in an execution plan. While these input may be tables, indexes, or even the results of a previous join, they are generally referred to as the **Outer Table** and **Inner Table**. The outer table is the first input accessed in the join algorithm and will appear on the top of the join. The inner table is accessed second and appears at the bottom of the join. The choice of which input should be the inner table and which should be the outer table is relevant in the join, because depending on the algorithm, it may influence the cost of the overall join and the order in which the rows are output.

Nested Loops joins

A **Nested Loops** join is a non-blocking operator. In a Nested Loops join, a row is fetched from the **Outer Table**, and the **Inner Table** is searched for a matching row. SQL Server loops on the **Inner Table** until no more rows are found, then it loops on the **Outer Table**. Because the number of iterations of the inner loop is determined by the number of rows in the **Outer Table**, SQL Server will generally choose the smaller of the two input to be the **Outer Table** in order to minimize the cost of the join. Also, since the outer table is the driver of the algorithm, the rows will be output from the Nested Loops join in the same order as they are input from the outer table.

The following diagram depicts the operation of a Nested Loops join:

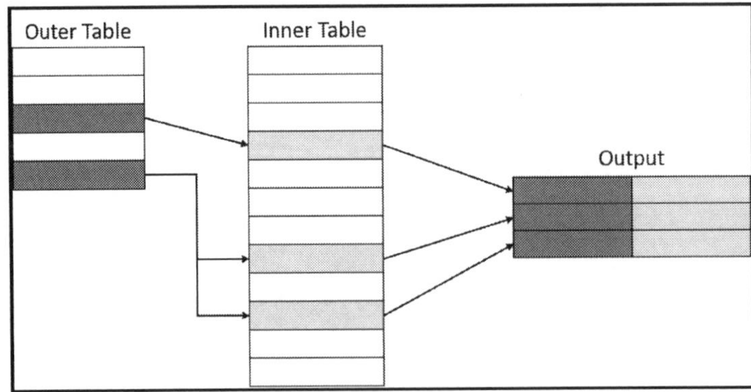

If used correctly, the Nested Loops join is generally the most efficient join algorithm for joining a small number of rows with supporting indexes as it requires a small amount of memory and CPU.

The following two additional concepts are applicable to Nested Loops during execution:

- **Rewind**: This concept is defined as an execution using the same value as the immediately preceding execution. In other words, while an Inner Table is being scanned for matches with the Outer Table, if a previously scanned value is found again, it is said the value is rewound.
- **Rebind**: This concept is defined as an execution using a different value. In other words, when a new value is picked from the Outer Table to be scanned in the Inner Table, it is said the value is rebound.

The following example shows a query executed in the **AdventureWorks** sample database with a Nested Loops operator:

```
SELECT p.LastName, p.FirstName, e.JobTitle
FROM Person.Person AS p
LEFT JOIN HumanResources.Employee AS e ON p.BusinessEntityID =
e.BusinessEntityID
WHERE p.LastName = N'Maxwell';
```

The query generates the following execution plan:

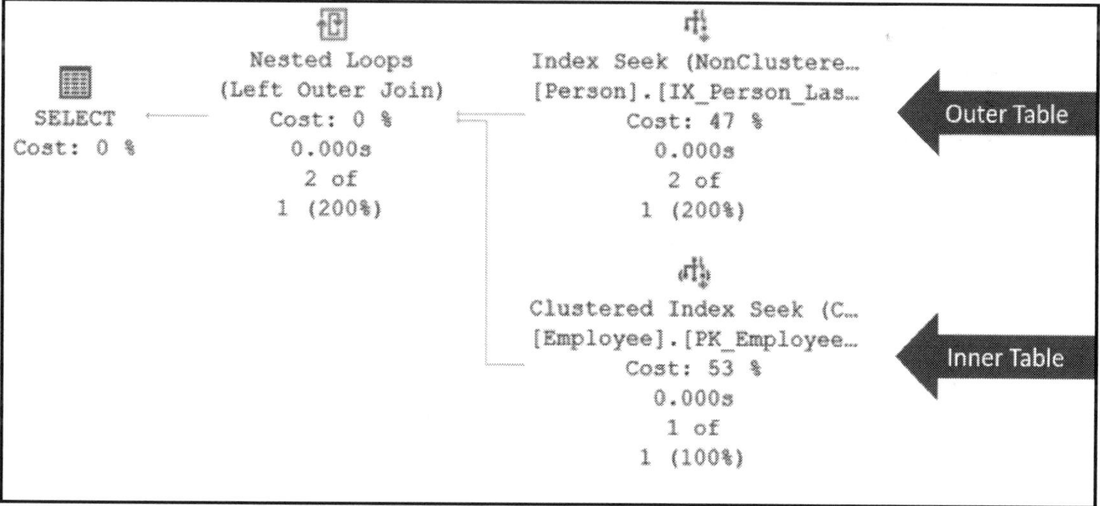

Merge Joins

A **Merge Join** operator represents a Merge Join in the execution plan. Merge joins are typically used to join two large input tables that have indexes to support the join. In a Merge Join, the size of the Outer and Inner Table doesn't affect the cost of the join, but both input tables must be sorted in the same order for the join to work. A row is retrieved from the Outer Table, then matched with rows from the Inner Table and the results output. Once all the matches have been exhausted on the Inner Table, SQL Server moves to the next row in the Outer Table. Since both the Inner and Outer Tables are sorted in the same order going into the merge join operation, the output is returned in the same order.

The following diagram depicts the operation of a Merge Join:

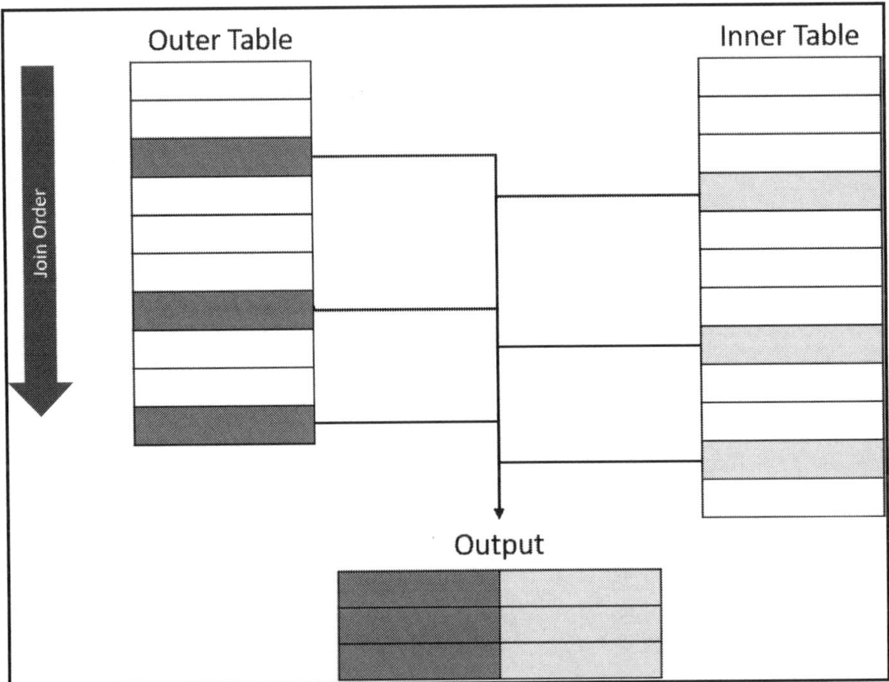

If there are indexes to support the join and the input are already sorted in the proper order, a merge operation is a very efficient way to join two large tables as it requires very little additional memory or CPU. This is often the method of choice when joining two tables on a primary key/foreign key relationship without a **WHERE** clause to limit the rows returned.

The following example shows a query executed in the **AdventureWorks** sample database with a merge join operator:

```
SELECT h.AccountNumber, d.ProductID, d.OrderQty
FROM Sales.SalesOrderHeader AS h
INNER JOIN Sales.SalesOrderDetail AS d ON h.SalesOrderID = d.SalesOrderID;
```

The query generates the following execution plan:

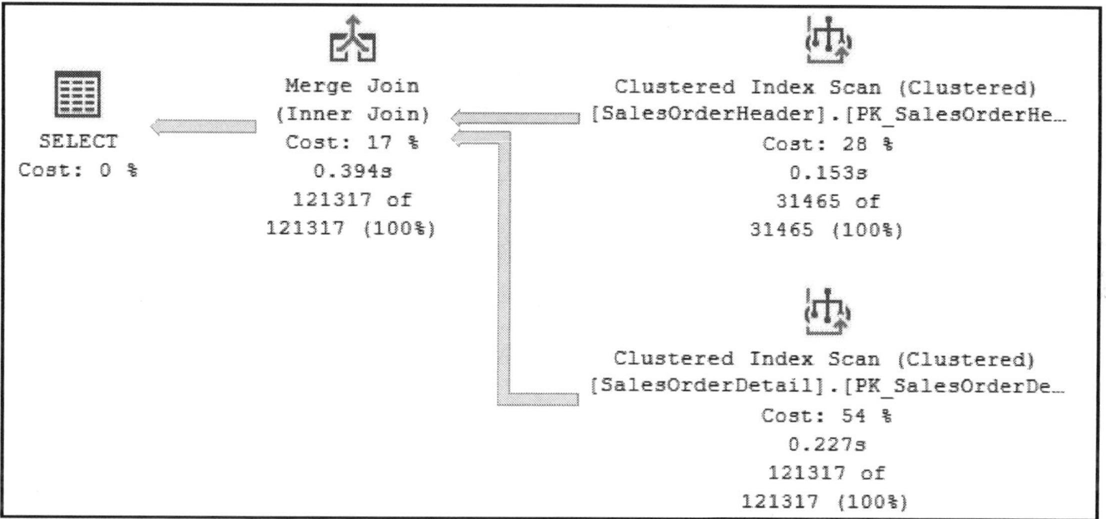

Hash Match joins

A **Hash Match** is a blocking operator that represents a Hash join operation in an execution plan. Hash joins are the most efficient way to join two large input that are not sorted and/or do not have any indexes that support the join. A Hash Match operation is expensive in that it consumes a significant amount of memory and CPU and may generate additional I/O if it does not fit in memory, but it is generally faster than both Nested Loops and Merge Joins when joining a large number of unsorted rows.

With a Hash Match, the Outer Table is also referred to as the **Build Table** and the Inner Table is referred to as the **Probe Table**. The smaller of the two input will be chosen as the **Build Table**, which will be used to build a hash table in memory. SQL Server will then apply a hash function to the join key of each row of the **Probe Table**, look it up in the hash table, and output the results if a match is found.

The following diagram depicts the operation of a Hash join:

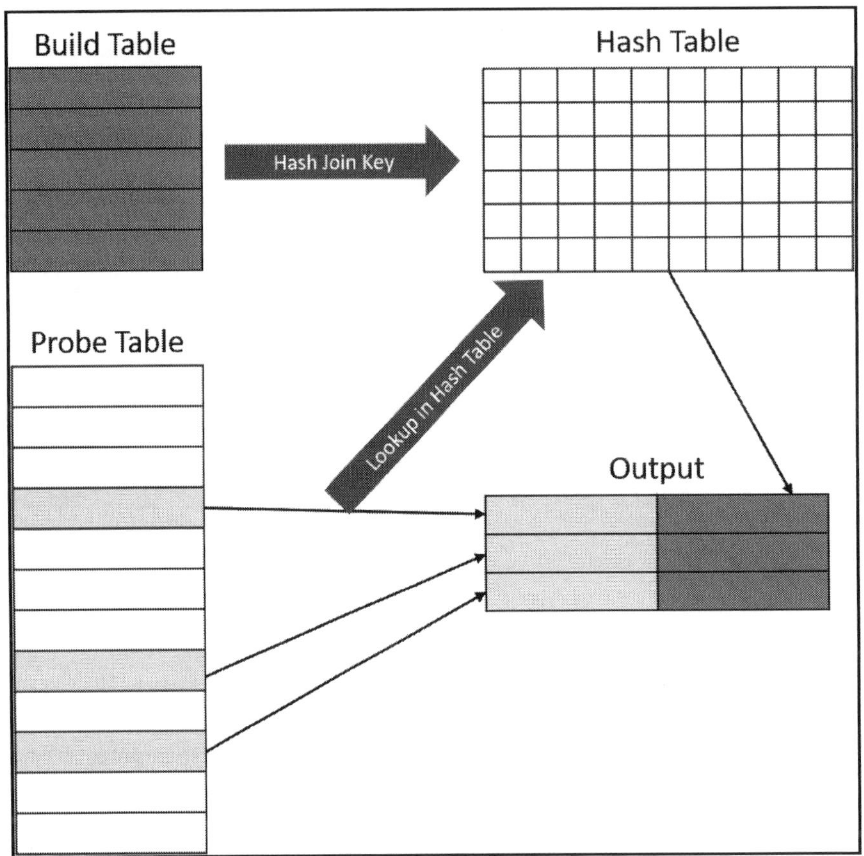

If the Build Table is too large for the entire hash table to fit in memory, intermediate results will be saved in a workfile in TempDB and the operation will have to be done recursively. This is called hash recursion and will generate a hash warning in the execution plan. We can see this as a yellow caution symbol in the following screenshot, and viewing the properties will tell us that a spill has occurred. In extreme cases, a hash bailout may occur. This happens when the maximum recursion level is reached but the hash table still does not fit in memory. A hash bailout will also show up as a hash warning; we'll need to look at the spill level specified in the properties of the plan to determine if a hash bailout has occurred.

There are two spill levels:

- **Spill level 1**: This indicates hash recursion. This happens when the build input requires surplus memory, which results in the splitting of input as multiple partitions that are processed individually. If any partitions are unable to fit in the free memory, it is split into sub-partitions, which are also processed individually. This continues until each partition fits into free memory or until the maximum recursion level is attained.
- **Spill level 2 or higher**: This indicates a hash bailout. This occurs when a hashing operation reaches its maximum recursion level and shifts to an alternate plan to process the remaining partitioned data.

The following query executed in the **AdventureWorksDW** database includes a Hash Match operator with a hash warning.

For this example, the query memory is purposefully limited using the **MAX_GRANT_PERCENT** query hint to produce a spill:

```
SELECT s.*, c.AverageRate
FROM FactResellerSales AS s
INNER JOIN FactCurrencyRate AS c ON c.CurrencyKey = s.CurrencyKey AND
c.DateKey = s.OrderDateKey
OPTION (MAX_GRANT_PERCENT = 0.01);
```

The query generates the following execution plan:

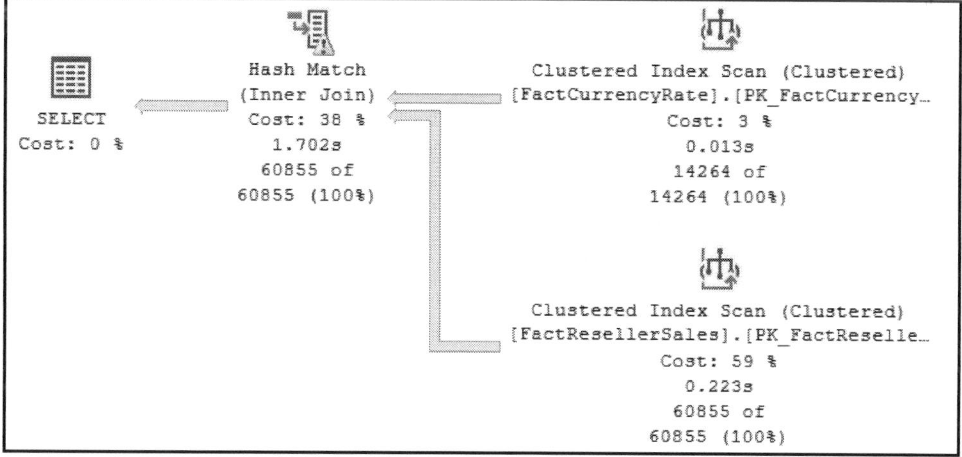

Hovering over the **Hash Match** operator reveals the properties of the operator with details on the warning, as shown in the following screenshot:

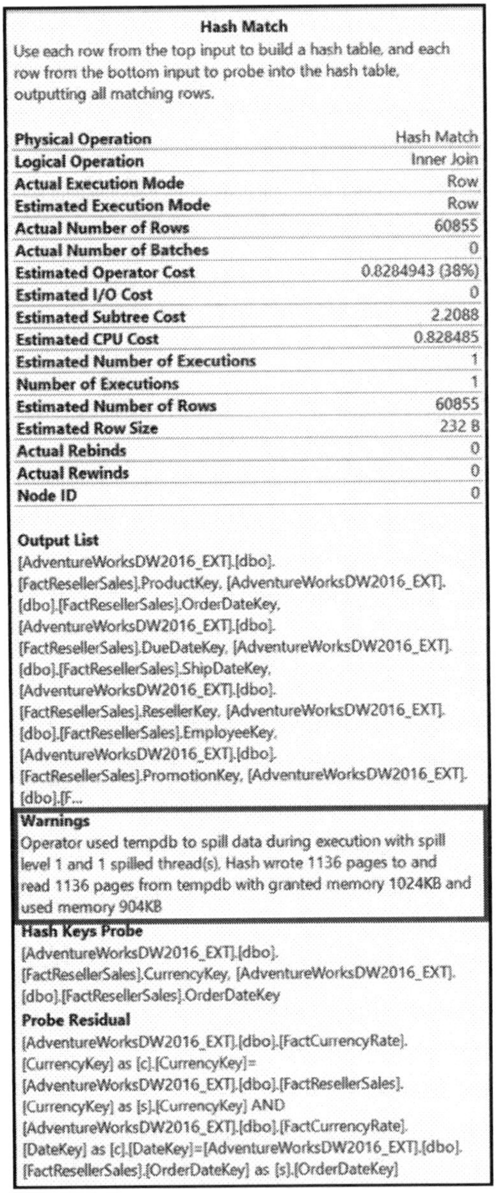

Hash Match

Use each row from the top input to build a hash table, and each row from the bottom input to probe into the hash table, outputting all matching rows.

Physical Operation	Hash Match
Logical Operation	Inner Join
Actual Execution Mode	Row
Estimated Execution Mode	Row
Actual Number of Rows	60855
Actual Number of Batches	0
Estimated Operator Cost	0.8284943 (38%)
Estimated I/O Cost	0
Estimated Subtree Cost	2.2088
Estimated CPU Cost	0.828485
Estimated Number of Executions	1
Number of Executions	1
Estimated Number of Rows	60855
Estimated Row Size	232 B
Actual Rebinds	0
Actual Rewinds	0
Node ID	0

Output List

[AdventureWorksDW2016_EXT].[dbo].[FactResellerSales].ProductKey, [AdventureWorksDW2016_EXT].[dbo].[FactResellerSales].OrderDateKey, [AdventureWorksDW2016_EXT].[dbo].[FactResellerSales].DueDateKey, [AdventureWorksDW2016_EXT].[dbo].[FactResellerSales].ShipDateKey, [AdventureWorksDW2016_EXT].[dbo].[FactResellerSales].ResellerKey, [AdventureWorksDW2016_EXT].[dbo].[FactResellerSales].EmployeeKey, [AdventureWorksDW2016_EXT].[dbo].[FactResellerSales].PromotionKey, [AdventureWorksDW2016_EXT].[dbo].[F...

Warnings

Operator used tempdb to spill data during execution with spill level 1 and 1 spilled thread(s), Hash wrote 1136 pages to and read 1136 pages from tempdb with granted memory 1024KB and used memory 904KB

Hash Keys Probe

[AdventureWorksDW2016_EXT].[dbo].[FactResellerSales].CurrencyKey, [AdventureWorksDW2016_EXT].[dbo].[FactResellerSales].OrderDateKey

Probe Residual

[AdventureWorksDW2016_EXT].[dbo].[FactCurrencyRate].[CurrencyKey] as [c].[CurrencyKey]=[AdventureWorksDW2016_EXT].[dbo].[FactResellerSales].[CurrencyKey] as [s].[CurrencyKey] AND [AdventureWorksDW2016_EXT].[dbo].[FactCurrencyRate].[DateKey] as [c].[DateKey]=[AdventureWorksDW2016_EXT].[dbo].[FactResellerSales].[OrderDateKey] as [s].[OrderDateKey]

We will further describe warnings in the *Query plan properties of interest* section.

Adaptive Joins

SQL Server 2017 introduces adaptive query processing, which includes, among other enhancements, **Batch Mode Adaptive Joins**. Batch mode refers to the query processing method used to process many rows in bulk, or batch. Batch mode execution is closely integrated with the columnstore storage format, although they are different technologies, and is best suited for analytical workloads because of its better parallelism and faster performance.

Normally if cardinality estimations are skewed, SQL Server may choose an inadequate physical join based on wrong data, which results in performance degradation. To avoid this, adaptive joins will defer the choice of using a Hash join or Nested Loops join until after the first join input has been scanned.

Adaptive joins are only used if the outer side of a join can run in batch mode. Depending on the type of physical join selected later, this outer side becomes either the outer table of a Nested Loops or the build table for a hash match.

This means that adaptive join implements both join types then adapts to runtime conditions by only continuing to execute the appropriate join type on the fly. As discussed in the previous sections, Nested Loops are suitable for small input, and Hash joins for large input.

SQL Server starts the adaptive join process by providing rows to a Spool-like structure called the **adaptive buffer** and defines a dynamic threshold that is used to decide when to use a hash match or a Nested Loops plan:

- If the threshold is hit, SQL Server will use a **Hash Match join** and the adaptive buffer becomes the Build Table.
- If the actual row count doesn't exceed the threshold, SQL Server uses a **Nested Loops** join and the adaptive buffer becomes the Outer Table.

The following screenshot illustrates the Adaptive Join processing flow:

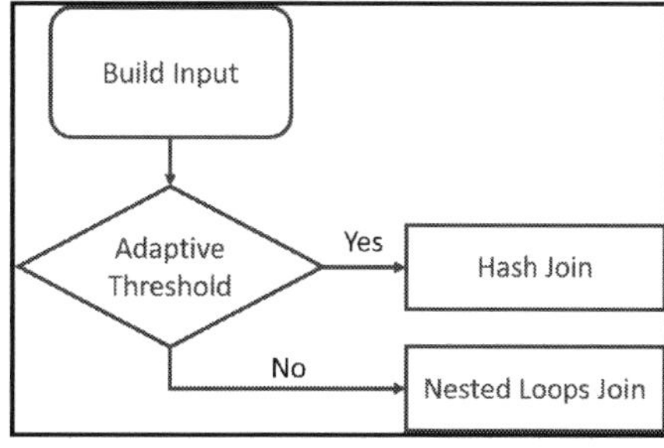

The following query executed in the **AdventureWorksDW** database includes an adaptive join operator. Because Adaptive Joins are only available when the database compatibility level is mapped to SQL Server 2017 level or higher, we need to set it with the following command:

```
USE [master]
GO
ALTER DATABASE [AdventureWorks2016DW_EXT] SET COMPATIBILITY_LEVEL = 140
GO
```

For this example, because the outer table of a join must run in batch mode for the Adaptive Join to be eligible, we are forcing a table with a clustered columnstore index to be on the outer side of the join using the **FORCE ORDER** query hint:

```
SELECT s.ProductKey,SUM(s.OrderQuantity)AS SumOrderQuantity,
       AVG(s.UnitPrice)AS AvgUnitPrice,AVG(s.DiscountAmount)AS
AvgDiscountAmount,
       c.AverageRate
FROM FactResellerSalesXL_CCI AS s
INNER JOIN FactCurrencyRate AS c ON c.CurrencyKey = s.CurrencyKey AND
c.DateKey = s.OrderDateKey
GROUP BY s.ProductKey, c.AverageRate
OPTION (FORCE ORDER);
```

The query generates the following execution plan:

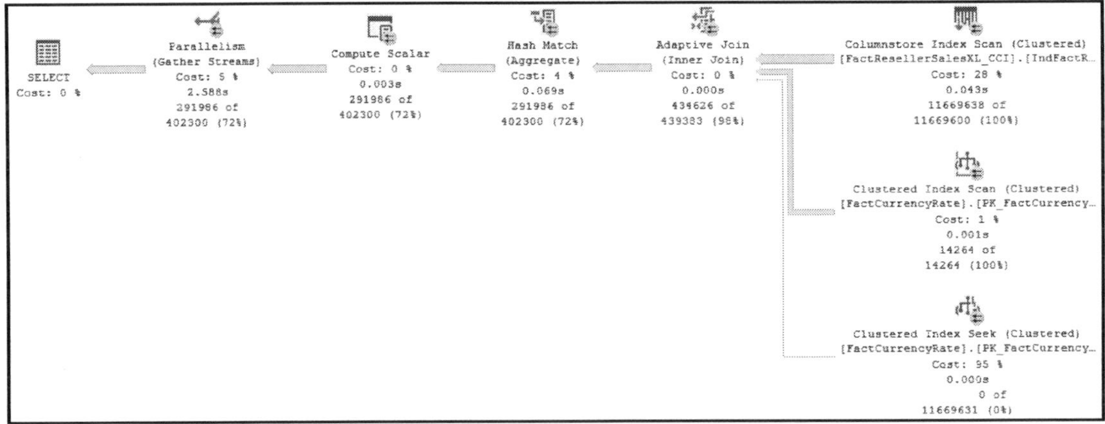

Hovering over the Adaptive Join operator reveals the properties of the operator with details on the adaptive threshold for this specific query, as well as the estimated and actual join type:

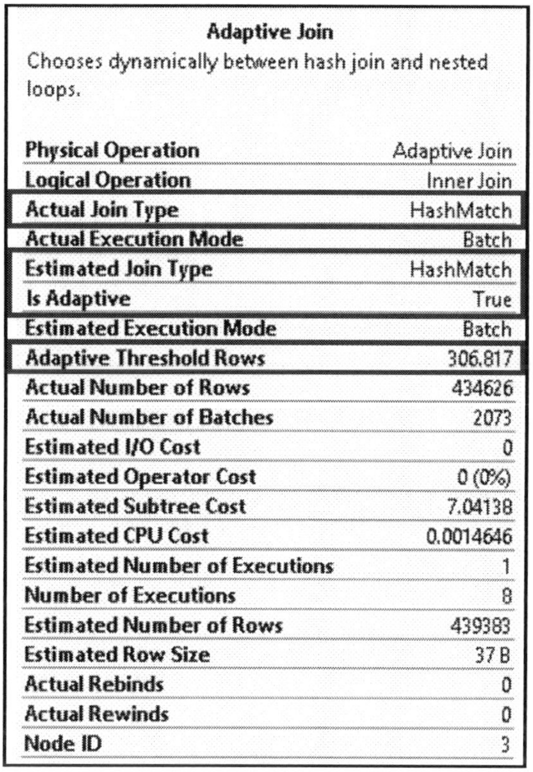

Adaptive Join

Chooses dynamically between hash join and nested loops.

Physical Operation	Adaptive Join
Logical Operation	Inner Join
Actual Join Type	HashMatch
Actual Execution Mode	Batch
Estimated Join Type	HashMatch
Is Adaptive	True
Estimated Execution Mode	Batch
Adaptive Threshold Rows	306.817
Actual Number of Rows	434626
Actual Number of Batches	2073
Estimated I/O Cost	0
Estimated Operator Cost	0 (0%)
Estimated Subtree Cost	7.04138
Estimated CPU Cost	0.0014646
Estimated Number of Executions	1
Number of Executions	8
Estimated Number of Rows	439383
Estimated Row Size	37 B
Actual Rebinds	0
Actual Rewinds	0
Node ID	3

Spools

Spools are expensive operators, but they are introduced in a query plan as an optimization, typically to compensate for inadequate indexes, or to optimize otherwise complex queries by significantly speeding up the overall runtime of a query. A Spool reads data and saves it in a worktable in TempDB. This process is used whenever the Query Optimizer knows that the density of a column is high (therefore having low selectivity) and the intermediate result is very complex to calculate. If this is the case, SQL Server computes the result once and stores it in a Spool so it can be searched later in the execution. Spools only exist while the query is being executed.

Conceptually, all physical Spool operators function the same way:

1. Read all rows from an input operator downstream
2. Store them in a worktable in TempDB
3. Allow upstream operators to read from this cache

There are the following three types of physical Spool operators:

- **Table Spool**: This Spool scans the input and places a copy of each row in a worktable. This is also called a performance spool, and it can be introduced to support a Nested Loops join upstream.
- **Index Spool**: A non-clustered index Spool contains a seek predicate. The index Spool operator scans the input rows, places a copy of each row in a worktable, and builds a non-clustered index on the rows. This allows SQL Server to use the seeking capability of indexes to output only those rows that satisfy the seek predicate, and is usually introduced when a proper index doesn't exist for the required predicates.
- **Row Count Spool**: This Spool scans the input and counts how many rows are present, and then returns the row count without any data attached to it. This allows SQL Server to check for the existence of rows when the data contained in the rows is not required and can be introduced by certain T-SQL constructs, such as an **EXISTS** clause dependent on a **COUNT** clause.

All the preceding three spools can implement one of the following two logical operations:

- **Eager Spool**: This Spool causes the physical Spool to become a non-blocking operator that will read all rows from the input operator at one time. It populates its worktable in an **eager** way. In other words, when the Spool's upstream operator asks for the first row, the Spool operator consumes all rows from its input operator and stores them in the worktable.
- **Lazy Spool**: This Spool causes the physical Spool to become a blocking operator that reads and stores data only when individual rows are required. It populates the worktable in a lazy fashion. In other words, each time the Spool's upstream operator asks for a row, the Spool operator gets a row from its input operator and stores it in the worktable, rather than consuming all rows at once. Because of this behavior, memory consumption for a lazy Spool is smaller than the memory needed for an eager Spool.

For both logical Spools, if the operator is rewound (for example, by a Nested Loops operator) but no rebinding is needed, the spooled data is used instead of re-scanning the input. If rebinding is needed, the spooled data is discarded, and the Spool object is rebuilt by re-scanning the input.

If a Spool is causing a bottleneck in a query, refactor it to try to eliminate the Spool. Creating and populating a temp table can sometimes perform better than a Spool and it can be indexed. If the same Spool is used several times, this method can yield better results.

SQL Server can introduce a Spool or Sort to enforce Halloween protection during a T-SQL statement that updates rows. We introduced Halloween protection in the *Query optimization essentials* section of `Chapter 2`, *Understanding Query Processing*.

Here is an example of a query executed in the **AdventureWorks** sample database with a **Table Spool** operator:

```
SELECT WO.WorkOrderID, WO.ProductID, WO.OrderQty, WO.StockedQty,
       WO.ScrappedQty, WO.StartDate, WO.EndDate, WO.DueDate,
       WO.ScrapReasonID, WO.ModifiedDate, WOR.WorkOrderID,
       WOR.ProductID, WOR.LocationID
FROM Production.WorkOrder AS WO
LEFT JOIN Production.WorkOrderRouting AS WOR
ON WO.WorkOrderID = WOR.WorkOrderID AND WOR.WorkOrderID = 12345;
```

The query generates the following execution plan:

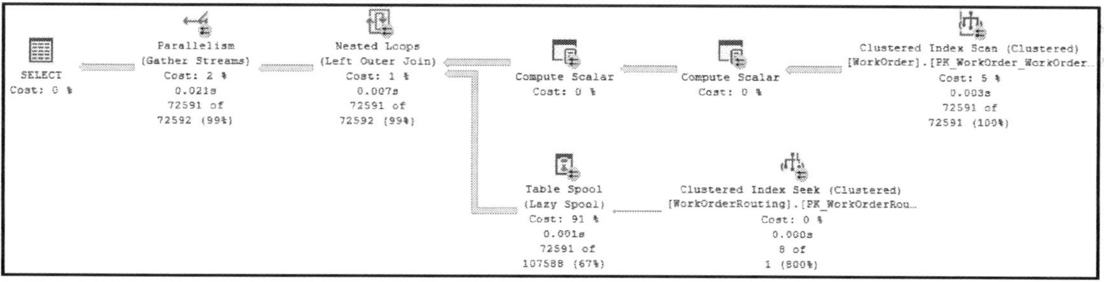

In the following screenshot, notice the difference between actual and estimated rows for the Spool (72,591 of 107,588). SQL Server doesn't hold statistics on worktables, so estimations are based on the estimated number of rows (1.48211) multiplied by the estimated number of executions (72,591). In turn, notice the number of rewinds and rebinds; these match the number of executions because executing a Spool is the action of rewinding and rebinding values as the Nested Loops required rows to process:

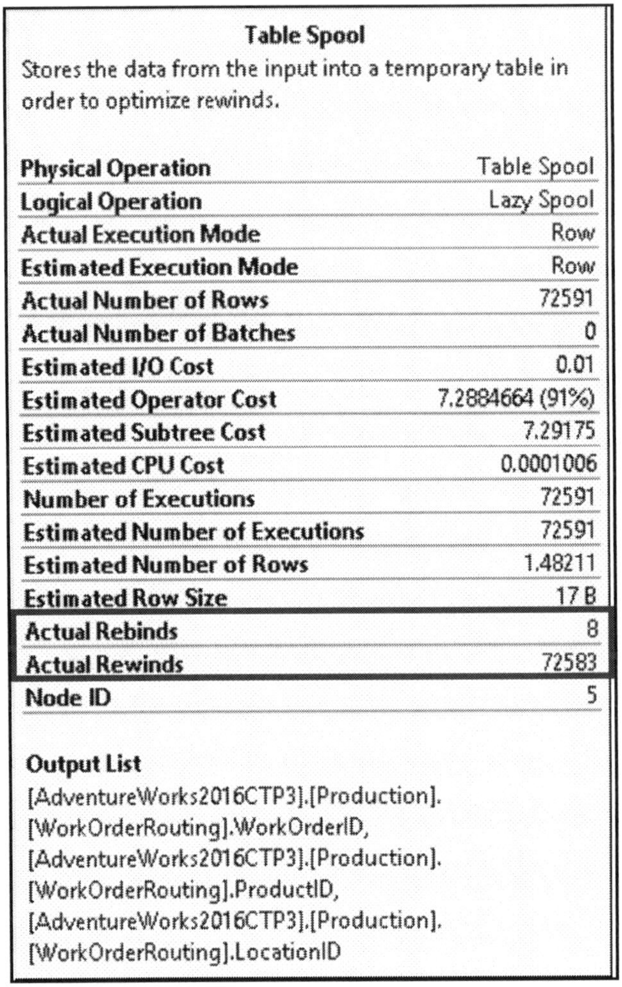

Table Spool

Stores the data from the input into a temporary table in order to optimize rewinds.

Physical Operation	Table Spool
Logical Operation	Lazy Spool
Actual Execution Mode	Row
Estimated Execution Mode	Row
Actual Number of Rows	72591
Actual Number of Batches	0
Estimated I/O Cost	0.01
Estimated Operator Cost	7.2884664 (91%)
Estimated Subtree Cost	7.29175
Estimated CPU Cost	0.0001006
Number of Executions	72591
Estimated Number of Executions	72591
Estimated Number of Rows	1.48211
Estimated Row Size	17 B
Actual Rebinds	8
Actual Rewinds	72583
Node ID	5

Output List

[AdventureWorks2016CTP3].[Production].[WorkOrderRouting].WorkOrderID, [AdventureWorks2016CTP3].[Production].[WorkOrderRouting].ProductID, [AdventureWorks2016CTP3].[Production].[WorkOrderRouting].LocationID

The Spool was included for performance reasons, to cache the result set from the inner side of the Nested Loops join. The idea is that if the next iteration of the Nested Loops join uses the same correlated parameters, the Spool can rewind – replaying the results from the prior execution. This saves the cost of evaluating the inner side subtree, at the cost of caching the result in a work table. As such, the **NO_PERFORMANCE_SPOOL** hint can apply to these scenarios to remove this type of Spool. As always, hints should be used only as a last resort, as they limit the Query Optimizer search space, and may preclude a query from leveraging future query optimization enhancements.

In `Chapter 7`, *Discovering T-SQL Anti-Patterns in Depth*, we will discuss some methods for avoiding Spool operators in our queries.

To prove that the Spool was beneficial, we can add the hint to the query:

```
SELECT WO.WorkOrderID, WO.ProductID, WO.OrderQty, WO.StockedQty,
WO.ScrappedQty, WO.StartDate,
       WO.EndDate, WO.DueDate, WO.ScrapReasonID, WO.ModifiedDate,
WOR.WorkOrderID,
       WOR.ProductID, WOR.LocationID
FROM Production.WorkOrder AS WO LEFT JOIN Production.WorkOrderRouting AS
WOR
ON WO.WorkOrderID = WOR.WorkOrderID
AND WOR.WorkOrderID = 12345
OPTION (NO_PERFORMANCE_SPOOL);
```

This generates the following execution plan:

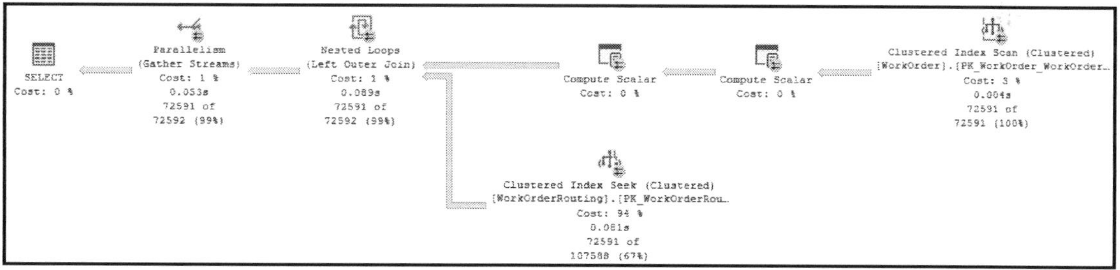

Instead of a Spool, SQL Server now accesses the clustered index for every single search on the inner table. We started this section by saying spools are expensive operators, but that they are also an optimization. That is proven here, where eliminating the Spool degrades query performance by using much more CPU.

Sorts and aggregation

Sort and aggregation operators are present in an execution plan when a query contains an **ORDER BY** and/or a **GROUP BY** clause. In some cases, SQL Server will introduce a sort in order to optimize the execution of a query, such as to enable a merge join or to improve the performance of a Nested Loops join. We may also see a Sort operator in an execution plan that contains `SELECT DISTINCT`. **DISTINCT** is effectively an aggregation as it requires grouping the rows and only returning one row per distinct set of values. A sort operation is a simple way to perform this type of aggregation. As discussed in the *Query Optimization Essentials* section of `Chapter 2`, *Understanding Query Processing*, SQL Server may also add a sort operator to an **UPDATE** plan in order to enforce Halloween protection.

Sorts

A **Sort** is a blocking operator that is used to order the input based on one or more columns. Sorts can be expensive operations since they require additional memory to store intermediate results and CPU to perform the sort. If the intermediate results do not fit in memory, sorts may also generate I/O as the results will be saved in a worktable in TempDB.

If any of these happens, a sort warning will be visible in the execution plan. As with a hash warning, it will appear as a yellow caution symbol in the plan and the properties will give more details on how much data was spilled. There are the following two spill levels:

- **Spill level 1**: This means one pass over the data was enough to complete the sort.
- **Spill level 2**: This means multiple passes over the data are required to sort the data.

The following query executed in the **AdventureWorksDW** database includes a sort operation with a sort warning:

```
SELECT *
FROM FactResellerSalesXL_PageCompressed s
ORDER BY ProductKey
```

The query generates the following execution plan:

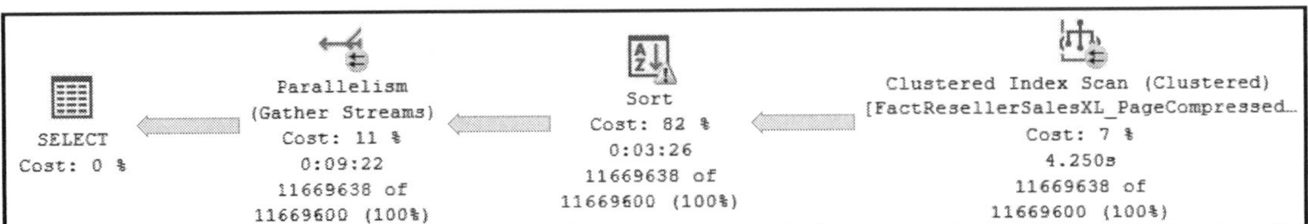

Hovering over the Sort icon will pop up the **Properties** window where we can see the **Sort** warning details:

Sort

Sort the input.

Physical Operation	Sort
Logical Operation	Sort
Actual Execution Mode	Row
Estimated Execution Mode	Row
Actual Number of Rows	11669638
Actual Number of Batches	0
Estimated Operator Cost	2265.6196 (88%)
Estimated I/O Cost	2053.36
Estimated CPU Cost	212.26
Estimated Subtree Cost	2336.45
Number of Executions	2
Estimated Number of Executions	1
Estimated Number of Rows	11669600
Estimated Row Size	224 B
Actual Rebinds	2
Actual Rewinds	0
Node ID	1

Output List

[AdventureWorksDW2016_EXT].[dbo].[FactResellerSalesXL_PageCompressed].ProductKey, [AdventureWorksDW2016_EXT].[dbo].[FactResellerSalesXL_PageCompressed].OrderDateKey, [AdventureWorksDW2016_EXT].[dbo].[FactResellerSalesXL_PageCompressed].DueDateKey, [AdventureWorksDW2016_EXT].[dbo].[FactResellerSalesXL_PageCompressed].ShipDateKey, [AdventureWorksDW2016_EXT].[dbo].[FactResellerSalesXL_PageCompressed].ResellerKey, [AdventureWorksDW2016_EXT].[dbo].[FactResellerSalesXL_PageCompressed].EmployeeKey, ...

Warnings

Operator used tempdb to spill data during execution with spill level 1 and 2 spilled thread(s), Sort wrote 315397 pages to and read 315397 pages from tempdb with granted memory 1571264KB and used memory 1571264KB

Order By

[AdventureWorksDW2016_EXT].[dbo].[FactResellerSalesXL_PageCompressed].ProductKey Ascending

We will further describe warnings in the *Query plan properties of interest* section.

Stream aggregation

As mentioned previously, aggregation is used to group rows together when a query contains a **GROUP BY** clause. With a **GROUP BY** clause, the **SELECT** list typically has one or more aggregate functions, such as **SUM**, **MIN**, or **MAX**. If the input to the aggregation operation is already sorted by the **GROUP BY** columns, a **Stream Aggregate** operator can be used. Stream aggregation is the more efficient of the two aggregation operators in that it does not require much additional CPU or memory, the rows are processed as they pass through the operator.

The following example shows a query executed in the **AdventureWorks** sample database with a stream aggregate operator:

```
SELECT SalesOrderID, COUNT(*) AS ItemCount
FROM Sales.SalesOrderDetail
GROUP BY SalesOrderID
```

The preceding query generates the following execution plan:

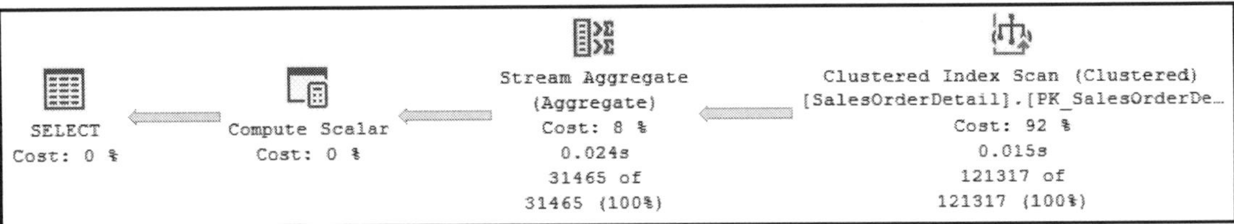

Hash aggregation

The **Hash Match (Aggregate)** operator also performs aggregation to support **GROUP BY**, but while stream aggregation requires the input to be sorted, Hash aggregation does not. Hash aggregation is effectively the same as a Hash join, the difference is that there is only a single input to process. As with a Hash join, Hash aggregation consumes additional CPU and memory to store the hash table and may be subject to hash recursion and additional I/O in the form of spills to TempDB.

The following example shows a query executed in the **AdventureWorks** sample database with a Hash Match (Aggregate) operator:

```
SELECT p.Name AS ProductName, SUM(OrderQty) AS TotalProductSales
FROM Sales.SalesOrderDetail sod
INNER JOIN Production.Product p on p.ProductID = sod.ProductID
GROUP BY p.Name
```

The preceding query generates the following execution plan:

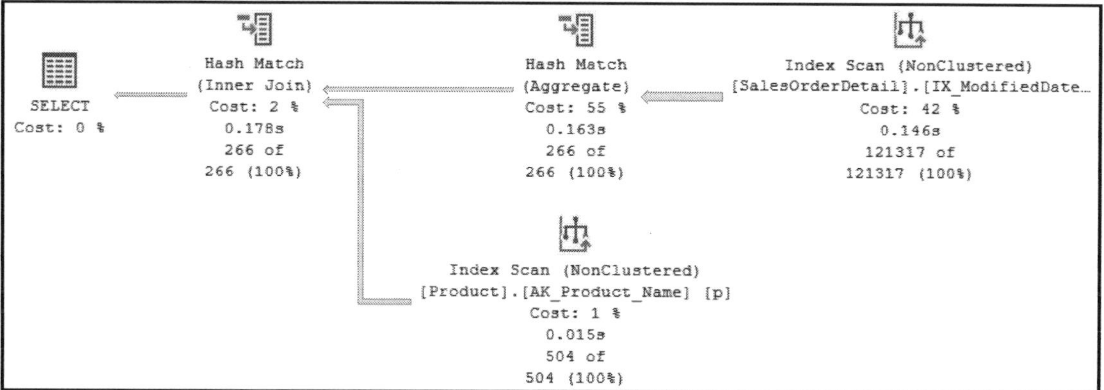

Query plan properties of interest

Each operator in a query execution plan has several properties that provide context and metrics around its compilation, optimization, and execution. The plans also have global properties to provide the overall context. Examining some key properties for the overall plan and some operators is especially relevant to writing T-SQL that scales well. We will look at these properties, understand their meaning, and become familiar with their significance, which will be important in the chapters where we explore T-SQL patterns and anti-patterns.

Plan-level properties

The root node of a plan has a few properties that are important for understanding the context of the execution. Different trace flags or **SET** options change the execution context and may drive query optimization choices, so having this information persisted in the showplan is a valuable tool.

The following example shows a query executed in the **AdventureWorks** sample database that allows us to examine most of these properties:

```
SELECT *
FROM Sales.SalesOrderDetail AS sod
INNER JOIN Production.Product AS p ON sod.ProductID = p.ProductID
ORDER BY Style DESC
OPTION (MAXDOP 1);
```

The preceding query generates the following execution plan:

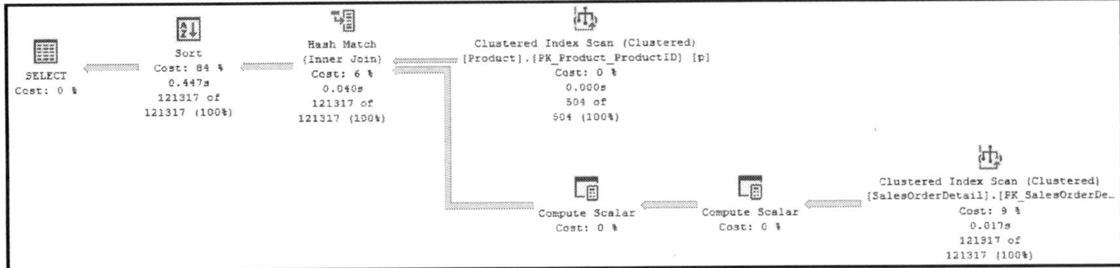

Right-click on the root node of the plan, open the context menu, and click on **Properties**:

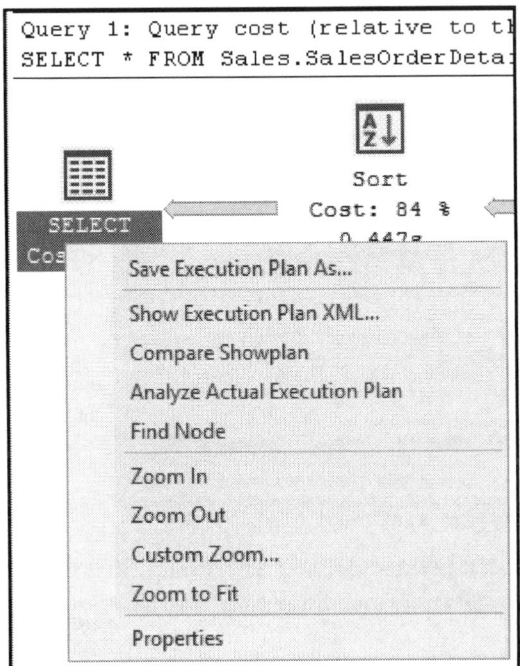

This opens the **Properties** window:

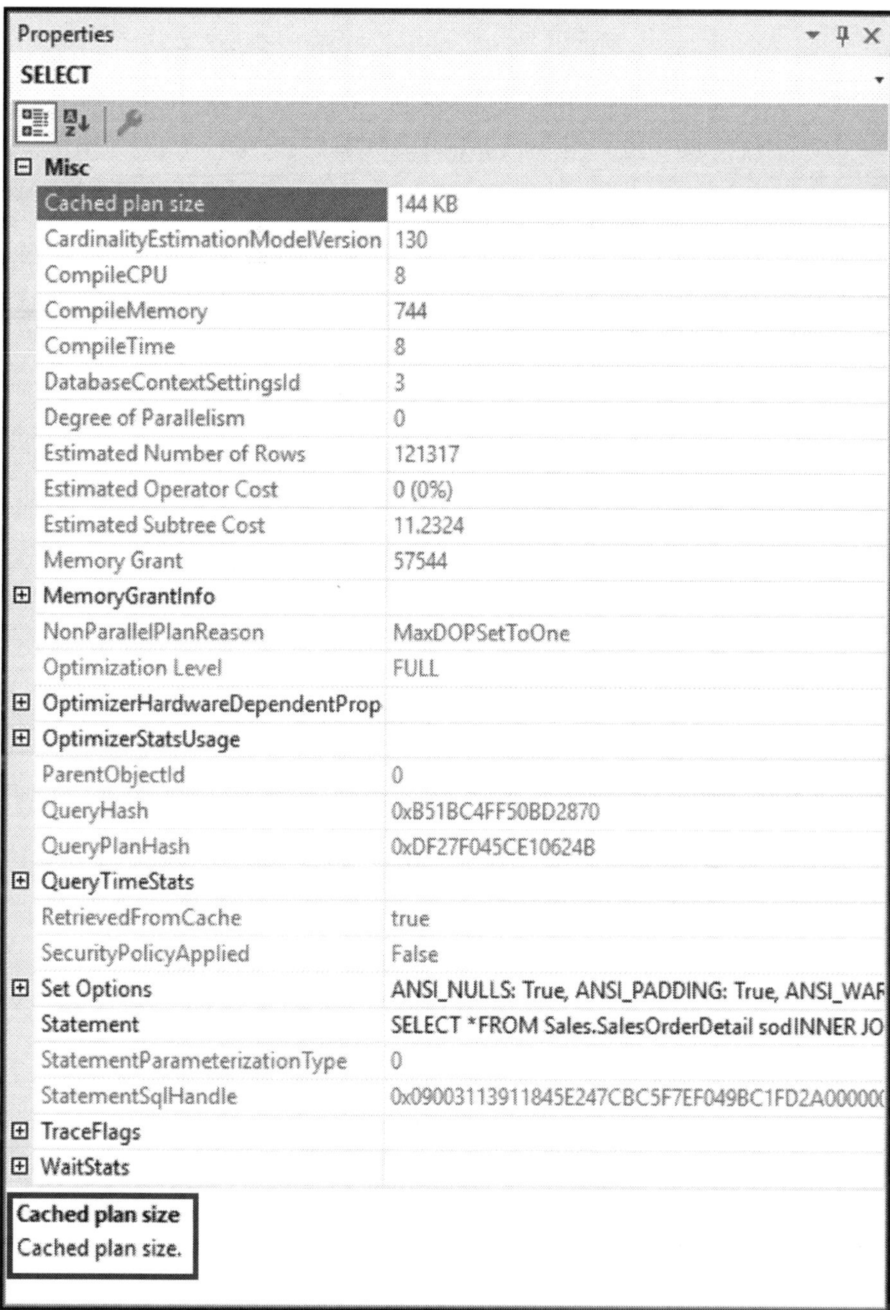

For each property selected, the lower part of the **Properties** window displays some informational text, such as the size of the plan in the plan cache.

The properties available depend on the version and build of SQL Server that the plan was captured on. At the time of writing of this book, all the plan-level properties described here exist in SQL Server 2016 **Service Pack 2 (SP2)**, SQL Server 2017 **Cumulative Update 3 (CU3)**, and SQL Server 2019. A subset of these properties will also be available in SQL Server 2016 SP1 and higher builds, SQL Server 2014 SP3, and SQL Server 2012 SP4.

Not all properties are available with an estimated plan, because this refers to a compiled plan that has not yet been executed. Some properties exist at runtime only and therefore are only available for an actual plan. However, all properties in an estimated plan are also available in an actual plan. In order to distinguish between compile time and runtime properties in this book, if a property only exists at runtime, we will use one asterisk after the property name, as in **Degree of Parallelism*** in the previous screenshot.

With this, let's look at some of the most important properties as seen in the previous **Properties** window screenshot.

Cardinality estimation model version

The **CardinalityEstimationModelVersion** property indicates the version with which the plan was compiled. In this case we see 130, mapping to the CE released with SQL Server 2016. While this query is being executed in a SQL Server 2017 database engine, the compatibility level of the **AdventureWorks** database is set to 130, because it hasn't been upgraded since being restored from a SQL Server 2016 system where it was first created. Because the CE version is a main driver for the query-optimization process, it represents vital information when database professionals analyze query plans. For more information on CE and database compatibility, refer to `Chapter 3`, *Mechanics of the Query Optimizer*.

Degree of Parallelism*

Degree of Parallelism* indicates the number of CPUs actually used to process a query that was eligible to execute in parallel. In this case, we see the value is zero (0) because the query was not executed in parallel. We have discussed how the query optimization process evaluates parallelism in the `Chapter 3`, *Mechanics of the Query Optimizer*. If the query had a cost that was high enough to go parallel but didn't, an extra property named **NonParallelPlanReason*** is also shown. In this case, we can see the reason was **MaxDOPSetToOne**, and indeed notice the query used the **MAXDOP 1** hint, forcing the Query Optimizer to not evaluate a parallel plan. Compare this with the **EstimatedAvailableDegreeOfParalellism** property; for example, if the actual parallelism was smaller than the estimated parallelism, this may indicate a CPU contention problem.

Memory Grant*

Memory Grant* indicates the amount of memory in **kilobytes (KB)** that SQL Server had to acquire to even start executing this query. In this case, we see 57,544 KB, roughly 56 **megabytes (MB)**. Being limited, memory is one of the most important resources for SQL Server. Even when our SQL Server has **terabytes (TB)** of memory at its disposal, it is most likely still less than the overall storage taken by all our databases. This means that making sure SQL Server can properly estimate the amount of memory to use for a given query to execute, and then use it without waste, it is a measure of scalability and enhanced concurrency in our database system. We will discuss this in detail later in this section as we look at possible warnings output by SQL Server during execution.

MemoryGrantInfo

MemoryGrantInfo can expand to show additional information on memory usage in KB, to report on all memory calculations accounted for during query optimization.

Here is the detail for this property for the example query:

Memory Grant	57544
⊟ MemoryGrantInfo	
DesiredMemory	57544
GrantedMemory	57544
GrantWaitTime	0
MaxQueryMemory	1908928
MaxUsedMemory	40648
RequestedMemory	57544
RequiredMemory	1536
SerialDesiredMemory	57544
SerialRequiredMemory	1536

The detailed elements of **MemoryGrantInfo** are as follows:

- **GrantedMemory***: This property indicates the memory acquired by the database engine at runtime.
- **GrantWaitTime***: This property indicates the time in seconds the query had to wait for a successful memory grant. This translates into **RESOURCE_SEMAPHORE** waits. If no waits occurred, the wait time will be zero.
- **MaxQueryMemory***: This property indicates the maximum memory allowed for a single query under the applicable **Resource Governor** pool's **MAX_MEMORY_PERCENT** configuration. If there are operators spilling and estimations are mostly correct, the query may be running into memory starvation.
- **MaxUsedMemory***: This property indicates the maximum memory used by the query during execution. If there is a large skew between the granted memory and the used memory, SQL Server will generate warnings.
- **RequiredMemory***: This property indicates the required memory for the chosen degree of parallelism when a query runs in parallel. If the query runs in serial mode, this is the same as **SerialRequiredMemory**. The query will not start without at least this much memory being available.
- **SerialRequiredMemory***: This element indicates the required memory for a serial query plan to execute. The query will not start without at least this much memory being available.

Optimization Level

Optimization Level refers to the Query Optimizer phase and can be either **TRIVIAL** or **FULL**. For more information on the Query Optimizer workflow, see `Chapter 3`, *Mechanics of the Query Optimizer*.

OptimizerHardwareDependentProperties

OptimizerHardwareDependentProperties can expand to show additional information on system-reported conditions that are accounted for during query optimization. Here is the detail for this property for the example query:

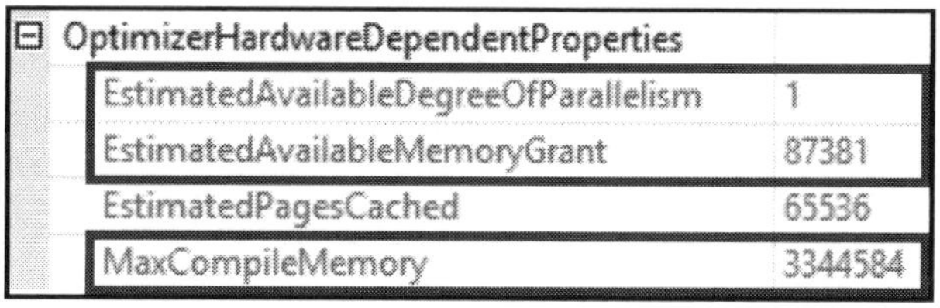

OptimizerHardwareDependentProperties	
EstimatedAvailableDegreeOfParallelism	1
EstimatedAvailableMemoryGrant	87381
EstimatedPagesCached	65536
MaxCompileMemory	3344584

The detailed elements of **OptimizerHardwareDependentProperties** are as follows:

- **EstimatedAvailableDegreeOfParalellism**: This indicates the expected number of schedulers available for query processing. One (**1**) means that no parallelism will be available, a number greater than one allows a parallel plan to be evaluated during query optimization. Compare this with the **Degree of Parallelism** property; for example, if the actual parallelism was smaller than the estimated parallelism, this may indicate a CPU contention problem.
- **EstimatedAvailableMemoryGrant**: This indicates the expected amount of memory (in KB) available for a single query under the applicable Resource Governor pool's **MAX_MEMORY_PERCENT** configuration.
- **MaxCompileMemory**: This indicates the maximum Query Optimizer memory available (in KB) during compilation under the applicable Resource Governor pool's **MAX_MEMORY_PERCENT** configuration. If the system is accumulating **RESOURCE_SEMAPHORE_QUERY_COMPILE** waits, queries are waiting to be compiled long before they can execute. This then surfaces as a high-compilation or recompilation scenario. We will further details about this scenario in `Chapter 7`, *Discovering T-SQL Patterns and Anti-Patterns in Depth.*

OptimizerStatsUsage

OptimizerStatsUsage can expand to show additional information on which statistics objects were used by the Query Optimizer for a given compilation. When analyzing a query plan that has performance problems, a database professional can use this information to see which statistics were loaded for use during query optimization, and also whether statistics need to be updated, which may be a root cause for performance problems grounded on CE issues.

Here is the detail for this property for the example query:

⊟ OptimizerStatsUsage	
⊟ [1]	
Database	[AdventureWorks2016_EXT]
LastUpdate	11/16/2015 1:04 PM
ModificationCount	0
SamplingPercent	100
Schema	[Sales]
Statistics	[PK_SalesOrderDetail_SalesOrderID_SalesOrderDetailID]
Table	[SalesOrderDetail]

The detailed elements of **OptimizerStatsUsage** are the following, and are repeated for every statistic object loaded for this plan:

- **Database**, **Schema**, **Table**, and **Statistics** refer to the respective four-part name of the statistic object.
- **LastUpdate** refers to the date and time the statistic object was last updated.
- **ModificationCounter** refers to the internal modification counter for each statistic that drives automatic updates. For more information on statistics, refer to the *Introducing the cardinality estimator* section in `Chapter 3`, *Mechanics of the Query Optimizer*.
- **SamplingPercent** refers to the sampling rate with which a statistic was last updated. It can reach 100%, meaning the statistic was updated as part of a full scan of the underlying table or indexed view.

QueryPlanHash

QueryPlanHash is a binary hash value calculated on the query plan and used to uniquely identify a query execution plan. In other words, this is a query plan fingerprint.

QueryHash

QueryHash is a binary hash value calculated on the query text and used to uniquely identify a query. In other words, this is a query fingerprint. We will see several examples of using the query hash in `Chapter 8`, *Building Diagnostics with DMVs and DMFs*.

Set options

Set options lists the **SET** options that were current as of compile time. These options determine the handling of specific information and may be different at runtime because they are based on the current session. The options tracked are **ANSI_NULLS, ANSI_PADDING, ANSI_WARNINGS, ARITHABORT, CONCAT_NULL_YIELDS_NULL, NUMERIC_ROUNDABORT**, and **QUOTED_IDENTIFIER**. These **SET** options affect estimations and query results, which means that if one option is changed inside of a batch, a recompilation must happen. Keep these options in mind when analyzing a query that may meet the expected performance in a development or pre-production system but performs poorly in a production system.

For example, **ANSI_NULLS** specifies the ISO-compliant behavior for **NULL** equality and inequality comparisons, which dramatically changes the resulting query plan.

The following examples executed in the **AdventureWorks** sample database differ only in the **ANSI_NULL** setting. First, by setting **ANSI_NULLS** to **ON** as recommended:

```
SET ANSI_NULLS ON
GO
SELECT *
FROM Sales.SalesOrderDetail AS sod
INNER JOIN Production.Product AS p ON sod.ProductID = p.ProductID
WHERE SellEndDate = NULL
ORDER BY Style DESC
OPTION (MAXDOP 1);
GO
```

The query generates the following execution plan:

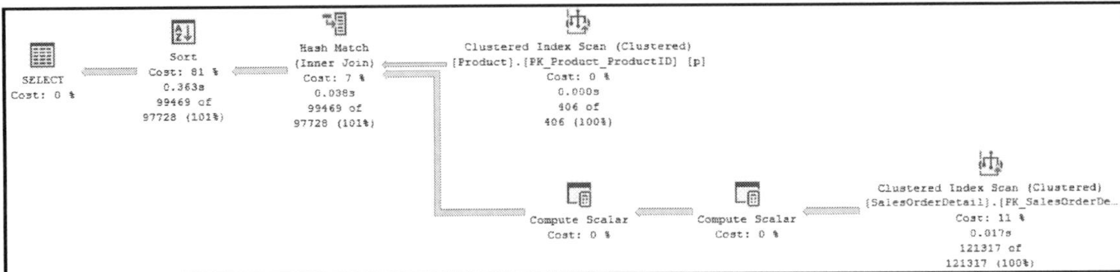

The first query returns 0 rows, and the second returns 99,469 rows, which has an obvious impact on resource usage.

The ISO-compliant statement for **NULL** equality should instead be the following:

```
SET ANSI_NULLS ON
GO
SELECT *
FROM Sales.SalesOrderDetail AS sod
INNER JOIN Production.Product AS p ON sod.ProductID = p.ProductID
WHERE SellEndDate IS NULL
ORDER BY Style DESC
OPTION (MAXDOP 1);
GO
```

The query generates the same execution plan as the preceding `ANSI_NULLS OFF` example. This is because when **ANSI_NULLS** is **ON**, a comparison to **NULL** must use the ISO convention that a **NULL** evaluates to an unknown value, and as such is not equal to another **NULL**. If `SET ANSI_NULLS` is not specified for the session or statement, the **ANSI_NULLS** database option stands.

Statement

Statement is the actual T-SQL statement that was executed. This is limited to 4,000 characters.

TraceFlags

TraceFlags can expand to show additional information on trace flags present during compilation and execution. Trace flags may change the behavior of SQL Server during query compilation and optimization, during query execution, or both. Therefore, during any query performance troubleshooting exercise, it's important to know which trace flags were influencing a given query at any stage.

Under the **TraceFlags** property, there are two lists that can be expanded:

- **[1] IsCompileTime | True**: This returns a list of all the trace flags active in the system when the query was undergoing the process of compilation and optimization
- **[2] IsCompileTime | False***: This returns a list of all the trace flags active in the system when the query was being executed

In the next screenshot, on the left side, we see two trace flags present at both compile and execution time: **7412** and **4199**.

These are documented trace flags. For more information, refer to the SQL Server documentation page at `http://aka.ms/traceflags`.

On the right side of the following screenshot, we see the same two trace flags present at compile time, but only one at execution time (**7412**). This means that between the time the query was compiled and the current query execution plan was captured, trace flag **4199** was disabled at the system level using the T-SQL command `DBCC TRACEOFF (4199, -1)`:

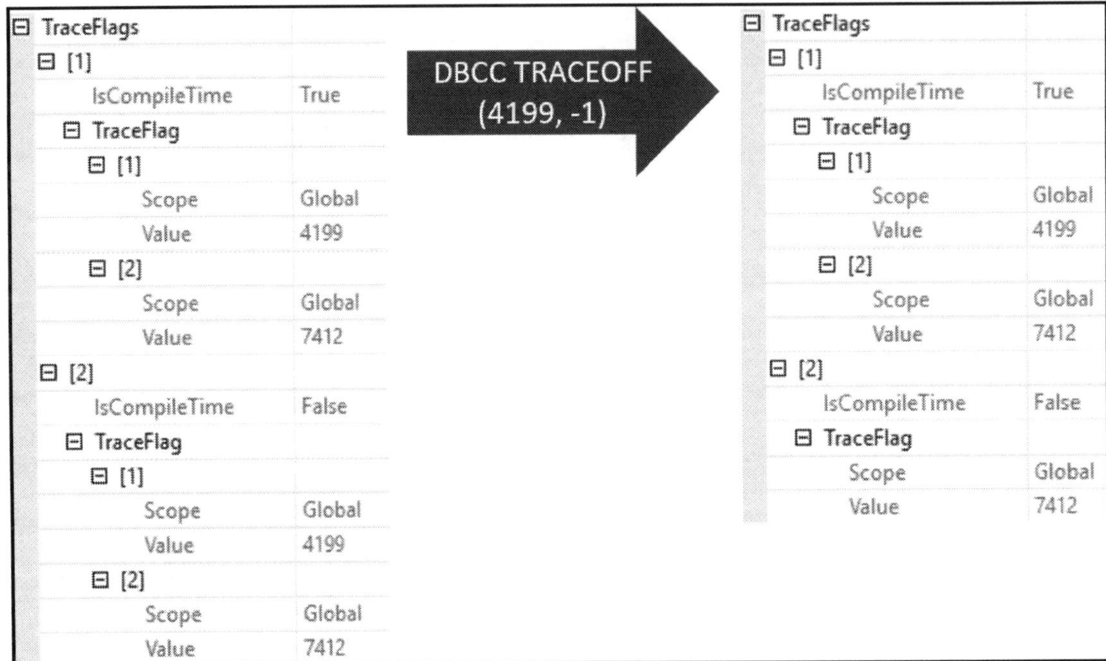

Because trace flag **4199** enables query optimizer hotfixes, we immediately know that the plan to which the left picture belongs was compiled using a non-default set of query optimization options. Because trace flag **4199** was disabled using the DBCC command, such options are not available for new incoming T-SQL queries that have not been compiled yet. This provides important context for the query performance troubleshooting exercise.

WaitStats

WaitStats* can expand to show additional information about the top 10 waits accrued while the query was executing in the scope of the current session, in descending order of wait time. For each wait, the following three properties are available:

- **WaitCount***: This refers to the number of times that tasks associated with this request had to wait for a required resource to become available
- **WaitTimeMs***: This refers to the overall wait time in milliseconds for the number of times a query had to wait during query execution
- **WaitType***: This refers the wait type as documented in the SQL Server documentation under the **sys.dm_os_wait_stats** DMV.

Here is the detail for this property for the example query:

⊟ WaitStats	
⊟ [1]	
WaitCount	1493
WaitTimeMs	1
WaitType	MEMORY_ALLOCATION_EXT
⊟ [2]	
WaitCount	5081
WaitTimeMs	7
WaitType	RESERVED_MEMORY_ALLOCATION_EXT
⊟ [3]	
WaitCount	21
WaitTimeMs	231
WaitType	PAGEIOLATCH_SH
⊟ [4]	
WaitCount	289
WaitTimeMs	2198
WaitType	SOS_SCHEDULER_YIELD
⊟ [5]	
WaitCount	53
WaitTimeMs	4102
WaitType	ASYNC_NETWORK_IO

QueryTimeStats*

QueryTimeStats* can expand to show additional information on time metrics for a given execution. The detailed elements in **QueryTimeStats** include **CpuTime*** and **ElapsedTime*** for the overall query. Both are measured in milliseconds and can replace the need to execute the query with `SET STATISTICS TIME` separately.

Here is the detail for this property for the example query:

QueryTimeStats	
CpuTime	557
ElapsedTime	3251

For queries that call **User-defined Functions (UDFs)**, the **UdfCpuTime*** and **UdfElapsedTime*** elements are also included under **QueryTimeStats**. These are available starting with SQL Server 2014 Service Pack 3, SQL Server 2016 Service Pack 2, and SQL Server 2017 Cumulative Update 3. Both are measured in milliseconds and provide insight into the cost of executing a UDF, which can otherwise go unnoticed by simply looking at a plan.

The following example creates a Scalar UDF in the **AdventureWorks** sample database:

```
CREATE FUNCTION ufn_CategorizePrice (@Price money)
RETURNS NVARCHAR(50)
AS
BEGIN
       DECLARE @PriceCategory NVARCHAR(50)
       IF @Price < 100 SELECT @PriceCategory = 'Cheap'
       IF @Price BETWEEN 101 and 500 SELECT @PriceCategory = 'Mid Price'
       IF @Price BETWEEN 501 and 1000 SELECT @PriceCategory = 'Expensive'
       IF @Price > 1001 SELECT @PriceCategory = 'Unaffordable'
       RETURN @PriceCategory
END;
```

Here's a query executed in the **AdventureWorks** sample database that uses the newly created UDF:

```
SELECT dbo.ufn_CategorizePrice(UnitPrice),
       SalesOrderID, SalesOrderDetailID, CarrierTrackingNumber,
       OrderQty, ProductID, SpecialOfferID, UnitPrice, UnitPriceDiscount,
       LineTotal, rowguid, ModifiedDate
FROM Sales.SalesOrderDetail;
```

In the generated execution plan, we can see the two additional properties under **QueryTimeStats**:

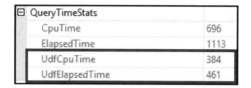

QueryTimeStats	
CpuTime	696
ElapsedTime	1113
UdfCpuTime	384
UdfElapsedTime	461

MissingIndexes

MissingIndexes refers to potentially missing indexes that may benefit the query's performance, as identified by the Query Optimizer during query compilation. During the compilation process, which we discussed in the *Query compilation essentials* section of Chapter 2, *Understanding Query Processing*, SQL Server matches existing indexes where any of the columns required for the query predicates, aggregates, and output are present. Then it chooses to access the existing index or set of indexes that minimize the cost of access to the required columns. In other words, which index or set of indexes are the cheapest to read data from.

As this matching process occurs, SQL Server can identify whether the current set of indexes already covers the query, partially or as a whole, or if a more optimized index could be created to lower the cost of accessing the required columns. For each table mentioned in the query, if SQL Server can find an index that might provide cheaper access to data, it will store that missing index recommendation in the cached plan.

The missing index recommendation builds the recommendation based on the following:

- Columns present in join or search equality predicates, such as WHERE column = value, WHERE column IS NULL for a nullable column, or a ON column = column join
- Columns present in join or search inequality predicates, such as WHERE column <> value, WHERE column > value, or WHERE column IS NOT NULL for a nullable column
- Columns present in the output, such as those in the **SELECT** clause or an UPDATE ... FROM clause

For all these conditions, the columns will be listed in the order that they appear in the underlying tables.

The query execution plan for which we have been examining all the previous properties doesn't have missing index recommendations, so we need to use a different query.

The following example is a query that executes in the **AdventureWorks** sample database with an existing non-clustered index scan and a clustered index scan:

```
SELECT p.FirstName, p.LastName, c.AccountNumbe
FROM Person.Person p
INNER JOIN Sales.Customer c ON c.PersonID = p.BusinessEntityID
WHERE p.FirstName = 'Robert';
```

The query generates the following execution plan:

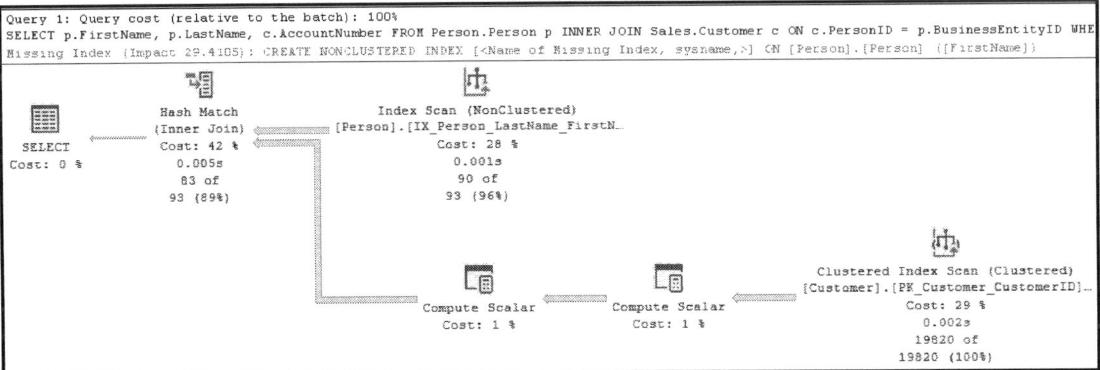

Recall what we discussed in the *Query Plan operators of interest* section under *NonClustered Index Scan*. In this case, SQL Server uses the following:

- An existing non-clustered index of the **Person** table that doesn't contain the **FirstName** column as a leading key column, but it is the second column in the index. Because the query is searching for **FirstName** only, SQL Server cannot seek the index.
- The clustered index of the **Customer** table because none of the existing non-clustered indexes contains **PersonID** as a key column. Because the query is joining on **PersonID** only, SQL Server cannot seek the index.

Note that in the graphical query plan, we can only see one index recommendation with an estimated impact of 29.4%. However, the query plan may have more than one index recommendation because the query uses several tables. To see all indexes, we need to see the XML of the plan. Alternatively, we can open the properties window by right-clicking the root node (**SELECT**), which we can see in the following screenshot:

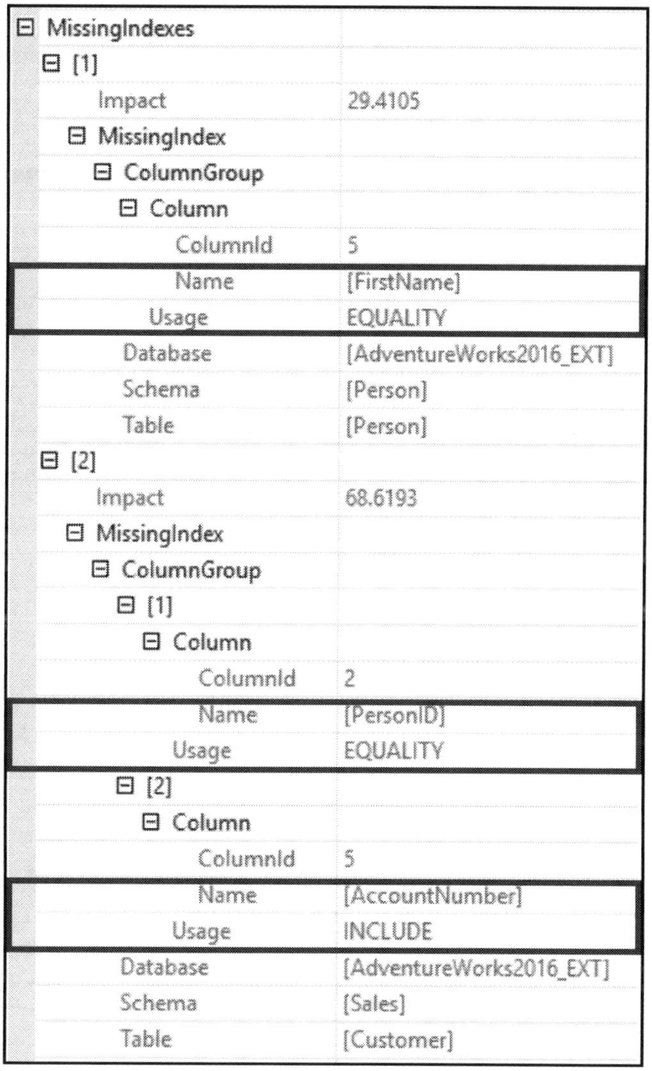

⊟ MissingIndexes	
⊟ [1]	
Impact	29.4105
⊟ MissingIndex	
⊟ ColumnGroup	
⊟ Column	
ColumnId	5
Name	[FirstName]
Usage	EQUALITY
Database	[AdventureWorks2016_EXT]
Schema	[Person]
Table	[Person]
⊟ [2]	
Impact	68.6193
⊟ MissingIndex	
⊟ ColumnGroup	
⊟ [1]	
⊟ Column	
ColumnId	2
Name	[PersonID]
Usage	EQUALITY
⊟ [2]	
⊟ Column	
ColumnId	5
Name	[AccountNumber]
Usage	INCLUDE
Database	[AdventureWorks2016_EXT]
Schema	[Sales]
Table	[Customer]

We can see that two index recommendations exist in the screenshot. Based on the order in which SQL Server builds index recommendations, we need to look at the **EQUALITY** columns, then the **INEQUALITY** columns (if any), and finally at any output columns (identified as **INCLUDE**). I can derive the following index-creation statements from this information—in fact, that is what SSMS did in the graphical query plan:

- One index recommendation for the **Person** table, with the following index creation statement: `CREATE INDEX IX_FirstName ON [Person].[Person] ([FirstName])`
- One index recommendation for the **Customer** table, with the following index creation statement: `CREATE INDEX IX_PersonID ON [Sales].[Customer] ([PersonID]) INCLUDE ([AccountNumber])`

Because there aren't any existing indexes that even closely match these definitions, we can create the indexes. Then we can execute the query again, which generates the following execution plan without missing index recommendations:

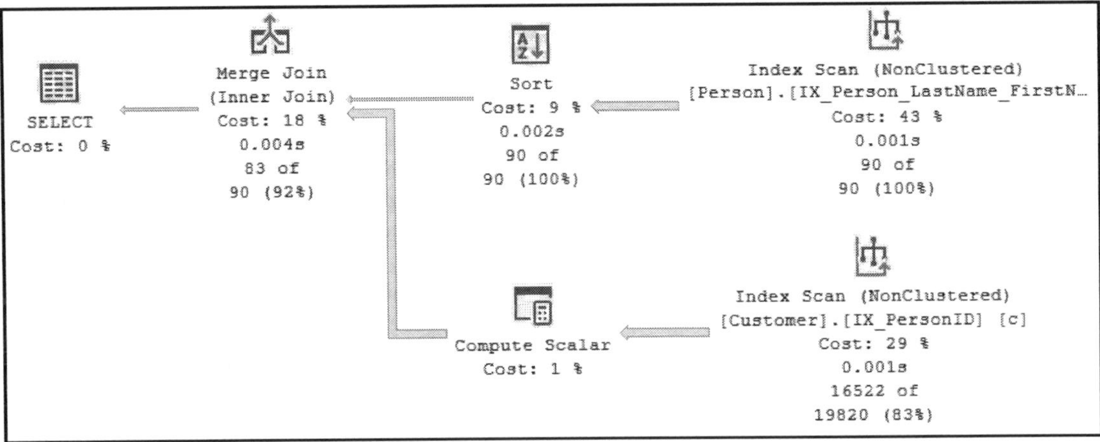

However, notice the new index on the **Person** table was not used. We created the new index with the key on the **FirstName** column as recommended, so why was the previous index used? The answer is that the new index doesn't include the other required column in the **Person** table, **LastName**. It was still cheaper to use the previous index than to use the new non-clustered index, which requires a lookup in the clustered index. Recreating the index to include the **LastName** column should allow the new index to be used. The following index creation statement does this: `CREATE INDEX IX_FirstName ON [Person].[Person] ([FirstName]) INCLUDE ([LastName])`.

Then we can execute the query again, which generates the following execution plan:

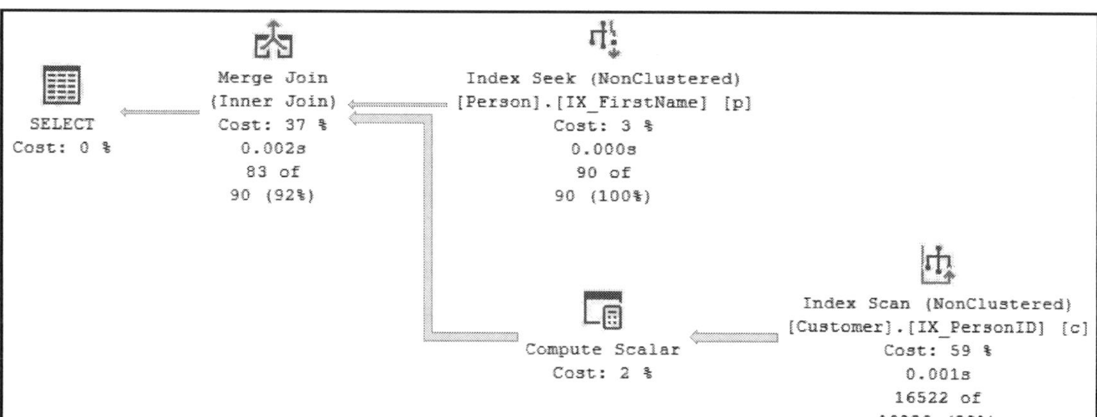

As expected, the revised index on the **Person** table is used. Look for missing index suggestions as one way to help optimize our queries. All the index types and options mentioned will be discussed in the *Basic index guidelines* section of `Chapter 5`, *Writing Elegant T-SQL Queries*.

In the *Troubleshooting common scenarios with DMV queries* section of `Chapter 8`, *Building Diagnostic Queries Using DMVs and DMFs*, we will see examples of how to leverage DMVs to programmatically access missing index information that our SQL Server may be storing.

Parameter List

Parameter List can expand to show additional information on which parameters the current plan was compiled with; it is available for parameterized queries only. This can be useful for troubleshooting issues such as parameter sniffing and data-type conversion issues from within showplan, without the need to access the database. That is very useful when the user that's analyzing the plan is working remotely or lacks the permission to access the database schema. For each parameter, the following four elements are available:

- **Column**: This element identifies the parameter name in the current plan
- **Parameter Compiled Value**: This element refers to the first incoming value for the parameter, which drove the process of query optimization
- **Parameter Data Type**: This element refers the the data type of the first incoming value for the parameter
- **Parameter Runtime Value***: This element refers to the last used value for the parameter, for a plan that had been previously compiled and cached

We will further detail implicit conversion issues in `Chapter 7`, *Discovering T-SQL Anti-Patterns in Depth*. Take the example of the following stored procedure created and executed in the **AdventureWorks** sample database:

```
CREATE OR ALTER PROCEDURE usp_SalesProds (@P1 NVARCHAR(10))
AS
SELECT *
FROM Sales.SalesOrderDetail AS sod
INNER JOIN Production.Product AS p ON sod.ProductID = p.ProductID
WHERE SalesOrderID = @P1
ORDER BY Style DESC
GO

EXEC usp_SalesProds @P1 = 49879
GO

EXEC usp_SalesProds @P1 = 48766
GO
```

In the generated execution plan, we can see the following information under **Parameter List**:

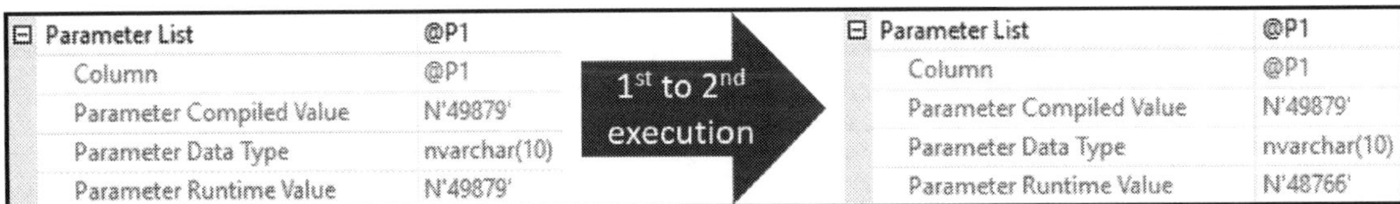

On the first execution of the stored procedure, SQL Server reads the incoming parameters and uses that information plus statistics to generate a plan that's optimized to retrieve the required set of data. This is the reason we see **Parameter Compiled Value** is equal to the **Parameter Runtime Value** property.

On the second execution, notice how the **Parameter Runtime Value** property changed but the **Parameter Compiled Value** property remained. This indicates that the query plan was reused from the cache.

Now let's see the example of the following query using **sp_prepare** in the **AdventureWorks** sample database:

```
DECLARE @P1 int;
EXEC sp_prepare @P1 output,
    N'@P1 int',
    N'SELECT *
FROM Sales.SalesOrderDetail AS sod
INNER JOIN Production.Product AS p ON sod.ProductID = p.ProductID
```

```
WHERE SalesOrderID = @P1
ORDER BY Style DESC
OPTION (MAXDOP 1);';

SELECT @P1;
GO
```

This returns the handle with a value of 1, which applications can use by executing **sp_execute**, before evicting the plan from the cache with **sp_unprepare**:

```
EXEC sp_execute 1, N'49879';
GO

EXEC sp_execute 1, N'48766';
GO

EXEC sp_unprepare1;
GO
```

In the generated execution plan, we can see the following information under **Parameter List**:

Notice that **Parameter Compiled Value** is absent. This is because the prepared plan was not parameterized, and so the cached plan does not retain any parameter information. Further, because unlike a stored procedure where a DBA can ultimately see the parameter data type by opening the T-SQL definition, a prepared query is not an object inside a database. So, having the information on the parameter data type becomes valuable for troubleshooting conversion issues that could otherwise only be found by tracing workload activity to detect the **sp_prepare** statement.

Warnings*

Warnings* can expand to show the type of warning, and additional information that helps the troubleshooting process. Plan-level warnings will show as a yellow triangle sign in the graphical query execution plan at the root-node level. Hovering over the operators that display such a triangle will also show details on the warning. At the time of writing this book, the existing plan-level warning types are the following.

PlanAffectingConvert

PlanAffectingConvert* happens when the Query Optimizer encounters the need to convert data types, and the conversion operation affects the CE process or the ability to seek an existing index. Because conversions occur at runtime, and query optimization happens before execution, the Query Optimizer cannot account for such information during compilation. This is a direct result of the developers' choices, either at the query or database schema level, but can usually be remediated.

The following example shows a query executed in the **AdventureWorks** sample database with a conversion warning about CEs:

```
CREATE TABLE #tmpSales (SalesOrderID CHAR(10) PRIMARY KEY CLUSTERED);
INSERT INTO #tmpSales
SELECT TOP 1000 SalesOrderID FROM Sales.SalesOrderHeader;
GO
SELECT * FROM #tmpSales WHERE SalesOrderID = 44360;
```

Next is the warning detail for the example query, where the two CE warning types are present:

⊟ Warnings	Type conversion in expression (CONVERT_IMPLICIT(int,[tempdb].[dbo].[#tmpSa
⊟ PlanAffectingConvert	
ConvertIssue	CardinalityEstimate
Expression	CONVERT_IMPLICIT(int,[tempdb].[dbo].[#tmpSales].[SalesOrderID],0)
⊟ PlanAffectingConvert	
ConvertIssue	SeekPlan
Expression	CONVERT_IMPLICIT(int,[tempdb].[dbo].[#tmpSales].[SalesOrderID],0)=(44360)

Looking at the query predicate and the table schema, we see the converted expression happens because of the mismatch between data types; the query predicate is passed as an integer, while the table's data type is a string. This affects the ability to do accurate estimations, but also prevents seeking on the clustered index for the same reason.

All warnings can also be seen in the generated execution plan by hovering over the **SELECT** clause:

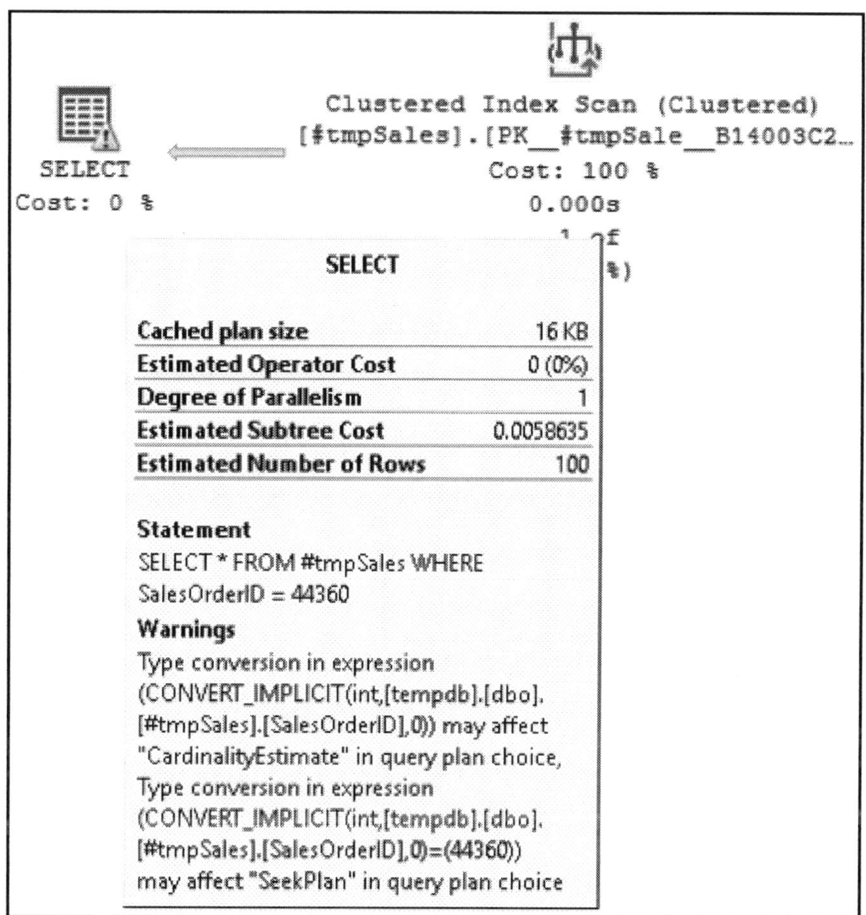

To fix this, simply change either the base table data type to integer, or the predicate to string. This eliminates both warnings because there will be no conversion, and therefore an index seek can be used rather than a scan.

WaitForMemoryGrant*

WaitForMemoryGrant* happens when a query waits more than one second to acquire a memory grant or when the initial attempt to get the memory fails. **RESOURCE_SEMAPHORE** waits may indicate an excessive number of concurrent queries, or an excessive amount of memory grant requests that the current resources cannot handle.

The warning reports the number of seconds the query had to wait for **MemoryGrant** during execution:

⊟ Warnings	The query memory grant detected "ExcessiveGrant", which may impact the reliability.
⊟ MemoryGrantWarning	
GrantedMemory	67808
GrantWarningKind	ExcessiveGrant
MaxUsedMemory	984
RequestedMemory	67808

MemoryGrantWarning*

MemoryGrantWarning* happens when SQL Server detects that memory grants were not estimated properly, as it relates to the comparison between the initial memory grant and the memory used throughout execution. This warning happens when one of the following three conditions occur:

- **ExcessiveGrant**: This warning is fired when the max used memory is too small when compared to the granted memory. This scenario can cause blocking and severely affect SQL Server's ability to run concurrent workload efficiently. For example, if a SQL Server has 10 GB of memory, and each request is granted 1 GB of memory but only uses a small fraction of that, then at most only 10 queries can be active simultaneously, but looking at the actual used memory, this number could be far greater. Here is the warning detail where the **ExcessiveGrant** condition is present:

⊟ Warnings	The query memory grant detected "ExcessiveGrant", which may impact the reliability.
⊟ MemoryGrantWarning	
GrantedMemory	67808
GrantWarningKind	ExcessiveGrant
MaxUsedMemory	984
RequestedMemory	67808

Memory estimations are directly related to the query-optimization process and the estimated plan. There are several ways to attempt remediation, and usually updating statistics can help improve estimations. Recent versions of SQL Server can administratively address these with the use of the **MIN_PERCENT_GRANT** and **MAX_PERCENT_GRANT** query hints.

- **GrantIncrease**: This warning is fired when the grant starts to increase too much, based on the ratio between the max used memory and initial requested memory grant. Unlike row mode, where the initial memory grant is not dynamic, batch mode allows for the initial grant to be exceeded to a point, before a spill occurs. This is done because spilling in batch mode has a greater cost than spilling in row mode. For example, consider a SQL Server with 10 GB of memory, where each request is running in batch mode and granted 512 MB of memory. If around 20 requests are executing simultaneously and can exceed that initial amount of memory, this can cause server instability and unpredictable workload performance.
- **UsedMoreThanGranted**: This warning is fired when the max used memory exceeds the initial granted memory. Much like the **GrantIncrease** scenario, this can cause **out-of-memory** (**OOM**) conditions on the server.

SpatialGuess*

SpatialGuess* happens when SQL Server must use a fixed selectivity estimation (also called **guess**) when optimizing a query that uses spatial data types and indexes. Here is the warning detail where the **SpatialGuess** condition is present:

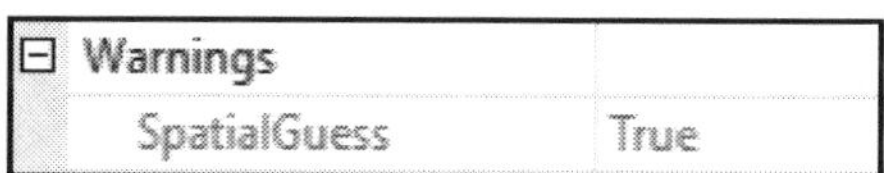

UnmatchedIndexes*

UnmatchedIndexes* happens when the Query Optimizer cannot match an existing filtered index with a query predicate due to parameterization.

SQL Server can use optimized non-clustered indexes that are defined using a WHERE clause. These are called **filtered indexes** and are especially suitable for narrow query coverage. Being defined on a subset of data, these indexes can significantly improve query performance.

The following example creates a filtered index in the **AdventureWorks** sample database, and then executes a query with an unmatched index warning:

```
CREATE NONCLUSTERED INDEX FIProductAccessories ON Production.Product (
    ProductSubcategoryID,
    ListPrice
)
INCLUDE (Name)
WHERE ProductSubcategoryID >= 27 AND ProductSubcategoryID <= 36;
GO

DECLARE @i int = 33
SELECT Name, ProductSubcategoryID, ListPrice
FROM Production.Product
WHERE ProductSubcategoryID = @i AND ListPrice > 25.00 ;
```

Next is the **UnmatchedIndexes** warning detail for the example query. Also notice the extra element, **UnmatchedIndexes**:

⊟ UnmatchedIndexes	
⊟ Parameterization	[AdventureWorks2016].[Production].[Product].[FIProductAccessories]
Database	[AdventureWorks2016]
Index	[FIProductAccessories]
Schema	[Production]
Table	[Product]
⊟ Warnings	
UnmatchedIndexes	True

It's clear that SQL Server was able to identify an eligible filtered index but was unable to use it because if a query is parameterized, that means that an incoming parameter with a value outside the defined filter would not produce a result.

In the following example, SQL Server can leverage the filtered index:

```
SELECT Name, ProductSubcategoryID, ListPrice
FROM Production.Product
WHERE ProductSubcategoryID = 33 AND ListPrice > 25.00;
```

This is because the query is not parameterized, which means SQL Server can match the incoming predicate with an existing filtered index and use it to read only the relevant subset of data.

One alternative to make SQL Server leverage the filtered index can be to build the variable into the string and then execute it:

```
DECLARE @i int = 33, @sqlcmd NVARCHAR(500)
SELECT @sqlcmd = 'SELECT Name, ProductSubcategoryID, ListPrice FROM
Production.Product WHERE ProductSubcategoryID = ' + CAST(@i AS NVARCHAR(5))
+ ' AND ListPrice > 25.00;'
EXECUTE sp_executesql @sqlcmd;
```

This way, SQL Server is executing a query that matches the non-parameterized version, and the filtered index predicate can be matched so the index is used.

FullUpdateForOnlineIndexBuild

FullUpdateForOnlineIndexBuild* happens when converting a partial index update to a full index update during an online index create or rebuild operation.

Operator-level properties

Analyzing the plan-level properties provides context for the overall plan and the system in which the query plan executed. After that step, it's very important to keep in mind some of the key properties that can be found in the query plan operators of interest that we discussed earlier in the *Query plan properties of interest* section in this chapter.

The following example shows a query executed in the **AdventureWorks** sample database that allows us to examine most of these properties:

```
SELECT *
FROM Sales.SalesOrderDetail AS sod
INNER JOIN Production.Product AS p ON sod.ProductID = p.ProductID
WHERE p.ProductID BETWEEN 850 AND 860
ORDER BY Style DESC
OPTION (USE HINT('ENABLE_PARALLEL_PLAN_PREFERENCE'));
```

The query generates the following execution plan:

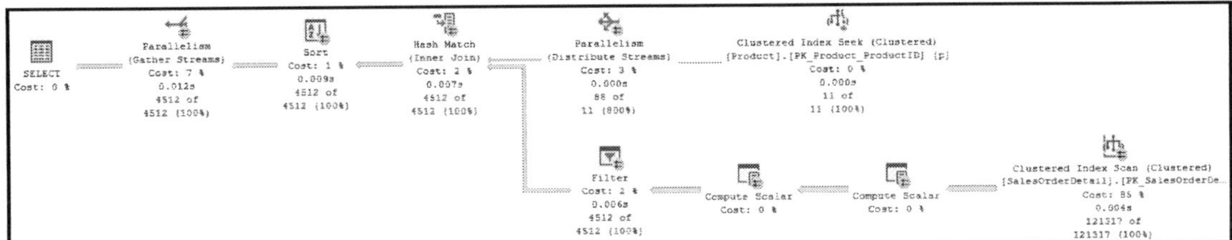

Right-click on the most expensive operator in the plan, open the context menu, and click on **Properties**:

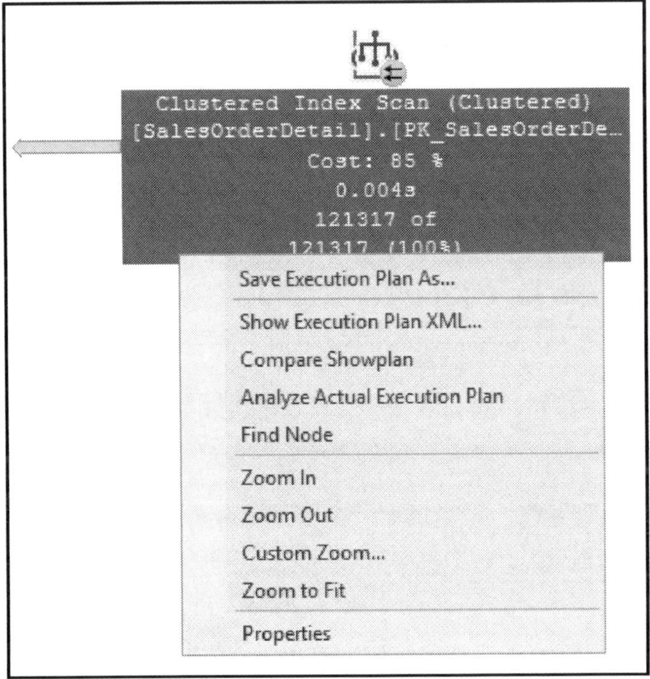

To identify the most expensive operators, follow the thickest arrows from left to right, top to bottom. Note that the **Cost** label in every operator refers to the estimated cost, not the actual execution cost. Therefore, do not use this label as a method of finding the most expensive operators in an actual execution plan.

This opens the **Properties** window:

The properties available depend on the version and build of SQL Server on which the plan was captured. At the time of writing, all the operator level properties described here exist in SQL Server 2016 Service Pack 1 (SP1), SQL Server 2017, and SQL Server 2019. SQL Server 2012 and SQL Server 2014 will have most of these properties available in their latest respective **Service Packs**.

RunTimeCountersPerThread

When troubleshooting query performance problems, having the right metrics available in the query plan avoids unnecessary roundtrips and delays, which can be critical. SQL Server stores several runtime statistics per operator and per thread under **RunTimeCountersPerThread***, providing great insights into performance metrics of various data-access operators.

Actual I/O Statistics*

Optimizing I/O is usually the best tuning approach, because with higher I/O comes higher memory consumption as SQL Server needs to store more data pages in the buffer pool, and higher CPU as cycles are spent processing I/O requests and data movement.

Actual I/O Statistics* provides information on **Large Object** (**LOB**), physical and logical reads allowing for immediate insight into the cost of an operator, without the need to collect or interpret the information from `SET STATISTICS IO`.

If the query was executed in parallel, we can see how many data pages were read by each thread. In the following screenshot, we see the detail for the most expensive operator in the preceding plan, a clustered index scan:

Actual I/O Statistics	
Actual Lob Logical Reads	0
Actual Lob Physical Reads	0
Actual Lob Read Aheads	0
Actual Logical Reads	1345
Thread 0	37
Thread 1	253
Thread 2	124
Thread 3	196
Thread 4	124
Thread 5	181
Thread 6	124
Thread 7	184
Thread 8	122
Actual Physical Reads	0
Actual Read Aheads	0
Actual Scans	9

Actual Number of Rows

Similarly, having information on the actual number of rows that flowed through the operators allows database professionals to track the most expensive areas of a plan. The **Actual Number of Rows** (**ActualRows*** in showplan XML) shows the number of rows output by an operator after any predicates were applied. The **Number of Rows Read** (**ActualRowsRead*** in showplan XML) shows the number of rows read before predicates were applied.

In the following screenshot, we see the detail for both properties in the same clustered index scan:

Actual Number of Rows	121317
Thread 0	0
Thread 1	23109
Thread 2	11174
Thread 3	18209
Thread 4	11421
Thread 5	17864
Thread 6	11469
Thread 7	16792
Thread 8	11279

Number of Rows Read	121317
Thread 1	23109
Thread 2	11174
Thread 3	18209
Thread 4	11421
Thread 5	17864
Thread 6	11469
Thread 7	16792
Thread 8	11279

Thread zero is the coordinating thread and does not accumulate I/O, which is handled by all the other threads for the request.

Actual Time Statistics

Time is an important measurement, not only by itself, but because these properties track the time in milliseconds an operator spent during execution. As such, comparing these with waits accrued during execution, and the overall query elapsed execution time, allows database professionals to pinpoint expensive areas of the plan with great accuracy.

The **Actual Elapsed CPU Time (ms)** (**ActualCPUms*** in showplan XML) shows the CPU time accumulated over all threads, with details on each thread for parallel queries. The **Actual Elapsed Time (ms)** (**ActualElapsedms*** in showplan XML) shows the elapsed time the operator took to execute. Although there is detail on each thread for parallel queries, the overall elapsed time is the same as the slowest thread time. Having this information in showplan removes the need to collect or interpret the information from `SET STATISTICS TIME`.

In the following screenshot, we see the detail for both properties in the same clustered index scan:

⊟ Actual Time Statistics	
⊟ Actual Elapsed CPU Time (ms)	20
Thread 0	0
Thread 1	2
Thread 2	2
Thread 3	4
Thread 4	2
Thread 5	4
Thread 6	2
Thread 7	2
Thread 8	2
⊟ Actual Elapsed Time (ms)	4
Thread 0	0
Thread 1	3
Thread 2	3
Thread 3	4
Thread 4	2
Thread 5	4
Thread 6	3
Thread 7	2
Thread 8	3

Estimated rows

When analyzing a plan retrieved from the plan cache, which is an estimated plan or query plan, only the estimations are available. In an actual plan, or query execution plan, this information is present, and it becomes useful to compare it with the actual rows we just discussed. This is because significant differences between estimated and actual rows usually expose CE issues, and whether queries are using underlying indexes efficiently.

We will discuss remediation techniques for cardinality estimation issues from `Chapter 10`, *Tracking Performance History with Query Store*, through `Chapter 12`, *Troubleshooting Live Queries*.

The **Estimated Number of Rows** (**EstimateRows** in showplan XML) shows the estimated number of rows output by an operator after any predicates are applied. The **Estimated Number of Rows to be Read** (**EstimatedRowsRead** in showplan XML) shows the estimated number of rows read before predicates are applied.

In the following screenshot, we see the detail for both properties in the same Clustered Index Scan:

Estimated Number of Rows	121317
Estimated Number of Rows to be Read	121317

EstimateRowsWithoutRowGoal

The **EstimateRowsWithoutRowGoal** property is available starting with SQL Server 2016 SP2 and SQL Server 2017 CU3, when the Query Optimizer uses an optimization technique called **row goal**. If the Query Optimizer used row goal, this property expresses the estimated number of rows that would be processed if row goal hadn't been used.

Normally, when the Query Optimizer estimates the cost of a query plan, it assumes that all qualifying rows from all tables must be processed. However, when a query uses a **TOP**, **IN**, or **EXISTS** clause, the **FAST** query hint, or a `SET ROWCOUNT` statement, this causes the Query Optimizer to search for a query plan that will quickly return a smaller number of rows. This makes the row goal a very useful optimization strategy for certain query patterns.

The following example shows a query executed in the **AdventureWorks** sample database that allows us to examine this property:

```
SELECT TOP (100)*
FROM Sales.SalesOrderHeader AS s
INNER JOIN Sales.SalesOrderDetail AS d ON s.SalesOrderID = d.SalesOrderID
WHERE s.TotalDue > 1000;
```

In the generated execution plan, we can see the **EstimateRowsWithoutRowGoal** property of the Clustered Index Scan operator on the **SalesOrderDetail** table:

EstimateRowsWithoutRowGoal	121317

These can be compared with the estimated rows we discussed in the *MissingIndexes* section to determine whether row goal is being used to the query's advantage. If the value of **Estimated Number of Rows** is significantly lower than that of **Estimated Number of Rows to be Read**, and row goal is used, it may be the case that row goal is not improving the plan quality. We will see more of this property and how to use it for troubleshooting in the *Query plan comparison* section of `Chapter 10`, *Comparative Analysis of Query Plans.*

Warnings*

Warnings* also surface on specific operators. These contain information that helps the troubleshooting process when drilling through a plan. As with plan-level warnings, operator level warnings show as a yellow triangle sign in the graphical query execution plan. Again, hovering over the operators that display this triangle will also show details on the warning. As of this writing, the existing operator level warning types were the following.

Columns With No Statistics*

Columns With No Statistics* happens when the Query Optimizer needs to load statistics on any given column that's relevant for the query, but none exist. If **Auto-Create Statistics** is disabled in the database, SQL Server cannot automatically create the missing statistics and this warning persists between executions.

The following example shows a query executed in the **AdventureWorks** sample database with a **Columns With No Statistics** warning:

```
USE [master]
GO
ALTER DATABASE [AdventureWorks] SET AUTO_CREATE_STATISTICS OFF
```

```
GO

SELECT [CarrierTrackingNumber]
FROM Sales.SalesOrderDetail
WHERE [OrderQty] > 10
ORDER BY OrderQty;
GO

ALTER DATABASE [AdventureWorks] SET AUTO_CREATE_STATISTICS ON
GO
```

In the generated execution plan, we can see the warning under the properties of the Clustered Index Scan operator that generated it:

⊟ Warnings	Columns With No Statistics: [AdventureWorks2016].[Sales].[SalesOrderDetail].Ord
⊟ Columns With No Statistics	
⊟ Column Reference	[AdventureWorks2016].[Sales].[SalesOrderDetail].OrderQty
Column	OrderQty
Database	[AdventureWorks2016]
Schema	[Sales]
Table	[SalesOrderDetail]

This warning is always present for the internal side of a Nested Loops join involving a spatial index. This is a by-design behavior.

If auto-create statistics is enabled as it is by default and a best practice, the database engine will create a single-column statistic on the column that triggered the warning condition if the column is eligible.

Because statistics cannot be created on a non-persisted computed column, auto-create statistics cannot automatically create a statistic object on these column types. Mark the computed column as persisted to allow auto-create statistics.

Starting with SQL Server 2019, the time spent creating the statistic triggered by this warning will also be visible as an accumulated wait with the **WAIT_ON_SYNC_STATISTICS_REFRESH** type.

Spill To TempDb

Spill To TempDb* happens when the available query memory (known as the **memory grant**) is not enough to run the required operation in memory, and rather than halting execution, the operation runs with the support of TempDB workfiles or worktables, depending on the type of spill. By resorting to I/O rather than being executed solely in memory, spills usually must be remediated as they can severely slow down query performance. We covered the common Sort and Hash spills, as follows, in the *Query plan operators of interest* section:

- **Sort Spill***
- **Hash Spill***
- **Exchange Spill***

No Join Predicate

No Join Predicate happens when SQL Server cannot identify a join predicate to apply to a join between two or more tables, and none has been specified in the T-SQL statement text.

The following example shows a query executed in the **AdventureWorks** sample database with a **No Join Predicate** warning:

```
SELECT*
FROM Sales.SalesOrderHeader AS h,
       Sales.SalesOrderDetail AS d,
       Production.Product AS p
WHERE h.SalesOrderID = 49879;
```

Unlike all other warnings, **No Join Predicate** is shown as a red circle with a white X in the graphical query execution plan:

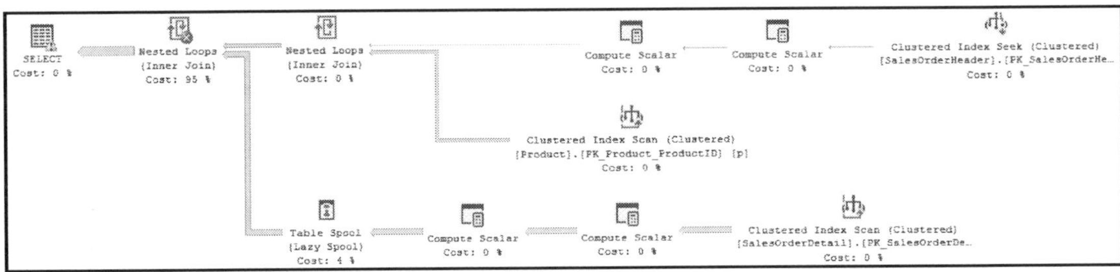

In the generated plan, we can see the warning under the properties of the Nested Loops operator that generated it:

⊟ Warnings	No Join Predicate
No Join Predicate	True

To remediate this case, rewrite the query to state the intended join operation and join predicates:

```
SELECT *
FROM Sales.SalesOrderHeader AS h
INNER JOIN Sales.SalesOrderDetail AS d ON h.SalesOrderID = d.SalesOrderID
INNER JOIN Production.Product AS p ON d.ProductId = p.ProductID
WHERE h.SalesOrderID = 49879;
```

The query then generates the following execution plan:

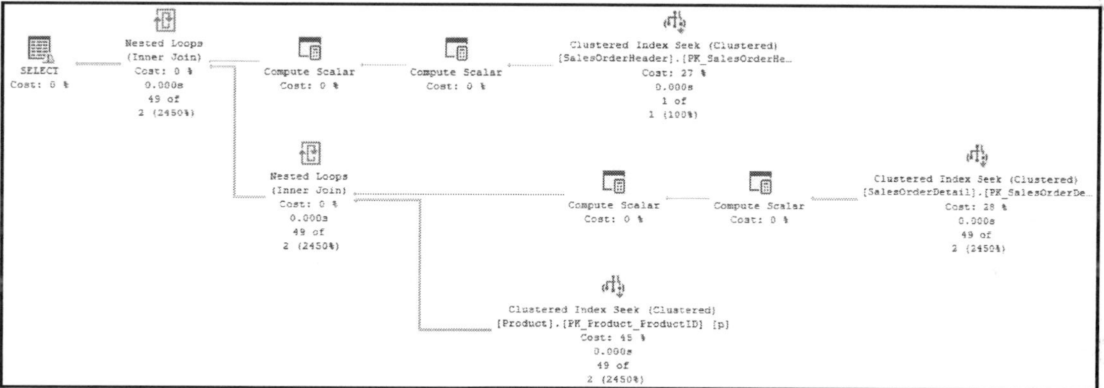

Summary

Hopefully, after reading this chapter, you have a good understanding of the various elements that make up a query execution plan in SQL Server. Nearly everything we need to understand and troubleshoot the performance of our T-SQL queries can be found somewhere in the plan, either in the visible part of the plan, or in the properties windows, which we can access by right-clicking the operators.

In the next chapter and throughout the rest of this book, we will use query execution plans to illustrate various T-SQL patterns and anti-patterns so we can identify and remediate them in our own code.

5 Writing Elegant T-SQL Queries

At this point, you should have a good understanding of how to build a T-SQL query, but how do we build an elegant T-SQL query? We want one that not only gets the job done but does so efficiently. There are a few guidelines that are important to keep in mind when writing T-SQL queries to ensure that they perform and scale well. For this purpose, this chapter discusses some basics of database physical design structure, such as indexes, as well as how the Query Optimizer estimates cost and chooses what data access methods must be used, based on how the query is written.

In this chapter, the following topics will be covered:

- Understanding predicate SARGability
- Basic index guidelines
- Best practices for T-SQL querying

Understanding predicate SARGability

A **predicate** is a filter that can be used to determine the set of conditions to apply to a query in order to trim the result set. As we have discussed in previous chapters, these are typically applicable to the following clauses:

- **JOIN** clauses, which filter rows matching the type of join
- **HAVING** clauses, which filter the results
- **WHERE** clauses, which filter source rows from a table or an index

Most queries will make use of predicates, usually through a **WHERE** clause. When a predicate is serviceable by an index, it is said the predicate is **SARGable**, which is an acronym for **Search ARGument-able**. Having SARGable predicates should be a goal for our T-SQL queries, because it can reduce the number of rows which need to be processed by a plan earlier in the execution, when the data is being read by the database engine. The implementation of this early row-count reduction is called a **predicate pushdown**, which is the action of using the predicate directly in the seek or scan operation and reading only the rows that match the given predicate. When predicate pushdown is not used, the cost implications are high: the database engine needs to read a larger number of rows from the source table or index, and only after that does it, filter down to the number of rows that match the predicate.

SQL Server always optimizes for Predicate Pushdown, sometimes even when part of the predicate cannot be serviced by an index, that is when part of the predicate is non-SARGable, even when it results in a higher number of rows being read; this optimization can eliminate the need for filter operators in a query plan.

We can see how to identify whether predicate pushdown is used efficiently with the following two examples of queries executing in the scope of the **AdventureWorks** sample database:

```
SELECT FirstName, LastName
FROM Person.Person
WHERE LastName like 'S%'AND FirstName = 'John';

SELECT FirstName, LastName
FROM Person.Person
WHERE LastName ='Smith' AND FirstName like 'J%';
```

The queries then generate the following result sets:

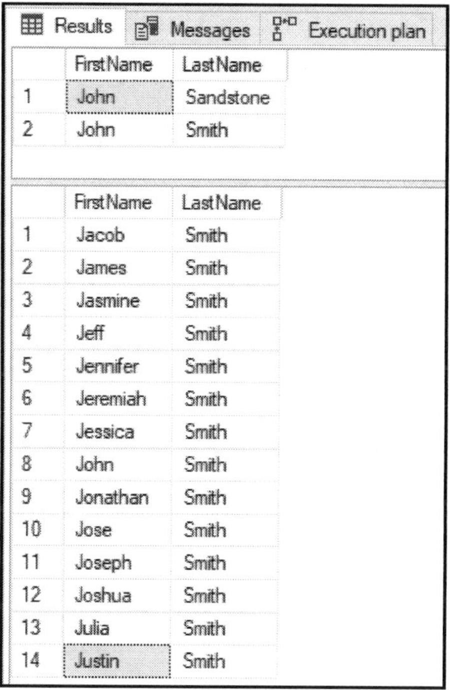

	FirstName	LastName
1	John	Sandstone
2	John	Smith

	FirstName	LastName
1	Jacob	Smith
2	James	Smith
3	Jasmine	Smith
4	Jeff	Smith
5	Jennifer	Smith
6	Jeremiah	Smith
7	Jessica	Smith
8	John	Smith
9	Jonathan	Smith
10	Jose	Smith
11	Joseph	Smith
12	Joshua	Smith
13	Julia	Smith
14	Justin	Smith

Also take a look at the following respective execution plans:

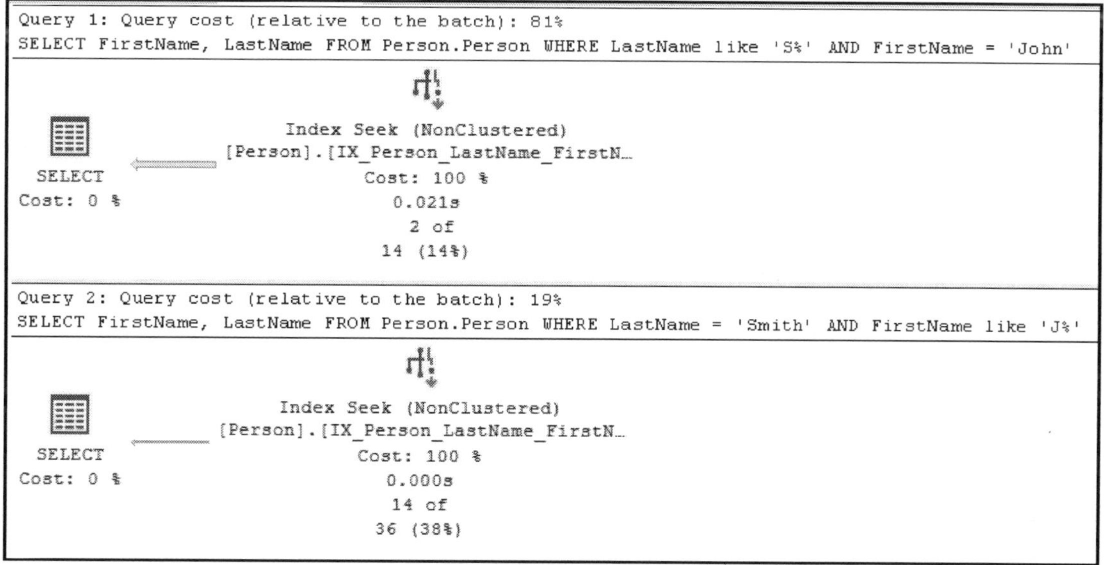

Notice how the plans look the same. However, the estimated cost for **Query 1** is much higher than **Query 2**, as it relates to the entire batch: 81 and 19 percent, respectively. This also translates into the time stats as seen in the plans shown in the preceding screenshot: 21 ms and <1 ms, respectively.

Why is there such a big difference? By looking at the **OptimizerStatsUsage** plan property in the following screenshot, we know the plans loaded the same statistics objects:

⊟ OptimizerStatsUsage	
⊟ [1]	
Database	[AdventureWorks2016_EXT]
LastUpdate	2/17/2019 11:21 AM
ModificationCount	0
SamplingPercent	41.5782
Schema	[Person]
Statistics	[_WA_Sys_00000005_7C4F7684]
Table	[Person]
⊟ [2]	
Database	[AdventureWorks2016_EXT]
LastUpdate	11/16/2015 1:04 PM
ModificationCount	0
SamplingPercent	100
Schema	[Person]
Statistics	[IX_Person_LastName_FirstName_MiddleName]
Table	[Person]

The **IX_Person_LastName_FirstName_MiddleName** statistic has its histogram on the **LastName** column, and the **_WA_Sys_00000005_7C4F7684** statistic has its histogram on the **FirstName** column. This makes sense because both queries have their predicates on those two columns, and the Query Optimizer requires this information to be able to produce an optimized query plan. Looking at the actual rows and estimated rows, we see **Query 1** returned two rows out of 15 estimated rows, and **Query 2** returned 14 rows out of 35 estimated rows. This is a low number of rows and the absolute difference is not significant, so it does not appear that the cost difference can be explained by an incorrect estimation of the number of rows.

Single-column statistics, created by the database engine automatically when auto-create statistics is enabled, are always named with the prefix **_WA_Sys**.

As we discussed in `Chapter 4`, *Exploring Query Execution Plans*, the **Actual Number of Rows** and **Estimated Number of Rows** properties refer to the number of rows output by an operator after any predicates were applied. While this can give us an indication of whether the query optimizer has accurately estimated the cost of the query, it is not really an accurate measure of whether predicate pushdown was effective. Instead, comparing the **Actual Number of Rows** and **Number of Rows Read** properties for an actual plan, or the **Estimated Number of Rows** and **Estimated Number of Rows to be Read** properties for an estimated plan, is the correct approach.

Those properties are available for the **IX_Person_LastName_FirstName_MiddleName** index in the seek operator, as illustrated in the following screenshot:

Query 1

Index Seek (NonClustered)

Scan a particular range of rows from a nonclustered index.

Property	Value
Physical Operation	Index Seek
Logical Operation	Index Seek
Actual Execution Mode	Row
Estimated Execution Mode	Row
Storage	RowStore
Number of Rows Read	2130
Actual Number of Rows	2
Actual Number of Batches	0
Estimated Operator Cost	0.0145016 (100%)
Estimated I/O Cost	0.0120139
Estimated Subtree Cost	0.0145016
Estimated CPU Cost	0.0024877
Estimated Number of Executions	1
Number of Executions	1
Estimated Number of Rows	14.8156
Estimated Number of Rows to be Read	2118.84
Estimated Row Size	74 B
Actual Rebinds	0
Actual Rewinds	0
Ordered	True
Node ID	0

Predicate
[AdventureWorks2016_EXT].[Person].[Person].[FirstName] =N'John' AND [AdventureWorks2016_EXT].[Person].[Person].[LastName] like N'S%'

Object
[AdventureWorks2016_EXT].[Person].[Person].[IX_Person_LastName_FirstName_MiddleName]

Output List
[AdventureWorks2016_EXT].[Person].[Person].FirstName, [AdventureWorks2016_EXT].[Person].[Person].LastName

Seek Predicates
Seek Keys[1]: Start: [AdventureWorks2016_EXT].[Person].[Person].LastName, [AdventureWorks2016_EXT].[Person].[Person].FirstName >= Scalar Operator(N'S'), Scalar Operator (N'John'), End: [AdventureWorks2016_EXT].[Person].[Person].LastName < Scalar Operator(N'T')

Query 2

Index Seek (NonClustered)

Scan a particular range of rows from a nonclustered index.

Property	Value
Physical Operation	Index Seek
Logical Operation	Index Seek
Actual Execution Mode	Row
Estimated Execution Mode	Row
Storage	RowStore
Number of Rows Read	14
Actual Number of Rows	14
Actual Number of Batches	0
Estimated Operator Cost	0.0033209 (100%)
Estimated I/O Cost	0.003125
Estimated Subtree Cost	0.0033209
Estimated CPU Cost	0.0001959
Estimated Number of Executions	1
Number of Executions	1
Estimated Number of Rows	35.3287
Estimated Number of Rows to be Read	35.3287
Estimated Row Size	74 B
Actual Rebinds	0
Actual Rewinds	0
Ordered	True
Node ID	0

Predicate
[AdventureWorks2016_EXT].[Person].[Person].[FirstName] like N'J%'

Object
[AdventureWorks2016_EXT].[Person].[Person].[IX_Person_LastName_FirstName_MiddleName]

Output List
[AdventureWorks2016_EXT].[Person].[Person].FirstName, [AdventureWorks2016_EXT].[Person].[Person].LastName

Seek Predicates
Seek Keys[1]: Prefix: [AdventureWorks2016_EXT].[Person].[Person].LastName = Scalar Operator(N'Smith'), Start: [AdventureWorks2016_EXT].[Person].[Person].FirstName >= Scalar Operator(N'J'), End: [AdventureWorks2016_EXT].[Person].[Person].FirstName < Scalar Operator(N'K')

For **Query 1,** we can see that 2,130 rows were read to return two rows after the **Seek Predicates** option (also in the preceding screenshot) was applied, so there is a significant difference. The predicate used for this query translates a seek condition where the **LastName** column values are greater than or equal to **S**, and **LastName** is smaller than **T**. We can also see that the database engine estimated that 2,118 rows would have to be read in order to return 14 rows, which is a similar ratio. This indicates that SQL Server worked with accurate statistics and came up with good estimations, and it just so happens that the index is not optimal for the query.

The non-SARGable predicate on the **FirstName** column was also pushed down for the condition when values equal **John**. Although no I/O was saved, this engine optimization avoided a filter operator being applied after the seek, saving CPU cycles.

If this query is executed often, then creating a better index for this query may be required, namely making **FirstName** the first key column: a full name such as **John** is more selective than one character followed by a wildcard.

For **Query 2,** only 14 rows were read to return 14 rows, meaning Predicate Pushdown read only the required number of rows for our query, which is also visible in the estimations: both **Estimated Number of Rows** and **Estimated Number of Rows to be Read** match at **35.3287** rows.

The predicates used by queries determine the database index design, and vice versa. Predicate Pushdown, namely SQL Server's ability to push down to the storage engine both SARGable and non-SARGable predicates, is an important performance feature that database professionals must be aware of when writing T-SQL queries that are expected to perform and scale well.

In summary, the next time you see a query that returns only a few rows but takes a relatively long time to execute and has relatively disproportionate CPU and I/O usage, investigate whether the query is making efficient use of our indexes. The next section discusses basic indexing guidelines that we must observe so that our T-SQL queries perform well from an I/O standpoint.

Basic index guidelines

The purpose of indexes in a database is to provide an efficient way to find and access data. Books provide a good analogy here. If we have a book of short stories and we want to find one that is about animals, without an index we would need to flip through every page of the book and read it to see whether any animals are mentioned.

If the book had an index on the subject, that would be a much more efficient way to find the story we are looking for. An index in a book is typically sorted alphabetically, so we wouldn't even need to read the entire index, we could just go to the **A** section and find **Animals** and then stories about animals would be listed with their page numbers. If all we want is to know is whether the book contains animal stories, we're done with just a quick glance at the index. If we want to actually read the story, we can flip to the page number listed in the index and start reading.

This is analogous to a non-clustered index seek with a lookup as we described in the *Query plan operators of interest* section in `Chapter 4`, *Exploring Query Execution Plans*. The seek operation is performed to find the page that contains the data we want based on the keys of the index, and then the lookup operation loads that page and reads the data from it.

We can use the book analogy to describe a **clustered index** as well. A clustered index contains data rows at the leaf level, so this means that the data is stored in the index itself. We can think of this as a dictionary. A dictionary is organized alphabetically, and sometimes a dictionary will have tabs or cutouts for each letter so that we can find the section we're looking for without having to flip through all the pages. There is no separate index in a dictionary because the book itself is organized as an index. This is how a clustered index works: we use the keys of the index to go directly to the page that contains the data we are looking for, so there is no need for the extra look-up step.

In SQL Server, table and index data is stored on pages, just like in a book. The cost of accessing data for a query is therefore measured by the number of page reads. As with a book, if no indexes exist on a table, the number of page reads for a query on that table will be high because each page must be scanned to find the data requested by the query. In general, the fewer reads a query must perform, the cheaper it is.

Keep in mind that the entire cost of the query is more than just the number of page reads; it also includes I/O, memory, and CPU required to join, sort, aggregate, and so on. In this case, we're talking about the cost of data access only—seeks, scans, and lookups—which typically accounts for most of the query cost.

Clustered indexes

As we discussed in the previous chapter, if a table does not have a clustered index, it is stored as a **heap**. While heap data structures allow for fast inserts, they are generally less efficient for data access, so it is recommended that most tables in a SQL Server database have a clustered index.

The clustered index defines the structure of the table itself. Once we create a clustered index, the data rows are stored in the index itself, ordered by the index keys. For this reason, there can be only one clustered index on a table. When choosing which column or columns should be used for the clustered index key, consider the following guidelines:

- **The key should be unique if possible**: While uniqueness is not required, because the data rows are stored in the index, SQL Server must have a way to uniquely identify each row. If the clustered index key is not unique, SQL Server will add a hidden 4-byte column to each row called a **uniqueifier**. This becomes part of the clustered index key in order to enforce uniqueness. This will of course increase the size of the rows, reduce the amount of user data that can fit in a row, reduce the number of rows that fit on a page, and cause the index to be larger than it needs to be, thus leading to more page reads.
- **The key should be narrow**: The entire tree structure of the index is built around the keys, so using a narrow key (in other words, a small data type) can dramatically reduce the size of the index rows, allowing more rows to fit on a page. This in turn minimizes page count and, again, reduces page reads.
- **The key should not be frequently updated**: An index is stored in the order of the keys, so if the key values change, the index must be re-arranged. This is particularly costly with a clustered index because the data rows are stored within the index, so not only is the index restructured when the key value changes, the entire data row will need to be relocated. Recall our discussion on lookups in `Chapter4`, *Exploring Query Execution Plans*. When there is a clustered index on the table, all the non-clustered indexes contain the clustered index key, which serves as a pointer to the data row. This means that if we change the value of a clustered index key, not only do we have to restructure the clustered index, but all the non-clustered indexes that contain this value must be updated.

- **The key should be useful for our queries, particularly wide queries**: Since the clustered index contains the data rows, it has the benefit of always being a covering index. If we frequently select all the columns, or many columns from the table, doing so based on the clustered index key allows us to avoid doing a costly lookup. This is also beneficial for updates and for joins to other tables.
- **The key should be self-ordering**: Since the data is contained at the leaf level of the clustered index, it must be ordered by the index key. If the index key is linearly increasing, each insert will have a key value that is greater than the previous key, so the rows will be inserted into the index structure in order with the new rows always being inserted at the end of the index. This ensures that the index structure stays neat and ordered. When SQL Server tries to insert a row on a page that is already full, the database engine adds a new page to the end of the index. If the insert is out of order, half the rows from the full page are relocated to the new page to leave two half-empty pages. Since the insert wasn't ordered, the full page may be anywhere within the index, so this new page will not be physically located next to the old page. This is called **fragmentation** and means that the physical order of the pages does not match the logical order. When this happens, it can reduce the efficiency of I/O against the index because SQL Server will not be able to leverage I/O optimizations such as the read-ahead mechanism. Page splits may also reduce the page density, which will increase the overall size of the index and lead to more I/O.

Given the preceding criteria, we might see why the primary key of a table often lends itself to being the clustered index key. It is unique, often self-ordering (via an identity column or sequence), typically narrow (**INT** or **BIGINT**), and often used to return an entire row or serve as the join column to other tables. Also, primary keys are rarely updated. For these reasons, when we create a primary key in SQL Server, the default behavior is to create a clustered index to support the key. We will talk more about primary and foreign keys later in this section.

Non-clustered indexes

While clustered indexes are typically chosen based on the structure of the data, **non-clustered indexes** are created to support the **WHERE** and **JOIN** clauses of our queries. Adding a non-clustered index on a column provides an efficient way to locate data based on values in that column. If we have simple queries with only one filter condition in the **WHERE** clause, a single-column non-clustered index may be sufficient, but if we have more complex queries, we may need more complex indexes. In some cases, SQL Server can use multiple single-column indexes to satisfy a **WHERE** clause that has more than one filter condition, but in many cases, it is more efficient to create multi-column, non-clustered indexes. The following rules apply when considering columns for multicolumn index keys:

- **Equality columns should appear before inequality columns**: An **equality column** is one that is used for equality comparisons such as `LastName = 'Smith'` or `ID = 1`. An **inequality column** is used for inequality comparisons such as `LastName LIKE 'Sm%'` or `ID > 10`. In general, equality comparisons will return fewer rows than inequality comparisons, so we want to satisfy those conditions first. The sooner we can narrow down the set of rows we need to search, the more efficient the query will be.
- **The equality column with the highest selectivity should appear first**: The equality column with the highest selectivity should appear first, followed by the rest of the equality columns. The **inequality column** with the highest selectivity should appear after the **last equality column**. The selectivity of a column is an indication of how many rows in the column have the same value. Filtering by a highly selective column will return fewer rows than a less selective column, so we want to perform these filters first in order to narrow down the set of rows quickly. This means the ideal first column in the index key is the most selective equality column. After that, the remaining equality columns should be added to the key, then the inequality columns in order of selectivity. Again, the goal is to narrow the set of rows quickly to make the query more efficient.

- **Columns used most frequently for filtering should appear first:** We can't create separate indexes for every filter condition in every query in the system, so thinking about which columns will be used most frequently for filter conditions can make the index useful for more than one query. If you have two columns that are both used for equality and have about the same selectivity, opt for the one that would be useful for a larger number of queries to appear first. An example is first name and last name. We may have queries that query by both first name and last name, but we may also have queries that query by last name only. It's very unlikely to query by first name only, so when creating an index containing both first names and last names, we would typically put last name first. Having an index where the last names are followed by the first names allows that index to be used by queries searching on both first name and last name or searching for last name alone.

INCLUDE columns

As we mentioned earlier, clustered indexes contain all the columns in the table because the data pages reside at the leaf level of the index. A non-clustered index on the other hand contains only columns that are part of the index definition. We have discussed some guidelines for choosing key columns for non-clustered indexes, but non-clustered indexes can contain another type of column called an **included column**. An included column is one that is added to the non-clustered index simply to make it a **covering index**—an index which contains all the columns necessary to satisfy the query without accessing the base table. Included columns are used to add columns that aren't used for filtering or joining, such as those in the **SELECT** list. They appear on the leaf level of the non-clustered index, but they are not part of the index key, so they are not used for sorting and don't typically appear in the non-leaf levels of the index. Adding a few included columns to a non-clustered index can make queries more efficient by allowing them to avoid a costly lookup.

Keep in mind that, while included columns do not add as much overhead to the index as key columns, they do still contribute to the size of the index and care must be taken to balance the cost of covering our queries with the additional cost of reading and maintaining the index. Adding many wide columns or columns that are heavily updated may increase the cost of the index so that a lookup would actually be more efficient in the long run, whereas adding narrow columns, especially columns that are not frequently updated, makes the index more useful without adding too much overhead.

For example, consider a table with a significant number of narrow columns such as **BIT** or **INT** data types, and a few wide columns such as large **VARCHAR** or **NVARCHAR** data types. Even though there are only a few large columns, size-wise, they represent the majority of the data in the table. If the **SELECT** statement requires that all the narrow columns are part of the result, but none of the wide columns, it may still be very efficient to create a covering index that includes all the narrow columns, since this is in fact a small subset of the data in the table, even though it is a large number of columns.

We will look at an example of using included columns in the *Indexing strategy* section later in this chapter.

Filtered indexes

It is also possible in SQL Server to create an index on a subset of the rows in a table based on some predicate. This is called a **filtered index**, as the rows on which the index is built have already been filtered by a predicate at the time the index was created. Filtered indexes can be useful because they may be much smaller than regular indexes and thus more efficient. They also have the benefit of pre-filtering common predicates so that they don't have to be applied at query time.

An example of where a filtered index might be useful is a database schema that supports **soft** deletes. A soft delete is where, rather than deleting an existing row when it is no longer needed, it is marked as deleted using some sort of Boolean value. If we are only interested in returning non-deleted rows, each one of our queries would have to contain the predicate `IsDeleted = 0` or something similar. This means that for our indexes to be useful, they all need to contain the **IsDeleted** column. Since we know ahead of time that we're only interested in returning rows where `IsDeleted = 0`, we can instead create a filtered index that includes the WHERE `IsDeleted =` clause. If our queries also contain this predicate, they will be able to use this filtered index and thus will be able to search and return only non-deleted rows without having to read deleted rows.

As we discussed in `Chapter 4`, *Exploring Query Execution Plans* under the *Query plan properties of interest* section, SQL Server may not be able to use filtered indexes if a query is parameterized. If you are considering using a filtered index, be sure that this predicate is not parameterized in your queries.

We will look at an example of using filtered indexes in the *Indexing strategy* section later in this chapter.

Unique versus non-unique

We already discussed why uniqueness is important for clustered indexes, but uniqueness is important for non-clustered indexes as well. In many cases, non-clustered indexes are not unique, but if they are, it's a good idea to specify the **UNIQUE** keyword. Not only does this help with the integrity of our data, it also makes for a more efficient index structure.

As with clustered indexes, SQL Server needs some way to uniquely identify each row of a non-clustered index. If the non-clustered index key is not unique by definition, SQL Server will add the clustered index key (including the uniqueifier if one exists), or the **row Identifier** (**RID**) if the table is a heap, to the non-clustered index key in order to make it unique.

The clustered index key or **RID** is always present at the leaf-level of all non-clustered indexes as it serves as the pointer to the data row, but when the non-clustered index is non-unique, this becomes part of the non-clustered index key and is therefore propagated throughout the entire index. This makes the index larger and can lead to additional page reads and thus more costly queries.

Columnstore indexes

In `Chapter 4`, *Exploring Query Execution Plans*, we introduced **columnstore indexes**. Columnstore indexes are different than rowstore indexes (clustered and non-clustered) in that all the data from a single column is stored together in a highly compressed format, rather than the entire row being stored together. This type of data storage is useful for data warehouse type queries—queries that need to search, aggregate, and return large amounts of data. Consider the following query against the **AdventureWorksDW** database:

```
SELECT s.ProductKey, p.EnglishProductName, SUM(s.OrderQuantity) as
TotalQuantity, SUM(s.TotalProductCost)as TotalSales,MAX(s.OrderDate)as
LastSaleDate
FROM FactResellerSalesXL_PageCompressed s
INNER JOIN DimProduct p ON p.ProductKey = s.ProductKey
GROUP BY s.ProductKey, p.EnglishProductName
ORDER BY TotalSales DESC
```

This is a typical data warehouse style query that is aggregating all 11,669,638 rows in the **FactResellerSalesXL_PageCompressed** table. The execution plan for the query is as follows:

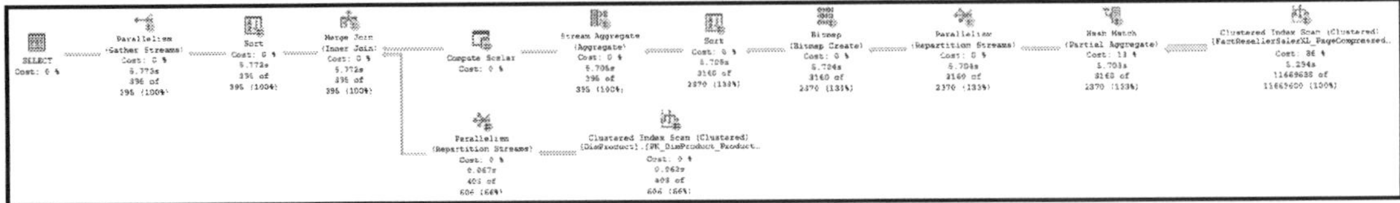

If we bring up the properties for this query, we can see it takes about 10 seconds of CPU time and almost 2 seconds of elapsed time to return:

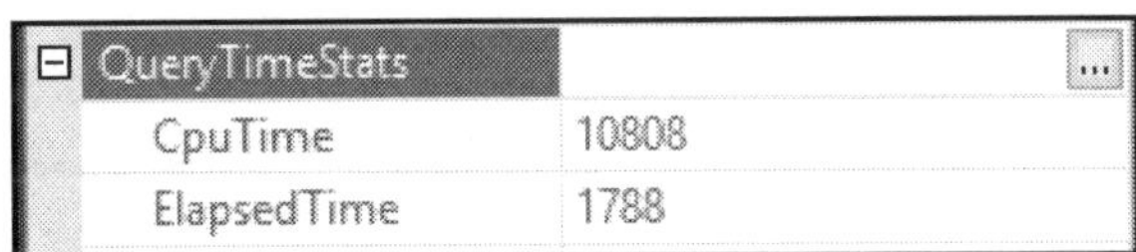

If we execute the same query against the **FactResellerSalesXL_CCI** table, which has a clustered columnstore index instead of a rowstore index, we get much better performance. The data is the same; the only difference is the presence of the clustered columnstore index in the table referenced in the following query:

```
SELECT s.ProductKey, p.EnglishProductName, SUM(s.OrderQuantity) as
TotalQuantity, SUM(s.TotalProductCost) as TotalSales, MAX(s.OrderDate) as
LastSaleDate
FROM FactResellerSalesXL_CCI s
INNER JOIN DimProduct p ON p.ProductKey = s.ProductKey
GROUP BY s.ProductKey, p.EnglishProductName
ORDER BY TotalSales DESC
```

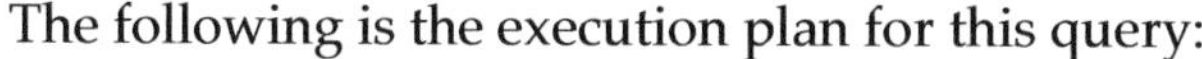

The following is the execution plan for this query:

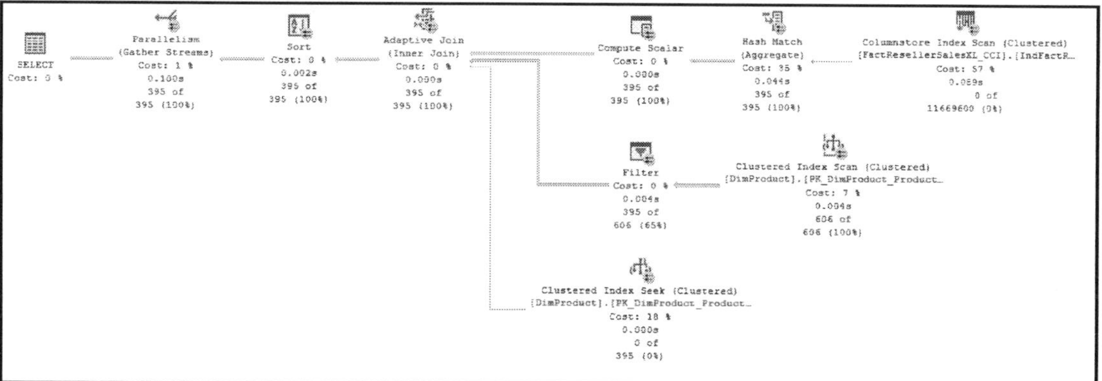

Using the clustered columnstore index, the same query runs with **526** ms of CPU time and only **101** ms of elapsed time:

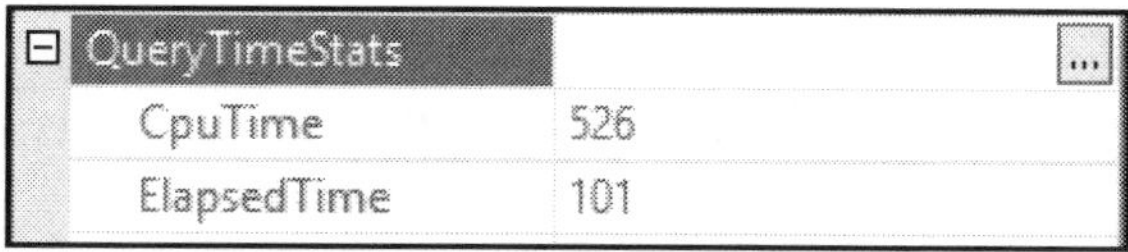

Given the large amount of data in the table (and the requirements of the query that contained aggregates on several columns and no **WHERE** clause to limit the rows before the aggregates were applied), a columnstore index is the best approach in this case.

Indexing strategy

Now that we have discussed the various types of indexes available, we need to put that together into an overall **indexing strategy**. There are many things to consider when it comes to creating indexes that are appropriate for our workload and identifying just the right combination of indexes is an ongoing process. We may create a series of indexes during the application development stage that work well, but then once the application is in production and users begin generating queries, a whole different set of indexes may become necessary. Let's start outlining this process by looking at the different considerations for building indexes.

Data structure considerations

When first designing our database, we decide how the data will be stored—which data resides in which tables, the data types of all the columns, and how the tables are related. At this stage, we will define the primary keys (PK) for all our tables, and then **foreign keys (FK)** can be added to define the relationships between the tables.

Generally, the primary key of a table is evident based on the data that is contained in the table, but if there's no natural key in the data itself, we may have to create a surrogate key by using some sort of unique value generated by the database. When we create a primary key on a table in SQL Server, a clustered index will be generated by default to support the key. As we discussed previously in this chapter, a primary key is typically well-suited to be the clustered index key of the table, but it is not a requirement. Some reasons why we might consider creating a non-clustered primary key and clustering a different column or set of columns are as follows:

- We are using a wide key such as a **GUID** or a multi-column natural key. The term GUID stands for **Globally Unique IDentifier** and it is used interchangeably with the **UNIQUEIDENTIFIER** data type.
- We have created a surrogate key that is only used within the database and most queries and joins will be against the natural key.
- We prefer the data to be stored and retrieved in a different order from the primary key. An example might be a table with a date column where the data is typically accessed and sorted by date. This may also be the case for GUID primary keys, since GUIDs are not useful for sorting.

Once we have our PKs and clustered indexes defined, we will create FKs that define how the tables are related, and often how they are joined. Unlike PKs, SQL Server does not automatically create an index for FKs.

The following screenshot displays the PK defined on column **BusinessEntityID** for each table as a yellow key icon, and the 1:Many FK relationship is displayed as the connector between the tables. The FK is created on the table **Person.PersonPhone** referencing the **Person.Person** table on the **BusinessEntityID** column.

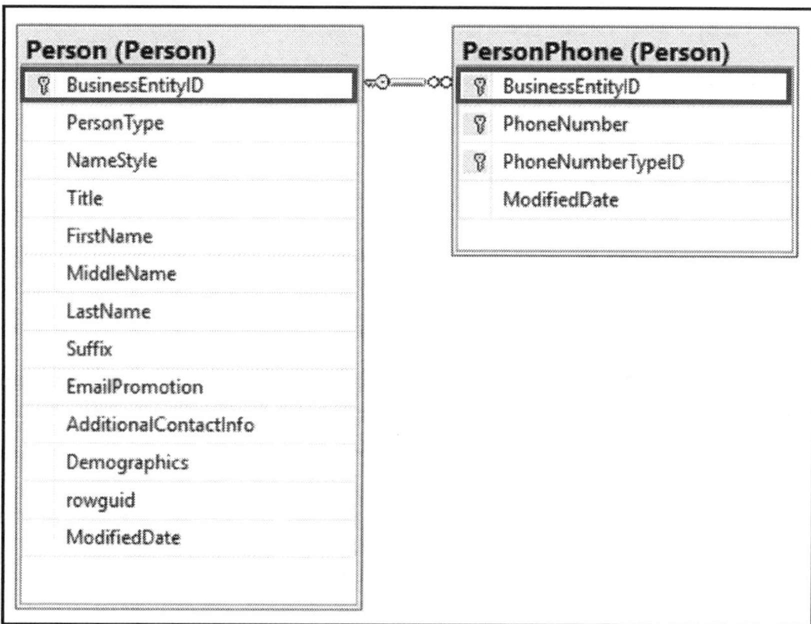

It's definitely a good idea to have indexes in place that can support our FKs, so consider creating non-clustered indexes on all your FK columns. This will improve the performance of queries that need to validate foreign keys, such as queries that delete rows from the PK table.

Database usage considerations

It's important to consider how the database is going to be used when creating indexes. While indexes improve the cost of data-access queries, they may increase the cost of queries that modify the data. Whenever we insert or update data in a table, that data must also be inserted or modified in the indexes on that table, which takes extra time and generates more I/O.

For **Online Transaction Processing** (**OLTP**) databases that have a mix of reads and writes, we will need to balance the needs of the read workload with the write workload. Avoid over-indexing tables and/or columns that are heavily updated. Tables that are not frequently updated may be able to support more indexes, but we need to consider queries when creating indexes. Don't add unnecessary columns to indexes just because we suspect they might be useful; focus on indexing columns that directly benefit our queries based on an analysis of query execution plans.

For **Online Analytical Processing (OLAP)** databases that are read-only or read-mostly, we can be less conservative with the number and size of the indexes. We may consider columnstore indexes for these types of databases, whereas OLTP databases, even if they have the occasional reporting query, would most likely not benefit from them.

Query considerations

Once we have primary and foreign key indexes in place, the next step is to create additional non-clustered indexes to support queries in the database. This is generally going to be done later in the development process because we won't know what queries will be executed against the database until the application is more mature. We may be able to anticipate which non-clustered indexes are needed in some cases, but, for the most part, the way to index for queries is to test the system with a dataset that is representative of the anticipated production data and analyze the query execution plans. Be sure that columns being used for joins and filter predicates are indexed, and follow the guidelines listed previously as to which columns should appear in the indexes and in which order.

Let's take the following query from the **AdventureWorks** database as an example:

```
SELECT p.LastName, p.FirstName, p.MiddleName, e.HireDate
FROM HumanResources.Employee e
INNER JOIN Person.Person p ON p.BusinessEntityID = e.BusinessEntityID
WHERE e.JobTitle = N'Sales Representative'
AND e.CurrentFlag = 1
ORDER BY p.LastName, p.FirstName, p.MiddleName
```

With the default structure of the **AdventureWorks** database, this query yields the following execution plan:

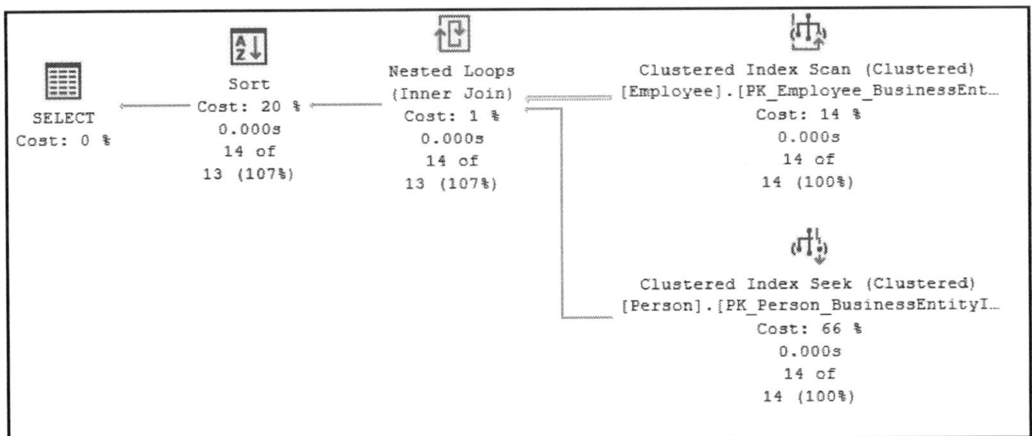

We notice here that **Clustered Index Scan** is on the **Employee** table. The clustered index on the **Employee** table is on the **BusinessEntitiyID** column, which is the primary key of the table. The query is joining on this field, but it's filtering on the **JobTitle** and **CurrentFlag** columns, and there are no indexes on these columns. We can see that SQL Server is able to apply the filter during the scan, but it's not able to use the filter to limit the number of rows scanned:

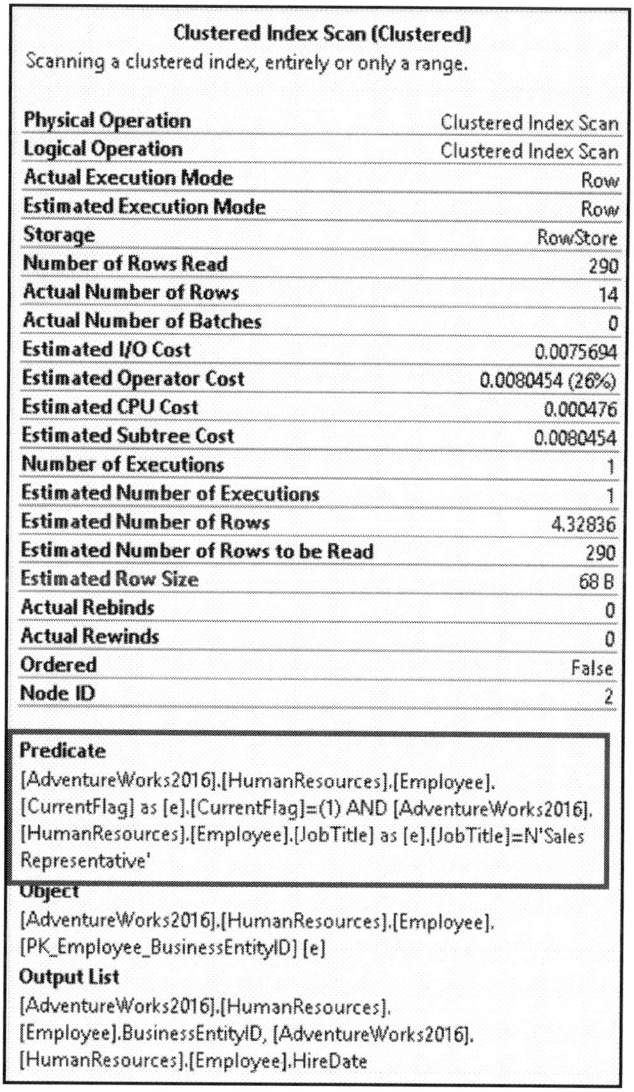

Clustered Index Scan (Clustered)

Scanning a clustered index, entirely or only a range.

Physical Operation	Clustered Index Scan
Logical Operation	Clustered Index Scan
Actual Execution Mode	Row
Estimated Execution Mode	Row
Storage	RowStore
Number of Rows Read	290
Actual Number of Rows	14
Actual Number of Batches	0
Estimated I/O Cost	0.0075694
Estimated Operator Cost	0.0080454 (26%)
Estimated CPU Cost	0.000476
Estimated Subtree Cost	0.0080454
Number of Executions	1
Estimated Number of Executions	1
Estimated Number of Rows	4.32836
Estimated Number of Rows to be Read	290
Estimated Row Size	68 B
Actual Rebinds	0
Actual Rewinds	0
Ordered	False
Node ID	2

Predicate

[AdventureWorks2016].[HumanResources].[Employee].[CurrentFlag] as [e].[CurrentFlag]=(1) AND [AdventureWorks2016].[HumanResources].[Employee].[JobTitle] as [e].[JobTitle]=N'Sales Representative'

Object

[AdventureWorks2016].[HumanResources].[Employee].[PK_Employee_BusinessEntityID] [e]

Output List

[AdventureWorks2016].[HumanResources].[Employee].BusinessEntityID, [AdventureWorks2016].[HumanResources].[Employee].HireDate

If we want a more efficient way of filtering these rows from the table, creating an index on these fields would be a good idea. We can create the following index:

```
CREATE NONCLUSTERED INDEX [IX_Employee_JobTitle_CurrentFlag] ON
[HumanResources].[Employee] (
        [JobTitle],
        [CurrentFlag]
);
```

We might think that the plan would change to use this new index instead of scanning the clustered index, but unfortunately, it does not. Even with the preceding index, SQL Server will still scan the clustered index. The reason for this is that this index is not a covering index—it does not include the **HireDate** column from the **SELECT** list.

In some cases, it might make sense to use the index, but in this case, the lookup we would have to do to retrieve the **HireDate** column when using the new non-clustered index makes the query too expensive; it's cheaper to just scan the clustered index. Remember from earlier in this chapter that we can easily make this a covering index by adding an included column. We can add the following index instead:

```
CREATE NONCLUSTERED INDEX [IX_Employee_JobTitle_CurrentFlag] ON
[HumanResources].[Employee] (
        [JobTitle],
        [CurrentFlag]
)
INCLUDE ([HireDate]);
```

SQL Server will use the new index and the plan changes to the following:

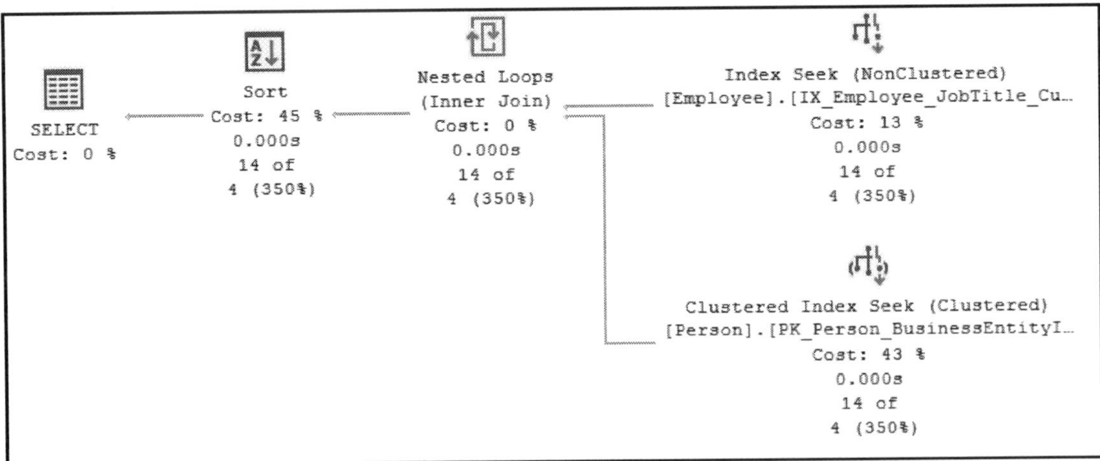

If we examine the properties of **Index Seek (NonClustered)**, we can see that both **JobTitle** and **CurrentFlag** are now being used as **Seek Predicates**:

Index Seek (NonClustered)

Scan a particular range of rows from a nonclustered index.

Physical Operation	Index Seek
Logical Operation	Index Seek
Actual Execution Mode	Row
Estimated Execution Mode	Row
Storage	RowStore
Number of Rows Read	14
Actual Number of Rows	14
Actual Number of Batches	0
Estimated I/O Cost	0.003125
Estimated Operator Cost	0.0032868 (13%)
Estimated CPU Cost	0.0001618
Estimated Subtree Cost	0.0032868
Estimated Number of Executions	1
Number of Executions	1
Estimated Number of Rows	4.32836
Estimated Number of Rows to be Read	4.32836
Estimated Row Size	14 B
Actual Rebinds	0
Actual Rewinds	0
Ordered	True
Node ID	2

Object

[AdventureWorks2016].[HumanResources].[Employee].[IX_Employee_JobTitle_CurrentFlag] [e]

Output List

[AdventureWorks2016].[HumanResources].[Employee].BusinessEntityID, [AdventureWorks2016].[HumanResources].[Employee].HireDate

Seek Predicates

Seek Keys[1]: Prefix: [AdventureWorks2016].[HumanResources].[Employee].JobTitle, [AdventureWorks2016].[HumanResources].[Employee].CurrentFlag = Scalar Operator(N'Sales Representative'), Scalar Operator((1))

We can even go one step further and use a filtered index for this query. The **WHERE** clause includes a predicate on a column called **CurrentFlag**. Let's assume that this table includes all the employees that have ever worked for the company and every position they have ever held. This means that a row with **CurrentFlag** set to `0` indicates that the employee no longer holds that position, either because they are no longer with the company or because they have moved on to a new position.

In this case, we are most likely only interested in the current state of employment, so most of our queries against this table will have `CurrentFlag = 1` in the **WHERE** clause. Rather than including **CurrentFlag** in all the non-clustered index keys on this table, we can instead create a filtered index that applies this predicate to the index:

```
CREATE NONCLUSTERED INDEX [IX_Employee_JobTitle_CurrentFlag] ON
[HumanResources].[Employee] (
        [JobTitle]
)
INCLUDE ([HireDate])
WHERE [CurrentFlag] = 1;
```

Creating this index doesn't change the plan shape, but notice how the estimated cost of the operators has shifted:

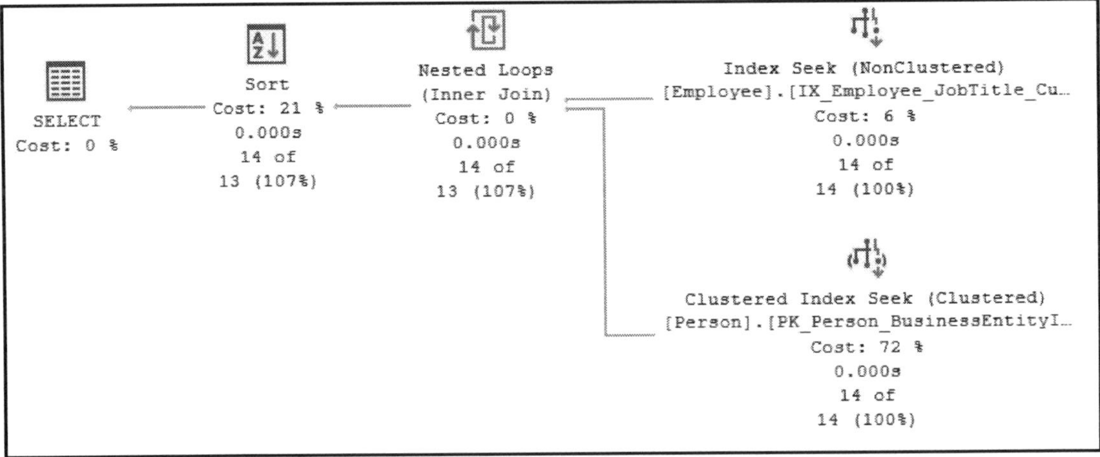

If we look at the properties of the **Index Seek (NonClustered)** on the **IX_Employee_JobTitle_CurrentFlag** index, we can see **Seek Predicates** is only on the **JobTitle** column; the **CurrentFlag** filter predicate is satisfied simply by our choosing to use the filtered index:

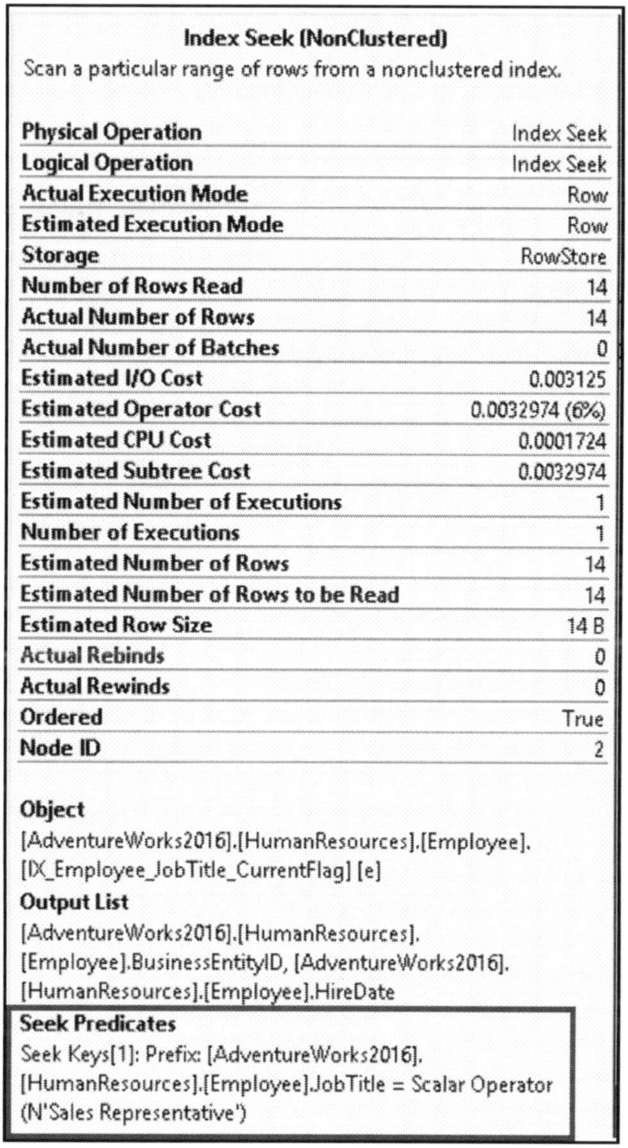

Index Seek (NonClustered)

Scan a particular range of rows from a nonclustered index.

Physical Operation	Index Seek
Logical Operation	Index Seek
Actual Execution Mode	Row
Estimated Execution Mode	Row
Storage	RowStore
Number of Rows Read	14
Actual Number of Rows	14
Actual Number of Batches	0
Estimated I/O Cost	0.003125
Estimated Operator Cost	0.0032974 (6%)
Estimated CPU Cost	0.0001724
Estimated Subtree Cost	0.0032974
Estimated Number of Executions	1
Number of Executions	1
Estimated Number of Rows	14
Estimated Number of Rows to be Read	14
Estimated Row Size	14 B
Actual Rebinds	0
Actual Rewinds	0
Ordered	True
Node ID	2

Object

[AdventureWorks2016].[HumanResources].[Employee].[IX_Employee_JobTitle_CurrentFlag] [e]

Output List

[AdventureWorks2016].[HumanResources].[Employee].BusinessEntityID, [AdventureWorks2016].[HumanResources].[Employee].HireDate

Seek Predicates

Seek Keys[1]: Prefix: [AdventureWorks2016].[HumanResources].[Employee].JobTitle = Scalar Operator (N'Sales Representative')

This makes sense because of the nature of the data; we're most often interested in rows where `CurrentFlag = 1`. If we had a different situation where we would also frequently query for rows where `CurrentFlag = 0` or without `CurrentFlag` in the **WHERE** clause at all, this index would not be useful. We can change our query to the following:

```
SELECT p.LastName, p.FirstName, p.MiddleName, e.HireDate
FROM HumanResources.Employee e
INNER JOIN Person.Person p ON p.BusinessEntityID = e.BusinessEntityID
WHERE e.JobTitle = N'Sales Representative'
ORDER BY p.LastName, p.FirstName, p.MiddleName
```

The index can no longer be used, and we go back to the **Clustered Index Scan** plan:

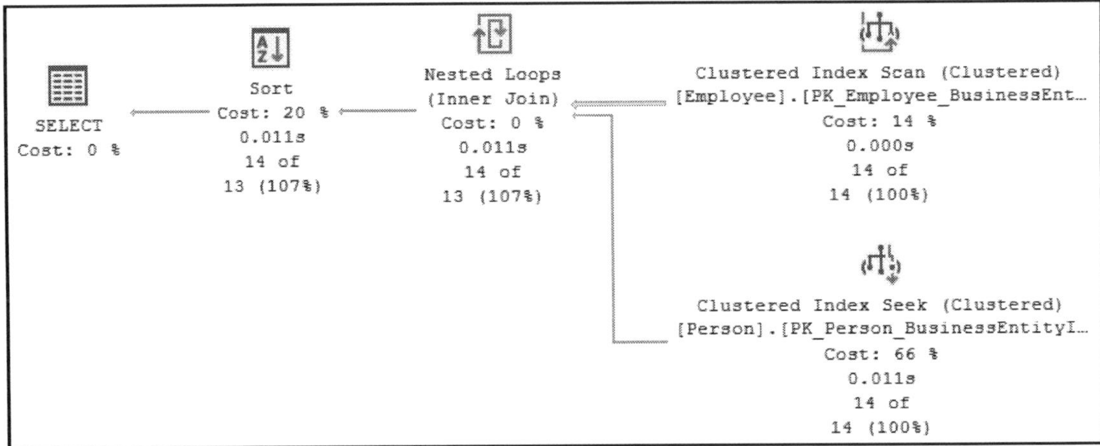

To summarize, use the following guidelines when developing an index strategy for a database:

- Create primary and foreign key indexes first based on the initial data schema:
  - If the primary key does not meet the requirements of a clustered index, consider creating a non-clustered primary key and create a clustered index on a different column.
  - Create non-clustered indexes on foreign key columns, as these are not created by default.
- Begin analyzing query execution plans to create additional non-clustered indexes based on the needs of the workload:
  - Create non-clustered indexes on join and filter columns.

    - Use included columns to create covering indexes wherever practical.
    - Consider filtered indexes for predicates that are used frequently such as filtering out soft deletes.
- Avoid adding too many indexes on heavily used tables and/or columns.
- Re-evaluate your indexing strategy on a regular basis to ensure that changes to your workload have not rendered your current indexing strategy obsolete.

Best practices for T-SQL querying

There are a number of best practices about writing good T-SQL that don't constitute a pattern or anti-pattern (this something we will discuss in upcoming chapters but that are important enough to observe when we want to write good queries. This section covers those practices.

Referencing objects

Always reference objects by their two-part name (`<schema>.<name>`) in T-SQL code because not doing so has some performance implications.

Using two-part object names avoids name resolution delays during query compilation: if the default schema for a user connecting to SQL Server is **dbo**, and that user attempts to execute the stored `HumanResources.uspUpdateEmployeePersonalInfo` procedure for which it also has permissions, but simply references `uspUpdateEmployeePersonalInfo`, SQL Server first searches the **dbo** schema for that stored procedure before searching other schemas, thus delaying resolution and therefore execution. When that stored procedure is used at scale, it may introduce unwarranted overhead.

Two-part object names also provide more opportunities for plan re-use, and less probability of failed executions if multiple objects with the same name exist across schemas. For cached query plans to be re-used, it is necessary that the objects referenced by the query don't require name resolutions. For example, referencing the **Sales.SalesOrderDetail** table does not require name resolution, but **SalesOrderDetail** does because there could be tables named **SalesOrderDetail** in other schemas.

Joining tables

When writing T-SQL queries, it's important to distinguish between proper join predicates and search predicates.

For inner joins, it is best to keep only join arguments in the **ON** clause, and move to a **WHERE** clause for all search arguments. Performance-wise, there is no difference if the generated query plan is the same, but the T-SQL is more readable. The following query examples can be executed in the scope of the **AdventureWorks** sample database, and yield the same query plans:

```
SELECT p.ProductID, p.Name, wo.StockedQty, wor.WorkOrderID
FROM Production.WorkOrder AS wo
INNER JOIN Production.Product AS p ON wo.ProductID = p.ProductID
INNER JOIN Production.WorkOrderRouting AS wor ON wo.WorkOrderID =
wor.WorkOrderID
WHERE p.ProductID = 771 AND wor.WorkOrderID = 852;


SELECT p.ProductID, p.Name, wo.StockedQty, wor.WorkOrderID
FROM Production.WorkOrder AS wo
INNER JOIN Production.Product AS p ON wo.ProductID = p.ProductID
       AND p.ProductID = 771
INNER JOIN Production.WorkOrderRouting AS wor ON wo.WorkOrderID =
wor.WorkOrderID
       AND wor.WorkOrderID = 852;
```

In the first query, it's immediately obvious which conditions are join predicates and which are search predicates.

For **LEFT** joins, add any search predicates for the table in the right side of the join. This is because adding references to the table in the right side of a join to the **WHERE** clause will convert the **OUTER** join to an **INNER** join. The following query examples can be executed in the scope of the **AdventureWorks** sample database:

```
SELECT wo.StockedQty, wor.WorkOrderID
FROM Production.WorkOrder AS wo
LEFT JOIN Production.WorkOrderRouting AS wor ON wo.WorkOrderID =
wor.WorkOrderID
WHERE wor.WorkOrderID = 12345;


SELECT wo.StockedQty, wor.WorkOrderID
FROM Production.WorkOrder AS wo
LEFT JOIN Production.WorkOrderRouting AS wor ON wo.WorkOrderID =
wor.WorkOrderID
WHERE wo.WorkOrderID = 12345;
```

These yield different query plans but the same result sets. In the first query, a reference to the **Production.WorkOrderRouting** table was added as a predicate. Since that table is on the right side of the join, this resulted in the left outer join becoming an inner join, as seen in the nested loops operator in the query plans:

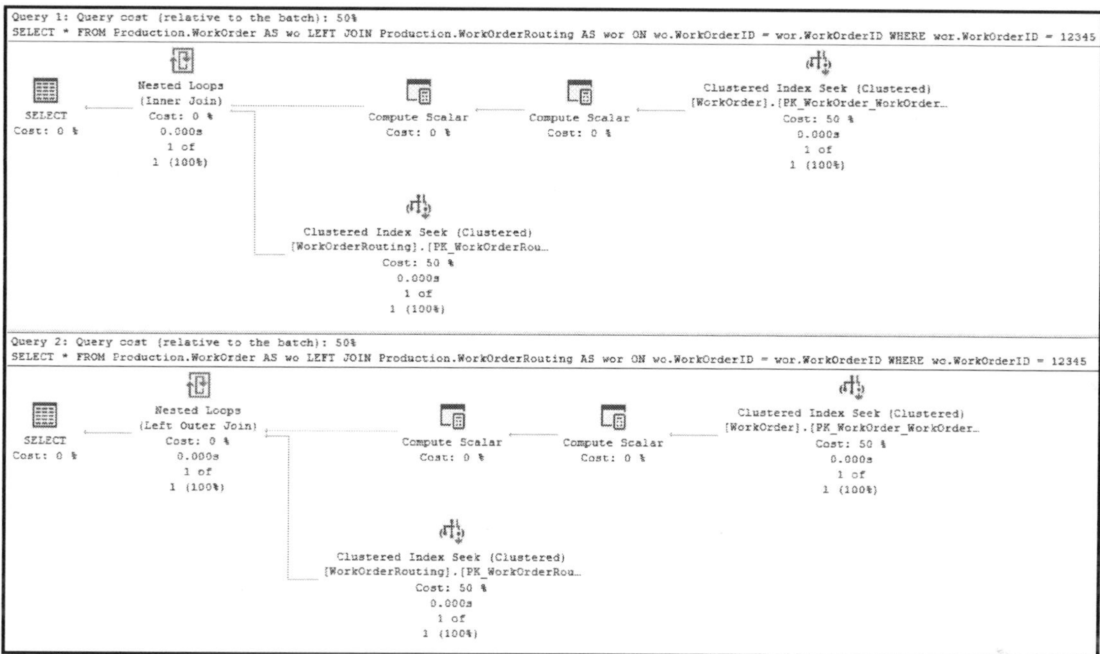

In some cases, this can result in different choices for physical joins, and can impact I/O, memory, and CPU resources. This also applies in the inverse case—adding a reference to the table on the left side of a **RIGHT JOIN**.

Using NOLOCK

SQL Server uses isolation levels to preserve the logical order of all transactions, and to protect transactions from the effects of updates performed by other concurrent transactions. The goal is to uphold the **atomicity, consistency, isolation, and durability** (**ACID**) properties of relational databases.

Read more about ACID in `http://en.wikipedia.org/wiki/ACID`.

Different isolation levels have trade-offs between concurrency and isolation requirements: using a more restrictive isolation means fewer concurrent transactions. In a nutshell, SQL Server complies with ANSI-99 standard isolation levels:

- **Read uncommitted**: In read uncommitted (lowest isolation level, maximum concurrency), statements can read rows that have been modified by other transactions but not yet committed
- **Read committed**: In read committed (the default isolation level in SQL Server), statements cannot read data that has been modified but not committed by other transactions
- **Repeatable read**: In repeatable read, statements cannot read data that has been modified but not yet committed by other transactions and no other transactions can modify data that has been read by the current transaction
- **Serializable**: In serializable (highest isolation level, no concurrency), statements cannot read data that has been modified but not yet committed by other transactions

SQL Server adds two Isolation Levels above the ANSI standard that are not discussed in this book: **Snapshot** and **Read Committed Snapshot Isolation** (**RCSI**).

The **NOLOCK** hint implements the same behavior as read uncommitted at the statement level. When this hint is used, it's possible to read uncommitted modifications, which are called dirty reads. This means that by using **NOLOCK**, a developer is explicitly allowing uncommitted data to be used for other transactions. Allowing dirty reads allows higher concurrency at the cost of reading data that can still be rolled back by other transactions. In turn, this may generate application errors, present uncommitted data to users, or cause users to see duplicate records, or no records at all. This is the sort of hint that should not be used in queries that require operational precision, such as banking or trade.

Using cursors

Cursor usage must be kept to a minimum. Depending on the cursor type, these may leverage TempDB worktables, which is an I/O penalty. Because cursors operate in a row-by-row fashion, they force the database engine to repeatedly fetch a new row, negotiate blocking and manage locks, and output each row result individually.

Consider whether set-based logic can be used. In some cases, cursors appear more straightforward, but leveraging T-SQL constructs such as **Common Table Expressions (CTEs)** or temporary tables may achieve the same results with less overhead. If a set-based approach is not possible, most cursors can be avoided by using a `WHILE` loop, that is, if there is a primary key or unique key in the table. However, there are scenarios where cursors are not only unavoidable but are actually needed. If this is the case, but they don't require updates to tables based on the cursor position, then the recommendation is to use **firehose** cursors, meaning forward-only and read-only cursors.

Summary

After reading this chapter, we should have a better understanding of some aspects that database professionals need to keep in mind to write good queries, and how to identify some inefficiencies that may surface if predicates expressed in queries are not supported by a suitable index design. These are all just a part of the intricacies of writing good, scalable T-SQL code.

In the next chapter, we will cover some easily identifiable T-SQL anti-patterns—some fairly common constructs that, while easy to identify and many times avoided, are still found too many times in critical application code that's required to scale and perform well.

6
Easily-Identified T-SQL Anti-Patterns

So far, we have been learning the building blocks of writing T-SQL code: T-SQL basics, query optimization fundamentals, reading and interpreting query plans, and some general best practices around indexing and writing efficient T-SQL code. By this point, we should have a good understanding of how to write an efficient query, but there are some common pitfalls that even experienced T-SQL developers can encounter that will make a query perform poorly.

In this chapter, we will examine some common T-SQL patterns and anti-patterns, specifically those that should be easily identified just by looking at the T-SQL code. We will cover the following topics:

- The perils of **SELECT** *
- Functions in our predicate
- Deconstructing table-valued functions
- Complex expressions
- Optimizing OR logic
- NULL means unknown
- Fuzzy string matching
- Inequality logic
- **EXECUTE** versus **sp_executesql**
- Composable logic

The perils of SELECT *

SELECT * should be avoided in stored procedures, views, and **multi-statement table-valued functions** (**MSTVF**) because our T-SQL code might break if there are any changes to the underlying schema. For example, applications that reference **SELECT** * may be relying on the ordinal position rather than column names and may encounter errors if the underlying table definition is changed. Instead, fully qualify the names of columns that are relevant for our result set.

This also has important performance implications. Some application patterns may rely on reading an entire dataset and applying filters in the client layer only. For example, imagine a web application where a sales supervisor can see a report of orders registered for a given month, with details per product. The application connects to the **AdventureWorks** sample database and runs a query:

```
Dim sqlConnection1 As New SqlConnection("Our Connection String")
Dim cmd As New SqlCommand
Dim reader As SqlDataReader
cmd.CommandText = "SELECT *
       FROM Sales.SalesOrderHeader AS h
       INNER JOIN Sales.SalesOrderDetail AS d ON h.SalesOrderID =
d.SalesOrderID
       INNER JOIN Production.Product AS p ON d.ProductId = p.ProductID
       WHERE h.OrderDate BETWEEN '2013-02-28 00:00:00.000'
AND '2013-03-30 00:00:00.000';"
cmd.CommandType = CommandType.Text
cmd.Connection = sqlConnection1

sqlConnection1.Open()

reader = cmd.ExecuteReader()
while (reader.Read())
{
       return reader["ProductLine"] as string;
       return reader["Name"] as string;
       return reader["OrderDate"] as DateTime;
       return reader["SalesOrderID"] as Int32;
       return reader["OrderQty"] as Int32;
       return reader["LineTotal"] as double;
       return reader["TotalDue"] as double;
}

reader.Close()
sqlConnection1.Close()
```

Let's observe the generated query execution plan:

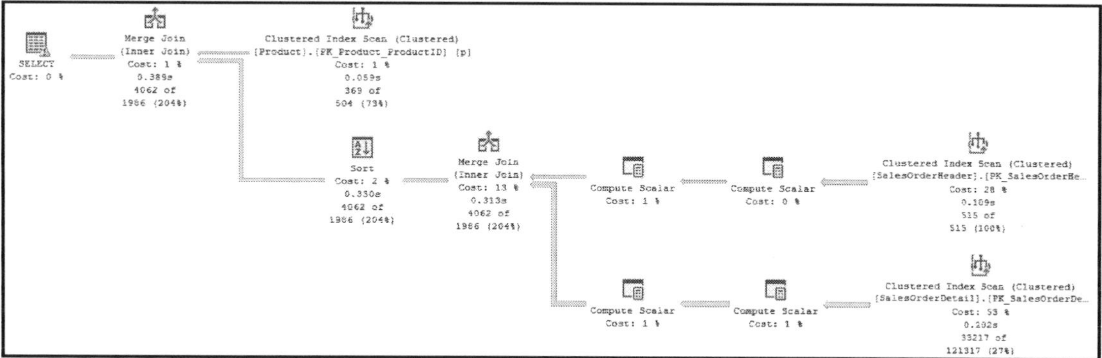

Notice that SQL Server chose to scan all clustered indexes, even on the table where a predicate exists. Given that we are retrieving all columns, there is no missing index suggestion about creating covering non-clustered indexes because these would be similar in size to the clustered indexes.

For reference, the **QueryTimeStats** property for this query execution plan are in the following screenshot:

QueryTimeStats	
CpuTime	90
ElapsedTime	430

And **MemoryGrantInfo** is the following screenshot:

MemoryGrantInfo	
DesiredMemory	2400
GrantedMemory	2400

Also notice in the application code that after getting the entire result set, only the relevant columns for our report are being used. So instead of selecting all columns in the table to then trim the number of columns in the client layer, it is preferable to issue a query that only retrieves the required columns from the table:

```
SELECT p.ProductLine, p.[Name], h.OrderDate,
    h.SalesOrderID, d.OrderQty, d.LineTotal, h.TotalDue
FROM Sales.SalesOrderHeader AS h
INNER JOIN Sales.SalesOrderDetail AS d ON h.SalesOrderID = d.SalesOrderID
INNER JOIN Production.Product AS p ON d.ProductId = p.ProductID
```

```
WHERE h.OrderDate BETWEEN '2013-02-28 00:00:00.000' AND '2013-03-30
00:00:00.000';
```

Let's observe the new query execution plan:

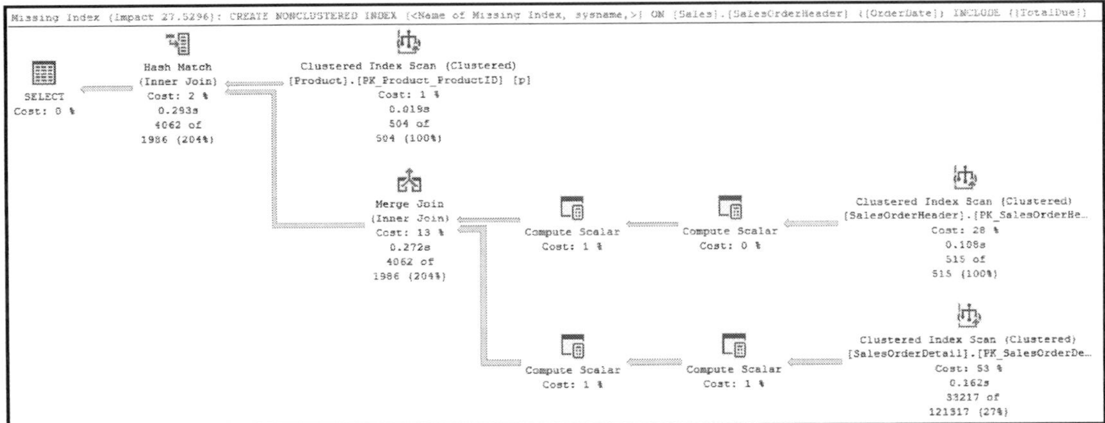

The **QueryTimeStats** property for this query execution plan is shown in the following screenshot:

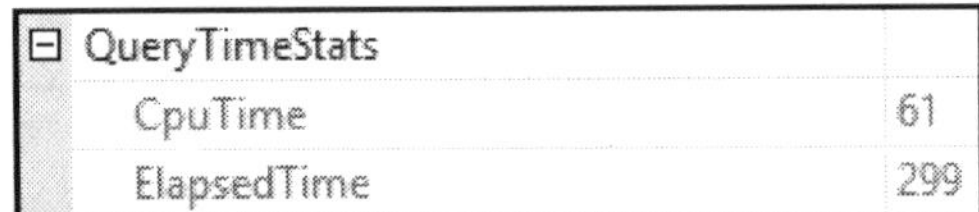

QueryTimeStats	
CpuTime	61
ElapsedTime	299

And the **MemoryGrantInfo** property in the following screenshot:

MemoryGrantInfo	
DesiredMemory	1312
GrantedMemory	1312

Even though the plan shape hasn't changed, we can clearly see a lower memory requirement (only 1.3 MB instead of 2.4 MB), and lower CPU use and execution time. Reading all columns from a table usually means accessing the underlying heap or clustered index directly, rather than leveraging narrower non-clustered indexes. Conversely, reading only the relevant subset of columns unlocks better usage of our existing index design, or allows for new covering indexes to be created, which can significantly improve read performance.

Precisely because we need fewer columns, SQL Server was able to identify an index suggestion that may yield even better results. This was not possible before because all the columns were being selected. As there is no current index that would be useful to even marginally change, we can create this index suggestion as follows:

```
CREATE NONCLUSTERED INDEX IX_OrderDate_TotalDue ON
[Sales].[SalesOrderHeader] (
        [OrderDate]
)
INCLUDE (
    [TotalDue]
);
```

Although it was not suggested, if we keep in mind the indexing guidelines we discussed in `Chapter 5`, *Writing Elegant T-SQL Queries*, we can create an additional covering index for the largest scan in the query execution plan:

```
CREATE NONCLUSTERED INDEX IX_SalesOrderID_ProductID_OrderQty_LineTotal ON
[Sales].[SalesOrderDetail] (
        [SalesOrderID],
        [ProductID]
)
INCLUDE (
        [OrderQty],
        [LineTotal]
);
```

The new query execution plan looks much better, and leverages the two new indexes:

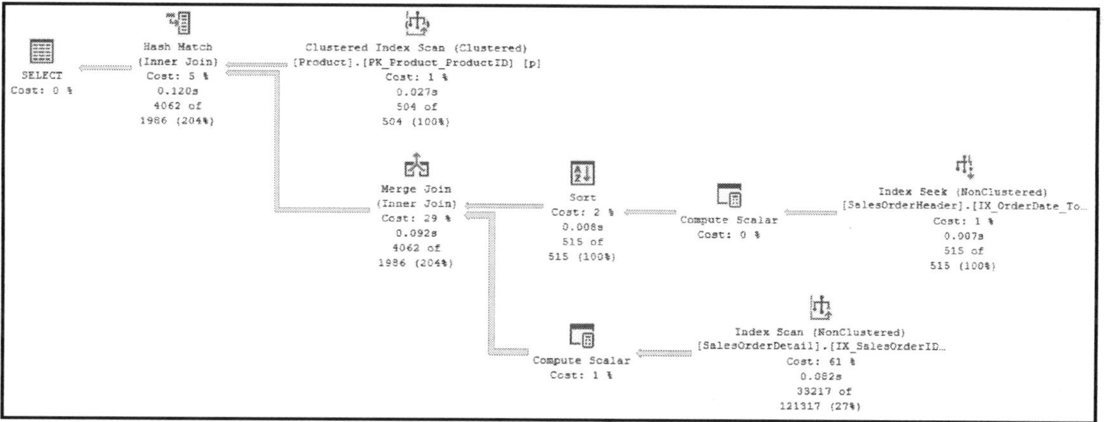

The **QueryTimeStats** property for this query execution plan confirm this: CPU time dropped from 61 ms to 24 ms (61% less), and execution time dropped from 299 ms to 57 ms (81% less):

⊟ QueryTimeStats	
CpuTime	24
ElapsedTime	57

And if using columnstore indexes, even without specifying any predicates, the same recommendation of not using **SELECT *** still applies. Selecting just the column names that are needed for the application can translate to significant I/O savings as well, because while still retrieving all the data in the columns without filters, being stored in columnar format means that only the columns required are indeed read. Also note that sending only the columns needed by the application to the client layer prevents unnecessary network I/O and reduces the memory footprint of the client. This can improve the overall performance and scalability of our application as well as the underlying T-SQL queries.

Functions in our predicate

Search predicates should not use deterministic function calls. Calls to deterministic functions with columns for parameters cause SQL Server to be unable to reference the selectivity of those columns, as the result of the function is unknown at compile time. Because of this, they cause unnecessary scans.

Keep in mind what was discussed in previous chapters: the Query Optimizer uses statistics and some internal transformation rules and heuristics at compile-time to determine a good-enough plan to execute a query; the **WHERE** clause is one of the first to be evaluated during logical query processing. The Query Optimizer depends on the estimated cost to resolve the search predicates in order to choose whether it seeks or scans over indexes.

The following example shows a query executed in the **AdventureWorks** sample database that uses non-deterministic function calls in the search predicate:

```
SELECT SalesOrderID, OrderDate
FROM Sales.SalesOrderHeader
WHERE YEAR(OrderDate) = 2013 AND MONTH(OrderDate) = 7;
```

Let's observe the query execution plan:

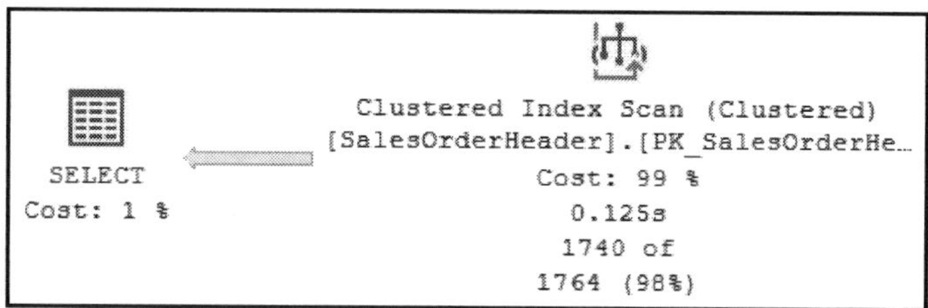

We have a scan of the clustered index. Notice that while we have a non-SARGable predicate, it was pushed down to be resolved during the **Clustered Index Scan** to return **1740** rows, but still the full **31465** rows were read as shown in the following screenshot:

Clustered Index Scan (Clustered)

Scanning a clustered index, entirely or only a range.

Physical Operation	Clustered Index Scan
Logical Operation	Clustered Index Scan
Actual Execution Mode	Row
Estimated Execution Mode	Row
Storage	RowStore
Number of Rows Read	31465
Actual Number of Rows	1740
Actual Number of Batches	0
Estimated I/O Cost	0.514977
Estimated Operator Cost	0.549745 (99%)
Estimated CPU Cost	0.0347685
Estimated Subtree Cost	0.549745
Number of Executions	1
Estimated Number of Executions	1
Estimated Number of Rows	1763.91
Estimated Number of Rows to be Read	31465
Estimated Row Size	19 B
Actual Rebinds	0
Actual Rewinds	0
Ordered	False
Node ID	1

Predicate

datepart(year,[AdventureWorks2016_EXT].[Sales].[SalesOrderHeader].[OrderDate])=(2013) AND datepart(month,[AdventureWorks2016_EXT].[Sales].[SalesOrderHeader].[OrderDate])=(7)

Object

[AdventureWorks2016_EXT].[Sales].[SalesOrderHeader].[PK_SalesOrderHeader_SalesOrderID]

Output List

[AdventureWorks2016_EXT].[Sales].[SalesOrderHeader].SalesOrderID, [AdventureWorks2016_EXT].[Sales].[SalesOrderHeader].OrderDate

Recall what we discussed in `Chapter 5`, *Writing Elegant T-SQL Queries*, under the *Predicate SARGability* section. What we see in the preceding screenshot calls for a better index, and knowing more about index tuning recommendations now, I can identify that the following index could be useful:

```
CREATE NONCLUSTEREDINDEX IX_OrderDate ON Sales.SalesOrderHeader(
       OrderDate
);
```

Let's execute the same query results in the following query execution plan:

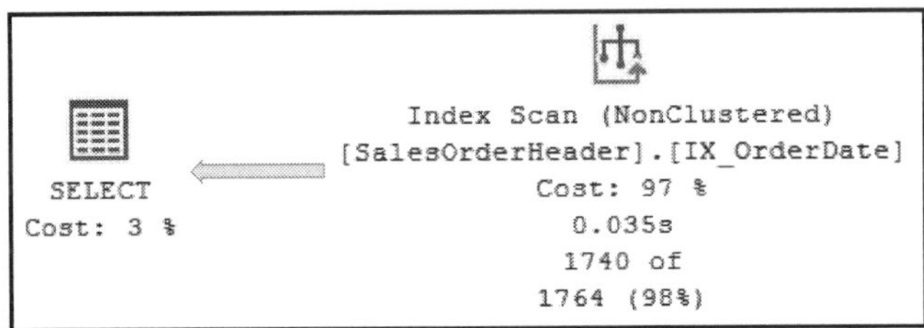

Still an index scan, although on the newly-created index. The new index is narrower, but the scan still read 31,645 rows. This is because the non-deterministic **YEAR** and **DATE** functions are being used in the predicate. The same result set can be achieved by rewriting the query to avoid these function calls in the search predicate and enable the Query Optimizer to consider other options. The following is just a quick example of how to express the same condition without the use of functions:

```
DECLARE @start DATETIME = '07/01/2013', @end DATETIME = '07/31/2013'
SELECT SalesOrderID, OrderDate
FROM Sales.SalesOrderHeader
WHERE OrderDate BETWEEN @start AND @end;
```

Let's observe the new query execution plan:

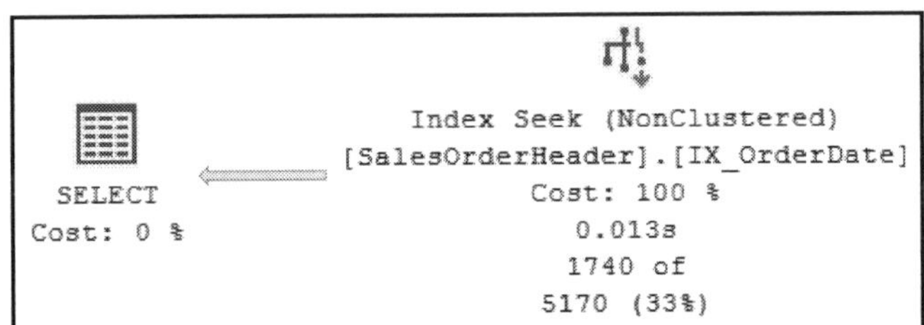

This is now a seek operation that only read the 1,740 rows that match the search predicate, because the query no longer needs to search based on non-deterministic functions. We could stop the rewrite here, but we are looking to write efficient T-SQL and one of the main goals is to ensure row estimations are always as close as possible to actual rows. Notice how the estimations are very skewed. The seek operation returned 1,740 rows of 5,170 estimated rows. The misestimation comes from the fact that the query uses local variables that inhibit the Query Optimizer from using the statistics histogram to get accurate estimations.

This can be addressed by using the **RECOMPILE** hint, or better yet, using **sp_executesql** as we discussed in the *Parameterization* section of `Chapter 2`, *Understanding Query Processing*. The following examples show both options; first, here's the **RECOMPILE** hint:

```
DECLARE @start DATETIME = '07/01/2013', @end DATETIME = '07/31/2013'
SELECT SalesOrderID, OrderDate
FROM Sales.SalesOrderHeader
WHERE OrderDate BETWEEN @start AND @end
OPTION (RECOMPILE);
```

And here's the **sp_executesql** method:

```
EXECUTE sp_executesql @stmt = N'SELECT SalesOrderID, OrderDate FROM
Sales.SalesOrderHeader
WHERE OrderDate BETWEEN @start AND @end;'
                    , @params = N'@start DATETIME, @end DATETIME'
                    , @start = '07/01/2013', @end = '07/31/2013';
```

We can observe the new query execution plan:

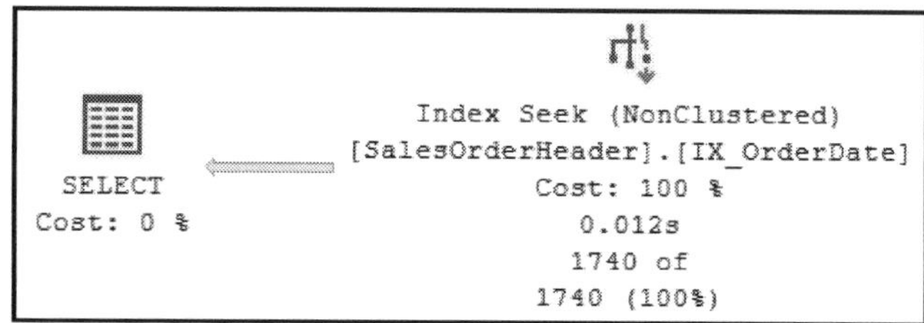

Notice that the estimation now matches the actual rows, denoting accurate estimations, and a perfect example of Predicate Pushdown, as we discussed in `Chapter 5`, *Writing Elegant T-SQL Queries*.

Deconstructing table-valued functions

A **user-defined function** (**UDF**) is like a stored procedure in that it is a block of T-SQL statements saved as an object, but it differs in that it does not generate a result set, it returns a value of a specified type. A scalar UDF is a function that returns a single value, a **table-valued function** (**TVF**) is a function that returns a table.

There are two types of TVFs in SQL Server:

- **Multi-statement TVFs (MSTVFs)**: MSTVFs declare a return table type, populates the table, then returns the table at the end of the function
- **Inline TVFs**: You can think of an inline TVF like a view that takes a parameter, the body of the function is a single query and the return value is the result of that query

The following is an example of a MSTVF that we can create in the **AdventureWorks** sample database:

```
CREATE OR ALTER FUNCTION dbo.ufn_FindReports (@InEmpID int)
RETURNS @retFindReports TABLE
(
    EmployeeID int primary key NOT NULL,
     FirstName nvarchar(255) NOT NULL,
    LastName nvarchar(255) NOT NULL,
    JobTitle nvarchar(50) NOT NULL,
    RecursionLevel int NOT NULL
)
--Returns a result set that lists all the employees who report to the
--specific employee directly or indirectly.*/
AS
BEGIN
    WITH EMP_cte(EmployeeID, OrganizationNode,
        FirstName, LastName, JobTitle, RecursionLevel) -- CTE name and
columns
    AS (
        -- Get the initial list of Employees for Manager n
        SELECT e.BusinessEntityID, e.OrganizationNode, p.FirstName,
p.LastName, e.JobTitle, 0
        FROM HumanResources.Employee e
        INNER JOIN Person.Person p
            ON p.BusinessEntityID = e.BusinessEntityID
        WHERE e.BusinessEntityID = @InEmpID
        UNION ALL
        -- Join recursive member to anchor
        SELECT e.BusinessEntityID, e.OrganizationNode, p.FirstName,
p.LastName, e.JobTitle,
```

```
            RecursionLevel + 1
        FROM HumanResources.Employee e
        INNER JOIN EMP_cte
            ON e.OrganizationNode.GetAncestor(1) = EMP_cte.OrganizationNode
        INNER JOIN Person.Person p
            ON p.BusinessEntityID = e.BusinessEntityID
        )
-- copy the required columns to the result of the function
   INSERT @retFindReports
   SELECT EmployeeID, FirstName, LastName, JobTitle, RecursionLevel
   FROM EMP_cte
   RETURN
END;
```

Since this function returns a table, we can reference it in a T-SQL query just like we would a table. The following is a sample query that uses this function:

```
SELECT EmployeeID, FirstName, LastName, JobTitle, RecursionLevel
FROM dbo.ufn_FindReports(25);
```

The problem with MSTVFs is the cost of the function can't be determined at compile time, so a fixed estimation of rows is used to create the query plan. Let's look at the query execution plan for the previous example in the following screenshot:

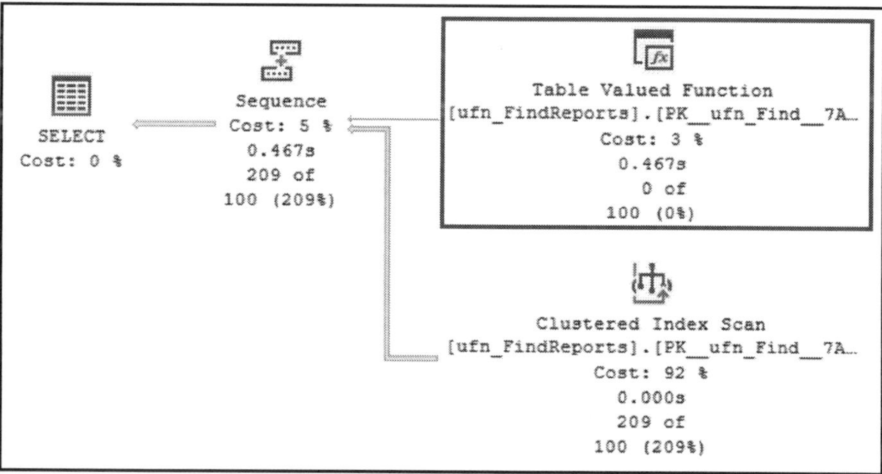

Notice that the TVF appears as an input to the join as if it were a table with an estimate of 100 rows, but an actual row count of one. This inaccurate cardinality estimate could cause the plan to be inefficient, but since the true cardinality can't be determined without executing the function, there is not much that can be done to improve this estimate.

Prior to SQL Server 2014, the fixed estimate for MSTVFs was one. In this case, it would have been a better estimate, but most MSTVFs return more than one row, so 100 is generally a better fixed estimate.

The **QueryTimeStats** property for this query are shown in the following screenshot:

QueryTimeStats	
CpuTime	261
ElapsedTime	468
UdfCpuTime	0
UdfElapsedTime	117

The query took 468 ms to execute, with 261 ms of CPU time. Note the **UdfElapsedTime** property is 117 ms and has to do with this query referencing the **GetAncestor** system function.

Starting with SQL Server 2017, a new feature called **interleaved execution** for MSTVFs was introduced. With interleaved execution, rather than using a fixed estimate, optimization is paused when a MSTVF is encountered, the function is materialized, and the actual row count is used to optimize the rest of the plan. The resulting plan is then cached so this process will not be repeated when subsequent executions reuse the plan. Using the previous example, if we change the database compatibility to level 140 which maps to the SQL Server 2017 release, we get an accurate row count for our query, as in the following screenshot:

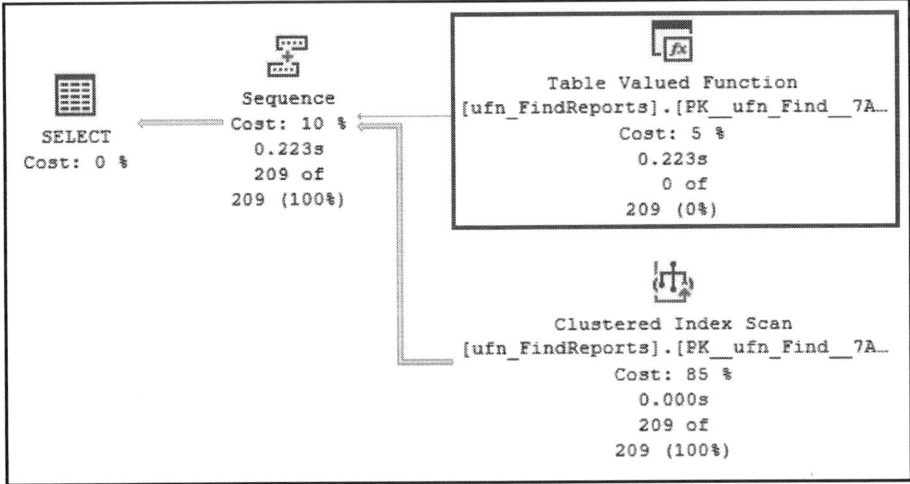

The **QueryTimeStats** property for this query are improved from the non-interleaved version: CPU time dropped from 261 ms to 223 ms (~14 percent less), and execution time dropped from 468 ms to 224 ms (~51 percent less), as seen in the following screenshot:

⊟ QueryTimeStats	
CpuTime	223
ElapsedTime	224
UdfCpuTime	0
UdfElapsedTime	115

An even better way to do this would be to write the function as an inline TVF. As we mentioned earlier in this section, inline TVFs behave like views, they can be folded into the query, allowing their cardinality to be known at compile time, thus generating a more efficient query plan. In the following example, let's look at how we can create an inline TVF that returns the same results as the MSTVF:

```
CREATE OR ALTER FUNCTION dbo.ufn_FindReports_inline (@InEmpID int)
RETURNS TABLE
AS
RETURN
    WITH EMP_cte(EmployeeID, OrganizationNode, FirstName,
        LastName, JobTitle, RecursionLevel) -- CTE name and columns
    AS (
        -- Get the initial list of Employees for Manager n
        SELECT e.BusinessEntityID AS EmployeeID, e.OrganizationNode,
p.FirstName, p.LastName, e.JobTitle,              0 AS RecursionLevel
        FROM HumanResources.Employee e
        INNER JOIN Person.Person p
            ON p.BusinessEntityID = e.BusinessEntityID
        WHERE e.BusinessEntityID = @InEmpID
        UNION ALL
        -- Join recursive member to anchor
        SELECT e.BusinessEntityID AS EmployeeID, e.OrganizationNode,
p.FirstName, p.LastName, e.JobTitle,              RecursionLevel + 1 AS
RecursionLevel
        FROM HumanResources.Employee e
        INNER JOIN EMP_cte
            ON e.OrganizationNode.GetAncestor(1) = EMP_cte.OrganizationNode
        INNER JOIN Person.Person p
            ON p.BusinessEntityID = e.BusinessEntityID
        )
SELECT EmployeeID, FirstName, LastName, JobTitle, RecursionLevel
FROM EMP_cte;
```

The plan shape for this query looks very different than the previous one:

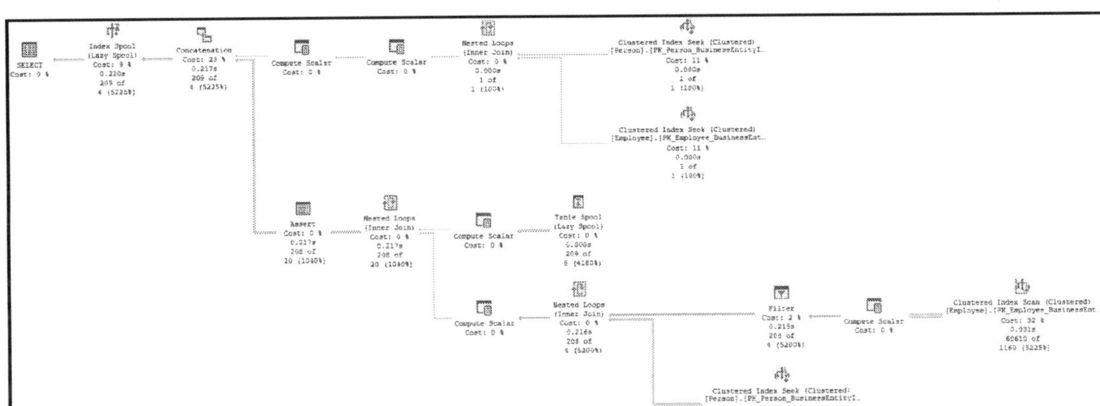

This is because the function is not being referenced as an object in this plan, the inline TVF is folded into the query as a table or view would be, allowing for a better overall plan and opening new opportunities for adjusting the indexes for an even better result. In this case, the performance of the query is like the interleaved MSTVF, CPU time dropped from 261 ms to 220 ms (~16 percent less), and execution time dropped from 468 ms to 221 ms (~52 percent less), as seen in the following screenshot:

⊟ QueryTimeStats	
CpuTime	220
ElapsedTime	221
UdfCpuTime	0
UdfElapsedTime	115

The takeaway here is to write TVFs as inline TVFs rather than MSTVFs where possible. If the logic is too complex to make an inline TVF feasible, upgrading to SQL Server 2017 to be able to leverage interleaved execution might improve query performance when leveraging TVFs.

Complex expressions

Search predicates should not use complex expressions. Much like the deterministic function calls we discussed in the *Functions in our predicate* section, complex expressions can also cause unnecessary scans.

As was discussed in previous chapters, the Query Optimizer uses statistics, internal transformation rules, and heuristics at compile-time to determine a good-enough plan to execute a query. This includes the ability to fold expressions, which is the process of simplifying constant expressions at compile-time. For example, a predicate such as `WHERE Column = 320 * 200 * 32` is computed at compile time to its arithmetic result and internally the predicate is evaluated as `WHERE Column = 2048000`. Unlike constants, calculations that involve column values, parameters, non-deterministic functions, or variables are only evaluated at runtime—this is another example of how the Query Optimizer can't accurately estimate row counts beforehand, resulting in an inefficient query plan.

The following example shows a query executed in the **AdventureWorks** sample database that uses a calculation with a table column in the search predicate. The query lists all ordered products where an additional 10% discount can be added if the final discount is less than or equal to 30%:

```
SELECT ProductID, [UnitPrice], [UnitPriceDiscount],
       [UnitPrice] * (1 - [UnitPriceDiscount]) AS FinalUnitPrice,
       [UnitPriceDiscount] + 0.10 AS NewUnitPriceDiscount,
       [UnitPrice] * (1 - 0.30) AS NewFinalUnitPrice
FROM Sales.SalesOrderDetail
WHERE [UnitPriceDiscount] + 0.10 <= 0.30
GROUP BY ProductID, [UnitPrice], [UnitPriceDiscount];
```

Let's observe the query execution plan:

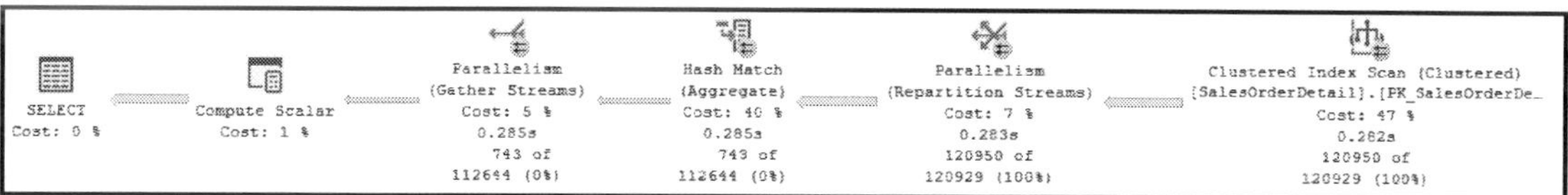

As we discussed in the *Functions in our predicate* section, we see a scan of the clustered index. The requirement for the query is to find ordered products where the company can add an additional 10% and still not go above a 30% discount, and the `[UnitPriceDiscount] + 0.10 <= 0.30` predicate accomplishes that.

But the same requirement can be expressed using a search predicate that does not use a complex expression, as seen in the following query:

```
SELECT ProductID, [UnitPrice], [UnitPriceDiscount],
       [UnitPrice] * (1 - [UnitPriceDiscount]) AS FinalUnitPrice,
       [UnitPriceDiscount] + 0.10 AS NewUnitPriceDiscount,
       [UnitPrice] * (1 - 0.30) AS NewFinalUnitPrice
FROM Sales.SalesOrderDetail
```

```
WHERE [UnitPriceDiscount] <= 0.20
GROUP BY ProductID, [UnitPrice], [UnitPriceDiscount];
```

Let's observe the new query execution plan:

And the **QueryTimeStats** property for this plan:

There is no discernible change, but that's because there isn't a better index to use in the current schema. However, SQL Server found an index suggestion that may yield better results, and this was possible because the search predicate could now be evaluated at compile time. We can create the index suggestion, as seen next:

```
CREATE NONCLUSTERED INDEX IX_UnitePriceDiscount ON
[Sales].[SalesOrderDetail] (
        [UnitPriceDiscount]
)
INCLUDE (
        [ProductID],
        [UnitPrice]
);
```

It's a good idea to assess the current index design after getting an index suggestion to determine whether an existing index is a subset of the suggested index. If such an index already exists, it is better to alter this index rather than creating a new index, which would be redundant with the existing one and unnecessarily increase index overhead.

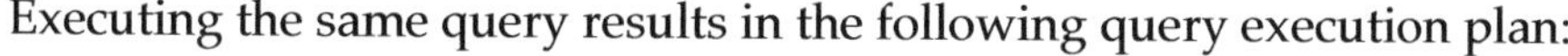

Executing the same query results in the following query execution plan:

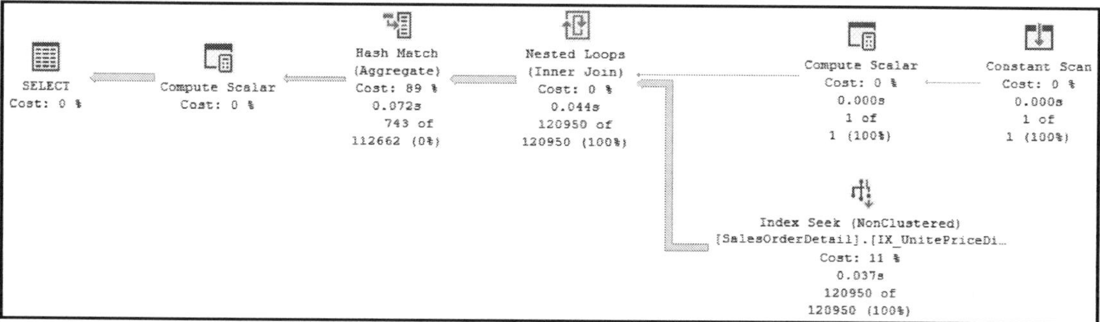

The new plan is much cheaper to execute, which is why it didn't even qualify for parallelism. And in fact, comparing the **QueryTimeStats** property from before and after the index was created, the improvements are also obvious: CPU time dropped from 140 ms to 67 ms (52% less), and execution time dropped from 276 ms to 74 ms (73% less):

⊟ QueryTimeStats	
CpuTime	67
ElapsedTime	74

Optimizing OR logic

A common query pattern involves the need to express several conditions of which at least one must be true to filter the result set, usually with OR logic. Expressing these OR conditions can have serious performance drawbacks and can often be replaced with other constructs that provide better scalability and performance.

The following example shows a query executed in the **AdventureWorks** sample database that uses an **OR** condition in the search predicate. The query lists all rows for a specific product, or where the price is set at a predetermined value:

```
SELECT ProductID, [UnitPrice], [UnitPriceDiscount],
       [UnitPrice] * (1 - [UnitPriceDiscount]) AS FinalUnitPrice,
       [UnitPriceDiscount] + 0.10 AS NewUnitPriceDiscount,
       [UnitPrice] * (1 - 0.30) AS NewFinalUnitPrice
FROM Sales.SalesOrderDetail
WHERE ProductID = 770
       OR UnitPrice = 3399.99
GROUP BY ProductID, [UnitPrice], [UnitPriceDiscount];
```

The preceding query displays the following query execution plan:

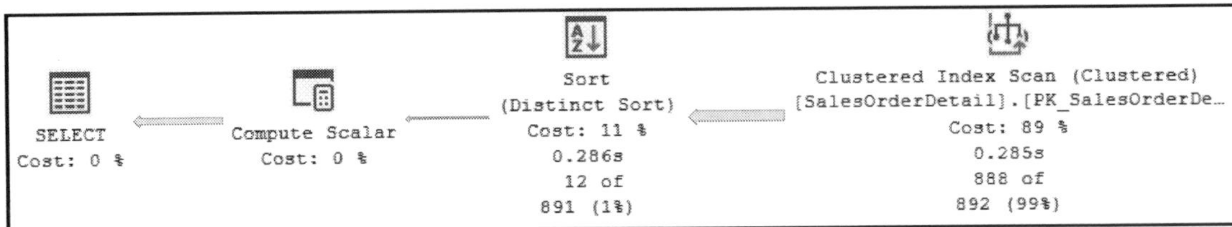

For reference, the **QueryTimeStats** property for this query execution plan are the following:

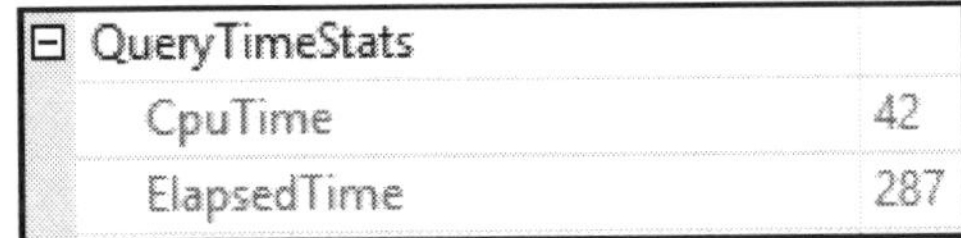

Looking at the search predicates, these are not necessarily mutually exclusive. Still they can effectively be expressed as two separate queries that are joined by a **UNION** operator, as in the following example:

```
SELECT ProductID, [UnitPrice], [UnitPriceDiscount],
       [UnitPrice] * (1 - [UnitPriceDiscount]) AS FinalUnitPrice,
       [UnitPriceDiscount] + 0.10 AS NewUnitPriceDiscount,
       [UnitPrice] * (1 - 0.30) AS NewFinalUnitPrice
FROM Sales.SalesOrderDetail
WHERE ProductID = 770
GROUP BY ProductID, [UnitPrice], [UnitPriceDiscount]
UNION
SELECT ProductID, [UnitPrice], [UnitPriceDiscount],
       [UnitPrice] * (1 - [UnitPriceDiscount]) AS FinalUnitPrice,
       [UnitPriceDiscount] + 0.10 AS NewUnitPriceDiscount,
       [UnitPrice] * (1 - 0.30) AS NewFinalUnitPrice
FROM Sales.SalesOrderDetail
WHERE UnitPrice = 3399.99
GROUP BY ProductID, [UnitPrice], [UnitPriceDiscount];
```

Let's observe the new query execution plan:

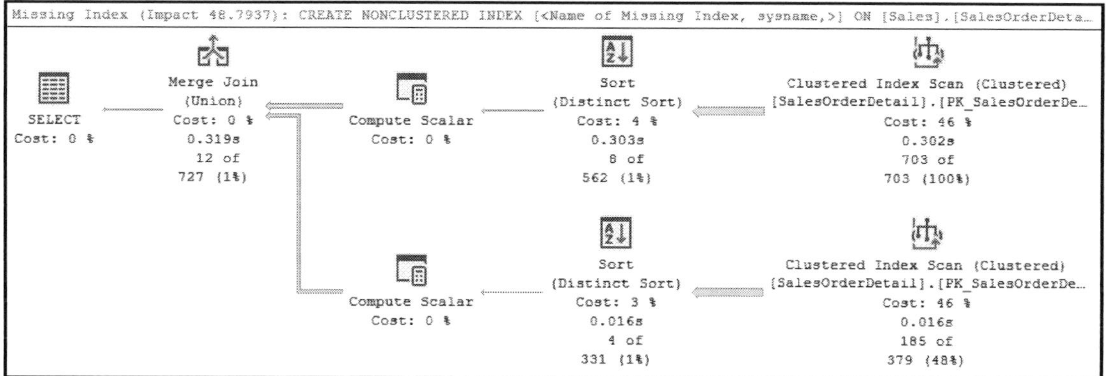

Since we now have separate queries, we see a missing index suggestion. The index being suggested is the following, which covers the second query in the union:

```
CREATE NONCLUSTERED INDEX IX_UnitPrice ON [Sales].[SalesOrderDetail] (
        [UnitPrice]
)
INCLUDE (
        [ProductID],
        [UnitPriceDiscount]
);
```

But I know we can also cover the first query in the union. There is already a non-clustered index on **ProductID**, but it is not covering **IX_SalesOrderDetail_ProductID**. However, I can change the existing index to make it a covering index with negligible effects on any query that was using the index before:

```
CREATE NONCLUSTERED INDEX IX_SalesOrderDetail_ProductID ON
[Sales].[SalesOrderDetail] (
        [ProductID]
)
INCLUDE (
        [UnitPrice],
        [UnitPriceDiscount]
)
WITH DROP_EXISTING;
```

The new query execution plan is the following:

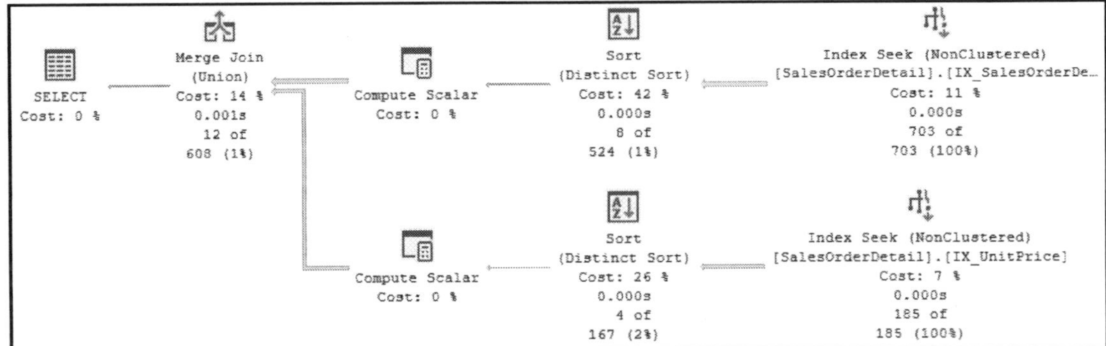

If we can verify that the predicates are mutually exclusive and that no repeated rows can exist in the result set, use **UNION ALL** instead of **UNION** and avoid the Sort operator seen in the plan. More information can be found in the *UNION ALL versus UNION* section of `Chapter 7`, *Discovering T-SQL Anti-Patterns in Depth.*

The **QueryTimeStats** property for this query execution plan confirms this improved performance: CPU time dropped from 42 ms to 23 ms (45 % less), and execution time dropped from 287 ms to 2 ms (~99 % less):

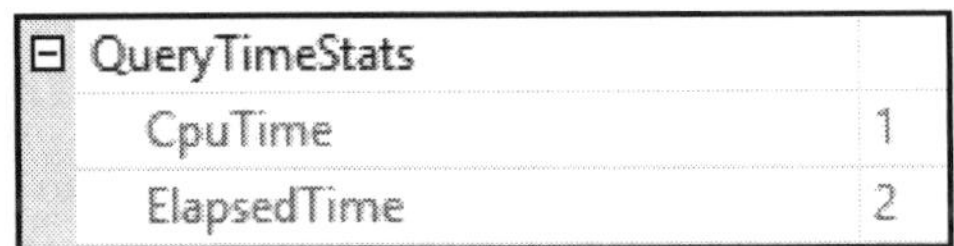

QueryTimeStats	
CpuTime	1
ElapsedTime	2

The query execution plan shape now seeks on non-clustered indexes. This is a more scalable and better-performing plan than the one that scanned the clustered index.

NULL means unknown

In the context of a database, if a column is set to **NULL**, it effectively means that value is unknown. If we compare any other value with **NULL**, the result of that comparison is also unknown. In other words, a value can never be equal to **NULL** as **NULL** is the absence of a value. This means the `ColumnValue = NULL` expression will never evaluate to true or false; even if **ColumnValue** is in fact **NULL**, it will always evaluate to unknown. To detect whether a column value is **NULL**, we must use the `IS NULL` or `IS NOT NULL` special expressions rather than = or <>.

This handling of `NULL` is not unique to SQL Server, it is based on the ANSI standard handling of NULL values.

Having NULL values in our database is not an anti-pattern in and of itself, but when we assign a meaning to the value NULL in our application, we may face some challenges when it comes to writing performant T-SQL due to the need for the special handling of NULL comparisons.

Let's look at an example like this in the **AdventureWorks** database. The **Product** table contains information about products that are sold in the shop, but it also contains information about parts that are kept in stock that are not goods for sale. These items will not have a category, so the **ProductSubcategoryID** column is **NULL** for these rows. This makes sense if there truly is no category for these items, but what if we were to say that a value of NULL in the **ProductSubcategoryID** column really means that these items are in the **Parts** category because they are unfinished goods? If we want to build a query that returns a list of all the products and includes their category and sub-category, since the sub-category column is **NULL** for all the parts, we need to embed a function in the join condition in order to handle the special **NULL** case. In fact, we need to get a bit creative with the T-SQL:

```
SELECT p.ProductID,
    p.Name AS ProductName,
    c.Name AS Category,
    s.Name AS SubCategory
FROM Production.Product AS p
LEFT JOIN Production.ProductSubcategory AS s
      ON p.ProductSubcategoryID = s.ProductSubcategoryID
INNER JOIN Production.ProductCategory AS c
      ON ISNULL(s.ProductCategoryID, 5) = c.ProductCategoryID
ORDER BY Category, SubCategory;
```

We need to perform `LEFT JOIN` between the **Product** and **ProductSubcategory** tables in order to include the rows that have a **NULL** value for **ProductSubcategoryID** in the **Product** table, but if we still want to join these **NULL** rows with the **ProductCategory** table, we must handle these **NULL** values in the join condition by using the **ISNULL()** function. We've hardcoded a value of **5**, which is **ProductCategoryID** for the new **Parts** category we added for this example. This would be even more complicated if the value we want to join on is **NULL** on both sides. In that case, we would need to have a function on both sides of the join to convert the **NULL** values into something that can be compared. In this case, there's a better way we could write this that would avoid **NULL** handling in the join. Since we know that all the rows with a **NULL** value for **ProductSubcategoryID** are in the **Parts** category, we can handle this in the **SELECT** list instead. Having an **ISNULL()** function in the **SELECT** list does not impact the performance as much because the function call does not interfere with the selectivity estimate, index usage, or plan selection, it's simply executed on the results after they are retrieved:

```
SELECT p.ProductID,
    p.Name AS ProductName,
    ISNULL(c.Name, 'Parts') AS Category,
    s.Name AS SubCategory
FROM Production.Product p
LEFT JOIN Production.ProductSubcategory AS s
    ON p.ProductSubcategoryID = s.ProductSubcategoryID
INNER JOIN Production.ProductCategory AS c
    ON s.ProductCategoryID = c.ProductCategoryID
ORDER BY Category, SubCategory;
```

Let's look at the query plan for these two queries and their estimated cost: **Query 1** is the bad query with **ISNULL()** in the join condition, and **Query 2** is the good query with **ISNULL()** in the **SELECT** list:

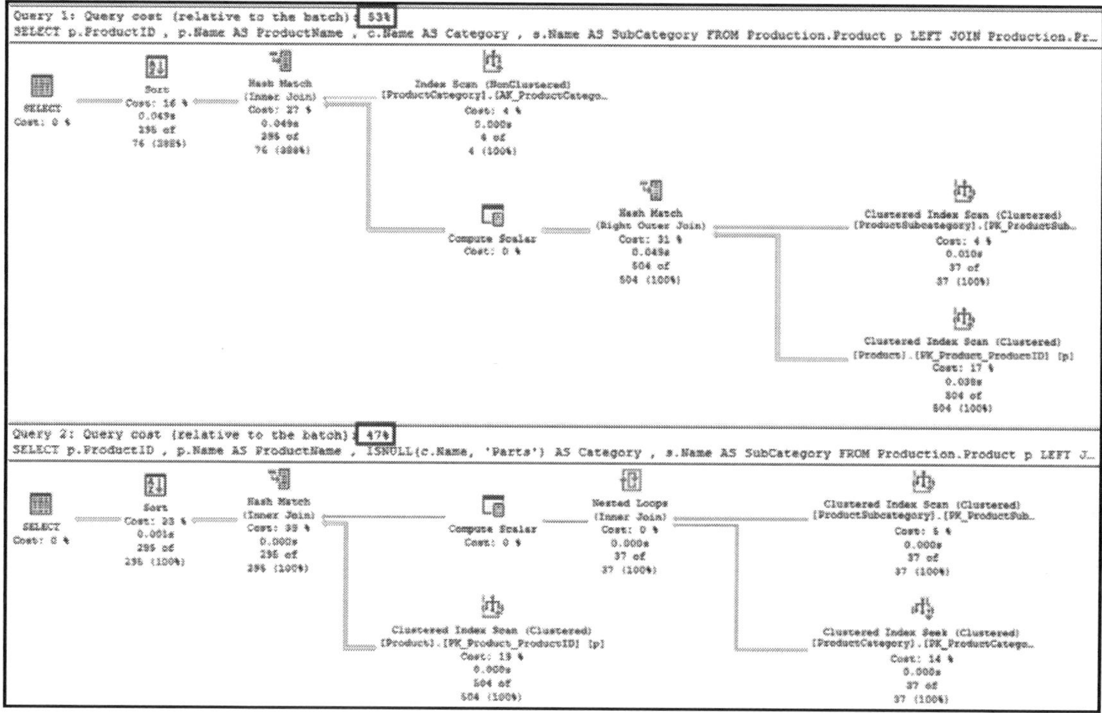

Looking at the **QueryTimeStats** property for these two queries, we can see that the **Query 1** uses three times as much CPU as **Query 2**:

Query 1		Query 2	
⊟ QueryTimeStats		⊟ QueryTimeStats	
CpuTime	3	CpuTime	1
ElapsedTime	50	ElapsedTime	1

We might notice that there is a scan of the **Product** table in both plans, which leads to an expensive Hash Match. This is because there is no index on the **ProductSubcategoryID** column in the **Product** table. Let's add a covering index to that column to see whether we can make the plan a little better:

```
CREATE NONCLUSTERED INDEX [IX_Product_ProductSubcategoryID] ON
[Production].[Product] (
        [ProductSubcategoryID]
)
INCLUDE (
    [Name]
);
```

Now if we run the queries again, we get the following plans and their estimated cost:

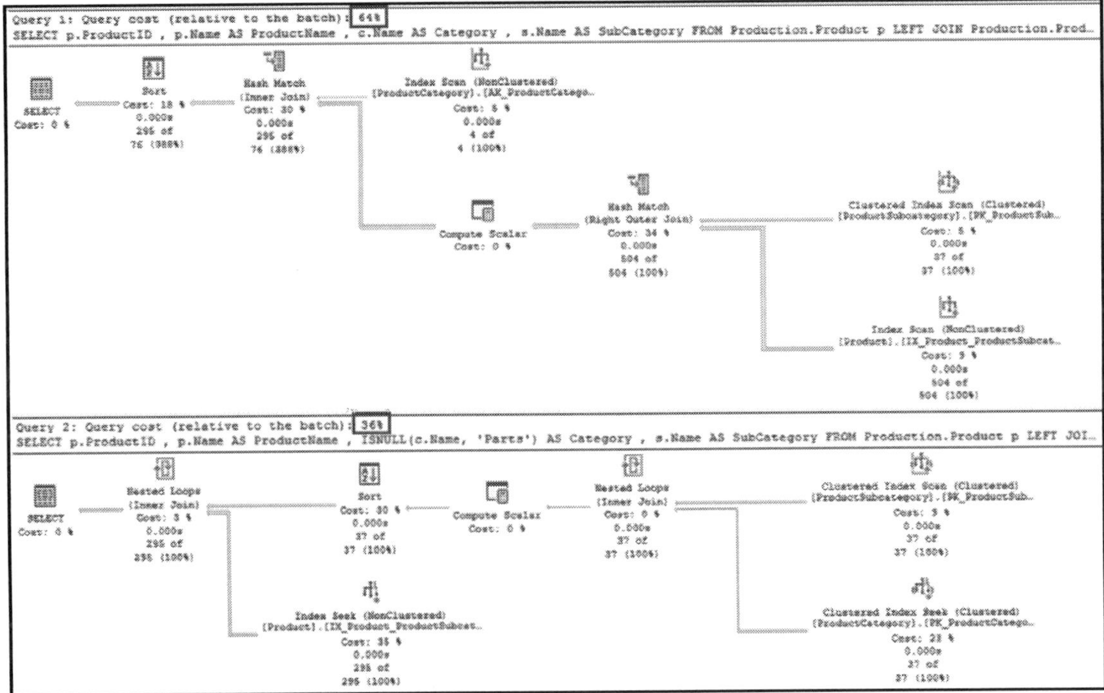

Query 1 uses the covering index, but because the **ISNULL()** function prevents SQL Server from using the predicate as a seek predicate, it has to scan it. **Query 2**, on the other hand, gets much better with seeks and nested loops joins. This is reflected in the **QueryTimeStats** property as well:

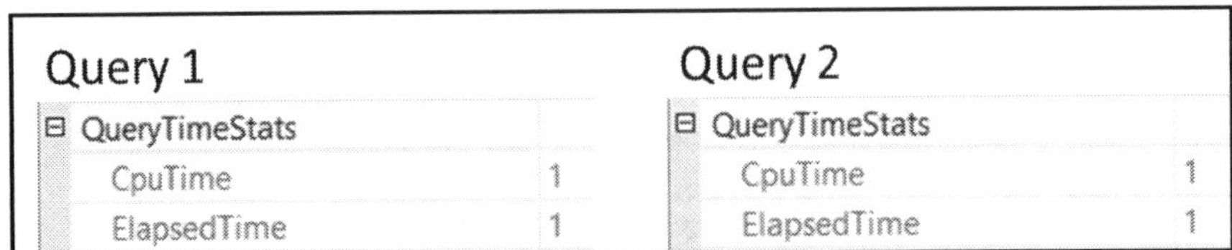

Query 1 goes down to 1 ms, whereas **Query 2** stays the same at **1** ms. Keep this in mind when using NULLs in our application. NULL means unknown or the absence of a value and requires special handling for comparisons; don't rely on it to represent something concrete.

Fuzzy string matching

When searching for strings in SQL Server using =, the strings must match exactly for the expression to evaluate to true. If we want to match only part of the string however, we must use a **LIKE** operator with wildcards. If we want to search for a pattern anywhere within a string, we need both leading and trailing wildcards. The problem with this is that it prevents us from being able to use an index or accurately estimate the cardinality . An index with a string key is sorted, starting with the first character of the string, but if we are searching for a pattern that may appear in the middle of the string, SQL Server must scan every value and search for the matching pattern in each string in the column. A **LIKE** operator with a leading wildcard (`"%a value"` or `"%a value%"`) almost always causes a scan operation.

Consider an example from the **AdventureWorks** database where we want to find all the flat washers in the **Product** table. We know they all start with **Flat Washer**, but there are several different names in the table. If we're not sure whether there are any characters before the words **Flat Washer**, we could write the following query:

```
SELECT ProductID, Name AS ProductName, ProductNumber
FROM Production.Product
WHERE Name LIKE '%Flat Washer%';
```

This query would yield the following execution plan:

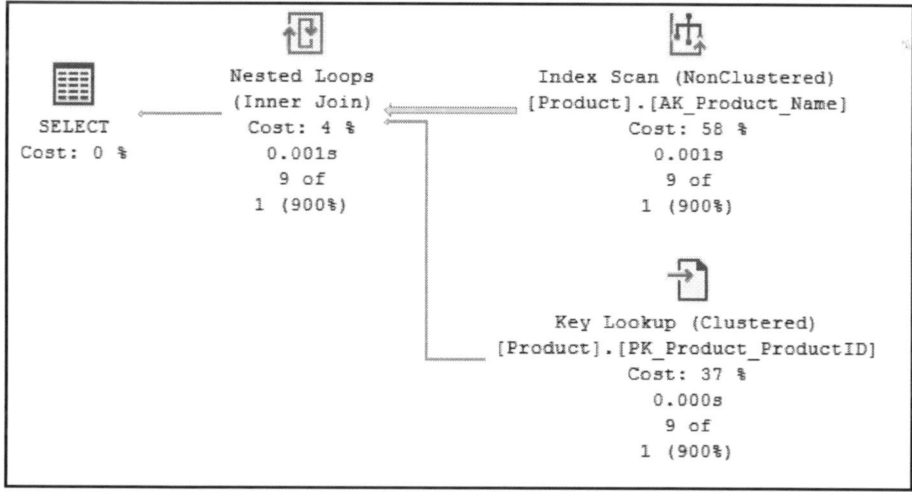

Notice there's an **Index Scan**, which is the most expensive operator in the plan.

If we look at the result set, we can see that the words **Flat Washer** always appear at the beginning of the string:

Results | Messages | Execution plan

	ProductID	ProductName	ProductNumber
1	341	Flat Washer 1	FW-1000
2	343	Flat Washer 2	FW-1400
3	346	Flat Washer 3	FW-5160
4	345	Flat Washer 4	FW-3800
5	348	Flat Washer 5	FW-7160
6	342	Flat Washer 6	FW-1200
7	349	Flat Washer 7	FW-9160
8	347	Flat Washer 8	FW-5800
9	344	Flat Washer 9	FW-3400

In this case, we don't really need the leading wildcard, so let's rewrite the query as follows:

```
SELECT ProductID, Name AS ProductName, ProductNumber
FROM Production.Product
WHERE Name LIKE 'Flat Washer%';
```

And then examine the execution plan:

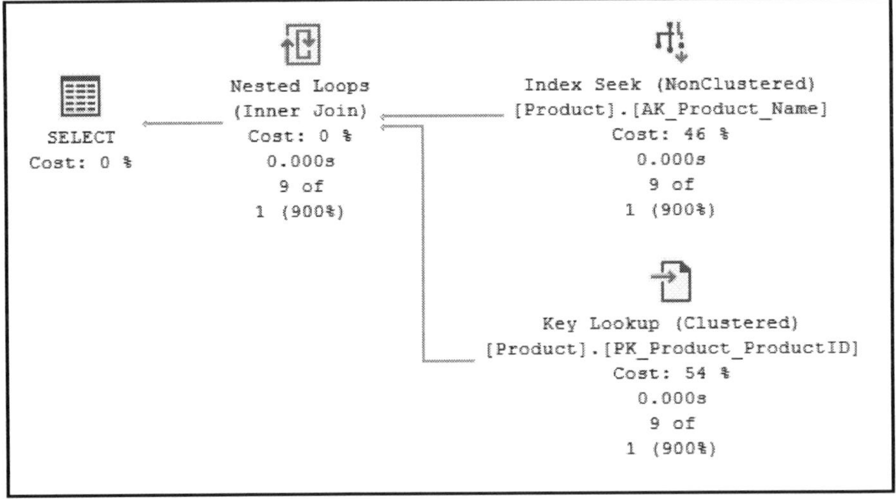

The expensive scan is replaced by a more efficient **Index Seek**.

If we must use a **LIKE** expression, try to avoid using a leading wildcard if possible. The **LIKE** expressions without a leading wildcard translates into a range scan. If it's not possible to avoid the leading wildcard, we might consider using full text indexes and their accompanying text functions, such as **CONTAINS**, to provide better performance for fuzzy string matching, particularly if this is the only filter condition on these queries.

Inequality logic

Inequality logic is logic that involves negative comparisons, such as **!=**, **<>**, **NOT IN**, or **NOT LIKE**. This type of predicate can be costly because it often results in evaluating each row, which translates to scan operations. Consider the following queries from the **AdventureWorks** database:

```
SELECT BusinessEntityID, FirstName, LastName
FROM Person.Person
WHERE PersonType NOT IN ('EM','SP','IN','VC','GC');

SELECT BusinessEntityID, FirstName, LastName
FROM Person.Person
WHERE PersonType = 'SC';
```

These queries are logically equivalent, since **SC** is the only **PersonType** that is not listed in the first query. Out of the box, the execution plans look like this:

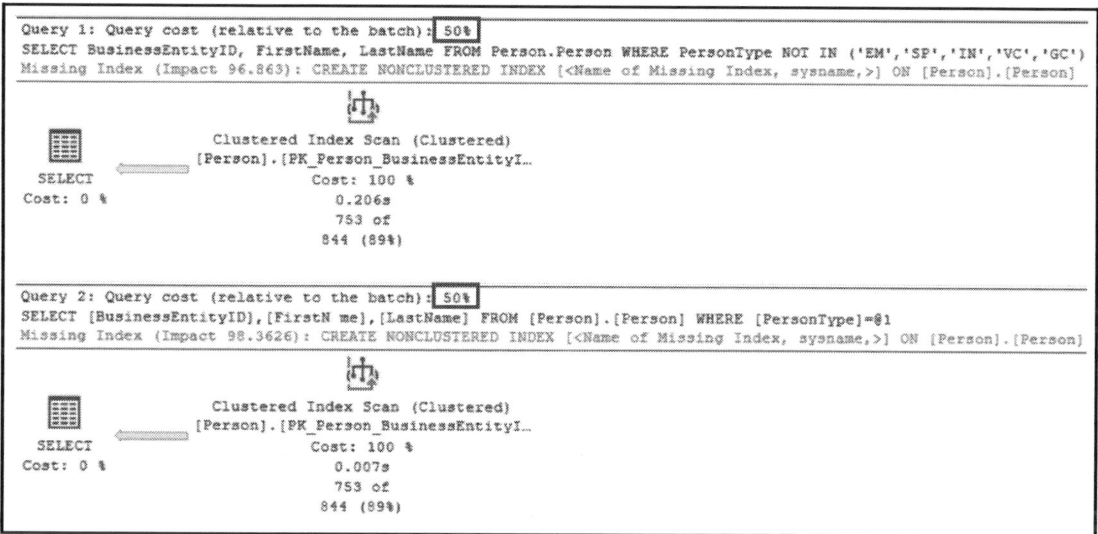

At this point, they appear to have the same estimated cost, but notice that both are doing a **Clustered Index Scan** and there is a missing index suggestion from SQL Server. This is because there is no index on the **PersonType** column to support the query. Let's add the following covering index to support this query:

```
CREATE NONCLUSTERED INDEX [IX_Person_PersonType] ON [Person].[Person] (
        [PersonType]
)
INCLUDE (
        [BusinessEntityID],
        [FirstName],
        [LastName]
);
```

Once we add the index, SQL Server can leverage it for both queries, but notice that for the first query, it results in a scan of the index, whereas the second query performs a seek. Also note the estimated cost difference between the plans, the first query is much more expensive than the second:

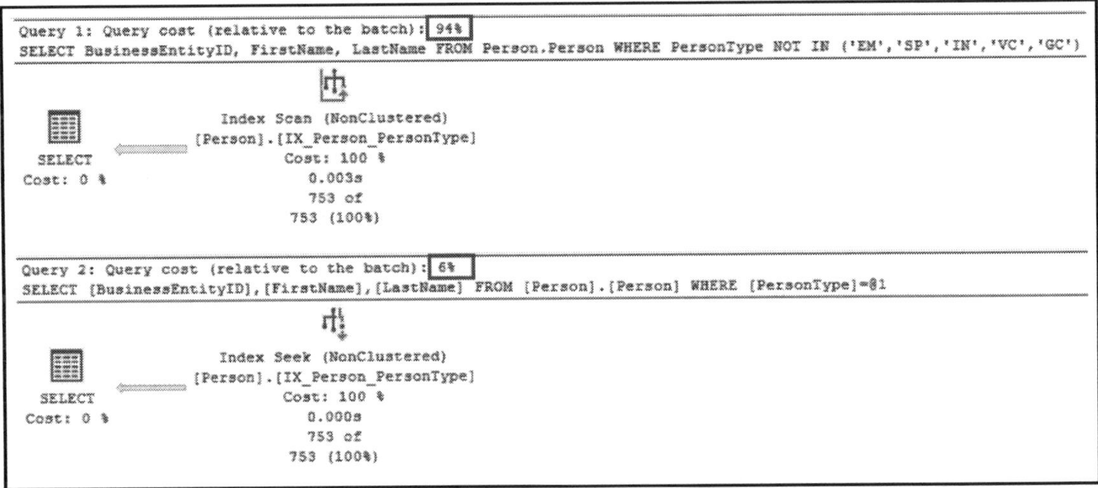

As we can see, while both queries are logically the same and return the same results, the second query is much more efficient than the first once the proper indexes are in place. If we have the option of writing a filter condition using an equality comparison versus an inequality comparison, using the equality comparison is generally better.

EXECUTE versus sp_executesql

There are times when an application must build a T-SQL statement dynamically before executing it on the server. In order to execute a dynamically-created T-SQL statement, we can use either the **EXECUTE** command or the **sp_executesql** stored procedure. The **sp_executesql** procedure is the preferred method for executing dynamic T-SQL because it allows we to add parameter markers and thus increases the likelihood that SQL Server will be able to reuse the plan and avoid costly query compilations.

Here's a sample script from the **AdventureWorks** database that builds a dynamic T-SQL statement and executes it via the **EXECUTE** command:

```
DECLARE @sql nvarchar(MAX), @JobTitle nvarchar(50) = N'Sales
Representative';

SET @sql = 'SELECT e.BusinessEntityID, p.FirstName, p.LastName
FROM HumanResources.Employee AS e
INNER JOIN Person.Person AS p ON p.BusinessEntityID = e.BusinessEntityID
WHERE e.JobTitle = N''' + @JobTitle + '''';

EXECUTE (@sql);
```

Notice that there is a variable for the **JobTitle** column, but the **EXECUTE** command does not allow for parameters, so this variable is appended to the T-SQL string in order to include it in the resulting query. We can reuse the same script by changing `Sales Representative` to `Accountant` and re-running it, but because the resulting query is not parameterized, SQL Server will have to compile and cache the query again. We can verify this by examining the **sys.dm_exec_query_stats** DMV. Recall from the *Query plan properties of interest* section of `Chapter 4`, *Exploring Query Execution Plans* that there is a property called **QueryHash** which contains a value that can identify a query in the cache and will return all the queries that are syntactically equivalent but have different query strings for some reason. Take a look at the following query:

```
SELECT st.text, qs.sql_handle, qs.execution_count
FROM sys.dm_exec_query_stats AS qs
CROSS APPLY sys.dm_exec_sql_text(qs.sql_handle) AS st
WHERE qs.query_hash = 0x3A17ADF596F7D5C9;
```

This query returns the following results:

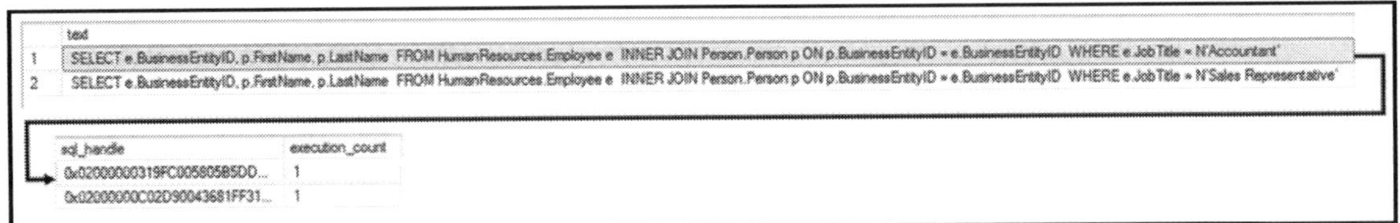

	text
1	SELECT e.BusinessEntityID, p.FirstName, p.LastName FROM HumanResources.Employee e INNER JOIN Person.Person p ON p.BusinessEntityID = e.BusinessEntityID WHERE e.JobTitle = N'Accountant'
2	SELECT e.BusinessEntityID, p.FirstName, p.LastName FROM HumanResources.Employee e INNER JOIN Person.Person p ON p.BusinessEntityID = e.BusinessEntityID WHERE e.JobTitle = N'Sales Representative'

sql_handle	execution_count
0x0200000319FC005805B5DD...	1
0x0200000C02D90043681FF31...	1

We can see that there are two different queries here, one for each of the different **JobTitle** values, that each have a single execution. Each execution of the preceding script resulted in a separate compilation and a separated cached query plan.

We will discuss **sys.dm_exec_query_stats** as well as other dynamic management views in more detail in `Chapter 8`, *Building Diagnostic Queries Using DMVs and DMFs.*

Let's see how we can rewrite this script using `sp_executesql` instead:

```
DECLARE @sql nvarchar(MAX), @JobTitle nvarchar(50) = N'Sales
Representative';

SET @sql = 'SELECT e.BusinessEntityID, p.FirstName, p.LastName
FROM HumanResources.Employee AS e
INNER JOIN Person.Person AS p ON p.BusinessEntityID = e.BusinessEntityID
WHERE e.JobTitle = @p1';

EXEC sp_executesql @sql, N'@p1 nvarchar(50)', @JobTitle;
```

Notice that in this case, we can leverage the **@JobTitle** variable as a parameter in the query. If we change the value of **@JobTitle** to **Accountant** and run the query again, SQL Server can reuse the existing execution plan from the cache. We can verify this by running the same query against **sys.dm_exec_query_stats** as mentioned previously with the **QueryHash** from this new query. This time, the results are different:

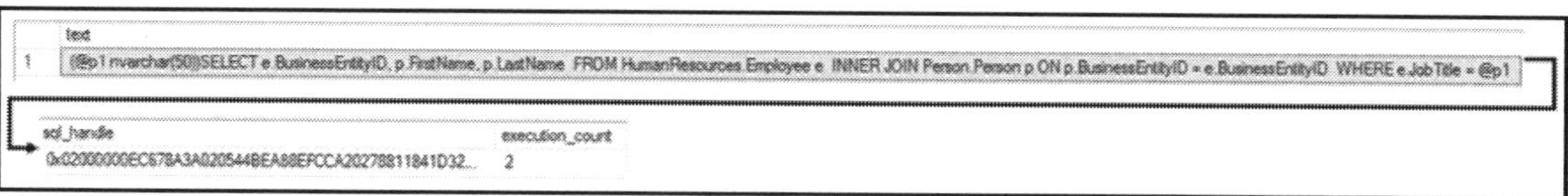

Notice that the query in the cache has a parameter marker, and the execution count is **2**, indicating that the query plan has been reused.

Whenever our application requires dynamic T-SQL for any reason, leveraging the **sp_executesql** procedure rather than the **EXECUTE** command is generally more efficient because it will increase the likelihood that SQL Server can reuse the query plan. Also recall that in the *The importance of parameters* section in `Chapter 2`, *Understanding Query Processing*, we mentioned that parameters and the use of **sp_executesql** can help avoid SQL Injection attacks, so it is more secure than using **EXECUTE**. For these reasons, **sp_executesql** is the recommended method for executing dynamic T-SQL.

Composable logic

Composable logic is what some developers use to make a single T-SQL statement do more than one thing, which allows us to reuse the same code for multiple tasks. When writing procedural code, reusability is desired because it makes the code more concise and maintainable. It allows developers to create libraries of modules that can be reused in other areas of the application, or even in other applications altogether. In T-SQL however, there can be a hefty performance penalty for writing generic reusable code.

For SQL Server to execute a query in the most efficient way, it needs to estimate the cost of the query and choose operators that will return the results in the cheapest way possible. This is all done at **compile time** based on how the query is written. With composable logic, however, the true cost of the query cannot be known until **runtime** because it is based on variables that change whenever the query is run. This type of generic code causes SQL Server to generate a generic plan at compile-time that will work no matter what the runtime values are. Typically, this plan will not perform well for any combination of runtime values, whereas a specific plan generated for the specific case that is being executed would likely perform much better. Writing T-SQL code for the specific case that is needed may result in some code duplication and less maintainability, what developers sometimes refer to as **spaghetti code**, but it will almost always provide better performance and scalability.

Consider the following stored procedure, which can be executed in the **AdventureWorks** sample database:

```
CREATE OR ALTER PROCEDURE GetSalesPersonOrders @SalesPerson INT NULL
AS
BEGIN
       SELECT SalesOrderID
            p.FirstName AS SalesFirstName,
            p.LastName AS SalesLastName,
       FROM Sales.SalesOrderHeader AS soh
       LEFT JOIN Person.Person AS p ON soh.SalesPersonID =
p.BusinessEntityID
       WHERE @SalesPerson IS NULL OR SalesPersonID = @SalesPerson;
END;
```

This is an example of composable logic. If a value is sent for the **@SalesPerson** parameter, we are effectively executing this query:

```
SELECT SalesOrderID, p.FirstName AS SalesFirstName, p.LastName AS
SalesLastName
FROM Sales.SalesOrderHeader AS soh
LEFT JOIN Person.Person AS p ON soh.SalesPersonID = p.BusinessEntityID
WHERE SalesPersonID = @SalesPerson
```

If **NULL** is sent for the **@SalesPerson** parameter, we are effectively executing this query:

```
SELECT SalesOrderID, p.FirstName AS SalesFirstName, p.LastName AS
SalesLastName
FROM Sales.SalesOrderHeader AS soh
LEFT JOIN Person.Person p ON soh.SalesPersonID = p.BusinessEntityID
```

Note that this second query has no **WHERE** clause, it will return the entire **SalesOrderHeader** table, including any matching rows from the **Person** table. This is naturally going to be much more expensive than the first query and should really have a different query plan. Let's look at the query plans and see how SQL Server would perform each query if written separately:

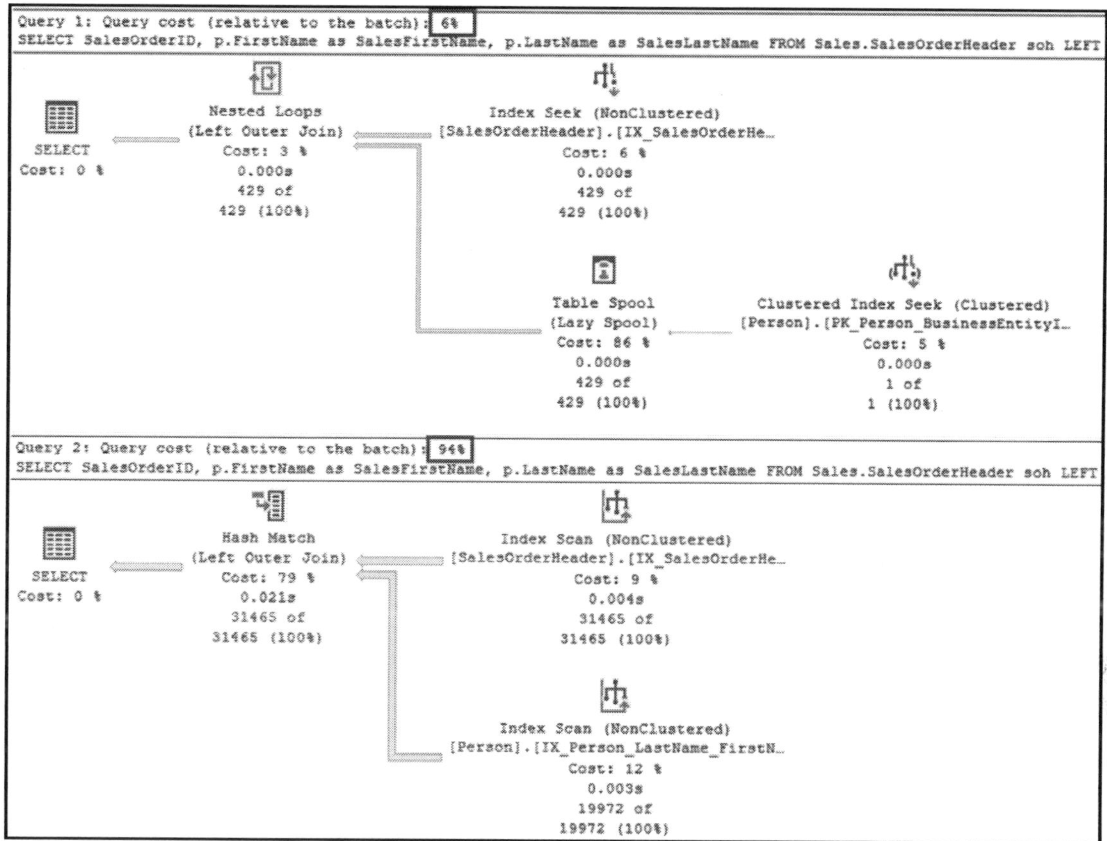

As we can see, the estimated cost for **Query 1**, which uses the **@SalesPerson** variable in the **WHERE** clause, is much cheaper than the estimated cost for **Query 2**, which returns every row in the **SalesOrderHeader** table. Also note that **Query 1** uses **Index Seeks** and a nested loops join, where **Query 2** uses **Index Scans** and a **Hash Match**. Here are the resulting **QueryTimeStats**:

Query 1		Query 2	
⊟ QueryTimeStats		⊟ QueryTimeStats	
CpuTime	1	CpuTime	27
ElapsedTime	29	ElapsedTime	114

Now let's try to execute **Query 1** by using the stored procedure that we created in the preceding code:

```
EXECUTE usp_GetSalesPersonOrders @SalesPerson = 279;
```

This yields the following query execution plan:

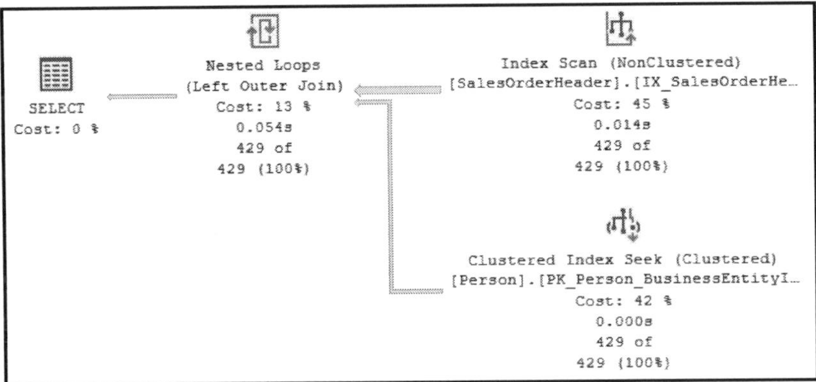

In this plan, SQL Server chooses to use a **Nested Loops** join, but one of the **Index Seeks** has become a scan. Also, if we look at the **QueryTimeStats** property of the plan, this plan used 5 ms of CPU time to execute, more than double the amount of time the standalone query used:

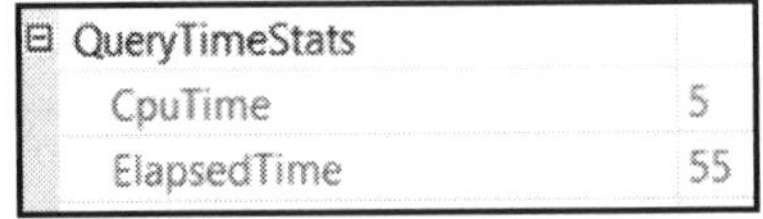

⊟ QueryTimeStats	
CpuTime	5
ElapsedTime	55

We can also execute the equivalent of **Query 2** using this stored procedure by sending a **NULL** value for **@SalesPerson**:

```
EXECUTE usp_GetSalesPersonOrders @SalesPerson = NULL;
```

This execution of the stored procedure will reuse the same plan from the cache, but the running time is very different:

QueryTimeStats	
CpuTime	28
ElapsedTime	100

While the difference isn't as much as with **Query 1**, **Query 2** used 28 ms of CPU time versus 27 ms when run as a standalone query. So, the plan generated by this generic stored procedure is worse for both queries than a plan generated for the specific queries.

The situation gets even worse if we happen to execute the stored procedure with `@SalesPerson = NULL` the first time. We introduced the concept of parameter sniffing in the section *The importance of parameters* of `Chapter 2`, *Understanding Query Processing*. Composable logic in stored procedures leaves our application even more vulnerable to parameter-sniffing issues. Let's look at the plan that is generated if we execute the preceding stored procedure for the first time with a **NULL** parameter:

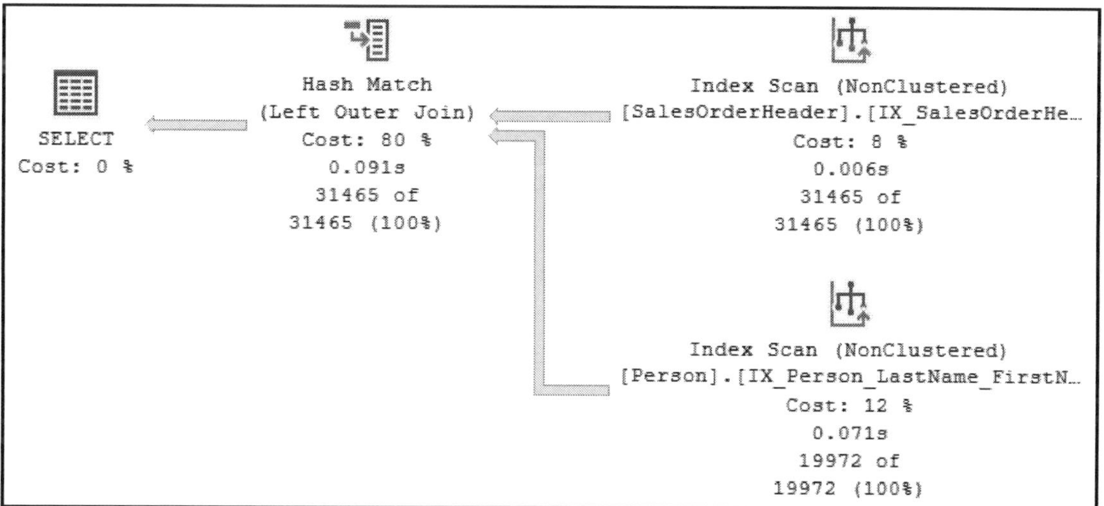

This is effectively the same plan that was generated for preceding **Query 2**, and the CPU time is similar. For **Query 2**, the impact of the composable logic is small, but what happens if we reuse this plan for the `@SalesPerson = 279` case? First, the CPU time is even higher than with the first stored procedure plan—8 ms versus 5 ms:

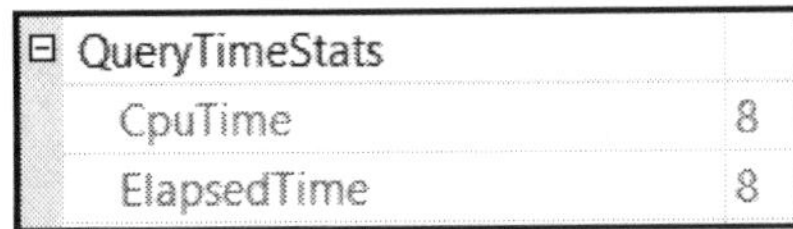

QueryTimeStats	
CpuTime	8
ElapsedTime	8

Also looking at the plan, we can see an excessive memory grant warning:

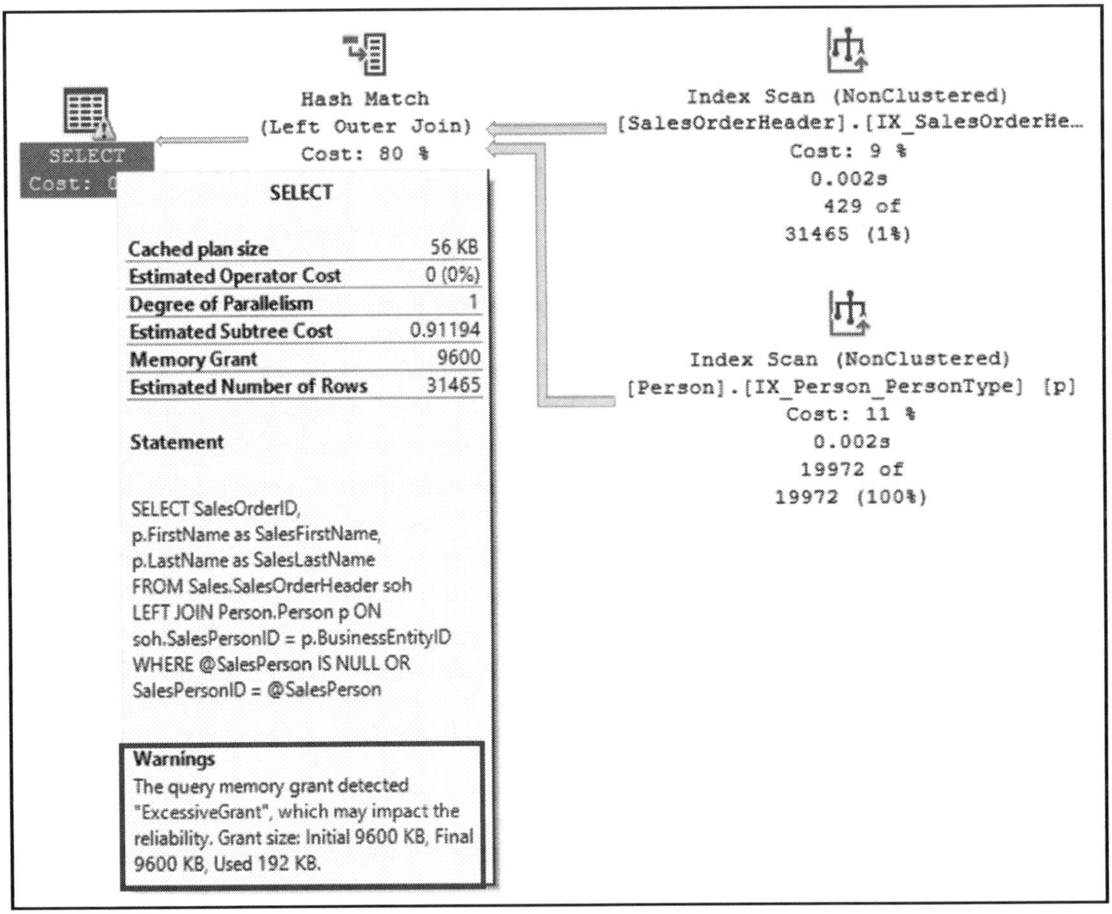

SELECT
Cost: 0

Hash Match
(Left Outer Join)
Cost: 80 %

Index Scan (NonClustered)
[SalesOrderHeader].[IX_SalesOrderHe...
Cost: 9 %
0.002s
429 of
31465 (1%)

Index Scan (NonClustered)
[Person].[IX_Person_PersonType] [p]
Cost: 11 %
0.002s
19972 of
19972 (100%)

SELECT

Cached plan size	56 KB
Estimated Operator Cost	0 (0%)
Degree of Parallelism	1
Estimated Subtree Cost	0.91194
Memory Grant	9600
Estimated Number of Rows	31465

Statement

```
SELECT SalesOrderID,
p.FirstName as SalesFirstName,
p.LastName as SalesLastName
FROM Sales.SalesOrderHeader soh
LEFT JOIN Person.Person p ON
soh.SalesPersonID = p.BusinessEntityID
WHERE @SalesPerson IS NULL OR
SalesPersonID = @SalesPerson
```

Warnings
The query memory grant detected "ExcessiveGrant", which may impact the reliability. Grant size: Initial 9600 KB, Final 9600 KB, Used 192 KB.

Because of parameter sniffing, the plan created the first time the procedure was run returned a much larger number of rows, which necessitated an expensive **Hash Match** that used a large amount of memory. When using a specific parameter value rather than **NULL**, the number of rows returned is much smaller, and thus neither the **Hash Match** nor the memory grant make sense. At compile-time, SQL Server must choose a plan that works for any parameter value that may be sent at runtime. Unfortunately, because of composable logic, the plan chosen is often the wrong one.

The best way to resolve this issue would be to have separate stored procedures for the two queries. The problem with this is that we can end up with many stored procedures that have similar queries and similar names, and code manageability can become an issue. One compromise is to have a single stored procedure with conditional logic outside the query in question. Here's an example of how that would look for these queries:

```
CREATE OR ALTER PROCEDURE usp_GetSalesPersonOrders_better @SalesPerson INT
NULL
AS
BEGIN
       IF @SalesPerson IS NULL
       BEGIN
              SELECT SalesOrderID,
                    p.FirstName AS SalesFirstName,
                    p.LastName AS SalesLastName
              FROM Sales.SalesOrderHeader AS soh
              LEFT JOIN Person.Person AS p ON soh.SalesPersonID =
p.BusinessEntityID
       END
       ELSE
       BEGIN
              SELECT SalesOrderID,
                    p.FirstName AS SalesFirstName,
                    p.LastName AS SalesLastName
              FROM Sales.SalesOrderHeader AS soh
              LEFT JOIN Person.Person AS p ON soh.SalesPersonID =
p.BusinessEntityID
              WHERE SalesPersonID = @SalesPerson;
       END
END;
```

The code is slightly less readable, but we get the benefit of the right plan at runtime:

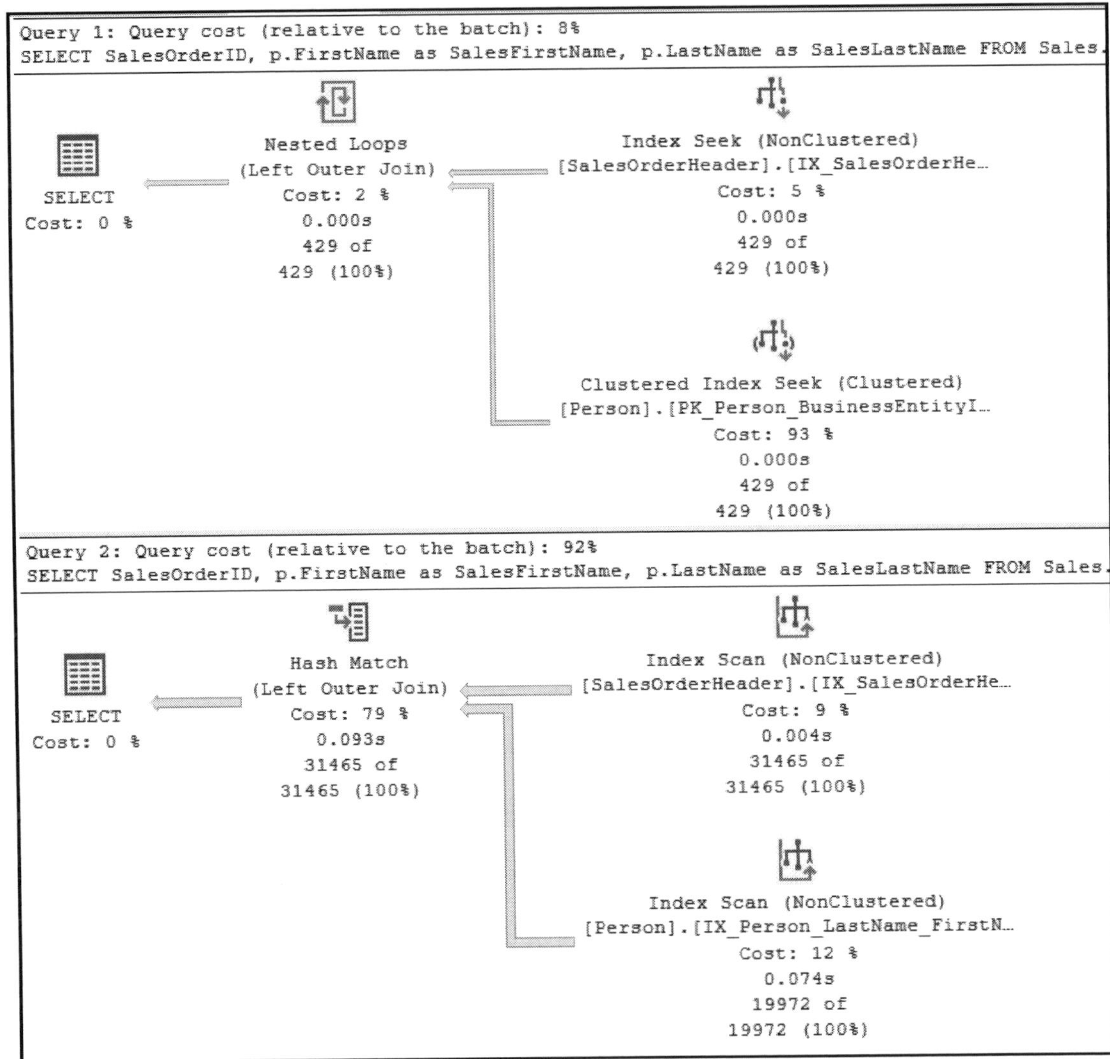

This is reflected in the **QueryTimeStats** property:

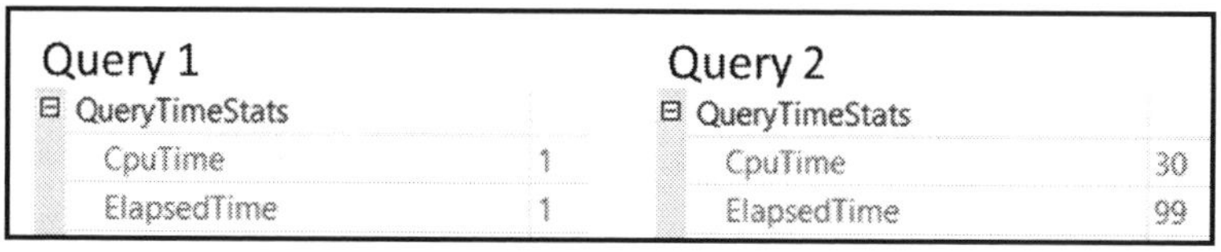

Query 1		Query 2	
⊟ QueryTimeStats		⊟ QueryTimeStats	
CpuTime	1	CpuTime	30
ElapsedTime	1	ElapsedTime	99

Another way to solve this problem would be to use dynamic T-SQL. In the previous section *EXECUTE versus sp_executesql*, we discussed using **sp_executesql** to execute dynamic T-SQL statements with parameter markers to allow SQL Server to cache and reuse the plans. If we have composable logic that involves many different options and would generate too many permutations to make conditional logic practical, leveraging dynamic T-SQL is likely the best option. Using the **sp_executesql** procedure allows we to programmatically generate code that is still reusable by SQL Server, so we get the right plan for the query every time without excessive compile time and cache bloat.

Summary

In this chapter, we reviewed a few T-SQL anti-patterns, such as **SELECT *** syntax, **OR** logic, and functions in our predicates, that are relatively easy to find simply by looking at our T-SQL code and how it is written. The scenarios covered in this chapter are some of the most common examples of patterns that prevent our T-SQL queries from scaling well and maintaining the expected level of performance throughout the lifetime of the applications. All are easy to detect, and most have easy workarounds. Therefore, when writing queries, try to avoid these anti-patterns by leveraging some of the techniques we outlined here.

In the next chapter, we will investigate some T-SQL anti-patterns that are a bit more difficult to identify as they require some additional research beyond simply reading the code.

7
Discovering T-SQL Anti-Patterns in Depth

In `Chapter 6`, *Easily-Identified T-SQL Anti-Patterns*, we covered some anti-patterns that may impact query performance that should be obvious just by reading the T-SQL code itself. Now we will move on to some anti-patterns that may require some more in-depth analysis to be identified. These often involve T-SQL that at first glance seems straightforward, but when we dig into the query plan, there may be hidden performance pitfalls, such as expensive operations or hidden practices that prevent predicate SARGability.

In this chapter, we will cover the following topics:

- Implicit conversions
- Avoiding unnecessary sort operations
- Avoiding UDF pitfalls
- Avoiding unnecessary overhead with stored procedures
- Pitfalls of complex views
- Pitfalls of correlated sub-queries
- Properly storing intermediate results

Implicit conversions

We introduced the concept of implicit conversions in `Chapter 4`, *Exploring Query Execution Plans*, particularly in the context of the **PlanAffectingConvert** warnings. An implicit conversion happens when SQL Server needs to compare two values that are not of the same data type. At this point, we should understand how to recognize an implicit conversion in our query plans, but what may not always be obvious is how they got there in the first place and how to correct them.

The most obvious cause of implicit conversions is to compare two columns that are not of the same data type. We can easily avoid this by making sure that columns that are related in our database, and thus may be joined, are of the same data type. A common mistake that can cause this situation is where we have some tables that have been created with **NVARCHAR** strings and some tables that have the **VARCHAR** strings. This may happen because a database was upgraded at some point to support Unicode UTF-16 strings so new tables have the **NVARCHAR** strings, but old tables still have **VARCHAR** strings, or perhaps some of the old tables were missed when data types were changed. The best solution in this case is to convert the **VARCHAR** columns to **NVARCHAR** so that the data types match.

Another cause of implicit conversions, which is not so obvious, but is perhaps the most common, is mismatched parameter data types. This is particularly common when using an **object-relational mapping** (**ORM**) such as **Entity Framework** (**EF**). EF sends queries to SQL Server as parameterized statements. By default, any strings that are sent as parameters are of the **NVARCHAR** type. This is fine, as long as the strings in the database are stored as **NVARCHAR**, but if they are stored as **VARCHAR**, this will lead to implicit conversions of the type that will make any comparisons using these parameters non-SARGable.

Let's look at an example from the **AdventureWorks** database that illustrates this situation. We will build a parameterized query using **sp_executesql** to simulate how an EF query would appear to SQL Server. All the strings in the **AdventureWorks** database are stored as **NVARCHAR**, so we'll need to do some setup to create our scenario here.

Using the following queries, let's set up a table called **Product_Narrow**, which will contain a subset of the data in the **Product** table, but with the **VARCHAR** strings instead of **NVARCHAR**:

```
CREATE TABLE [Production].[Product_Narrow](
      [ProductID] [int] NOT NULL,
      [Name] [varchar](50) NOT NULL,
      [ProductNumber] [varchar](25) NOT NULL,
      [Color] [varchar](15) NULL,
      [StandardCost] [money] NOT NULL,
```

```
        [ListPrice] [money] NOT NULL,
        [Size] [varchar](5) NULL,
        [SizeUnitMeasureCode] [char](3) NULL,
        [WeightUnitMeasureCode] [char](3) NULL,
        [Weight] [decimal](8, 2) NULL,
        [Class] [char](2) NULL,
        [Style] [char](2) NULL,
        [ProductSubcategoryID] [int] NULL,
        [ProductModelID] [int] NULL,
        CONSTRAINT [PK_Product_Narrow_ProductID] PRIMARY KEY CLUSTERED
([ProductID]));

INSERT Production.Product_Narrow
        (ProductID, Name, ProductNumber, Color, StandardCost, ListPrice,
Size, SizeUnitMeasureCode,
         WeightUnitMeasureCode, Weight, Class, Style, ProductSubcategoryID,
ProductModelID)
SELECT ProductID, Name, ProductNumber, Color, StandardCost, ListPrice,
Size, SizeUnitMeasureCode,
        WeightUnitMeasureCode, Weight, Class, Style, ProductSubcategoryID,
ProductModelID
FROM Production.Product;

CREATE UNIQUE NONCLUSTERED INDEX [AK_Product_Narrow_Name] ON
[Production].[Product_Narrow]
([Name]);
```

First, let's start with an implicit conversion example that would not trigger a **PlanAffectingConvert** warning. We'll use the original **Product** table for this query:

```
EXEC sp_executesql N'SELECT ProductID, Name, ListPrice, StandardCost
                     FROM Production.Product
                     WHERE Name = @ProductName',
                   N'@ProductName VARCHAR(50)', 'Long-Sleeve Logo Jersey,
XL';
```

The **Name** column in the **Product** table is stored as a user-defined type called **Name**, which maps to **NVARCHAR(50)**. Using **sp_executesql**, we sent **VARCHAR(50)** instead. Here's the plan:

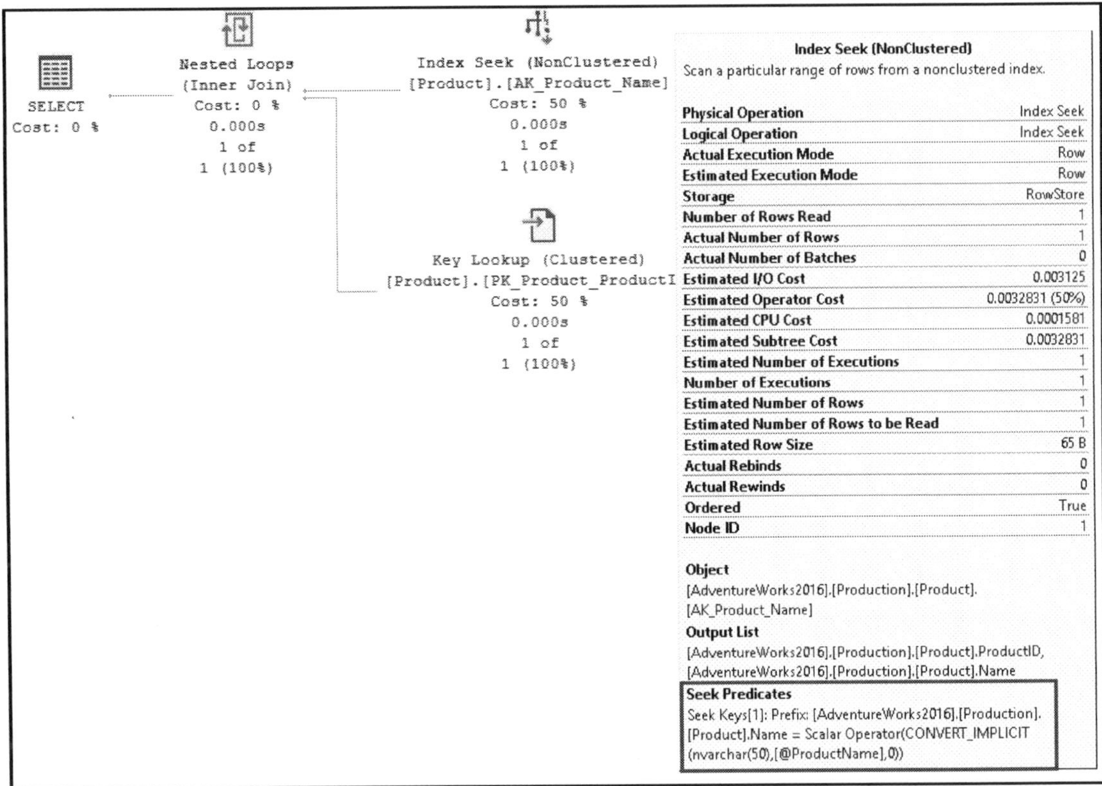

Notice that there is an implicit conversion here, but it didn't produce a warning. This is because SQL Server converted the parameter, rather than the column. This conversion happened only one time against the literal side of the comparison, so it doesn't affect the plan at all.

We can verify this by sending the correct parameter data type:

```
EXEC sp_executesql N'SELECT ProductID, Name, ListPrice, StandardCost
                    FROM Production.Product
                    WHERE Name = @ProductName',
                    N'@ProductName nvarchar(50)', N'Long-Sleeve Logo
Jersey, XL';
```

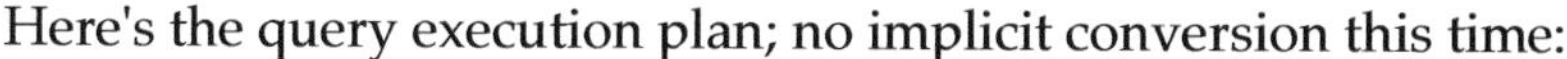

Here's the query execution plan; no implicit conversion this time:

SELECT
Cost: 0 %

Nested Loops
(Inner Join)
Cost: 0 %
0.000s
1 of
1 (100%)

Index Seek (NonClustered)
[Product].[AK_Product_Name]
Cost: 50 %
0.000s
1 of
1 (100%)

Key Lookup (Clustered)
[Product].[PK_Product_ProductI
Cost: 50 %
0.000s
1 of
1 (100%)

Index Seek (NonClustered)

Scan a particular range of rows from a nonclustered index.

Physical Operation	Index Seek
Logical Operation	Index Seek
Actual Execution Mode	Row
Estimated Execution Mode	Row
Storage	RowStore
Number of Rows Read	1
Actual Number of Rows	1
Actual Number of Batches	0
Estimated I/O Cost	0.003125
Estimated Operator Cost	0.0032831 (50%)
Estimated CPU Cost	0.0001581
Estimated Subtree Cost	0.0032831
Estimated Number of Executions	1
Number of Executions	1
Estimated Number of Rows	1
Estimated Number of Rows to be Read	1
Estimated Row Size	65 B
Actual Rebinds	0
Actual Rewinds	0
Ordered	True
Node ID	1

Object
[AdventureWorks2016].[Production].[Product].
[AK_Product_Name]
Output List
[AdventureWorks2016].[Production].[Product].ProductID,
[AdventureWorks2016].[Production].[Product].Name
Seek Predicates
Seek Keys[1]: Prefix [AdventureWorks2016].[Production].
[Product].Name = Scalar Operator([@ProductName])

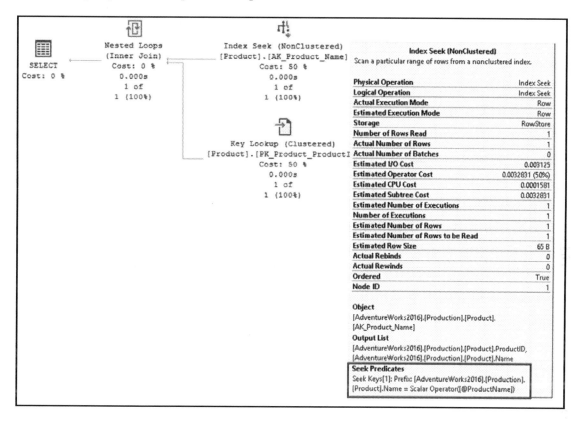

Now let's use our new **Product_Narrow** table to illustrate an implicit conversion that will cause a warning. We'll use the same query, but this time remember that the **Name** column is stored as **VARCHAR(50)** rather than **NVARCHAR(50)**:

```
EXEC sp_executesql N'SELECT ProductID, Name, ListPrice, StandardCost
                      FROM Production.Product_Narrow
                      WHERE Name = @ProductName',
                      N'@ProductName nvarchar(50)', N'Long-Sleeve Logo
Jersey, XL';
```

Here is the query execution plan, including a warning this time:

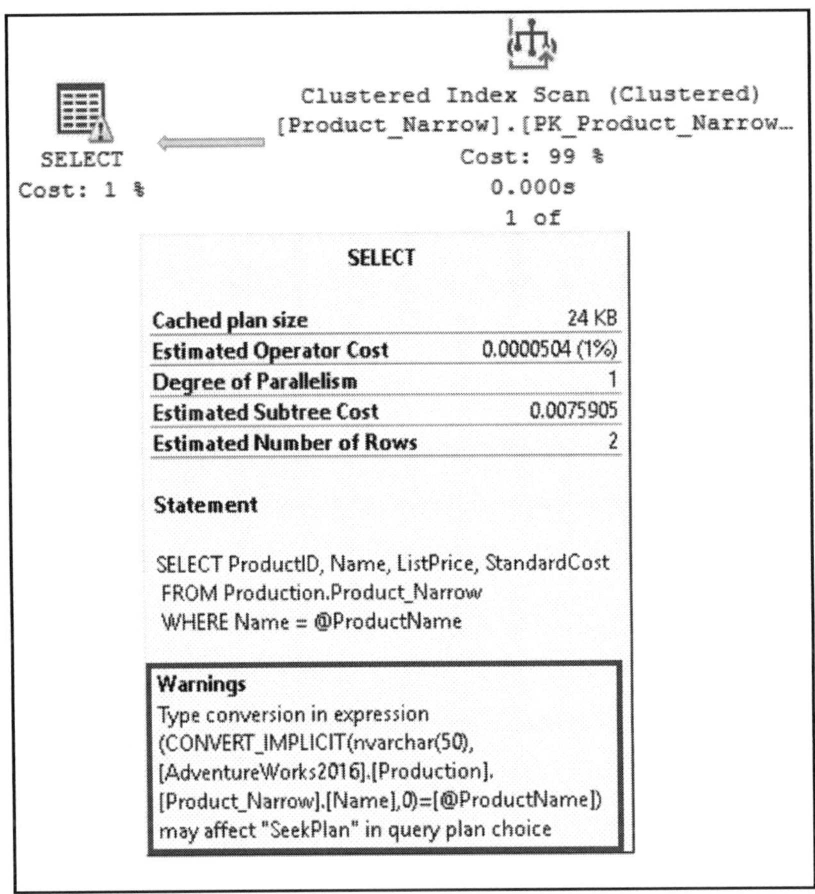

If we look at the properties of the scan, we'll see there's an implicit conversion, but this time SQL Server converted the column side of the comparison rather than the literal side as it did in the previous query against the **Product** table, making the predicate non-SARGable:

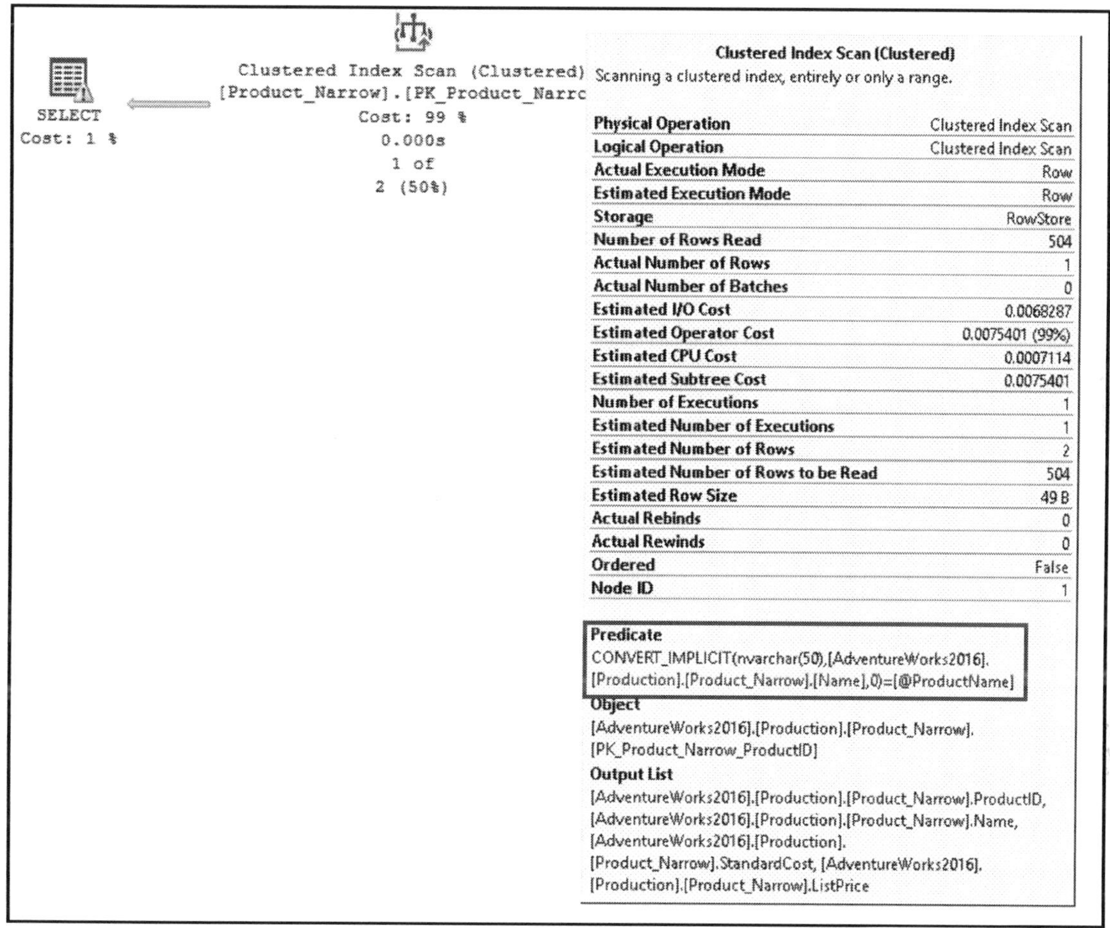

We might be wondering why SQL Server would choose to do this conversion when it is obviously more expensive than converting the literal side of the comparison. The reason is that SQL Server must follow the rules of data type precedence when performing an implicit conversion. SQL Server will convert all the data types involved in the comparison to the data type that has the highest precedence if the conversion is possible at all. For example, a **DATETIME2** type only implicitly converts to strings and other date and time-related types.

Here's the list of SQL Server data types in order of their precedence:

1. **user-defined data types (highest)**	16. **int**
2. **sql_variant**	17. **smallint**
3. **xml**	18. **tinyint**
4. **datetimeoffset**	19. **bit**
5. **datetime2**	20. **ntext**
6. **datetime**	21. **text**
7. **smalldatetime**	22. **image**
8. **date**	23. **timestamp**
9. **time**	24. **uniqueidentifier**
10. **float**	25. **nvarchar (including nvarchar(max))**
11. **real**	26. **nchar**
12. **decimal**	27. **varchar (including varchar(max))**
13. **money**	28. **char**
14. **smallmoney**	29. **varbinary (including varbinary(max))**
15. **bigint**	30. **binary (lowest)**

Notice that **NVARCHAR** has a higher precedence than **VARCHAR**. This means that no matter which side of the comparison the **VARCHAR** value is on, it will always be converted to **NVARCHAR**, even if it makes the predicate non-SARGable. The solution here is simple: send the correct parameter data type and the conversion will be unnecessary. See the following example with the correct parameter data type:

```
EXEC sp_executesql N'SELECT ProductID, Name, ListPrice, StandardCost
                      FROM Production
.Product_Narrow
                      WHERE Name = @ProductName',
                      N'@ProductName varchar(50)', 'Long-Sleeve Logo
Jersey, XL';
```

When sending the correct data type of **VARCHAR(50)** for the parameter, no implicit conversion is needed and SQL Server is able to choose a better plan:

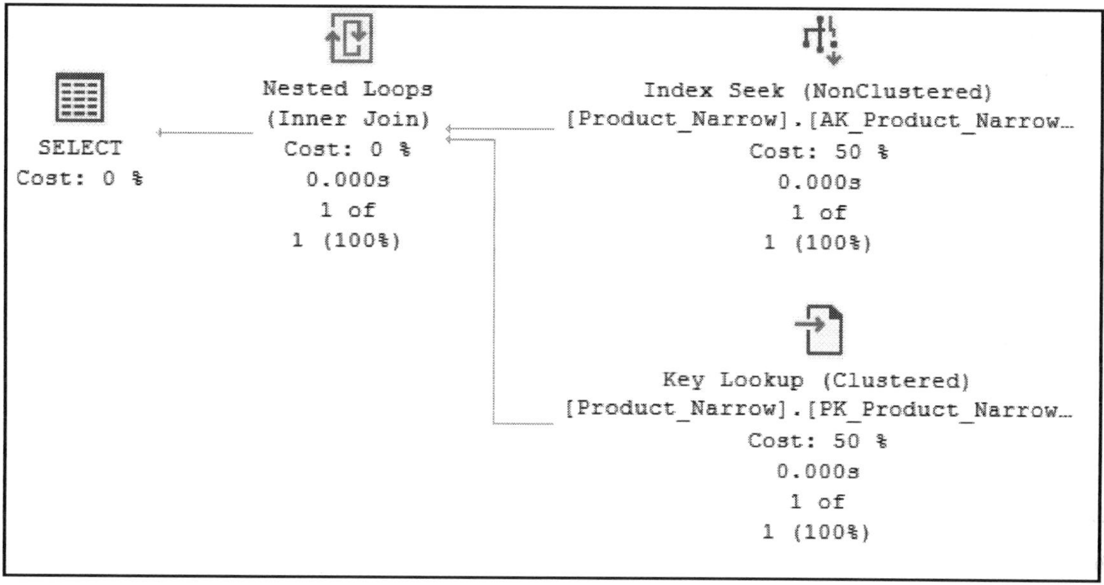

This problem is easy to see when the code is all in the database in the form of Stored Procedures, but when the database code is generated on the client, it may be more difficult to identify. If we see a conversion warning in a query execution plan, be sure to check the **ParameterList** property and verify that the data types of all the parameters are correct. See `Chapter 4`, *Exploring Query Execution Plans*, for more information on the **ParameterList** property.

EF is one example of a database-code generator that is vulnerable to this problem, but it is not the only one. With the increasing popularity of code-first database design, this problem is also becoming more and more common. It's important to take the time to ensure that the data types chosen for the database match the needs of the application, and even more important to ensure that when possible, the database code is strictly typed based on the actual data types rather than the defaults.

Avoiding unnecessary sort operations

Sort operations in a query plan are very expensive, and hence we need to avoid anything that might introduce a sort where it is not needed. Using **ORDER BY** in our query practically guarantees a sort unless we happen to be able to leverage an index and an ordered scan.

If our query needs to produce an ordered result set and uses a covering index, ensure the index sort order is the same as the query's desired order. This will increase the likelihood that SQL Server can leverage the index to order the rows rather than having to do a sort.

This may be necessary if we need our result set to be returned in a specific order, but if the order is not important, this is just overhead.

In this section, we will look at a few examples that may introduce an unnecessary sort operation.

UNION ALL versus UNION

The **UNION** and **UNION ALL** operators are used to combine the results of two separate queries into a single result set. If it is possible for rows to be duplicated between the two queries and we do not want to return duplicate rows, using the **UNION** operator will cause SQL Server to filter out any duplicate rows in the two sets. Doing this requires a Sort operation, however, so it is important to only use **UNION** when necessary. If duplicate values are allowed in the final result set, or if the source results sets cannot have duplicates to begin with, for example, both input have unique constraints or primary keys and the sets don't overlap, using a **UNION ALL** is more efficient. This avoids introducing implicit sort operations that increase the query cost.

Let's look at an example from the **AdventureWorks** database. The store is going to have a friends and family sale and we'd like to invite all our customers and vendors to get a special discount on this day. We need to build an email list to send out the promotion, but the information about customers is stored separately from vendors. The easiest way to do this is to create two separate queries and join them with a **UNION** operator.

Here's what the query might look like:

```
SELECT 'Customer' AS ContactType, p.FirstName, p.LastName, e.EmailAddress
FROM Sales.Customer c
INNER JOIN Person.Person p ON c.PersonID = p.BusinessEntityID
INNER JOIN Person.EmailAddress e ON e.BusinessEntityID = p.BusinessEntityID
WHERE EmailPromotion > 0
UNION
SELECT 'Vendor' AS ContactType, v.FirstName, v.LastName, v.EmailAddress
FROM Purchasing.vVendorWithContacts v
WHERE EmailPromotion > 0;
```

If we use a **UNION** operator, as with the preceding query, this is what the plan looks like:

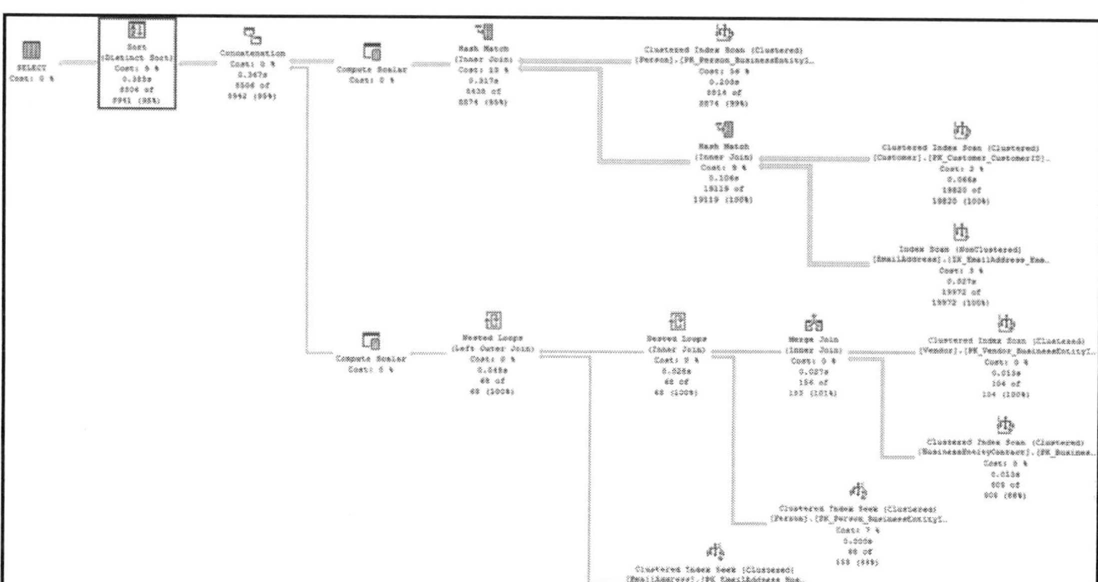

Here is the **QueryTimeStats** property for this query:

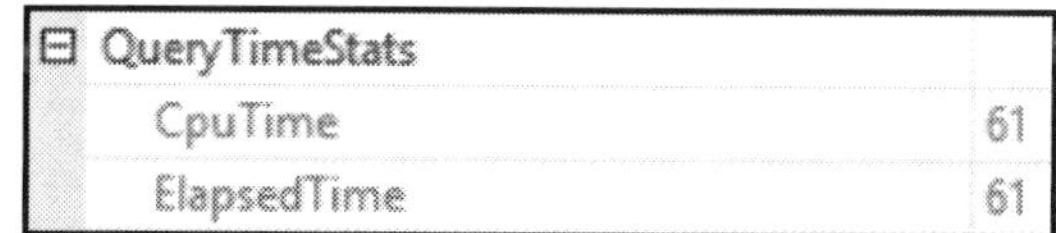

QueryTimeStats	
CpuTime	61
ElapsedTime	61

There is obviously some opportunity for tuning here as we have several scans and hash matches that may be eliminated with the addition of an index or two; but notice there is also a sort operation that is taking up 9 percent of the estimated cost. This is something that can be eliminated by simply changing the **UNION** operator to **UNION ALL**. Unlike **UNION**, **UNION ALL** assumes that there is no overlap between the result sets that are being combined – if there are overlaps, then the duplicates will not be eliminated as they would by using UNION. We know that there is no overlap between our vendors and customers, and even there were, we are fine with sending duplicate emails, especially because vendors may receive a different email than customers.

Here's the plan for the same query with **UNION ALL** instead of **UNION**:

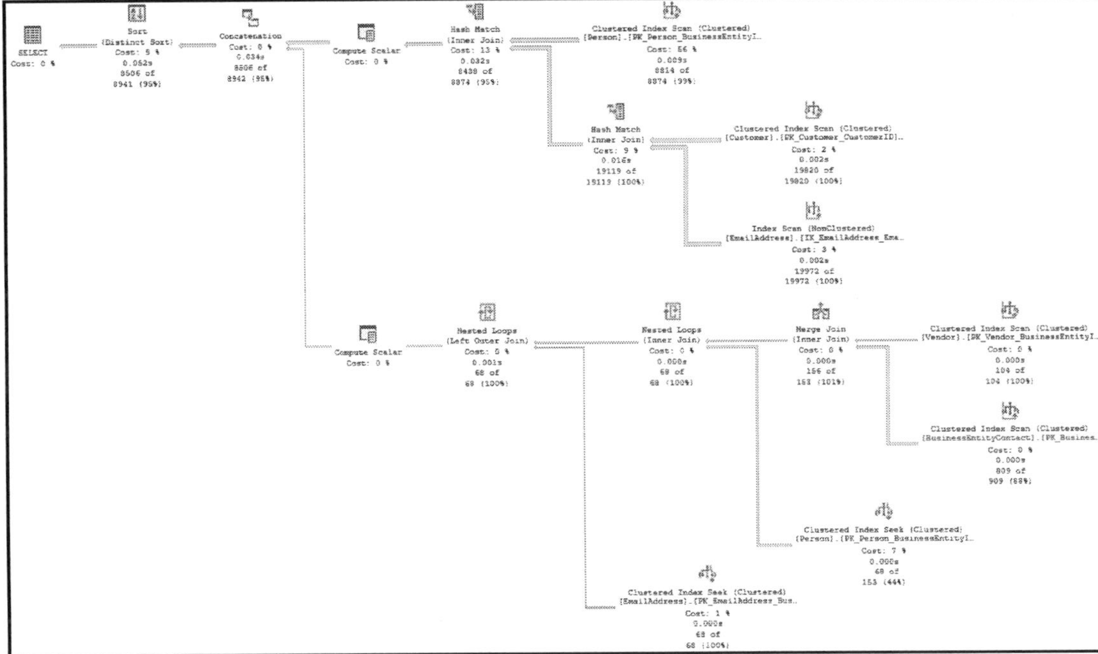

Notice the sort operator is gone now, and the results are the same, but the **QueryTimeStats** property has improved:

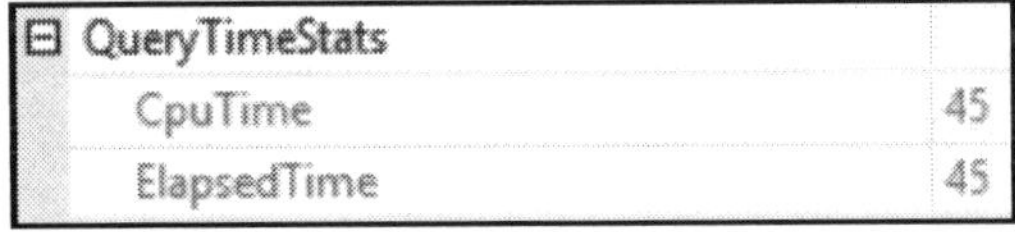

Both CPU and elapsed time were reduced from 61 ms to 45 ms (~26 percent improvement). When we need to join two or more result sets together, leveraging **UNION ALL** rather than **UNION** wherever possible will make our queries more efficient with very little effort on our part.

SELECT DISTINCT

Like the **UNION** operator, using **DISTINCT** in our **SELECT** query directs SQL Server to filter out any duplicate rows that may be in the results, which it typically does by introducing a sort operation. If we already have an **ORDER BY** clause in the query, the sort may be necessary anyway so this would not be additional overhead, but if order is not important, and neither are duplicates, the **DISTINCT** clause is unnecessary and the query would likely be cheaper without it.

Rather than blindly applying a **DISTINCT** operator to our query, it's worth taking some time to investigate why there are duplicate rows in the results. It may be expected and intentional, but if we are getting duplicates in our results when they are not expected often indicates an error condition. It could be due to an incorrectly formed **JOIN** condition, bad data in the table (for example, incorrect ETL that causes duplicate or missing values, or the lack of a unique or primary key to allow duplicate rows), or selecting columns from a table that together are not unique. The outcome is that using **DISTINCT** can hide these conditions but doesn't solve them. Even if the duplicates are expected, there may be a cheaper way to get the desired results rather than applying **DISTINCT**.

Going back to the **AdventureWorks** database, let's assume that we want to get a list of all the categories and subcategories for products that haven't been discontinued.

The most basic way to do that would be the following query:

```
SELECT c.Name AS Category,
s.Name AS SubCategory
FROM Production.Product p
INNER JOIN Production.ProductSubcategory s ON p.ProductSubcategoryID =
s.ProductSubcategoryID
INNER JOIN Production.ProductCategory c ON s.ProductCategoryID =
c.ProductCategoryID
WHERE p.DiscontinuedDate IS NULL;
```

Unfortunately, this query by itself will return a lot of duplicate rows because there are many products that have the same category and subcategory. The simplest way to fix this problem is to add **DISTINCT** to the query:

```
SELECT DISTINCT c.Name AS Category, s.Name AS SubCategory
FROM Production.Product p
INNER JOIN Production.ProductSubcategory s
ON p.ProductSubcategoryID = s.ProductSubcategoryID
INNER JOIN Production.ProductCategory c ON s.ProductCategoryID =
c.ProductCategoryID
WHERE p.DiscontinuedDate IS NULL;
```

This solves the problem, but it also requires SQL Server to sort all the rows and keep only the unique category and subcategory combinations. Another way to do this would be use an **IN** or **EXISTS** predicate in the **WHERE** clause. Here's an example of what that query might look like:

```
SELECT c.Name AS Category, s.Name AS SubCategory
FROM Production.ProductSubcategory s
INNER JOIN Production.ProductCategory c ON s.ProductCategoryID =
c.ProductCategoryID
WHERE s.ProductSubcategoryID IN (SELECT ProductSubcategoryID
                                  FROM Production.Product
                                 WHERE DiscontinuedDate IS NULL);
```

This may look more complicated and, on the surface, may seem more expensive, but if we examine the plans, we can see that it's cheaper:

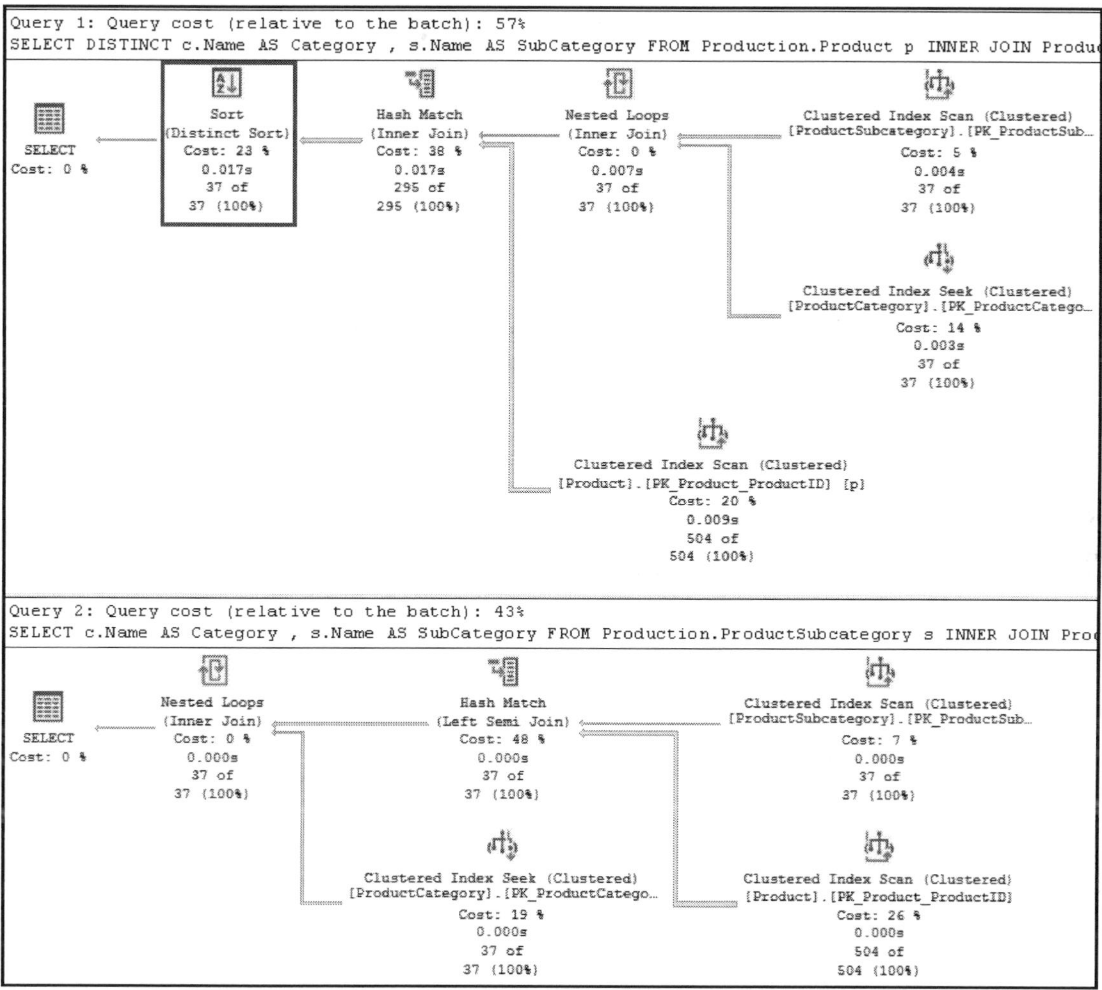

Query 1 with **DISTINCT** in the **SELECT** clause contains a sort operator that accounts for 23% of the estimated cost. **Query 2**, which uses the **IN** clause, does not require a sort operation. This query returns the same results but does so with less effort. While it may be more effort for us to take the time to investigate the query plan and determine whether there's an alternative to adding **DISTINCT**, we only need to spend that effort once, whereas SQL Server will have to spend it every time it executes the query.

SELECT TOP 1 with ORDER BY

A very common way to return the maximum or minimum row in a set is to perform a `SELECT TOP 1` with an **ORDER BY** clause. The problem with this pattern is that it may result in an unnecessary sort operation. SQL Server will need to sort all the rows to order them by the desired column, but then return only the first (or last) row in the set. In some cases, it is more efficient to find the minimum or maximum value first, then select the row that is equal to this value.

Let's look at an example from the **AdventureWorks** database.

The following query returns the row with the highest sub-total from the **Sales.SalesOrderHeader** table:

```
SELECT TOP 1 soh.CustomerID, SalesPersonID, SubTotal, OrderDate,
cust.LastName as CustomerLastName, cust.FirstName as CustomerFirstName
FROM Sales.SalesOrderHeader soh
INNER JOIN sales.Customer c ON c.CustomerID = soh.CustomerID
LEFT JOIN Person.Person cust ON cust.BusinessEntityID = c.CustomerID
ORDER BY SubTotal DESC;
```

Alternatively, for this sample database we could write the query the following way, when we know the sub-query can only return one row:

```
SELECT soh.CustomerID, SalesPersonID, SubTotal, OrderDate,
cust.LastName as CustomerLastName, cust.FirstName as CustomerFirstName
FROM Sales.SalesOrderHeader soh
INNER JOIN sales.Customer c ON c.CustomerID = soh.CustomerID
LEFT JOIN Person.Person cust ON cust.BusinessEntityID = c.CustomerID
WHERE SubTotal = (SELECT MAX(SubTotal) FROM Sales.SalesOrderHeader);
```

Examining the two query plans, we can see that **Query 1** (the `TOP 1` plan) is significantly more expensive than **Query 2**, and it includes a costly **SORT** operator:

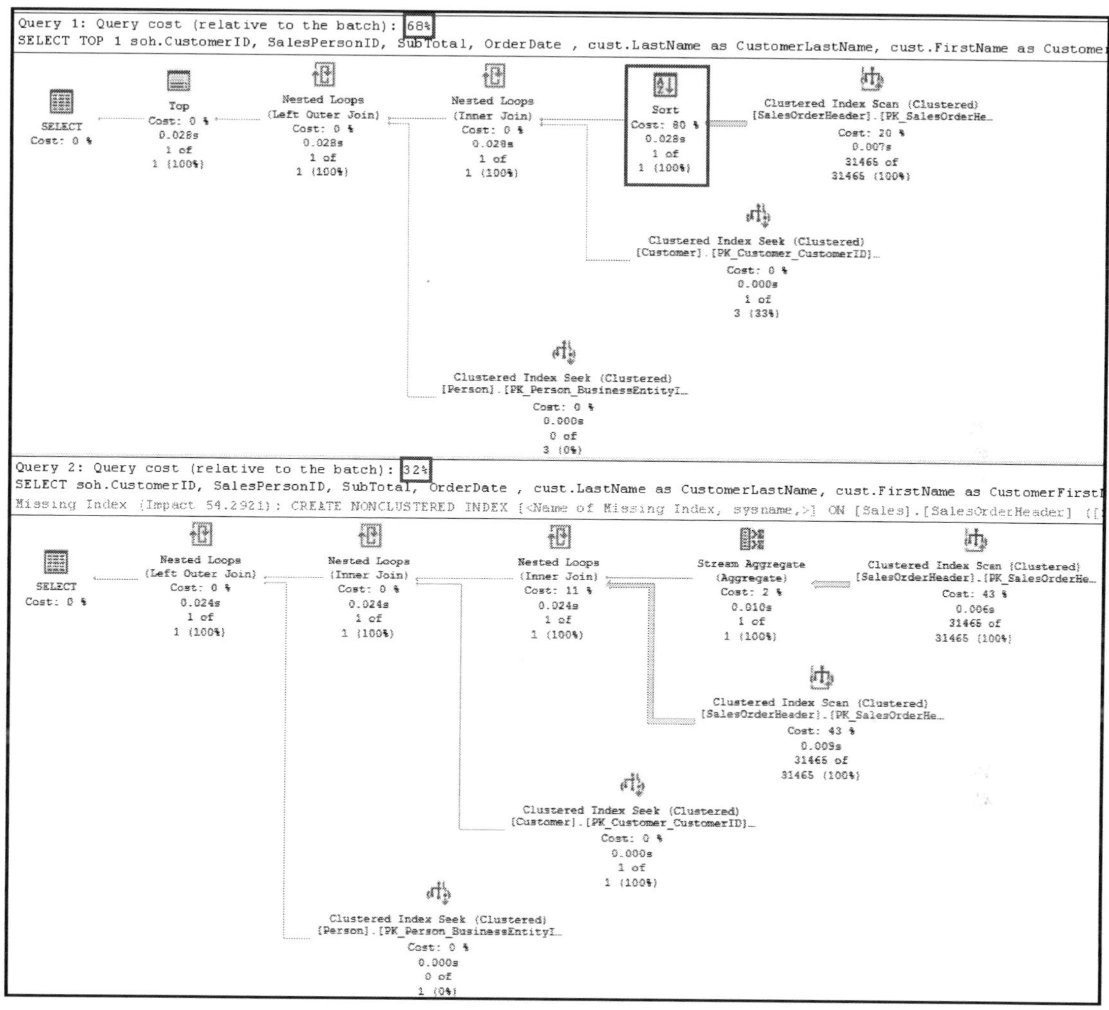

Notice there is a missing index suggestion for **Query 2** in the preceding plan. If we add this index, it can be leveraged by both plans and it will eliminate the sort in **Query 1**, but **Query 2** will still be significantly cheaper because it can perform the **TOP** operation earlier in the plan. The following query plan does not include the expensive **SORT** operator:

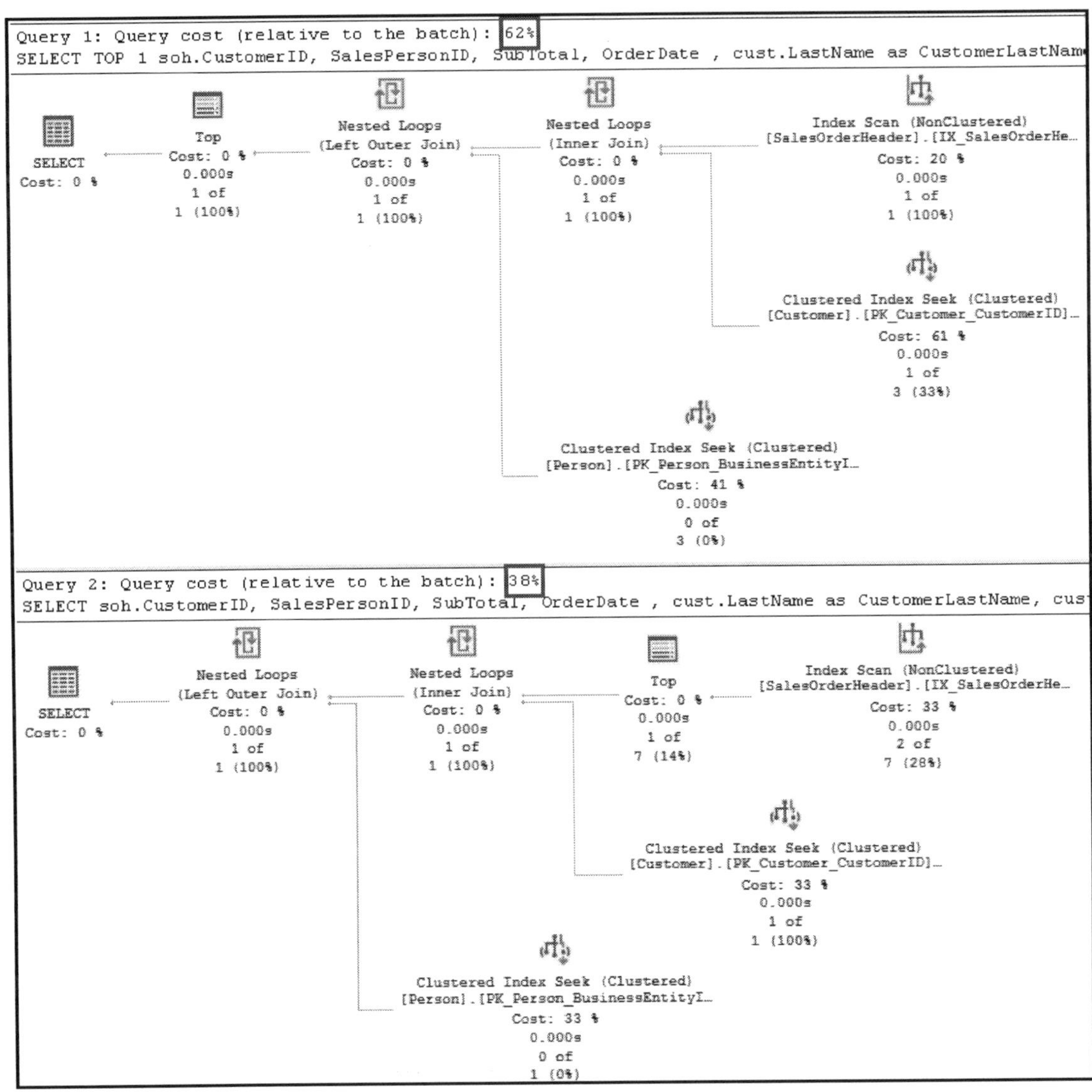

Keep in mind that not all queries will benefit from removing the `TOP 1`, but it's worth looking into, especially if the query in question is already very expensive and/or runs frequently.

Avoiding UDF pitfalls

Scalar **User-defined Functions (UDFs)** are a very useful T-SQL programming artifact because they allow a specific routine to be reused very easily. However, these seemingly harmless constructs can be detrimental to performance, because the Query Optimizer does not account for any T-SQL logic inside a UDF, and UDFs are executed for every row in the result set, just like a cursor. When using scalar UDFs, there are specific recommendations that apply to UDFs that access system or user data, and recommendations that apply to all UDFs.

An example of a scalar UDF that does not access data was referenced in `Chapter 4`, *Exploring Query Execution Plans*, under the *Query plan properties of interest* section, as shown in the following query:

```
CREATE FUNCTION ufn_CategorizePrice (@Price money)
RETURNS NVARCHAR(50)
AS
BEGIN
       DECLARE @PriceCategory NVARCHAR(50)
       IF @Price < 100 SELECT @PriceCategory = 'Cheap'
       IF @Price BETWEEN 101 and 500 SELECT @PriceCategory = 'Mid Price'
       IF @Price BETWEEN 501 and 1000 SELECT @PriceCategory = 'Expensive'
       IF @Price > 1001 SELECT @PriceCategory = 'Unaffordable'
       RETURN @PriceCategory
END;
```

An example of a query that uses that UDF in the **AdventureWorks** sample database looks like the following query:

```
SELECT dbo.ufn_CategorizePrice(UnitPrice),       SalesOrderID,
SalesOrderDetailID, CarrierTrackingNumber,
       OrderQty, ProductID, SpecialOfferID, UnitPrice, UnitPriceDiscount,
       LineTotal, rowguid, ModifiedDate
FROM Sales.SalesOrderDetail;
```

Notice the resulting query execution plan:

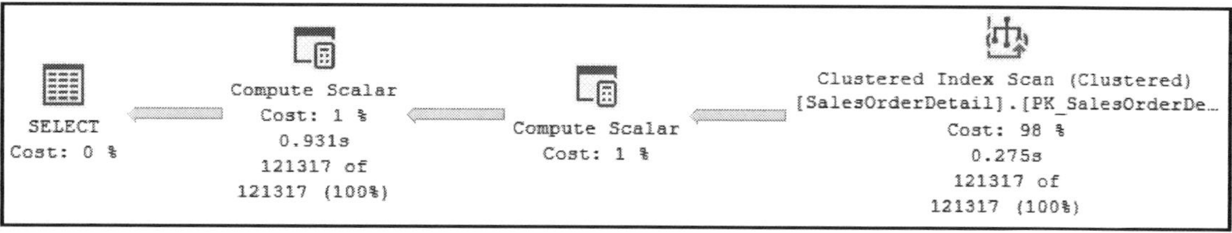

Evaluating the performance impact of running a UDF in our T-SQL code was not an easy task until very recently. We see that the UDF execution is identified only by the presence of the **compute scalar** operator, and its logic is obfuscated from the query plan. We also observe that it took almost four times as much time to execute the UDF (859 ms) than to read the data from the table (223 ms).

Also note that the preceding plan is not being executed in parallel. This is because, by design, UDFs inhibit the use of parallelism, which may also add to performance problems with certain queries that would be otherwise eligible for parallelism.

We know this scalar UDF doesn't access data by looking at its definition, but SQL Server doesn't expand the UDF definition at compile time, so the assumption is that the UDF does access data. This adds overhead to UDF execution.

The following query example allows us to see the UDF properties:

```
-- Object accesses system data, system catalogs or virtual system tables,
in the local instance of SQL Server?
SELECT OBJECTPROPERTYEX(OBJECT_id('dbo.ufn_CategorizePrice'),
'SystemDataAccess') AS AccessesSystemData
-- Object accesses user data, user tables, in the local instance of SQL
Server?
SELECT OBJECTPROPERTYEX(OBJECT_id('dbo.ufn_CategorizePrice'),
'UserDataAccess') AS AccessesUserData
-- The precision and determinism properties of the object can be verified
by SQL Server?
SELECT OBJECTPROPERTYEX(OBJECT_id('dbo.ufn_CategorizePrice'),
'IsSystemVerified') AS HasBeenSystemVerified;
```

Executing the above query yields the following resultset:

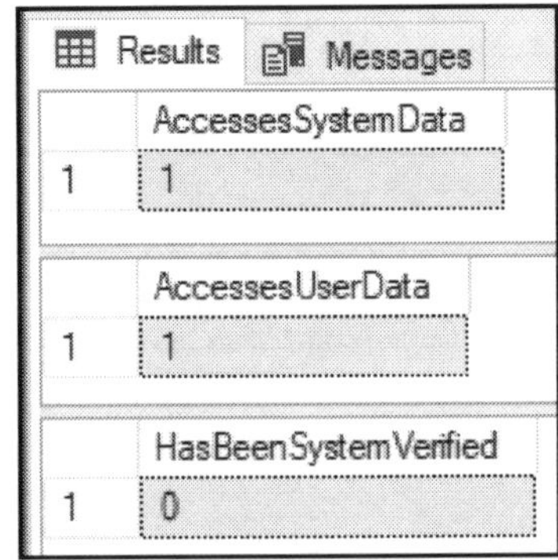

We see SQL Server takes a pessimistic approach and assumes the scalar UDF we created might access both system and user data, and it has not been system-verified.

Especially for UDFs that do not access data (such as the case in this example), always specify the **SCHEMABINDING** option during the UDF creation, as seen in the following example:

```
CREATE OR ALTER FUNCTION ufn_CategorizePrice (@Price money)
RETURNS NVARCHAR(50)
WITH SCHEMABINDING
AS
BEGIN
       DECLARE @PriceCategory NVARCHAR(50)
       IF @Price < 100 SELECT @PriceCategory = 'Cheap'
       IF @Price BETWEEN 101 and 500 SELECT @PriceCategory = 'Mid Price'
       IF @Price BETWEEN 501 and 1000 SELECT @PriceCategory = 'Expensive'
       IF @Price > 1001 SELECT @PriceCategory = 'Unaffordable'
       RETURN @PriceCategory
END;
```

This will make the UDF schema-bound and mark the UDF as a deterministic object in the system, allowing SQL Server to verify the UDF and properly derive its data-access properties.

For UDFs that are schema-bound, any attempt to change the underlying schema that depends on the UDF will result in an error. But this option ensures that the UDF will not inadvertently break due to schema changes.

We can use the preceding query example to see the new UDF properties, which now yields the following resultset:

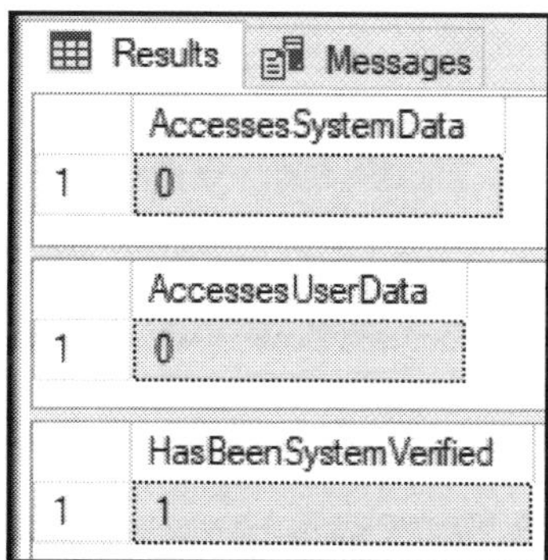

In the previous screenshot we can see that the new schema-bound UDF has been system-verified and does not access neither system nor user data. When schema-binding scalar UDFs, SQL Server can determine in advance whether the UDF accesses system catalogs or virtual system tables, and whether the UDF accesses user tables. In turn, this ensures that the Query Optimizer does not generate any unnecessary operations for query plans involving UDFs that don't access data and avoids having to derive the underlying schema properties for each execution of the UDF.

This schema-bound UDF was verified to not access user tables, and notice the resulting query execution plan:

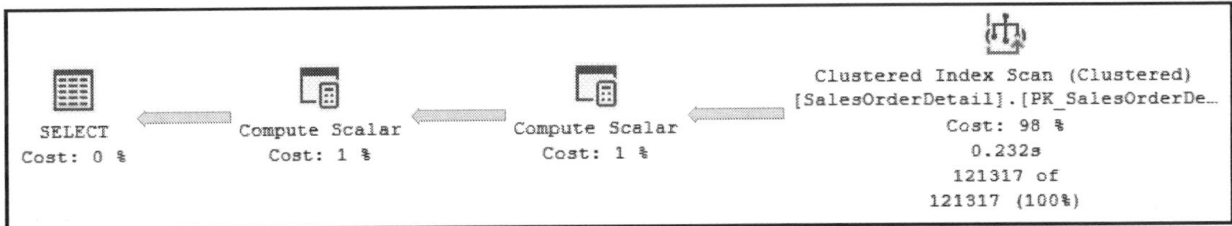

In `Chapter 4`, *Exploring Query Execution Plans*, under the *Query plan properties of interest* section, we referenced an improvement introduced in recent versions of SQL Server, where showplan started to include UDF runtime stats under the **QueryTimeStats** property.

Looking at those UDF runtime stats, we see the UDF still has a significant cost (500 ms elapsed time), although less than the non-schema-bound UDF.

Note that the aforementioned object properties can be determined using the following sample query:

```
SELECT OBJECTPROPERTY(object_id, 'IsDeterministic'),
       OBJECTPROPERTY(object_id, 'IsSystemVerified'),
       OBJECTPROPERTY(object_id, 'SystemDataAccess'),
       OBJECTPROPERTY(object_id, 'UserDataAccess'),
       OBJECTPROPERTY(object_id, 'IsSystemVerified')
FROM sys.objects WHERE name = 'ufn_CategorizePrice';
```

When a scalar UDF accesses data, the potential performance implications under SQL Server 2017 or an earlier version are considerable. The following example can be executed in the scope of the **AdventureWorks** sample database:

```
CREATE OR ALTER FUNCTION dbo.ufn_GetTotalQuantity (@SalesOrderID INT)
RETURNS INT
WITH SCHEMABINDING
AS
BEGIN
```

```
    DECLARE @Qty INT
    SELECT @Qty = SUM(OrderQty)
    FROM Sales.SalesOrderDetail
    WHERE SalesOrderID = @SalesOrderID
    RETURN (@Qty)
END;
GO

SELECT TOP 5000 *,
       dbo.ufn_GetTotalQuantity (SalesOrderID) AS TotalQty
FROM Sales.SalesOrderHeader;
```

The query generates the following execution plan:

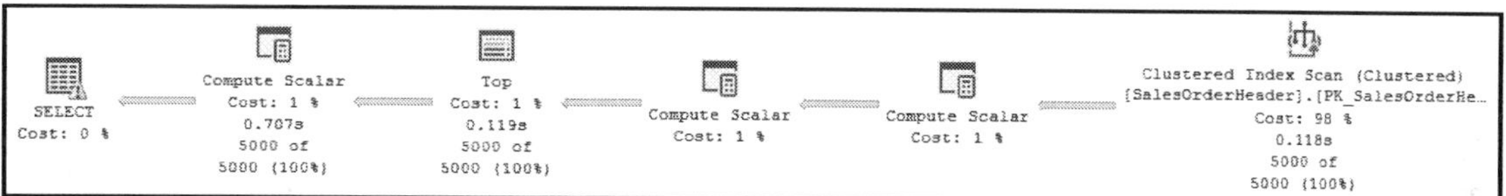

We can make similar observations regarding the obfuscation of the T-SQL logic inside the UDF. Here is the **QueryTimeStats** property for this query execution plan:

QueryTimeStats	
CpuTime	365
ElapsedTime	912
UdfCpuTime	323
UdfElapsedTime	582

The recommended action to attempt to improve the plan is to surface the expressions inside the UDF to the query itself, in an exercise called inlining the expression. Doing this across all queries that reference the scalar UDF may be hard work, but the effort may be warranted if the performance gains are considerable.

Starting with SQL Server 2019, however, and only under database compatibility level 150, SQL Server can automatically inline certain UDF expressions, and account for the UDF logic during query optimization to yield better query plans.

The goal of the **scalar UDF inlining** feature is to improve performance for queries that invoke scalar UDFs, where the UDF execution is a bottleneck, without any code changes.

A team of researchers at Microsoft's Gray Systems Lab developed the Froid framework for inlining UDF constructs into parent queries. The Froid paper can be accessed at `http://www.vldb.org/pvldb/vol11/p432-ramachandra.pdf`.

By simply changing the **AdventureWorks** database compatibility level from 130 to 150, notice the resulting query execution plan where all the scalar UDF logic is now visible:

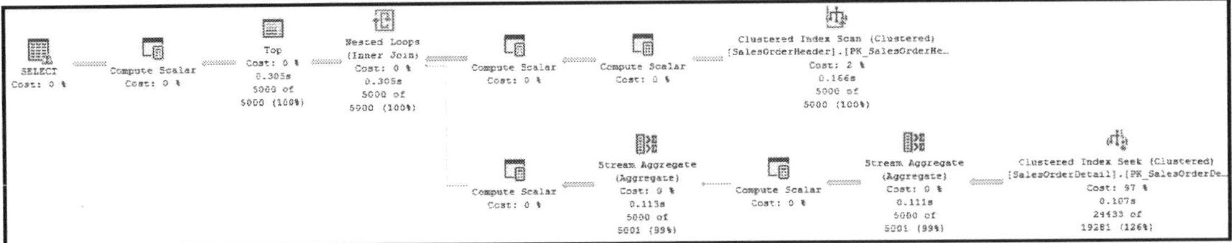

The **QueryTimeStats** property for this inlined execution plan is considerably better than before, both in CPU time and elapsed time:

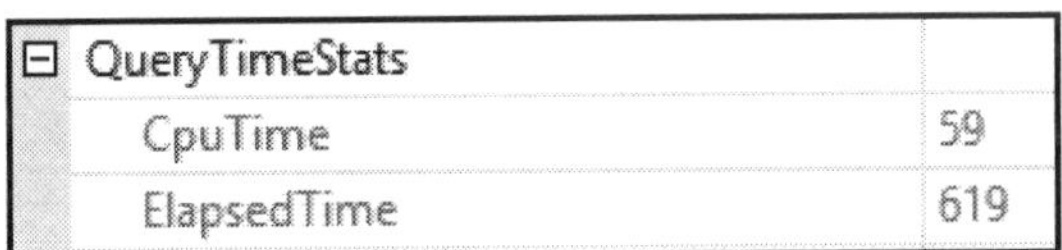

Avoiding unnecessary overhead with stored procedures

In stored procedures, use the `SET NOCOUNT ON` notation even when there's a requirement to return current row count during execution, like in the following example:

```
CREATE OR ALTER PROCEDURE [dbo].[uspStocksPerWorkOrder] @WorkOrderID [int]
AS
BEGIN
SET NOCOUNT ON;
       SELECT wo.StockedQty, wor.WorkOrderID
       FROM Production.WorkOrder AS wo
       LEFT JOIN Production.WorkOrderRouting AS wor ON wo.WorkOrderID =
wor.WorkOrderID
       WHERE wo.WorkOrderID = @WorkOrderID;
END;
```

When **SET NOCOUNT** is **ON**, the count indicating the number of rows affected by a T-SQL statement is not returned to the application layer, which provides a performance boost.

The **@@ROWCOUNT** function will still be incremented even with `SET NOCOUNT ON`.

To put this to a test, we can use the **ostress** utility and simulate a client application that executes the same stored procedure 1,000 times over 10 concurrent connections, as seen in the following command:

```
ostress.exe -S<my_server_name> -E -dAdventureWorks -Q"EXEC
[dbo].[uspStocksPerWorkOrder] 117" -n10 -r1000
```

ostress is a free command-line tool that is part of the **Replay Markup Language (RML) Utilities** for SQL Server. This tool can be used to simulate the effects of stressing a SQL Server instance by using ad hoc queries or pre-saved `.sql` script files.

Executing the preceding command three times yields the following elapsed time information:

```
OSTRESS exiting normally, elapsed time: 00:00:31.057
OSTRESS exiting normally, elapsed time: 00:00:31.484
OSTRESS exiting normally, elapsed time: 00:00:31.476
```

We can see a stable elapsed time between executions. Now if we recreate the stored procedure to remove `SET NOCOUNT ON` and execute the same command three times, this yields the following elapsed time information:

```
OSTRESS exiting normally, elapsed time: 00:00:33.771
OSTRESS exiting normally, elapsed time: 00:00:33.824
OSTRESS exiting normally, elapsed time: 00:00:34.097
```

Again, we get consistent results but higher elapsed time throughout the test runs. For stored procedures that do not return large datasets, such as the case here, or for stored procedures that contain T-SQL loops, setting **NOCOUNT** to **ON** can provide a significant performance boost. Network traffic is reduced because SQL Server doesn't send the **DONE_IN_PROC** token stream for each statement in the code. This may not be noticeable in singleton executions, but when a stored procedure is executed multiple times, the scale effect is usually measurable.

Also, strive to validate input parameters early in the T-SQL code. Doing this allows early determination of whether data-access operations can run, instead of encountering issues after much work has already been done, wasting resources.

Using the previous example, adding an IF condition prevents data access if the incoming parameter is null for a column that doesn't accept null values by design:

```
CREATE OR ALTER PROCEDURE [dbo].[uspStocksPerWorkOrder] @WorkOrderID [int]
AS
BEGIN
SET NOCOUNT ON;
        IF @WorkOrderID IS NOT NULL
        BEGIN
                SELECT wo.StockedQty, wor.WorkOrderID
                FROM Production.WorkOrder AS wo
                LEFT JOIN Production.WorkOrderRouting AS wor ON
wo.WorkOrderID = wor.WorkOrderID
                WHERE wo.WorkOrderID = @WorkOrderID;
        END;
END;
```

Pitfalls of complex views

Views are often used with the same intent as UDFs, to allow easy reuse of what could be otherwise a complex expression to inline in our T-SQL query. Often developers build a view that will serve multiple queries, and then just select from that view with different **SELECT** statements and different filters, be those joins or search predicates. However, what may look like a seemingly harmless T-SQL construct may be detrimental for query performance if the underlying view is complex.

Imagine that in the **AdventureWorks** sample database, a developer built an all-encompassing view that gets data on all company employees, as in the following example:

```
CREATE OR ALTER VIEW [HumanResources].[vEmployeeNew]
AS
SELECT e.[BusinessEntityID], p.[Title], p.[FirstName], p.[MiddleName],
        p.[LastName], p.[Suffix], e.[JobTitle], pp.[PhoneNumber],
        pnt.[Name] AS [PhoneNumberType], ea.[EmailAddress],
p.[EmailPromotion],
        a.[AddressLine1], a.[AddressLine2], a.[City], sp.[Name] AS
[StateProvinceName],
        a.[PostalCode], cr.[Name] AS [CountryRegionName]
FROM [HumanResources].[Employee] AS e
INNER JOIN [Person].[Person] AS p ON p.[BusinessEntityID] =
e.[BusinessEntityID]
INNER JOIN [Person].[BusinessEntityAddress] AS bea ON
bea.[BusinessEntityID] = e.[BusinessEntityID]
INNER JOIN [Person].[Address] AS a ON a.[AddressID] = bea.[AddressID]
INNER JOIN [Person].[StateProvince] AS sp ON sp.[StateProvinceID] =
```

```
a.[StateProvinceID]
INNER JOIN [Person].[CountryRegion] AS cr ON cr.[CountryRegionCode] =
sp.[CountryRegionCode]
INNER JOIN [Person].[PersonPhone] AS pp ON pp.BusinessEntityID =
p.[BusinessEntityID]
INNER JOIN [Person].[PhoneNumberType] AS pnt ON pp.[PhoneNumberTypeID] =
pnt.[PhoneNumberTypeID]
INNER JOIN [Person].[EmailAddress] AS ea ON p.[BusinessEntityID] =
ea.[BusinessEntityID];
```

This view may have been built as an encapsulation for a recurrent query, making it just an easily-referenceable artifact. But later, another developer needs to build a report with a simplified org chart, and the following query is executed, using the pre-existing view:

```
SELECT Title, FirstName, MiddleName, LastName, Suffix, JobTitle
FROM [HumanResources].[vEmployeeNew];
```

Notice the resulting query execution plan:

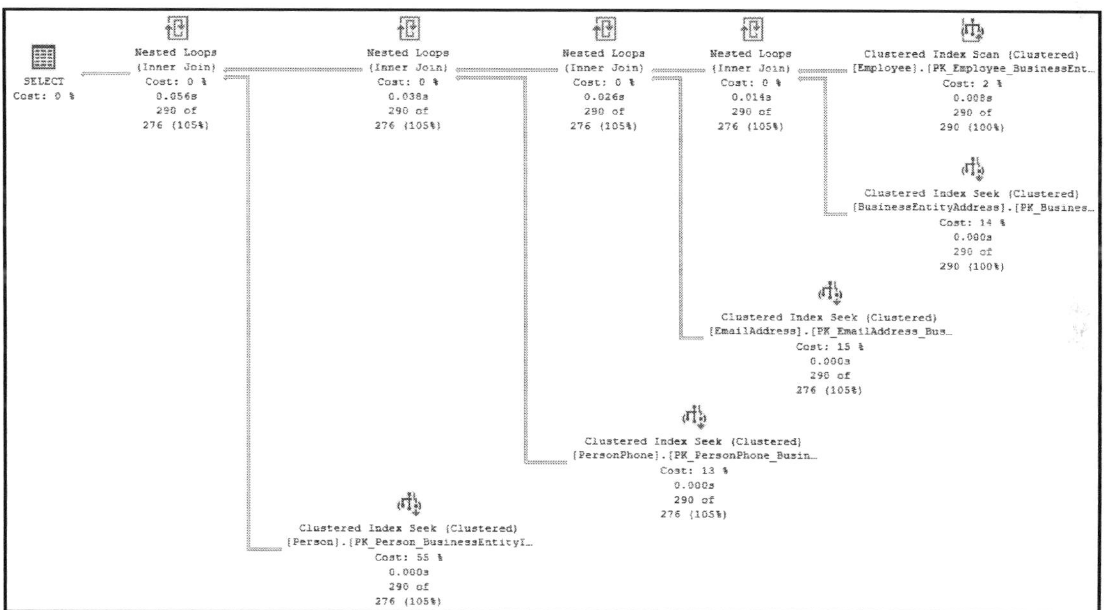

And its **QueryTimeStats** property:

⊟ QueryTimeStats	
CpuTime	6
ElapsedTime	56
Reason For Early Termination Of Statement Optimization	Time Out

Also notice the information about how the Query Optimizer got to this plan (seen in the **Reason For Early Termination Of Statement Optimization** property in showplan): a timeout means that the best available plan found before the Query Optimizer timeout hit was used. The immediate conclusion is that the query is probably too complex and the optimization space too wide to run through it all before the internal timeout is reached.

The fact is the plan accesses five tables to retrieve data from each one, even though the columns in the **SELECT** clause are present in a small subset of the tables (two in this case). Each table in the query execution plan output 290 rows, therefore incurring I/O for each table.

What if we could simplify the query? And have the report query only the required data? For that, we replaced the query referencing the view with a query that only accesses the required tables:

```
SELECT Title, FirstName, MiddleName, LastName, Suffix, JobTitle
FROM HumanResources.Employee AS e
INNER JOIN [Person].[Person] AS pp ON e.BusinessEntityID =
pp.BusinessEntityID;
```

Notice the resulting query execution plan:

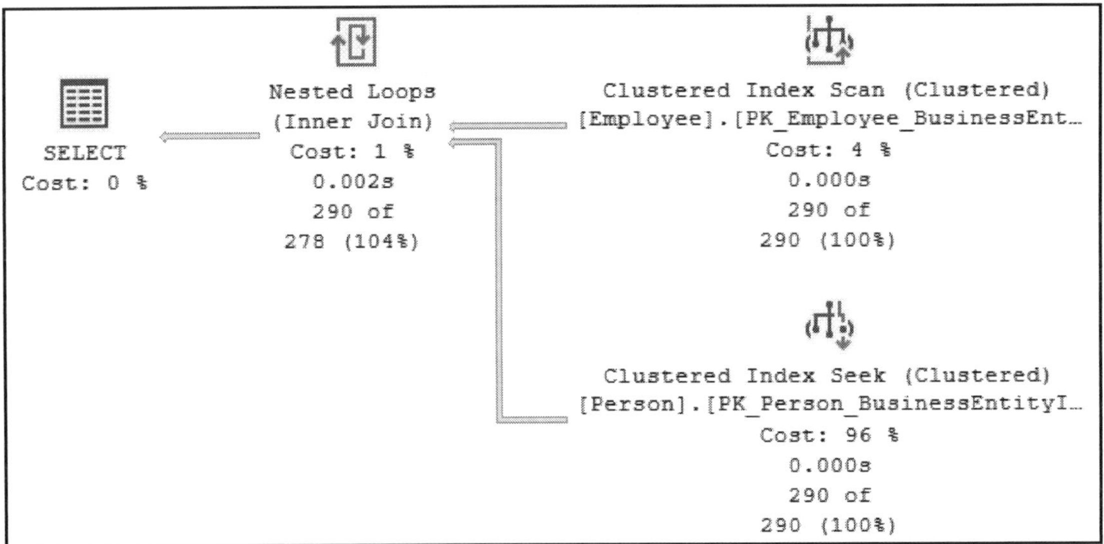

And its **QueryTimeStats** property:

⊟ QueryTimeStats	
CpuTime	2
ElapsedTime	3
Reason For Early Termination Of Statement Optimization	Good Enough Plan Found

The result was a simpler and faster plan. Also notice the information seen in the **Reason For Early Termination Of Statement Optimization** showplan property: the optimization search space was smaller and so covered inside the internal timeout period, resulting in the good-enough plan seen earlier.

This is an example of how our SQL Server workload may be incurring higher costs because at development time certain shortcuts were used – in this case, using an all-encompassing view that doesn't fit all usage scenarios, which may even limit the Query Optimizer ability to search for a more optimal plan. Simplifying is the key action in these cases – only query for what we want to query, and not more. The performance and scalability of our workload will speak for itself. This is similar to what we discussed in the *Composable logic* section of `Chapter 6`, *Easily-Identified T-SQL Anti-Patterns*; writing generic code saves development time, but the potential trade-off is poor performance during execution.

Another less efficient but valid option could be to create a unique clustered index on the view, and ensure SQL Server accesses the view itself, rather than expanding it.

Expanding the view is the action of opening the view definition and using the tables defined inside the view, rather than the view itself. This is done for every view but can be optionally skipped for indexed views, also known as **materialized views**.

To create an indexed view, we must first recreate the view as schema-bound, by adding the `WITH SCHEMABINDING` keyword to the view definition:

```
CREATE OR ALTER VIEW [HumanResources].[vEmployeeNew]
WITH SCHEMABINDING
AS
(...)
```

Then create the following index:

```
CREATE UNIQUE CLUSTERED INDEX IX_vEmployeeNew
ON [HumanResources].[vEmployeeNew] (
      [BusinessEntityID]
);
```

A view without an index contains no data, it's simply the definition of a query that is stored as an object. Once an index is created on the view, the results of the view are physically stored as a database object, as if we had created a new table. This results in additional storage requirements and overhead when updating data in the base tables that are referenced by the view.

To ensure the view is used directly by the Query Optimizer, we can add the **NOEXPAND** table hint, as seen as in the following example:

```
SELECT Title, FirstName, MiddleName, LastName, Suffix, JobTitle
FROM [HumanResources].[vEmployeeNew] WITH (NOEXPAND);
```

Notice the resulting query execution plan and **QueryTimeStats**:

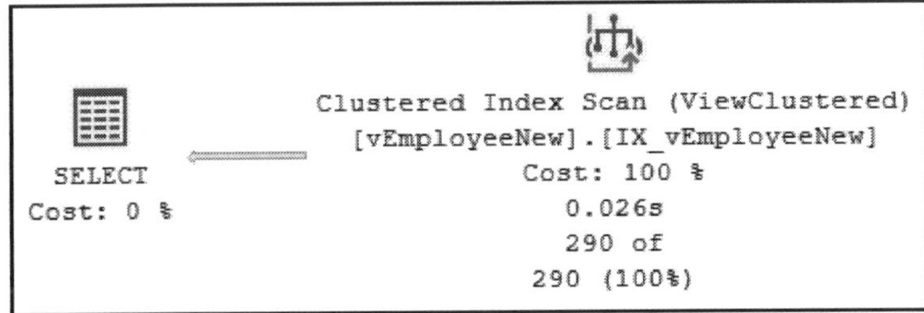

Take a look at the following screenshot:

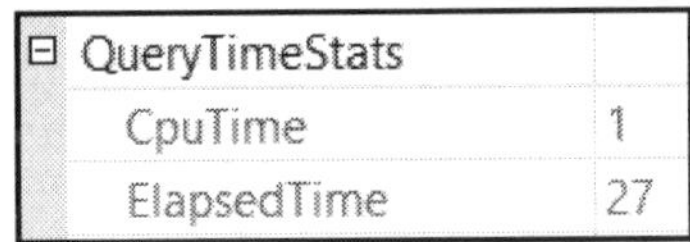

While this is not as optimal as querying only for the data we need for the report, creating an indexed view is a valid strategy to improve query performance, as we compare the preceding **QueryTimeStats** property with **QueryTimeStats** in the first query using the non-indexed view. There, CPU time dropped from 6 ms to 1 ms (~84 percent less), and execution time dropped from 56 ms to 27 ms (~52 percent less). The estimated cost for each plan is also clearly different, as seen next – using the indexed view in **Query 1** is significantly more efficient than **Query 2**:

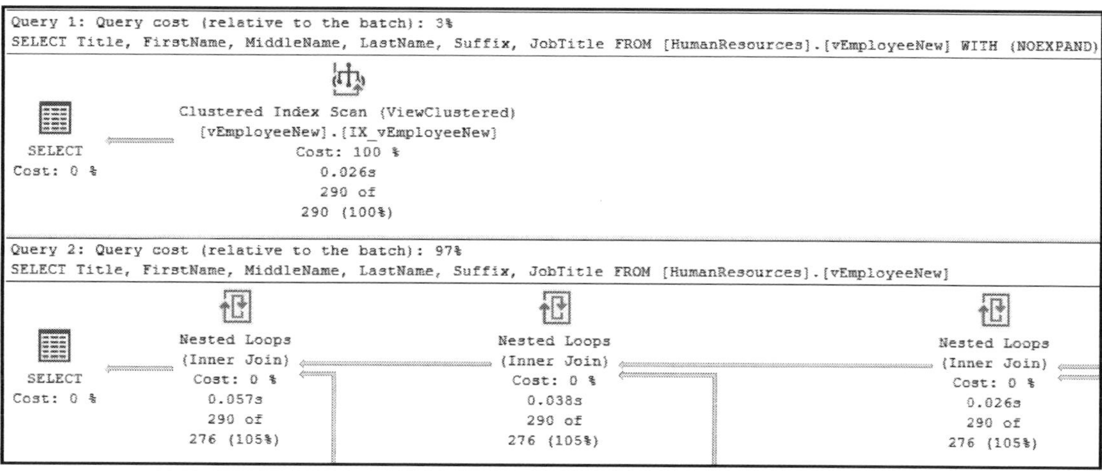

While in this case we used the **NOEXPAND** table hint, if a view is indexed, the Query Optimizer may choose to do **indexed view matching** automatically, which is the process by which the view is used directly rather than expanding it to access the underlying tables. This process can also be forced by using the **NOEXPAND** table hint as we did in this example.

Before SQL Server 2016 Service Pack 1, only Enterprise Edition was capable of doing indexed view matching; the **NOEXPAND** hint was required to use indexed views in Standard Edition. Azure SQL database doesn't require the **NOEXPAND** hint to make use of indexed view matching.

SQL Server will automatically create statistics on an indexed view when the **NOEXPAND** table hint is used. If we see a plan that is using indexed views and notice a plan warning about missing statistics, we should either use the hint or manually create the missing statistics.

Pitfalls of correlated sub-queries

It is not uncommon to use sub-queries to express certain predicates inline in queries, but developers must keep in mind that joins are frequently better than correlated sub-queries.

The following query examples can be executed in the scope of the **AdventureWorks** sample database:

```
SELECT wo.StockedQty, wo.WorkOrderID, wor.ActualCost
FROM Production.WorkOrder AS wo
INNER JOIN Production.WorkOrderRouting AS wor ON wo.WorkOrderID =
wor.WorkOrderID
WHERE wor.WorkOrderID = 12345;

SELECT wo.StockedQty, wo.WorkOrderID,
       (SELECT wor.ActualCost
              FROM Production.WorkOrderRouting AS wor
              WHERE wor.WorkOrderID = 12345)
FROM Production.WorkOrder AS wo
WHERE wo.WorkOrderID IN
       (SELECT wor.WorkOrderID
              FROM Production.WorkOrderRouting AS wor
              WHERE wor.WorkOrderID = 12345);
```

These yield different query plans but the same result sets, where the plan with the correlated sub-queries is more expensive:

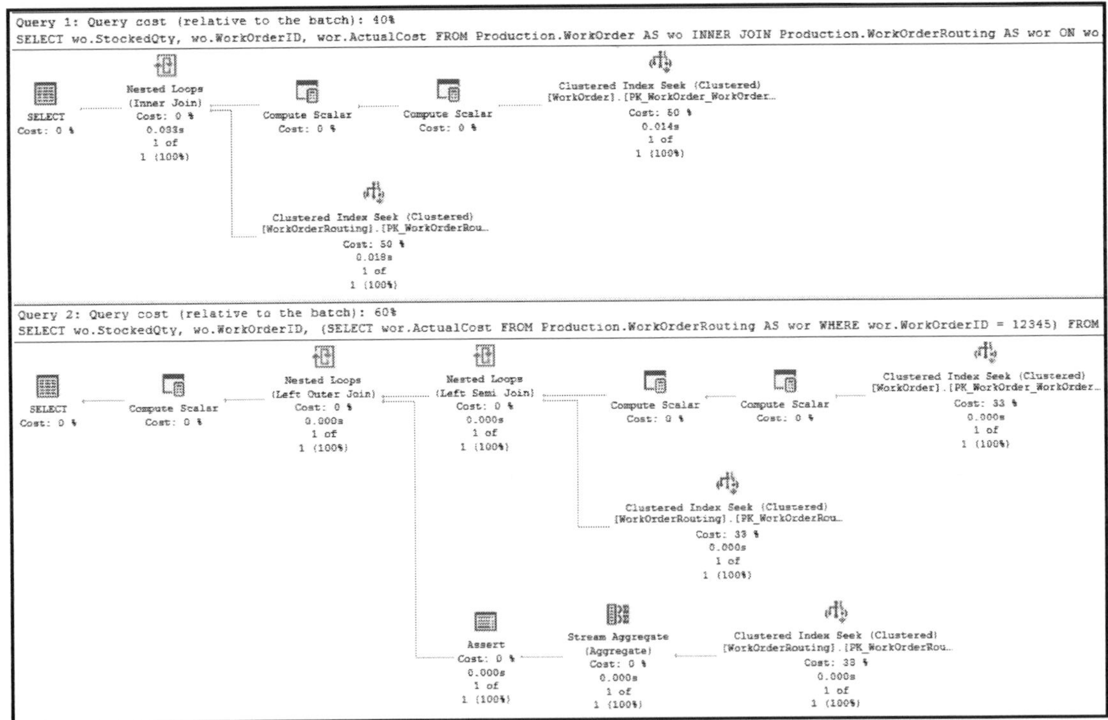

The estimated cost for each plan is clearly different, and favors using the join, which is significantly more efficient than the correlated sub-query.

Properly storing intermediate results

There are times when a query can become very complex, either because of a complicated database schema or because of complex business logic in the query, or both. In these cases, it may be easier to write the query in parts and store intermediate query results so that they can be used in a later query. This can make the query more readable, but it can also help SQL Server create a better query execution plan. There are different ways to store intermediate query results in SQL Server; this section will look at a few different options along with some of the considerations for when and where to use them.

Using table variables and temporary tables

Table variables and temporary tables serve the same basic purpose: to store an intermediate resultset to be used by a subsequent query. Database developers use these to break down complex joined queries that typically are not very efficient.

We have mentioned before how the way a query is written can severely compromise SQL Server's ability to optimize a query efficiently in the little time it has to do it.

This means that a complex T-SQL query can be broken down into simpler T-SQL statements that store intermediate results before being used to join with other tables. Imagine a developer needs to build a query in the **AdventureWorks** sample database that returns the sales quota data by year for each salesperson. This requires intermediate calculations that cannot be easily expressed with a joined query.

Instead, a developer can use table variables to store intermediate results and then use as a simple joined query, as seen in the following example:

```
DECLARE @Sales_TV TABLE (
 SalesPersonID intNOTNULL,
 TotalSales money,
 SalesYear smallint
);

-- Populate the first Table Variable
INSERT INTO @Sales_TV
SELECT SalesPersonID,SUM(TotalDue)AS TotalSales,
 YEAR(OrderDate) AS SalesYear
FROM Sales.SalesOrderHeader
WHERE SalesPersonID ISNOTNULL
GROUP BY SalesPersonID, YEAR(OrderDate);

-- Define the second Table Variable, which stores sales quota data by year
for each sales person.
DECLARE @Sales_Quota_TV TABLE (
 BusinessEntityID intNOTNULL,
 SalesQuota money,
 SalesQuotaYear smallint
);

INSERT INTO @Sales_Quota_TV
SELECT BusinessEntityID,SUM(SalesQuota)AS SalesQuota,
 YEAR(QuotaDate) AS SalesQuotaYear
FROM Sales.SalesPersonQuotaHistory
GROUPBY BusinessEntityID,YEAR(QuotaDate)

-- Define the outer query by referencing columns from both Table Variables.
SELECTCONCAT(FirstName,' ', LastName)AS SalesPerson, SalesYear,
 FORMAT(TotalSales,'C','en-us')AS TotalSales, SalesQuotaYear,
 FORMAT(SalesQuota,'C','en-us')AS SalesQuota,
 FORMAT (TotalSales -SalesQuota, 'C','en-us') AS Amt_Above_or_Below_Quota
FROM @Sales_TV AS Sales_TV
INNER JOIN @Sales_Quota_TV AS Sales_Quota_TV
 ON Sales_Quota_TV.BusinessEntityID = Sales_TV.SalesPersonID
 AND Sales_TV.SalesYear = Sales_Quota_TV.SalesQuotaYear
INNER JOIN Person.Person
 ON Person.BusinessEntityID = Sales_Quota_TV.BusinessEntityID
ORDER BY SalesPersonID, SalesYear;
```

Notice the resulting query execution plan with three queries:

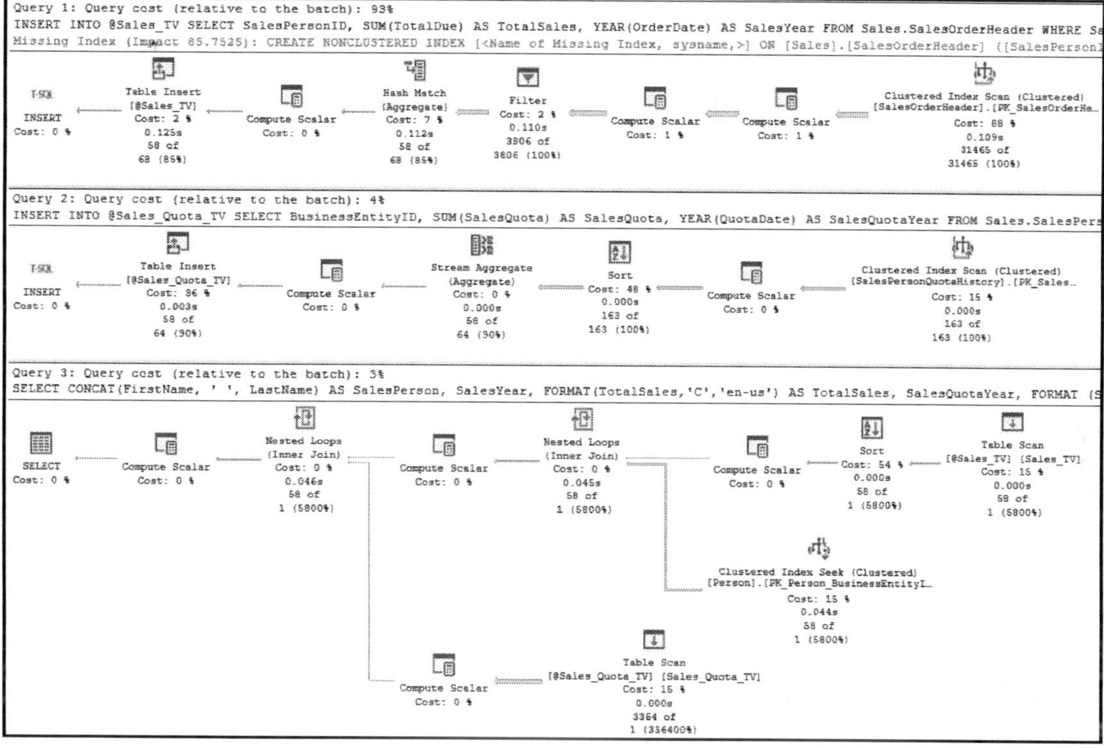

Alternatively, we can use temporary tables, as seen in this example:

```
DROP TABLE IF EXISTS #Sales_TT;
CREATE TABLE #Sales_TT (
       SalesPersonID intNOTNULL,
       TotalSales money,
       SalesYear smallint
);

-- Populate the first Temp Table
INSERT INTO #Sales_TT
SELECT SalesPersonID,SUM(TotalDue)AS TotalSales,
       YEAR(OrderDate) AS SalesYear
FROM Sales.SalesOrderHeader
WHERE SalesPersonID ISNOTNULL
GROUP BY SalesPersonID, YEAR(OrderDate);

-- Define the second Temp Table, which stores sales quota data by year for
each sales person.
DROP TABLE IF EXISTS #Sales_Quota_TT;
CREATE TABLE #Sales_Quota_TT (
       BusinessEntityID intNOTNULL,
       SalesQuota money,
       SalesQuotaYear smallint
);

INSERT INTO #Sales_Quota_TT
SELECT BusinessEntityID,SUM(SalesQuota)AS SalesQuota,
       YEAR(QuotaDate) AS SalesQuotaYear
FROM Sales.SalesPersonQuotaHistory
GROUPBY BusinessEntityID,YEAR(QuotaDate)

-- Define the outer query by referencing columns from both Temp Tables.
SELECTCONCAT(FirstName,' ', LastName)AS SalesPerson, SalesYear,
 FORMAT(TotalSales,'C','en-us')AS TotalSales, SalesQuotaYear,
 FORMAT(SalesQuota,'C','en-us')AS SalesQuota,
 FORMAT (TotalSales -SalesQuota, 'C','en-us') AS Amt_Above_or_Below_Quota
FROM #Sales_TT AS Sales_TT
INNER JOIN #Sales_Quota_TT AS Sales_Quota_TT
       ON Sales_Quota_TT.BusinessEntityID = Sales_TT.SalesPersonID
       AND Sales_TT.SalesYear = Sales_Quota_TT.SalesQuotaYear
INNER JOIN Person.Person
       ON Person.BusinessEntityID = Sales_Quota_TT.BusinessEntityID
ORDER BY SalesPersonID, SalesYear;
```

Notice the resulting query execution plan with three queries. Comparing **Query 1** and **Query 2** from the table variable example and temporary table example, we see that the plan is the same on both, except for the type of object where the data is inserted:

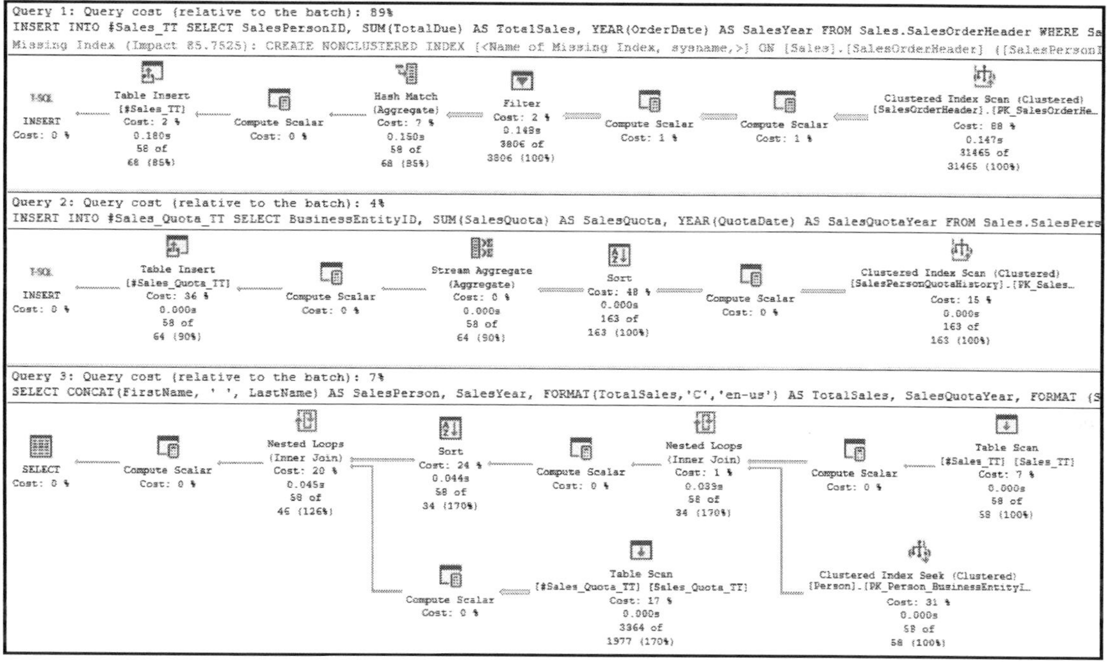

However, notice how the plans for **Query 3** in both examples are different. Notice especially the differences in the information of how many actual rows versus estimated rows flowed through the operators in each plan.

In the table variable case, we see the estimations are always **1**, whereas in the temporary table case they are either completely accurate (actual rows and estimated rows match) or are much closer to each other (3,364 actual of 1,977 estimated rows):

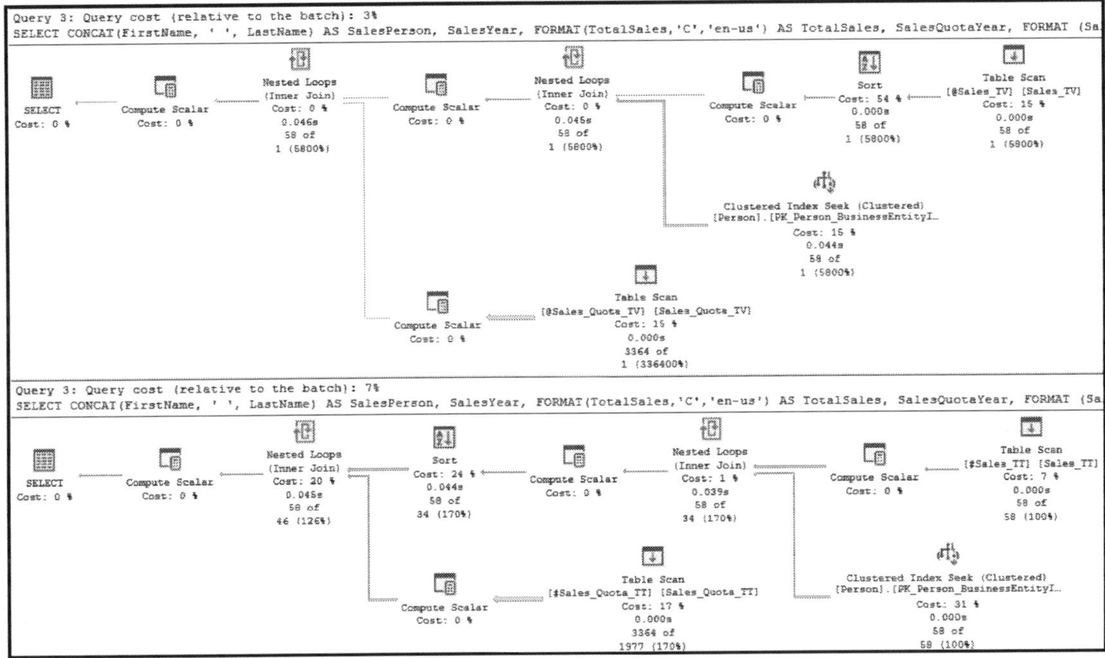

This is because SQL Server supports automatic statistics creation on temporary tables, as well as manual statistics creation and update, which the Query Optimizer can use. Up to and including SQL Server 2017, table variables are runtime objects only and are compiled together with all other statements, before any of the statements that populate the table variables even execute. For this reason, the Query Optimizer uses a default estimation of one row for table variables, since the row count is not available at compile-time.

However, in SQL Server 2019 and under Database Compatibility Level 150, the compilation of a statement that references a table variable that doesn't exist is deferred until the first execution of the statement, just as it is done for temporary tables. In effect, this means that table variables are materialized on their first use, and the Query Optimizer uses the row count in the first materialization of the table variable to create a query plan. The following is the example of **Query 3** running in SQL Server 2017, and then in SQL Server 2019:

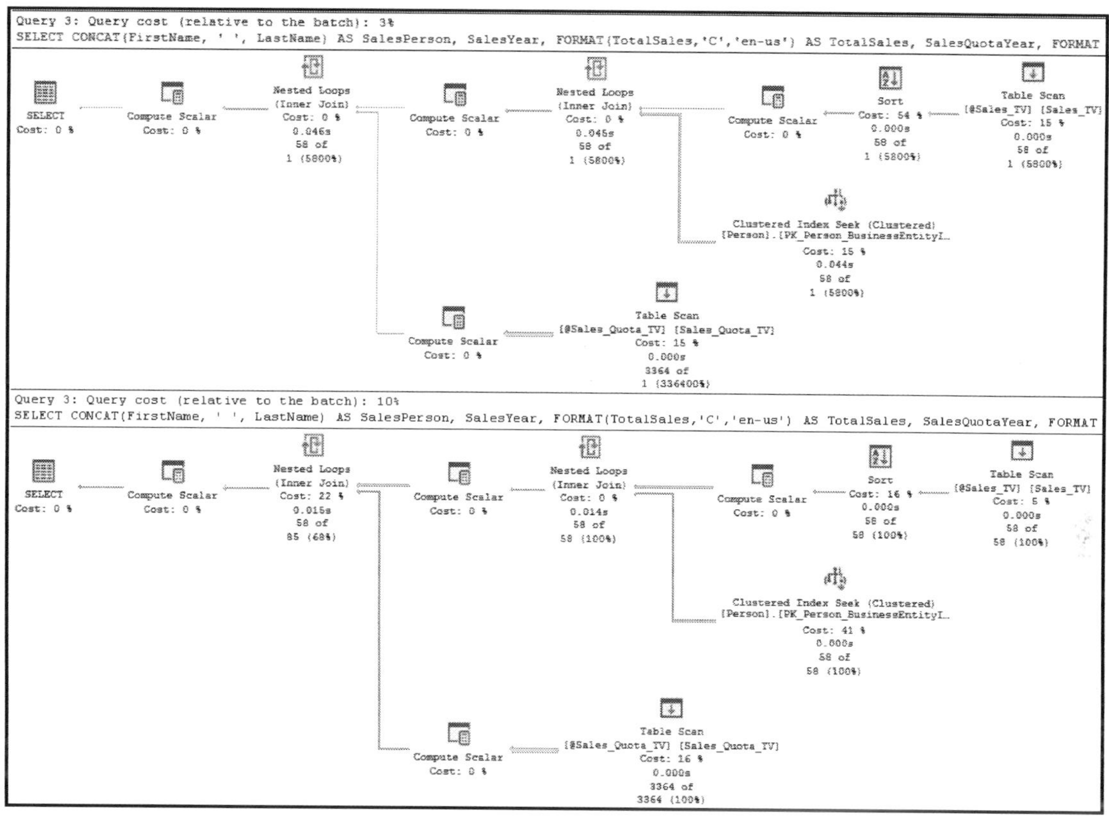

While in this case the plan doesn't materially change, the estimated and actual rows match when using SQL Server 2019's deferred compilation of table variables, providing the Query Optimizer the opportunity to create a query plan with better estimate memory requirements, which translates into improved resource usage.

Using Common Table Expressions

Common Table Expressions (CTEs) are runtime constructs to derive an inline intermediate result set from a query. This means that a complex T-SQL query can be broken down into simpler T-SQL statements that store intermediate results before joining with other tables or other CTEs that had been previously defined in the T-SQL statement. For example, take the two following queries that can be executed in the **AdventureWorks** sample database:

```
WITH Sales_CTE(SalesPersonID, SalesOrderID, SalesYear)
AS
(
```

```
    SELECT SalesPersonID, SalesOrderID, YEAR(OrderDate) AS SalesYear
    FROM Sales.SalesOrderHeader
    WHERE SalesPersonID IS NOT NULL
  )
  SELECT SalesPersonID, COUNT(SalesOrderID) AS TotalSales, SalesYear
  FROM Sales_CTE
  GROUP BY SalesYear, SalesPersonID
  ORDER BY SalesPersonID, SalesYear;

  SELECT SalesPersonID, COUNT(SalesOrderID) AS TotalSales, YEAR(OrderDate) AS
  SalesYear
  FROM Sales.SalesOrderHeader
  WHERE SalesPersonID IS NOT NULL
  GROUP BY YEAR(OrderDate), SalesPersonID
  ORDER BY SalesPersonID, SalesYear;
```

The queries generate the following execution plans:

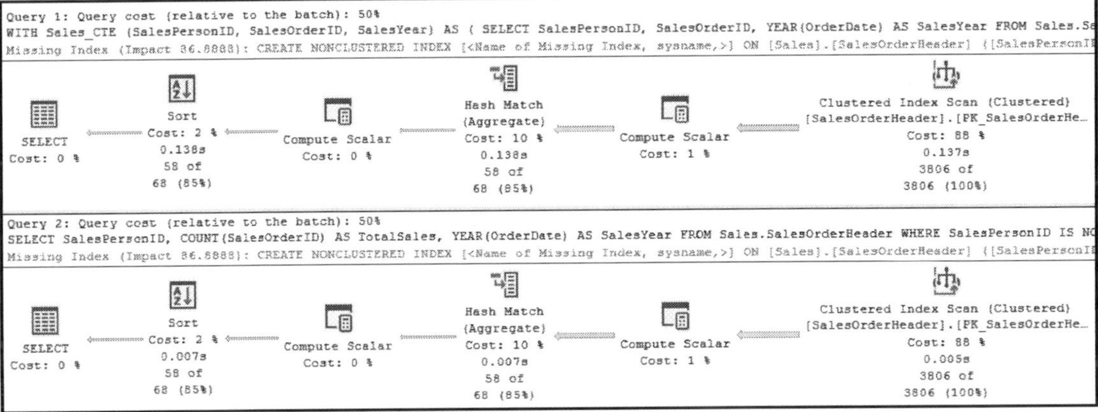

These yield matching query plans because they express the same set of conditions and were optimized in the same way. However, CTEs can be very useful to express conditions that become impossible to express with a joined query, such as recursive queries or queries that reference nested result sets.

The following example is a different way of building a query can be executed in the **AdventureWorks** sample database and builds a CTE that is then referenced by another CTE before being joined with the **Person.Person** table:

```
WITH Sales_CTE(SalesPersonID, TotalSales, SalesYear)
AS
-- Define the first CTE query.
(
```

```
  SELECT SalesPersonID, SUM(TotalDue) AS TotalSales, YEAR(OrderDate) AS
SalesYear
  FROM Sales.SalesOrderHeader
  WHERE SalesPersonID IS NOT NULL
  GROUP BY SalesPersonID, YEAR(OrderDate)
),
-- Define the second CTE query, which returns sales quota data by year for
each sales person.
Sales_Quota_CTE(BusinessEntityID, SalesQuota, SalesQuotaYear)
AS
(
       SELECT BusinessEntityID,SUM(SalesQuota)AS SalesQuota,
YEAR(QuotaDate) AS SalesQuotaYear
       FROM Sales.SalesPersonQuotaHistory
       GROUP BY BusinessEntityID, YEAR(QuotaDate)
)
-- Define the outer query by referencing columns from both CTEs and a
Table.
SELECT CONCAT(FirstName,' ', LastName)AS SalesPerson, SalesYear,
 FORMAT(TotalSales,'C','en-us')AS TotalSales, SalesQuotaYear,
 FORMAT(SalesQuota,'C','en-us')AS SalesQuota,
 FORMAT (TotalSales -SalesQuota, 'C','en-us') AS Amt_Above_or_Below_Quota
FROM Sales_CTE
INNER JOIN Sales_Quota_CTE
    ON Sales_Quota_CTE.BusinessEntityID = Sales_CTE.SalesPersonID
    AND Sales_CTE.SalesYear = Sales_Quota_CTE.SalesQuotaYear
INNER JOIN Person.Person
    ON Person.BusinessEntityID = Sales_Quota_CTE.BusinessEntityID
ORDER BY SalesPersonID, SalesYear;
```

Notice the resulting query execution plan with one single query, unlike the table variable and temporary table variants:

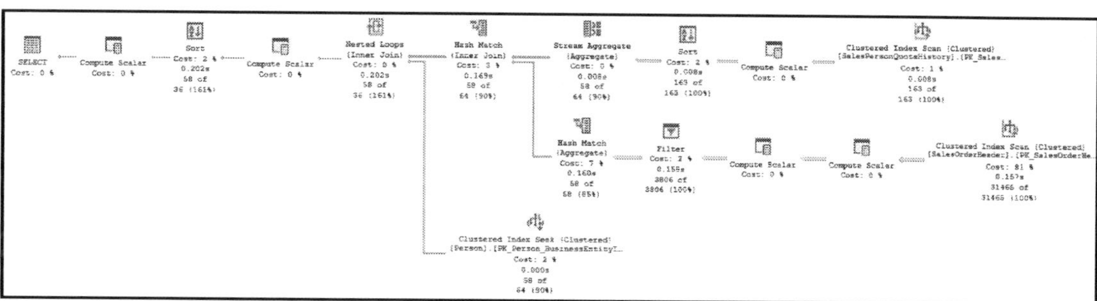

CTEs can be a very efficient alternative of driving Query Optimizer choices that improve performance. In `Chapter 4`, *Exploring Query Execution Plans*, under the *Query plan operators of interest* section, we had the following example of a query executed in the **AdventureWorks** sample database:

```
SELECT WO.WorkOrderID, WO.ProductID, WO.OrderQty, WO.StockedQty,
        WO.ScrappedQty, WO.StartDate, WO.EndDate, WO.DueDate,
        WO.ScrapReasonID, WO.ModifiedDate, WOR.WorkOrderID,
        WOR.ProductID, WOR.LocationID
FROM Production.WorkOrder AS WO
LEFT JOIN Production.WorkOrderRouting AS WOR
        ON WO.WorkOrderID = WOR.WorkOrderID AND WOR.WorkOrderID = 12345;
```

The query generates the following execution plan:

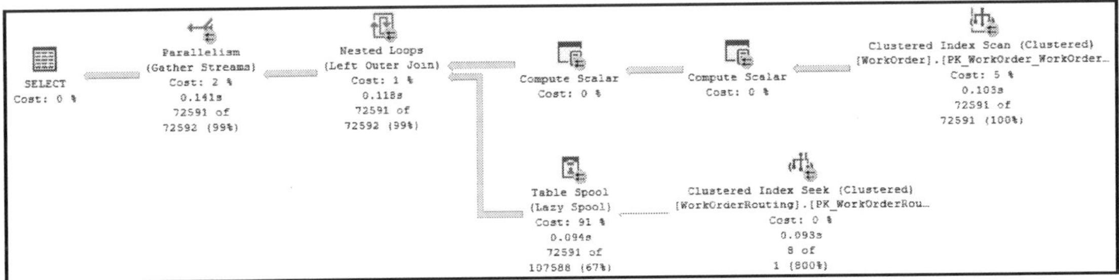

Where we can see its **QueryTimeStats** property:

QueryTimeStats	
CpuTime	247
ElapsedTime	713

Notice the Table Spool operator, which we know is something developers must attempt to avoid. We can't always avoid these, for example a Spool that enforces Halloween protection is unlikely to be removable. But in this case, refactoring the query to move the part that required the spool to a CTE, and including the join predicate seeking on the scalar value **12345**, allows us can eliminate the Spool:

```
;WITH cte AS (
    SELECT WorkOrderID, ProductID, LocationID
    FROM Production.WorkOrderRouting WHERE WorkOrderID = 12345
)
SELECT WO.WorkOrderID, WO.ProductID, WO.OrderQty, WO.StockedQty,
        WO.ScrappedQty, WO.StartDate, WO.EndDate, WO.DueDate,
        WO.ScrapReasonID, WO.ModifiedDate, WOR.WorkOrderID,
```

```
        WOR.ProductID, WOR.LocationID
FROM Production.WorkOrder AS WO LEFT JOIN cte AS WOR ON WO.WorkOrderID =
WOR.WorkOrderID;
```

Verify the new execution plan:

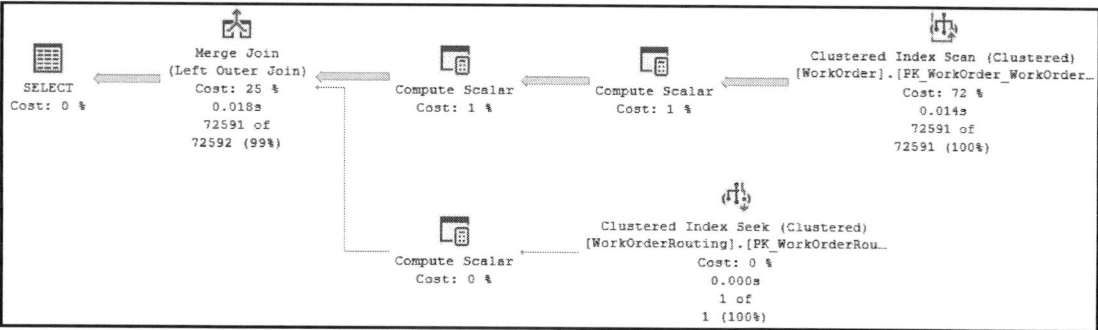

And its **QueryTimeStats** property:

⊟ QueryTimeStats	
CpuTime	46
ElapsedTime	46

Because of the CTE use, the Query Optimizer found that a merge join is a good-enough join algorithm, and better than a nested loop, which is why the spool is eliminated in this case. The plan becomes cheap enough not to exceed the cost threshold for parallelism configuration, which means it is executed in serial.

Let's compare the preceding **QueryTimeStats** with the **QueryTimeStats** in the first query using the non-indexed view: CPU time dropped from 247 ms to 46 ms (~81 percent less), and execution time dropped from 713 ms to 46 ms (~93 percent less). For such a simple query, this means we not only improved the singleton execution and CPU time, but also removed any use of TempDB. In turn, this improved the scalability of the workload by using fewer resources and reducing the overall concurrency in the workload.

Summary

This chapter covered some performance pitfalls that are not always obvious when writing T-SQL queries. Using the knowledge and tools covered in earlier chapters, together with the anti-patterns discussed in this chapter, we should now be able to dig deeper into our query execution plans and uncover issues that have the potential to impact performance and scalability before they reach production. So far, we have been focusing on how to write efficient, performant T-SQL code, but what if the code is already written, and we are faced with identifying these issues in an existing system?

In the next and final part of the book, we will investigate some of the tools available in SQL Server that will help us to identify and troubleshoot issues with our T-SQL query performance.

3

Section 3: Assemble Your Query Troubleshooting Toolbox

This section introduces some of the diagnostics artifacts and tools that ship with SQL Server for query performance troubleshooting.

The following chapters are included in this section:

- `Chapter 8`, *Building Diagnostic Queries Using DMVs and DMFs*
- `Chapter 9`, *Building xEvent Profiler Traces*
- `Chapter 10`, *Troubleshooting Live Queries*
- `Chapter 11`, *Comparative Analysis of Query Plans*
- `Chapter 12`, *Tracking Query Performance History with the Query Store*

8

Building Diagnostic Queries Using DMVs and DMFs

Dynamic Management Views (DMVs) and **Dynamic Management Functions (DMFs)** expose relevant real-time information that can unlock the secrets of T-SQL execution and SQL Server health, even on a live production server. There are hundreds of DMVs and DMFs (collectively referred to as DMVs) available in SQL Server, and while they are mostly documented, it may not be obvious how they can be used by database developers and administrators to troubleshoot performance both in production systems and during the development process.

In this chapter, we will start by enumerating some of the DMVs that are most relevant for both T-SQL developers and database administrators alike to troubleshoot T-SQL query performance. Building on this information, we will provide real-world examples in order to explore how to use DMVs to troubleshoot different poor-performance scenarios, as well as to give us the information needed to begin building our own DMV scripts.

This chapter covers the following topics:

- Introducing Dynamic Management Views
- Exploring query execution DMVs
- Exploring query plan cache DMVs
- Troubleshooting common scenarios with DMV queries

Introducing Dynamic Management Views

SQL Server 2005 introduced a new concept in the Database Engine—the **SQL Operating System** (**SQLOS**). The SQLOS is an abstraction layer that encapsulates all the low-level resource management and monitoring tasks that the Database Engine must perform, while providing an **application programming interface** (**API**) for other components of the Database Engine to leverage these services. Not only does this centralization of resource management code make the Database Engine more efficient, it also provides a central location for monitoring various aspects of Database Engine performance. Dynamic Management Views (DMVs) take advantage of this centralized architecture by providing the user with a mechanism to view this information in a way that is lightweight and accurate.

DMVs allow the user to query memory structures in the SQLOS. Some DMVs show information that is only relevant for the specific point in time at which they are queried, while other DMVs show cumulative information that goes back to the last time the SQL Server service was started. Because they are querying in-memory structures, most DMVs do not persist any information between restarts of the SQL Server service.

There are hundreds of DMVs that can be used to monitor everything from memory consumption to query performance, as well as features of the Database Engine such as **Replication**, **Resource Governor**, **Availability Groups**, and others. In this chapter, we will be focusing on DMVs that are relevant for troubleshooting T-SQL query performance, as well as some other performance issues that are relevant when monitoring query execution.

Exploring query execution DMVs

There are several different DMVs that might be relevant when analyzing the activity that is currently happening on a SQL Server. In this section, we will cover a few of the most common DMVs, along with some examples of the information that they can provide.

sys.dm_exec_sessions

The **sys.dm_exec_sessions** DMV lists information about all the sessions that are currently active in the server. This includes both user sessions and system sessions, and it also includes idle sessions that are connected but are not currently executing any queries.

Idle sessions can be identified by looking for rows that have a status of **sleeping**. When using connection pooling especially, it is common to have several user sessions in **sleeping** status.

This DMV can be used to view information that is relevant to the session, such as **login_name**, **host_name**, **program_name**, and other properties that would be set at the session level. This can be helpful when trying to identify which applications might be connected to the server, and which databases those applications are connected to. It shows current information only, so once a session is no longer active, it will not be visible in the view.

Here is a sample query that can be executed against **sys.dm_exec_sessions**:

```
SELECT session_id, login_time, host_name, program_name, login_name, status,
    last_request_start_time, db_name(database_id) AS [db_name]
FROM sys.dm_exec_sessions
WHERE session_id = 93
```

The following screenshot shows an example of the results when running this query from SQL Server Management Studio (SSMS):

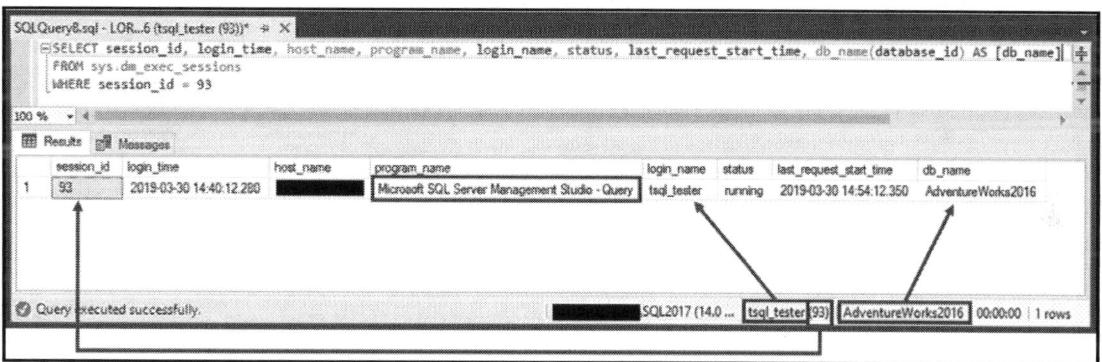

There are a few interesting things to note here. First is the **session_id**. This is important because it will help identify this session in other DMVs.

You can use the **is_user_process** column of **sys.dm_exec_sessions** to determine whether a session is generated by the system (`is_user_process = 0`) or by a user (`is_user_process = 1`), but most system sessions have a session_id of less than 50. This is a shortcut that can help us distinguish between user and system sessions in other views that contain **session_id**. In newer versions of SQL Server, there may be system sessions greater than 50, but they will typically have a status of **background**.

When we run a query in SSMS, we might notice that the status bar at the bottom contains information such as our login name and the server we are connected to, along with the database name. The number in parentheses next to our login name is our **session_id**. We can see this same information in **sys.dm_exec_sessions**, along with the **program_name** "Microsoft SQL Server Management Studio – Query" indicating the session is coming from a query window in SSMS. If we are investigating a long-running query in a production SQL Server, this information can help us identify where that query is coming from and who is executing it.

sys.dm_exec_requests

When we execute a query on the server, it is called a **request**. This DMV lists all the requests that are currently active on the server. Once a query completes and the results have been consumed by the client who made the request, it will no longer appear in this view, even if the session that generated it is still active. You can join this view to **sys.dm_exec_sessions** through the **session_id** column in order to obtain both information about the session, such as **program_name**, **login_time**, and so on, as well as information about the query execution, such as **cpu_time**, **total_elapsed_time**, **logical_reads**. This DMV displays information that is current for the moment in time at which it was queried, so the results returned will likely be different each time it is run.

For example, the following query will give us information about queries that are currently executing:

```
SELECT r.session_id, r.start_time, s.program_name, r.status, r.command,
       r.sql_handle, r.statement_start_offset, r.statement_end_offset,
r.database_id
FROM sys.dm_exec_requests r
INNER JOIN sys.dm_exec_sessions s ON s.session_id = r.session_id
WHERE r.session_id > 50 AND r.status IN ('running', 'runnable',
'suspended')
```

As we can see in the following screenshot, there are two queries currently executing from SSMS:

	session_id	start_time	program_name	status	command
1	93	2019-03-30 16:32:11.080	Microsoft SQL Server Management Studio - Query	running	SELECT
2	101	2019-03-30 16:32:07.780	Microsoft SQL Server Management Studio - Query	suspended	SELECT

sql_handle	statement_start_offset	statement_end_offset	database_id
0x020000002FD31338CFAA1C9D87AF90E16372F6A26330882...	0	652	30
0x0200000012B271257D955C46339A0A23FFA5C49BE0DE31...	0	3460	26

Refer to `Chapter 2`, *Understanding Query Processing*, for a discussion of the various states that a query will cycle through during execution. Filtering out sessions that have a status other than **running**, **runnable**, or **suspended** will allow us to focus on user sessions only.

You can gain a lot of information from this view about the performance of a request as well, such as CPU consumption, elapsed time in milliseconds, and I/O. The following query shows some of the relevant performance-related columns:

```
SELECT session_id, status, cpu_time, total_elapsed_time, logical_reads,
reads, writes
FROM sys.dm_exec_requests
WHERE session_id > 50
AND status IN ('running', 'runnable', 'suspended')
```

The following screenshot shows the results of this query:

	session_id	status	cpu_time	total_elapsed_time	logical_reads	reads	writes
1	62	running	4306	4306	233878	0	241
2	63	running	2487	2507	162912	9	245
3	64	runnable	6059	6085	291462	9	241
4	65	running	2	2	228	0	0

sys.dm_exec_sql_text

The **sys.dm_exec_sql_text** DMF is a helper function that can be used in conjunction with any DMV that contains the **sql_handle** column to retrieve the text of a query. You can select from this table-valued function by passing a valid **sql_handle** as a parameter, but it is most commonly used via the **CROSS APPLY** operator in combination with queries against either **sys.dm_exec_requests** or **sys.dm_exec_query_stats**.

Building on our example from the previous section, we can use the **CROSS APPLY** operator to retrieve the text of the queries that are running, as in the following query:

```
SELECT r.session_id, r.start_time, s.program_name, r.status,
    st.text AS statement_text, r.statement_start_offset,
r.statement_end_offset, r.database_id
FROM sys.dm_exec_requests r
INNER JOIN sys.dm_exec_sessions s ON s.session_id = r.session_id
CROSS APPLY sys.dm_exec_sql_text(r.sql_handle) st
WHERE r.session_id > 50
    AND r.status IN ('running', 'runnable', 'suspended')
```

This query yields the results illustrated in the following screenshot:

	session_id	start_time	program_name	status
1	93	2019-03-30 16:41:54.417	Microsoft SQL Server Management Studio - Query	running
2	101	2019-03-30 16:41:50.060	Microsoft SQL Server Management Studio - Query	suspended

statement_text	statement_start_offset	statement_end_offset	database_id
SELECT r.session_id, r.start_time, s.program_nam...	0	758	30
SELECT e.[BusinessEntityID], p.[Title], ...	0	3460	26

Alternatively, we can copy one of the values for **sql_handle** that we obtained from the first sample query in the *sys.dm_exec_requests* section and execute this DMF as a standalone query:

```
SELECT * FROM
sys.dm_exec_sql_text(0x020000002EED8B2B6539C6D9CB85FAAA57145FECF54E1DA70000
0000000000000000000000000000000000000)
```

This query yields the following results:

	dbid	objectid	number	encrypted	text
1	NULL	NULL	NULL	0	SELECT r.session_id, r.start_time, s.program_name, r.status, st.text AS statement_text, r....

As we can see, the **text** column contains the text of the first sample query we executed in the *sys.dm_exec_requests* section.

sys.dm_os_waiting_tasks

Every request that is submitted to SQL Server is broken down into one or more **tasks**, depending on whether parallelism is involved. As we mentioned previously, in the *Query execution essentials* section of `Chapter 2`, *Understanding Query Processing*, each task that is involved in processing the query is assigned to a worker thread, and these threads are used to complete the work of the query on the CPUs. Throughout the execution of a query, the various threads will cycle through the **running**, **runnable**, and **suspended** statuses as they process the different operations required to complete the query. When a task needs to wait for a resource, it goes into the suspended state. This is relevant information when troubleshooting query performance, because it indicates contention for a resource of some kind. The **sys.dm_os_waiting_tasks** DMV lists all the tasks that are active within the server, but are in the **suspended** state, meaning they are waiting for a resource. This view contains information such as **wait_type**, which is helpful when analyzing what is contributing to a query's execution time. This information is also available at the request level via **sys.dm_exec_requests**, as we discussed earlier in this chapter, but when a query is running in parallel, the information listed at the request level may not be giving us a full picture of what is going on on the individual thread level.

Let's change the columns we select from **sys.dm_exec_requests** to show more information about the current status of the queries that are executing:

```
SELECT r.session_id, r.start_time, r.status, r.sql_handle,
       r.wait_type, r.wait_time, r.wait_resource
FROM sys.dm_exec_requests r
WHERE r.session_id > 50
AND r.status IN ('running', 'runnable', 'suspended')
```

The following screenshot illustrates the results of this query:

	session_id	start_time	status	sql_handle	wait_type	wait_time	wait_resource
1	93	2019-03-30 16:51:43.440	running	0x020000007AF71800029A4291F7CA5C915B33445EDB18C13...	NULL	0	
2	101	2019-03-30 16:51:25.067	suspended	0x0200000012B271257D955C46339A0A23FFA5C498E0DE31...	CXPACKET	18025	

Note that **session_id 101** is currently in the suspended state, which means it is waiting for a resource. The **wait_type** column contains the **CXPACKET** value. This wait type indicates that the query is running in parallel, but we're only getting information from one of the threads in **sys.dm_exec_requests**, the coordinator thread.

If we want to know what all the suspended threads that are involved in this query execution are doing, we need to join to the **sys.dm_os_waiting_tasks** DMV to get the task-level detail:

```
SELECT r.session_id, t.exec_context_id, t.blocking_exec_context_id,
       r.start_time, r.status, r.sql_handle, t.wait_type,
t.wait_duration_ms
FROM sys.dm_exec_requests r
LEFT JOIN sys.dm_os_waiting_tasks t ON r.session_id = t.session_id
WHERE r.session_id > 50
    AND r.status IN ('running', 'runnable', 'suspended')
ORDER BY t.exec_context_id
```

Note that a **LEFT JOIN** is used in this query because it is possible to have rows in **sys.dm_exec_requests** that have no waiting tasks, but we still want them to appear in our results.

This yields the following results:

	session_id	exec_context_id	blocking_exec_context_id	start_time	status	sql_handle	wait_type	wait_duration_ms
1	93	NULL	NULL	2019-03-30 17:05:31.207	running	0x02000000E0B2B83399C76C847B5AE78710EE50522B9CB9B...	NULL	NULL
2	101	0	18	2019-03-30 17:05:26.297	suspended	0x0200000012B271257D955C46339A0A23FFA5C49BE0DE31...	CXPACKET	4612
3	101	1	12	2019-03-30 17:05:26.297	suspended	0x0200000012B271257D955C46339A0A23FFA5C49BE0DE31...	CXCONSUMER	481
4	101	2	13	2019-03-30 17:05:26.297	suspended	0x0200000012B271257D955C46339A0A23FFA5C49BE0DE31...	CXCONSUMER	526
5	101	3	11	2019-03-30 17:05:26.297	suspended	0x0200000012B271257D955C46339A0A23FFA5C49BE0DE31...	CXCONSUMER	118
6	101	4	15	2019-03-30 17:05:26.297	suspended	0x0200000012B271257D955C46339A0A23FFA5C49BE0DE31...	CXCONSUMER	4255
7	101	5	9	2019-03-30 17:05:26.297	suspended	0x0200000012B271257D955C46339A0A23FFA5C49BE0DE31...	CXCONSUMER	37
8	101	6	13	2019-03-30 17:05:26.297	suspended	0x0200000012B271257D955C46339A0A23FFA5C49BE0DE31...	CXCONSUMER	335
9	101	7	13	2019-03-30 17:05:26.297	suspended	0x0200000012B271257D955C46339A0A23FFA5C49BE0DE31...	CXCONSUMER	300
10	101	8	9	2019-03-30 17:05:26.297	suspended	0x0200000012B271257D955C46339A0A23FFA5C49BE0DE31...	CXCONSUMER	148

We can see that session **93** was in the running state, so the fields from **sys.dm_os_waiting_tasks** are **NULL** for this row. For session **101**, the parallel query, there are several rows returned with different values for **exec_context_id** and **blocking_exec_context_id**. These show the various tasks that make up the request, and which tasks are blocking them, along with the **wait_type** and **wait_duration_ms**. Note that while **sys.dm_exec_requests** showed only **CXPACKET** for the wait type, there are in fact several tasks waiting on **CXCONSUMER** as well. The task with `exec_context_id = 0` is the coordinator thread; the rest of the tasks are the ones doing the actual work.

A detailed discussion about waits is outside the scope of this book, but if we would like more information about wait types, search the SQL Server documentation for the DMV **sys.dm_os_wait_stats**. This DMV shows cumulative wait information since the server was last started. The documentation for this DMV contains a reference for the various wait types and what they mean.

Exploring query plan cache DMVs

Another set of DMVs that are helpful when troubleshooting T-SQL query performance are the query plan cache related DMVs. While the execution DMVs we discussed in the previous section contain point-in-time information that changes frequently, these DMVs contain information about queries that are currently in the plan cache, which can contain information all the way back to when the server was last restarted, depending on how long query plans remain in the cache.

The amount of time a plan remains in the cache depends on several factors, such as memory pressure, recompilation, schema changes, and so on. Provided that the server has been online for some time and no cache-flushing events have occurred, such as changing MAXDOP, or manually clearing the plan cache by running `ALTER DATABASE SCOPED CONFIGURATION CLEAR PROCEDURE_CACHE`, these plan cache DMVs should give a good idea of the overall query performance on the server.

Before describing the DMVs in more detail, it's important to understand how query execution plans are stored. Query execution plans are stored as a batch, which means that all the statements that were submitted to the server as a single request are stored as a single plan object. An example of a batch might be a single stored procedure, or a group of T-SQL queries submitted in a single request.

If running a query from SSMS, a batch is everything between **GO** statements.

A plan object will have a **plan_handle**, which is a hexadecimal value that uniquely identifies the object. The text of the batch will also have a handle called the **sql_handle**, which can be used to identify the T-SQL query itself and retrieve the batch text. Within that batch, there will be one or more **statements**. Each statement is identified by **statement_start_offset** and **statement_end_offset**, which are byte offsets from the beginning of the batch text that point to the beginning and end of the statement within the batch. You can use these offsets to extract the individual queries from a batch, typically by using a **SUBSTRING** function. Keep these concepts in mind as we explore the various plan cache DMVs.

sys.dm_exec_query_stats

The **sys.dm_exec_query_stats** DMV displays cumulative query execution statistics for all the queries that are currently in the cache. As we observed in the previous section, the DMV **sys.dm_exec_requests** shows query performance while the query is executing. Once the query is complete, **sys.dm_exec_query_stats** is incremented with this new execution information. While query execution plans are stored as a batch, this DMV lists one row per statement, so there may be multiple rows with the same **plan_handle** and **sql_handle**. statements. These rows will have a different **statement_start_offset** and **statement_end_offset** to distinguish between the statements in the same batch.

There are many different query performance metrics that can be gathered with this DMV. This sample query highlights a few of the more common ones:

```
SELECT st.text, qs.plan_handle, qs.last_execution_time, qs.execution_count,
       qs.total_worker_time AS total_cpu_time,
       qs.total_worker_time/qs.execution_count AS average_cpu_time,
       qs.total_logical_reads, qs.total_logical_reads/qs.execution_count AS
average_logical_reads,
       qs.total_elapsed_time,
       (qs.total_elapsed_time/qs.execution_count)/1000000 AS
average_elapsed_time_sec
FROM sys.dm_exec_query_stats qs
CROSS APPLY sys.dm_exec_sql_text(qs.sql_handle) st
WHERE qs.sql_handle =
0x0200000022D4D930BD648A1C5BA9320D2448C8F7CFCEF3D6000000000000000000000000
000000000000000
```

In this case, we've used the **sql_handle** that we retrieved earlier from the sample query against **sys.dm_exec_requests**. This query yields the following results:

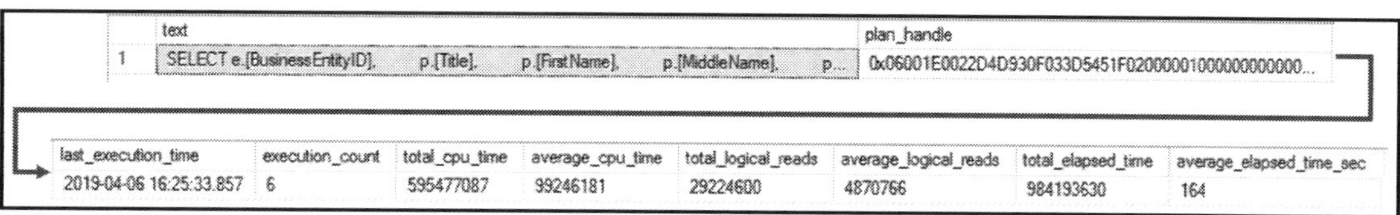

	text	plan_handle
1	SELECT e.[BusinessEntityID], p.[Title], p.[FirstName], p.[MiddleName], p...	0x06001E0022D4D930F033D5451F0200000100000000000...

last_execution_time	execution_count	total_cpu_time	average_cpu_time	total_logical_reads	average_logical_reads	total_elapsed_time	average_elapsed_time_sec
2019-04-06 16:25:33.857	6	595477087	99246181	29224600	4870766	984193630	164

Based on **execution_count** in the results, we can see that this query plan has been executed six times since it entered the cache. The columns that start with **total_** are cumulative for all six executions, so we can calculate the average by dividing by **execution_count**. Also note that all times are in microseconds, so in order to get the average execution time in seconds, we calculated the average first by dividing **total_elapsed_time** by **execution_count**, then we divided by 1,000,000 to convert microseconds to seconds. In addition to totals, each metric also has columns for minimum and maximum values across all executions, as well as the value for the last execution.

In the *Troubleshooting Common Scenarios with DMV Queries* section, we will cover some additional columns that are specific to certain performance scenarios, but a comprehensive list of the columns returned by this DMV can be found by searching for the **sys.dm_exec_query_stats** documentation page.

sys.dm_exec_procedure_stats

The **sys.dm_exec_procedure_stats** DMV is like **sys.dm_exec_query_stats** in that it contains cumulative execution statistics for query plans in the cache, but at the stored procedure level rather than the query level. Stored procedures may contain T-SQL code constructs other than queries, such as conditional logic, variable assignments, and function calls. These constructs consume resources, but they aren't accounted for in **sys.dm_exec_query_stats** because they aren't queries. This DMV can be used to determine the total resource consumption of the procedure as a whole, including code that is not accounted for in **sys.dm_exec_query_stats**.

The following example shows a stored procedure that contains some conditional logic as well as a **WAITFOR** command that causes the execution to wait for the specified amount of time before proceeding to the next statement in the procedure:

```
CREATE OR ALTER PROCEDURE uspGetEmployeeByDepartment @Department
nvarchar(50)
AS
SELECT *
FROM HumanResources.vEmployeeDepartment
WHERE Department = @Department
IF @Department = N'Engineering'
       WAITFOR DELAY '00:00:10'
GO
```

We can execute this stored procedure a few times in the **AdventureWorks** sample database with a few different values for **@Department**, and then use the following query to see the execution statistics:

```
SELECT object_name(object_id, database_id) AS proc_name, plan_handle,
       execution_count, min_elapsed_time, max_elapsed_time
FROM sys.dm_exec_procedure_stats
WHERE object_id = object_id('uspgetEmployeeByDepartment')
```

This query returns the following results:

	proc_name	plan_handle	execution_count	min_elapsed_time	max_elapsed_time
1	uspGetEmployeeByDepartment	0x05001E008116D84AA0BC768B1F0200000100000000000...	22	2119	10008883

Notice the difference between the minimum and maximum elapsed time. This is because the **WAITFOR** command only executes when `@Department = N'Engineering'` so these executions take over 10 seconds, whereas other parameter values take much less time, only about the time it takes to execute the query.

We can confirm this by using the value from the **plan_handle** column to look up the statements in **sys.dm_exec_query_stats**:

```
SELECT st.text, qs.statement_start_offset, qs.statement_end_offset,
       qs.execution_count, qs.min_elapsed_time, qs.max_elapsed_time
FROM sys.dm_exec_query_stats qs
CROSS APPLY sys.dm_exec_sql_text(qs.sql_handle) st
WHERE plan_handle =
0x05001E008116D84AA0BC768B1F020000010000000000000000000000000000000000000
000000000000000
```

This query returns the following results:

	text	statement_start_offset	statement_end_offset	execution_count	min_elapsed_time	max_elapsed_time
1	CREATE PROCEDURE uspGetEmployeeByDepartment @Dep...	152	316	22	2061	211117

Notice that, while the minimum elapsed time for the query alone is close to the minimum elapsed time of the entire procedure, the maximum elapsed time is an order of magnitude smaller. This is because the **WAITFOR** command is not part of the query, and thus its execution time is not included here.

There are two other DMVs that are like **sys.dm_exec_procedure_stats**, called **sys.dm_exec_trigger_stats** and **sys.dm_exec_function_stats**. These DMVs can be used to view execution statistics for triggers and functions respectively, in the same way **sys.dm_exec_procedure_stats** is used for stored procedures.

sys.dm_exec_query_plan

The **sys.dm_exec_query_plan** DMF is another helper function like **sys.dm_exec_sql_text** that retrieves the estimated execution plan based on **plan_handle**. You can call **sys.dm_exec_query_plan** on its own with a valid **plan_handle**, or you can leverage **CROSS APPLY** with views like **sys.dm_exec_query_stats** that contain a **plan_handle** column.

The value that is returned in the **query_plan** column is in XML format but querying this view in SSMS will show the XML as a link. When clicked, the link will open as a graphical plan in a new tab.

We can use the **plan_handle** we found earlier in the *sys.dm_exec_procedure_stats* section to retrieve the estimated plan for the **uspGetEmployeeByDepartment** stored procedure, as in the following example:

```
SELECT query_plan
FROM
sys.dm_exec_query_plan(0x05001E008116D84AA0BC768B1F0200000100000000000000000000
00000000000000000000000000000000000000)
```

The following screenshot shows the results of this query:

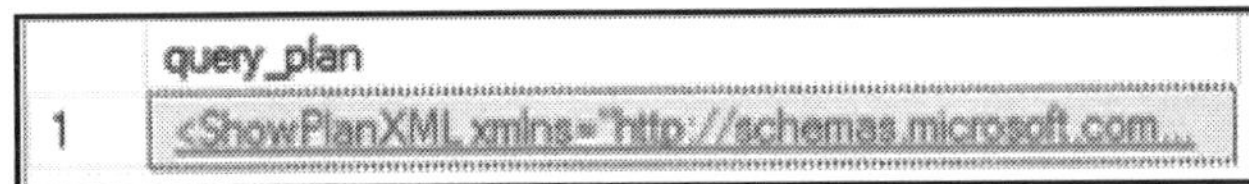

If we click the link displayed in the results, the following query execution plan opens in a new window:

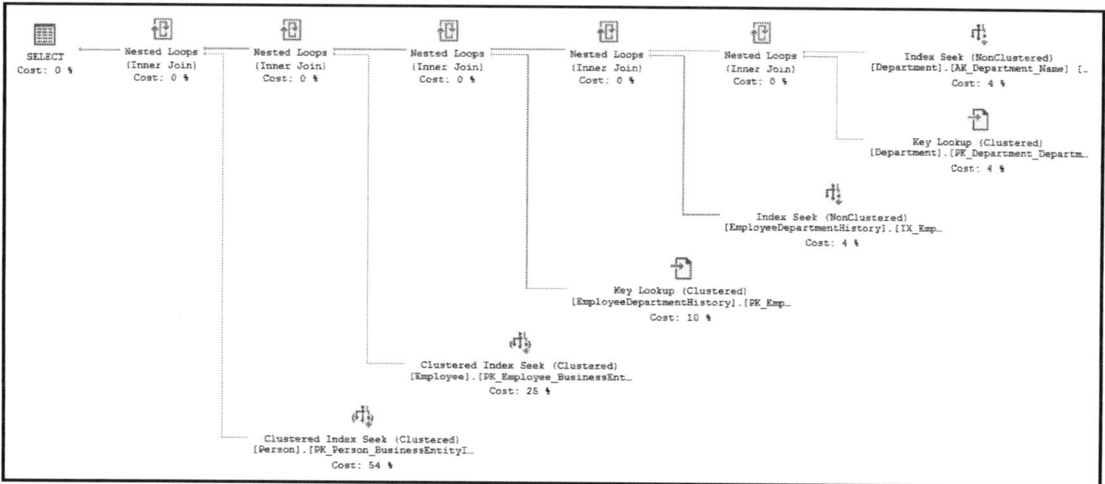

There are some cases where even if the plan is still in the cache and we have a valid **plan_handle**, **sys.dm_exec_query_plan** returns a NULL value for the plan. In most cases, the reason for this is that the query that generated the plan is very complex and has many nested elements within it. Due to a limitation of the XML data type that only allows 128 levels of nested elements, these complex plans cannot be returned via **sys.dm_exec_query_plan**. If we face this situation, we can attempt to use the **sys.dm_exec_text_query_plan** function instead. This function returns the plan as **NVARCHAR(max)** rather than XML. The text returned is XML data, but since the **NVARCHAR(max)** datatype doesn't have any formatting, it isn't affected by the nesting limitation. Query plans retrieved in this way will not be clickable, so we will need to copy the XML data from the column, paste it into a new window (either SSMS or some other text editor) and save it as a `.sqlplan` file. Once we have this file, we can double-click it and SSMS will open it as a graphical plan.

The following query can be used to retrieve the same plan using **sys.dm_exec_text_query_plan**:

```
SELECT query_plan
FROM
sys.dm_exec_text_query_plan(0x05001E008116D84AA0BC768B1F020000010000000000
0000000000000000000000000000000000000000000, 152, 316)
```

Note that this function takes two additional parameters, these are **statement_start_offset** and **statement_end_offset**. These values can also be obtained from **sys.dm_exec_query_stats**. This query returns the following results:

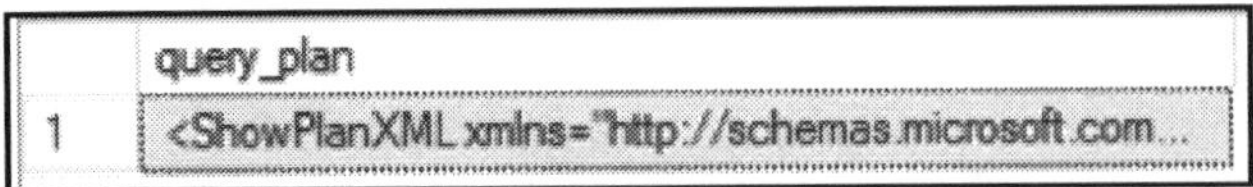

	query_plan
1	<ShowPlanXML xmlns="http://schemas.microsoft.com...

As we can see, the results are essentially the same as **sys.dm_exec_query_plan**, except there is no hyperlink.

sys.dm_exec_cached_plans

The **sys.dm_exec_cached_plans** DMV can be used to view all the query execution plans that are currently in the cache. Unlike **sys.dm_exec_query_stats**, which contains information about the execution of the query, this DMV contains information about the plan object itself, including things like the size of the plan, the type of plan (for example, stored procedure, prepared statement, ad hoc query, and so on), and the number of times the plan has been used. Also, since plans are stored as a batch, this DMV will have only one row per plan, rather than one row per statement as in **sys.dm_exec_query_stats**.

Here's an example of a query against **sys.dm_exec_cached_plans**:

```
SELECT TOP 10 plan_handle, usecounts, size_in_bytes, objtype, query_plan
FROM sys.dm_exec_cached_plans
CROSS APPLY sys.dm_exec_query_plan(plan_handle)
ORDER BY size_in_bytes DESC
```

Note in the preceding query example that we can cross apply the **sys.dm_exec_query_plan** DMF with this DMV, in order to retrieve the plan. This query yields the following results, ordered by the size of the plan, largest first:

	plan_handle	usecounts	size_in_bytes	objtype	query_plan
1	0x06000100EE9461139082C37DB9010000001000000000000...	15	2138112	Adhoc	<ShowPlanXML xmlns="http://schemas.microsoft.com...
2	0x06000900237690050051C27DB9010000001000000000000...	107	835584	Prepared	NULL
3	0x06000400FE012E12B0DDB0E7B8010000001000000000000...	2	819200	Prepared	<ShowPlanXML xmlns="http://schemas.microsoft.com...
4	0x06001E00FE012E1260BFFAC0B8010000001000000000000...	38	819200	Prepared	<ShowPlanXML xmlns="http://schemas.microsoft.com...
5	0x06001A002376900590C2C27DB9010000001000000000000...	1	770048	Prepared	NULL
6	0x0600010044A7DF07104AC37DB9010000001000000000000...	15	679936	Adhoc	NULL
7	0x05000400BD2C136AB033669FB8010000001000000000000...	1	630784	Proc	<ShowPlanXML xmlns="http://schemas.microsoft.com...
8	0x0500FF7F99F756F09031C27DB9010000001000000000000...	31	598016	Proc	<ShowPlanXML xmlns="http://schemas.microsoft.com...
9	0x0600040056CDA83760DF8396B8010000001000000000000...	10	573440	Prepared	<ShowPlanXML xmlns="http://schemas.microsoft.com...
10	0x0600010056CDA837603F26BAB8010000001000000000000...	4	565248	Prepared	<ShowPlanXML xmlns="http://schemas.microsoft.com...

This is just a simple example that returns the 10 largest plans in the cache. In the next section, we will look at a few more comprehensive queries that leverage **sys.dm_exec_cached_plans**.

Troubleshooting common scenarios with DMV queries

Now that we have reviewed some of the DMVs that are relevant to examining query performance, we can look at how to combine these views into larger queries that target specific troubleshooting scenarios.

Many of the examples in this chapter are derived from queries on the Tiger Toolbox on GitHub (`https://aka.ms/tigertoolbox`). For more examples and comprehensive DMV scripts, be sure to download and explore this repository.

Investigating blocking

Blocking is a very common scenario in many database systems. This is what happens when one query is holding exclusive access to a resource that another query also requires. It is normal for some blocking to occur, but severe blocking can cause major performance issues and should be investigated. When troubleshooting query performance, it's a good idea to check for blocking first, to see if queries are slow because they are expensive, or because they are being blocked by some other workload.

The key DMVs for investigating blocking are **sys.dm_exec_requests** and **sys.dm_os_waiting_tasks**. As we discussed previously, these DMVs show us which queries are currently running and what state they are in. They also have columns that will indicate which sessions may be causing blocking.

The following example shows a simple query that can be used to look for blocking on the system:

```
SELECT s.session_id, s.last_request_end_time,IS NULL(r.status,s.status) AS
status,
    s.database_id, r.blocking_session_id, r.wait_type, r.wait_time,
    r.wait_resource, s.open_transaction_count
FROM sys.dm_exec_sessions s
LEFT JOIN sys.dm_exec_requests r ON r.session_id = s.session_id
WHERE s.is_user_process = 1
```

The following screenshot shows an example of the results this query might generate on a system that has blocking:

	session_id	last_request_end_time	status	database_id	blocking_session_id	wait_type	wait_time	wait_resource	open_
1	51	2019-04-07 11:14:30.527	running	30	0	NULL	0		0
2	54	2019-04-07 11:08:42.263	sleeping	1	NULL	NULL	NULL	NULL	0
3	61	2019-04-06 17:44:40.757	sleeping	30	NULL	NULL	NULL	NULL	0
4	62	2019-04-06 17:28:33.773	sleeping	1	NULL	NULL	NULL	NULL	0
5	63	2019-04-06 15:48:51.190	sleeping	26	NULL	NULL	NULL	NULL	0
6	73	2019-04-07 11:13:16.480	sleeping	30	NULL	NULL	NULL	NULL	0
7	97	2019-04-07 10:19:30.173	suspended	26	0	WAITFOR	3300229		0
8	99	2019-04-07 10:54:09.127	suspended	30	109	LCK_M_S	1221379	KEY: 30:72057594048086016 (61a06abd401c)	0
9	100	2019-04-07 11:14:30.530	sleeping	26	NULL	NULL	NULL	NULL	0
10	101	2019-04-07 11:11:18.217	sleeping	1	NULL	NULL	NULL	NULL	0
11	102	2019-04-07 11:13:36.327	suspended	26	0	WRITELOG	0		1
12	103	2019-04-07 11:13:36.327	suspended	26	125	PAGELATCH_EX	0	26:1:157921	2
13	104	2019-04-06 17:32:39.947	sleeping	26	NULL	NULL	NULL	NULL	0
14	105	2019-04-07 11:13:36.327	suspended	26	0	WRITELOG	0		1
15	106	2019-04-06 17:04:05.573	sleeping	1	NULL	NULL	NULL	NULL	0
16	107	2019-04-07 11:13:36.330	suspended	26	0	WRITELOG	0		1
17	108	2019-04-07 11:13:36.327	suspended	26	111	PAGELATCH_EX	0	26:1:157921	2
18	109	2019-04-07 10:54:06.477	sleeping	30	NULL	NULL	NULL	NULL	1

Notice that session 99 has a status of **suspended**, which indicates it's waiting for something. The **wait_type** column shows a value of **LCK_M_S**, which means the session is waiting on a shared lock. The **wait_resource** column gives some information about what resource the session is trying to lock—it's a key (as in a key of an index), in database **30**, with an **hobt_id** of **72057594048086016**.

The identifier **hobt_id** stands for Heap or B-tree ID. This is the identifier for a single partition of an object, either a table, an index, or columnstore segments.

You can reference system catalog views in the database to determine which object the lock request is for. The following query will return the index that is causing this blocking situation:

```
SELECT object_name(p.object_id)AS [object_name], p.index_id,
       i.name AS index_name, partition_number
FROM sys.partitions p
INNER JOIN sys.indexes i ON i.object_id = p.object_id AND i.index_id =
p.index_id
WHERE p.hobt_id = 72057594048086016
```

This will return the following results in the **AdventureWorks** sample database:

	object_name	index_id	index_name	partition_number
1	Product	1	PK_Product_ProductID	1

The **blocking_session_id** column shows a value of 109, which means that session **109** is the session that is currently holding this resource and therefore blocking session **99**. Interestingly, session **99** has a status of **sleeping**, which means it is not currently executing a query, but **open_transaction_count** is **1**, which means it started a transaction but hasn't committed or rolled back the transaction. This is what is sometimes referred to as an orphaned session; it can happen when an application generates an unhandled exception and the transaction doesn't get cleaned up. In this case, there's not much we can do to resolve the blocking situation naturally, so we typically need to kill the orphaned session (session **109**), which should allow the blocked session (session **99**) to proceed.

There are other wait types which may cause blocking, such as **PAGELATCH_EX**, which can be seen in the previous screenshot. These wait types are not user objects such as tables and indexes; they are pages that are an internal resource. You can still get more information about these resources using a new DMF in SQL Server 2019 called **sys.dm_db_page_info**. Using the **wait_resource** 26:1:157921 from the previous screenshot, we can generate the following query to determine which page this resource references: `SELECT * FROM sys.dm_db_page_info (26,1,157921,'LIMITED')`.

In this case, the blocking scenario was quite simple: one session was blocking another session. In some cases, blocking can be very complex and can form what's called a **blocking chain**. A blocking chain is hierarchical: one session blocks another session, and that session in turn blocks another session, and so forth. In this case, the session that starts the blocking chain is called the **head blocker**. This complex blocking is difficult to diagnose using a simple query such as the one we referenced here. In this case, we can use a more comprehensive query such as can be found in the Tiger Toolbox (`http://aka.ms/uspWhatsUp`), or by using a tool such as Activity Monitor in SSMS. You can read more about Activity Monitor in `Chapter 12`, *Troubleshooting Live Queries*.

You may notice in the preceding screenshot showing a blocking situation, that there are other sessions that are **suspended** but have a value of 0 for **blocking_session_id**. These sessions are waiting for a resource, but it's not considered blocking because the resource is not one that is owned by another session. These are typically system resources such as disk, memory, or CPU. In this case, **wait_type** is **WRITELOG**, which means the session is waiting to write to the transaction log.

Cached query plan issues

As we discussed earlier, in the *sys.dm_exec_query_stats* section, SQL Server maintains execution statistics for all the queries that are currently in the cache. There is a wealth of information in this DMV that we can use to troubleshoot several different query performance related issues. We will cover a few issues here, but be sure to reference the *BPCheck* script in the Tiger Toolbox (`https://aka.ms/bpcheck`) for a more comprehensive example of queries to identify these scenarios and others.

Single-use plans (query fingerprints)

In the *EXECUTE versus sp_executesql* section of *Chapter 6, Easily Identified T-SQL Anti-Patterns,* we discussed how to send ad hoc T-SQL queries to SQL Server in a way that allows for plan reuse (also see the *Plan caching and re-use* section in `Chapter 2`, *Understanding Query Processing,* for the importance of plan reuse). If we are not sure whether or not our application is successfully parameterizing queries and leveraging plan reuse, we can use the **query_hash** column in **sys.dm_exec_query_stats** (known as the query fingerprint) to identify queries that are logically equivalent, but have different entries in the cache. Queries that have the same **query_hash** but different values for the **sql_handle** column are stored as separate objects but are effectively the same query.

The following sample query can be used to identify single-use or low-use plans:

```
SELECT qs.query_hash
       , Query_Count = COUNT(DISTINCT sql_handle)
       , Executions = SUM(execution_count)
       , CPU = SUM(qs.total_worker_time)
       , Reads = SUM(qs.total_logical_reads)
       , Duration = SUM(qs.total_elapsed_time)
       , Sample_Query = MAX(st.text)
FROM sys.dm_exec_query_stats qs
       CROSS APPLY sys.dm_exec_sql_text(qs.sql_handle) st
GROUP BY qs.query_hash
HAVING COUNT(DISTINCT sql_handle) > 5 --> Can be any number, depending on
our tolerance for duplicate queries
ORDER BY Query_Count DESC
```

The results of this query are shown in the following screenshot:

	query_hash	Query_Count	Executions	CPU	Reads	Duration	Sample_Query
1	0x952BEAE65388AE04	8	22	246903	86509	285116	SELECT p.BusinessEntityID, p.FirstName, p.LastNa...

The results show a single row where **Query_Count** is **8**. This means that the cache currently contains eight different queries that have this same **query_hash** and therefore are effectively the same query.

If we look at the **Sample_Query** column, we'll find the following query:

```
SELECT p.BusinessEntityID, p.FirstName, p.LastName, e.EmailAddress
FROM Person.Person p
INNER JOIN Person.EmailAddress e ON p.BusinessEntityID = e.BusinessEntityID
WHERE PersonType = 'IN'
AND EmailPromotion = 1
```

As we can see, this query does not have any parameter markers. There are the following three different ways we can fix this:

1. Create a stored procedure and have the application call that instead
2. Parameterize the query by using **sp_executesql** or parameter objects from the database connection library
3. Turn on **Forced Parameterization**

If there's only one or two queries like this, it may be easy enough to fix them by modifying the code using either method *1* or *2*. If there are hundreds of queries that need to be parameterized, it might be worth turning on **Forced Parameterization** to temporarily correct the issue until the application can be re-written, using the following T-SQL command:

```
ALTER DATABASE CURRENT SET PARAMETERIZATION FORCED WITH NO_WAIT
```

It may also be worth to enable the **Optimize for Ad hoc Workloads** server setting to prevent plan cache bloating for workloads that contain many single use ad hoc batches, using the following T-SQL command:

```
EXEC sys.sp_configure N'optimize for ad hoc workloads', N'1'
GO
RECONFIGURE WITH OVERRIDE
GO
```

These are also useful if the application is developed by a third-party software vendor and we do not have the ability to change the code.

Finding resource intensive queries

If SQL Server is experiencing resource contention such as high CPU consumption or heavy I/O, or we simply want to find queries that are resource intensive, we can use **sys.dm_exec_query_stats** to list the top resource consuming queries that are currently in the cache. There are several different metrics available via **sys.dm_exec_query_stats**, such as CPU, logical reads, and elapsed time, which we can sort by to obtain a list of queries that consume large amounts of these resources.

The following query will list the top 10 queries by average CPU consumption in the cache:

```
SELECT st.[text], qp.query_plan, q.*
FROM
(SELECT TOP 10
       [execution_count], [total_worker_time]/[execution_count] AS
[Avg_CPU_Time],
       [total_elapsed_time]/[execution_count] AS [Avg_Duration],
       [total_logical_reads]/[execution_count] AS [Avg_Logical_Reads],
       ISNULL([Total_grant_kb]/[execution_count], -1) AS [Avg_Grant_KB],
       ISNULL([Total_used_grant_kb]/[execution_count], -1) AS
[Avg_Used_Grant_KB],
       plan_handle,sql_handle
       FROM sys.dm_exec_query_stats WITH (NOLOCK)
       ORDER BY [Avg_CPU_Time] DESC
) as q
OUTER APPLY sys.dm_exec_query_plan(q.plan_handle) AS qp
OUTER APPLY sys.dm_exec_sql_text(q.sql_handle) AS st
```

This query yields the following results:

	text	query_plan	execution_count
1	SELECT e.[BusinessEntityID], p.[Title], p.[First...	<ShowPlanXML xmlns="http://schemas.microsoft.com...	1
2	SELECT e.[BusinessEntityID], p.[Title], p.[First...	<ShowPlanXML xmlns="http://schemas.microsoft.com...	1
3	SELECT e.[BusinessEntityID], p.[Title], p.[First...	<ShowPlanXML xmlns="http://schemas.microsoft.com...	1
4	SELECT target_data FROM sys.dm_xe_session_ta...	<ShowPlanXML xmlns="http://schemas.microsoft.com...	1
5	SELECT st.[text], qp.query_plan, q.* FROM (SELECT T...	<ShowPlanXML xmlns="http://schemas.microsoft.com...	1
6	SELECT st.[text], qp.query_plan, q.* FROM (SELECT T...	<ShowPlanXML xmlns="http://schemas.microsoft.com...	1
7	(@used_memory_count_ratio float) select /* {5552be2b-...	NULL	2
8	(@ph varbinary(64))select query_plan from sys.dm_exec_...	<ShowPlanXML xmlns="http://schemas.microsoft.com...	1
9	WITH profiled_sessions as (SELECT DISTINCT sessio...	<ShowPlanXML xmlns="http://schemas.microsoft.com...	47
10	(@_msparam_0 nvarchar(4000),@_msparam_1 nvarchar...	<ShowPlanXML xmlns="http://schemas.microsoft.com...	1

Avg_CPU_Time	Avg_Duration	Avg_Logical_Reads	Avg_Grant_KB	Avg_Used_Grant_KB	plan_handle	sql_handle
247019338	332544264	4870724	115520	7056	0x060005009292E20390A2...	0x020000009292E2038A...
191279733	418772142	4870753	115520	7056	0x060005009292E2039042...	0x020000009292E2038A...
190289745	417717910	4870738	115520	7056	0x060005009292E203F048...	0x020000009292E2038A...
437101	811505	226	1200	104	0x060001008604D91CE068...	0x020000008604D91CA9...
215396	706739	70	1024	16	0x06001E00E2D5B9318069...	0x02000000E2D5B931C9...
199686	643946	56	1024	16	0x06001E00A411CC156077...	0x02000000A411CC15C5...
17927	17928	1043	1248	32	0x06000D00A0BC3739106A...	0x02000000A0BC3739D6...
13321	37580	4	0	0	0x06000100DDDAB12810B...	0x02000000DDDAB128B...
9512	37428	80	0	0	0x06000200C37C8B1110D9...	0x02000000C37C8B117D...
8054	69519	1496	1024	16	0x06001E0056CDA837E0B...	0x0200000056CDA8373E...

Notice that many of the queries in the results have only a single execution. Tuning these queries would make them faster, but if they're only executed occasionally, this may not have a large impact on the overall server performance. If we want to reduce CPU consumption on the server as a whole, we might consider changing the query to sort by **total_worker_time** rather than the calculated **Avg_CPU_Time** column. This would bring queries to the top that are both high-CPU consumers and are executed frequently.

You can use this same query to examine other aspects of server performance. If you want to find slow queries, sort by **Avg_Duration**. If you want to find I/O intensive queries, sort by **Avg_Logical_Reads** or **total_logical_reads**. If you want to find queries that use a large amount of memory, sort by **Avg_Grant_KB** or **total_grant_kb**. You can find more queries like these in the *BPCheck* script in the Tiger Toolbox (`https://aka.ms/bpcheck`), or we can experiment with our own queries using the example in this section as a starting point.

Queries with excessive memory grants

In `Chapter 4`, *Exploring Query Execution Plans,* we covered a few different topics regarding memory grants, particularly in the *Query plan properties of interest* section. It is important for SQL Server to get memory grants correct. If a query asks for more memory than it needs, other queries may be stuck waiting for a memory grant even though this memory is not actually being used. Similarly, if the query asks for less memory than it needs, it could end up spilling to disk, which will slow it down significantly. In the previous section, *Finding resource intensive queries,* we explored the different ways to sort results from **sys.dm_exec_query_stats** to surface queries that consume a large amount of resources. We can also use these columns to do more complex computations that will allow us to identify queries that have an excessive memory grant.

The following query is a modification of the example we gave in the *Finding resource intensive queries* section:

```
SELECT st.[text], qp.query_plan, q.*
FROM
(SELECT TOP 10
        [execution_count], [total_worker_time]/[execution_count] AS
[Avg_CPU_Time],
        [total_elapsed_time]/[execution_count] AS [Avg_Duration],
        [total_logical_reads]/[execution_count] AS [Avg_Logical_Reads],
        ISNULL([Total_grant_kb]/[execution_count], -1) AS [Avg_Grant_KB],
        ISNULL([Total_used_grant_kb]/[execution_count], -1) AS
[Avg_Used_Grant_KB],
        COALESCE((([Total_used_grant_kb] * 100.00)/
         NULLIF([Total_grant_kb],0)), 0) AS [Grant2Used_Ratio],
        plan_handle, sql_handle
        FROM sys.dm_exec_query_stats WITH (NOLOCK)
        WHERE total_grant_kb/execution_count > 1024
               AND execution_count > 1
        ORDER BY [Grant2Used_Ratio]
) as q
OUTER APPLY sys.dm_exec_query_plan(q.plan_handle) AS qp
OUTER APPLY sys.dm_exec_sql_text(q.sql_handle) AS st
```

In this query, we added a new column called **Grant2Used_Ratio**, which is a calculation of the percent of the memory grant that was actually used. The lower this ratio, the further off the memory grant estimate was, which means a large amount of memory is being wasted. Looking at the **WHERE** clause in the example, we can see that we are filtering out single execution queries and queries that have a very small memory grant (1 KB or less).

The following screenshot shows sample results from this query:

	text	query_plan	execution_count
1	DECLARE @xmlMessage XML DECLARE @x XML SELECT ...	<ShowPlanXML xmlns="http://schemas.microsoft.com...	30
2	SELECT DISTINCT Name FROM Production.Product WHERE ...	<ShowPlanXML xmlns="http://schemas.microsoft.com...	2
3	SELECT DISTINCT Name FROM Production.Product WHERE ...	<ShowPlanXML xmlns="http://schemas.microsoft.com...	19
4	SELECT DISTINCT Name FROM Production.Product AS p W...	<ShowPlanXML xmlns="http://schemas.microsoft.com...	13
5	SELECT DISTINCT Name FROM Production.Product WHERE ...	<ShowPlanXML xmlns="http://schemas.microsoft.com...	3
6	SELECT ProductID, AVG(UnitPrice) AS 'Average Price' FROM ...	<ShowPlanXML xmlns="http://schemas.microsoft.com...	8
7	SELECT ProductID FROM Sales.SalesOrderDetail GROUP BY...	<ShowPlanXML xmlns="http://schemas.microsoft.com...	4
8	SELECT ProductID FROM Sales.SalesOrderDetail WHERE U...	<ShowPlanXML xmlns="http://schemas.microsoft.com...	2
9	SELECT AVG(OrderQty) AS 'Average Quantity', NonDiscountS...	<ShowPlanXML xmlns="http://schemas.microsoft.com...	13
10	SELECT ProductID, SpecialOfferID, AVG(UnitPrice) AS 'Average...	<ShowPlanXML xmlns="http://schemas.microsoft.com...	16

Avg_CPU_Time	Avg_Duration	Avg_Logical_Reads	Avg_Grant_KB	Avg_Used_Grant_KB	Grant2Used_Ratio	plan_handle	sql_handle
1311	1397	0	1517744	0	0.000000000000000	0x06001A000151451C90A2C...	0x0200000000151451C51C5...
926	927	17	1056	104	9.848484848484848	0x06001A005C2E4725C0A7F...	0x020000005C2E47254813...
1024	1024	17	1056	104	9.848484848484848	0x06001A005C2E472560DF5...	0x020000005C2E47254813...
1041	13490	17	1056	104	9.848484848484848	0x06001A00163F4C0050DAA...	0x0200000163F4C00F1A1...
1051	1051	17	1056	104	9.848484848484848	0x06001A005C2E472560DF9...	0x020000005C2E47254813...
18587	22375	1266	1632	328	20.098039215686274	0x06001A009A588104E09A1...	0x020000009A588104D026...
76778	101549	1266	1616	328	20.297029702970297	0x06001A00910D5C12909C1...	0x0200000910D5C12355...
79075	79743	1266	1616	328	20.297029702970297	0x06001A00863A5632B0516...	0x0200000863A5632A3D2...
109090	169823	1266	3792	920	24.261603375527426	0x06001A007E8D690830B6E...	0x020000007E8D6908C614...
272490	490791	1266	2704	688	25.443786982248520	0x06001A00032AC613B0AEE...	0x0200000032AC613EF1A...

The top query in this result has a **Grant2Used_Ratio** of **0**, which is the worst it can possibly be. In this case, the query requested 1.5 GB of memory and didn't use any of it! This is a query that we would want to tune as soon as possible. The rest of the queries in the list have low percentages, but their **Avg_Grant_KB** values are not very high, so they may not be as big of a problem as the first query. You can experiment with different predicates in the **WHERE** clause and different sorting columns to find different issues with memory grants using the sample query in this section as a starting point.

Mining XML query plans

As we mentioned in the *sys.dm_exec_query_plan* section, query execution plans are stored as XML, and the **sys.dm_exec_query_plan** DMV returns them as a proper **XML** datatype. This allows us to leverage **XML Path Language** (**XPath**) to generate queries that can search for elements and attributes within the query execution plans. Using these XPath queries, or **XQueries**, we can search for common query performance issues across all the query execution plans in the cache, rather than having to examine each graphical plan individually. In this section, we will cover a few common scenarios, but be sure to reference the *Mining-PlanCache* section of the TIGER toolbox (`https://aka.ms/tigertoolbox`) for more examples.

The queries shown in this section can be used individually to search for specific issues, but running the entire *BP Check* script from the TIGER toolbox (`https://aka.ms/bpcheck`) will gather all this information and more in a single result set.

Plans with missing indexes

In the *Query plan properties of interest* section of `Chapter 4`, *Exploring Query Execution Plans,* we discussed the **MissingIndexes** property. If this property exists in a query execution plan, it means that there is at least one index that SQL Server could have benefited from that does not exist.

The following query uses DMVs to list all the missing index suggestions on the server:

```
SELECT DB_NAME(d.database_id) as [database_name],
              OBJECT_NAME(d.object_id, d.database_id)ASobject_name,
              total_cost_savings =
                ROUND(s.avg_total_user_cost * s.avg_user_impact
*(s.user_seeks + s.user_scans),0)/100,
              s.avg_total_user_cost, s.avg_user_impact, s.user_seeks,
s.user_scans,
              d.equality_columns, d.inequality_columns, d.included_columns
FROM sys.dm_db_missing_index_groups g
INNER JOIN sys.dm_db_missing_index_group_stats s on s.group_handle =
g.index_group_handle
INNER JOIN sys.dm_db_missing_index_details d on d.index_handle =
g.index_handle
ORDER BY total_cost_savings DESC
```

Sample results for this query can be seen in the following screenshot:

	database_name	object_name	total_cost_savings	avg_total_user_cost	avg_user_impact
1	AdventureWorks2016CTP3	SalesOrderDetailBulk	23434.52	67.2765925805513	78.63
2	AdventureWorks2016_EXT	SalesOrderDetail	297.72	3.59327503977793	36.5
3	AdventureWorks2016_EXT	SalesOrderDetail	180.29	1.69672937411795	57.75
4	AdventureWorks2016	Person	157.11	3.10548731539778	90.34
5	AdventureWorks2016_EXT	SalesOrderDetail	100.23	1.17768299416184	88.65
6	AdventureWorks2016_EXT	SalesOrderDetail	98.06	1.21672150262773	83.95
7	AdventureWorks2016_EXT	SalesOrderDetail	98.06	1.32619431562189	77.02
8	AdventureWorks2016_EXT	SalesOrderDetail	86.42	1.83201991110446	53
9	AdventureWorks2016	Person	5.6	2.85557850074074	98.05
10	AdventureWorks2016	Person	5.58	2.88154210074074	96.86

user_seeks	user_scans	equality_columns	inequality_columns	included_columns
443	0	NULL	[ProductID]	[OrderQty], [UnitPrice], [UnitPriceDiscount]
227	0	[ProductID]	NULL	[OrderQty], [UnitPrice], [UnitPriceDiscount]
184	0	NULL	[UnitPrice]	[ProductID], [LineTotal]
56	0	[PersonType], [EmailPromotion]	NULL	[FirstName], [LastName]
96	0	NULL	[CarrierTrackingNumber]	NULL
96	0	NULL	[OrderQty]	[ProductID], [UnitPrice]
96	0	NULL	[UnitPrice]	[OrderQty], [ProductID]
89	0	NULL	[UnitPrice]	[OrderQty], [ProductID], [LineTotal]
2	0	[PersonType]	NULL	[FirstName], [LastName]
2	0	NULL	[PersonType]	[FirstName], [LastName]

This is useful for getting an overall idea of all the missing index suggestions across all the queries on the server, but on a busy server with many applications and databases, this may be overwhelming. Also, while this gives us the ability to sort the index suggestions by potential impact, there is no way to determine which queries may benefit from these indexes. Also, in some cases, the index suggestion may not be practical. Looking at the query execution plan that generated the missing index suggestion may reveal an even better index that would improve the query performance even more, and perhaps be usable by multiple queries.

Use the *BP Check* script from the TIGER toolbox (`https://aka.ms/bpcheck`) to know about missing indexes that may be required in a database. *BP Check* can optionally generate the index creation scripts for the missing indexes that are expected to have a very high impact using a scoring method. *BP Check* can warn if two missing indexes would be redundant if created, for example, if one suggested index is already a subset of another suggested index.

The following query can be used to look for any query execution plans that have the **MissingIndex** property:

```
WITH
XMLNAMESPACES(DEFAULT'http://schemas.microsoft.com/sqlserver/2004/07/showpl
an'),
       PlanMissingIndexes AS (SELECT query_plan, cp.usecounts,
cp.refcounts, cp.plan_handle
                              FROM sys.dm_exec_cached_plans cp WITH (NOLOCK)
                              CROSS APPLY
sys.dm_exec_query_plan(cp.plan_handle) tp
                              WHERE cp.cacheobjtype ='Compiled Plan'
                                     AND
tp.query_plan.exist('//MissingIndex')=1
                               )
SELECT c1.value('(//MissingIndex/@Database)[1]', 'sysname') AS
database_name,
       c1.value('(//MissingIndex/@Schema)[1]', 'sysname') AS [schema_name],
       c1.value('(//MissingIndex/@Table)[1]', 'sysname') AS [table_name],
       c1.value('@StatementText', 'VARCHAR(4000)') AS sql_text,
       c1.value('@StatementId', 'int') AS StatementId,
       pmi.usecounts,
       pmi.refcounts,
       c1.value('(//MissingIndexGroup/@Impact)[1]', 'FLOAT') AS impact,
       REPLACE(c1.query('for $group in //ColumnGroup for $column in
$group/Column where $group/@Usage="EQUALITY" return
string($column/@Name)').value('.', 'varchar(max)'),'] [', '],[') AS
equality_columns,
       REPLACE(c1.query('for $group in //ColumnGroup for $column in
$group/Column where $group/@Usage="INEQUALITY" return
string($column/@Name)').value('.', 'varchar(max)'),'] [', '],[') AS
inequality_columns,
       REPLACE(c1.query('for $group in //ColumnGroup for $column in
$group/Column where $group/@Usage="INCLUDE" return
string($column/@Name)').value('.', 'varchar(max)'),'] [', '],[') AS
include_columns,
       pmi.query_plan,
       pmi.plan_handle
FROM PlanMissingIndexes pmi
CROSS APPLY pmi.query_plan.nodes('//StmtSimple') AS q1(c1)
WHERE pmi.usecounts > 1
ORDER BY c1.value('(//MissingIndexGroup/@Impact)[1]', 'FLOAT') DESC
OPTION(RECOMPILE,MAXDOP 1);
```

The following screenshot shows sample results for this query:

	database_name	schema_name	table_name	sql_text	StatementId	usecounts	refcounts	impact
1	[AdventureWorks2016]	[Person]	[Person]	SELECT BusinessEntityID, FirstName, LastN...	1	4	2	96.8582
2	[AdventureWorks2016]	[Person]	[Person]	; SELECT BusinessEntityID, FirstName, Las...	2	4	2	96.8582

equality_columns	inequality_columns	include_columns	query_plan	plan_handle
[PersonType]	[PersonType]	[FirstName],[LastName],[FirstName],[LastName]	<ShowPlanXML xmlns="http://schemas.microsoft.com...	0x06001E000DA44507203D4...
[PersonType]	[PersonType]	[FirstName],[LastName],[FirstName],[LastName]	<ShowPlanXML xmlns="http://schemas.microsoft.com...	0x06001E000DA44507203D4...

As the results show, this query allows us to gather the same information that the DMVs provide, but including the query execution plan so that further analysis can be done before we create any of the indexes suggested.

Executing XQueries can be very expensive, particularly on a busy server that has a very large procedure cache. Avoid running this type of query directly on a production server. If you would like to analyze a production workload, it is best to dump the XML query plans into a table on the production server, and then back up or detach the database and restore or attach it on a test server for analysis.

Plans with warnings

In the *Query plan properties of interest* section of `Chapter 4`, *Exploring Query Execution Plans,* we covered warnings that can occur in a query execution plan at either the plan level or the operator level. We can leverage XQueries to identify plans with warnings as well.

The following query will find query execution plans that have a plan-level warning:

```
WITH
XMLNAMESPACES(DEFAULT'http://schemas.microsoft.com/sqlserver/2004/07/showpl
an'),
       WarningSearch AS (SELECT qp.query_plan, cp.usecounts, cp.objtype,
                            wn.query('.') AS StmtSimple, cp.plan_handle
                        FROM sys.dm_exec_cached_plans cp WITH (NOLOCK)
                        CROSS APPLY
sys.dm_exec_query_plan(cp.plan_handle) qp
                        CROSS APPLY qp.query_plan.nodes('//StmtSimple')
AS p(wn)
                        WHERE wn.exist('//Warnings') = 1
                             AND wn.exist('@QueryHash') = 1
                       )
SELECT StmtSimple.value('StmtSimple[1]/@StatementText', 'VARCHAR(4000)') AS
sql_text,
       StmtSimple.value('StmtSimple[1]/@StatementId', 'int') AS
```

```
StatementId,
        CASE WHEN c2.exist('@UnmatchedIndexes[. = "1"]') = 1
              THEN 'UnmatchedIndexes'
             WHEN (c4.exist('@ConvertIssue[. = "Cardinality Estimate"]') = 1
                   OR c4.exist('@ConvertIssue[. = "Seek Plan"]')= 1)
              THEN'ConvertIssue_'+ c4.value('@ConvertIssue','sysname')
         END AS warning,
        ws.objtype,
        ws.usecounts,
        ws.query_plan,
        ws.plan_handle
FROM WarningSearch ws
CROSS APPLY StmtSimple.nodes('//QueryPlan') AS q1(c1)
CROSS APPLY c1.nodes('./Warnings') AS q2(c2)
CROSS APPLY c1.nodes('./RelOp') AS q3(c3)
OUTER APPLY c2.nodes('./PlanAffectingConvert') AS q4(c4)
OPTION(RECOMPILE, MAXDOP 1);
```

The following screenshot shows sample results for this query:

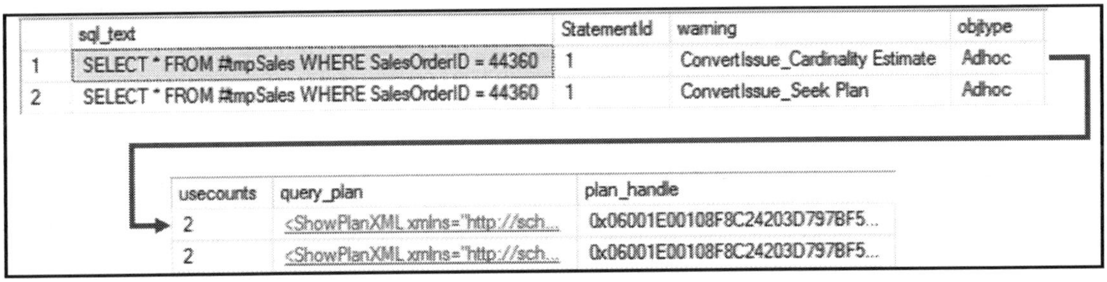

	sql_text	StatementId	warning	objtype
1	SELECT * FROM #tmpSales WHERE SalesOrderID = 44360	1	ConvertIssue_Cardinality Estimate	Adhoc
2	SELECT * FROM #tmpSales WHERE SalesOrderID = 44360	1	ConvertIssue_Seek Plan	Adhoc

usecounts	query_plan	plan_handle
2	<ShowPlanXML xmlns="http://sch...	0x06001E00108F8C24203D797BF5...
2	<ShowPlanXML xmlns="http://sch...	0x06001E00108F8C24203D797BF5...

We can also use a similar query to find warnings at the operator level. The following query will find query execution plans that have an operator-level warning:

```
WITH
XMLNAMESPACES(DEFAULT'http://schemas.microsoft.com/sqlserver/2004/07/showpl
an'),
       WarningSearch AS (SELECT qp.query_plan, cp.usecounts, cp.objtype,
                            wn.query('.') AS StmtSimple, cp.plan_handle
                            FROM sys.dm_exec_cached_plans cp WITH (NOLOCK)
                            CROSS APPLY
sys.dm_exec_query_plan(cp.plan_handle) qp
                            CROSS APPLY qp.query_plan.nodes('//StmtSimple')
AS p(wn)
                            WHERE wn.exist('//Warnings') = 1
                                 AND wn.exist('@QueryHash') = 1
                          )
SELECT StmtSimple.value('StmtSimple[1]/@StatementText', 'VARCHAR(4000)') AS
```

```
sql_text,
       StmtSimple.value('StmtSimple[1]/@StatementId', 'int') AS
StatementId,
       c1.value('@PhysicalOp','sysname') AS physical_op,
       c1.value('@LogicalOp','sysname') AS logical_op,
       CASE WHEN c2.exist('@NoJoinPredicate[. = "1"]') = 1
                THEN 'NoJoinPredicate'
            WHEN c3.exist('@Database') = 1
                THEN'ColumnsWithNoStatistics'
       END AS warning,
       ws.objtype,
       ws.usecounts,
       ws.query_plan,
       ws.plan_handle
FROM WarningSearch ws
CROSS APPLY StmtSimple.nodes('//RelOp') AS q1(c1)
CROSS APPLY c1.nodes('./Warnings') AS q2(c2)
OUTER APPLY c2.nodes('./ColumnsWithNoStatistics/ColumnReference') AS q3(c3)
OPTION(RECOMPILE, MAXDOP 1);
```

The following screenshot shows sample results for this query:

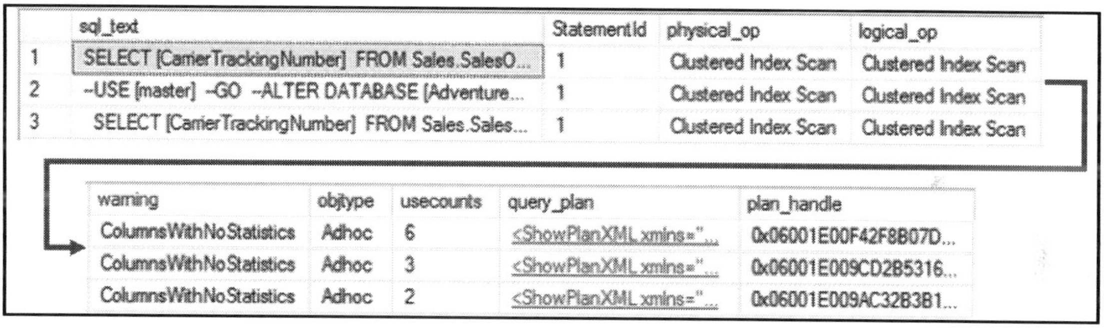

	sql_text	StatementId	physical_op	logical_op
1	SELECT [CarrierTrackingNumber] FROM Sales.SalesO...	1	Clustered Index Scan	Clustered Index Scan
2	--USE [master] --GO --ALTER DATABASE [Adventure...	1	Clustered Index Scan	Clustered Index Scan
3	SELECT [CarrierTrackingNumber] FROM Sales.Sales...	1	Clustered Index Scan	Clustered Index Scan

warning	objtype	usecounts	query_plan	plan_handle
ColumnsWithNoStatistics	Adhoc	6	<ShowPlanXML xmlns="...	0x06001E00F42F8B07D...
ColumnsWithNoStatistics	Adhoc	3	<ShowPlanXML xmlns="...	0x06001E009CD2B5316...
ColumnsWithNoStatistics	Adhoc	2	<ShowPlanXML xmlns="...	0x06001E009AC32B3B1...

Use these queries to start experimenting with finding different warnings in your query plans. You can change the predicates in these queries to look for any of the warnings outlined in `Chapter 4`, *Exploring Query Execution Plans*.

Plans with implicit conversions

In the previous section, *Plans with warnings*, we looked at an XQuery that will find plans that have conversion warnings at the plan level. If we want to find query execution plans that have implicit conversions anywhere in the plan, whether or not they generate a **PlanAffectingConvert** warning, we can use an XQuery that looks specifically for implicit conversions.

The following query will find query execution plans that have implicit conversions in any of the operators within the plan:

```
WITH
XMLNAMESPACES(DEFAULT'http://schemas.microsoft.com/sqlserver/2004/07/showpl
an'),
       Convertsearch AS (SELECT qp.query_plan, cp.usecounts, cp.objtype,
                                cp.plan_handle, cs.query('.') AS StmtSimple
                         FROM sys.dm_exec_cached_plans cp WITH (NOLOCK)
                         CROSS APPLY
sys.dm_exec_query_plan(cp.plan_handle) qp
                         CROSS APPLY qp.query_plan.nodes('//StmtSimple')
AS p(cs)
                         WHERE cp.cacheobjtype ='Compiled Plan'
                            AND cs.exist('@QueryHash') = 1
                            AND
cs.exist('.//ScalarOperator[contains(@ScalarString,
                                            CONVERT_IMPLICIT")]') = 1
                            AND cs.exist('.[contains(@StatementText,
"Convertsearch")]') = 0
                       )
SELECT c2.value('@StatementText', 'VARCHAR(4000)') AS sql_text,
       c2.value('@StatementId', 'int') AS StatementId,
       c3.value('@ScalarString[1]','VARCHAR(4000)') AS expression,
       ss.usecounts,
       ss.query_plan,
       ss.plan_handle
FROM Convertsearch ss
CROSS APPLY query_plan.nodes('//StmtSimple') AS q2(c2)
CROSS APPLY c2.nodes('.//ScalarOperator[contains(@ScalarString,
"CONVERT_IMPLICIT")]') AS q3(c3)
OPTION(RECOMPILE, MAXDOP 1);
```

The following screenshot shows sample results for this query:

	sql_text	StatementId	expression
1	BEGIN DELETE TOP(@batch_size) sys.syscom...	20	CONVERT_IMPLICIT(bigint,[@batch_size],0)
2	BEGIN DELETE TOP(@batch_size) sys.syscom...	20	CONVERT_IMPLICIT(bigint,[@batch_size],0)
3	BEGIN DELETE TOP(@batch_size) sys.syscom...	20	CONVERT_IMPLICIT(bigint,[@batch_size],0)
4	BEGIN DELETE TOP(@batch_size) sys.syscom...	20	CONVERT_IMPLICIT(bigint,[@batch_size],0)
5	BEGIN DELETE TOP(@batch_size) sys.syscom...	20	CONVERT_IMPLICIT(bigint,[@batch_size],0)

usecounts	query_plan	plan_handle
1	<ShowPlanXML xmlns="htt...	0x0500FF7F99F756F0B0...
1	<ShowPlanXML xmlns="htt...	0x0500FF7F99F756F0A0...
1	<ShowPlanXML xmlns="htt...	0x0500FF7F99F756F010...
1	<ShowPlanXML xmlns="htt...	0x0500FF7F99F756F0B0...
1	<ShowPlanXML xmlns="htt...	0x0500FF7F99F756F050...

Leveraging this query will help us identify queries that are comparing two values with different data types, either because of incorrect parameter types, or mismatched data types in the database schema itself.

Plans with lookups

One of the quickest ways to tune a query is to add a covering index. As we discussed in `Chapter 4`, *Exploring Query Execution Plans*, the presence of a lookup in a query execution plan indicates that a query is not covered. We can leverage this same XQuery method to find query execution plans that contain a lookup anywhere in the plan.

The following query will find query execution plans that have a lookup:

```
WITH
XMLNAMESPACES(DEFAULT'http://schemas.microsoft.com/sqlserver/2004/07/showpl
an'),
        Lookupsearch AS (SELECT qp.query_plan, cp.usecounts, ls.query('.')
AS StmtSimple, cp.plan_handle
                        FROM sys.dm_exec_cached_plans cp (NOLOCK)
                        CROSS APPLY sys.dm_exec_query_plan(cp.plan_handle) qp
                        CROSS APPLY qp.query_plan.nodes('//StmtSimple') AS
p(ls)
                        WHERE cp.cacheobjtype = 'Compiled Plan'
                                AND ls.exist('//IndexScan[@Lookup = "1"]') = 1
                                AND ls.exist('@QueryHash') = 1
```

```
                        )
SELECT StmtSimple.value('StmtSimple[1]/@StatementText', 'VARCHAR(4000)') AS
sql_text,
       StmtSimple.value('StmtSimple[1]/@StatementId', 'int') AS
StatementId,
       c1.value('@NodeId','int') AS node_id,
       c2.value('@Database','sysname') AS database_name,
       c2.value('@Schema','sysname') AS [schema_name],
       c2.value('@Table','sysname') AS table_name,
       'Lookup - '+ c1.value('@PhysicalOp','sysname')AS physical_operator,
       c2.value('@Index','sysname') AS index_name,
       c3.value('@ScalarString','VARCHAR(4000)') AS predicate,
       ls.usecounts,
       ls.query_plan,
       ls.plan_handle
FROM Lookupsearch ls
CROSS APPLY query_plan.nodes('//RelOp') AS q1(c1)
CROSS APPLY c1.nodes('./IndexScan/Object') AS q2(c2)
OUTER APPLY c1.nodes('./IndexScan//ScalarOperator[1]') AS q3(c3)
-- Below attribute is present either in Index Seeks or RID Lookups so it
can reveal a Lookup is executed
WHERE c1.exist('./IndexScan[@Lookup = "1"]') = 1
       AND c2.value('@Schema','sysname') <> '[sys]'
OPTION(RECOMPILE, MAXDOP 1);
```

The following screenshot shows sample results from this query:

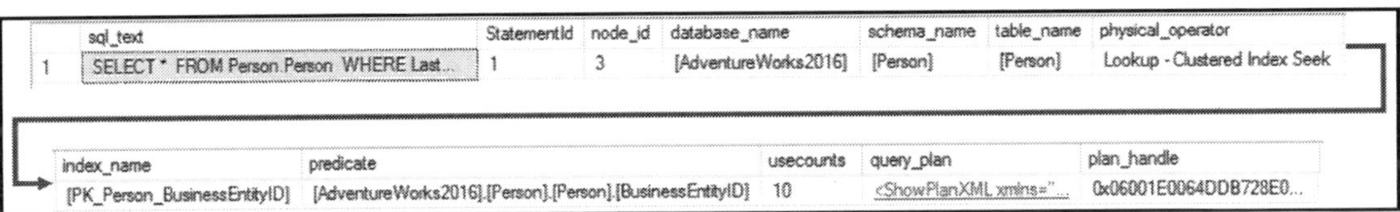

	sql_text	StatementId	node_id	database_name	schema_name	table_name	physical_operator
1	SELECT * FROM Person.Person WHERE Last...	1	3	[AdventureWorks2016]	[Person]	[Person]	Lookup - Clustered Index Seek

index_name	predicate	usecounts	query_plan	plan_handle
[PK_Person_BusinessEntityID]	[AdventureWorks2016].[Person].[Person].[BusinessEntityID]	10	<ShowPlanXML xmlns="...	0x06001E0064DDB728E0...

While we can't add covering indexes to all queries, this sample XQuery can help us identify areas where our index strategy could be improved, and hopefully reveal targeted indexes that may benefit multiple queries.

Summary

While the examples in this chapter are only a small sample, hopefully, at this point, we can see how DMVs and DMFs can be a powerful troubleshooting tool when it comes to diagnosing query performance issues. They are lightweight, easy to use, and provide a breadth of information that is useful for zeroing in on the performance issues that were covered in `Chapter 6`, *Easily Identified T-SQL Anti-Patterns*, and `Chapter 7`, *Discovering T-SQL Anti-Patterns in Depth*.

While DMVs are great for point in time and cumulative analysis, there are some issues that can only be diagnosed by catching queries and related data in real time. This is where tracing with **Extended Events (XEvents)** is useful.

In the next chapter, we will introduce XEvents and discuss how to set up the new XEvent Profiler trace, which can capture all the queries that are executed against a server in real time.

9
Building XEvent Profiler Traces

In `Chapter 8`, *Building Diagnostic Queries Using DMVs and DMFs,* we learned how to gain insight into query performance using the built-in system views. This information is valuable, but because these views mostly represent the current point in time, they are not always sufficient to answer every question we have about the performance of our queries. In this chapter, we will introduce **Extended Events** (**XEvents**), the lightweight infrastructure that exposes relevant just-in-time information from every component of SQL Server, focusing on those related to T-SQL execution. We will explore real-world examples of how to use these XEvents to troubleshoot different poor-performance scenarios; leverage collection and analysis tools such as the XEvent Profiler, SQL Diag; use **Replay Markup Language** (**RML**) for event analysis; and drop a note on the infamously deprecated SQL Server profiler.

In this chapter, we will cover the following topics:

- Introducing XEvents
- SQL Server Profiler—deprecated but not forgotten
- Getting up and running with the XEvent profiler
- Remote collection with PSSDiag and SQLDiag
- Analyzing traces with RML utilities

Introducing Extended Events

When we connect to SQL Server and run a query, it fires a series of events—a user logs in, a connection is established, a query begins executing, a plan is found in the cache, a plan is recompiled, a query completes execution—these are just a few examples. Virtually everything that happens within the database engine is an event.

While **Dynamic Management Views (DMVs)** are powerful tools, they don't always give a complete picture of what is going on within the engine. Most DMVs provide a snapshot in time, a picture of what is going on the moment they are queried. They may have some history that goes back to the last time the server was restarted, but, even then, the information is typically cumulative, and they can't tell us what the server looked like a few minutes before, and they can't tell us the events that led up to the current state. This is where **tracing** comes in. Tracing allows us to capture all the occurrences of one or more events on the server over a period of time, and store that data in a target location, typically a file on disk, for later analysis.

The SQL Server XEvents engine provides a mechanism to consume events, collect related data, and direct them to a target for later analysis. The events themselves are defined at various points in the database engine code that are significant for some reason.

Using XEvents to trace these significant database events can give you a much greater level of detail than DMVs, but the cost is higher to the server. While the XEvents engine is relatively lightweight compared to other tracing mechanisms such as SQL Trace, it still generates overhead on the server and should only be used when this level of detail is required.

There are a few terms that are important to understand before we begin creating XEvent traces:

- A **package** is a container for a group of XEvents objects. There are three packages in SQL Server—**package0** (the default package), **sqlserver**, **sqlos**.
- An **event** is a point of interest in the SQL Server database engine code. When an event fires, it means that the code in question was reached, and any information that is relevant to that event is captured. There are hundreds of events in SQL Server, far too many to list here, but we will cover some T-SQL performance-related events in this chapter and a few of the remaining chapters in the book.
- A **channel** is a categorization of events by intended audience. There are four channels in SQL Server:
    - **Admin**: General events that are targeted to administrators such as **cpu_threshold_exceeded** and **xml_deadlock_report**.
    - **Operational**: Events used to diagnose a problem such as **blocked_process_report** and **server_memory_change**.
    - **Analytic**: Events that are used in performance investigations such as **sql_batch_completed** and **rpc_completed**.

    - **Debug**: Events that are used for deep troubleshooting and debugging such as **inaccurate_cardinality_estimate**. These events are generally reserved for use when working with Microsoft Support. They can be especially expensive to consume and should be used with caution.
- A **category** (also known as a **keyword**) is a finer grain categorization used to identify events that pertain to a specific component or area of the database engine.
- A **target** is where the event output is directed. SQL Server supports the following six targets:
    - **Event file**: This is a file on disk. This is the most common, and the one we will use most often when creating XEvent traces.
    - **Ring buffer**: This is a circular in-memory buffer, meaning when the buffer is full, the oldest events are overwritten.
    - **Event counter**: This target simply counts the occurrences of an event, rather than capturing the data for the event.
    - **Histogram**: This is like the event counter target in that it counts occurrences, but the histogram target allows us to sort events into buckets based on data available in the event. This is useful for something such as the **wait_info** event where we might want to count the number of waits by the **wait_type** event field.
    - **Event pairing**: This target allows us to pair events such as login and logout so that we can identify events that don't occur as a matched set.
    - **Event Tracing for Windows (ETW)**: ETW is a common framework that is used to correlate traces across applications running on Windows, or with the operating system itself.
- An **action** is a response to an event firing. Typically, this is additional data that we want to collect that's not a part of the event data itself.
- A **session** is the definition of the XEvent collection that we want to perform. In a session, we define the events where we want to collect the target, the actions, and any predicates we might want to apply to filter the events that are captured.

Now that we've got our terms defined, let's look at an example of how we can use XEvents to analyze database activity. Assume that a group within our company is about to release a new application that it wants us to validate. The developers have used some sort of database code generator, so there are no stored procedures in the database for us to review. In order to get an idea of the queries that the application generates and the performance of those queries, we want to trace all the query activity against the server while the application is being tested in pre-production.

For this example, we'll use SSMS to create and analyze an XEvent session. To get started, expand the **Extended Events** section under the **Management** folder in **Object Explorer**.

Right-click on **Sessions** and choose **New Session...** as shown in the following screenshot:

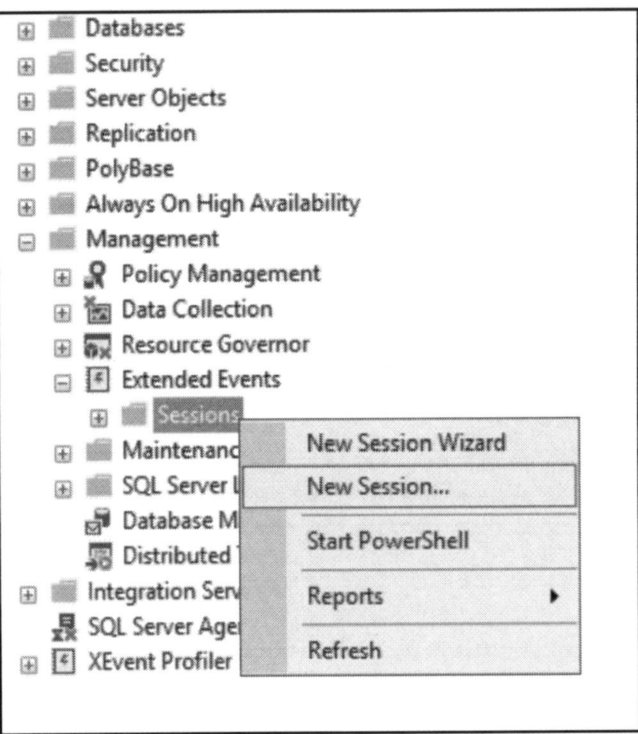

In the **New Session** window, type in a name for our session, as in the following screenshot:

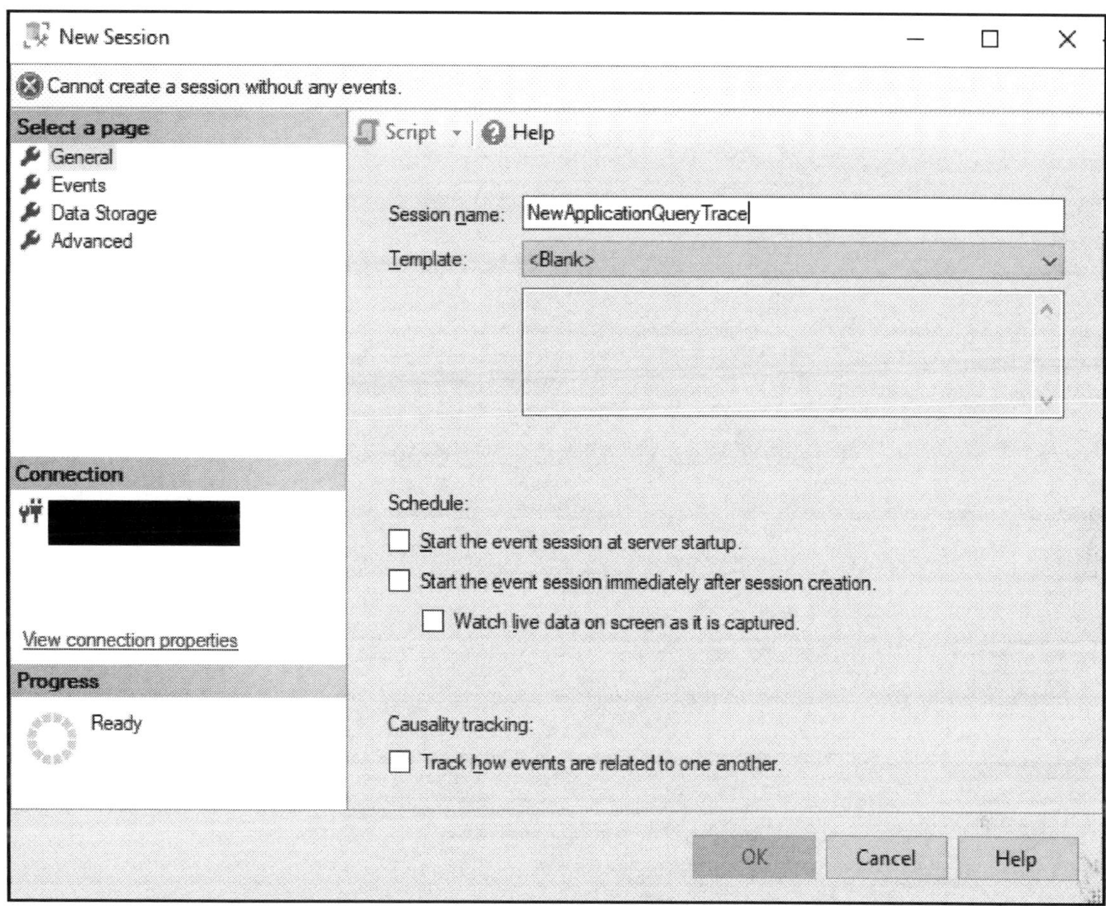

Click on the **Events** page to add events, and then optionally add actions and filter predicates.

Since we want to capture all the queries that are executing against the server, we'll need two events at a minimum: **rpc_completed** and **sql_batch_completed**. **RPC** stands for **Remote Procedure Call**. When an application executes a stored procedure using a procedure object, it comes through as an RPC. This is also the event we would see if we ran a query via **sp_executesql**, or if we built a parameterized query from client code using a database connectivity library such as **Open Database Connectivity** (**ODBC**). If we send an ad hoc query to the server using **EXECUTE**, or by sending a text query string, the query will be an SQL batch rather than an RPC. There are events for both starting and completing a batch or an RPC, but if all we want to know is the queries that are executing and the performance metrics for those queries, the completed events are enough.

In the following screenshot, we are typing **completed** into the search box to find the desired events:

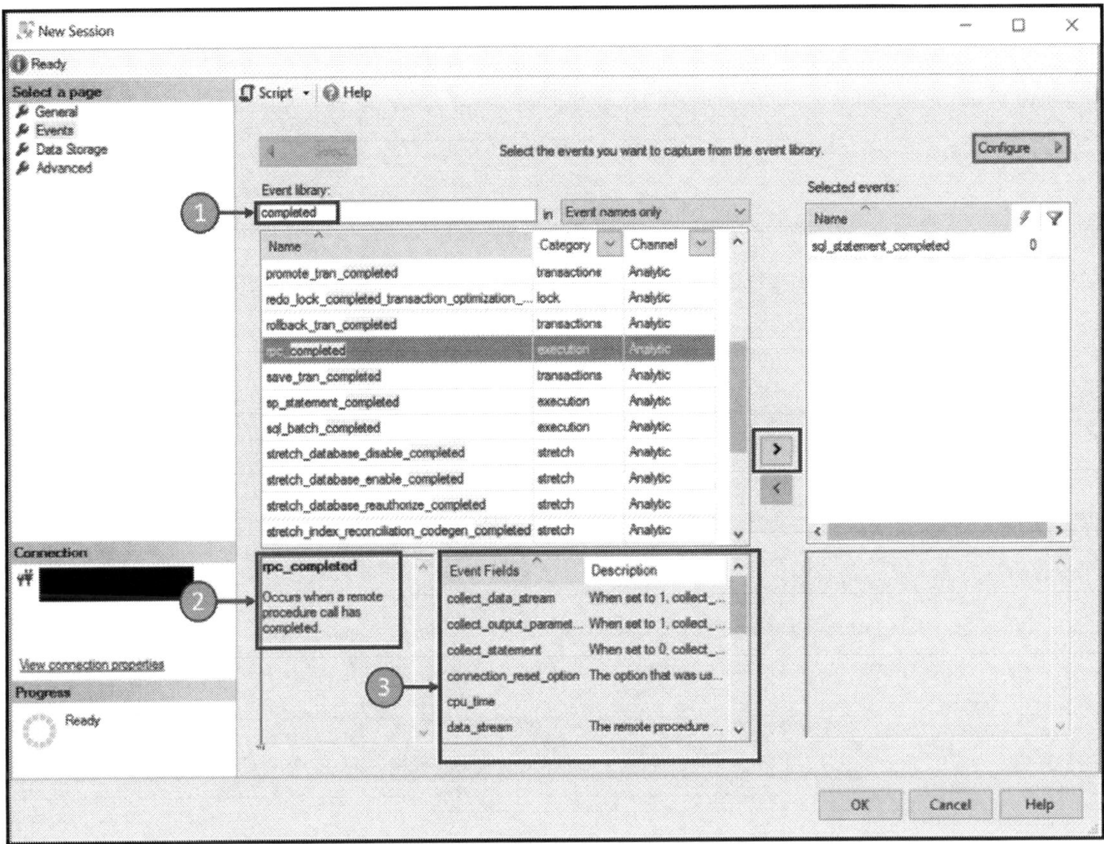

In this screenshot, we can see the following:

1. The search box used to locate events that contain the search term in the name—this is where we typed `completed`
2. The name and description of the selected event
3. The **Event Fields** that the selected event collects by default, including a description of each field

After we select the events we want, we then click the right arrow to add them to the session. Once we have added all the events, we can click the **Configure** button to add any actions and filter predicates that we might want.

In the event configuration window, we can add any additional fields that we'd like to collect (Actions) when the event fires. Since we are not familiar with the applications working on the server, it might be worthwhile to gather **client_app_name** so we can see the various applications that are running queries against the server.

Each event is configured separately, so if we want to collect the same actions for all the events, we need to select all the events in the **Selected Events** box shown in the following screenshot:

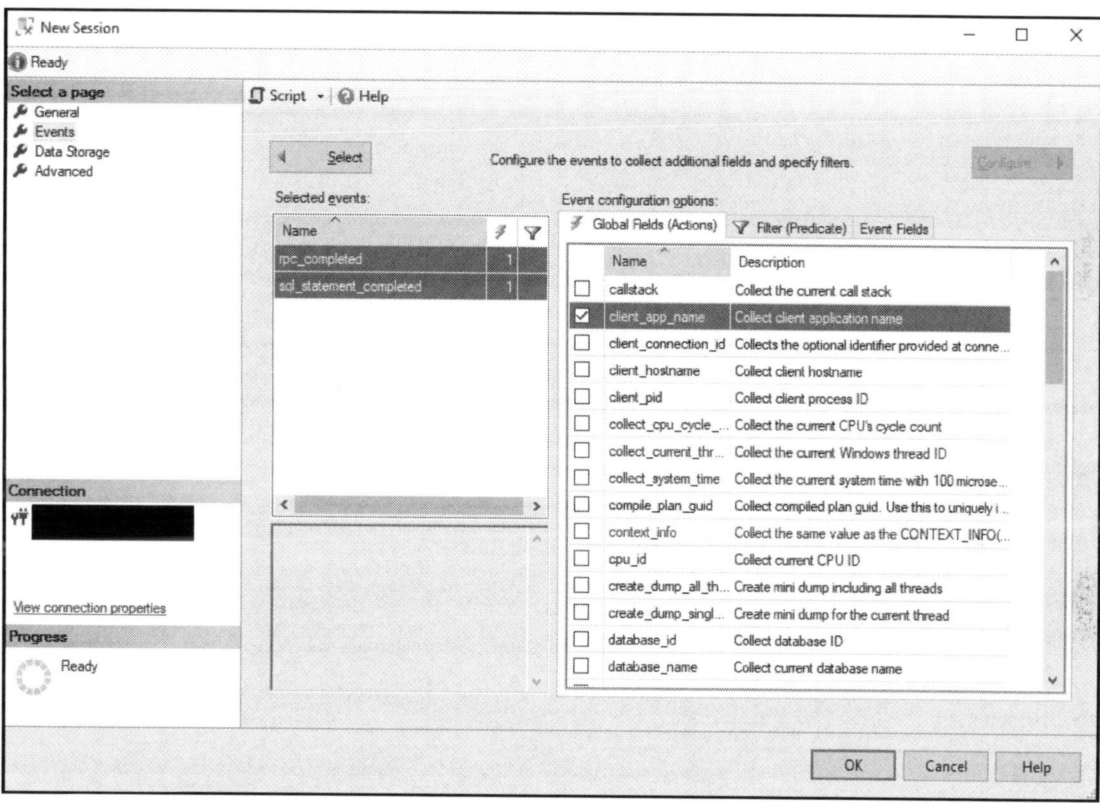

In most cases, the **Event Fields** that are part of the event are enough to provide the data needed for analysis. Try to avoid adding a large number of **Actions** if possible. Gathering this data is extra work that must be done for each event whenever it fires, so adding too many actions can cause extra overhead on the server.

Once we have added the desired actions, click on the **Filter (Predicate)** tab to add any predicates. This allows us to filter the events that will be passed to the target. While filtering out events can keep the size of our target down, it does not reduce the overhead of the session as each event must be processed to apply the filter. In this case, we're only interested in the queries that are coming from the application, not system sessions. To keep system sessions out of our trace, we can add a filter to both events to capture only events where `is_system = 0`.

Again, the events are configured separately, so we can apply different filters to each event. In this case, we want the same filter for both so we will select both events, as in the following screenshot:

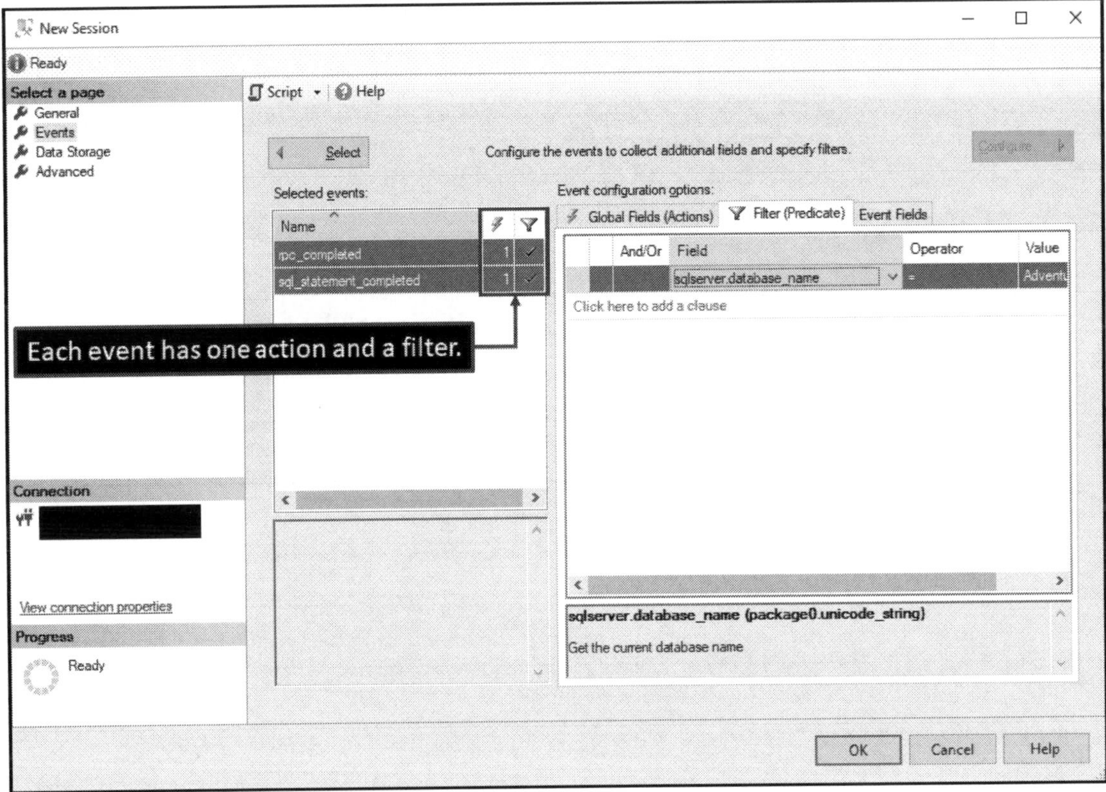

As we can see from the preceding screenshot, we've added our filter to both events. The lightning bolt column indicates actions and the funnel column indicates filters. Each event has one action configured and a filter applied.

At this point, we could click on **OK** and start the session, but then the only way to view the events would be to watch the session live in real time. This wouldn't allow us to do much analysis on the data, so we want to add a target to the session before we create it. We will add a file target so that we can save the event data and then analyze it on another server later. To do this, click on the **Data Storage** page in the **Select a page** window, then click on **Click here to add a target**, and finally choose **event_file** from the **Type** drop-down list under **Targets**. Once we choose **event_file**, several configurable properties appear below the **Targets** window. We can choose the file name and location, maximum size, whether a new file should be created when the file is full (file rollover) and the maximum number of files. In this case we will keep the default values and the files will be created in the default log directory for SQL Server, for example, `C:\Program Files\Microsoft SQL Server\MSSQL14.SQL2017\MSSQL\Log`. This is shown in the following screenshot:

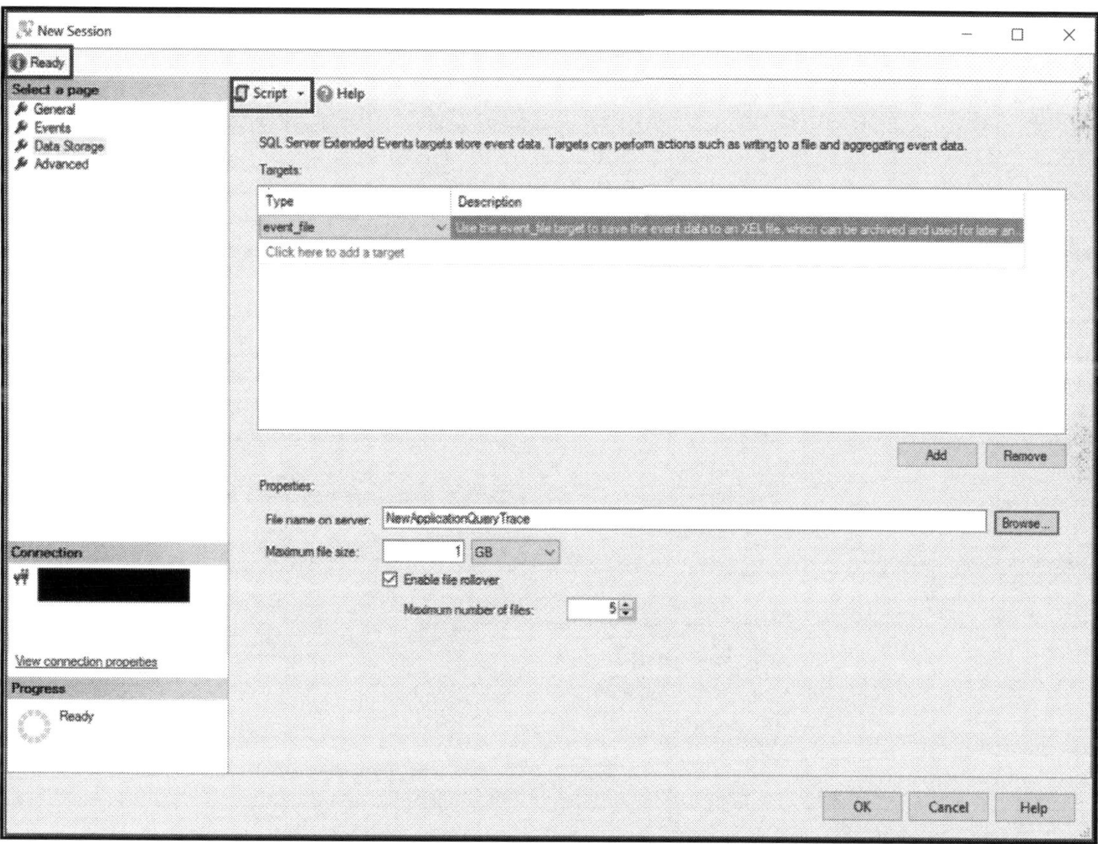

As we can see in the previous screenshot, all the required elements have been configured so the session is marked as **Ready** and will be created once we click on **OK.** Before we do that, it's worth clicking the **Script** button so we can see what the equivalent T-SQL is to create this session. Using T-SQL to configure a session is another option that allows us to save the definition of the session for use on other servers.

The following code block shows the T-SQL script that will create this event session:

```
CREATE EVENT SESSION [NewApplicationQueryTrace] ON SERVER
ADD EVENT sqlserver.rpc_completed(
    ACTION(sqlserver.client_app_name)
    WHERE ([sqlserver].[is_system]=(0))),
ADD EVENT sqlserver.sql_batch_completed(
    ACTION(sqlserver.client_app_name)
    WHERE ([sqlserver].[is_system]=(0)))
ADD TARGET package0.event_file(SET filename=N'NewApplicationQueryTrace')
GO
```

At this point, we can either run the script or click on **OK** on the **New Session** window to create the session. Since we did not choose to start the session immediately upon creation, we'll now need to manually start and stop it once we're ready to test the application. Again, we can do this either via T-SQL or through SSMS. From SSMS, find the session under the **Management** | **Extended Events** | **Sessions** folder, right-click, and choose **Start Session** as shown in the following screenshot:

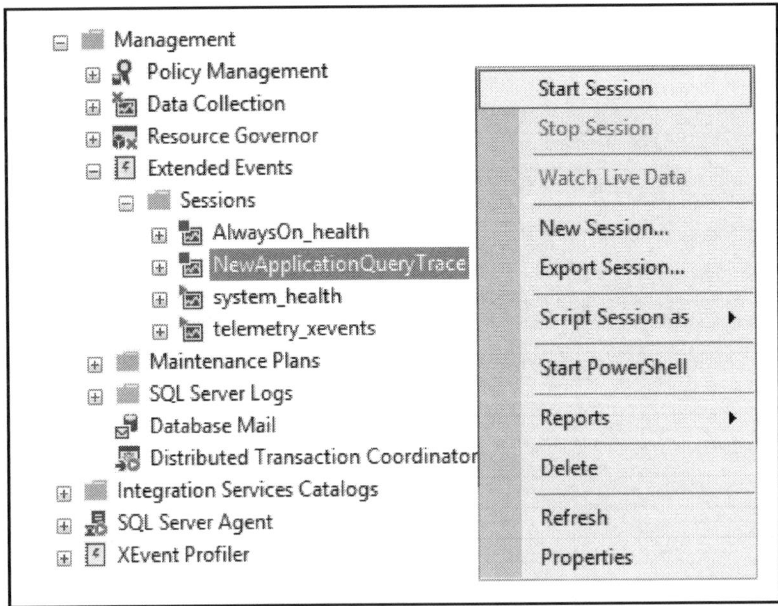

The following script will start the session via T-SQL:

```
ALTER EVENT SESSION NewApplicationQueryTrace ON SERVER
STATE = start;
```

Once the session has started, we can instruct the testing team to begin testing the application. Once the team has notified us that it has completed its test, we can stop the session in a similar manner: right-click on the session and click on **Stop Session** or run the following T-SQL script:

```
ALTER EVENT SESSION NewApplicationQueryTrace ON SERVER
STATE = stop;
```

At this point, we are ready to do some analysis on the collected data. Expand the **NewApplicationQueryTrace** session and there should be a single target, **package0.event_file**. Right-click on this file and click on **View Target Data...** as shown in the following screenshot:

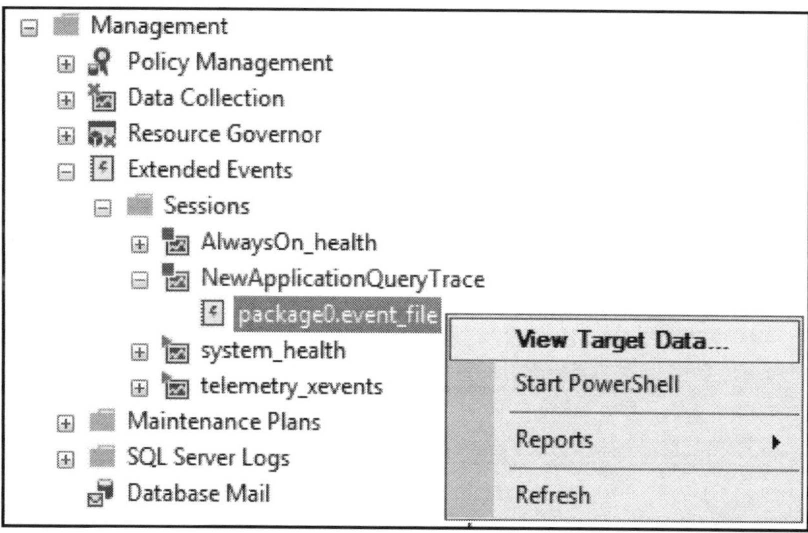

This opens the event file as a new tab in SSMS. The tab has a summary view at the top that shows the list of events ordered by their timestamps. Clicking any of the events in the summary view displays the details of that event in the **Details** tab. By default, only the **name** (event name) and **timestamp** columns are displayed in the summary view, but you can right-click on any of the fields in the **Details** tab and click on **Show Column in Table** in order to display the field as a column in the summary view above. This is all shown in the following screenshot:

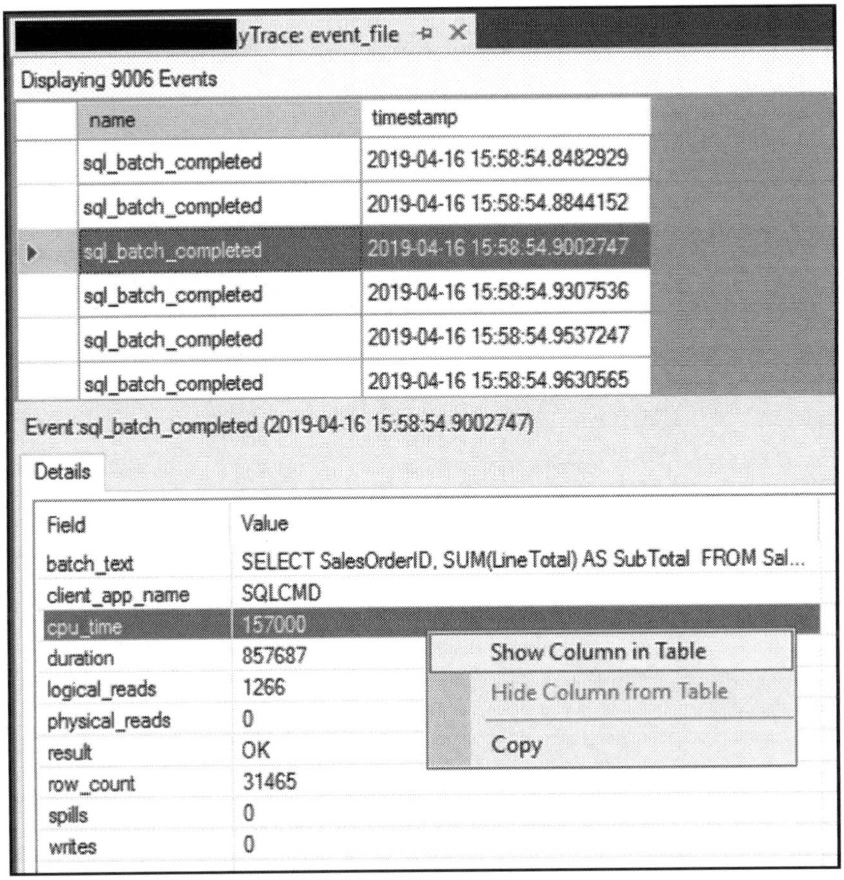

Once you have the desired fields displayed, you can use either the **Extended Events** menu, or the toolbar to filter, group, aggregate, and search for data within the XEvent results, as shown in the following screenshot:

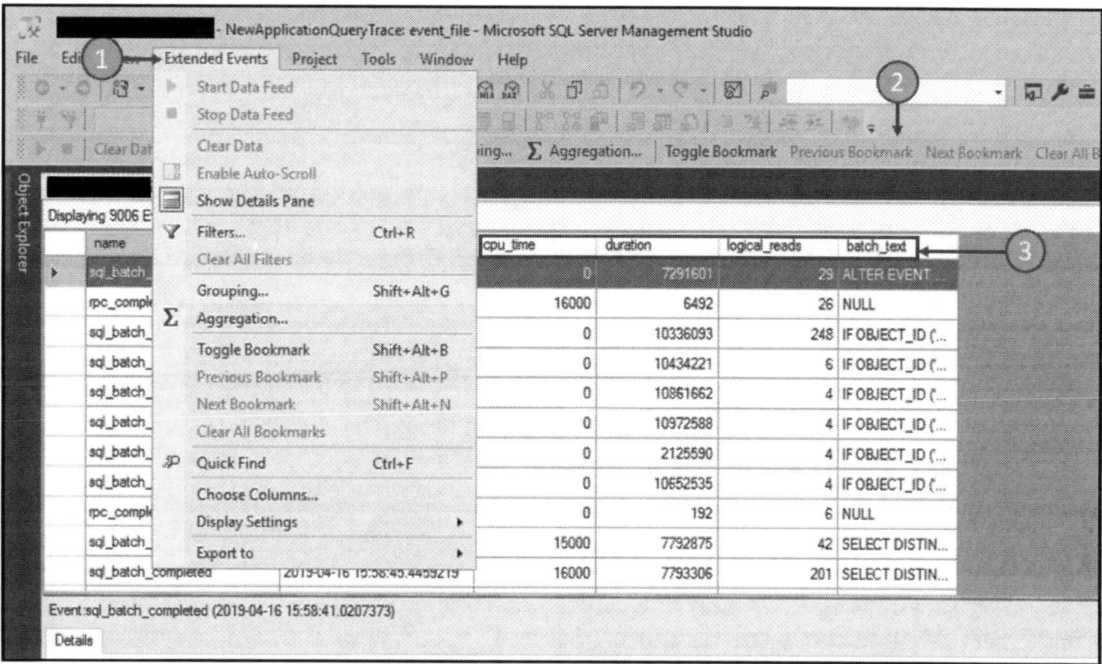

In the preceding screenshot, we can see the following:

1. The **Extended Events** menu that appears when an XEvent data viewer tab is opened
2. The XEvent toolbar that appears when an XEvent data viewer tab is opened
3. Additional fields that were added from the **Details** tab

Depending on the screen resolution and the width of the SSMS window, we may be able to see the entirety of the XEvents toolbar. If only one or two buttons are visible, we can use the mouse to pull the toolbar down to a new line so that the entire bar is visible.

While SSMS has a rich set of features that allows you to analyze XEvent data within the UI, when there is a large number of events, or when we need to do more extensive analysis on the trace as a whole, it may be easier and more efficient to use another tool to do the analysis for us. In the *Analyzing traces with RML Utilities* section later in this chapter, we will introduce such a tool.

In this section, we have done a very high-level introduction to tracing with XEvents. Many of the scenarios we have described throughout the book can be detected and analyzed by collecting events such as **query_post_execution_showplan** to retrieve an actual execution plan, **statement_recompile** to detect statements that are recompiling frequently, **blocked_process_report** to detect blocking, and many, many more. We will cover a few more events in the remainder of the book, but a great way to get started is to open the **New Session** window in SSMS and begin browsing the available events along with their descriptions, to get an idea of the breadth of information that can be collected using this method.

SQL Server Profiler – deprecated but not forgotten

Those of us who have been working with SQL Server for some time likely have experience with **SQL Server Profiler**. Profiler is a tool that has been around since the early versions of SQL Server and leverages the SQL Trace infrastructure to provide event-based monitoring of SQL Server. While it has been deprecated since SQL Server 2012, many users still prefer it over XEvents due to its ease of use, familiarity, and the rich set of tools that have been built over the years to capture, analyze, and replay trace data.

While SQL Server Profiler is still available in the product, its use has declined over the years as XEvents gained feature parity. Starting with SQL Server 2012, all the events that could be captured with Profiler could also be captured with XEvents, and with less overhead on the server. In fact, XEvents have a much wider range of events than Profiler, and a rich set of actions that can be captured along with the events to provide much more detail than Profiler. Also, XEvents have more flexibility in configuration with the ability to apply filters at the event level, more complex targets, and the ability to support multiple targets in a single session.

Given that XEvents are a more powerful and lighter weight way to monitor SQL Server, why are users still using SQL Server Profiler? The answer is most often either ease of use, or lack of knowledge about XEvents. Since Profiler has been available for much longer, the tools that go along with it have been as well, and users have become familiar with them. The good news is that most of these tools now support XEvents as well, so we can continue to use all the tools we are familiar with, but still leverage the power and performance of XEvents.

In the last few sections of this chapter, we will discuss some of the complementary tools that help us work with XEvents to profile our applications and servers.

Getting up and running with XEvent Profiler

One of the benefits of SQL Server Profiler was that it was very easy to get a trace going quickly. With all its built-in templates, we can open the tool, click on **Start**, and we're up and running. This is very handy if there's an ongoing problem that we need to diagnose quickly.

All the templates that were available in Profiler are available in XEvents, and we can access them from the **New Session** window as in the following screenshot:

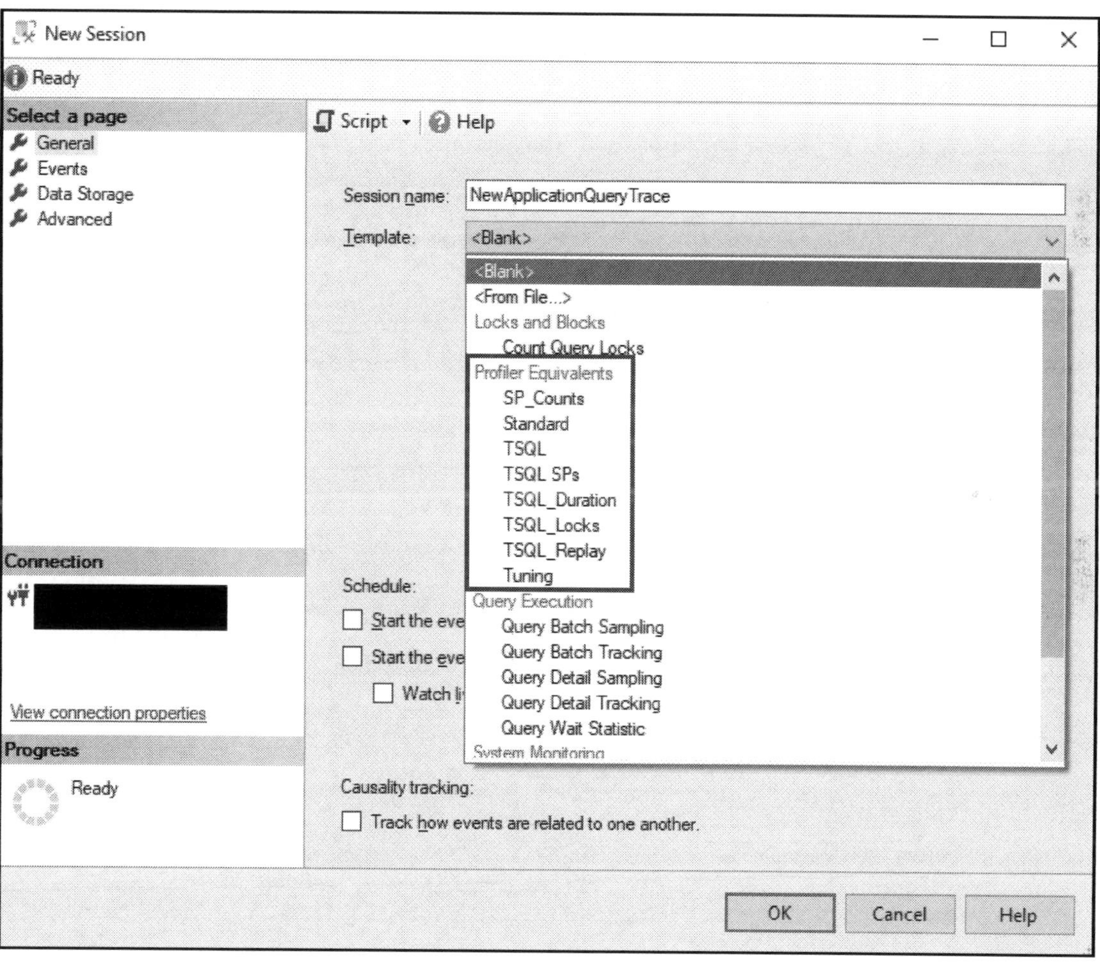

The only problem with setting up an XEvent session is that it requires a few more steps than creating a live Profiler trace. Once we add the template, we then need to check the boxes for **Start the event session immediately after session creation** and **Watch live data on screen as it is captured**, or add a target. Once the session is running, only the **name** and **timestamp** fields will be visible in the viewer, so we'll need to select the events and add any additional fields we want to view. This can take quite a bit of time, so if we're trying to catch something quickly, by the time we get this set up, we could miss it.

By leveraging the XEvent Profiler in SSMS, with a few clicks we can be up and running with a live XEvent trace that gives us a similar experience to SQL Server Profiler. At the bottom of the **Object Explorer** tab in SSMS we'll see a folder called **XEvent Profiler**. Expanding this folder will show us two options for traces—**Standard** and **TSQL** which map to the Profiler templates with the same names.

Simply right-click the desired template and click on **Launch Session** as in the following screenshot:

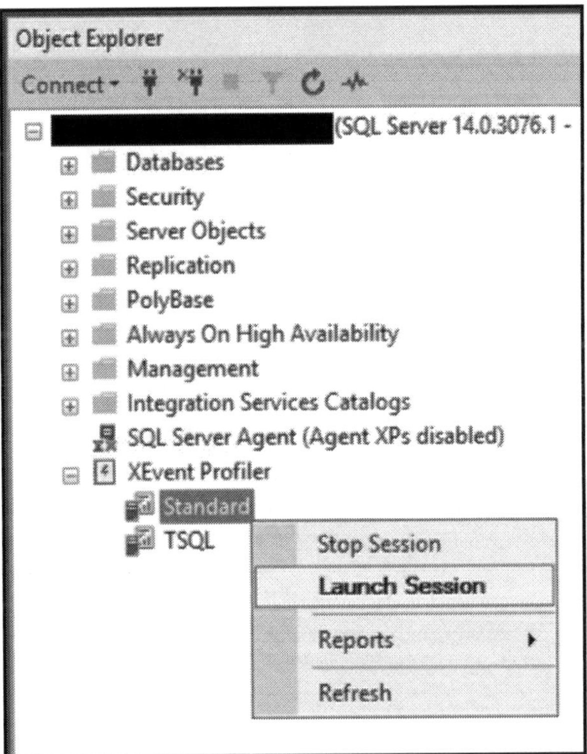

This will start up the session using the selected template, open a live data XEvent viewer that contains the same columns we would see in Profiler, and start displaying events as in the following screenshot:

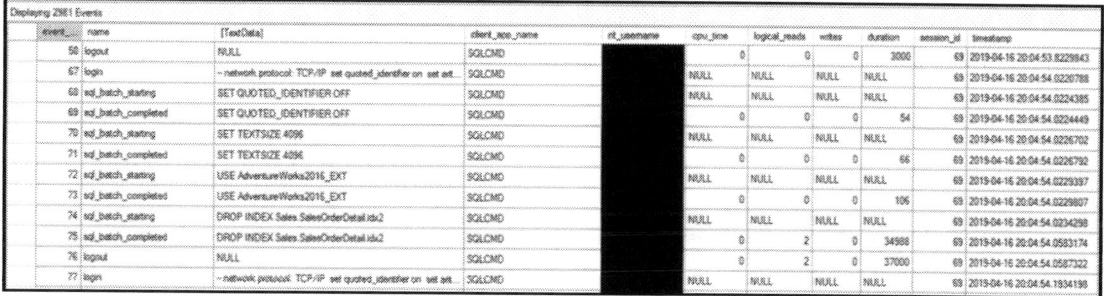

In short, XEvent Profiler gives us a quick and easy way to see what's happening on a server in real time, with less overhead than SQL Server Profiler.

Remote collection with PSSDiag and SQLDiag

While configuring an XEvent session is simple enough when you have access to the server, if you find yourself in a situation where you need to analyze server or application performance remotely, XEvents can be a challenge. As we discussed in the *Introducing Extended Events* section, we can save the XEvent session as a script file and send it to someone to run, but in order to analyze the data we'll need a file target, and configuring one requires knowledge of the disk layout of the system. Also, we would need to ensure that the person we send the script to has at least basic SQL Server knowledge such as how to open, edit, and execute a T-SQL script along with the rights to create an XEvent session. If the person who has access to the server is not a database professional, this might be a challenge.

This is the type of troubleshooting that Microsoft Support must do every day. To make the job easier, it created a tool called **PSSDiag**.

PSS stands for **Product Support Services**, which is what the group was called at the time the tool was created.

PSSDiag is a configurable tool that can collect various diagnostic information from SQL Server, and from the server on which it is running (either Windows or Linux). It can be used to collect things such as performance monitor, DMV output, errorlogs, Windows event logs, custom T-SQL scripts and more, including XEvents. The tool does not require installation; it's just a folder that is copied to the server, then an executable file is started and stopped via Command Prompt. Everything it collects is written to a folder called **output** in the same directory it runs from. This folder can then be zipped and sent to us for analysis.

The tool became so popular with customers that Microsoft decided to begin shipping it with SQL Server 2005, at which point it became known as **SQLDiag**. Since SQLDiag is now part of the product, you can be sure that it's available on any SQL Server instance you need to analyze, so you can configure it to collect what you need, and send simple instructions that anyone who has administrator access to the server should be able to follow.

The **SQLDiag.exe** executable file can be found in the SQL Server installation directory, for example, `C:\Program Files\Microsoft SQL Server\140\Tools\Bin`. The first time the tool is executed on a server, an XML configuration file, **SQLDiag.XML**, is created. By default, this configuration file doesn't capture much aside from event logs and error logs, but it can be modified to collect various data such as Profiler traces, XEvent traces, performance monitoring, and other data including custom collectors.

We can modify the XML file manually, but the easiest way to configure an SQLDiag collection is to use the **Pssdiag/Sqldiag Manager** graphic configuration tool from Microsoft's GitHub repository (`https://github.com/Microsoft/DiagManager`). This is a quick and easy way to configure the collector, and it includes some additional data collectors that the built-in SQLDiag does not include.

The following screenshot shows the **Pssdiag/Sqldiag Manager** UI:

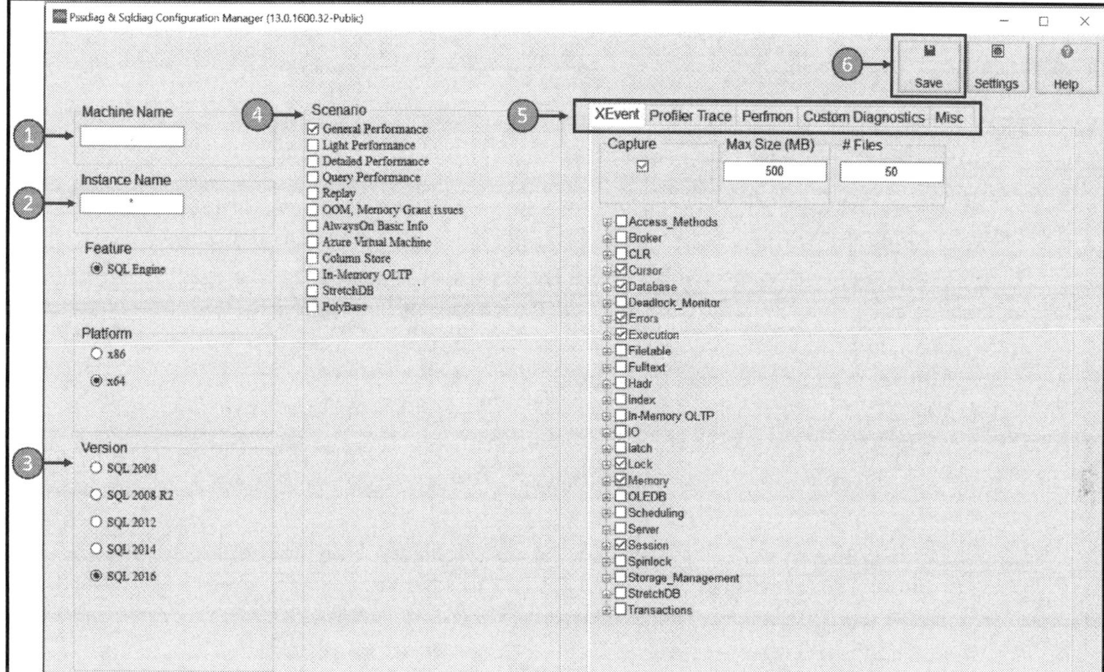

Let's examine the various options that can be configured using this tool:

1. The **Machine Name** field is populated with (.), which refers to the local machine. This won't need to be changed unless the SQL Server that we want to analyze is a **Failover Cluster Instance** (**FCI**). If it is an FCI, this should be populated with the **Virtual Server Name** (**VSN**) of the target instance of SQL Server.
2. The **Instance Name** field is populated with (*), which collects all instances of SQL Server found on the server indicated in the **Machine Name** field. If there is more than one instance on the server, this should be the name of the target instance, such as **SQL2017** for a named instance, or **MSSQLSERVER** for the default instance.

3. The **Version** field refers to the version of the target SQL Server instance.

While the current version of the tool does not include SQL 2017 or SQL 2019, you can modify the version in the resulting **PSSDiag.XML** file to make the collector work for these versions. Simply find the attribute `ssver="13"` in the file and replace it with `ssver="14"` for SQL 2017 and `ssver="15"` for SQL 2019.

4. The **Scenario** list allows us to choose one or more troubleshooting scenarios that will enable various collectors in the tool. The default **General Performance** will get what is needed to troubleshoot most common scenarios. **Light Performance** will configure a very lightweight XEvent trace such as the one we collected in the *Introducing Extended Events* section of this chapter. **Detailed Performance** will configure a much heavier trace that includes the **query_post_execution_showplan** event. This gives us everything we need to troubleshoot a query performance issue, but it can consume a large amount of resources on the server and shouldn't be run for more than a few minutes at a time.
5. On the right side of the window are a series of tabs that contain configuration options for the various collectors. It's worthwhile to explore these and see what is available, but unless there's a specific item that we want to collect, choosing a scenario should be enough.
6. Once everything is configured as desired, click on the **Save** button to save the collector as a `.zip` file that can be sent to the person who will run the collector.

Now that we have the `.zip` file, we can instruct the user to copy the file to the server and unzip it to a folder on a disk that has plenty of space available. XEvent traces can become large depending on how busy the server is, so there should be several gigabytes of space available. Also, it is a good idea to avoid putting the collector on a drive that hosts SQL Server data or transaction log files, as we do not want to generate unnecessary I/O on these drives and potentially cause a performance issue on the server. Once the folder is in place, the user should open Command Prompt and browse to the location of the collector, then type `pssdiag` and hit the *Enter* key to start the collector.

Once the collector is started, the SQLDIAG window should look like the following screenshot:

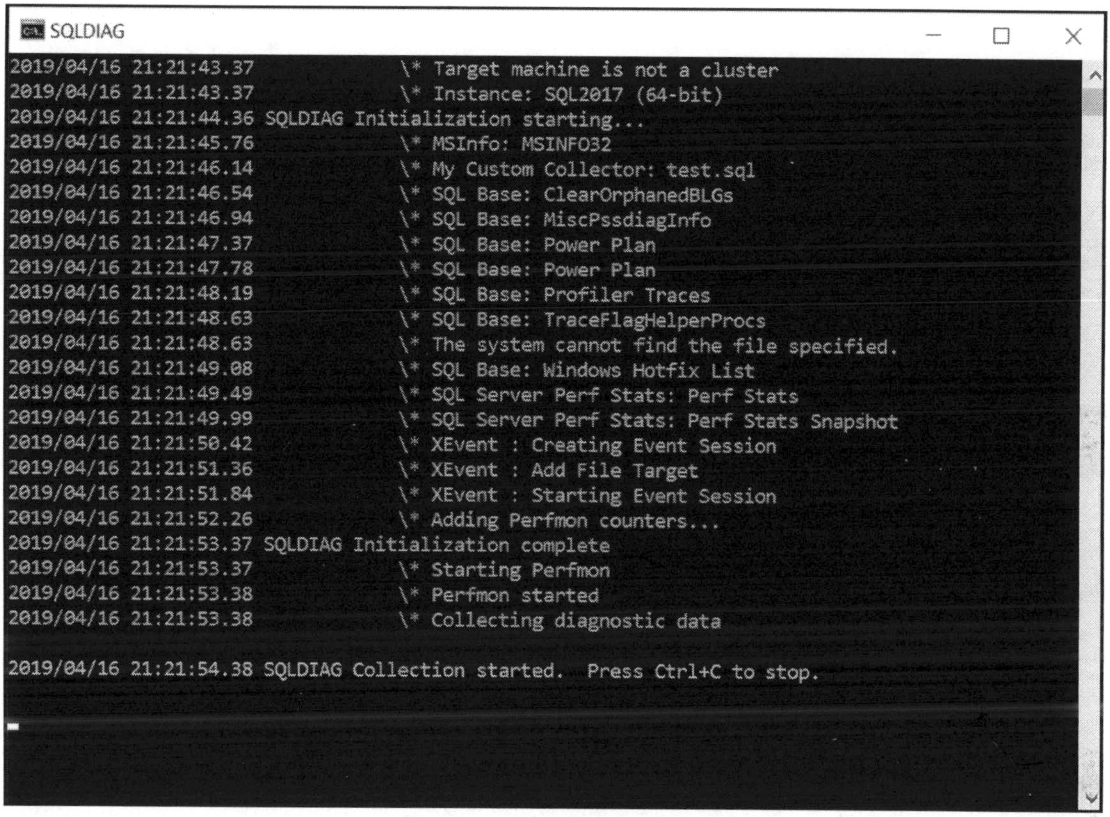

```
SQLDIAG
2019/04/16 21:21:43.37           \* Target machine is not a cluster
2019/04/16 21:21:43.37           \* Instance: SQL2017 (64-bit)
2019/04/16 21:21:44.36 SQLDIAG Initialization starting...
2019/04/16 21:21:45.76           \* MSInfo: MSINFO32
2019/04/16 21:21:46.14           \* My Custom Collector: test.sql
2019/04/16 21:21:46.54           \* SQL Base: ClearOrphanedBLGs
2019/04/16 21:21:46.94           \* SQL Base: MiscPssdiagInfo
2019/04/16 21:21:47.37           \* SQL Base: Power Plan
2019/04/16 21:21:47.78           \* SQL Base: Power Plan
2019/04/16 21:21:48.19           \* SQL Base: Profiler Traces
2019/04/16 21:21:48.63           \* SQL Base: TraceFlagHelperProcs
2019/04/16 21:21:48.63           \* The system cannot find the file specified.
2019/04/16 21:21:49.08           \* SQL Base: Windows Hotfix List
2019/04/16 21:21:49.49           \* SQL Server Perf Stats: Perf Stats
2019/04/16 21:21:49.99           \* SQL Server Perf Stats: Perf Stats Snapshot
2019/04/16 21:21:50.42           \* XEvent : Creating Event Session
2019/04/16 21:21:51.36           \* XEvent : Add File Target
2019/04/16 21:21:51.84           \* XEvent : Starting Event Session
2019/04/16 21:21:52.26           \* Adding Perfmon counters...
2019/04/16 21:21:53.37 SQLDIAG Initialization complete
2019/04/16 21:21:53.37           \* Starting Perfmon
2019/04/16 21:21:53.38           \* Perfmon started
2019/04/16 21:21:53.38           \* Collecting diagnostic data

2019/04/16 21:21:54.38 SQLDIAG Collection started.  Press Ctrl+C to stop.
```

After the green line is shown on the screen, the collector is gathering data. Once the issue has been reproduced, or the required data is collected, press *Ctrl* + *C* to stop the collector.

When the collector is stopped, some additional data will be gathered, then the script will complete, and the SQLDIAG window should look like the following screenshot:

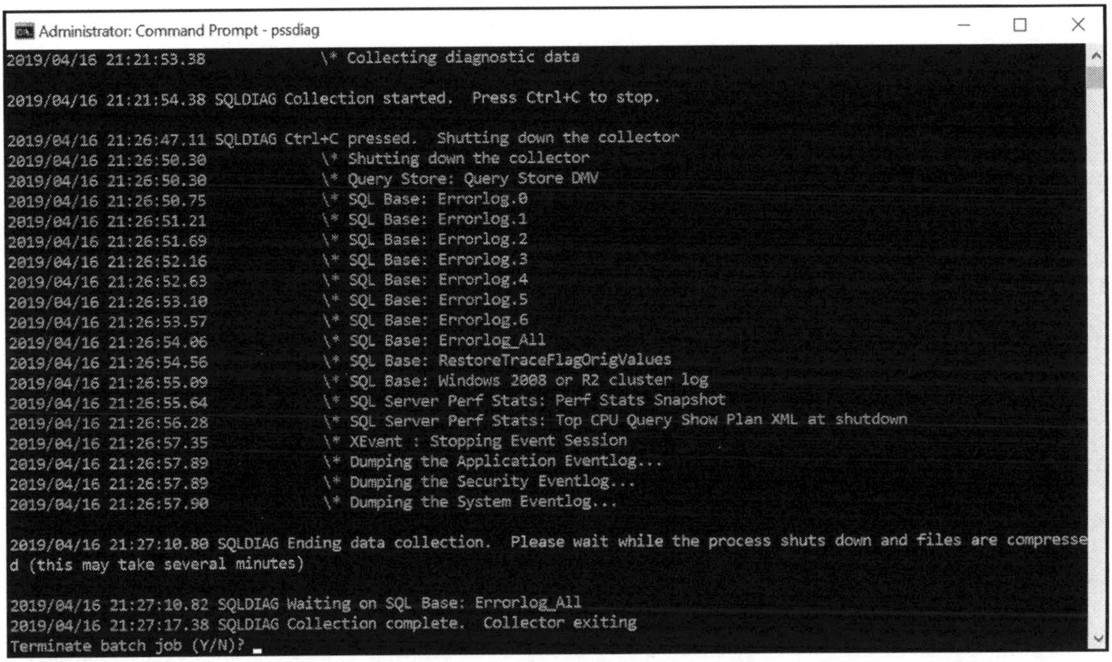

```
Administrator: Command Prompt - pssdiag
2019/04/16 21:21:53.38            \* Collecting diagnostic data

2019/04/16 21:21:54.38 SQLDIAG Collection started.  Press Ctrl+C to stop.

2019/04/16 21:26:47.11 SQLDIAG Ctrl+C pressed.  Shutting down the collector
2019/04/16 21:26:50.30            \* Shutting down the collector
2019/04/16 21:26:50.30            \* Query Store: Query Store DMV
2019/04/16 21:26:50.75            \* SQL Base: Errorlog.0
2019/04/16 21:26:51.21            \* SQL Base: Errorlog.1
2019/04/16 21:26:51.69            \* SQL Base: Errorlog.2
2019/04/16 21:26:52.16            \* SQL Base: Errorlog.3
2019/04/16 21:26:52.63            \* SQL Base: Errorlog.4
2019/04/16 21:26:53.10            \* SQL Base: Errorlog.5
2019/04/16 21:26:53.57            \* SQL Base: Errorlog.6
2019/04/16 21:26:54.06            \* SQL Base: Errorlog_All
2019/04/16 21:26:54.56            \* SQL Base: RestoreTraceFlagOrigValues
2019/04/16 21:26:55.09            \* SQL Base: Windows 2008 or R2 cluster log
2019/04/16 21:26:55.64            \* SQL Server Perf Stats: Perf Stats Snapshot
2019/04/16 21:26:56.28            \* SQL Server Perf Stats: Top CPU Query Show Plan XML at shutdown
2019/04/16 21:26:57.35            \* XEvent : Stopping Event Session
2019/04/16 21:26:57.89            \* Dumping the Application Eventlog...
2019/04/16 21:26:57.89            \* Dumping the Security Eventlog...
2019/04/16 21:26:57.90            \* Dumping the System Eventlog...

2019/04/16 21:27:10.80 SQLDIAG Ending data collection.  Please wait while the process shuts down and files are compresse
d (this may take several minutes)

2019/04/16 21:27:10.82 SQLDIAG Waiting on SQL Base: Errorlog_All
2019/04/16 21:27:17.38 SQLDIAG Collection complete.  Collector exiting
Terminate batch job (Y/N)? _
```

Press *Y* to stop the collector. The user can then go to the location of the collector and find the folder named `output`, zip the folder, and send us the results for analysis. We can then manually review the data by opening the XEvent trace files in SSMS and the other various files in a text editor, or we can use a tool such as RML Utilities to automatically analyze the XEvent data and produce a report that we can review instead.

In the next section, we will explore RML Utilities and see how we can use it to quickly and easily analyze XEvent trace files.

Analyzing traces with RML Utilities

Replay Markup Language Utilities, or **RML Utilities** as it's more commonly known, is a suite of tools that can be used to analyze and replay SQL Server workloads. We first introduced the RML Utilities in `Chapter 7`, *Discovering T-SQL Anti-Patterns in Depth* in the *Avoiding unnecessary overhead with stored procedures* section where we used the **ostress** tool to simulate a multi-threaded workload on the server. The input to ostress can be a single query or T-SQL script, but ostress can also take a prepared trace file (either SQL Trace or XEvents) as input. This allows you to capture a workload from a production server, and then replay that workload on a test server so that you can experiment with various settings or performance tuning options, or even to test how a new version of SQL Server would perform with the same workload.

The **Database Experimentation Assistant** (**DEA**) is another free tool from Microsoft that uses RML Utilities to facilitate A/B testing of the same workload against two different targets. This is a wizard-like experience that can help automate the testing process when planning for an upgrade, migration, or other major change to your environment.

Another tool that is part of RML Utilities is **ReadTrace**. The ReadTrace tool is used to analyze and prepare traces for replay via ostress, but it can also be used to do a general analysis of an XEvent trace. Together with its native **Reporter** tool, RML Utilities can be used to extract and aggregate relevant data from the trace, and then present it in a way that allows you to quickly zero in on poor-performing queries, or other potential performance issues on the server and/or with the application.

In this section, we will explore using ReadTrace and Reporter to analyze the XEvent trace we captured via SQLDiag in the previous section *Remote collection with PSSDiag and SQLDiag*.

The first thing we need to do to begin the analysis is to run the ReadTrace tool with the XEvents output from our SQLDiag collection.

Once we have downloaded and installed RML Utilities, we find some helpful shortcuts in the Start menu, as seen in the following screenshot:

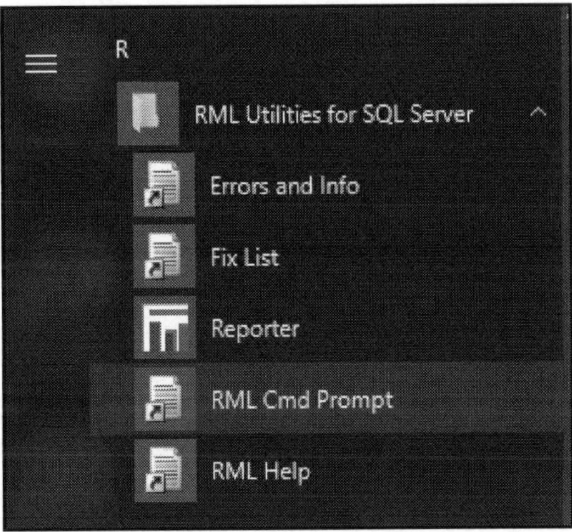

ReadTrace is a command-line tool, but there is a shortcut called **RML Cmd Prompt**, which will automatically open Command Prompt in the correct location. From here, you can run the `ReadTrace /?` command to get some information about the various commands and switches that are available, as well as some examples of how to run the tool.

We are doing a basic analysis of XEvent data for the purpose of performance troubleshooting, not to replay the trace, so the following sample command can be used:

```
ReadTrace -S<servername>\<instancename> -E
-
IC:\PSSDIAG\output\SERVERNAME_SQL2017_pssdiag_xevent_0_131999485123190000.x
el -f -dNewApplicationPerf
-T28 -T29
```

Let's look at the following switches used in the example:

- **-S** is the SQL Server that ReadTrace will connect to for the purposes of loading and aggregating the trace data.
- **-E** indicates we should connect to the server with a trusted connection (Windows authentication).
- **-I <filename>** is the first `.xel` trace file to be imported. If the trace rolled over and multiple files were generated, ReadTrace will automatically read all the `.xel` files in the same sequence.
- **-f** indicates that individual session-level RML files should not be created. These are required for replay, but not for analyzing the trace for performance.
- **-d** is the database name that will be created and will contain the trace analysis data once the process is complete.
- **-T28** and **-T29** are trace flags that disable validation of events collected. As long as we are using PSSDiag or SQLDiag to collect the traces, we should have the events we need for performance analysis, and using these trace flags can help avoid some validation errors that may prevent a successful import of the files.

RML Utilities can be installed on any Windows machine, client or server, but it needs to connect to either a local or remote SQL Server database to perform and save its analysis. Installing on a production server is not recommended.

Depending on the size of the trace file(s), this may take several minutes to complete. Once it is complete, review the output to look for any errors that may have occurred, then close the RML Command Prompt window.

If you are running RML Utilities on trace files from SQL Server 2016 or 2017, you may need to download a newer version of ReadTrace. The new version can be obtained by downloading the DEA tool and copying the new ReadTrace files to your RML Utilities installation folder. Instructions on how to do so can be found at `https://github.com/Microsoft/SqlNexus/issues/49`).

If the trace files were successfully processed, the **Reporter** tool will automatically open and display the **Performance Overview** report. If it does not open for some reason, or to view reports for a collection that was done in the past, we can open **Reporter from the Start** menu. When it is opened this way, the first screen is a configuration screen where we can enter connection information.

In the **Server Name** and **Baseline Database** fields, we enter the SQL Server instance name and database name where we had directed the ReadTrace output, as shown in the following screenshot:

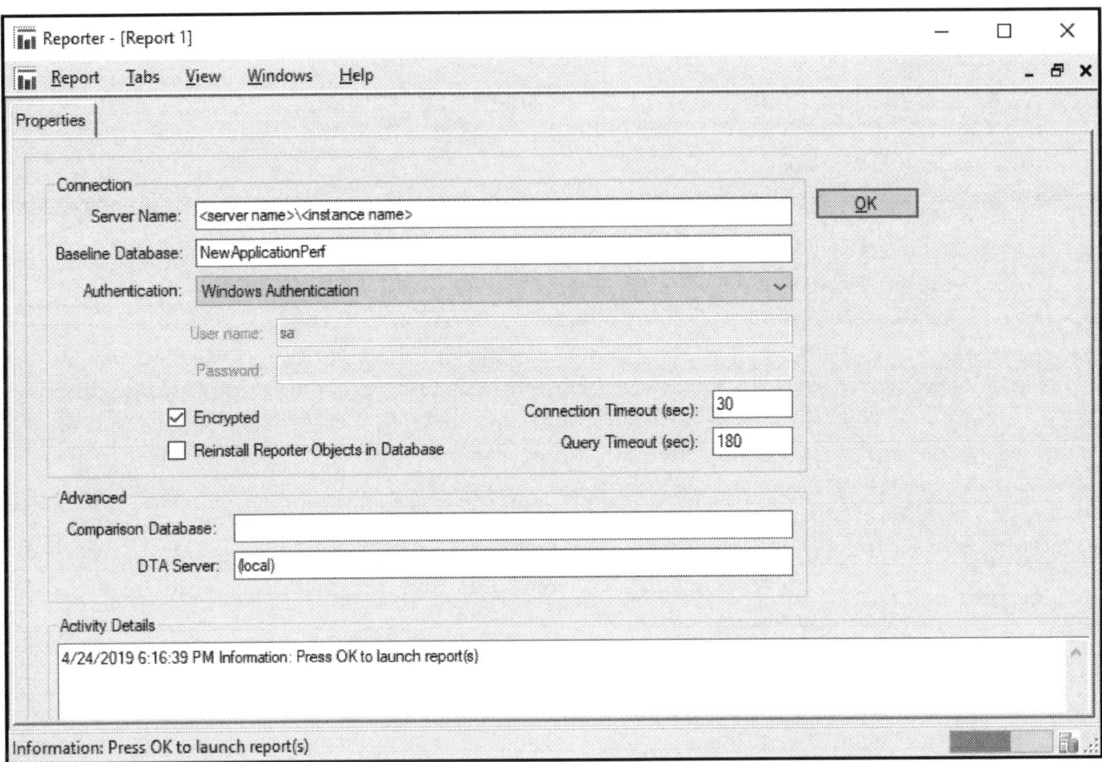

When we click on **OK**, the reporter will open to the **Performance Overview** report as shown in the following screenshot:

Properties M..

100% Find | Next

Performance Overview

NewApplicationPerf

Parameters	Value
Start Time:	4/17/2019 9:55:52 PM
End Time:	4/17/2019 10:01:46 PM

Resource Consumption by ...

Application Name | Unique Batches
Database ID | Unique Statements
Login Name

Additional Reports

Interesting Events
Data Lineage

Cumulative Resource Usage

Value

Completed Time

4/17 21:56:00 | 4/17 21:57:00 | 4/17 21:58:00 | 4/17 21:59:00 | 4/17 22:00:00 | 4/17 22:01:00

Show/Hide	Scale	Counter	Average	Minimum	Maximum	Total
▶	0.1	Batches Started	140.30	0	483	15,433
▶	0.1	Batches Completed	140.25	0	491	15,427
▶	1	Attentions	0.00	0	0	0
▶	0.0000001	Duration (µs)	20,098,558.25	260	265,511,933	2,210,841,408
▶	0.001	CPU	1,824.23	0	57,932	200,665
▶	0.00001	Reads	208,676.58	0	2,815,274	22,954,424
▶	0.01	Writes	2,958.96	0	5,560	325,486

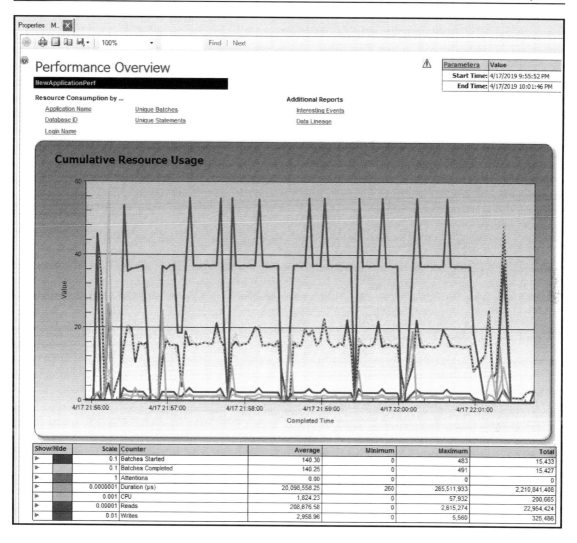

This report gives us some overall statistics about the workload such as the number of batches started and batches completed, along with resource consumption. This information is graphed over time so we can get an idea of the overall workload pattern. At the top, there are several hyperlinks that will open other more detailed reports in new tabs. This allows us to switch between the reports as we analyze the data.

If the links do not work, you may need to install a hotfix for the Visual Studio Report Viewer that is one of RML's dependencies. This hotfix can be found at `https://support.microsoft.com/kb/2549864`.

Exploring the various reports will give us a good picture of what was happening on the server while the trace was running. Covering all the reports is outside the scope for this book, but it is one worth mentioning, and perhaps the most useful one is the **Unique Batches** report. This report presents the top unique batches that ran during the trace, along with several metrics for each query.

The following screenshot shows an example of this report:

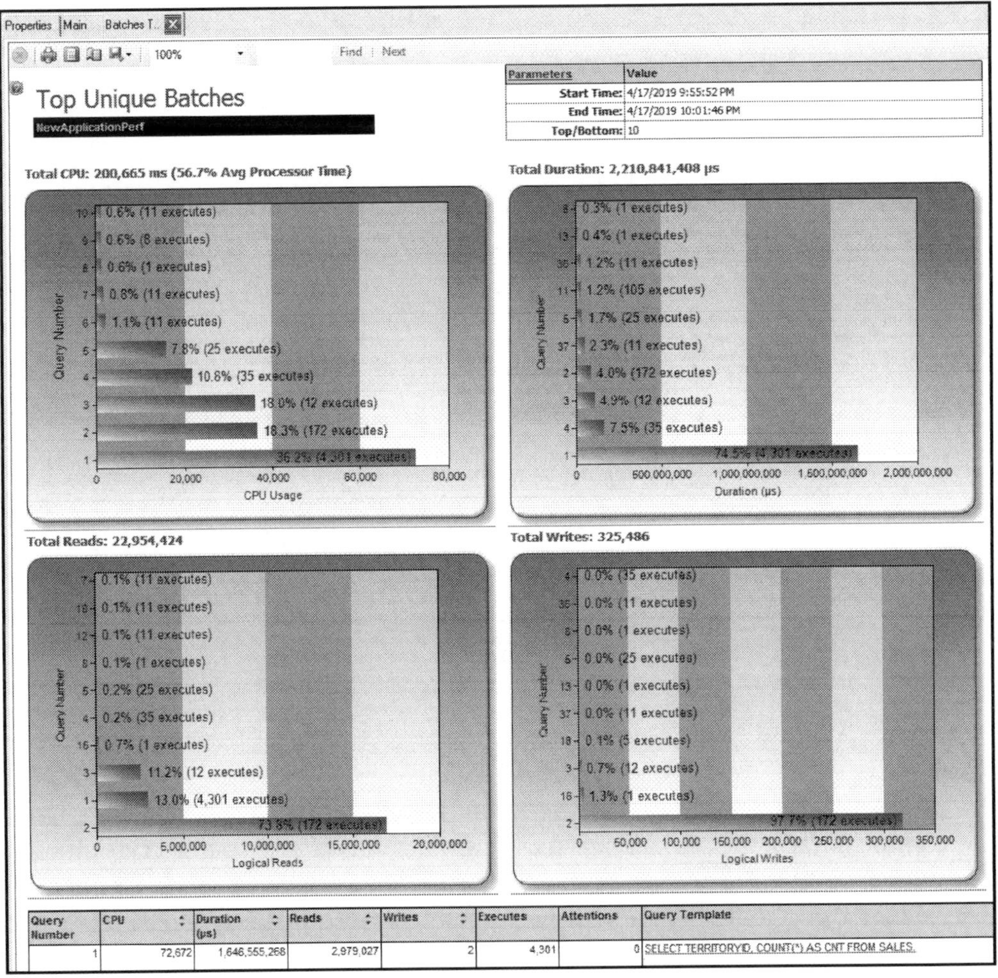

Query Number	CPU	Duration (µs)	Reads	Writes	Executes	Attentions	Query Template
1	72,672	1,646,555,268	2,979,027	2	4,301	0	SELECT TERRITORYID, COUNT(*) AS CNT FROM SALES.

The graphs at the top of the report show the top queries by each metric: **CPU**, **Duration (ps)**, **Reads**, and **Writes**. The list of queries is first sorted by CPU and assigned a number based on their position in the list. **Query Number 1** has the highest total CPU, **Query Number 2** the next, and so on.

The other three graphs sort the list by their respective metrics using the numbers assigned based on the CPU ranking. As you can see in the previous screenshot, **Query Number 1** had the highest total **CPU** and total **Duration**, but did not have the highest **Reads** or **Writes**. Also note that these metrics are a total across all executions of the query. The number of executions is also indicated in the graph.

Each of the queries is listed below the graphs ordered by CPU ranking, and as we can see at the bottom of the previous screenshot, the text of the query is a hyperlink.

Clicking this hyperlink opens a detailed report for that query as seen in the following screenshot:

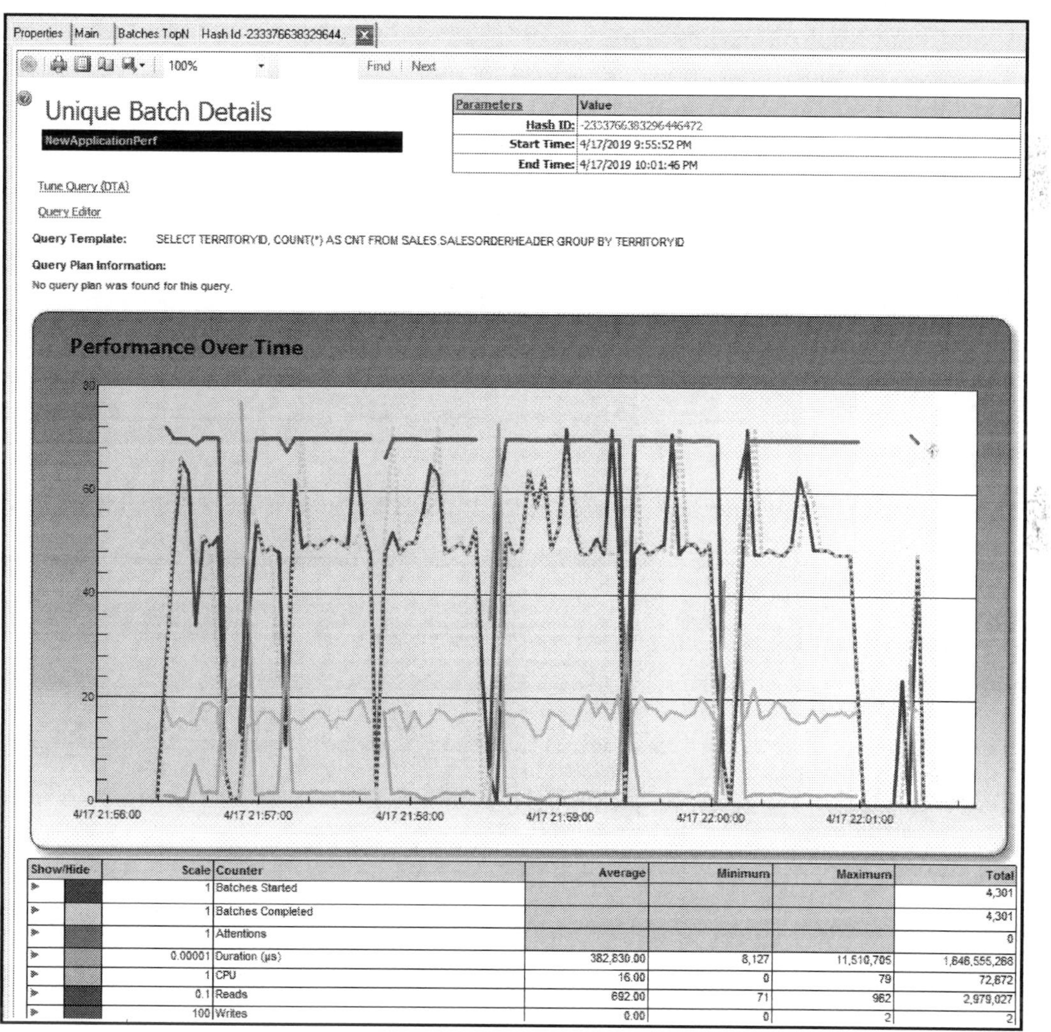

This report allows us to see more detailed metrics for the query in question, including **Average**, **Minimum**, and **Maximum** numbers for each of the various metrics, as well as the performance of the query graphed over the time of the collection. The Query Editor hyperlink at the top of the report allows us to open the query in an SSMS Query Editor window so we can examine the T-SQL and begin tuning the query using the knowledge we have gained in this book.

In the GitHub TIGER Toolbox (`http://aka.ms/tigertoolbox`) under the `SQL Nexus and ReadTrace Analysis Scripts` folder, we can find scripts that allow us to extract interesting information from the ReadTrace database that is not available through the default reports.

As we can see, RML Utilities provides us with a few simple tools that make the work of analyzing XEvent traces quick and easy. Together with SQLDiag, we can easily gather the data we need to diagnose any number of T-SQL performance issues, even without direct access to the server where the queries are running.

For even more quick and easy analysis of SQLDiag collections, check out SQL Nexus, another free tool from Microsoft that leverages RML Utilities and other analysis to import and report on all the data collected by SQLDiag. You can find SQL Nexus at `https://github.com/Microsoft/SqlNexus`.

Summary

In this chapter, we reviewed the XEvents engine in SQL Server and how you can leverage XEvent traces to gather detailed data about query execution and performance. We also discussed the various free tools from Microsoft that can be used to quickly and easily configure, capture, and analyze XEvent traces. Together with DMVs, we now have several tools in our toolbelt that can be used to diagnose and troubleshoot the various issues covered throughout the book.

In the next chapter, we will review yet another tool that is part of SQL Server designed to help diagnose query performance issues using SSMS for the analysis of query plans.

10
Comparative Analysis of Query Plans

In `Chapter 4`, *Exploring Query Execution Plans,* we discussed how to access query plans, how to navigate a query plan, and what properties we can look for when analyzing query performance issues. That was a manual process until recently. Back in 2015, SSMS introduced rich-UI features to make query plan analysis easier. This chapter will introduce the query plan comparison and query plan analysis functionalities in SSMS, to help streamline the process of troubleshooting certain classes of issue with query performance.

In this chapter, we will cover the following tools for query plan analysis:

- Query Plan Comparison
- Query Plan Analyzer

Query Plan Comparison

Throughout their careers, database professionals are likely to encounter some of the following scenarios:

- Troubleshooting point-in-time performance regressions. In other words, the scenario where a query had been meeting performance expectations, but after an event it started to slow down. Finding the root cause may uncover opportunities to prevent queries that avoid regressions from reoccurring.
- Determining what the impact is of rewriting a T-SQL query. For example, when tuning a query, you may be required to rewrite it in part entirely. Does it actually perform better?

- Determining the impact of changing or adding a schema object such as an index. We discussed how these may be required in the *Indexing strategy* section of `Chapter 5`, *Writing Elegant T-SQL Queries*.

For all these scenarios, typically, we must compare query plans to determine what differences may help explain what changed between the plans, for example, between plan A—a plan from a query that has regressed in the production system and plan B—a plan from the same query that was tuned in a **development** (**dev**) machine using a copy of the same database.

In the following example, we captured the plan for a query that was not performing as expected in production—as compared to dev tests. The plan was captured using one of the methods described in the *Exploring query plan cache DMVs* section of `Chapter 8`, *Building Diagnostic Queries Using DMVs and DMFs*. That query plan was saved as a `.sqlplan` file, and we open it with SSMS in the development environment.

The following screenshot shows the captured query plan:

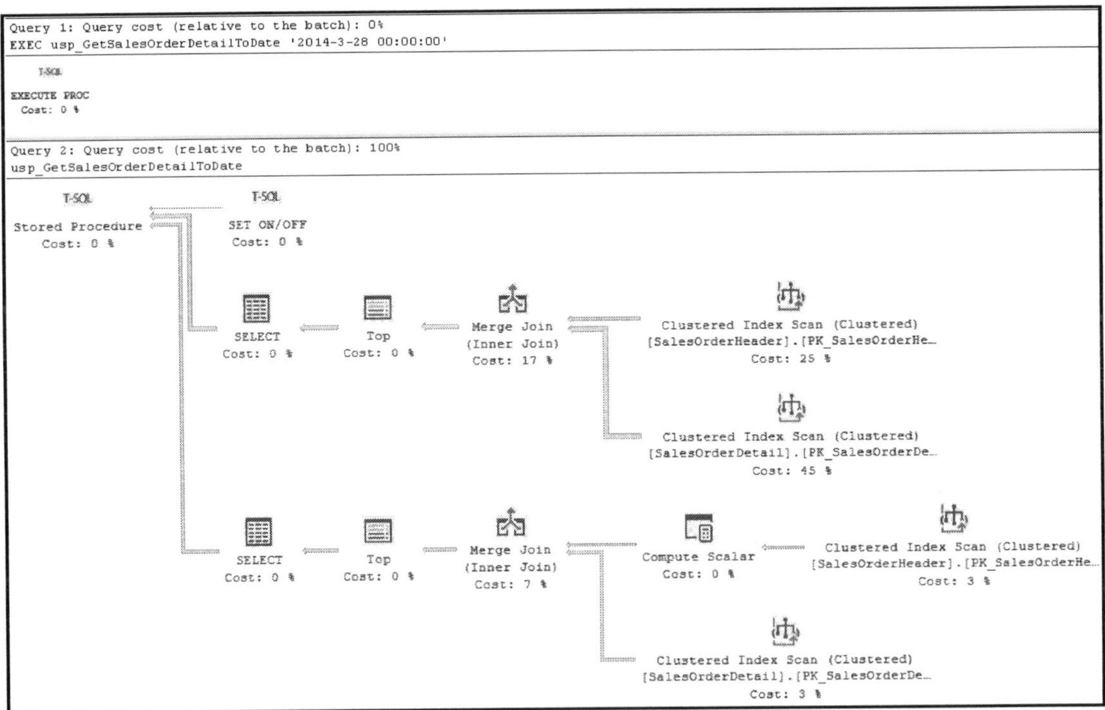

And in the following screenshot, we focus in more detail on queries inside the stored procedure:

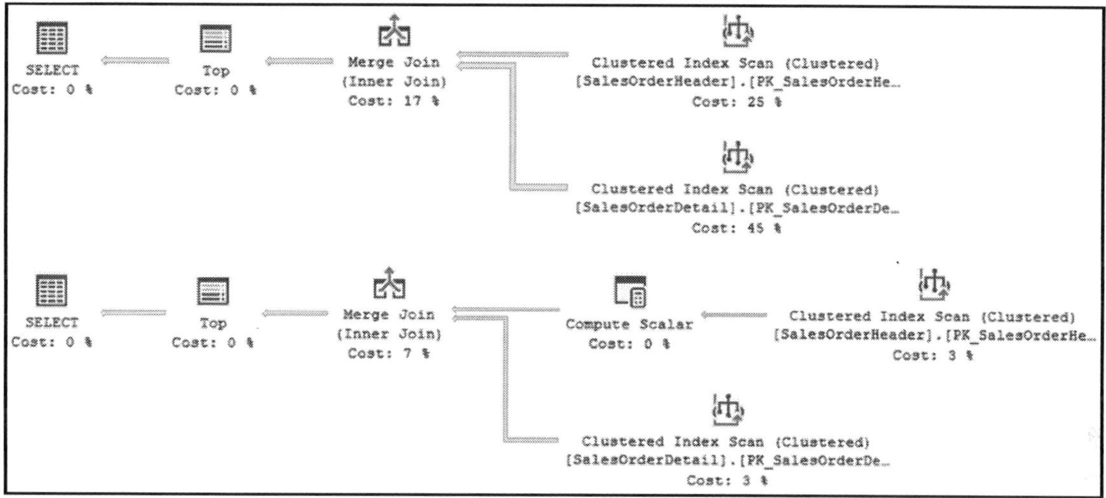

The stored procedure in the preceding query plan is executing in the **AdventureWorks** sample database, and is created as in the following example:

```
CREATE OR ALTER PROCEDURE usp_GetSalesOrderDetailToDate @FromDate DATETIME
AS
SET NOCOUNT ON;
SELECT TOP 1500 h.SalesOrderID, h.RevisionNumber, h.OrderDate,
       h.OnlineOrderFlag, h.PurchaseOrderNumber, h.DueDate,
       h.ShipDate, h.Status, h.AccountNumber, h.CustomerIDFROM
Sales.SalesOrderHeader AS h
INNER JOIN Sales.SalesOrderDetail AS d ON h.SalesOrderID = d.SalesOrderID
WHERE h.OrderDate >= @FromDate;

SELECT TOP 100 h.SalesOrderID, h.RevisionNumber, h.OrderDate,
       h.OnlineOrderFlag, h.PurchaseOrderNumber, h.DueDate,
       h.ShipDate, h.Status, h.AccountNumber, h.CustomerID
FROM Sales.SalesOrderHeader AS h
INNER JOIN Sales.SalesOrderDetail AS d ON h.SalesOrderID = d.SalesOrderID
WHERE h.TotalDue > 1000;
```

Only the first query in the stored procedure depends on parameters. We can see the parameter with which this stored procedure was compiled in the **Parameter List** property of the plan's properties. This provides us with our first hypothesis to test: is this a parameter sniffing related issue? And, if so, would updating the statistics provide a different plan?:

Parameter List	@FromDate
Column	@FromDate
Parameter Compiled Value	'2014-03-28 00:00:00.000'
Parameter Data Type	datetime

We discussed parameter sniffing in the *The importance of parameters* section in `Chapter 2`, *Understanding Query Processing,* and in the *Query plan properties on interest* section in `Chapter 4`, *Exploring Query Execution Plans.*

In a production-like dev machine, we can execute a stored procedure with the compiled value **'2014-3-28 00:00:00'** using the following T-SQL command:

```
EXECUTE usp_GetSalesOrderDetailToDate '2014-3-28 00:00:00'
```

This yields the following query execution plan:

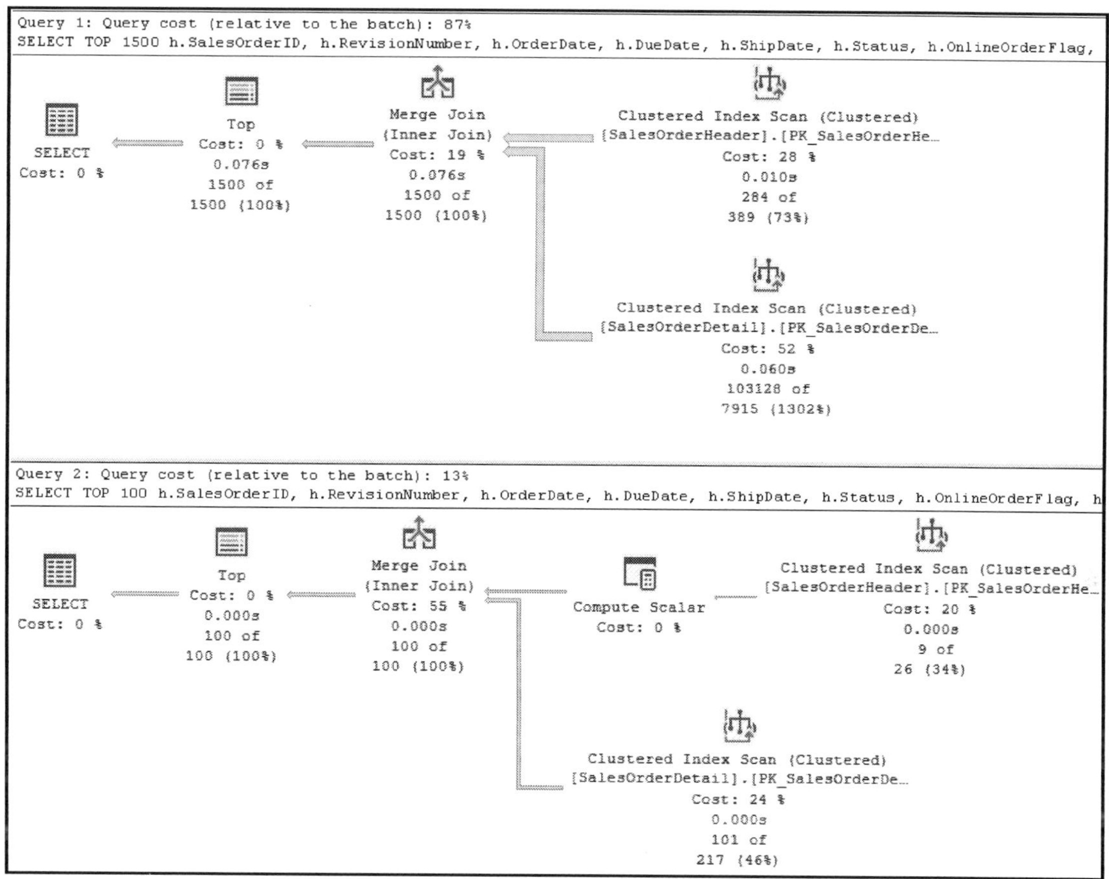

We want to compare this query execution plan (an actual execution plan) with the query plan from production (an estimated execution plan). We need to determine whether this was a valid execution as it relates to production. Are plans in both environments being compiled the same way? The plan shapes are similar, but we need to have evidence beyond the plan shape.

In the past, we would have needed two monitors for this comparison, but we don't in the more recent versions of SSMS. To compare the plan we just received with the previously saved `.sqlplan` file, right-click anywhere in the query execution plan and the following menu pops up:

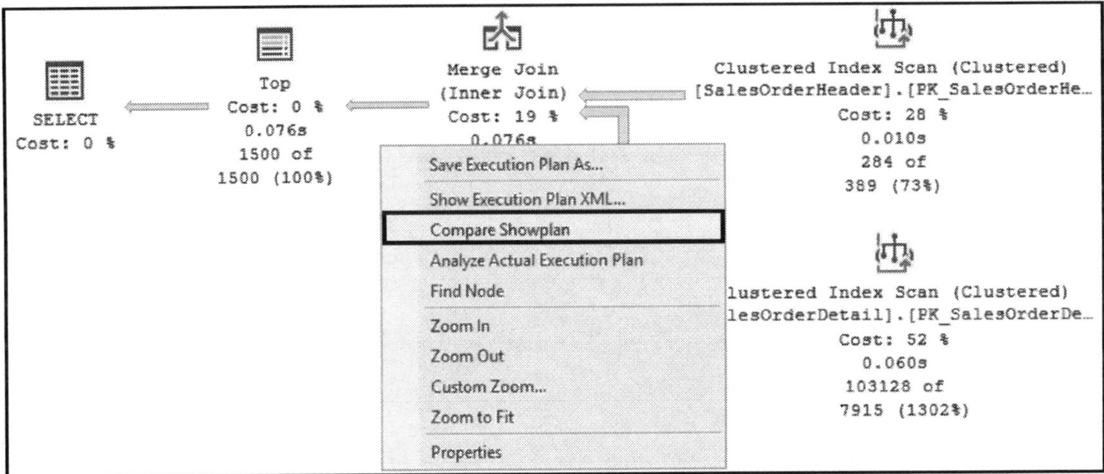

Clicking the **Compare Showplan** menu option opens an **Open file** dialog, where we can search and open the required `.sqlplan` file. In turn, doing this opens the new **Showplan Comparison** tab:

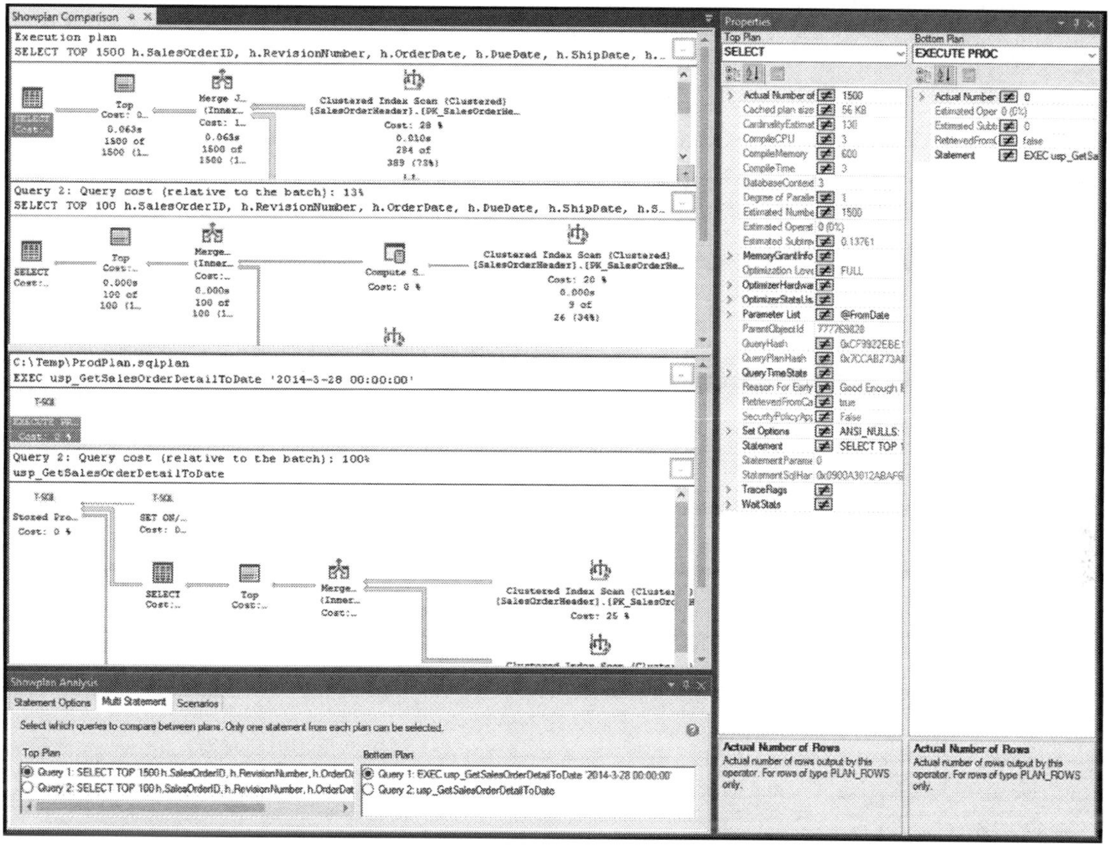

The SSMS Query Plan Comparison feature can open `.sqlplan` files from any version of SQL Server starting with SQL Server 2008. Also, this feature can be used in a completely disconnected way from any SQL Server, when comparing two previously saved `.sqlplan` files.

What are the components of **Query Plan Comparison** we see on the screen? We will go through each one:

First there's the **split window showing the compared plans**. On the top, we have the query execution plan (the actual execution plan), identified as **Execution plan**, and on the bottom we have the **ProdPlan.sqlplan** file that had been previously saved (the estimated execution plan):

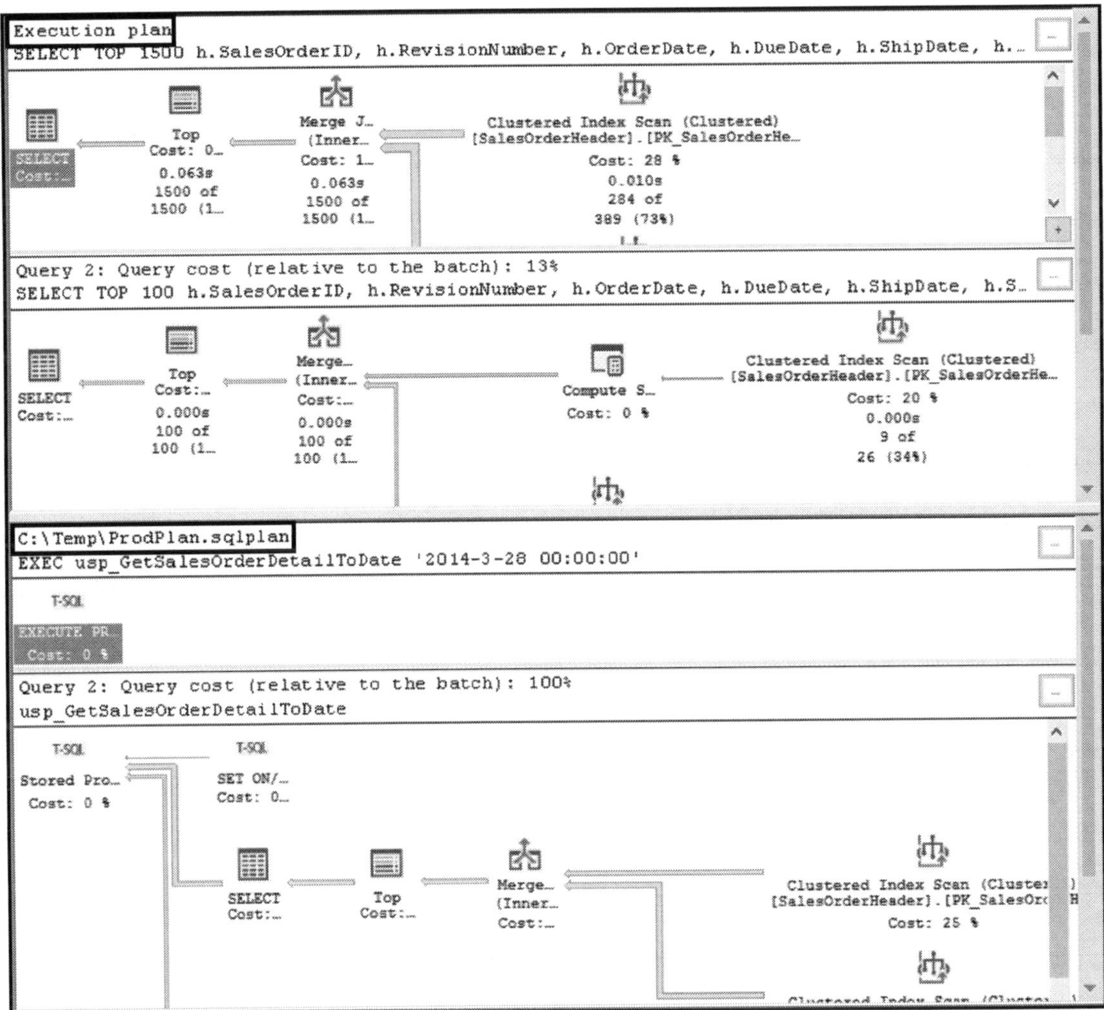

Normally, when two query execution plans are compared, the same region on each plan is highlighted with the same color and outline pattern. When we click on one colored region in any compared plan, the UI will center the other plan on the matching region. In this case, we can't see that behavior just yet; we'll see why later.

Also, depending on whether we use a tall/vertical monitor instead of a wide/horizontal monitor, right-clicking any area of a plan shows the following menu, where the split comparison tab can be toggled from the default **Top/Bottom** to **Left/Right**:

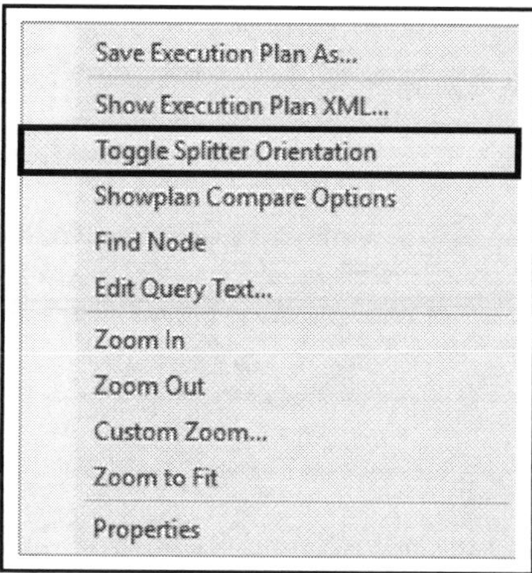

Second, the **Showplan Analysis** window will open in the scope of the **Multi Statement** tab. Here, we can select which statement pair to compare. By default, each plan opens in the scope of **Query 1**. The default nomenclature of the plans is **Top Plan** and **Bottom Plan**, signifying their position in the comparison tab. If the comparison window orientation has been toggled from the default, then this will show as **Left Plan** and **Right Plan**:

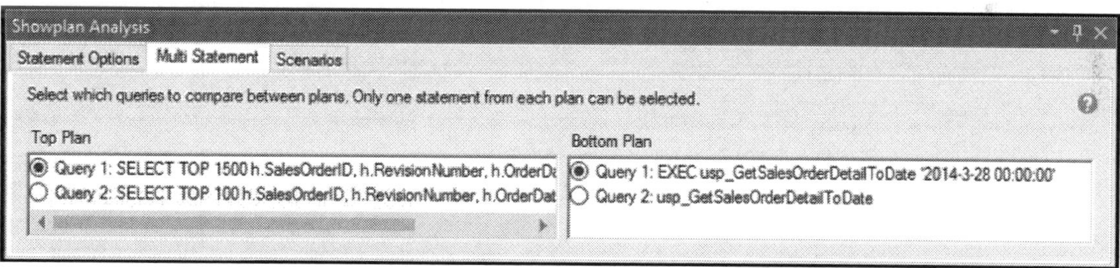

The **Statement Options** tab allows us to configure the plan comparison experience, for example, we can decide whether to ignore database names when comparing plans, which is useful when comparing plans between a production environment and dev, where the dev database has a different name, for example, when the production database is called **AdventureWorks** but **AdventureWorksDev** in the dev environment, and the schema of both databases is the same.

The **Properties** comparison window opens in the scope of the root node for the compared statements. The nomenclature of the plans here is also **Top Plan** and **Bottom Plan**, or **Left Plan** and **Right Plan** if the comparison window orientation has been toggled from the default. Each property on either side that is either not matched to a counterpart on the other side, or whose existing counterpart has a different value, will show the mathematical symbol for difference (≠). Only top-level and first-level nested properties are compared. Beyond the first nesting level, properties are not compared and must be manually expanded and compared:

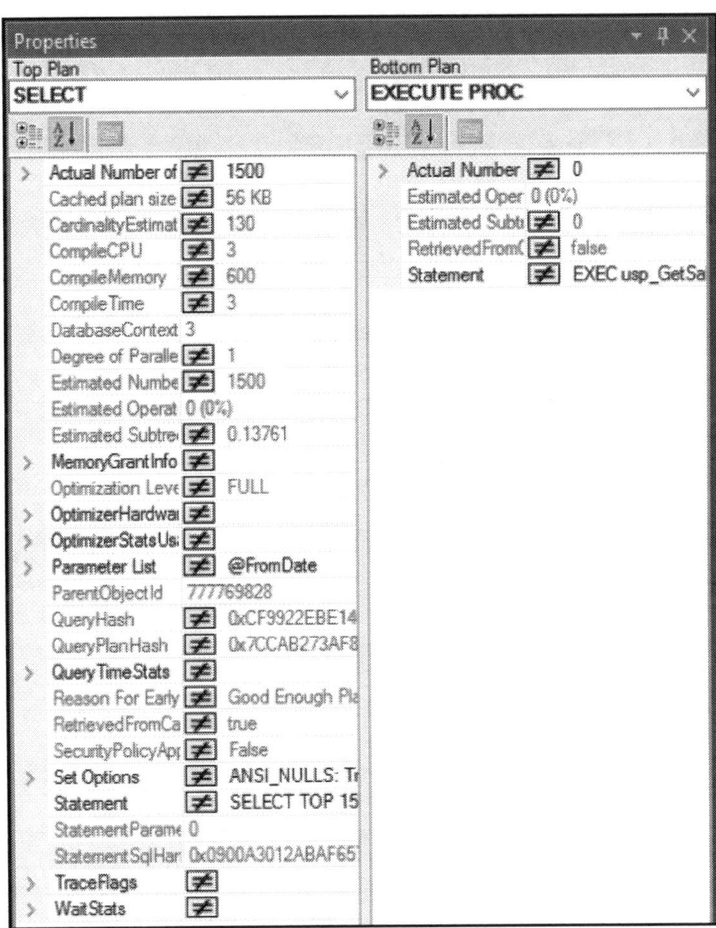

Notice that, in the preceding screenshot, hardly any property is actually comparable because the starting point for any plan comparison—the root node of the first query in both plans—is different in both plans. On **Top Plan**, the root node is **SELECT** and, in the **Bottom Plan**, the root node is an `EXECUTE PROC` statement. Why?

That is because the query plan captured in production is a cached plan from a stored procedure and as such it has extra elements, compared to the actual execution plan for the stored procedure we got from the dev environment. Notice in the following screenshot that the top plan shows the two query statements separately as **Query 1** and **Query 2**, whereas the bottom plan has both query statements consolidated under **Query 2** and the execute command under **Query 1**. The latter is what we see for cached plans from stored procedure or user-defined functions:

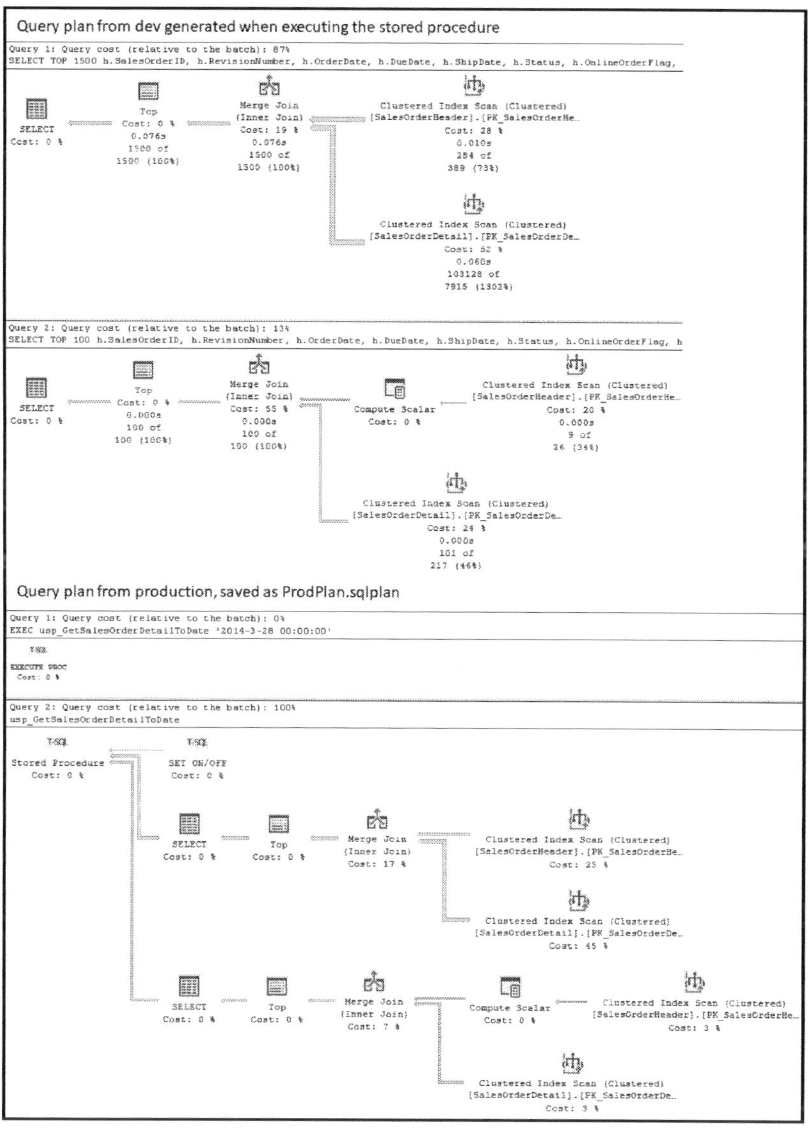

To compare correct statements in this case—comparing the estimated plan and the actual plan for a stored procedure—we need to use a multi-step process. First, we need to go back to the **Multi Statement** tab, and select **Query 1** from **Top Plan**, and **Query 2** from the **Bottom Plan**, as seen in the following screenshot:

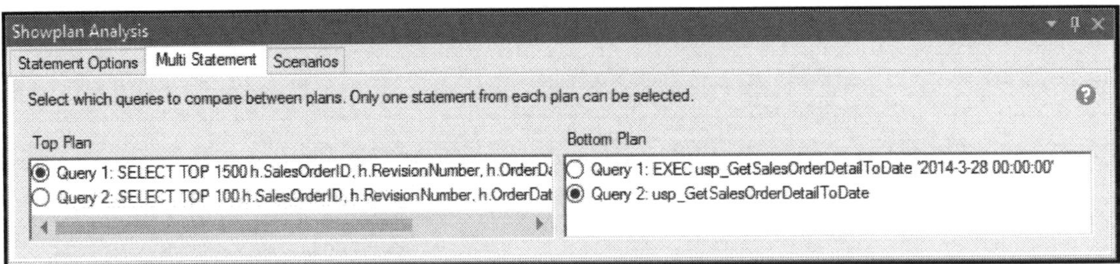

This resets the comparison window to highlight similar areas in both plans, so we can start comparing what has happened in the same context for both plans. Only data-processing operators such as seeks, scans, and joins are accounted for when searching for similar regions. Also, the same table must be used in the matching region of the plan.

In the following screenshot, we can see matched regions between the compared plans. On the top plan, we previously selected **Query 1** to compare. On the bottom plan, we selected **Query 2,** which actually contains two separate queries and thus has two matching regions. We know these two regions don't belong to the same query in this example—only one relates to the first query in the stored procedure, but they both have a join with two inputs on the same tables (remember, plan comparison ignores compute scalar), making them similar enough to be matched:

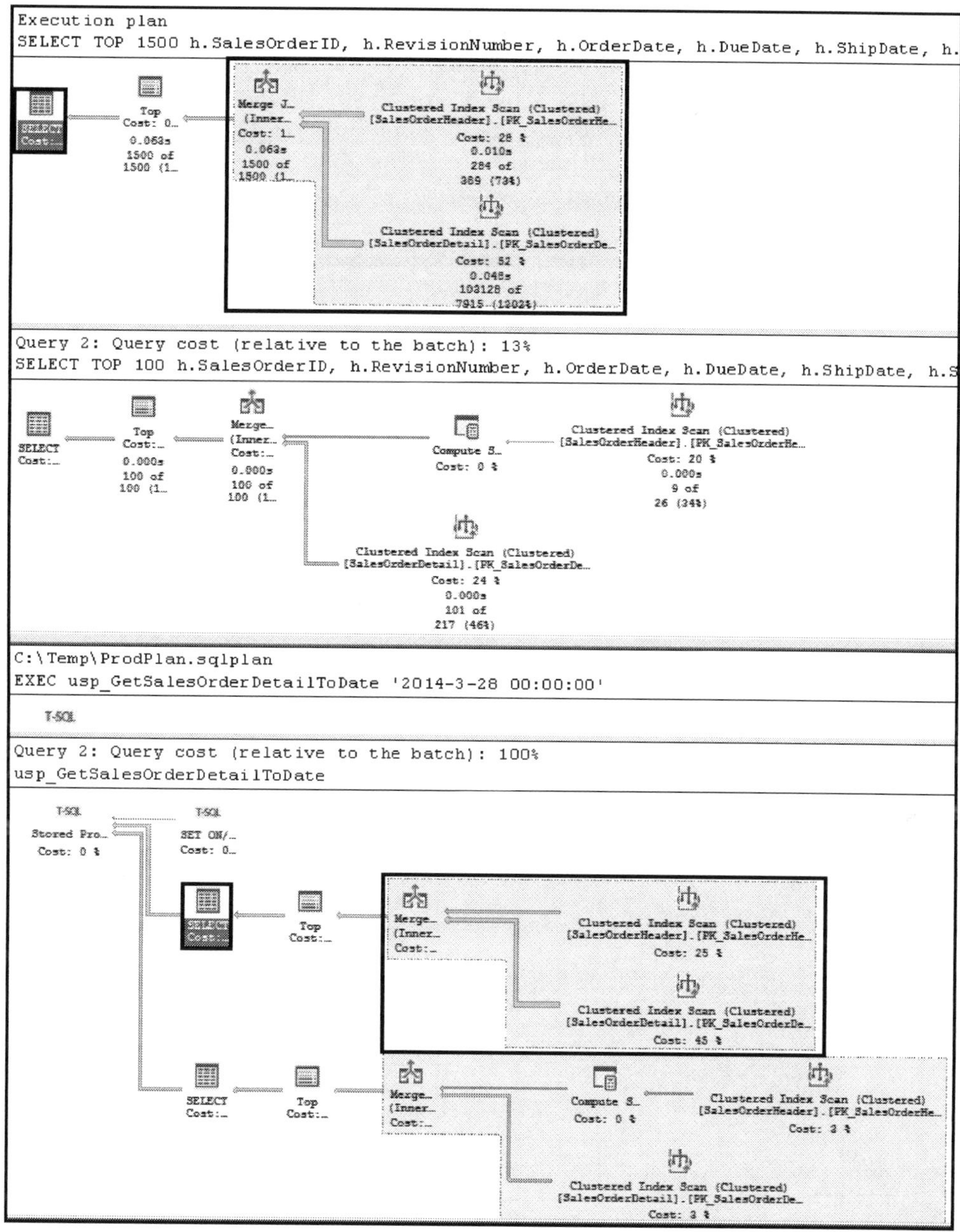

Execution plan
SELECT TOP 1500 h.SalesOrderID, h.RevisionNumber, h.OrderDate, h.DueDate, h.ShipDate, h.
Query 2: Query cost (relative to the batch): 13%
SELECT TOP 100 h.SalesOrderID, h.RevisionNumber, h.OrderDate, h.DueDate, h.ShipDate, h.S
C:\Temp\ProdPlan.sqlplan
EXEC usp_GetSalesOrderDetailToDate '2014-3-28 00:00:00'
Query 2: Query cost (relative to the batch): 100%
usp_GetSalesOrderDetailToDate

If we wanted to compare the second queries in each batch, we would need to return to the **Multi Statement** tab and choose **Query 2** from **Top Plan** and **Query 2** again from **Bottom Plan**.

We'll focus on comparing the highlighted regions on both plans as shown in the previous screenshot. But before doing that, we want to know whether there were any compilation differences between production and dev that can lead us down the wrong investigation path. For that, we compare the root nodes (**SELECT**) on both plans. Click on the root node (**SELECT**) of **Top Plan**, and manually click on the corresponding **SELECT** option of **Bottom Plan** as seen in the previous screenshot.

Looking at the following **Properties** window, we can compare properties that can help answer our question: are we looking at equivalent query plans?

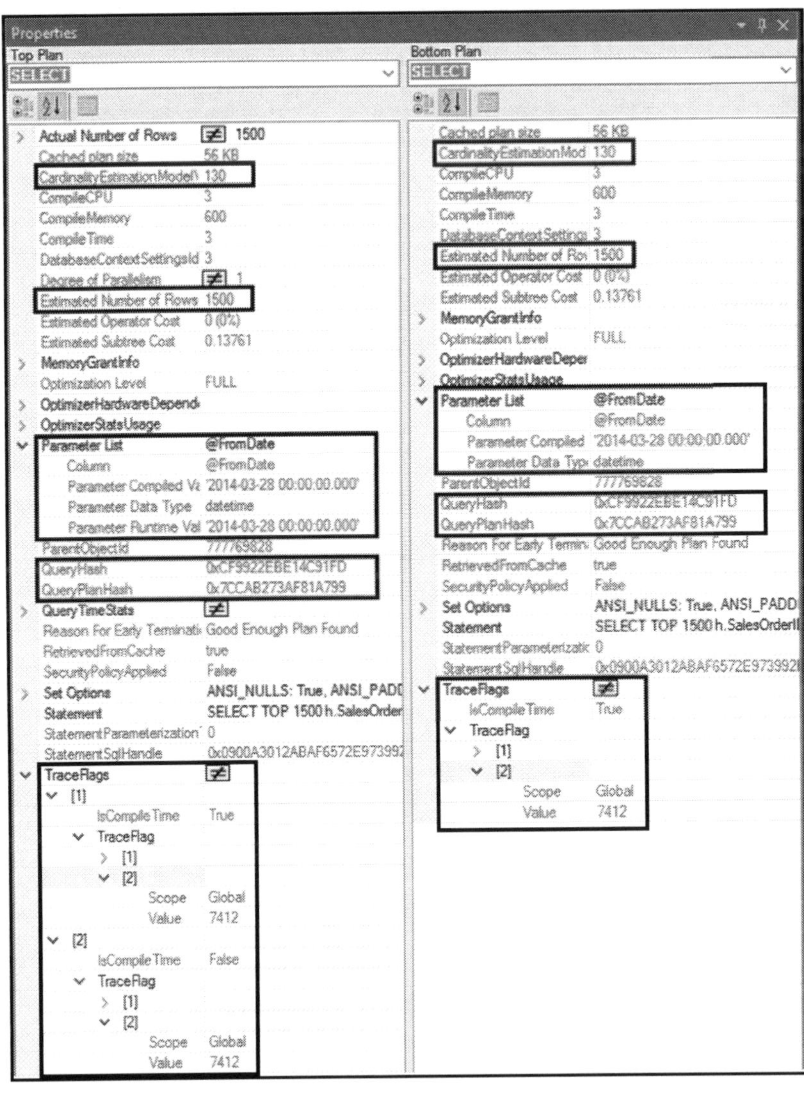

Both plans have the same **CardinalityEstimationModelVersion** (130) and the same number of **EstimatedRows**. The **TraceFlags** property is signaled as being different between plans. Expanding them reveals that's not the case; it's just that the top plan is an actual execution plan, and thus it has both **IsCompileTime | True** and **IsCompileTime | False**, whereas the bottom plan—a cached plan or estimated execution plan—only has **IsCompileTime | True**. But the actual trace flags are the same on both environments (only trace flag 7412 in the preceding screenshot) and none impact the Query Optimizer.

Refer to the *Query plan properties of interest* section in `Chapter 4`, *Exploring Query Execution Plans*, for a run-down of most of the relevant showplan properties.

More importantly, **QueryHash** and **QueryPlanHash** are the same. This means that the plan we are analyzing in dev is equivalent to production, which shows that the dev environment is good enough to dig deeper into the standing hypothesis: are we experiencing a parameter sniffing issue? And are statistics outdated?

A quick look in the **OptimizerStatsUsage** property in both plans shows that both plans used the same set of statistics objects (only three statistics are expanded in the following screenshot) and that no statistics require updating. Notice that **ModificationCount** is zero and **SamplingPercent** is **100,** so in principle we can rule out outdated statistics as a problem:

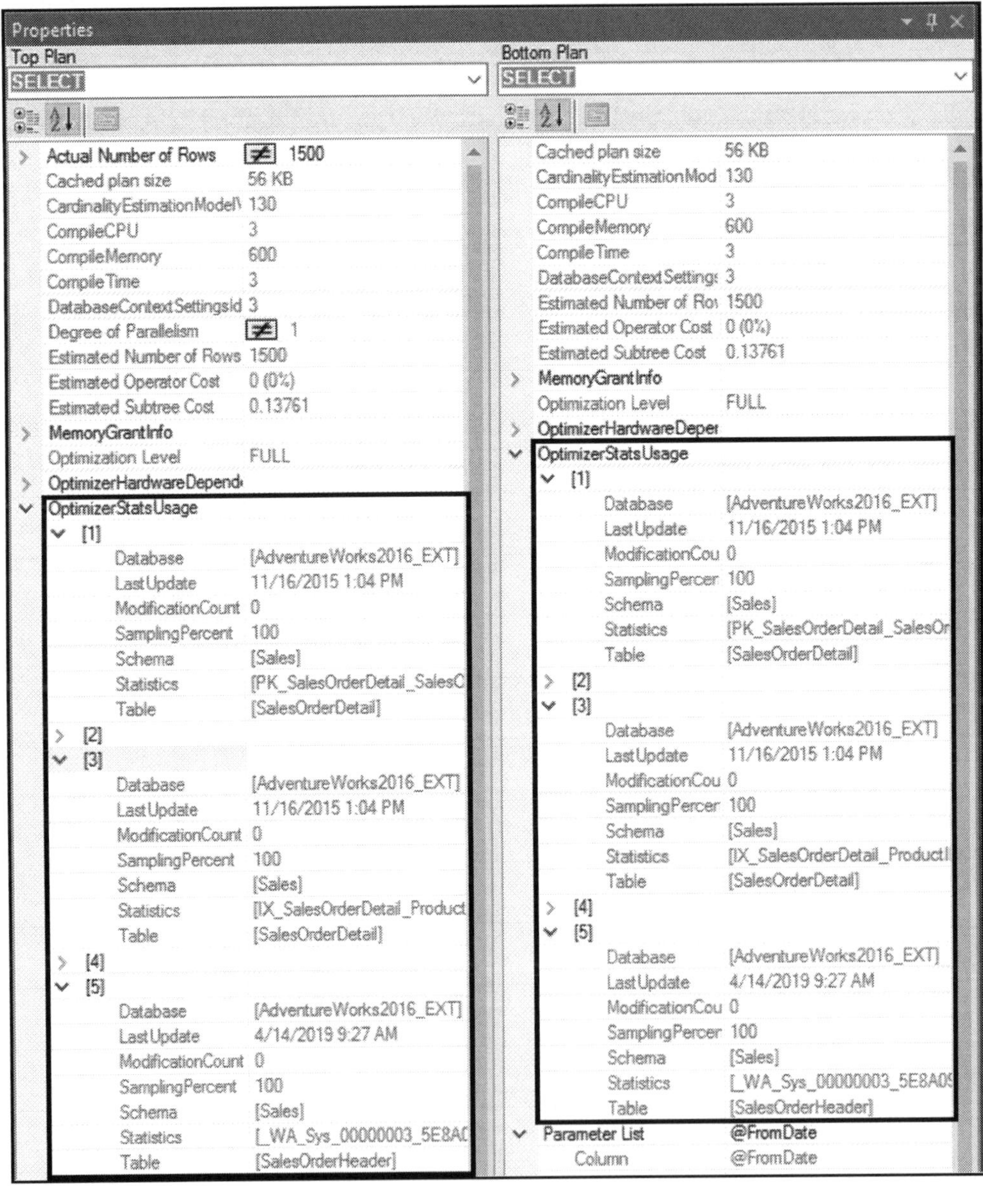

Now we can have confidence that whatever investigations and recommendations we do in the dev environment are likely to be applicable to production. Looking back at the actual execution plan, it's evident that the **Clustered Index Scan** on the **SalesOrderDetail** table has skewed estimations—it returned **103,128** of **7,915** rows, which is over 1,300 percent of what was previously estimated, as shown in the following screenshot:

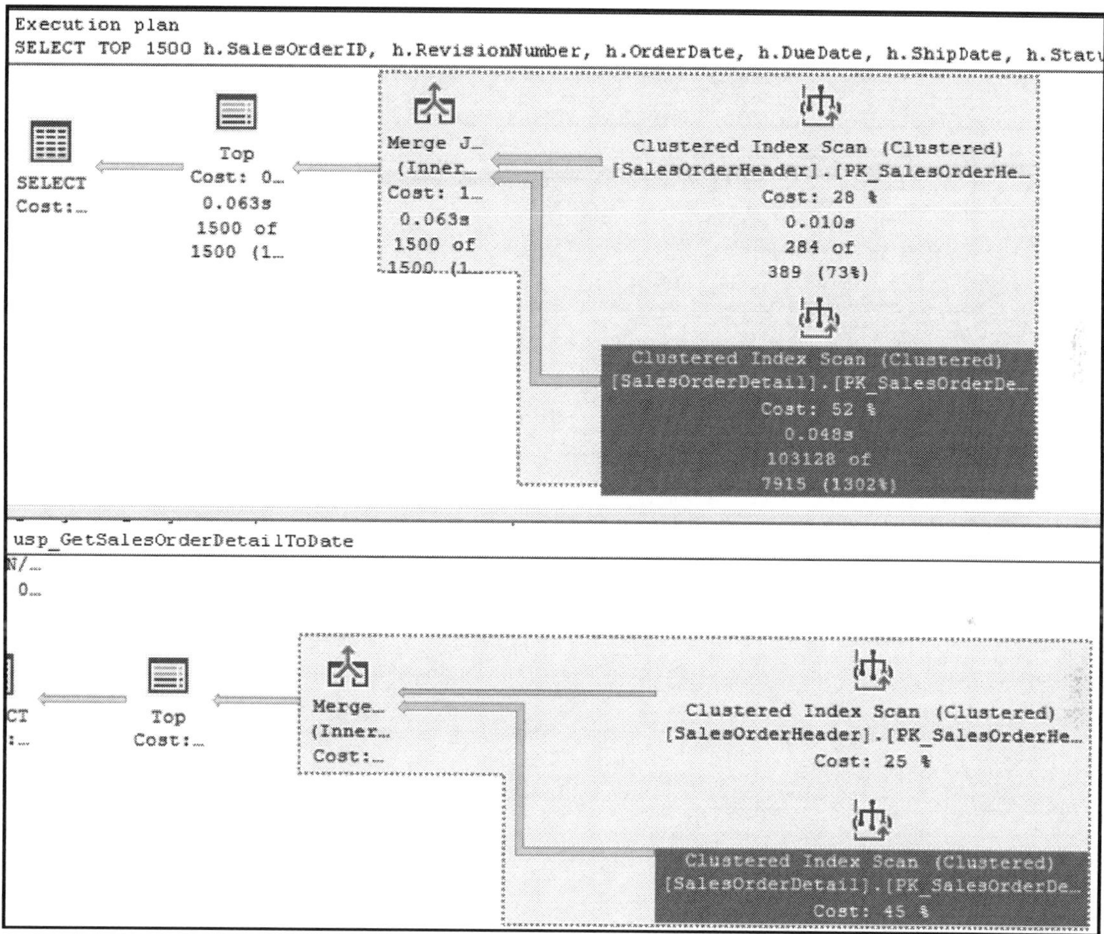

This may very well be a parameter sniffing issue. So, next we clear the plans from the plan cache, and apply different parameters as seen in the following examples:

```
ALTER DATABASE SCOPED CONFIGURATION CLEAR PROCEDURE_CACHE;
GO
EXEC usp_GetSalesOrderDetailToDate '2014-5-28 00:00:00'
GO
```

```
ALTER DATABASE SCOPED CONFIGURATION CLEAR PROCEDURE_CACHE;
GO
EXEC usp_GetSalesOrderDetailToDate '2013-5-28 00:00:00'
GO
```

These examples yield the following query execution plans, which do not differ from the query plan we saved from the production environment, nor from the query execution plan produced for the first compiled value:

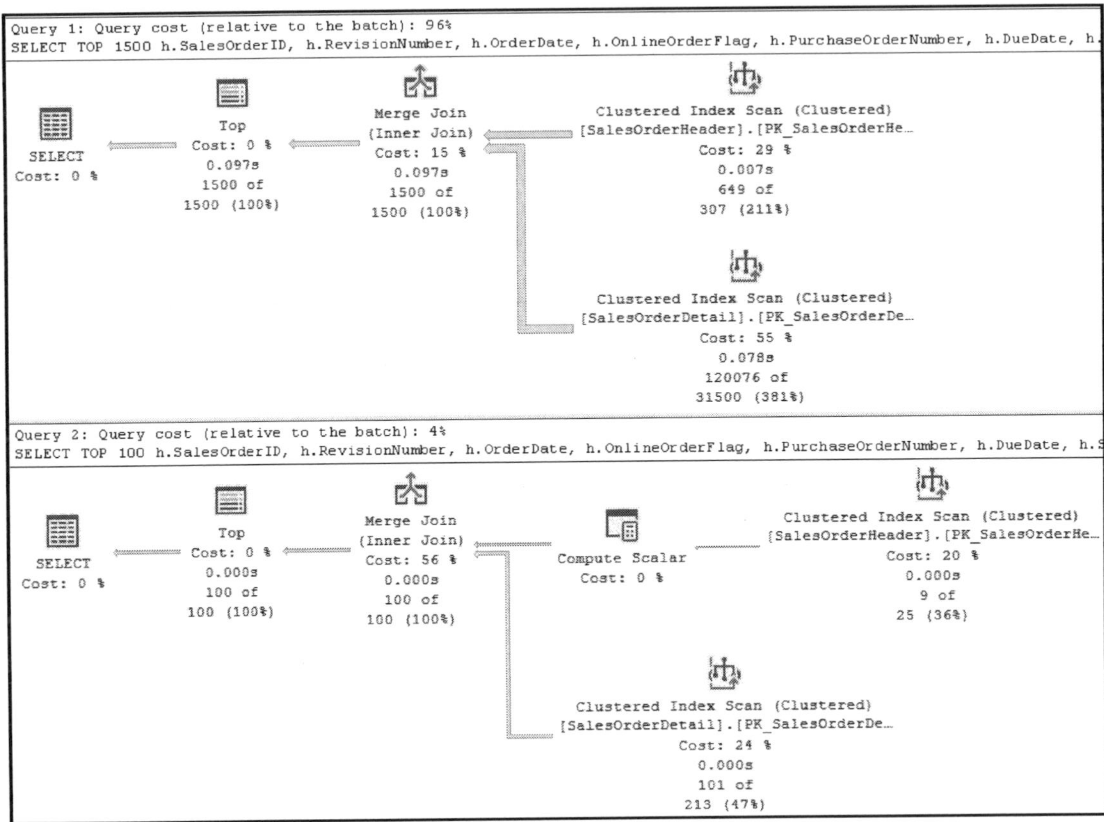

It is not parameter sniffing, but the answer lies somewhere in the query plan. Focus on the overly skewed **Clustered Index Scan** and its properties. As seen in the following screenshot, the **Bottom Plan** (production) has a severe skew between the **Estimated Number of Rows** and the **Estimated Number of Rows to be Read** (7,915 of 121,317 rows). The **Top Plan** (dev) has the same estimation skews, but these are not confirmed by runtime data: comparing **Actual Number of Rows** with **Number of Rows Read** shows these are equal. We have seen this pattern before in the *Understanding predicate SARGability* section of `Chapter 5`, *Writing Elegant T-SQL Queries*. Could this be a predicate pushdown related problem? Notice there are no Seek Predicate properties in the **Clustered Index Scan** so there isn't any predicate involved here:

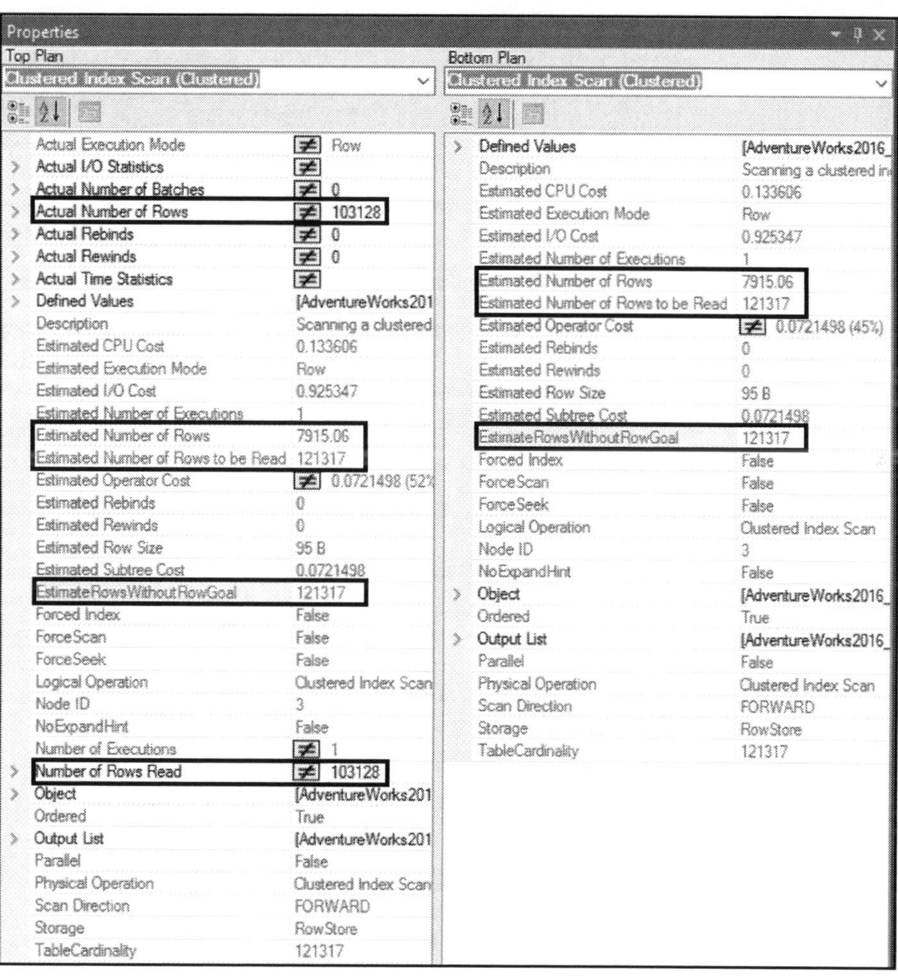

However, notice another property: **EstimateRowsWithoutRowGoal**. We discussed this property in the *Query plan properties of interest* section of `Chapter 4`, *Exploring Query Execution Plans*.

EstimateRowsWithoutRowGoal shows that, if row goal wasn't used, the Query Optimizer would account for **103,128** rows being processed rather than just **7,915**. That would be much closer to the **121,317** rows that were actually read.

When a query uses a **TOP**, **IN** or **EXISTS** clause, the **FAST** query hint, or a **SET ROWCOUNT** statement, this causes the Query Optimizer to search for a query plan that will quickly return a smaller number of rows—this is called row goal optimization.

When the row goal is very low and a join is required, the Query Optimizer will leverage nested loop joins because its initial cost (the cost to produce the first row) is relatively low. However, when the row goal is larger, other types of join might be preferred. For example, a hash-match join is usually a good choice when SQL Server needs to join larger inputs. Although it has a higher initial cost because it must build a hash table before any rows can be returned, once the hash table is built, the hash match join is generally cheaper. But if the two join inputs are sorted on their join predicate, a merge join is usually the cheapest.

We can disable the Query Optimizer row goal technique and see whether that has a positive effect. Starting with SQL Server 2016 Service Pack 1, this can be done at the query level using the **DISABLE_OPTIMIZER_ROWGOAL** use hint, or trace flag 4138 for earlier versions.

Before we change the stored procedure to add the hint, save the actual execution plan from the stored procedure execution in the dev environment to a `.sqlplan` file. We will need it to do a final comparison.

Then change the stored procedure as seen in the following example:

```
ALTER PROCEDURE usp_GetSalesOrderDetailToDate @FromDate DATETIME
AS
SET NOCOUNT ON;
SELECT TOP 1500 h.SalesOrderID, h.RevisionNumber, h.OrderDate,
       h.OnlineOrderFlag, h.PurchaseOrderNumber, h.DueDate,
       h.ShipDate, h.Status, h.AccountNumber, h.CustomerID
FROM Sales.SalesOrderHeader AS h
INNER JOIN Sales.SalesOrderDetail AS d ON h.SalesOrderID = d.SalesOrderID
WHERE h.OrderDate >= @FromDate
OPTION (USE HINT('DISABLE_OPTIMIZER_ROWGOAL'));

SELECT TOP 100 h.SalesOrderID, h.RevisionNumber, h.OrderDate,
       h.OnlineOrderFlag, h.PurchaseOrderNumber, h.DueDate,
       h.ShipDate, h.Status, h.AccountNumber, h.CustomerID
FROM Sales.SalesOrderHeader AS h
INNER JOIN Sales.SalesOrderDetail AS d ON h.SalesOrderID = d.SalesOrderID
WHERE h.TotalDue > 1000;
```

Then we execute the stored procedure again as in the following example:

```
ALTER DATABASE SCOPED CONFIGURATION CLEAR PROCEDURE_CACHE;
GO
EXECUTE usp_GetSalesOrderDetailToDate '2014-3-28 00:00:00';
```

We now need to compare the resulting query execution plan with the **DevPlan.sqlplan** file we saved earlier. The **Plan Comparison** window opens as seen in the following screenshot, in the scope of **Query 1** and the first occurrence of a similar region or operator:

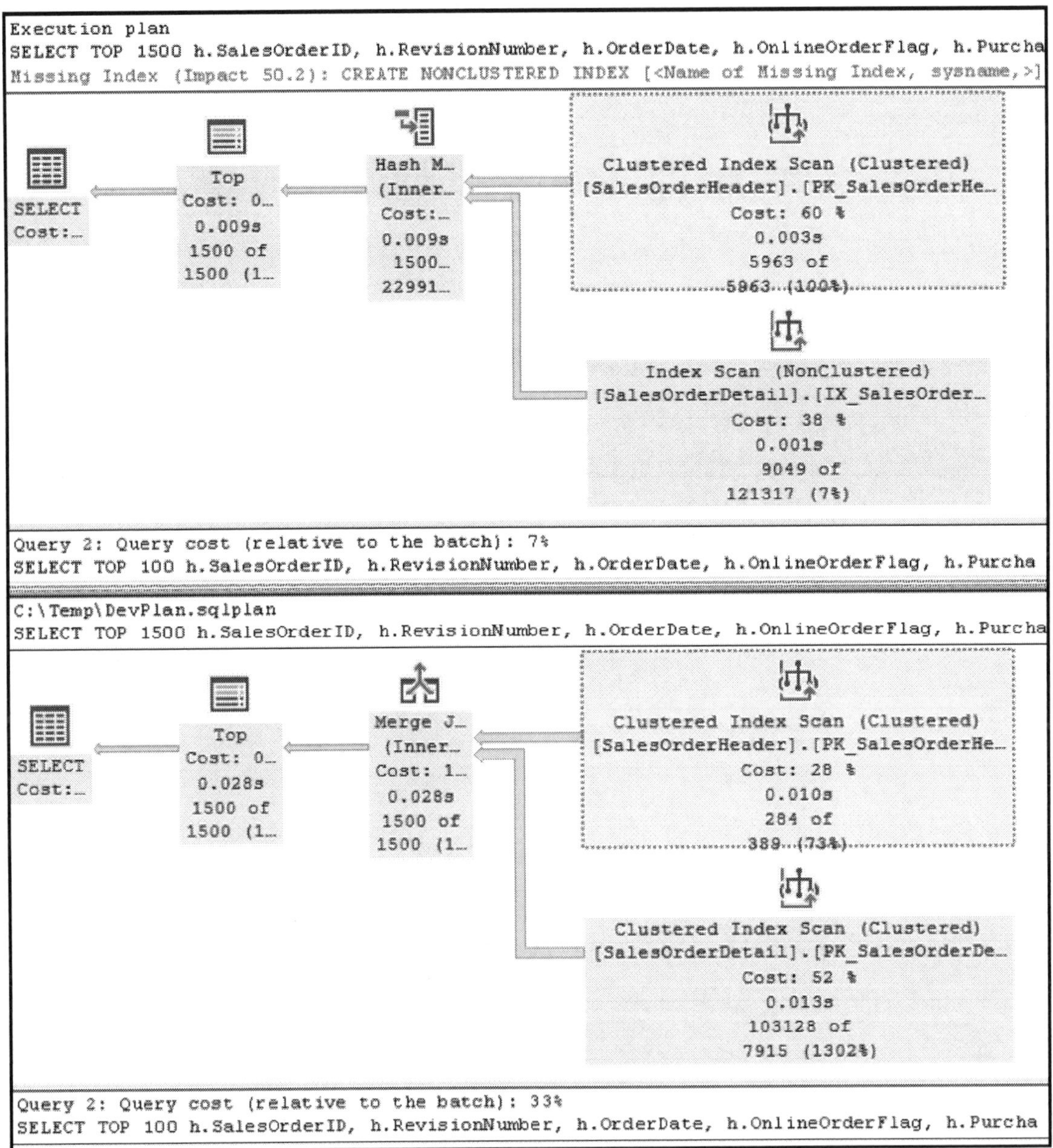

Note that for this comparison we also want to highlight differences, not only default similar regions or operators. For that purpose, we can go to the **Statement Options** tab in the **Showplan Analysis** window and check the **Highlight operators not matching similar segments** option, after which operators that don't match between plans are highlighted in yellow:

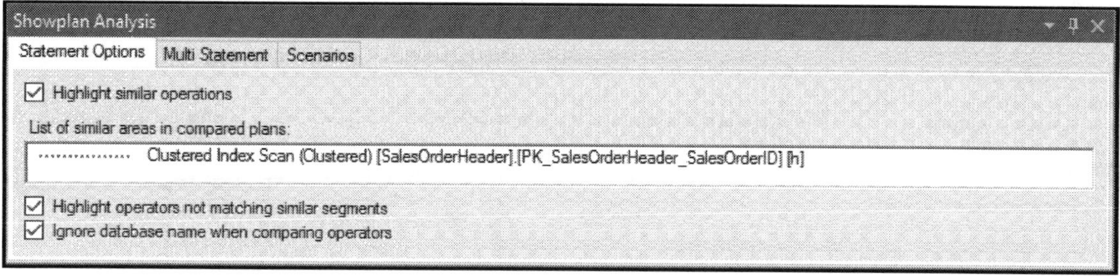

If we go back to the previous Plan Comparison window, we can see the execution plans for **Query 1** are different. The join type between both tables has changed from a merge join to a hash-match join, which executes much faster (9 ms instead of 28 ms). Hash matches are usually a good choice when SQL Server needs to join larger inputs that, now that we have removed row goal optimization, we can verify here.

The only similar region between plans is the **Clustered Index Scan** on the **SalesOrderHeader** table, but where as before it was the outer table for a merge join, it's now the **Build** table for the Hash Match join. And while this operator returns fewer rows in the **Bottom Plan** (the original query) than in the **Top Plan** (the hinted query), it also takes longer to execute (10 ms instead of 3 ms).

This can be explained by looking at the compared properties of both operators in the following screenshot:

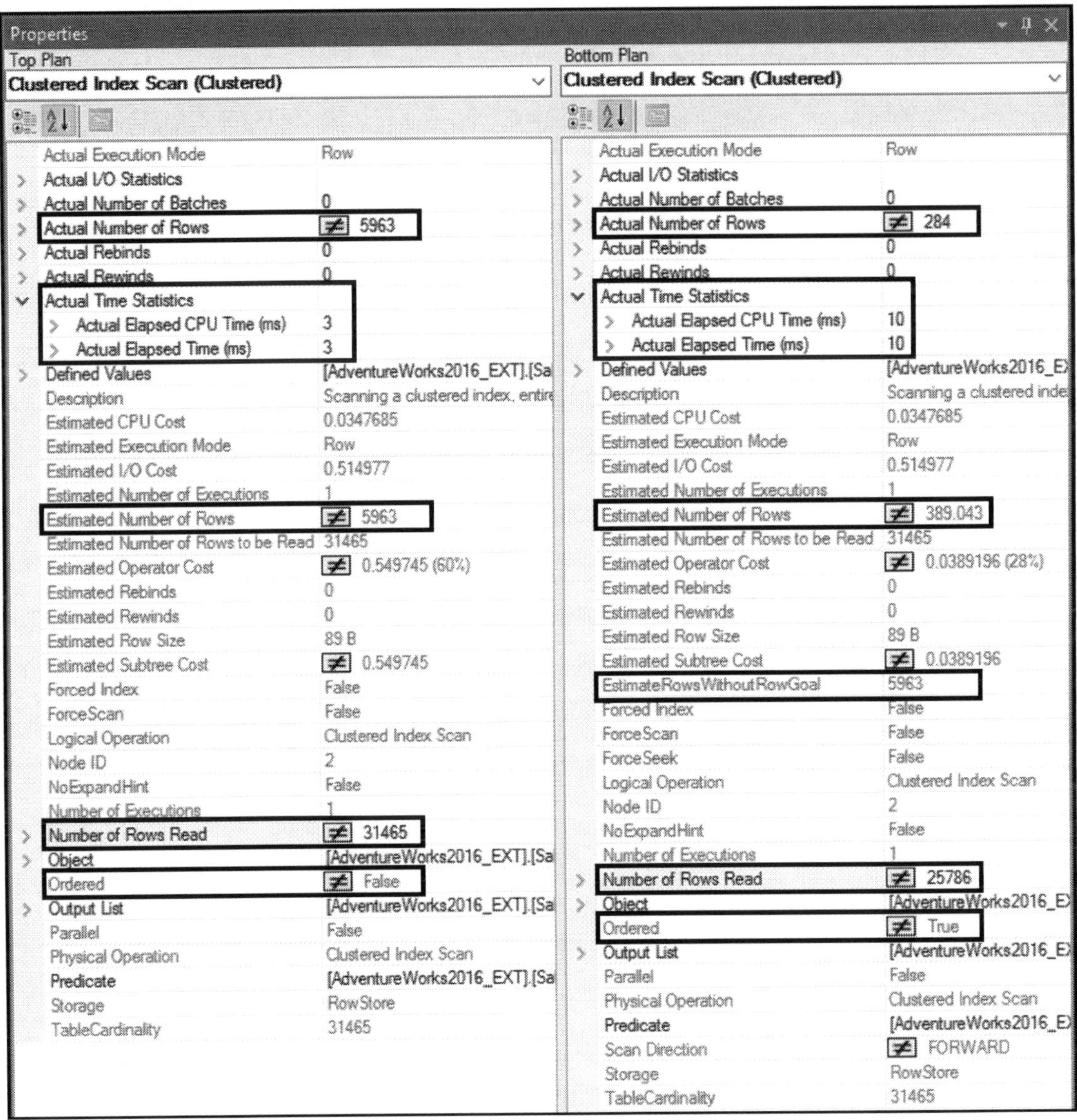

In the preceding screenshot we can observe that:

- The **Actual Number of Rows** after the predicate `[h].[OrderDate]>=[@FromDate]` is applied and changed from **284** in the **Bottom Plan** to **5,963** in the **Top Plan**.
- The **Number of Rows Read** (before the predicate is applied) has changed from **25,786** in the **Bottom Plan** to **31,465** in the **Top Plan** (this is the full **TableCardinality**).
- Yet we see in the **Actual Time Statistics** that the scan is faster in **Top Plan**. Why?
- Both the **Actual Number of Rows** and **Estimated Number of Rows in the Top Plan** match the **EstimateRowsWithoutRowGoal** property in the **Bottom Plan**. This was expected when we purposefully hinted out the row goal optimization.
- The scan of the **Bottom Plan** is slower because it has the **Ordered** property set to **True**, which indicates that the scan needs to enforce an explicit order to guarantee that the merge join has the required sorted input. At the storage engine level, this means enforcing that all rows are read in their logical order—following a linked list of index leaf-level pages ordered by index key order rather than their physical order—the page allocation order.
- The scan of the **Top Plan** has the **Ordered** property set to **False**, which indicates the rows are read following the index leaf-level pages' physical order. This explains that while the scan in the **Top Plan** reads more rows than the **Bottom Plan**, it is faster by reading all pages in order of physical allocation.

And what about the other index that is now identified as a difference? The **Clustered Index Scan** on the **SalesOrderDetail** table was replaced by a **NonClustered Index Scan**.

In the following plan comparison screenshot, we can observe that:

- While in the **Bottom Plan** (the original query) has drastically underestimated of the actual number of rows (103,128 of 7,915 estimated rows), the **Top Plan** (the hinted query) has an overestimation (9,049 actual rows of 121,317 estimated rows).

- Yet, the scan in the **Top Plan** executed in 1 ms, whereas the scan in the **Bottom Plan** executed in 13 ms.

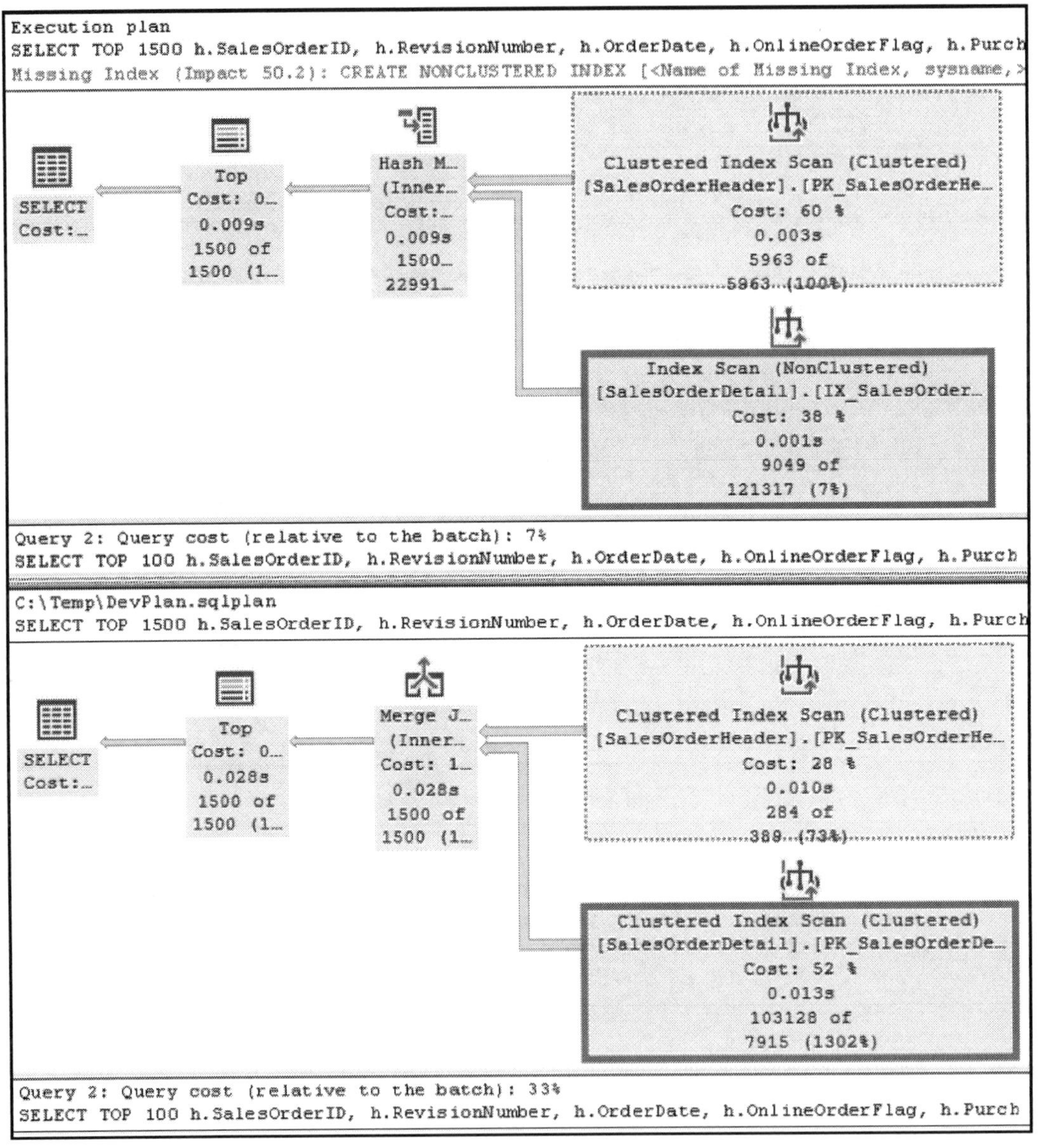

But even if SQL Server had to scan the entire non-clustered index as it did with the clustered index in the previous plan, it would still be faster with the new plan. Why?

We can see information about the indexes in **SalesOrderDetail** using the following T-SQL query example:

```
SELECT t.name AS TableName, i.name AS IndexName,
       i.type_desc, p.rows, a.total_pages, a.used_pages,
       CONVERT(DECIMAL(19,2),ISNULL(a.used_pages,0))*8/1024 AS DataSizeMB,
       ips.index_depth, ips.avg_record_size_in_bytes
FROM sys.allocation_units AS a
INNER JOIN sys.partitions AS p ON p.hobt_id = a.container_id AND a.type = 1
INNER JOIN sys.indexes AS i ON i.object_id= p.object_id
       AND i.index_id = p.index_id
INNER JOIN sys.tables AS t ON t.object_id = p.object_id
CROSS APPLY sys.dm_db_index_physical_stats (DB_ID(), p.object_id,
i.index_id, NULL, 'SAMPLED') AS ips
WHERE t.name = 'SalesOrderDetail';
```

The following screenshot shows the result set for the query example:

	TableName	IndexName	type_desc	rows	total_pages	used_pages	DataSizeMB	index_depth	avg_record_size_in_bytes
1	SalesOrderDetail	PK_SalesOrderDetail_SalesOrderID...	CLUSTERED	121317	1505	1290	10.0781250	3	80.06
2	SalesOrderDetail	AK_SalesOrderDetail_rowguid	NONCLUSTERED	121317	657	495	3.8671875	3	28
3	SalesOrderDetail	IX_SalesOrderDetail_ProductID	NONCLUSTERED	121317	424	308	2.4062500	2	16

When compared to the clustered index, we can see that, even if SQL Server had to scan the full non-unique, non-clustered **IX_SalesOrderDetail_ProductID** index, that would amount to 2.4 MB of I/O instead of 10 MB for a full scan of the clustered index, which would be consistently better. The size difference is explained by the average record size for the non-clustered index being 16 bytes versus 80 bytes for the clustered index.

Query Plan Analyzer

So far, we have had to analyze query plans by correlating information in plan and operator properties to create working hypotheses on how to solve query performance issues. One constant throughout all these troubleshooting scenarios has to do with comparing estimated rows with actual rows flowing through the operators in a query plan. This is because significant differences between estimated and actual rows usually expose **Cardinality Estimator** (**CE**) issues, which indicate several possible causes, from outdated statistics, to parameter sniffing or even out-of-model constructs such as **User-defined Functions** (**UDF**) or **Multi-Statement Table-valued Functions** (**MSTVF**).

And depending on the query performance problem, it may not be easy to even start troubleshooting, especially in complex plans. This is exactly why SSMS has a plan analysis tool, and this can jump-start our query performance troubleshooting efforts.

In the following example, we will examine a query that was not performing as expected in production. Specifically, one stored procedure that's executed many times a minute was thought to be abnormally slow, because the application that used it was not responding properly.

First, we tried running the stored procedure in the dev environment using sample data and couldn't find any major issue with the resulting query plan nor its performance. This must mean that whatever is happening can only be found in production. What is needed to proceed with troubleshooting is an actual execution plan, and so we used XEvents to capture the query execution plan for the offending stored procedure using the **query_post_execution_showplan** XEvent—not an easy proposition given collecting this XEvent itself generates overhead. We will discuss several other ways of collecting the actual execution plan in a much more lightweight fashion in `Chapter 12`, *Troubleshooting Live Queries*.

The captured query execution plan is shown in the following screenshot:

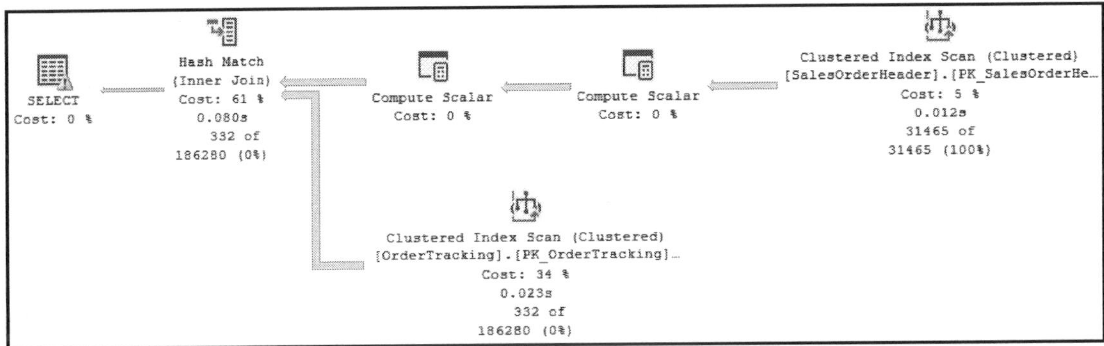

The stored procedure in the preceding query execution plan is in the **AdventureWorks** sample database, and is created as the following example:

```
CREATE OR ALTER PROCEDURE usp_SalesTracking @UpdatedOn datetime
AS
SET NOCOUNT ON;
SELECT *
FROM Sales.SalesOrderHeader AS soh
INNER JOIN Sales.OrderTracking AS ot ON ot.SalesOrderID = soh.SalesOrderID
WHERE ot.EventDateTime >= @UpdatedOn;
GO
```

With the plan open, right-click anywhere in in the query execution plan and the following menu pops up:

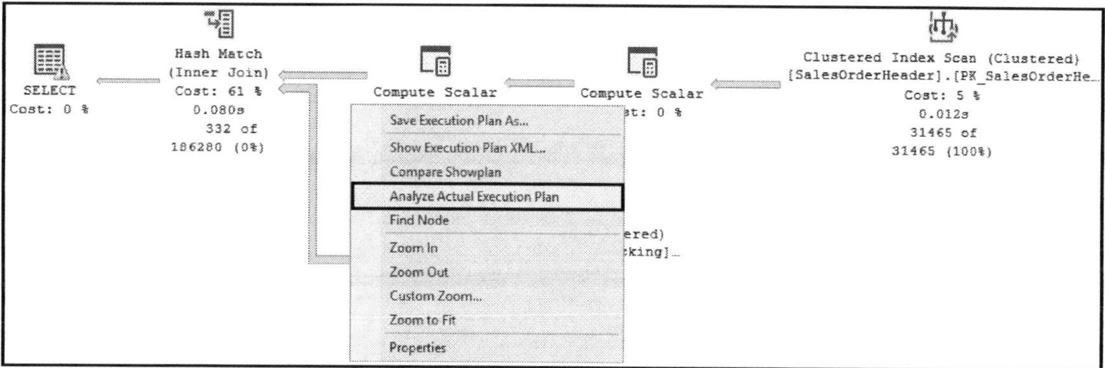

Clicking the **Analyze Actual Execution Plan** menu option opens a new window docked on the bottom—**Showplan Analysis**:

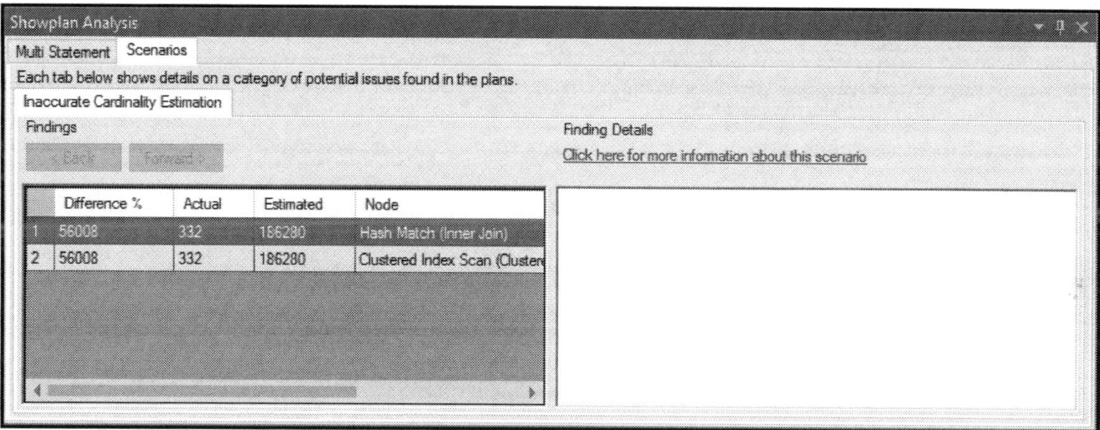

Inside the window there is a **Scenarios** tab—a placeholder to facilitate adding future scenarios if there's user demand for them—on which we find the **Inaccurate Cardinality Estimation** tab.

If we click on the link to the right under **Finding Details**, we get a popup that explains what this scenario is all about:

"One of the most important inputs for the Query Optimizer to choose an optimal execution plan is the estimated number of rows to be retrieved per operator. These estimations model the amount of data to be processed by the query, and therefore drive cost estimation. Changes in the estimated number of rows is one of the most frequent reasons for the Query Optimizer to pick different query plans.

This scenario helps you to find differences in estimated number of rows between two execution plans, scoped to the operators that perform similar data processing, and suggests possible causes for those differences, as well as possible workarounds to improve the estimates. Note that this automation may not identify all operators, their differences, or all possible root causes. So while the information displayed here is a tentative mitigation opportunity to resolve an issue identified by this scenario, it should still help in analyzing root causes of plan difference."

As previously suggested, it will try to find hotspots in the query execution plan that have to do with patterns of inaccurate CE, and two such findings are already on the left side of the window.

As seen in the following screenshot, selecting any of the findings will center the plan on the offending operator—in this case, the **Clustered Index Scan**:

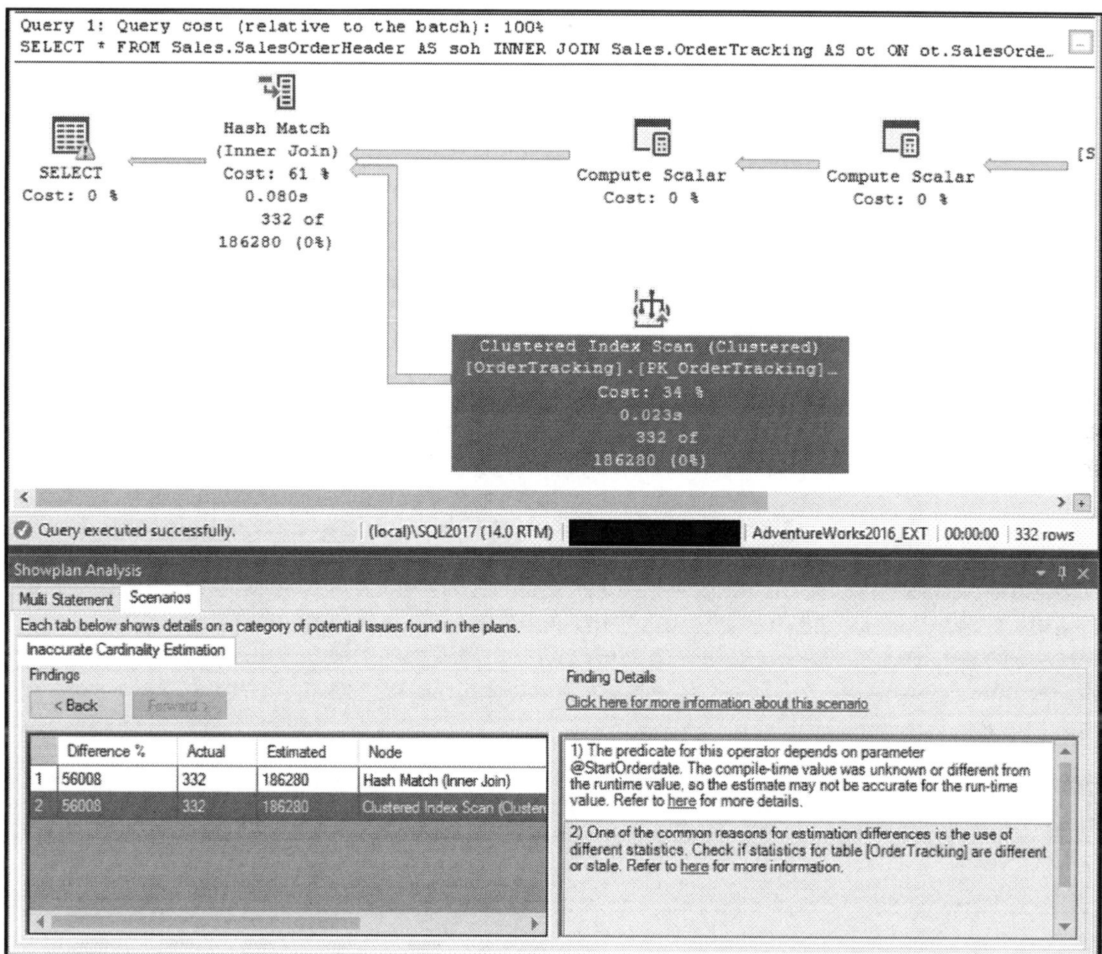

We should always start by analyzing findings that are related to data-reading operators such as seeks and scans, and then move up the query plan tree to aggregates and joins. The **Clustered Index Scan** in the plan has a 56,000 percent difference between actual and estimated rows (332 of 186,280). Notice **Finding Details** to the right. The following are two possible reasons for the incorrect estimation presented:

- The plan analyzer found a predicate in this scan that depends on a parameter whose runtime value is different than the compile time value, or the compile time value is **NULL**. This constitutes a case of bad parameter sniffing. Clicking the link at the end of the result of the search (the word **here**) opens a pop-up window with detailed background information about bad parameter sniffing and how to mitigate it.
- Because it's common to have incorrect estimations based on wrong or outdated statistics, the plan analyzer suggests we need to look at whatever statistics are loaded for this plan and verify whether they need to be updated. Again, clicking the link at the end of the finding (the word **here**) opens a pop-up window with background information.

We can start with suggestion 2 because this very easy to determine using an actual execution plan. On the plan root node (**SELECT**), open the properties window to analyze the **OptimizerStatsUsage** property. As seen in the following screenshot, no statistics require updating—notice that **ModificationCount** is zero; however, several statistics related to the **OrderTracking** table have only 30 percent sampling. This may be an issue—if it's possible to update statistics with a higher sampling ratio, especially for tables whose data distribution is not uniform, that is always a good choice:

OptimizerStatsUsage	
[1]	
Database	[AdventureWorks2016_EXT]
LastUpdate	4/14/2019 10:41 PM
ModificationCount	0
SamplingPercent	30.5933
Schema	[Sales]
Statistics	[IX_OrderTracking_SalesOrderID]
Table	[OrderTracking]
[2]	
[3]	
Database	[AdventureWorks2016_EXT]
LastUpdate	4/14/2019 10:41 PM
ModificationCount	0
SamplingPercent	30.5933
Schema	[Sales]
Statistics	[IX_OrderTracking_CarrierTrackingNumber]
Table	[OrderTracking]
[4]	
Database	[AdventureWorks2016_EXT]
LastUpdate	4/14/2019 10:42 PM
ModificationCount	0
SamplingPercent	30.5933
Schema	[Sales]
Statistics	[_WA_Sys_00000006_770B9E7A]
Table	[OrderTracking]

If updating statistics with a larger sample is not doable for now (maybe the tables have millions of rows and updating with a larger sample could cause problems), we can move on to suggestion 1, which points to bad parameter sniffing.

We discussed the topic of parameter sniffing in the *The importance of parameters* section in `Chapter 2`, *Understanding Query Processing*, and in the *Query plan properties of interest* section in `Chapter 4`, *Exploring Query Execution Plans*.

This is also easy enough to investigate: open the properties window to analyze the **Parameter List** property. As seen in the following screenshot, the parameter with which the stored procedure was compiled and optimized is not the same as the parameter run-time value:

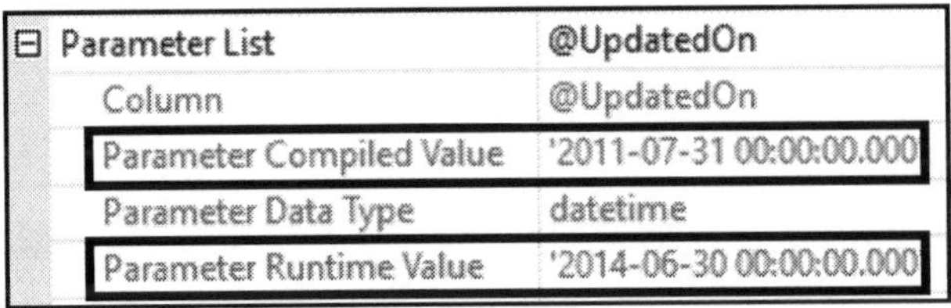

Parameter List
@UpdatedOn
Column
@UpdatedOn
Parameter Compiled Value
'2011-07-31 00:00:00.000
Parameter Data Type
datetime
Parameter Runtime Value
'2014-06-30 00:00:00.000

This means that at its first execution, the plan was optimized for a date value **'2011-07-31 00:00:00.000'** and was cached for subsequent use.

Before moving on, save the current plan to a `.sqlplan` file because we may need it later for comparison with other plans.

Executing the stored procedure with the compiled value yields the following query execution plan:

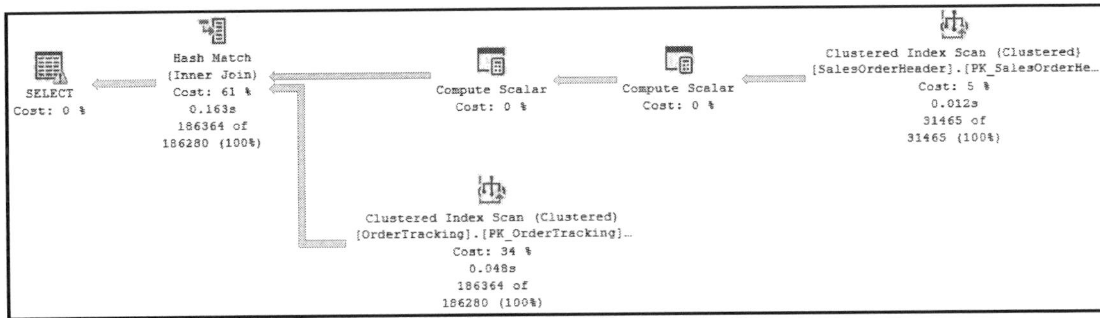

A quick analysis shows that all operators have perfect estimations—the actual rows are the same as the estimated rows. This confirms that the currently cached plan is optimized for the first incoming parameter, which is an older date. But if the parameter used in the first compilation wasn't the most frequently used, but instead more recent dates are often used as parameters, a reasonable hypothesis is that compiling the stored procedure and executing it for the first time using a common parameter will yield a different plan.

We can test this using the following example, which creates a new test-stored procedure that is not called by the application:

```
CREATE OR ALTER PROCEDURE usp_SalesTracking_Test @UpdatedOn datetime
AS
SET NOCOUNT ON;
SELECT *
FROM Sales.SalesOrderHeader AS soh
INNER JOIN Sales.OrderTracking AS ot ON ot.SalesOrderID = soh.SalesOrderID
WHERE ot.EventDateTime >= @UpdatedOn;
GO
EXECUTE usp_SalesTracking_Test '2014-6-30 00:00:00'
GO
```

Executing the new stored procedure with a common value yields the following query execution plan:

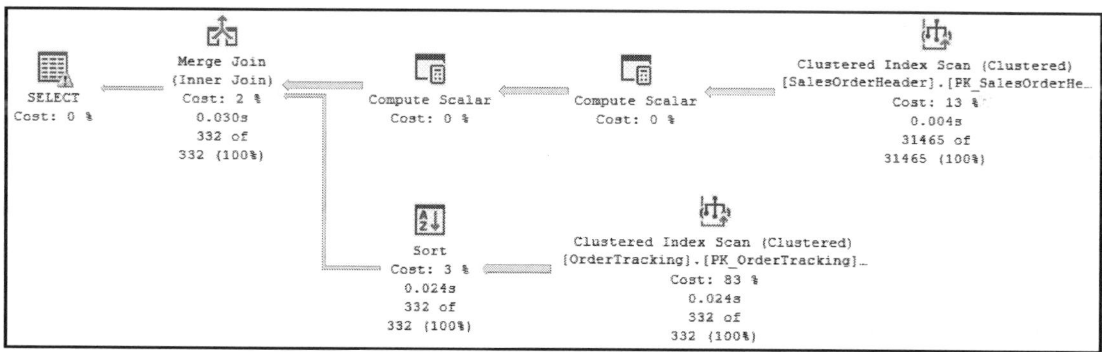

This is a very different plan that also executed quicker. We can use the plan comparison feature we discussed in the previous section to quickly find the main differences between the plan we just got and the previously saved **ParamSniffingInvestigation.sqlplan** file. The comparison window looks like the following screenshot:

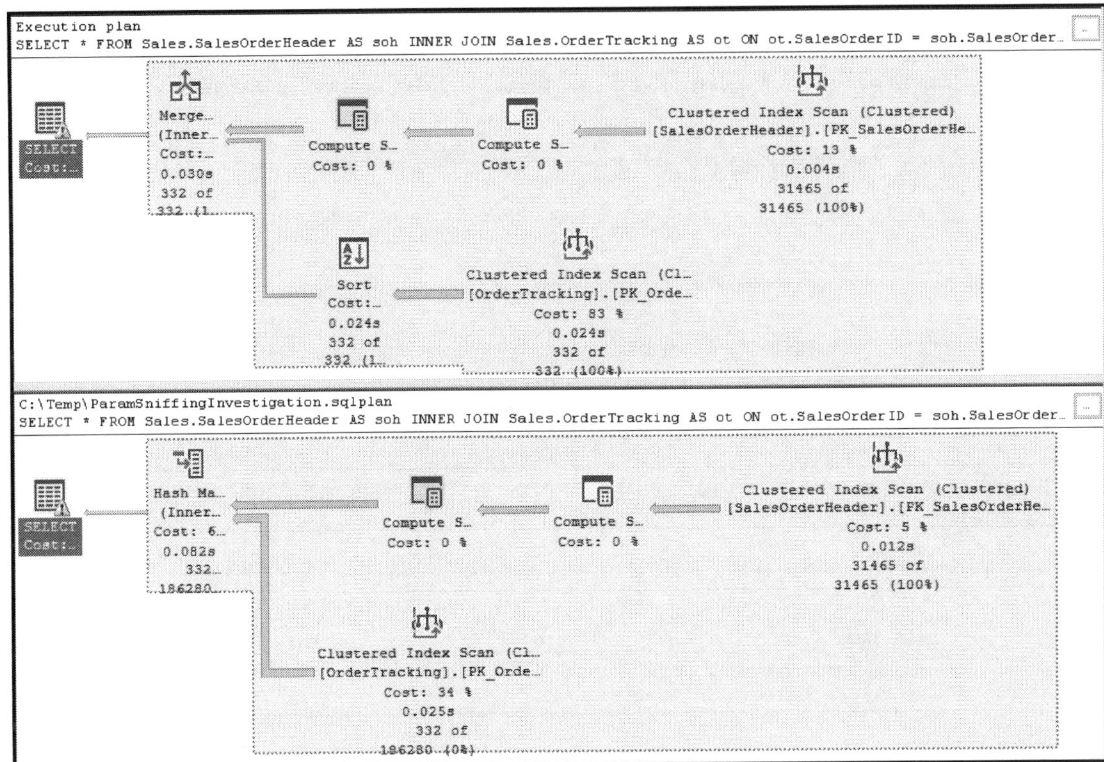

The plans are similar, with a couple of interesting observations to be made:

- The **Clustered Index Scan** on the **OrderTracking** table has **accurate estimations** that match the common case of returning fewer records—the estimated rows match the actual rows returned.
- The **previous Hash Match** join (**Bottom Plan** compiled with the **'2011-7-31 00:00:00'** parameter value) **turned in to a Merge Join** (**Top Plan** compiled with the **'2014-6-30 00:00:00'** parameter value), due to the corrected estimations.

Opening the properties of the root nodes (**SELECT**) shows additional relevant information that flags the need to optimize for the common case, as seen in the following screenshot:

- The **QueryTimeStats** property for each query shows that optimizing for the common value (**Top Plan**) executes quicker than reusing the plan from production (**Bottom Plan**) compiled with an older date: 32 ms instead of 81 ms.
- The **Memory Grant** property is also much lower in the **Top Plan** (1.9 MB) than in the **Bottom Plan** (76 MB). Expanding the **MemoryGrantInfo** section would reveal that, of the 76 MB, the **Bottom Plan** only used 7 MB.

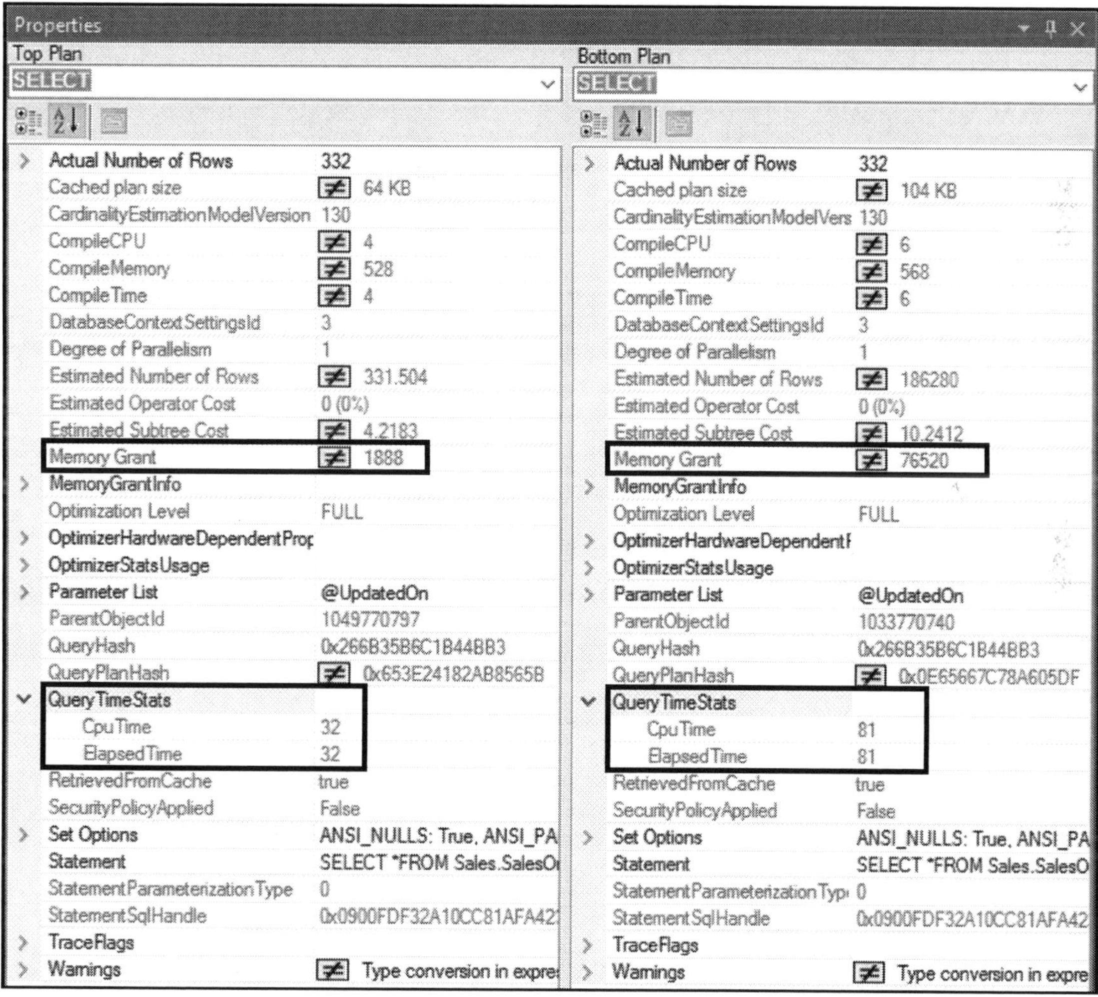

We discussed the effects on concurrency of having memory grant incorrect estimations in the *Query plan properties of interest* section of `Chapter 4`, *Exploring Query Execution Plans*, and how to mine the plan cache for other such concurrency inhibitors in the *Troubleshooting common scenarios with DMV queries* section of `Chapter 8`, *Building Diagnostic Queries Using DMVs and DMFs*.

Having proven this is a case of bad parameter sniffing, a few options are available to remediate the issue in production:

- Rewrite the stored procedure to add the `OPTION (RECOMPILE)` hint. With this hint, a plan is calculated every time the stored procedure is executed and optimized for the current incoming parameter value.
- Rewrite the stored procedure to add the `OPTION (OPTIMIZE FOR (@UpdatedOn = '2014-6-30 00:00:00'))` hint. With this hint, even after recompiling, the stored procedure will be optimized for the common value—a recent date that we chose.
- Rewrite the stored procedure to add the `OPTION (OPTIMIZE FOR UNKNOWN)` hint. This will create a generic plan that may not necessarily be optimized for any incoming parameter.

This currently has the same effect as rewriting the stored procedure to assign the parameter value to a local variable and using that within the query rather than the parameter directly. However, this is simply a side-effect of the way local variables affect the optimization process, and not of explicitly directing the Query Optimizer to turn off parameter sniffing.

- If most queries in a database had a bad parameter sniffing issue, then disabling parameter sniffing may be a mitigation when hinting all the code is not a feasible option. To do this at the database level, use the database-scoped configuration **PARAMETER_SNIFFING** in the following T-SQL command: `ALTER DATABASE SCOPED CONFIGURATION SET PARAMETER_SNIFFING = OFF;`

- To do this at the system level, use the following T-SQL command to enable trace flag **4136** globally. Note that enabling a global trace flag requires sysadmin privileges and can't be used on Azure: `DBCC TRACEON (4136, -1);`

Summary

In the *Query Plan Comparison* section, we were able to take a query plan from the production environment that was not performing as expected and validate that, when running the same query in the development (dev) environment with a production-like database, we were able consistently response the issue. And then, through comparative analysis of the cached query plan from production (an estimated execution plan) and the actual execution plan from dev, we created hypotheses from the data we observed, until we found the root cause. Last, we tested a fix for the root cause of the issue by hinting the query, which, again by comparing plans, determined that the new plan was better than the old plan, and should now be implemented in production.

In the *Query Plan Analyzer* section, we were able to take a query plan that had been captured in the production environment through an XEvent trace and get started with finding out what could be negatively affecting performance by using this new feature. This allowed us to find significant differences between estimated and actual rows in the affected query execution plan and led us to suspect a bad parameter sniffing problem, which turned out to be confirmed. After that, we were given several strategies to deal with the problem to bring back to production, and definitively mitigate, the issue.

In the next chapter, we will look at a tool called **Query Store** that can help capture query plans and identify query performance regressions.

11
Tracking Performance History with Query Store

This chapter will introduce the Query Store, which is effectively a flight recorder for SQL Server T-SQL executions, allowing performance tracking over time and analysis of workload trends through rich UI reports that are included with SSMS.

We will also see how the Query Store integrates with the Query Plan Comparison, which was covered in `Chapter 10`, *Comparative Analysis of Query Plans*, for a complete UI-driven workflow for query performance insights.

This chapter covers the following topics:

- The Query Store
- Tracking expensive queries
- Fixing regressed queries

The Query Store

The requirement to track query performance statistics over time had been a long-time request by SQL Server users, because it unlocks the ability to go back in time and understand trends, but also point-in-time occurrences. Maybe our company website glitched because there was a point-in-time issue with the database, or a critical application sometimes slows down without a predictable pattern, or we upgrade from an older version of SQL Server and suddenly part of our workload is much slower. Barring any hardware problems, all these scenarios can usually be boiled down to one common cause—query plan optimization choices. This led to the creation of the **Query Store** (**QS**)—an effective flight recorder for our databases that's available in SQL Server (starting with SQL Server 2016) and Azure SQL Database, including Managed Instance.

Recall what we discussed about the process of query optimization in `Chapter 2`, *Understanding Query Processing*, and specifically the role of cardinality estimation that we discussed in `Chapter 3`, *Mechanics of the Query Optimizer*: SQL Server can consider many plans during the query optimization process and so, when a problem occurs, being able to backtrack historical information to understand if there were changes to the query plans of slow queries is fundamental.

We have seen queries that allow us to mine the plan cache to get all types of important information in the *Exploring Query Plan Cache DMVs* section of `Chapter 8`, *Building Diagnostic Queries Using DMVs and DMFs*, but those alone are not enough to help answer three pressing questions during a performance troubleshooting exercise:

- Which query or set of queries slowed down from a previous moment in time?
- What was the previous query plan that worked better than the current plan in the cache?
- Is there a way that I can force the plan to look more like the good plan? Can I use a plan guide, for example? We will see how a plan guide can be used in `Chapter 12`, *Troubleshooting Live Queries*, under the *Activity Monitor gets new life* section.

To answer these questions, the Query Store captures query plans and runtime execution statistics in the user database. Storing information on-disk means that, unlike most DMVs, its information is available after a restart, database upgrade, and query plan recompilations. With all of this, Query Store makes it easier to find performance regressions and mitigate them literally with one click of a button—we'll show this later in this chapter—which is a process that can take hours or days with other means, such as collecting traces and analyzing them manually. Query Store also unlocks the ability to identify top resource consuming queries, and analyze performance trends across workloads, putting database professionals in the driving seat when it comes to learning about recurring patterns and finding tuning opportunities to optimize our T-SQL queries.

Inner workings of the Query Store

When a query is compiled, its query text and plan (the same plan that gets stored in the plan cache) are captured in Query Store's memory structures to minimize the I/O overhead. When the query's first execution completes (and any subsequent execution), runtime execution statistics are also stored in memory. In the background, an asynchronous process runs to bucketize the information in time window aggregates and stores all this data in internal tables that reside in the user database. Both the aggregation time intervals and storage for on-disk tables are configurable, and we will cover them in the *Inner workings of the Query Store* section of this chapter.

Storing internal tables in the user database means that the QS is a single-database performance tracking system that stays with database backups and database clones. This in itself is a powerful capability, because we can get a database backup that includes its Query Store from one system and analyzes the performance data in another system.

Database clones refer to schema-only databases that are created with the DBCC **CLONEDATABASE** command. This operation creates a database with empty tables and indexes but maintains all programmability objects such as stored procedures and functions, as well as statistics objects and the Query Store. This becomes a powerful tool during cases of remote assistance for query optimization-related issues.

On top of the Query Store's memory and disk tables, there are system views to access all the information that is stored on both dimensions of data that's collected: query compilation and query execution time information. The QS system views exist in Azure SQL Database and SQL Server.

The SQL Server 2017 QS system views can be seen in the following screenshot, which we will use throughout this chapter:

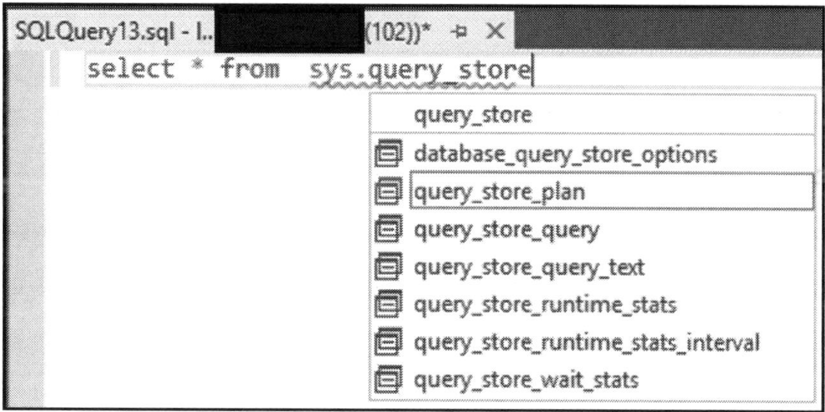

In turn, SSMS has a rich UI experience on the Query Store that's built on top of the system views. The available SSMS Query Store reports can be accessed under each database in the **Query Store** folder, as seen in the following screenshot:

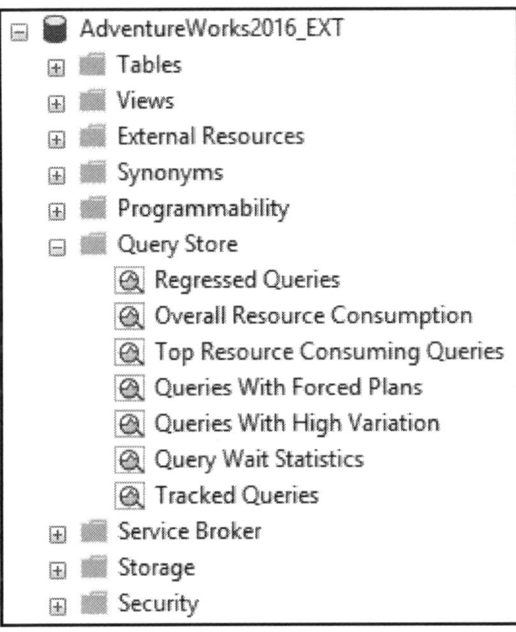

The following diagram outlines the Query Store architecture we discussed in this section:

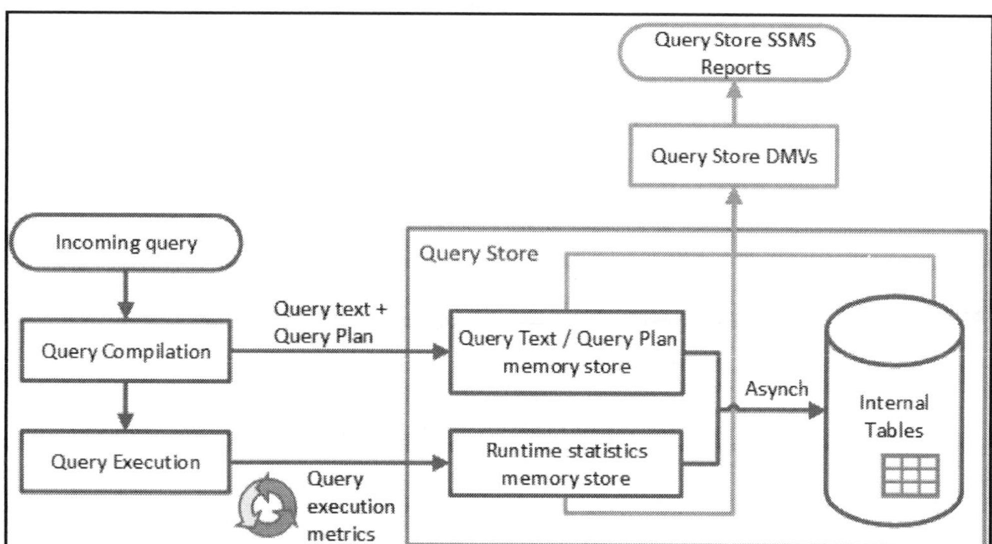

Configuring the Query Store

Azure SQL Database has the Query Store enabled by default. However, on SQL Server, it must be enabled manually. This can be done in two different ways:

- Using T-SQL, as seen in the following example for the **AdventureWorks2016** sample database:

```
USE [master]
GO
ALTER DATABASE [AdventureWorks2016]
SET QUERY_STORE = ON
GO
ALTER DATABASE [AdventureWorks2016]
SET QUERY_STORE (OPERATION_MODE = READ_WRITE)
GO
```

- Using SSMS, when we right-click on a database name in **Object Explorer**, select **Properties**, select the **Query Store** page, and change **Operation Mode** from **Off** to **Read Write**, as shown in the following screenshot:

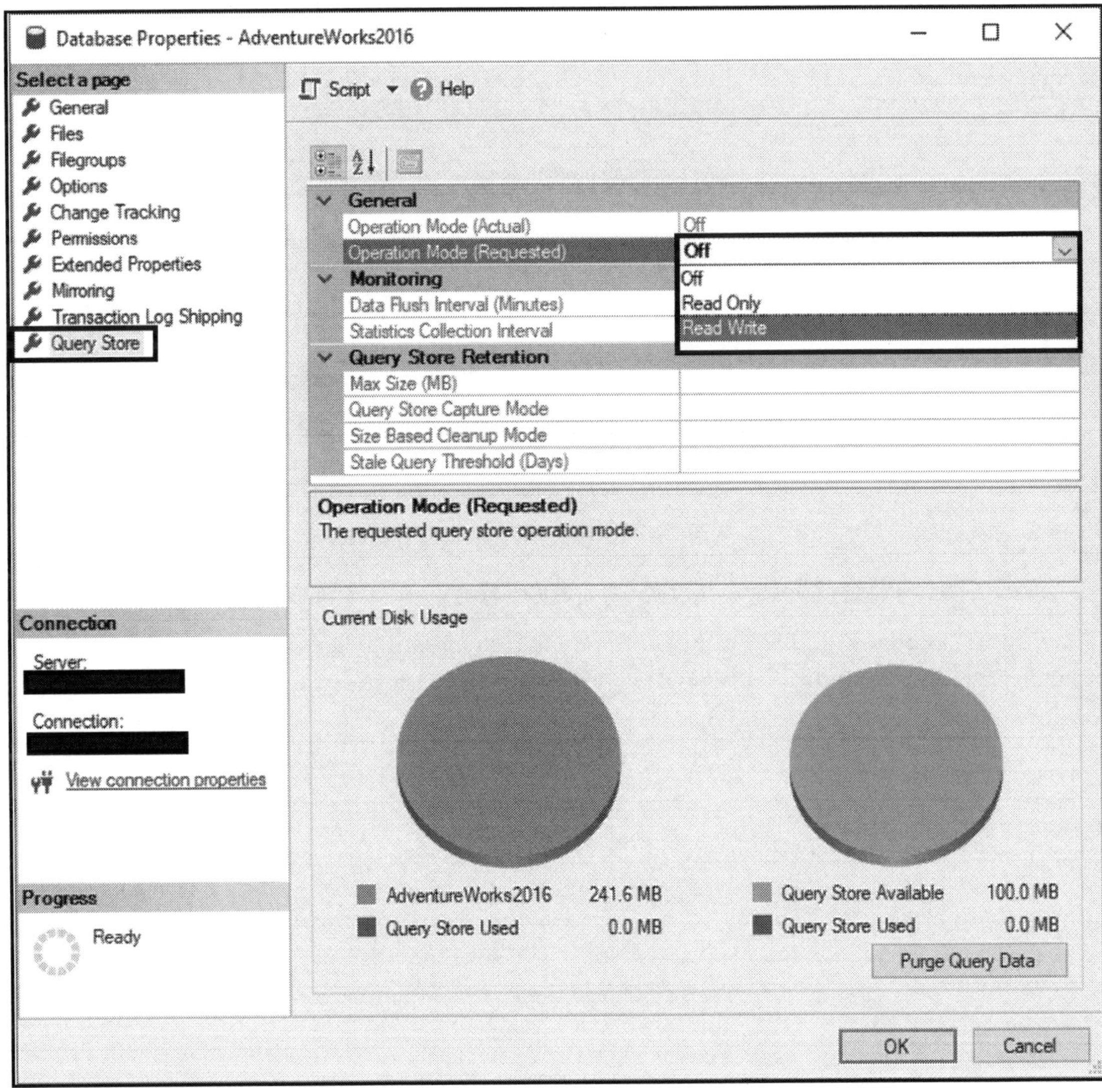

In the previous screenshot, we can see the full size of the database (241.6 MB) and how much of that size is used by the Query Store (0.0 MB). From the current Query Store size limit (100.0 MB), we can also see how much is being used (0.0 MB).

While the Query Store is disabled by default in SQL Server, it can be enabled via the **model** database. This would ensure that each new database will inherit the enabled Query Store settings from the model database.

However, the QS options cannot be set for the model database via SSMS. T-SQL must be used, as seen in the following example:

```
USE [master]
GO
ALTER DATABASE [model] SET QUERY_STORE = ON
GO
ALTER DATABASE [model] SET QUERY_STORE (OPERATION_MODE = READ_WRITE)
GO
```

As for the available settings to control the QS behavior through SSMS, these are as follows:

- **Operation Mode**: Defines the current operational status of QS, such as if it is currently collecting data. Can be disabled (**Off**), disabled but not cleared (**Read Only**), and enabled for data collection (**Read Write**).
- **Data Flush Interval (Minutes)**: Defines the frequency to persist collected runtime statistics from memory to disk tables. The default is **15** minutes (**900** seconds internally), which is what Microsoft recommends for most systems.
- **Statistics Collection Interval**: Defines the time interval aggregation buckets. The default is **1** hour (**60** minutes internally). Microsoft doesn't recommend a lower value for 24/7 operation.
- **Max Size (MB)**: Defines the maximum size up to which the Query Store can grow inside the user database, before it starts to clean up older information. If the cleanup process cannot keep up before the QS space is full, then QS operation mode will turn to **Read Only**. The default **up to SQL Server 2017 is 100 MB** increased to **1 GB in SQL Server 2019**.
- **Query Store Capture Mode**: Defines the amount of query information collected. Query store can collect information on all queries (**All**), only queries that execute regularly (**Auto**), or no queries whatsoever (**None**). The default is **All up to SQL Server 2017** (but it is highly recommended that you use Auto instead), and changes to **Auto in SQL Server 2019**—the same as Azure SQL Database. The **All** setting can be used sporadically for point-in-time troubleshooting, but we have other methods of collecting query plan information that don't aggregate data, which we will discuss in `Chapter 12`, *Troubleshooting Live Queries*.

- **Size Based Cleanup Mode**: Defines whether the internal cleanup task removes the oldest queries and their related runtime statistics from the Query Store using a **least recently used** (**LRU**) algorithm. The cleanup task wakes up when the size of QS on-disk tables reaches 90 percent of the defined maximum. The cleanup task stops when approximately 20 percent of the defined maximum is free. The default is **Auto** but can be turned **Off**, in which case the QS operation mode will turn to Read Only when the size limit is reached.
- **Stale Query Threshold (Days)**: Defines the duration that runtime statistics must be kept per collected query. For queries that haven't been executed over the defined time, its runtime statistics are evicted. The default is **30 days**. Consider the time that we need to reasonably keep query execution history. For example, if our workload roughly repeats itself every other week, we can lower this configuration value to 15 days because we should only need to keep about 2 weeks of data to investigate any issues.

All the previous **QS** options can also be set using T-SQL, plus two additional **QS** settings that are only available through T-SQL:

- **Max Plans per Query**: This setting defines the maximum number of plans maintained for each query. The default is **200**, and when the limit is reached, QS stops capturing new plans for that query. This can be the case for stored procedures that recompile often, for example.
- **Wait Stats Capture Mode**: Defines whether wait stats should be captured (**ON**) or not (**OFF**). The default is **ON**. A detailed discussion about waits is outside the scope of this book, but if you would like more information about the various wait types, the SQL Server documentation about waits is in the page for the DMV, **sys.dm_os_wait_stats**. This DMV shows cumulative wait information since the server was last started. However, QS does not collect detailed information per individual wait type name. Instead, QS groups wait types are per category, such as Lock, CPU, Tran Log IO, Network IO, Buffer IO, Latch, and so on. The mapping between Query Store wait categories and real wait type names is available in the SQL Server documentation page for the system view, **sys.query_store_wait_stats**.

Microsoft also recommends enabling two global trace flags that improve QS behavior on typical production systems:

- **Trace flag 7745**: Used to prevent QS data from having to be written to disk in case of a failover or shutdown, which would otherwise delay the failover or shutdown. However, this causes QS data that has not been persisted to disk yet to be lost (up to the time that was defined by **Data Flush Interval**), but typically this is not critical. This is the default behavior in Azure SQL Database.

- **Trace flag 7752**: Up to SQL Server 2017, this trace flag is used to allow an asynchronous load of the Query Store during database startup operations. The default synchronous load can delay database startup until the Query Store is fully available, which may not be warranted for production databases where uptime is more valuable than synchronous availability of monitoring data. **Starting with SQL Server 2019, this trace flag is not needed** because the asynchronous load becomes the default behavior. This is also the default behavior in Azure SQL Database.

We can see the options in the following screenshot, where the defaults were changed to the recommended values, just after we changed **Operation Mode** to **Read Write**:

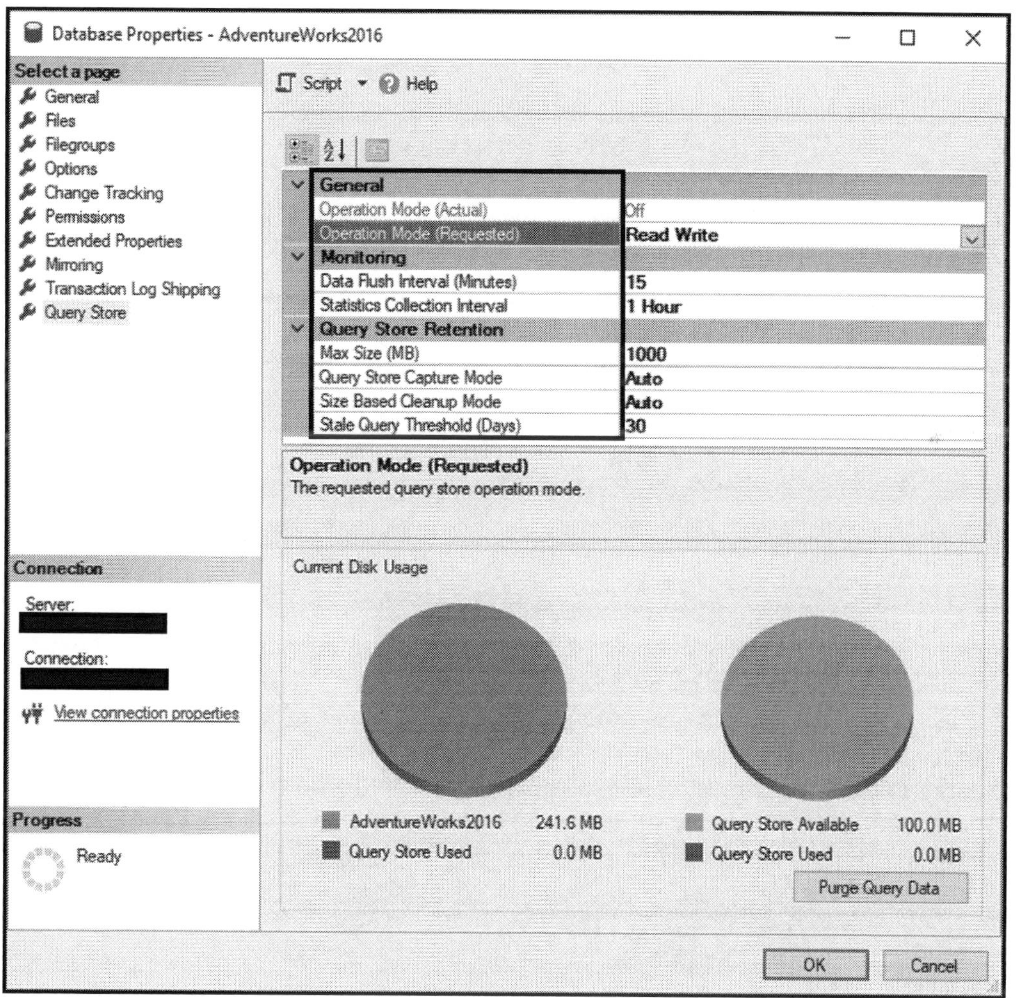

We can also use T-SQL, as shown in the following example:

```
USE [master]
GO
ALTER DATABASE [AdventureWorks2016] SET QUERY_STORE = ON
GO
ALTER DATABASE [AdventureWorks2016] SET QUERY_STORE (
        OPERATION_MODE=READ_WRITE,
        DATA_FLUSH_INTERVAL_SECONDS = 900,
        INTERVAL_LENGTH_MINUTES = 60,
        MAX_STORAGE_SIZE_MB= 1000,
        QUERY_CAPTURE_MODE = AUTO,
        SIZE_BASED_CLEANUP_MODE=AUTO,
        MAX_PLANS_PER_QUERY = 200,
        WAIT_STATS_CAPTURE_MODE = ON,
        CLEANUP_POLICY = (STALE_QUERY_THRESHOLD_DAYS = 90)
        );
```

In this chapter, we have been primarily usually SQL Server 2017. However, if you're using SQL Server 2016, ensure that the Cumulative Update 2 of Service Pack 2 is installed at a minimum. This update included several scalability fixes for the Query Store that were already part of SQL Server 2017.

When the Query Store is configured according to the best practices we discussed in this chapter, it can be enabled 24/7. When QS is always enabled, it can start providing value to every database professional that ever had to invest countless hours into query performance troubleshooting that resulted from plan changes related to data distribution changes, or even configuration changes with SQL Server.

Tracking expensive queries

The Query Store only collects plans for **data manipulation language** (**DML**) statements, such as **SELECT**, **INSERT**, **UPDATE**, **DELETE**, **MERGE**, and **BULK INSERT**, as these are the T-SQL statements that will be responsible for most of our SQL Server's resource usage. Most **database administrators** (**DBAs**) are constantly looking for ways to optimize resource usage—after all, if T-SQL queries are using just the amount of resources they need (CPU, I/O, and memory), then SQL Server is operating at peak efficiency and allows for maximum concurrency with its current hardware resources.

This brings us to one of the main benefits of Query Store: tracking our workload heavy hitters—the most resource consuming queries. With this exercise, we may be able to uncover tuning opportunities that, if successful, further improve the efficiency of the server's resource usage.

To generate enough workload in our **AdventureWorks** database, we will be using an application called **QueryStoreSimpleDemo.exe**, available in the Microsoft GitHub sample repository at `https://github.com/Microsoft/sql-server-samples/blob/master/samples/features/query-store`. When this executable is started, we are prompted to enter the SQL Server instance we want to connect to, and one of several sample workloads that are available, as seen in the following screenshot. For now, we will use option **L**:

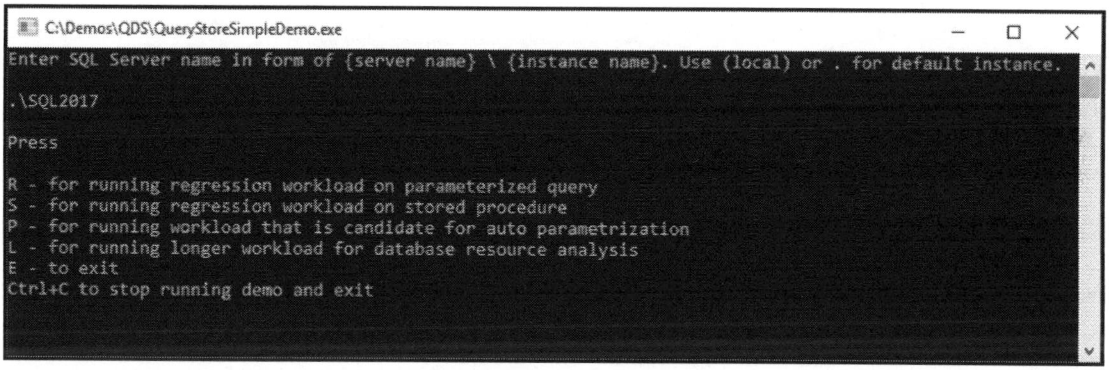

```
C:\Demos\QDS\QueryStoreSimpleDemo.exe
Enter SQL Server name in form of {server name} \ {instance name}. Use (local) or . for default instance.

.\SQL2017

Press

R - for running regression workload on parameterized query
S - for running regression workload on stored procedure
P - for running workload that is candidate for auto parametrization
L - for running longer workload for database resource analysis
E - to exit
Ctrl+C to stop running demo and exit
```

So that we have relevant data for our exercise, we need to leave the workload executing for about one hour at a minimum. This allows considerable resources to be used and tracked and have a production-like data collection available in Query Store. Then, we can start by using some of the reports and system views to understand the behavior of the workload over our **AdventureWorks** sample database.

We will start by double-clicking on the **Top Resource Consuming Queries** SSMS report, which is highlighted in the following screenshot:

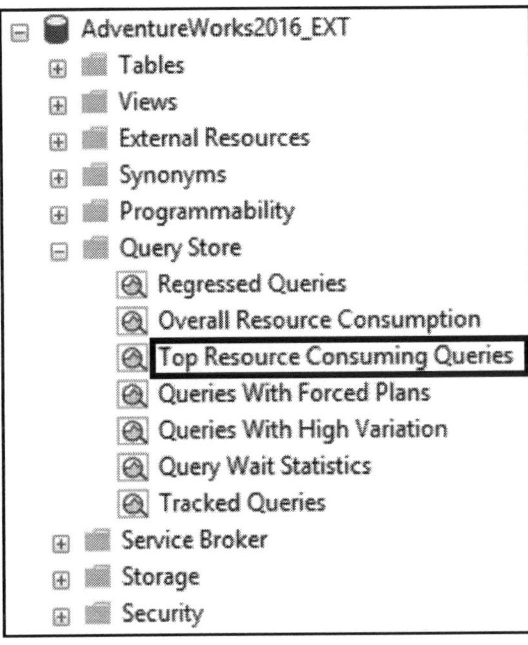

This opens the report in a new window tab, as seen in the following screenshot:

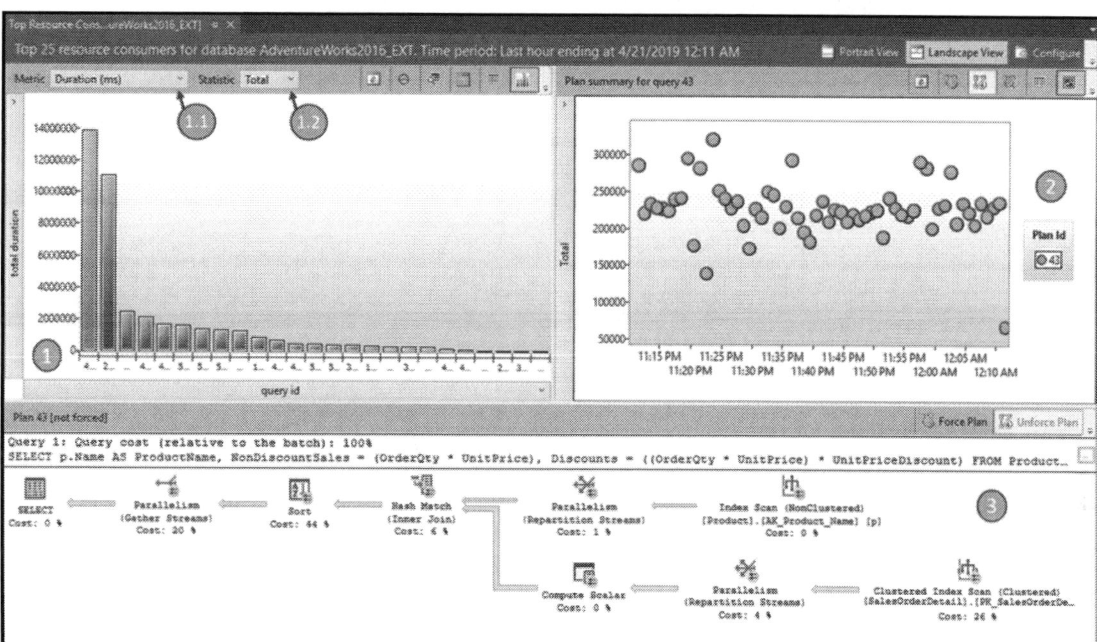

Let's explore what this report can show us. The top left quadrant (marked as **1** in the preceding screenshot) displays the top 25 resource consumers for our database. Just above it, we can see two dropdowns that allow us to change the following settings:

- **Metric**: It's the setting by which the charts are drawn (marked as **1.1** in the preceding screenshot), from the default **Duration (ms)** to any other metric available, as seen in the following screenshot detail.

- **Statistic**: The aggregation used for the chosen metric (marked as **1.2** in the preceding screenshot) with the default being **Total**, but other are available, such as **average (Avg)**, **maximum (Max)**, **minimum (Min)**, and **standard deviation (Std Dev)**:

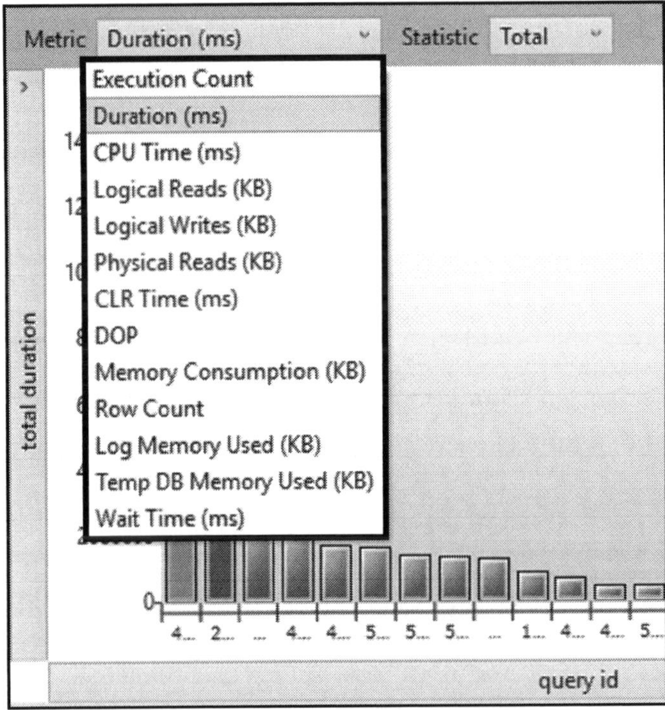

For example, let's assume that our server is CPU-bound: it makes sense to change the metric to **CPU Time (ms)** so that we can take those queries and analyze them for tuning opportunities. Other scenarios are possible, for example, if we've detected waiting queries and suspect parallelism may have been misused in the workload, then we change the metric to **DOP** to find queries that operate with a high degree of parallelism and may be waiting too much. Or perhaps memory is the concern, and so using the **Memory Consumption (KB)** metric is the starting point.

The top right quadrant (marked as **2** in the preceding screenshot) displays the **plan summary** for the chosen query, namely its distribution throughout the timeline. If more than one plan exists for the query in scope, we'll see different colors for each **plan Id**. We will explore the other options that are available here later in this section.

The bottom (marked as **3** in the preceding screenshot) displays the **query plan**—the same as the cached query plan. Given that we know that query plan choices drive resource usage, this is an important resource to have available. There are no runtime metrics in the query plan—this is not an actual execution plan, but we can explore runtime information about this plan by playing with the top left quadrant view.

The top left quadrant can also be displayed in a tabular format organized by the chosen metric, which makes it easier to see actual numbers to correlate with the query plans. To change the view, we click the button that's highlighted in the following screenshot:

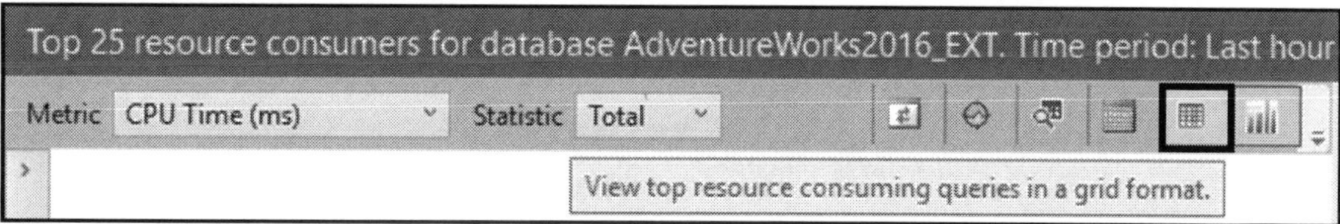

This changes the report to the following view (notice that we also changed the metric to **CPU Time**):

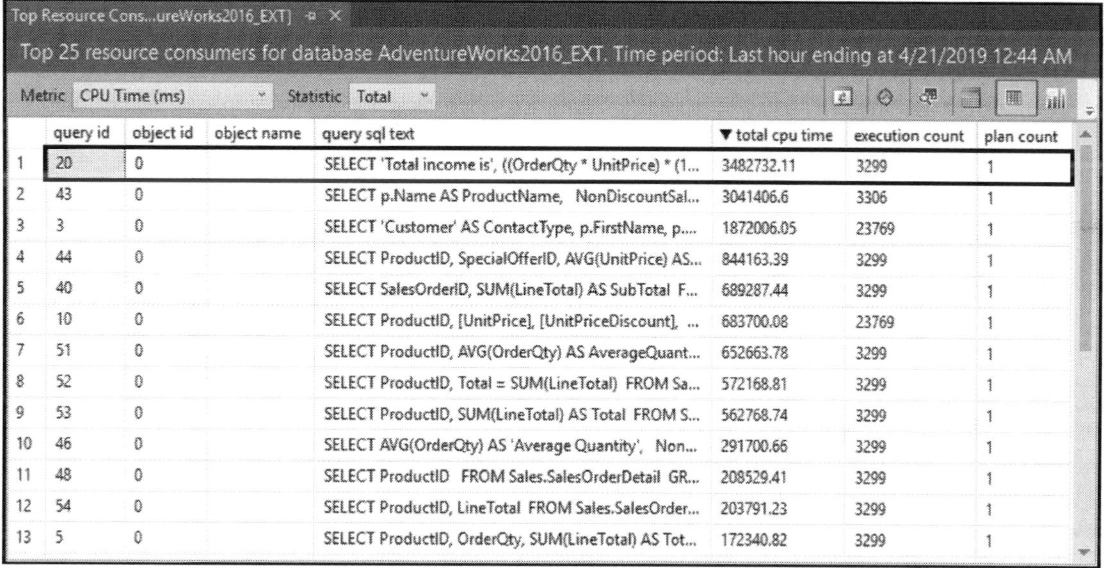

Top Resource Cons...ureWorks2016_EXT]

Top 25 resource consumers for database AdventureWorks2016_EXT. Time period: Last hour ending at 4/21/2019 12:44 AM

Metric CPU Time (ms) Statistic Total

	query id	object id	object name	query sql text	▼total cpu time	execution count	plan count
1	20	0		SELECT 'Total income is', ((OrderQty * UnitPrice) * (1...	3482732.11	3299	1
2	43	0		SELECT p.Name AS ProductName, NonDiscountSal...	3041406.6	3306	1
3	3	0		SELECT 'Customer' AS ContactType, p.FirstName, p....	1872006.05	23769	1
4	44	0		SELECT ProductID, SpecialOfferID, AVG(UnitPrice) AS...	844163.39	3299	1
5	40	0		SELECT SalesOrderID, SUM(LineTotal) AS SubTotal F...	689287.44	3299	1
6	10	0		SELECT ProductID, [UnitPrice], [UnitPriceDiscount], ...	683700.08	23769	1
7	51	0		SELECT ProductID, AVG(OrderQty) AS AverageQuant...	652663.78	3299	1
8	52	0		SELECT ProductID, Total = SUM(LineTotal) FROM Sa...	572168.81	3299	1
9	53	0		SELECT ProductID, SUM(LineTotal) AS Total FROM S...	562768.74	3299	1
10	46	0		SELECT AVG(OrderQty) AS 'Average Quantity', Non...	291700.66	3299	1
11	48	0		SELECT ProductID FROM Sales.SalesOrderDetail GR...	208529.41	3299	1
12	54	0		SELECT ProductID, LineTotal FROM Sales.SalesOrder...	203791.23	3299	1
13	5	0		SELECT ProductID, OrderQty, SUM(LineTotal) AS Tot...	172340.82	3299	1

Notice that **query id 20** is the heaviest in terms of total CPU time. We can also see the same information programmatically, using the system views that the report also leverages, as shown in the following sample query:

```
SELECT TOP 25 q.query_id, qt.query_sql_text,
    SUM(rs.count_executions) AS total_execution_count,
       AVG(rs.avg_rowcount) AS avg_rowcount,
       CAST(AVG(rs.avg_duration/1000) AS decimal(8,2)) AS avg_duration_ms,
       CAST(AVG(rs.avg_cpu_time/1000) AS decimal(8,2)) AS avg_cpu_time_ms,
       CAST(AVG(rs.avg_query_max_used_memory/8) AS decimal(8,2)) AS
avg_query_max_used_memory_KB,
       CAST(AVG(rs.avg_physical_io_reads/8) AS decimal(8,2)) AS
avg_physical_io_reads_KB,
       CAST(AVG(rs.avg_logical_io_reads/8) AS decimal(8,2)) AS
avg_logical_io_reads_KB,
       CAST(AVG(rs.avg_logical_io_writes/8) AS decimal(8,2)) AS
avg_logical_io_writes_KB
FROM sys.query_store_query_text AS qt
INNER JOIN sys.query_store_query AS q ON qt.query_text_id = q.query_text_id
INNER JOIN sys.query_store_plan AS p  ON q.query_id = p.query_id
INNER JOIN sys.query_store_runtime_stats AS rs ON p.plan_id = rs.plan_id
WHERE execution_type = 0
GROUP BY q.query_id, qt.query_sql_text
ORDER BY avg_cpu_time_ms DESC;
```

This returns the following resultset ordered by average CPU time. Not surprisingly, **query id 20** is the heaviest:

Results | Messages

	query_id	query_sql_text	total_execution_count	avg_rowcount	avg_duration_ms	avg_cpu_time_ms	avg_query_max_used_memory_KB	avg_physical_io_reads_KB	avg_logical_io_reads_KB	avg_logical_io_writes_KB
1	20	SELECT 'Total income is', ((OrderQty * UnitPrice) * (1.0 - ...	11338	121317	3384.34	1061.00	525.00	0.00	169.75	0.00
2	89	SELECT u.name AS [Name], u.principal_id AS [ID], ISN...	4	22	1107.48	1033.33	0.00	0.00	24.00	0.00
3	119	SELECT q.query_id, qt.query_text_id, qt.query_sql_text, ...	1	8136	3086.32	974.10	485.25	62.75	16929.50	2071.50
4	43	SELECT p.Name AS ProductName, NonDiscountSales...	11337	121317	4241.63	927.36	523.00	0.00	169.75	0.00
5	131	SELECT TOP 25 q.query_id, qt.query_sql_text, SU...	1	25	846.22	614.09	408.88	0.00	186.38	0.00
6	121	SELECT q.query_id, qt.query_sql_text, wait_category_d...	1	225	979.92	611.17	335.50	0.00	134.00	0.00
7	135	SELECT TOP 25 q.query_id, qt.query_sql_text, SU...	1	25	750.58	594.03	424.00	0.00	191.00	0.00
8	120	SELECT q.query_id, qt.query_text_id, qt.query_sql_text, ...	1	223	640.94	588.11	485.25	0.00	21284.88	2390.25
9	127	SELECT q.query_id, qt.query_sql_text, wait_category_d...	1	236	1054.82	573.53	346.50	0.00	172.75	0.00
10	147	SELECT 'Total income is', ((OrderQty * UnitPrice) * (1.0 - ...	1	121317	705.61	515.47	525.00	0.00	169.75	0.00

We can also see the top 25 queries by their average wait time using the following sample query:

```
SELECT TOP 25 q.query_id, qt.query_sql_text, wait_category_desc,
       SUM(ws.total_query_wait_time_ms) AS total_query_wait_time_ms,
       AVG(ws.avg_query_wait_time_ms) AS avg_query_wait_time_ms
FROM sys.query_store_query_text AS qt
INNER JOIN sys.query_store_query AS q ON qt.query_text_id = q.query_text_id
INNER JOIN sys.query_store_plan AS p  ON q.query_id = p.query_id
INNER JOIN sys.query_store_wait_stats AS ws ON p.plan_id = ws.plan_id
WHERE ws.wait_category_desc NOT IN ('Unknown', 'Idle') AND
ws.execution_type = 0
GROUP BY q.query_id, qt.query_sql_text, ws. wait_category_desc
ORDER BY avg_query_wait_time_ms DESC;
```

This returns the following resultset, where **query id 20** is the second query with the most wait time. Notice that it's a parallelism-related wait:

Results | Messages

	query_id	query_sql_text	wait_category_desc	total_query_wait_time_ms	avg_query_wait_time_ms
1	43	SELECT p.Name AS ProductName, NonDiscountSales ...	Parallelism	340353788	28911.5003290672
2	20	SELECT 'Total income is', ((OrderQty * UnitPrice) * (1.0 - ...	Parallelism	259237557	22032.4774165844
3	147	SELECT 'Total income is', ((OrderQty * UnitPrice) * (1.0 - ...	Parallelism	4899	4899
4	119	SELECT q.query_id, qt.query_text_id, qt.query_sql_text, ...	Other Disk IO	1406	1406
5	89	SELECT u.name AS [Name], u.principal_id AS [ID], ISNU...	Preemptive	4413	1103.25
6	130	SELECT TOP 25 q.query_id, qt.query_sql_text, SU...	CPU	1035	1035
7	122	SELECT q.query_id, qt.query_sql_text, SUM(rs.cou...	CPU	941	941
8	138	SELECT TOP 25 q.query_id, qt.query_sql_text, SU...	CPU	802	802
9	43	SELECT p.Name AS ProductName, NonDiscountSales ...	CPU	8681128	737.939639723995
10	43	SELECT p.Name AS ProductName, NonDiscountSales ...	Network IO	7769547	659.022727884016

While using the system view can prove to be a powerful tool, if the rich UI experience that's available in SSMS reports is preferred, a **Query Wait Statistics** report is also available. Opening it provides the view that's shown in the following screenshot, where we confirm that parallelism waits are the most prevalent in the workload:

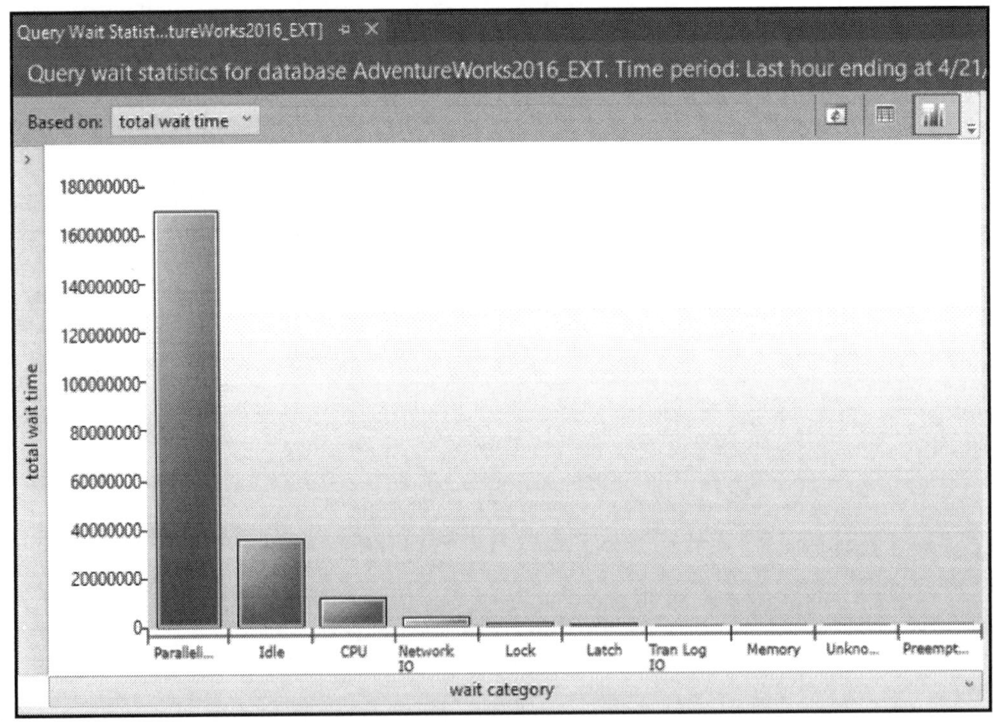

Clicking in the first bar (parallelism) opens a second view with the details for that wait category, as seen in the following screenshot. It confirms what we'd seen in the waits DMV—**query 20** is the second highest in wait times:

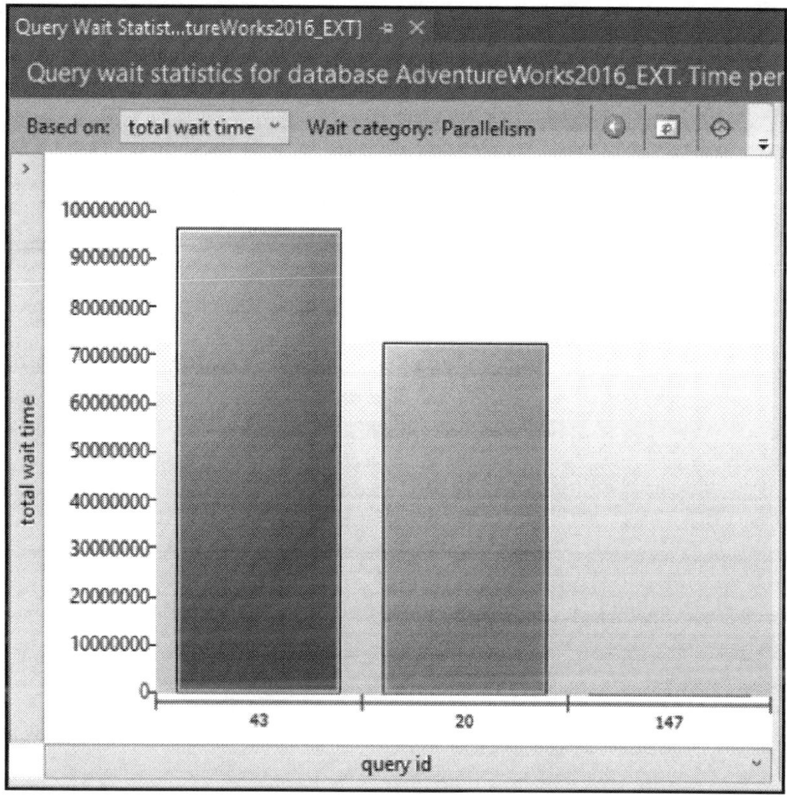

Now, we have a clear notion of the heavy hitters that need investigation, and the working hypothesis that tuning these will drive down CPU usage and alleviate our CPU-bound server. Back in the QS report, let's take the first query (20) and investigate. In the bottom section, we have the query plan. We can click the magnifier button, as shown in the following screenshot, to open the query text:

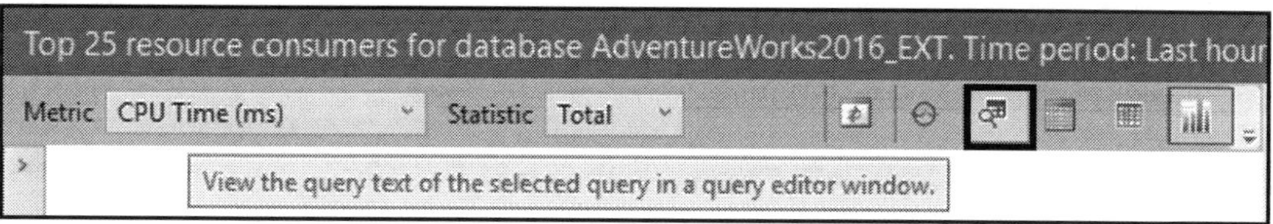

Alternatively, we can click the ellipsis button on the right-hand side for the same purpose:

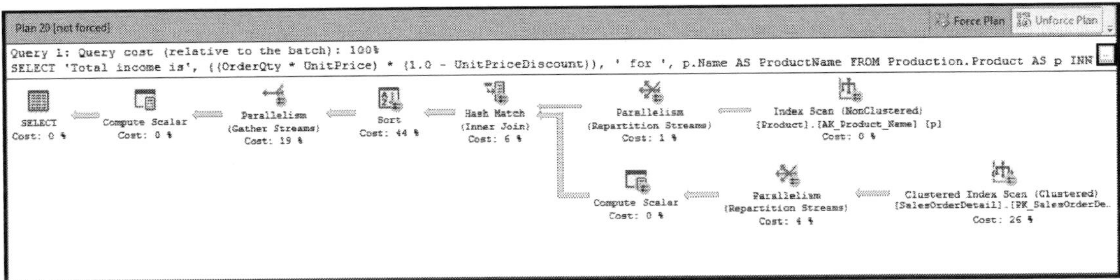

Once the query opens in a new session window, we can execute it to the get the following actual execution plan:

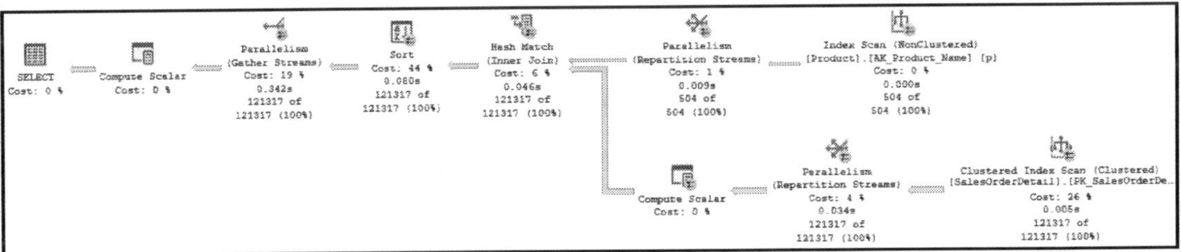

The **QueryTimeStats** property for this plan is as follows:

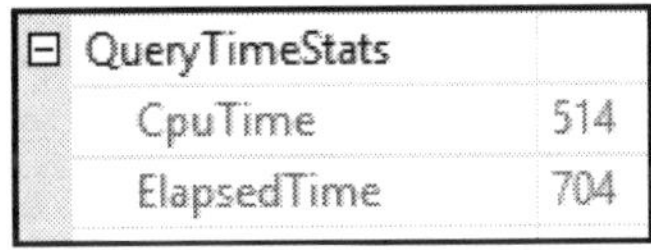

QueryTimeStats	
CpuTime	514
ElapsedTime	704

Now that we have the query execution plan, we can confirm in the **WaitStats** property that this query waited mostly on **CXPacket**, which is a parallelism wait, just like it was reported in the Query Store:

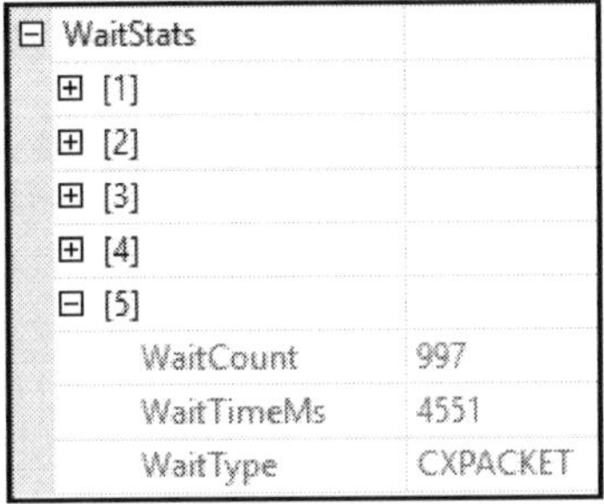

WaitStats	
[1]	
[2]	
[3]	
[4]	
[5]	
WaitCount	997
WaitTimeMs	4551
WaitType	CXPACKET

We also have a Clustered Index Scan on the **SalesOrderDetail** table. The query only needs three columns from this table, so it is a relevant subset, but there's no index that can cover the query. However, we can see that the existing index, **IX_SalesOrderDetail_ProductID**, already covers the join predicate on the **ProductID** column. Given that there are no other predicates on the query, and we need three extra columns just for the **SELECT**, we can add them to this index as **INCLUDE** columns. The hypothesis is that if SQL Server uses a narrower index, it can optimize I/O, which in turn has tangible effects on CPU usage. Given that the new columns are not interfering with the key of the existing index, any other queries that need it won't be too affected and we should be able to address our current heavy hitter query.

The index can be changed using the following query example:

```
CREATE NONCLUSTERED INDEX IX_SalesOrderDetail_ProductID ON
[Sales].[SalesOrderDetail] (
       [ProductID] ASC
)
INCLUDE (
       [OrderQty],
       [UnitPrice],
       [UnitPriceDiscount]
) WITH DROP_EXISTING;
```

After creating the index, we execute the query again to get the following actual execution plan, using the new index. Notice that the plan no longer executes in parallel because it became cheap enough not to exceed the **Cost Threshold for Parallelism** configuration. And because of the lower cost to access data in both tables, the Hash Match was replaced with **Nested Loops**, which is cheaper, and the sort is gone now because both indexes have been sorted on the required key order as shown in the following screenshot:

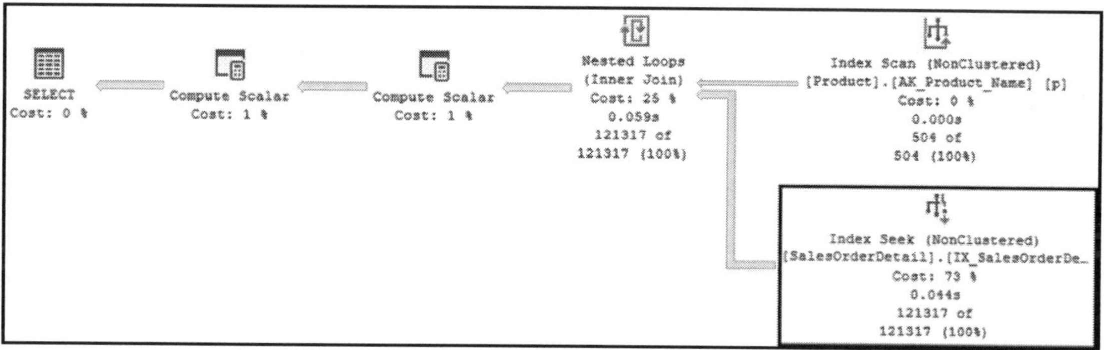

The **QueryTimeStats** for this plan reflect the lower resource usage: **CpuTime** dropped from 514ms to 265ms (~49 percent less), and **ElapsedTime** dropped from 704 ms to 570 ms (20 percent less):

⊟ QueryTimeStats	
CpuTime	265
ElapsedTime	570

Without parallelism, there are no more parallelism waits for this query. By cutting CPU usage in half, we were successful in tuning this query. The next step would be to continue with the other heavy hitters until the CPU is reduced to an acceptable level.

Fixing regressed queries

Parameters are fundamental drivers of the query optimization process. We discussed the topic of parameter sensitivity, known as parameter sniffing, in the *The importance of parameters* section of `Chapter 2`, *Understanding Query Processing*, and the *Query plan properties of interest* section in `Chapter 4`, *Exploring Query Execution Plans*.

This brings us to the other main benefit of the Query Store: tracking plan changes over time—in other words, regressions from parameter-sensitive plans. With this exercise, we want to make sure that the volatility that can come with parameter-sensitive plans is addressed, and that the plan that is used is the one that's best for most uses, if not all. If successful, we will address the complaints we've been getting that sometimes the application just slows down for a few minutes, and then recovers.

To generate enough workload in our **AdventureWorks** database, we will use the **QueryStoreSimpleDemo.exe** application, available in the Microsoft GitHub sample repository at `https://github.com/Microsoft/sql-server-samples/blob/master/samples/features/query-store`. When this executable is started, we are prompted to enter the SQL Server instance we want to connect to, and one of several sample workloads that are available, as shown in the following screenshot. For now, we will use option `S`:

```
C:\Demos\QDS\QueryStoreSimpleDemo.exe
Enter SQL Server name in form of {server name} \ {instance name}. Use (local) or . for default instance.

.\SQL2017

Press

R - for running regression workload on parameterized query
S - for running regression workload on stored procedure
P - for running workload that is candidate for auto parametrization
L - for running longer workload for database resource analysis
E - to exit
Ctrl+C to stop running demo and exit
```

To get the relevant data for our exercise, we leave the workload executing for about 15 to 20 minutes at least, although less than that already produces visible results. Then, we can start to understand the behavior of the workload over the **AdventureWorks** sample database. We can start by double-clicking on the **Queries with High Variation** SSMS report, as highlighted in the following screenshot:

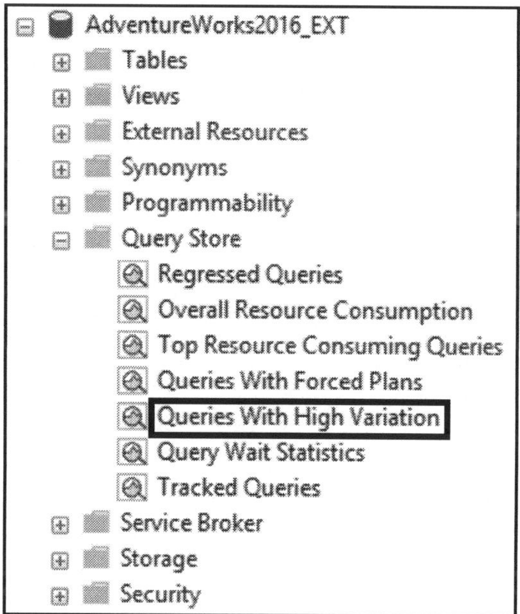

Then, the report opens in a new window tab, as seen in the following screenshot, on which we changed to the **standard deviation (Std Dev)** statistic:

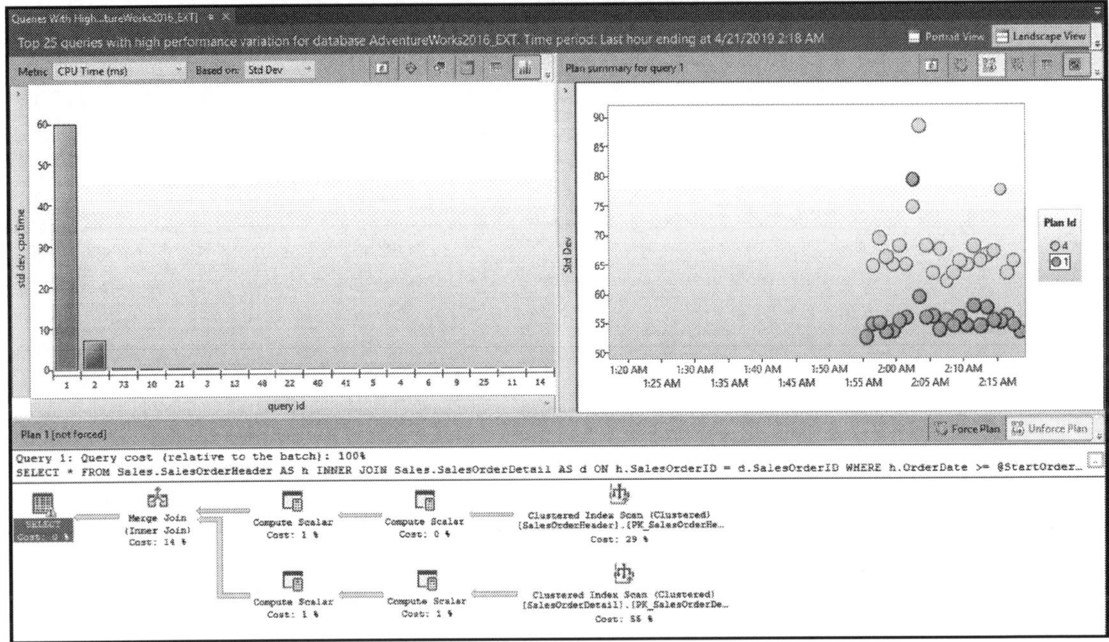

Immediately, we can see that **query id 1** has two plans being tracked (top right quadrant) with widely different performance. **query id 1** is the query with the widest variance between executions (top left quadrant) running in our SQL Server.

We can click on each plan (4 and 1), but we can also use **Plan Comparison** for this job. We discussed this tool as a standalone tool in `Chapter 10`, *Comparative Analysis of Query Plans*, but it can also be used from within the Query Store. To do that, hold down the *Shift* key and click on both IDs in the **Plan Id** legend. After they've been selected, click on the **Plan Comparison** button:

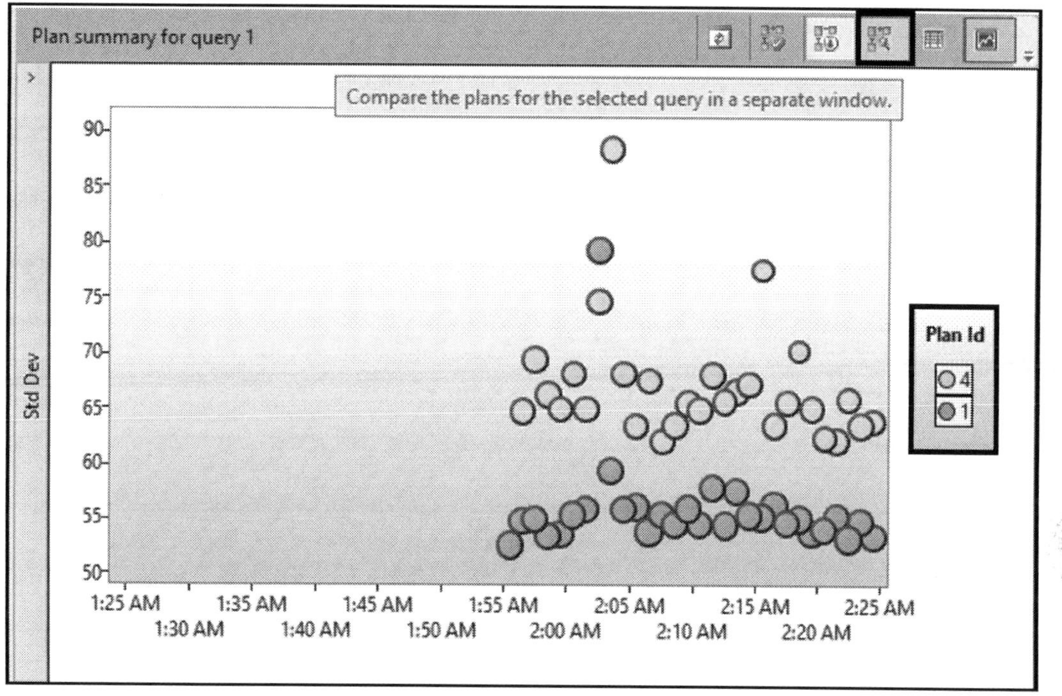

The comparison window appears as seen in the following screenshot:

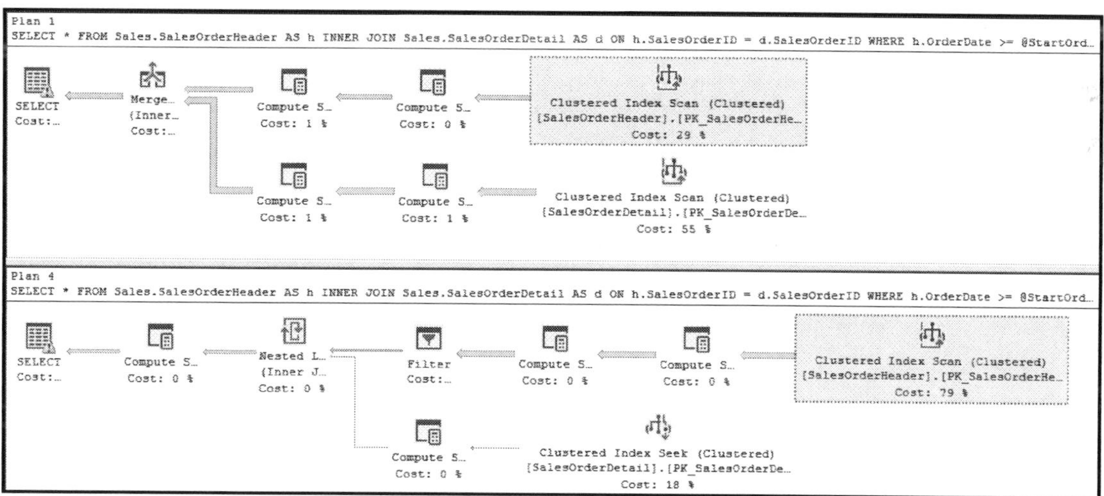

Notice that the only similarity between the plans is the **Clustered Index Scan** on the **SalesOrderHeader** table. Everything else is different: the data reader on the **SalesOrderDetail** tables changes from **Clustered Index Scan** in Plan Id 1 to **Clustered Index Seek** on Plan Id 4, which affects the type of join. Plan Id 1 has **Merge Join** that changes to **Nested Loops** on Plan Id 1. Looking at the compared **Properties** window, we can see why the plans are different: both plans were compiled with different parameters, so this is a case of parameter sensitivity.

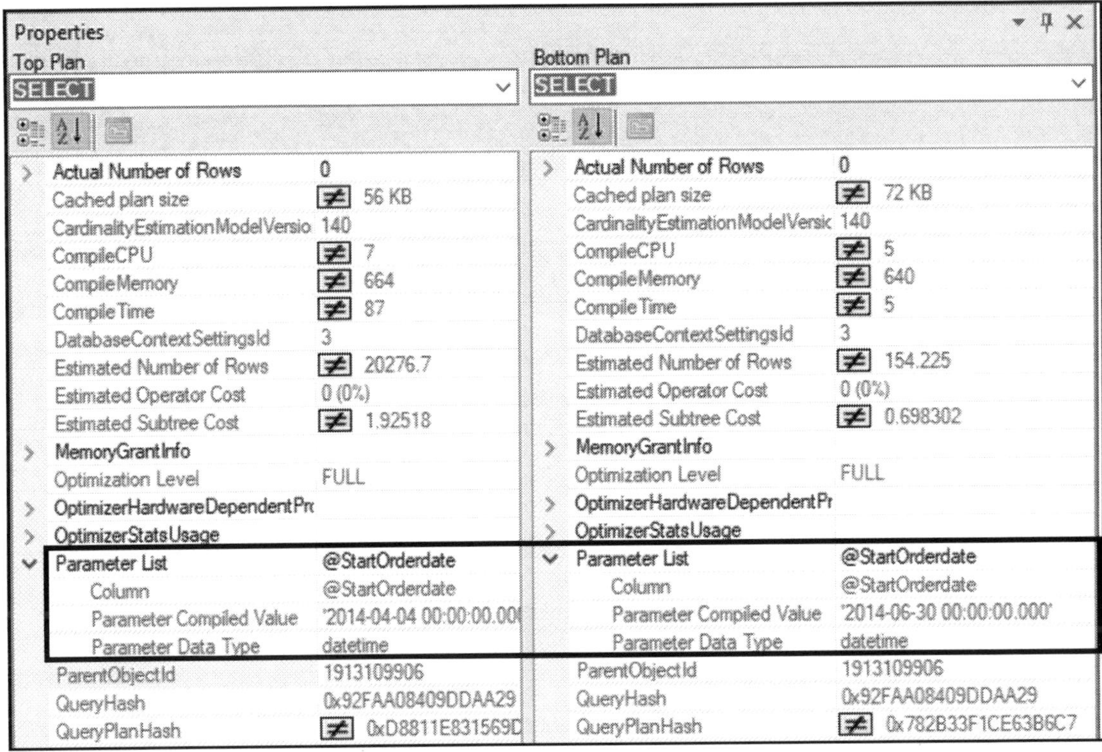

Because we have the **ParentObjectId** in the query plan, the following example tells us that the queries in the comparison are executed in context of the **usp_SalesFromDate** stored procedure:

```
SELECT OBJECT_NAME(1913109906);
```

We have covered several techniques to deal with this scenario in the *Query Plan Comparison* section of `Chapter 10`, *Comparative Analysis of Query Plans*, but in the meantime, the application is unstable. This is where the Query Store proves its worth again. We can select plan ID 1, which is consistently better (as seen in the report), and click the **Force Plan** button, as shown in the following screenshot:

With just one click, we stabilized the application by forcing the better plan, and minutes later we refreshed the report to see that plan ID 4 is no longer being used. Notice in the following screenshot that the forced plan shows a checkmark to signal that it's been forced. Also notice that the **Unforce Plan** button became available in case we ever need to let the query optimization process run again, for example, if we applied one of the mitigation techniques by making code changes with `CREATE OR ALTER PROCEDURE`:

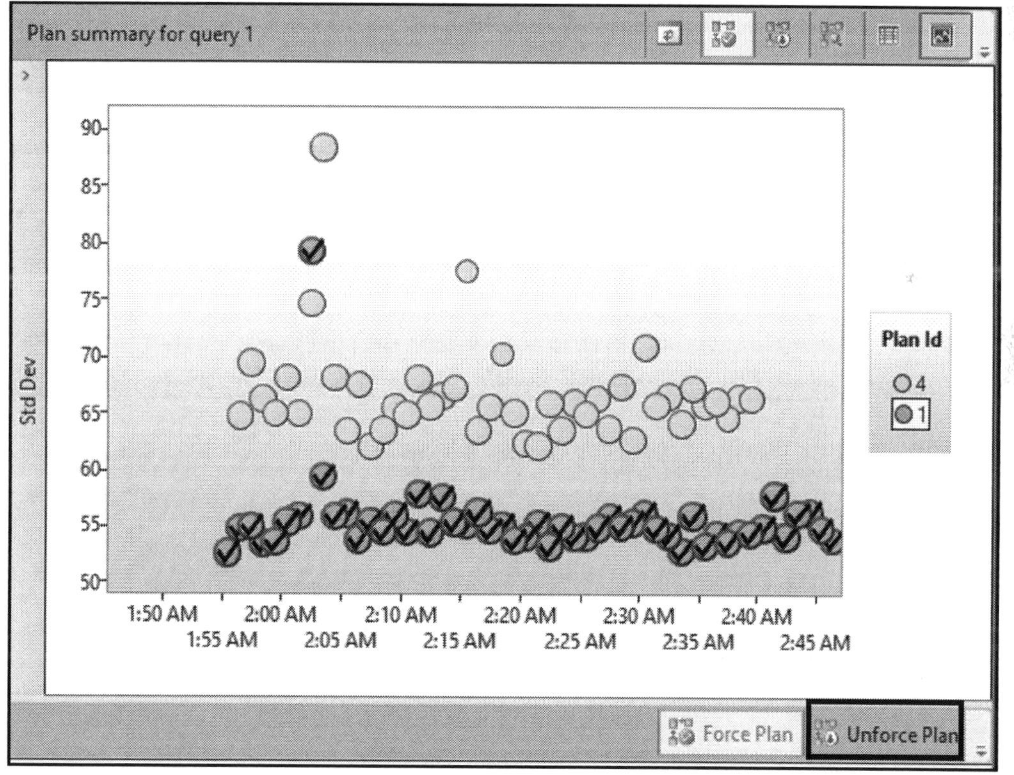

In case we have to force several plans in our work to minimize application issues over time, it could be easy to lose track of what plans are forced. That's why, in the last few releases of SSMS, a new **Queries with Forced Plans** report was included, which looks as follows:

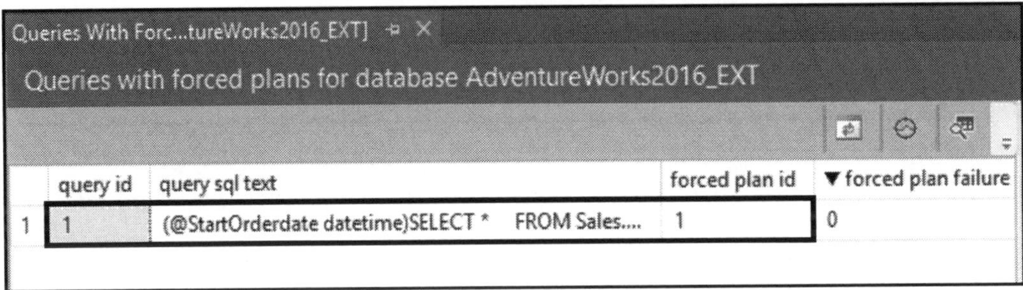

Summary

This chapter covered the important topic of storing query performance statistics in the flight recorder that is the Query Store, which allows us to access query plans and their runtime statistics, along with how they change over time. With what we've learned so far in all the previous chapters of this book, especially in `Chapter 4`, *Exploring Query Execution Plans*, about what information lies inside query plans, we can now more easily find resolutions for performance problems. We can easily identify plans that must be tuned for a quick mitigation, just to return a known good plan that had been stored in the Query Store.

We covered how to use either system views or SSMS to uncover the highest resource consuming queries that are executing in our databases and help us quickly find and fix query performance issues that are related to plan changes, which greatly simplifies query performance troubleshooting.

However, this also provides performance stability across SQL Server upgrades when following the recommended database compatibility-level upgrade process, which we will discuss in the *Understanding where QTA is needed* section of `Chapter 13`, *Managing Optimizer Changes with the Query Tuning Assistant*.

In the next chapter, we will investigate how to troubleshoot a different kind of query performance issue that the tools and methods we have covered so far may not be helpful for: long-running queries.

12
Troubleshooting Live Queries

During our career as a database professional we likely encounter cases where a runaway query takes hours to complete or doesn't even complete by any reasonable time measurement. How do we troubleshoot such cases?

A query execution plan can help provide a conclusive explanation of query performance issues. But to get a query execution plan there is one requirement a long-running query can't easily meet: **query completion**.

If a query takes a long time to complete or never actually does, then how can we troubleshoot those cases? And assume we take that production query back to our development server and it will run well? That means there is some set of conditions that can only be reproduced in the production server, be that the size of the database, the data distribution statistics, or even the availability of resources such as memory or CPU. Therefore, the ability to analyze a query execution plan while a query is executing is something many SQL Server professionals have been requesting for a long time.

This chapter will introduce the **Query Profiling Infrastructure** that exposes real-time query execution plans, which enable scenarios such as production systems troubleshooting. We will explore real-world examples of how to leverage rich-UI tools for query performance troubleshooting: **Live Query Statistics** as a standalone case, or as part of the **Activity Monitor** functionality of **SQL Server Management Studio (SSMS)**.

This chapter covers the following topics:

- Using Live Query Statistics
- Understanding the need for Lightweight Profiling
- Activity Monitor gets a new life

Using Live Query Statistics

To meet the need to analyze a query execution plan while the query is executing, **Live Query Statistics (LQS)** was introduced with the SQL Server 2016 release of SSMS, adding rich visuals by animating the in-flight execution plan to allow more immediate and precise identification of hot spots in a plan during query execution.

To see LQS in action, open a new query window in SSMS, in which we can use the following example query from `Chapter 3`, *Mechanics of the Query Optimizer*. This is a previously identified long-running query that I'm tasked to troubleshoot and tune:

```
SELECT e.[BusinessEntityID], p.[Title], p.[FirstName],p.[MiddleName],
       p.[LastName], p.[Suffix], e.[JobTitle],
       pp.[PhoneNumber], pnt.[Name] AS [PhoneNumberType],
       ea.[EmailAddress], p.[EmailPromotion], a.[AddressLine1],
       a.[AddressLine2], a.[City], sp.[Name] AS [StateProvinceName],
       a.[PostalCode], cr.[Name] AS [CountryRegionName],
       p.[AdditionalContactInfo]
FROM [HumanResources].[Employee] AS e
INNER JOIN [Person].[Person] AS p
       ON RTRIM(LTRIM(p.[BusinessEntityID])) =
RTRIM(LTRIM(e.[BusinessEntityID]))
INNER JOIN [Person].[BusinessEntityAddress] AS bea
       ON RTRIM(LTRIM(bea.[BusinessEntityID])) =
RTRIM(LTRIM(e.[BusinessEntityID]))
INNER JOIN [Person].[Address] AS a
       ON RTRIM(LTRIM(a.[AddressID])) = RTRIM(LTRIM(bea.[AddressID]))
INNER JOIN [Person].[StateProvince] AS sp
       ON RTRIM(LTRIM(sp.[StateProvinceID])) =
RTRIM(LTRIM(a.[StateProvinceID]))
INNER JOIN [Person].[CountryRegion] AS cr
       ON RTRIM(LTRIM(cr.[CountryRegionCode])) =
RTRIM(LTRIM(sp.[CountryRegionCode]))
LEFT OUTER JOIN [Person].[PersonPhone] AS pp
       ON RTRIM(LTRIM(pp.BusinessEntityID)) =
RTRIM(LTRIM(p.[BusinessEntityID]))
LEFT OUTER JOIN [Person].[PhoneNumberType] AS pnt
       ON RTRIM(LTRIM(pp.[PhoneNumberTypeID])) =
RTRIM(LTRIM(pnt.[PhoneNumberTypeID]))
LEFT OUTER JOIN [Person].[EmailAddress] AS ea
       ON RTRIM(LTRIM(p.[BusinessEntityID])) =
RTRIM(LTRIM(ea.[BusinessEntityID]));
```

To see the query progress for the query while it executes on the **AdventureWorks** sample database, click on the button to **Include Live Query Statistics**, as shown in the following screenshot:

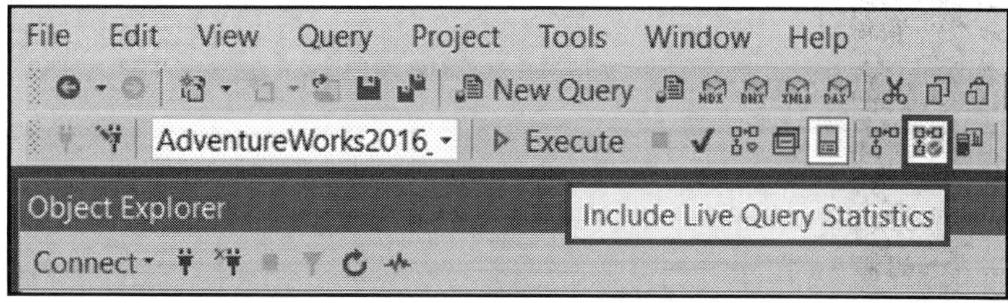

When the query execution starts, then the **Live Query Statistics** tab appears, showing the in-flight query execution plan.

As the query execution progresses in the following plan, we can see the following:

1. **Solid lines** connecting two operators, indicating areas of the plan that have completed.
2. **Dotted and animated lines** connecting two operators, indicating areas of the plan that are still in-flight.
3. Operators with their **elapsed time stopped**, indicating that they have completed processing rows.
4. Operators with their **elapsed time continuing to tick**, indicating that they are still processing rows.
5. What the **overall query elapsed time** is.

6. The **estimated query progress displayed as a percentage**. This is an on-the-fly calculation based on the estimated rows versus the actual rows that have already been processed. This calculation is just an indicator that can be accurate enough if the plan doesn't have severe skews between the estimated and actual number of rows. However, for severely skewed estimations, this can be inaccurate, and might not show the expected linear progress:

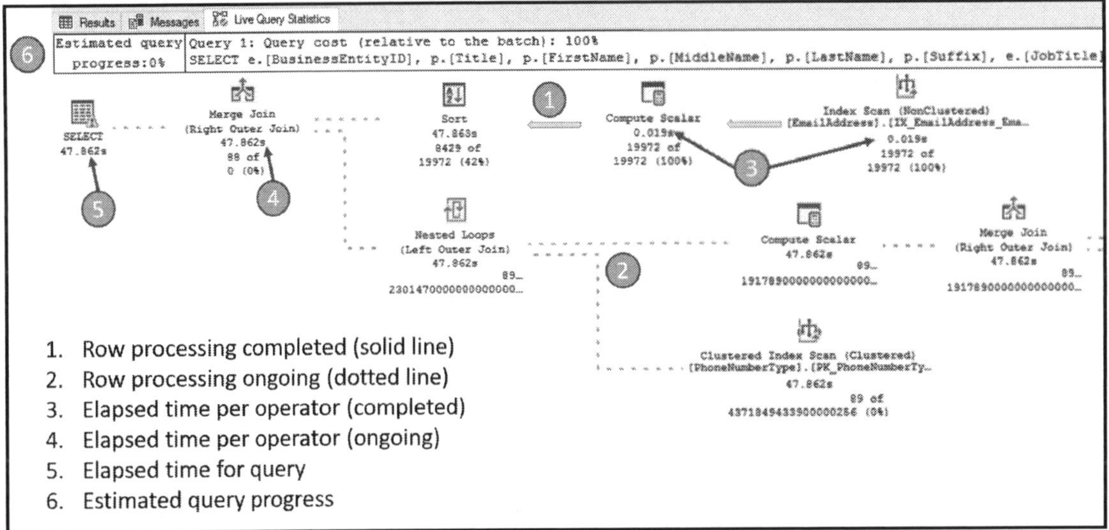

For all query plan operators, we can also see the actual number of rows processed versus the estimated number of rows, together with the percentage of actual rows versus estimated rows.

For example, in the **Index Scan** of the previous plan, this reads 19,972 of 19,972 (100%), which means that estimations were completely accurate compared to the actual rows processed by that operator. But for the Clustered Index Scan, we see that it is currently in progress, and reading row 89 of 1,371,849,433,900,000,256 estimated rows (yes, over one quintillion rows). Given that the **PhoneNumberType** table has only 290 rows and the scan happens once, the misestimation is obvious.

Even though LQS was released with SQL Server 2016's SSMS, we can use any modern version of SSMS such as version 17 or version 18 to connect to any SQL Server instance and use LQS, starting with SQL Server 2014.

LQS is an SSMS UI feature that provides the visualization of data stored in the **sys.dm_exec_query_profiles** DMV. The following query is an example that allows programmatic access to the same information SSMS rendered as a graphical showplan. Note that the long-running query was executing in session ID **97**; therefore, the predicate is on `session_id = 97`:

```
SELECT node_id, physical_operator_name,SUM(row_count)AS row_count,
       SUM(estimate_row_count)AS estimate_row_count,
       CAST(SUM(row_count)*100 AS float) / SUM(estimate_row_count) AS
operator_progress
FROM sys.dm_exec_query_profiles
WHERE session_id = 97
GROUP BY node_id, physical_operator_name
ORDER BY node_id;
```

The result set for the query shows the following information:

- Each individual operator in the plan (node IDs) that processes rows of data. This excludes operators such as **Compute Scalar**. Note that node ID zero (**0**) corresponds to the top-left operator (**Merge Join**) just before the root node (**SELECT**) in the graphical query plan; node ID **1** is the sort at the outer side of the merge join, node ID **2** is the NonClustered index scan leading up to that sort, node ID 3 is the nested loops join at the inner side of the merge join, and so on and so forth.
- A snapshot of the current row count for the moment the DMV was invoked.
- The estimated row count for each operator.
- A calculation that provides the current operator progress.

The following screenshot shows the resultset for the **sys.dm_exec_query_profiles** example:

	node_id	physical_operator_name	row_count	estimate_row_count	operator_progress
1	0	Merge Join	59	9223372036854775807	6.39679281766448E-16
2	1	Sort	5520	19972	27.6386941718406
3	3	Index Scan	19972	19972	100
4	4	Nested Loops	60	2301473268204480000	2.60702571821786E-15
5	6	Merge Join	60	1917894385407257856	3.12843086963098E-15
6	7	Sort	5626	19972	28.1694372120969
7	9	Index Scan	19972	19972	100
8	10	Merge Join	61	959859044513641	6.3550997772708E-12
9	11	Sort	5732	19972	28.7001802523533
10	13	Clustered Index Scan	19972	19972	100
11	14	Merge Join	62	480602358407	1.29004776850252E-08
12	15	Sort	63	290	21.7241379310345
13	17	Clustered Index Scan	290	290	100
14	18	Nested Loops	5812	16572494870	3.50701571826765E-05
15	19	Nested Loops	5812	696323303	0.000834669753972028
16	20	Nested Loops	5812	38470900	0.0151075228289434
17	21	Sort	5813	19614	29.6369939838891
18	23	Index Scan	19614	19614	100
19	24	Table Spool	114002424	384708996	29.6334177743013
20	26	Index Scan	19614	19614	100
21	27	Table Spool	1051972	6963232900	0.0151075228289434
22	29	Clustered Index Scan	181	181	100
23	30	Table Spool	1383256	165724946114	0.000834669753972028
24	32	Index Scan	238	238	100
25	33	Clustered Index Scan	60	3835788770814515714	1.56421543481549E-15

In summary, using the LQS feature is extremely useful for a scenario where we have a previously identified query that runs with poor performance in a production **Very Large Database** (**VLDB**), but has no issues running on a development machine with a smaller data dataset. Often, restoring a VLDB outside a production environment is a non-starter, and so troubleshooting in production is the only viable option.

Understanding the need for Lightweight Profiling

If you are asking yourself why you would want to know about an obscure **Database Engine** component named **Query Profiling Infrastructure**, then read on. Not many database professionals know it by name, but most have dealt with it when there's a need to troubleshoot query performance issues in a production environment. When a SQL Server performance issue hits, one of the first requirements is to understand which queries are executing and how system resources are being used. And one of the most important artifacts anyone can use to know more about queries that are executing are query plans.

Analyzing a query plan, also known as an **estimated execution plan**, means that we're only looking at what SQL Server *estimated* should be a good-enough plan to return the intended results efficiently. But since an estimated plan is missing runtime data for analysis, it can't truly provide a conclusive explanation for many query performance issues. Recall what we covered about the query compilation and optimization process in `Chapter 2`, *Understanding Query Processing*, and more specifically how SQL Server estimates work, as discussed in `Chapter 3`, *Mechanics of the Query Optimizer*. Estimations drive optimizer choices, and when these estimations are wrong, then the generated plans are inefficient.

So, what is needed is a query execution plan, also known as an **actual execution plan**. This allows us to see runtime data that is crucial to uncover hot spots in the plan, such as the actual number of rows processed by a query operator.

This runtime information has been accessible for many years and on many different versions of SQL Server, but at a very high cost. Collecting runtime data on queries adds overhead to the query execution itself—the SQL Server team measured a 75 percent overhead with a TPC-C-like workload, which is why this information is not readily available all the time.

TPC-C is a standard OLTP workload that is used to benchmark database systems. We can read more about TPC-C at `http://www.tpc.org/tpcc`.

The high cost of this data collection is grounded in the need to enable enable the standard version of the Query Profiling Infrastructure, the **Standard Query Execution Statistics Profile Infrastructure**, or **Standard Profiling**, for short, which must be enabled to collect information about query execution plans, namely the number of actual rows flowing through operators, as well as CPU and I/O usage. Standard Profiling can be enabled globally to collect information for all queries, or for a single session and query.

To collect query execution plans for a single query using Standard Profiling, the following methods are available:

- Use `SET STATISTICS XML ON` or `SET STATISTICS PROFILE ON` before a T-SQL query is executed. We covered these commands in the *Accessing a query plan* section of `Chapter 4`, *Exploring Query Execution Plans.*
- **LQS**: This feature was covered in the previous section of this chapter.

To collect query execution plans for all queries using Standard Profiling, one of the following methods can be used:

- Using the **query_post_execution_showplan** XEvent in an XEvent trace. We discussed XEvents in `Chapter 9`, *Building XEvent Profiler Traces.*
- Using the **Showplan XML** trace event in SQL Trace and SQL Server Profiler. However, these methods are deprecated and should not be used in modern versions of SQL Server where the more complete and less intrusive XEvents are available.

SQL Server 2014 SP2 and SQL Server 2016 introduced a lightweight version of the Query Profiling Infrastructure that exists side-by-side with Standard Profiling, the new **Lightweight Query Execution Statistics Profiling Infrastructure**, or **Lightweight Profiling** (**LWP**) for short. LWP has evolved over time to hold true to its name and concentrate on the fundamental task of democratizing access to the equivalent of an actual execution plan, which is an essential artifact for query performance troubleshooting. The SQL Server team measured a 1.5 to 2 percent overhead with a TPC-C like workload—a significant improvement from Standard Profiling. Lightweight profiling can also be enabled globally to collect information for all queries, or for a single session and query.

To collect query execution plans for a single query using Lightweight Profiling, use the **QUERY_PLAN_PROFILE** query hint in conjunction with a trace that captures the **query_plan_profile** XEvent. We will show how this XEvent can be used in more detail later in this section.

Clicking the **Live Query Statistics** button in SSMS enables **Standard Profiling** for that single query, irrespective of whether Lightweight Profiling is enabled globally and already populating the `sys.dm_exec_query_profiles` DMV. In this case, the DMV is populated using Standard Profiling for that query only, and lightweight profiling for all other queries.

To collect query execution plans for all queries using lightweight profiling, one of the following methods can be used:

- Enabling **trace flag 7412 globally** in SQL Server 2016 and SQL Server 2017. If our SQL Server is not already CPU-bound and can withstand the 1.5 to 2 percent overhead as a trade-off to having always available runtime data for every query in every session, then it is a recommended best practice to enable this trace flag at startup. To enable the trace flag globally, but not at startup, use the , `DBCC TRACEON (7412, -1)` T-SQL command. When Lightweight Profiling is enabled globally, the **sys.dm_exec_query_profiles** DMV is populated for all queries that are being executed.
- Using the **query_thread_profile** or the **query_post_execution_plan_profile** XEvents in an XEvent trace. We will discuss how to use these XEvents in more detail later in this section.

Starting with SQL Server 2019, LWP is enabled by default and trace flag 7412 is not needed. However, LWP can be disabled at the database level setting the database scoped configuration **LIGHTWEIGHT_QUERY_PROFILING** to **OFF** using the following T-SQL command: `ALTER DATABASE SCOPED CONFIGURATION SET LIGHTWEIGHT_QUERY_PROFILING = OFF;`.

So, what is available in a query execution plan that is obtained through LWP? How is that plan different than the one obtained using Standard Profiling? Why is the term **equivalent of an actual execution plan** being used here? These are all pertinent questions that we will answer in this chapter.

From SQL Server 2014 through SQL Server 2017, the noticeable difference between Standard Profiling and LWP is that LWP did not collect per-operator CPU runtime information, because tracking CPU usage across queries is one of the aspects that added so much overhead to Standard Profiling. Per-operator CPU usage isn't necessarily fundamental information when we are troubleshooting a query performance issue. And for these SQL Server versions, LWP still collects per-operator I/O usage information and actual row counts—this is the important information. At the query level, LWP still collects information about the overall CPU and the elapsed time, memory grant usage, runtime warnings, and actual **Degree of Parallelism (DOP)**.

If both Query Profiling infrastructures are enabled simultaneously, then Standard Profiling takes precedence over LWP, for the scope in which each is enabled. For example, if LWP is enabled globally, but then we use `SET STATISTICS XML ON` for a specific query, that query's execution plan will use Standard Profiling instead.

Starting with SQL Server 2019, LWP was revised to specifically exclude per-operator I/O runtime information by default—only per-operator row counts are reported. This was done after finding that in very extreme cases even tracking I/O could introduce overhead that would make LWP not stay true to its principle of being lightweight. LWP still collects the same query level information as it did in previous versions.

If we require per-operator I/O information to be collected with LWP and have tested its impact on our SQL Server, we can enable trace flag 7415 to restore per-operator I/O metrics, as available in SQL Server 2016 and SQL Server 2017.

Diagnostics available with Lightweight Profiling

Because it became cheaper to collect information about query execution plans with LWP, this allowed several diagnostics artifacts to be added to SQL Server: **XEvents** and **Dynamic Management Functions** (**DMFs**). We will discuss all these new diagnostics and how to use them in the remainder of this section.

The query_thread_profile XEvent

SQL Server 2016 Service Pack 1 introduced a new XEvent named **query_thread_profile**. Unlike the **query_post_execution_showplan** XEvent, which uses only Standard Profiling, **query_thread_profile** uses lightweight profiling by default. Also, unlike **query_post_execution_showplan**, **query_thread_profile** doesn't output a query execution plan as a single showplan XML—it outputs one event per-operator and thread with the same execution statistics that are expected in a query execution plan. This means that it can be quite verbose, but since it's based on lightweight profiling rather than Standard Profiling, it can be used for a longer period of time than was possible with **query_post_execution_showplan**.

The following example shows a session that uses this XEvent:

```
CREATE EVENT SESSION [PerfStats_Node] ON SERVER
ADD EVENT sqlserver.query_thread_profile(
       ACTION(sqlos.scheduler_id, sqlserver.database_id,
sqlserver.is_system, sqlserver.plan_handle,
              sqlserver.query_hash_signed,
sqlserver.query_plan_hash_signed,
              sqlserver.server_instance_name,sqlserver.session_id,
sqlserver.session_nt_username,
              sqlserver.sql_text)
              )
       ADD TARGET package0.event_file(
              SET filename=N'C:\Temp\PerfStats_Node.xel',
              max_file_size=(50), max_rollover_files=(2)
       )
WITH (MAX_MEMORY=4096 KB, EVENT_RETENTION_MODE=ALLOW_SINGLE_EVENT_LOSS,
      MAX_DISPATCH_LATENCY=30 SECONDS, MAX_EVENT_SIZE=0 KB,
MEMORY_PARTITION_MODE=NONE,
     TRACK_CAUSALITY=OFF,STARTUP_STATE=OFF);
```

To see the output this XEvent produces, execute the following query in the **AdventureWorks** sample database:

```
ALTER EVENT SESSION [PerfStats_Node] ON SERVER STATE = start;
GO
SELECT COUNT(*)
FROM Sales.SalesOrderDetail AS sod
INNER JOIN Sales.SalesOrderHeader AS soh ON soh.SalesOrderID =
sod.SalesOrderID
GROUP BY soh.Status;
GO
ALTER EVENT SESSION [PerfStats_Node] ON SERVER STATE = stop;
GO
```

The resulting file can be opened using SSMS, as seen in the following screenshot. Note that the same XEvent session and query was executed in SQL Server 2017 and SQL Server 2019 for comparison between the versions:

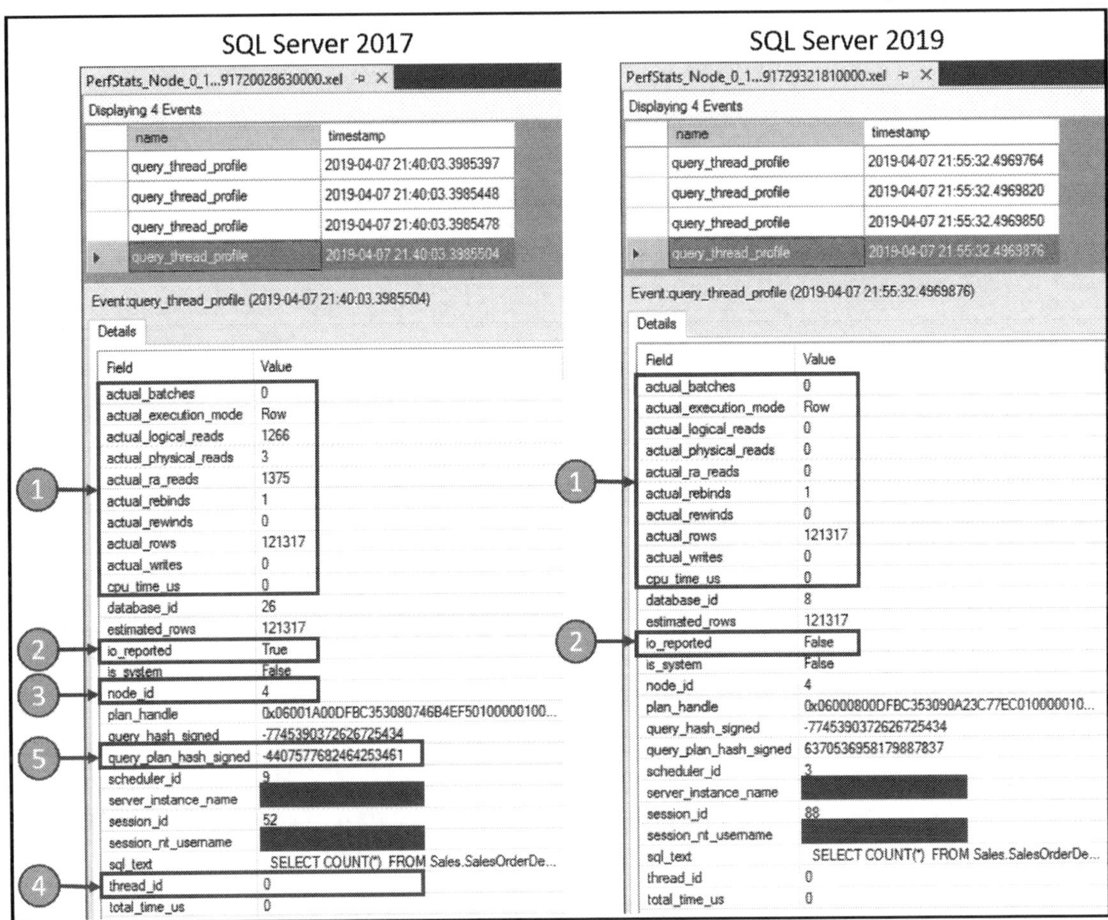

Notice that, for one single query execution, this XEvent fired four times, once for each operator that processes data in the query plan. Let's focus on the last XEvent fired for this session. In it, we can find the following information:

1. Runtime data that includes the number of actual rows read by this operator (node ID) that matches the **RunTimeCountersPerThread** showplan element we discussed in the *Operator-level properties* section of `Chapter 4`, *Exploring Query Execution Plans*. Notice that the CPU time is zero because LWP doesn't collect per-operator CPU metrics. As expected in the SQL Server 2019 example, the per-operator I/O metrics are not populated either.
2. The **io_reported** action indicates whether I/O is reported in the XEvent. As expected, it's **True** for SQL Server 2014 through SQL Server 2017, and **False** starting with SQL Server 2019.
3. The current node ID in this case is 4. This information will be used to map this node ID when we look at a graphical query plan.
4. As mentioned, this XEvent fires once per operator and thread. In this example trace, we only have one XEvent per node ID, and each node ID shows a thread ID zero. When an operator only fires one XEvent, this thread ID will always be zero and means the operator executed in serial, meaning on a single scheduler. If an operator executes in parallel, for example, with a **Degree of Parallelism** (**DOP**) 4, then five such XEvents are fired for a single operator: one for the coordinator thread and one for each of the four child threads.
5. The query plan hash that is needed to retrieve the query plan from cache, which is useful for mapping the text-only XEvent data to a graphical query plan.

Starting with SQL Server 2014 SP2 and SQL Server 2016, use the **query_hash_signed** and **query_plan_hash_signed** actions instead of the **query_hash** and **query_plan_hash** actions to correlate data from XEvent collections with DMVs such as **sys.dm_exec_requests** and **sys.dm_exec_query_stats**. The **query_hash** and **query_plan_hash** actions are not the same data types as the respective columns in the DMVs, which don't allow the expected correlation.

The node IDs can be searched in the graphical execution plan so we can get better clarity on all the operator types in this plan. We can use the query plan hash to get the graphical plan from the cache, using the query in SSMS:

```
SELECT qp.query_plan
FROM sys.dm_exec_query_stats qs
CROSS APPLY sys.dm_exec_query_plan(qs.plan_handle) qp
WHERE CAST(qs.query_plan_hash AS BIGINT) = -4407577682464253461;
```

This returns the following result set:

Clicking on the link in the **Results** tab opens the graphical plan, and now it's time to start mapping the XEvent session runtime information with the cached plan. To do this, we use the **Node Search** feature in SSMS. Right-click anywhere in the plan and click on **Find Node**, as seen in the following screenshot:

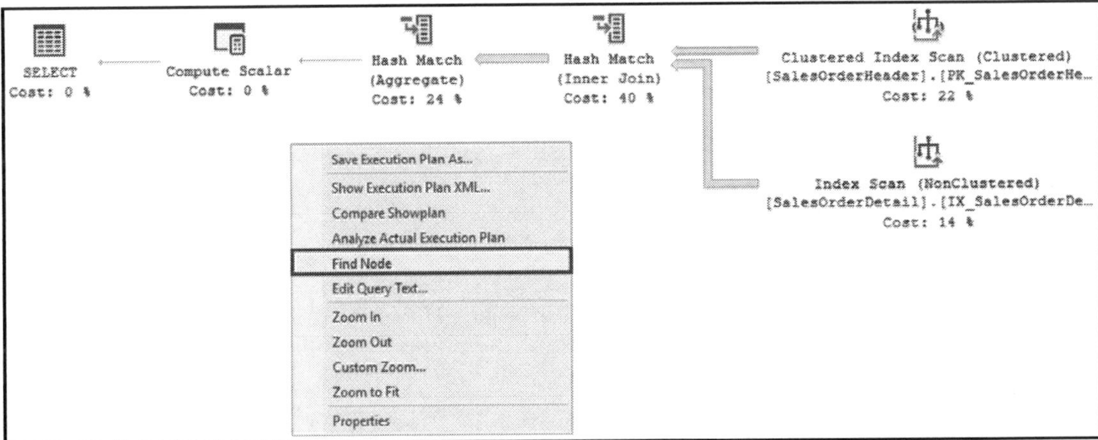

This feature allows me to search for any property that exists in the showplan XML, as seen in the following screenshot:

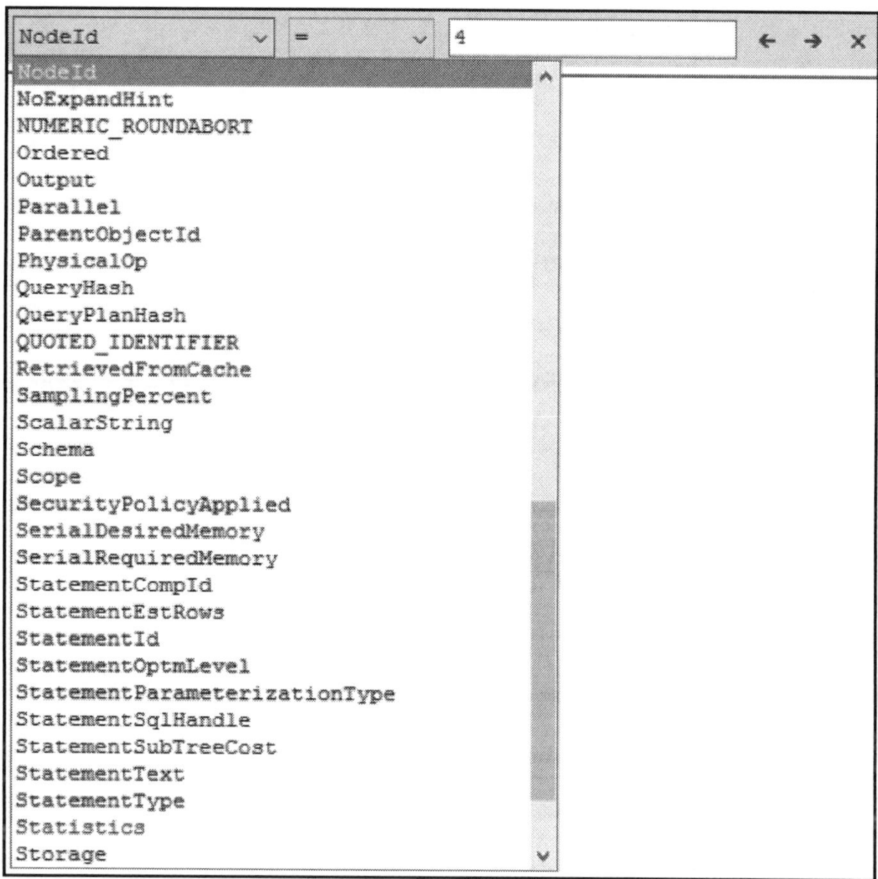

Searching for **NodeId** = **4** immediately focuses on the NonClustered Index Scan that represents node ID 4 in the following query plan:

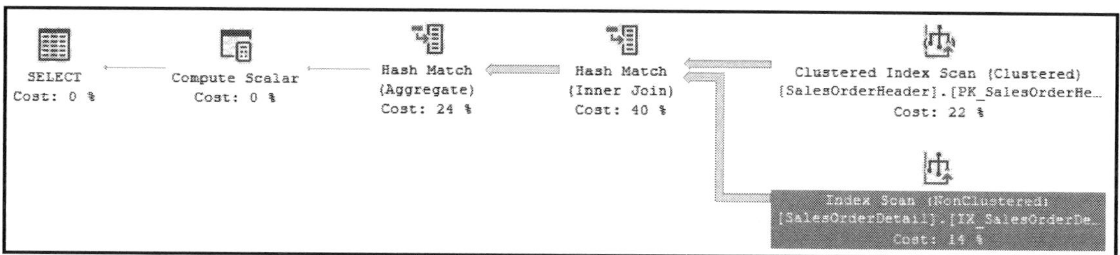

Correlating with the data in the XEvent, I now know that this index scan read 121,317 rows, in 1,266 logical reads and 1,375 read-aheads. This XEvent is very useful for collecting runtime query data at scale, which may be worth the time-consuming task of doing this correlation exercise.

The query_plan_profile XEvent

SQL Server 2016 SP2 CU3 and SQL Server 2017 CU11 introduced a new XEvent named **query_plan_profile**. This XEvent outputs the equivalent of a query execution plan such as the **query_post_execution_showplan** XEvent. Unlike the **query_post_execution_showplan** XEvent, which uses Standard Profiling, **query_plan_profile** uses lightweight profiling by default.

The **query_plan_profile** XEvent allows a very targeted plan collection that can be used for a longer period of time to gather data for a specific query execution and doesn't require any object or statement filtering in the XEvent session. This is because the XEvent only fires for a query or queries that are using the `USE HINT ('QUERY_PLAN_PROFILE')` hint.

The following is an example session that uses this XEvent:

```
CREATE EVENT SESSION [PerfStats_LWP_Plan_Single] ON SERVER
ADD EVENT sqlserver.query_plan_profile(
       ACTION(sqlos.scheduler_id, sqlserver.database_id,
sqlserver.is_system, sqlserver.plan_handle,
              sqlserver.query_hash_signed,
sqlserver.query_plan_hash_signed,
              sqlserver.server_instance_name,sqlserver.session_id,
              sqlserver.session_nt_username, sqlserver.sql_text)
       )
       ADD TARGET package0.event_file(
              SET filename=N'C:\Temp\PerfStats_LWP_Plan_Single.xel',
              max_file_size=(50), max_rollover_files=(2)
       )
WITH (MAX_MEMORY=4096 KB, EVENT_RETENTION_MODE=ALLOW_SINGLE_EVENT_LOSS,
      MAX_DISPATCH_LATENCY=30 SECONDS, MAX_EVENT_SIZE=0 KB,
MEMORY_PARTITION_MODE=NONE,
      TRACK_CAUSALITY=OFF,STARTUP_STATE=OFF);
```

To see the output this XEvent produces, we need to set up our example. Creating the following stored procedure in the **AdventureWorks** sample database allows us to later use this XEvent as we would probably do in a production environment:

```
CREATE OR ALTER PROCEDURE [Sales].[CountSalesOrderByStatus]
AS
SELECT COUNT(*)
FROM Sales.SalesOrderDetail AS sod
INNER JOIN Sales.SalesOrderHeader AS soh
       ON soh.SalesOrderID = sod.SalesOrderID
GROUP BY soh.Status;
```

In a production system, it is most likely we will not be able to alter the existing stored procedure to add the required hint. The same would happen if a query we want to track is geneeerated by an application and we can't change the query at its origin. The solution is to use a plan guide to add the hint, as seen in the following example, created for the **Sales.CountSalesOrderByStatus** stored procedure:

```
EXEC sp_create_plan_guide
@name = N'Guide1',
@stmt = 'SELECT COUNT(*)
FROM Sales.SalesOrderDetail AS sod
INNER JOIN Sales.SalesOrderHeader AS soh
       ON soh.SalesOrderID = sod.SalesOrderID
GROUP BY soh.Status;',
@type = N'OBJECT',
@module_or_batch = N'Sales.CountSalesOrderByStatus',
@params = NULL,
@hints = N'OPTION (USE HINT (''QUERY_PLAN_PROFILE''))';
```

Now we can execute the following example query in the **AdventureWorks** sample database:

```
ALTER EVENT SESSION [PerfStats_LWP_Plan_Single] ON SERVER STATE = start;
GO
EXEC Sales.CountSalesOrderByStatus;
GO
ALTER EVENT SESSION [PerfStats_LWP_Plan_Single] ON SERVER STATE = stop;
GO
```

The resulting file can be opened using SSMS, as seen in the following screenshot:

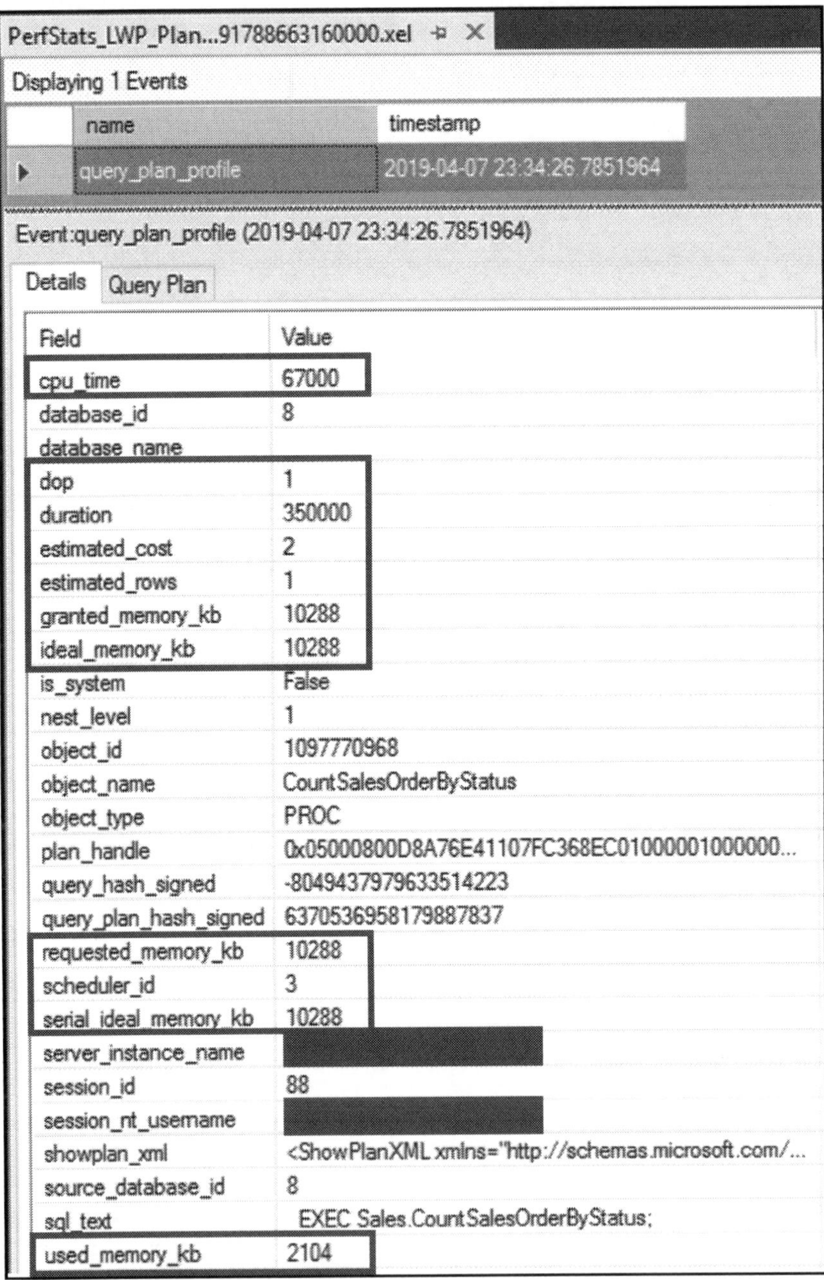

The XEvent contains runtime data for the overall query, including duration in microseconds, memory grant information, and the actual DOP (degree of parallelism) that was used, which in this case is 1, meaning the query executed in serial.

To see the plan itself, we click in the **Query Plan** tab. Note that the same XEvent session and query was executed in SQL Server 2017 and SQL Server 2019 for comparison between the versions:

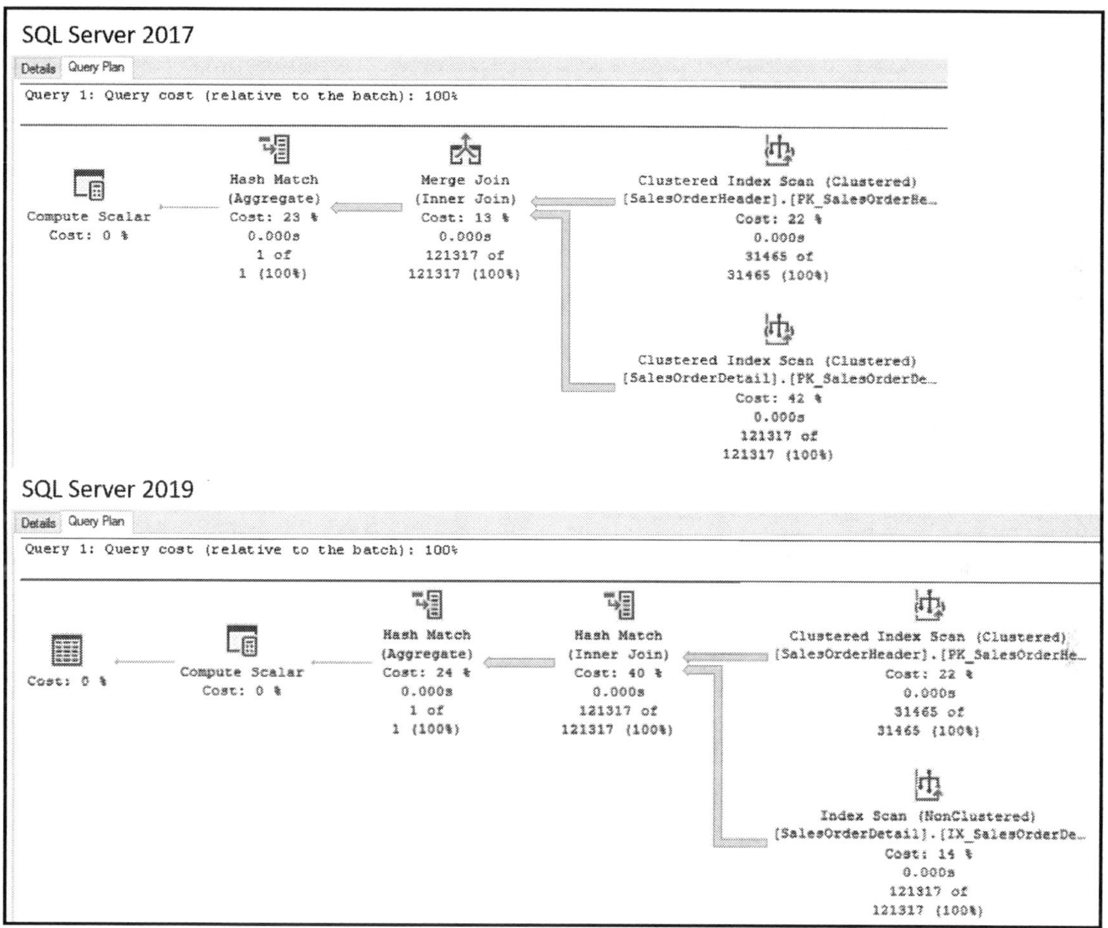

Notice that the plans don't have any reference to the statement text that was executed: this is already present in the XEvent itself, and so this information can be removed from the captured plan and make the collection more lightweight. Furthermore, the SQL Server 2019 plan contains one extra operator—the Cost root node, which has information that is usually found in a root node of a query execution plan, which was discussed in the *Query plan properties section of interest* section in `Chapter 4`, *Exploring Query Execution Plans.*

When we look at the properties for node ID 4—the NonClustered Index Scan—these include the number of actual rows read by this operator (node ID), which can also be seen below the operator icon as the number of actual rows versus the number of estimated rows that flowed through the operator (121,317 of 121,317). However, in the SQL Server 2019 example, we see the I/O metrics are not present because LWP in SQL Server 2019 doesn't collect I/O information by default, as seen in the following screenshot:

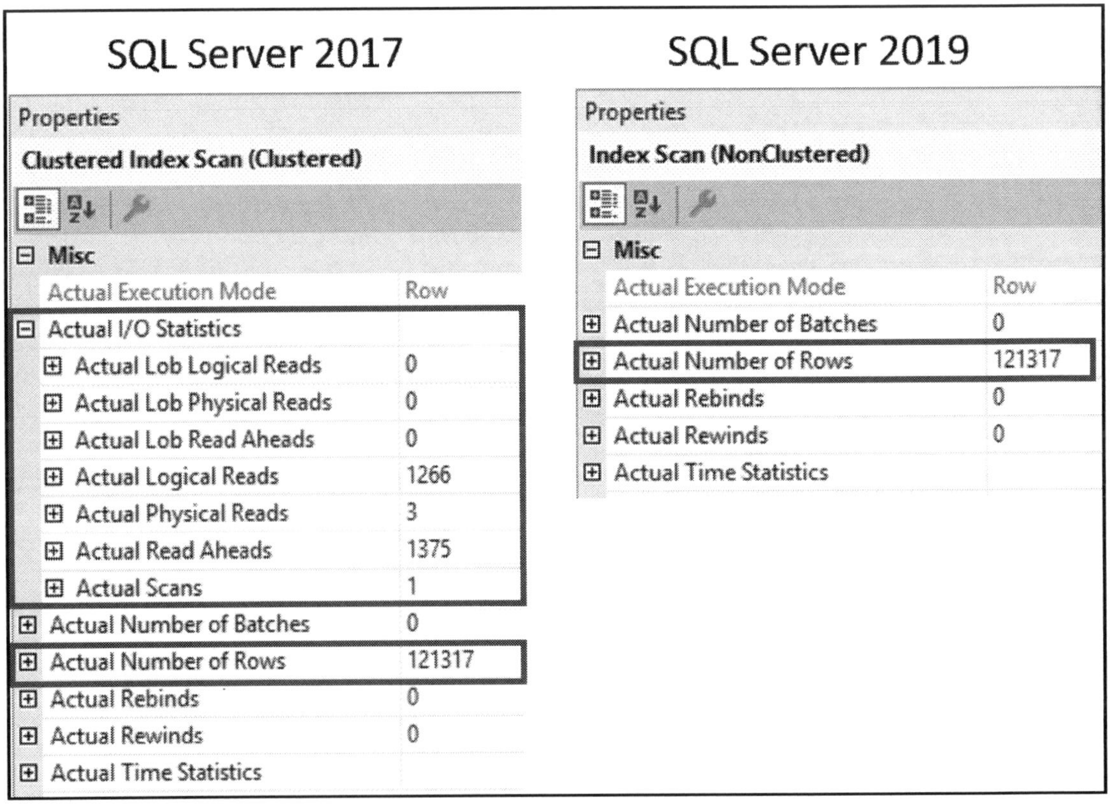

SQL Server 2017

Properties

Clustered Index Scan (Clustered)

Misc	
Actual Execution Mode	Row
Actual I/O Statistics	
Actual Lob Logical Reads	0
Actual Lob Physical Reads	0
Actual Lob Read Aheads	0
Actual Logical Reads	1266
Actual Physical Reads	3
Actual Read Aheads	1375
Actual Scans	1
Actual Number of Batches	0
Actual Number of Rows	121317
Actual Rebinds	0
Actual Rewinds	0
Actual Time Statistics	

SQL Server 2019

Properties

Index Scan (NonClustered)

Misc	
Actual Execution Mode	Row
Actual Number of Batches	0
Actual Number of Rows	121317
Actual Rebinds	0
Actual Rewinds	0
Actual Time Statistics	

The query_post_execution_plan_profile XEvent

SQL Server 2017 Cumulative Update 14 and SQL Server 2019 introduced a new XEvent named **query_post_execution_profile**, which can be used to collect the equivalent of an actual execution plan for all queries, much like the **query_post_execution_showplan** XEvent. Unlike the **query_plan_profile** XEvent, **query_post_execution_profile** is not bound to a query hint, but it also uses lightweight profiling by default. The following is an example session that uses this XEvent:

```
CREATE EVENT SESSION [PerfStats_LWP_Plan_All] ON SERVER
ADD EVENT sqlserver.query_post_execution_plan_profile(
        ACTION(sqlos.scheduler_id, sqlserver.database_id,
sqlserver.is_system,
sqlserver.plan_handle, sqlserver.query_hash_signed,
sqlserver.query_plan_hash_signed,
sqlserver.server_instance_name,sqlserver.session_id,
sqlserver.session_nt_username, sqlserver.sql_text)
        )
        ADD TARGET package0.event_file(
                SET filename=N'C:\Temp\PerfStats_LWP_Plan_All.xel',
                max_file_size=(50), max_rollover_files=(2)
        )
WITH (MAX_MEMORY=4096 KB, EVENT_RETENTION_MODE=ALLOW_SINGLE_EVENT_LOSS,
    MAX_DISPATCH_LATENCY=30 SECONDS, MAX_EVENT_SIZE=0 KB,
MEMORY_PARTITION_MODE=NONE,
    TRACK_CAUSALITY=OFF,STARTUP_STATE=OFF);
```

To see the output this XEvent produces, execute the following example query in the **AdventureWorks** sample database:

```
ALTER EVENT SESSION [PerfStats_LWP_Plan_All] ON SERVER STATE = start;
GO
SELECT COUNT(*)
FROM Sales.SalesOrderDetail AS sod
INNER JOIN Sales.SalesOrderHeader AS soh
        ON soh.SalesOrderID = sod.SalesOrderID
GROUP BY soh.Status;
GO
ALTER EVENT SESSION [PerfStats_LWP_Plan_All] ON SERVER STATE = stop;
GO
```

The resulting file can be opened using SSMS, as seen in the following screenshot:

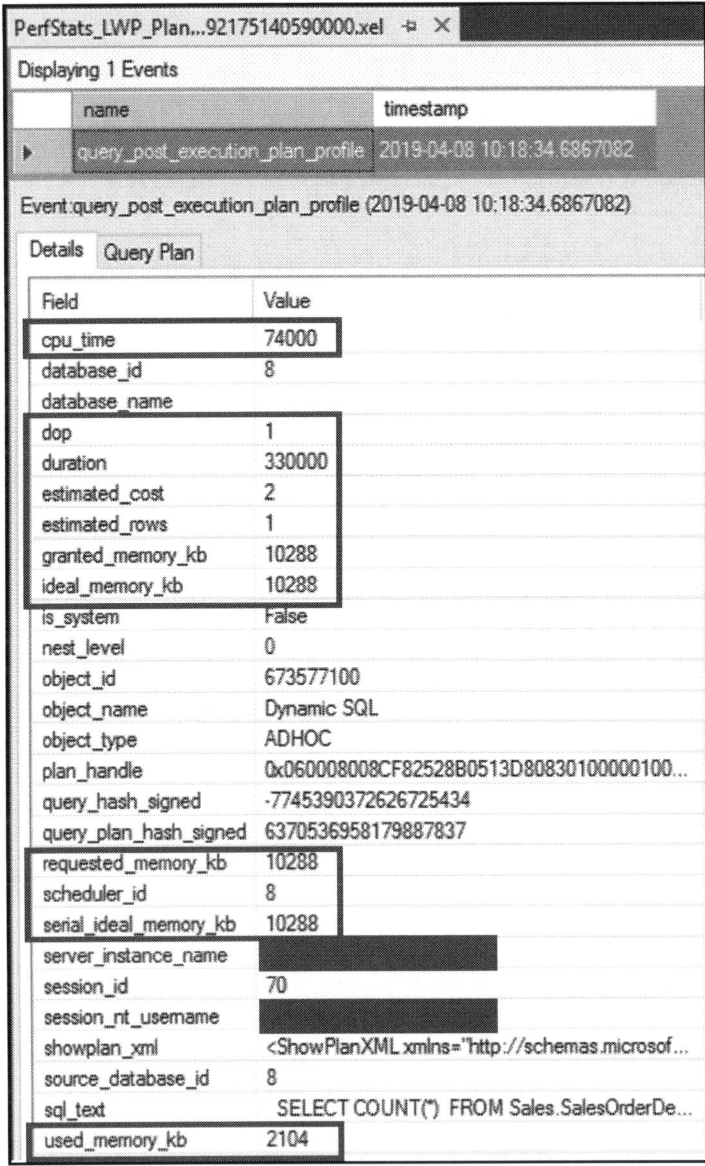

The XEvent contains the same runtime data we had observed for the **query_plan_profile** XEvent. This makes sense because these XEvents are very close implementations, minus the binding to a query hint on **query_plan_profile**. Therefore, as expected, when we click in the **Query Plan** tab, the observations for SQL Server 2017 and SQL Server 2019 query execution plans are also the same as in the previous chapter for the **query_plan_profile** XEvent.

The sys.dm_exec_query_statistics_xml DMF

SQL Server 2016 SP1 introduced a new DMF named **sys.dm_exec_query_statistics_xml**, which leverages LWP by default, but it also works if Standard Profiling is enabled. This DMF outputs the query execution plan as a snapshot of the current in-flight request. As such, this query execution plan will have transient runtime statistics captured at the moment the DMF was invoked.

The ability to programmatically access the query execution plan for any running request is a leap forward for scenarios in which we must troubleshoot a long-running query. In this case, we can use this DMF, or LQS, which we discussed in the first section of this chapter.

Let's look at a practical example of using this new DMF. The following example was used in `Chapter 3`, *Mechanics of the Query Optimizer*, and was saved in a file named **ProblemQuery.sql**:

```
SELECT e.[BusinessEntityID], p.[Title], p.[FirstName],
       p.[MiddleName], p.[LastName], p.[Suffix], e.[JobTitle],
       pp.[PhoneNumber], pnt.[Name] AS [PhoneNumberType],
       ea.[EmailAddress], p.[EmailPromotion], a.[AddressLine1],
       a.[AddressLine2], a.[City], sp.[Name] AS [StateProvinceName],
       a.[PostalCode], cr.[Name] AS [CountryRegionName],
p.[AdditionalContactInfo]
FROM [HumanResources].[Employee] AS e
INNER JOIN [Person].[Person] AS p
       ON RTRIM(LTRIM(p.[BusinessEntityID])) =
RTRIM(LTRIM(e.[BusinessEntityID]))
INNER JOIN [Person].[BusinessEntityAddress] AS bea
       ON RTRIM(LTRIM(bea.[BusinessEntityID])) =
RTRIM(LTRIM(e.[BusinessEntityID]))
INNER JOIN [Person].[Address] AS a
       ON RTRIM(LTRIM(a.[AddressID])) = RTRIM(LTRIM(bea.[AddressID]))
INNER JOIN [Person].[StateProvince] AS sp
       ON RTRIM(LTRIM(sp.[StateProvinceID])) =
RTRIM(LTRIM(a.[StateProvinceID]))
INNER JOIN [Person].[CountryRegion] AS cr
       ON RTRIM(LTRIM(cr.[CountryRegionCode])) =
RTRIM(LTRIM(sp.[CountryRegionCode]))
```

```
LEFT OUTER JOIN [Person].[PersonPhone] AS pp
       ON RTRIM(LTRIM(pp.BusinessEntityID)) =
RTRIM(LTRIM(p.[BusinessEntityID]))
LEFT OUTER JOIN [Person].[PhoneNumberType] AS pnt
       ON RTRIM(LTRIM(pp.[PhoneNumberTypeID])) =
RTRIM(LTRIM(pnt.[PhoneNumberTypeID]))
LEFT OUTER JOIN [Person].[EmailAddress] AS ea
       ON RTRIM(LTRIM(p.[BusinessEntityID])) =
RTRIM(LTRIM(ea.[BusinessEntityID]));
```

We can use the **ostress** utility and simulate a client application executing the same long-running query over 10 concurrent connections, as seen in the following command:

```
ostress.exe -S<my_server_name> -E -dAdventureWorks2016_EXT -
iProblemQuery.sql -n10 -r1000
```

ostress is a free command-line tool that is part of the **Replay Markup Language (RML)** Utilities for SQL Server. This tool can be used to simulate the effects of stressing a SQL Server instance by using ad hoc queries or `.sql` script files.

While the workload is executing, we can join **sys.dm_exec_query_statistics_xml** with other DMVs such as **sys.dm_exec_requests**, **sys.dm_exec_sessions**, and **sys.dm_exec_connections**. The following query uses the **sys.dm_exec_requests** DMV as a starting point, since I'm looking to get the current state of the execution plan for an in-flight request:

```
SELECT er.session_id, er.start_time, er.status, er.database_id,
       er.wait_type, er.last_wait_type, er.cpu_time, er.total_elapsed_time,
       er.logical_reads, er.granted_query_memory, er.dop,
       st.text, qsx.query_plan
FROM sys.dm_exec_requests AS er
CROSS APPLY sys.dm_exec_sql_text(plan_handle) AS st
CROSS APPLY sys.dm_exec_query_statistics_xml(session_id) AS qsx;
```

This query returns the following results:

	session_id	start_time	status	database_id	wait_type	last_wait_type	cpu_time	total_elapsed_time	logical_reads	granted_query_memory	dop	text	query_plan
1	66	2019-04-08 17:59:42.517	runnable	26	NULL	SOS_SCHEDULER_YIELD	24	48	235	3422	1	SELECT e.[BusinessEntityID], ...	<ShowPlanXML xmlns="http://schema...
2	75	2019-04-08 17:59:42.497	runnable	26	NULL	SOS_SCHEDULER_YIELD	32	91	272	3422	1	SELECT e.[BusinessEntityID], ...	<ShowPlanXML xmlns="http://schema...
3	77	2019-04-08 17:59:42.377	running	26	NULL	SOS_SCHEDULER_YIELD	78	228	4427	3422	1	SELECT e.[BusinessEntityID], ...	<ShowPlanXML xmlns="http://schema...
4	81	2019-04-08 17:59:42.610	running	26	NULL	SOS_SCHEDULER_YIELD	20	20	204	3422	1	SELECT e.[BusinessEntityID], ...	<ShowPlanXML xmlns="http://schema...
5	83	2019-04-08 17:59:42.637	running	26	NULL	RESERVED_MEMORY_AL...	10	18	98	3422	1	SELECT e.[BusinessEntityID], ...	<ShowPlanXML xmlns="http://schema...
6	84	2019-04-08 17:59:42.597	running	26	NULL	SOS_SCHEDULER_YIELD	32	93	263	3422	1	SELECT e.[BusinessEntityID], ...	<ShowPlanXML xmlns="http://schema...
7	85	2019-04-08 17:59:42.703	runnable	26	NULL	SOS_SCHEDULER_YIELD	11	21	125	3422	1	SELECT e.[BusinessEntityID], ...	<ShowPlanXML xmlns="http://schema...
8	86	2019-04-08 17:59:42.687	runnable	26	NULL	SOS_SCHEDULER_YIELD	28	55	281	3422	1	SELECT e.[BusinessEntityID], ...	<ShowPlanXML xmlns="http://schema...
9	88	2019-04-08 17:59:42.680	running	26	NULL	RESERVED_MEMORY_AL...	43	83	471	3422	1	SELECT e.[BusinessEntityID], ...	<ShowPlanXML xmlns="http://schema...
10	112	2019-04-08 17:59:42.567	running	1	NULL	SOS_SCHEDULER_YIELD	81	223	0	0	1	SELECT er.session_id, er.start...	<ShowPlanXML xmlns="http://schema...

Each row is an in-flight request. To see a snapshot of the ongoing query execution plan, click the link in the **query_plan** column, as seen in the following screenshot:

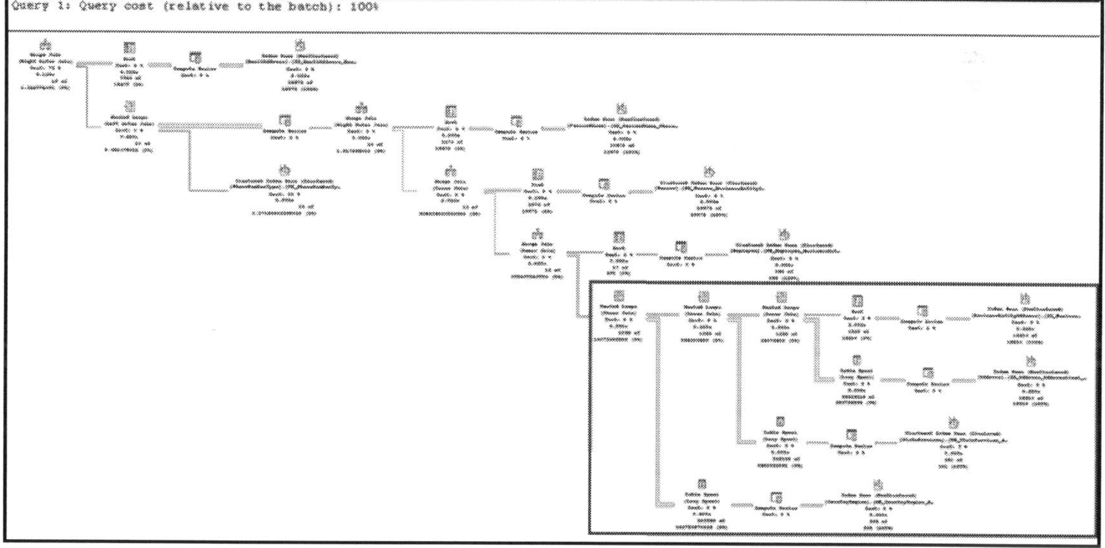

If we zoom into the bottom-right quadrant of the query execution plan, as seen in the following screenshot, we see some slow progress building two Table Spools—we discussed Spools in in the *Query plan operators of interest* section of `Chapter 4`, *Exploring Query Execution Plans,* and the focus of analysis should be this section of the plan, which we did in the *Using Live Query Statistics* section of this chapter:

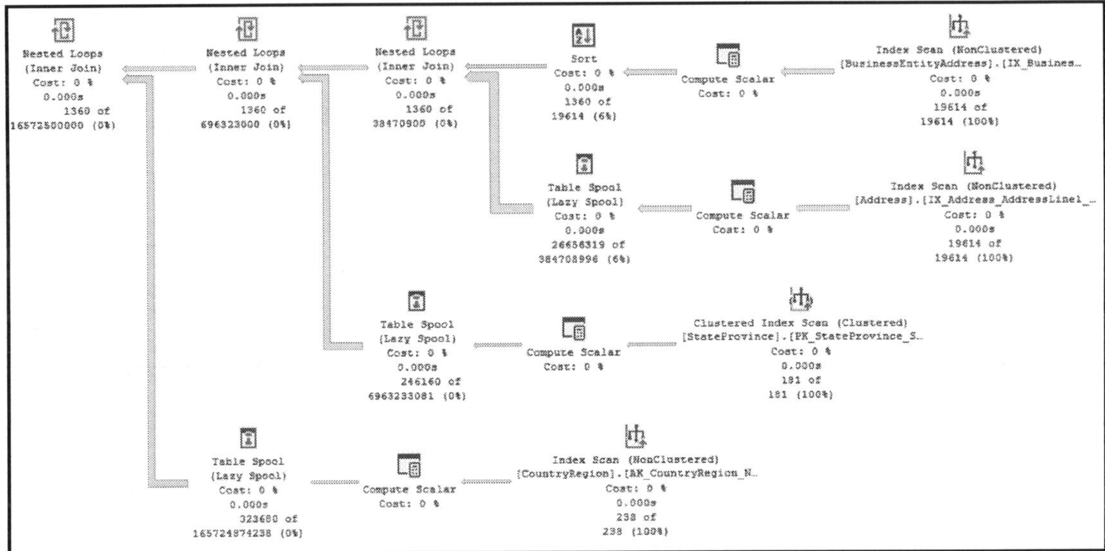

In the GitHub TIGER toolbox (`http://aka.ms/tigertoolbox`), we can find a comprehensive script that can quickly help us diagnose performance issues with in-flight requests and blocking scenarios (`http://aka.ms/uspWhatsUp`). This script uses a combination of DMVs that includes **sys.dm_exec_query_statistics_xml**.

The sys.dm_exec_query_plan_stats DMF

SQL Server 2019 introduced a new DMF named **sys.dm_exec_query_plan_stats**, which leverages LWP by default, and like the DMF in the previous section, it also works if Standard Profiling is enabled. This DMF outputs the last known equivalent of a query execution plan for any given query whose query plan can still be found in the plan cache. In other words, every data professional can now have the last actual execution plan always available for any query.

This DMF only maintains a subset of what is available through XEvents using lightweight profiling. The available information for plans accessed through this DMF is operator level row count, spill warnings (without I/O detail), and query level CPU time and elapsed time. Wait type statistics and operator-level I/O statistics are not included due to potential overhead.

There are two methods to enable this DMF to be populated:

- Enable trace flag 2451 (at the session level or globally, adding the **-1** parameter) using the following T-SQL command: `DBCC TRACEON(2451, -1);`
- Set the database scoped **LAST_QUERY_PLAN_STATS** configuration to **ON** using the following T-SQL command:
  `ALTER DATABASE SCOPED CONFIGURATION SET LAST_QUERY_PLAN_STATS = ON;`

The concept of always having the last known query execution plan always available is a game changer for troubleshooting just-in-time scenarios where a query's performance has suddenly regressed and you are the database professional that gets a call informing you that the application has poor performance as a result and that you must provide a root-cause analysis.

If it's a long running query, then we can use LQS or the DMF in the previous section. But if it's a case of a query that has been executing (to completion) repeatedly in the last few minutes, then accessing the last known actual execution plan allows us to start troubleshooting immediately, without the need to set up any kind of tracing.

SQL Trace and SQL Server Profiler are deprecated and should not be used in modern versions of SQL Server where the more complete and less intrusive XEvents are available.

If we are familiar with **Query Store (QS)**, which we discussed in `Chapter 10`, *Tracking Performance History with the Query Store*, then that may be our first go-to feature to troubleshoot our current scenario. However, QS aggregates performance data in configurable time periods, which is excellent for doing performance troubleshooting over time (analogous to a time series) and analyzing workload trends, but for just-in-time scenarios where the requirement is to get the query's execution plan that just executed, then this DMF is a welcome diagnostic.

If any query profiling infrastructure is enabled, the DMF captures and saves the query execution plan data for all query plans in the cache. If the query is canceled, the query execution plan will have data up to the point when the query was canceled.

Let's look at a practical example of using this new DMF. The following sample query can be executed in the scope of the **AdventureWorks** sample database:

```
SELECT TOP 1000 *
FROM [dbo].[DimProduct] AS dp
INNER JOIN [dbo].[DimProductCategory] AS dpc ON dp.ProductSubcategoryKey =
dpc.ProductCategoryKey;
```

We can then join with other DMVs, such as **sys.dm_exec_cached_plans**, **sys.dm_exec_query_stats**, **sys.dm_exec_requests**, **sys.dm_exec_procedure_stats**, and **sys.dm_exec_trigger_stats**. Next, we have examples of queries that can retrieve information on the specific query, including the last known equivalent of a query execution plan from **sys.dm_exec_query_plan_stats**.

The following query uses the **sys.dm_exec_cached_plans** DMV as a starting point, since the **sys.dm_exec_query_plan_stats** DMF can only report on query plans that are cached:

```
SELECT qps.dbid, st.text, qps.query_plan,
       cp.refcounts, cp.usecounts, cp.cacheobjtype, cp.objtype
FROM sys.dm_exec_cached_plans AS cp
CROSS APPLY sys.dm_exec_sql_text(plan_handle) AS st
CROSS APPLY sys.dm_exec_query_plan_stats(plan_handle) AS qps
WHERE st.text LIKE '%SELECT TOP 1000%';
```

This query returns the following results:

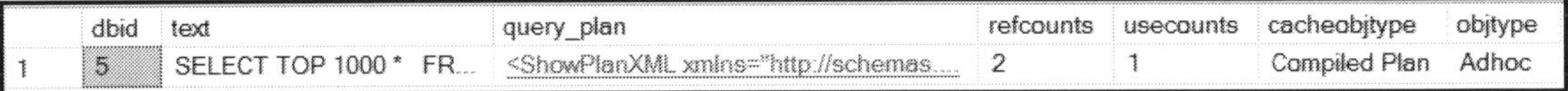

	dbid	text	query_plan	refcounts	usecounts	cacheobjtype	objtype
1	5	SELECT TOP 1000 * FR...	<ShowPlanXML xmlns="http://schemas....	2	1	Compiled Plan	Adhoc

If the corresponding runtime plan information is not available, the **query_plan** column shows **NULL**.

The following query uses the **sys.dm_exec_query_stats** DMV as a starting point in order to see performance metrics for all queries that have executed since the last SQL Server startup, where the query plan is still in the plan cache:

```
SELECT qps.dbid, st.text, qps.query_plan,
       qs.last_dop, qs.last_elapsed_time, qs.last_execution_time,
```

```
        qs.last_grant_kb, qs.last_used_grant_kb, qs.last_logical_reads,
        qs.last_logical_writes, qs.last_physical_reads,
        qs.last_rows, qs.last_spills, qs.last_worker_time
FROM sys.dm_exec_query_stats AS qs
OUTER APPLY sys.dm_exec_sql_text(plan_handle) AS st
OUTER APPLY sys.dm_exec_query_plan_stats(plan_handle) AS qps
WHERE st.text LIKE '--%';
```

This query returns the following results:

	dbid	text	query_plan	last_dop	last_elapsed_time	last_execution_time
1	5	SELECT TOP 1000 * FR...	<ShowPlanXML xmlns="http://schemas....	1	382986	2019-04-08 15:08:47.640

last_grant_kb	last_used_grant_kb	last_logical_reads	last_logical_writes	last_physical_reads	last_rows	last_spills	last_worker_time
1192	248	1146	0	595	139	0	13453

Again, if the corresponding runtime plan information is not available, the **query_plan** column is **NULL**. On both results, click the link in the **query_plan** column to open the last known query execution plan, as seen in the following screenshot:

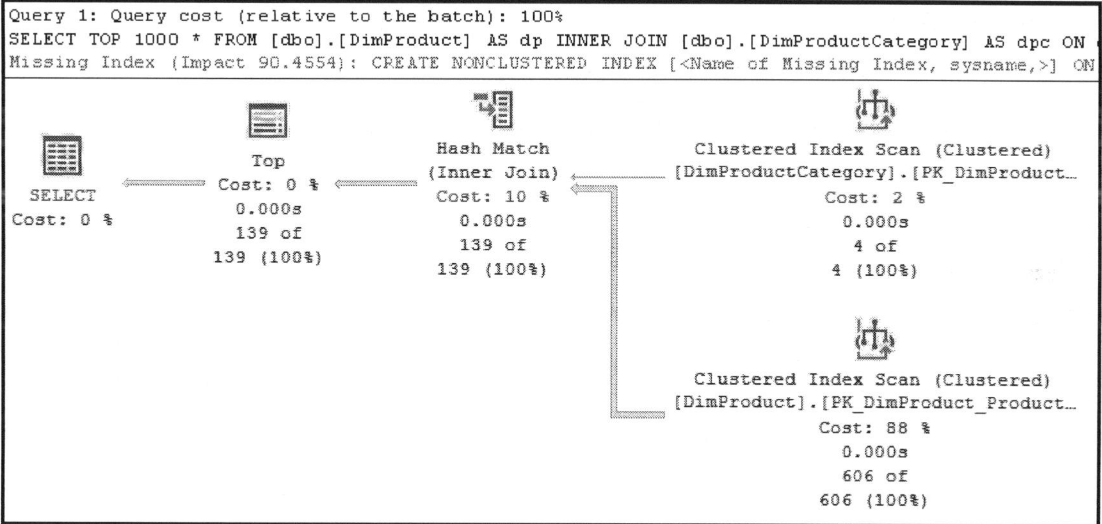

In the GitHub TIGER toolbox (`http://aka.ms/tigertoolbox`), we can find a comprehensive script that can quickly help us diagnose performance issues with in-flight requests and blocking scenarios (`http://aka.ms/uspWhatsUp`). This script uses a combination of DMVs that includes **sys.dm_exec_query_plan_stats**.

Activity Monitor gets a new life

LQS has its viable use case as we discussed in the *Using Live Query Statistics* section of this chapter—a previously identified long-running query. But what if we haven't identified an offending query yet? What if we are the database professional who got that middle-of-the-night call asking them to solve an issue with a business-critical ETL process that runs every night, but is unusually slow today?

ETL is an acronym for **Extract-Transform-Load** which is the name given to a process that extracts data from a data source, enacts transformations in that data such as aggregations or calculations, and loads the results into a destination such as a database. A typical example of an ETL process is a SQL Server Agent job that schedules the execution of a **SQL Server Integration Services** (**SSIS**) package.

That is where **Activity Monitor** (**AM**) comes in. AM is a SSMS feature that's been there for a long time and has probably gone unnoticed by many SSMS users. AM can be enabled by right-clicking the instance name in **Object Explorer**, and then clicking on **Activity Monitor** as seen in the following screenshot:

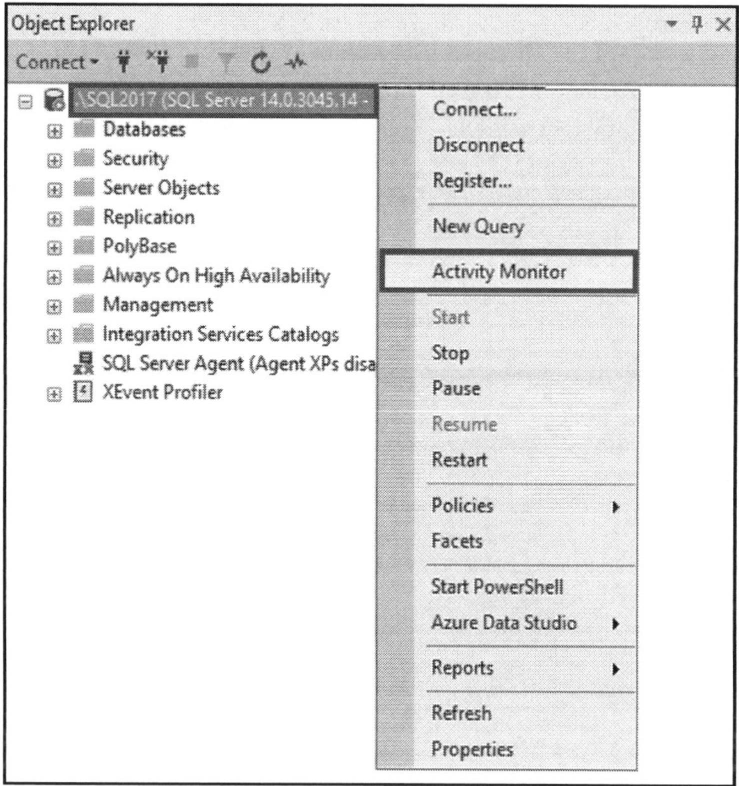

A new tab will be displayed which contains the following information sections:

- An **Overview** of a few key performance counters: CPU usage, number of waiting tasks, database I/O measured in MB/sec, and the number of **Batch Requests/sec**. Notice the CPU is running at 80 percent now that the ETL is executing. I'm also doing six **Batch Requests/sec,** which is a very low number:

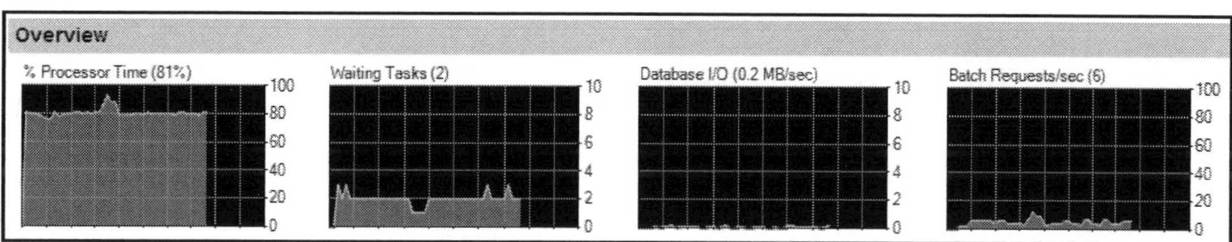

- The current processes or sessions active in SQL Server, including useful information such as the login and database that set the context for that session; the current task state (running, runnable, suspended) as defined in the *Query execution essentials* section of `Chapter 2`, *Understanding Query Processing;* wait information that shows details if the task is in a suspended state; the calling application and host machine; and whether the current session is a head blocker of a blocking chain. This is all information coming from DMVs that was thoroughly discussed in `Chapter 8`, *Building Diagnostic Queries Using DMVs and DMFs*:

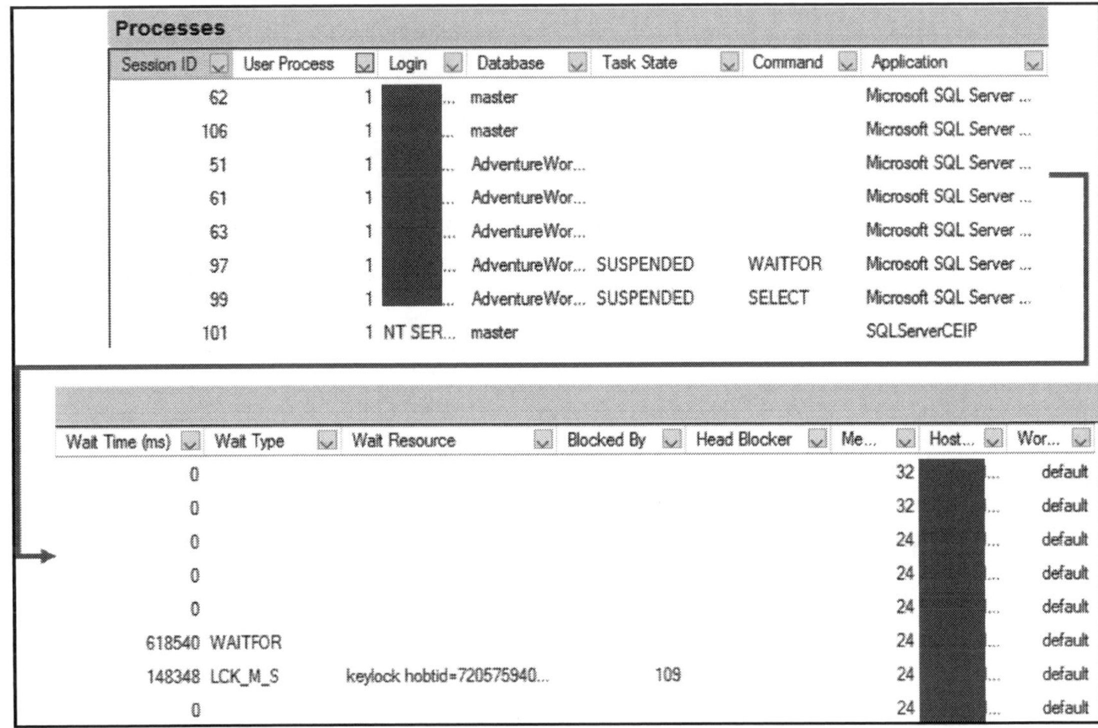

- The current **Resource Waits**, including **Wait Category** and **Metrics** such as the cumulative wait time accrued for the wait type:

Resource Waits

Wait Category	Wait Time (ms/sec)	Recent Wait Time (ms/sec)	Average Waiter Count	Cumulative Wait Time (sec)
Logging	16479	20878	16.5	8259
Buffer Latch	2985	1449	3.0	479
Latch	4229	1231	4.2	308
Lock	1002	996	1.0	5798
Buffer I/O	16	1	0.0	4619
Compilation	0	0	0.0	0
Memory	0	0	0.0	0
Network I/O	0	0	0.0	1642

- The **Data File I/O** related to the read and write I/O, including access latency for each file:

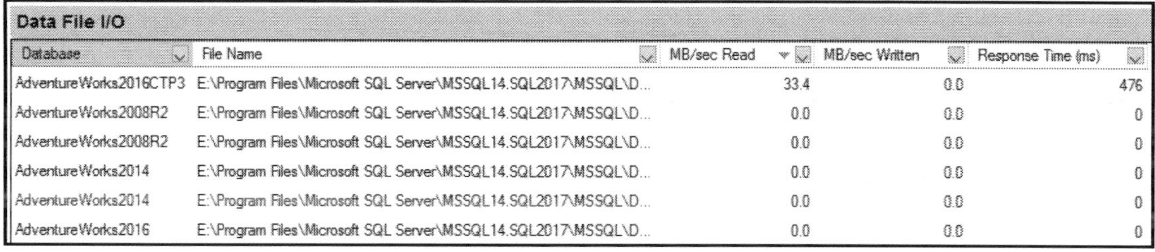

Data File I/O

Database	File Name	MB/sec Read	MB/sec Written	Response Time (ms)
AdventureWorks2016CTP3	E:\Program Files\Microsoft SQL Server\MSSQL14.SQL2017\MSSQL\D...	33.4	0.0	476
AdventureWorks2008R2	E:\Program Files\Microsoft SQL Server\MSSQL14.SQL2017\MSSQL\D...	0.0	0.0	0
AdventureWorks2008R2	E:\Program Files\Microsoft SQL Server\MSSQL14.SQL2017\MSSQL\D...	0.0	0.0	0
AdventureWorks2014	E:\Program Files\Microsoft SQL Server\MSSQL14.SQL2017\MSSQL\D...	0.0	0.0	0
AdventureWorks2014	E:\Program Files\Microsoft SQL Server\MSSQL14.SQL2017\MSSQL\D...	0.0	0.0	0
AdventureWorks2016	E:\Program Files\Microsoft SQL Server\MSSQL14.SQL2017\MSSQL\D...	0.0	0.0	0

- The **Recent** and **Active Expensive Queries** tabs allowing to pinpoint queries with long elapsed times and CPU usage:

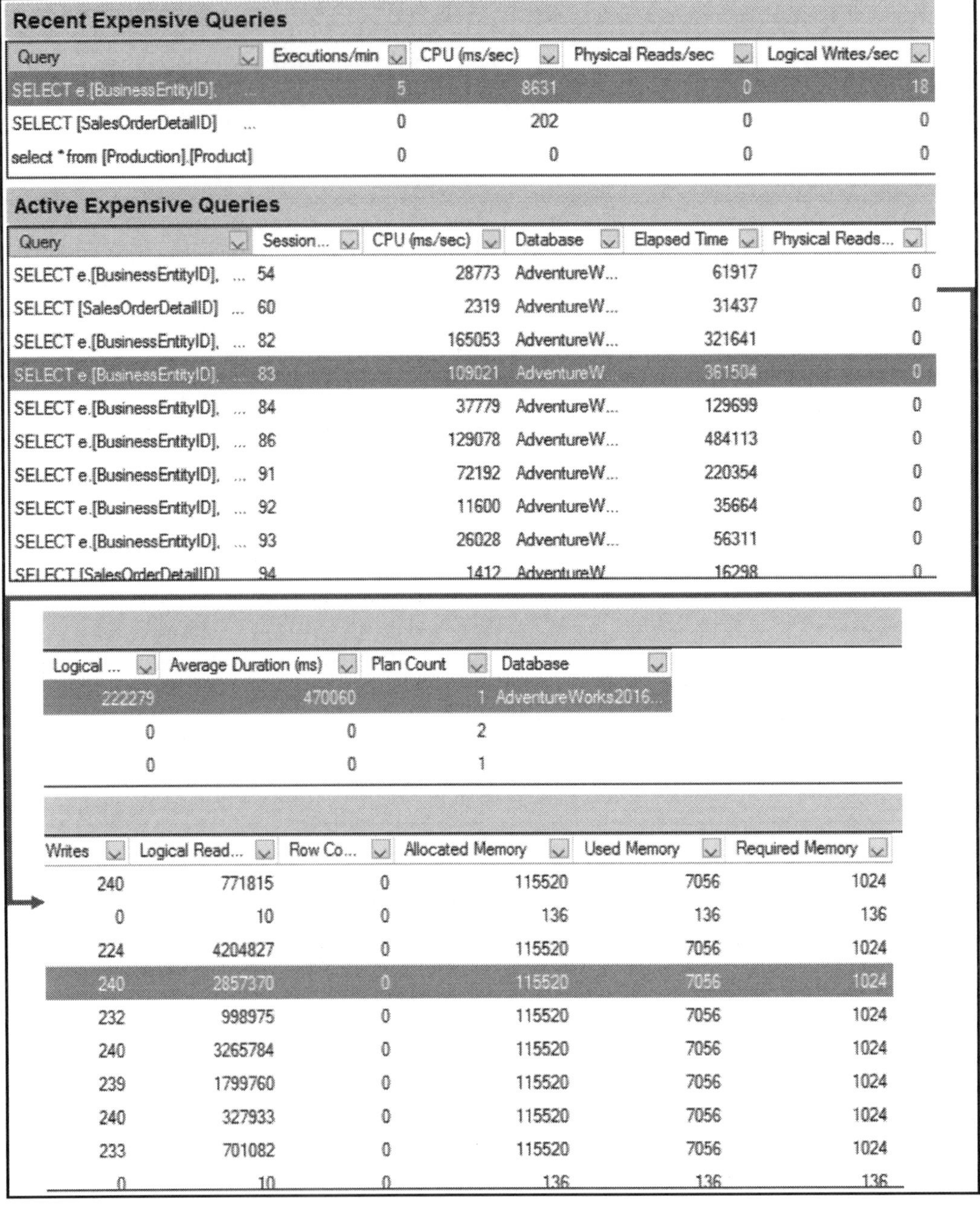

Recent Expensive Queries

Query	Executions/min	CPU (ms/sec)	Physical Reads/sec	Logical Writes/sec	Logical ...	Average Duration (ms)	Plan Count	Database
SELECT e.[BusinessEntityID]. ...	5	8631	0	18	222279	470060	1	AdventureWorks2016...
SELECT [SalesOrderDetailID] ...	0	202	0	0	0	0	2	
select * from [Production].[Product]	0	0	0	0	0	0	1	

Active Expensive Queries

Query	Session...	CPU (ms/sec)	Database	Elapsed Time	Physical Reads...	Writes	Logical Read...	Row Co...	Allocated Memory	Used Memory	Required Memory
SELECT e.[BusinessEntityID]. ...	54	28773	AdventureW...	61917	0	240	771815	0	115520	7056	1024
SELECT [SalesOrderDetailID] ...	60	2319	AdventureW...	31437	0	0	10	0	136	136	136
SELECT e.[BusinessEntityID]. ...	82	165053	AdventureW...	321641	0	224	4204827	0	115520	7056	1024
SELECT e.[BusinessEntityID]. ...	83	109021	AdventureW...	361504	0	240	2857370	0	115520	7056	1024
SELECT e.[BusinessEntityID]. ...	84	37779	AdventureW...	129699	0	232	998975	0	115520	7056	1024
SELECT e.[BusinessEntityID]. ...	86	129078	AdventureW...	484113	0	240	3265784	0	115520	7056	1024
SELECT e.[BusinessEntityID]. ...	91	72192	AdventureW...	220354	0	239	1799760	0	115520	7056	1024
SELECT e.[BusinessEntityID]. ...	92	11600	AdventureW...	35664	0	240	327933	0	115520	7056	1024
SELECT e.[BusinessEntityID]. ...	93	26028	AdventureW...	56311	0	233	701082	0	115520	7056	1024
SELECT [SalesOrderDetailID]	94	1412	AdventureW...	16298	0	0	10	0	136	136	136

Here is the interesting part about why AM should be part of our toolbox: when one of the query profiling infrastructures we discussed in `Chapter 11`, *Tracking Performance History with Query Store* is enabled globally, the **sys.dm_exec_query_profiles** DMV is populated for every query that is executing—this has been mentioned before, which means that unlike LQS that can only show the live plan for the query running in my own session, AM can show live plans for queries in any session.

When the **query_post_execution_showplan** XEvent is in use, the **sys.dm_exec_query_profiles** DMV is populated for all queries using Standard Profiling. This means that using AM or directly querying the DMV has a higher impact than when LWP is used. In the previous chapter, we covered the many ways in which LWP can be enabled.

So, when I got that middle-of-the-night call, I accessed the ETL process and looked at which queries are being used. Then I used AM to easily pinpoint the query being executed by the ETL process and see its live plan. How? For example, using the **Active Expensive Queries** tab in AM, right-click a long-running query, and selecting the **Show Live Execution Plan** option as seen in the following screenshot:

Active Expensive Queries

Query	Session...	CPU (ms...
SELECT e.[BusinessEntityID], p.[Title], ...	54	28773
SELECT [SalesOrderDetailID] ,[OrderQty] ...	60	2319
SELECT e.[BusinessEntityID], p.[Title], ...	82	165053
SELECT e.[BusinessEn...		109021
SELECT e.[BusinessEn		37779
SELECT e.[BusinessEn		129078
SELECT e.[BusinessEn		72192
SELECT e.[BusinessEntityID], p.[Title], ...	92	11600
SELECT e.[BusinessEntityID], p.[Title], ...	93	26028

Edit Query Text
Show Live Execution Plan
Show Execution Plan

If the menu option **Show Live Execution Plan** is grayed-out, this means that neither Standard Profiling nor Lightweight Profiling are enabled globally. To enable LWP globally for all queries, see the *Understanding the need for Lightweight Profiling* section.

For this query that has been executing for over 100 seconds now, a new tab will display the live execution plan as seen in the following screenshot:

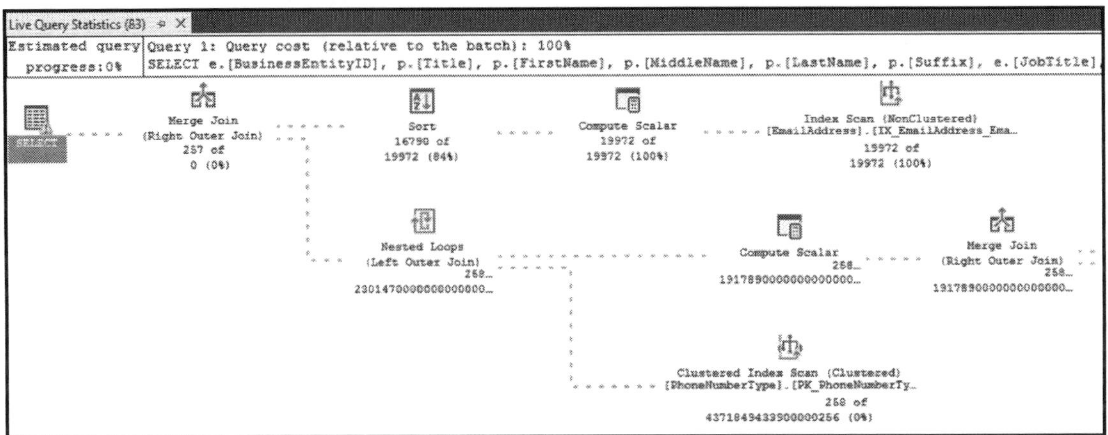

Notice this is the same query used in the previous section on LQS, but when it's displayed in AM, the operator times are missing. Why? Remember that LQS leverages Standard Profiling, which tracks operator-level information such as the CPU and the elapsed time. However, in this example, we are using LWP, which does not include that per-operator information.

As the database professional who got that middle-of-the-night call, how can I analyze and possibly solve the ongoing performance issue? I start by opening the plan properties by right-clicking the root node and selecting **Properties**—refer to `Chapter 4`, *Exploring Query Execution Plans* under the *Plan-level properties* and *Operator-level properties* sections for more information on the available showplan properties that are useful for troubleshooting query performance.

It's best to first try to understand if there are any server-wide configurations that may be impacting query execution. One good place to start are trace flags. Are there trace flags impacting this query's execution? Looking at the trace flag information in the plan I notice two trace flags, as seen in the following screenshot:

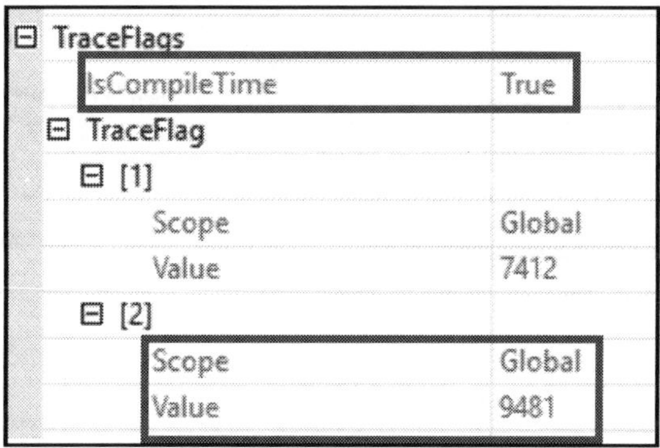

There are the following two data points I can extract from here:

1. There were global (server-wide) trace flags present at the time this query was compiled.
2. Of the two trace flags, we know now that **7412** enables the LWP by default, which allowed me to use AM to troubleshoot in the first place. So, we need to research trace flag **9481** to see whether it's impacting query optimization choices that would affect the plan.

Looking in the documentation about trace flags (`http://aka.ms/traceflags`), here is the explanation for what trace flag 9481 does: it enables us to "*set the query optimizer cardinality estimation model to the SQL Server 2012 (11.x) and earlier versions, irrespective of the compatibility level of the database.*".

This is a good starting point: although this ETL is executing in a SQL Server 2017 instance and the **AdventureWorks** database is in database compatibility level 130, which maps to using CE 130, the query was optimized with CE 70 instead, as seen in the following screenshot:

Properties

SELECT

Misc	
Actual Number of Rows	286
Cached plan size	160 KB
CardinalityEstimationModelVersion	70
CompileCPU	162
CompileMemory	2144
CompileTime	449
CompletionEstimate	6.564727453204526E-17
DatabaseContextSettingsId	5
ElapsedTime	0
Estimated Number of Rows	4598570000000000000000

So, here is a working hypothesis: using CE 130 most likely will yield a different query plan. Will it improve the query performance over the current plan?

We can refer to the *Introducing the Cardinality Estimator* section of `Chapter 3`, *Mechanics of the Query Optimizer*, for further context on the potentially enormous impact this CE change carries for the query optimization process.

Let's experiment overriding the global trace flag at a query level, so to experiment what is the effect of using the default CE model for database compatibility level 130. For that, I will take the query from the execution plan, open a new query window in SSMS, add the hint `OPTION (USE HINT('FORCE_DEFAULT_CARDINALITY_ESTIMATION'))` to my query, and execute it in **AdventureWorks**:

```
SELECT e.[BusinessEntityID], p.[Title], p.[FirstName],
       p.[MiddleName], p.[LastName], p.[Suffix], e.[JobTitle],
       pp.[PhoneNumber], pnt.[Name] AS [PhoneNumberType],
       ea.[EmailAddress], p.[EmailPromotion], a.[AddressLine1],
       a.[AddressLine2], a.[City], sp.[Name] AS [StateProvinceName],
       a.[PostalCode], cr.[Name] AS [CountryRegionName],
p.[AdditionalContactInfo]
```

```
FROM [HumanResources].[Employee] AS e
INNER JOIN [Person].[Person] AS p
       ON RTRIM(LTRIM(p.[BusinessEntityID])) =
RTRIM(LTRIM(e.[BusinessEntityID]))
INNER JOIN [Person].[BusinessEntityAddress] AS bea
       ON RTRIM(LTRIM(bea.[BusinessEntityID])) =
RTRIM(LTRIM(e.[BusinessEntityID]))
INNER JOIN [Person].[Address] AS a
       ON RTRIM(LTRIM(a.[AddressID])) = RTRIM(LTRIM(bea.[AddressID]))
INNER JOIN [Person].[StateProvince] AS sp
       ON RTRIM(LTRIM(sp.[StateProvinceID])) =
RTRIM(LTRIM(a.[StateProvinceID]))
INNER JOIN [Person].[CountryRegion] AS cr
       ON RTRIM(LTRIM(cr.[CountryRegionCode])) =
RTRIM(LTRIM(sp.[CountryRegionCode]))
LEFT OUTER JOIN [Person].[PersonPhone] AS pp
       ON RTRIM(LTRIM(pp.BusinessEntityID)) =
RTRIM(LTRIM(p.[BusinessEntityID]))
LEFT OUTER JOIN [Person].[PhoneNumberType] AS pnt
       ON RTRIM(LTRIM(pp.[PhoneNumberTypeID])) =
RTRIM(LTRIM(pnt.[PhoneNumberTypeID]))
LEFT OUTER JOIN [Person].[EmailAddress] AS ea
       ON RTRIM(LTRIM(p.[BusinessEntityID])) =
RTRIM(LTRIM(ea.[BusinessEntityID]))
OPTION (USE HINT('FORCE_DEFAULT_CARDINALITY_ESTIMATION'));
```

This hinted query executed in 291 ms, while the original query is still running at almost 3 minutes elapsed time.

The shape for the ETL original plan and the new plan using the hint can be seen in the *Introducing the Cardinality Estimator* section in `Chapter 3`, *Mechanics of the Query Optimizer*.

At this point, I have several possible actions:

1. Disable the trace flag globally, unless the trace flag had been enabled as a result of workload tests that showed most queries benefit from CE 70. Even so, it's recommended to *not* use the trace flag, but rather the corresponding database scoped configuration to set that behavior at the database level, using the following T-SQL command:

   ```
    ALTER DATABASE SCOPED CONFIGURATION SET
   LEGACY_CARDINALITY_ESTIMATION = ON;
   ```

2. If the decision of disabling the trace flag warrants further system-wide tests, then at least for the offending query, we know that using CE 130 yields better results. Change the ETL to add the `USE HINT('FORCE_DEFAULT_CARDINALITY_ESTIMATION')` hint.
3. If changing the ETL code is not possible now, consider creating a plan guide that adds the required hint on the fly for any incoming execution of that query, as seen in the following example. This allows new incoming execution to use the new optimized plan, while not making any immediate change to the ETL code:

   ```
   EXEC sp_create_plan_guide
   @name = N'Guide1',
   @stmt = 'SELECT e.[BusinessEntityID], p.[Title], p.[FirstName],
       p.[MiddleName], p.[LastName], p.[Suffix], e.[JobTitle],
       pp.[PhoneNumber], pnt.[Name] AS [PhoneNumberType],
       ea.[EmailAddress], p.[EmailPromotion], a.[AddressLine1],
       a.[AddressLine2], a.[City], sp.[Name] AS [StateProvinceName],
       a.[PostalCode], cr.[Name] AS [CountryRegionName],
   p.[AdditionalContactInfo]
   FROM [HumanResources].[Employee] AS e
   INNER JOIN [Person].[Person] AS p
       ON RTRIM(LTRIM(p.[BusinessEntityID])) =
   RTRIM(LTRIM(e.[BusinessEntityID]))
   INNER JOIN [Person].[BusinessEntityAddress] AS bea
       ON RTRIM(LTRIM(bea.[BusinessEntityID])) =
   RTRIM(LTRIM(e.[BusinessEntityID]))
   INNER JOIN [Person].[Address] AS a
       ON RTRIM(LTRIM(a.[AddressID])) = RTRIM(LTRIM(bea.[AddressID]))
   INNER JOIN [Person].[StateProvince] AS sp
       ON RTRIM(LTRIM(sp.[StateProvinceID])) =
   RTRIM(LTRIM(a.[StateProvinceID]))
   INNER JOIN [Person].[CountryRegion] AS cr
       ON RTRIM(LTRIM(cr.[CountryRegionCode])) =
   RTRIM(LTRIM(sp.[CountryRegionCode]))
   LEFT OUTER JOIN [Person].[PersonPhone] AS pp
       ON RTRIM(LTRIM(pp.BusinessEntityID)) =
   ```

```
RTRIM(LTRIM(p.[BusinessEntityID]))
LEFT OUTER JOIN [Person].[PhoneNumberType] AS pnt
    ON RTRIM(LTRIM(pp.[PhoneNumberTypeID])) =
RTRIM(LTRIM(pnt.[PhoneNumberTypeID]))
LEFT OUTER JOIN [Person].[EmailAddress] AS ea
    ON RTRIM(LTRIM(p.[BusinessEntityID])) =
RTRIM(LTRIM(ea.[BusinessEntityID]));',
@type = N'SQL',
@module_or_batch = NULL,
@params = NULL,
@hints = N'OPTION (USE HINT
(''FORCE_DEFAULT_CARDINALITY_ESTIMATION''))';
```

With this change, look at AM's **Overview** section current status:

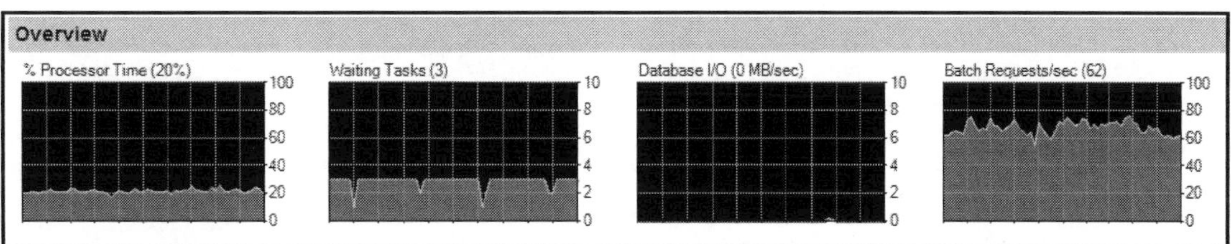

Notice the CPU is now running at 20 percent and the ETL is still executing. I'm also doing 60 **Batch Requests/sec**, which is significantly better than my starting point of 6 Batch **Requests/sec**.

Summary

This chapter covered the important topic of tracking query progress, and how to use either LQS to see the live progress of a single query in SSMS, or Activity Monitor to access the live progress of any running query. We also covered how these tools and the underlying Database Engine features are invaluable to troubleshoot and solve query performance issues, namely for those queries that take hours to complete, or never do complete.

The Query Profiling Infrastructures available in SQL Server depend on the Database Engine version. The following table summarizes the available options to enable either of the Query Profiling Infrastructures and the minimum required version for each option:

<table>
<tr><th>Where to enable</th><th>Standard Profiling</th><th>Lightweight Profiling</th></tr>
<tr><td rowspan="3">Globally</td><td>XEvent session with query_post_execution_showplan XE;
Starting with SQL Server 2012</td><td>XEvent session with query_thread_profile XE;
Starting with SQL Server 2014 SP2</td></tr>
<tr><td rowspan="2">Showplan XML trace event in SQL Trace and SQL Server Profiler;
Starting with SQL Server 2000</td><td>XEvent session with query_post_execution_plan_profile XE;
Starting with SQL Server 2019</td></tr>
<tr><td>Trace Flag 7412;
Starting with SQL Server 2016 SP1</td></tr>
<tr><td rowspan="3">Single session</td><td>Use <code>SET STATISTICS XML ON</code>;
Starting with SQL Server 2000</td><td rowspan="3">QUERY_PLAN_PROFILE query hint + XEvent session with query_plan_profile XE;
Starting with SQL Server 2016 SP2 CU3 and 2017 CU11</td></tr>
<tr><td>Use <code>SET STATISTICS PROFILE ON</code>;
Starting with SQL Server 2000</td></tr>
<tr><td>Click LQS button in SSMS;
Starting with SQL Server 2014 SP2</td></tr>
</table>

This analysis was possible because, at this point, we know how to the create reasonable hypotheses about potential query performance issues by analyzing query plan properties, and what those say about the query optimization choices during compilation time.

In the next and final chapter of the book, we will investigate a tool available to us in SSMS that will help identify and remediate issues with our T-SQL query performance that arise due to changes in the CE, specifically when upgrading our database compatibility level. This tool is invaluable when upgrading our database to a new version of SQL Server.

13
Managing Optimizer Changes with the Query Tuning Assistant

In this chapter, we will discuss a recently introduced feature: the **Query Tuning Assistant (QTA)**. QTA aims to address some of the most common causes of **cardinality estimation** related performance regressions that may affect our T-SQL queries after an upgrade from an older version of SQL Server to a newer version, namely SQL Server 2016 and above.

At the time this book is being written, SQL Server 2008 and 2008 R2 are months away from completing their 10-year life cycle and reaching the end of their support; SQL Server 2014 reaches end of mainstream support at the same time; and SQL Server 2012 is no longer in mainstream support. This can raise concerns for all those still running applications supported by these legacy SQL Server versions.

But modernizing the database platform, another word for upgrading in this context, is not a risk-free proposition: the risk that after upgrading and leaping so many years and versions, a part of the application's workload can experience performance regressions due to CE changes is very real. This is why Microsoft has invested over the years in building features that can greatly mitigate much of this regression risk: Query Store, Auto Tuning, and now QTA.

This chapter covers the following topics:

- Understanding where QTA is needed
- Understanding QTA fundamentals
- Exploring the QTA workflow

Understanding where QTA is needed

We discussed how the CE version is tied to the concept of database compatibility level in the *Introducing the Cardinality Estimator* section of `Chapter 3`, *Mechanics of the Query Optimizer*. The CE version that our databases use influences how query plans are calculated for queries that will execute in those databases. And we have seen first-hand the effects of the CE every time we compared the estimated number of rows with the actual number of rows throughout the book—for example in the *Query plan comparison* section of `Chapter 10`, *Comparative Analysis of Query Plans*, where we dealt with the row goal optimization.

When upgrading from older versions of SQL Server to Azure SQL Database and SQL Server 2016, or higher versions, we need to be conscious of how upgrading from CE 70 to a newer CE can affect our workloads—benefits are expected for the most part, but regressions can happen. For example, we have discussed in `Chapter 7`, *Discovering T-SQL Anti-Patterns in Depth*, how SQL Server 2017 and 2019 solve classic anti-patterns with little to no code changes—these are welcomed changes.

We also need to be conscious of the difference between upgrading SQL Server as a Database Engine and upgrading the **Database Compatibility Level** setting of the user databases. For the sake of what we're discussing in this chapter, upgrading the database compatibility means upgrading to a recent CE version, but the CE version doesn't change by upgrading the Database Engine version itself. In other words, upgrading SQL Server binaries doesn't necessarily mean we must upgrade the database compatibility—in fact, we shouldn't—not immediately after we upgrade the binaries. Decoupling the two upgrade moments—SQL Server Database Engine and database compatibility level—allows us to keep workloads stable after the SQL Server upgrade. And how can we do that? How do we take charge of upgrade risks?

Microsoft recommends the following plan that is built on this difference between upgrading the SQL Server platform, and upgrading a database:

1. **Upgrade SQL Server** from any older version (for example, SQL Server 2008 to SQL Server 2017), and **keep databases in the same Database Compatibility Level as the source** SQL Server version:
    - If we do an in-place upgrade, all databases keep the same database compatibility level as before the upgrade: 100. This was the highest and native compatibility level in SQL Server 2008
    - If we do a side-by-side upgrade (a migration), then all databases that are moved through attach/detach or backup/restore also keep the same database compatibility level as before the upgrade

2. **Enable Query Store**. We discussed the Query Store feature in `Chapter 11`, *Tracking Performance History with Query Store*.
3. Let Query Store **collect a baseline for the workload** that represents the typical business cycle. For example, if the workload belongs to a payroll application, then the baseline may have to cover a pay cycle. If we are going through this process in production, this means allowing the production workload to just execute. If we are doing this in a pre-production or development (dev) environment, then we need to ensure that whatever test workload we have is a valid representation of the production workload.

4. Once we know enough time has passed and the Query Store has accrued enough information about our workloads, **plan to change the database compatibility level to our chosen target level**. In this case, it will be **140**, which is the highest compatibility level in the SQL Server 2017 release—this is a per-database operation. We can do this using the T-SQL command, `ALTER DATABASE CURRENT SET COMPATIBILITY_LEVEL = 140;`, or by using the database options menu in SSMS, as shown in the following screenshot:

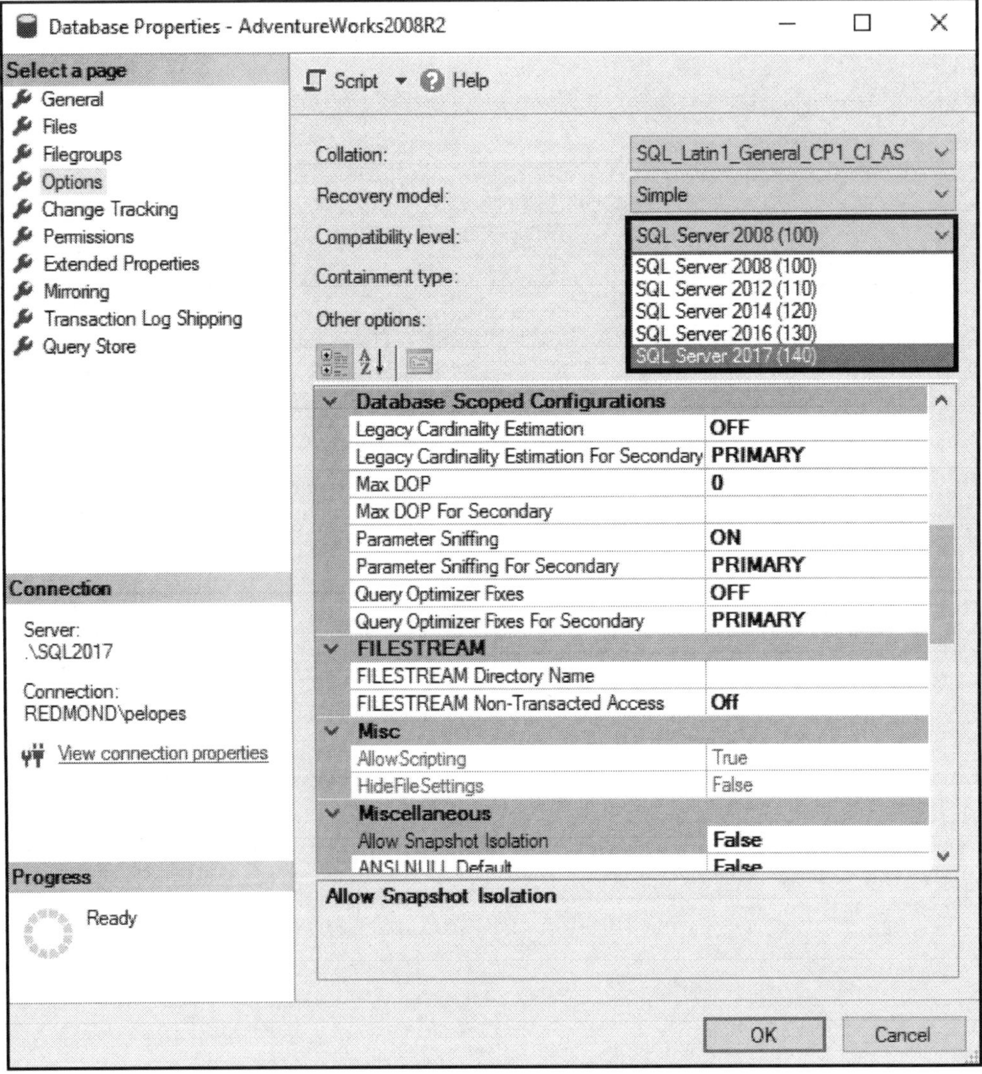

5. Monitor the **Regressed Queries** report in Query Store to quickly find and fix regressions with the **Force Plan** feature, as seen in the following screenshot:

Forcing a previously known good plan becomes possible precisely because we collected a baseline of query plans that were produced using CE 70—the same that drove Query Optimizer choices in SQL Server 2008. From there, any regressions that occur due to the change in the CE version become trackable and actionable.

In our current scenario, because we have upgraded to SQL Server 2017 in this case, we can enable the **Automatic Tuning** feature and this last step of forcing the plan becomes automated.

Automatic tuning is a database feature that was released with SQL Server 2017 and is also in Azure SQL Database. One of its functionalities is **automatic plan correction**, which identifies query execution plan regressions based on CPU time. In the scope of CE upgrades, **automatic plan correction** will revert to the last known good query plan, provided the recommended baseline with the source database compatibility level was collected.

The following diagram summarizes the recommended steps to minimize risk with CE upgrades, discussed earlier in this chapter:

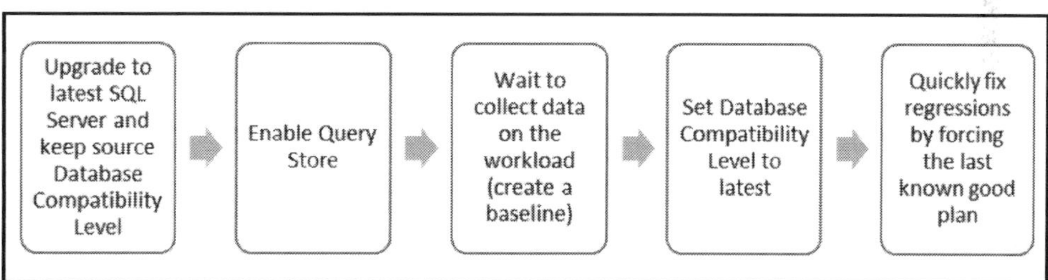

At this point, we may ask: if Query Store and automatic plan correction can mitigate query regression problems when I upgrade the database compatibility level, why would Microsoft create the QTA tool?

The main problem is that too many database professionals skip the recommended process and go rogue, upgrading to the latest database compatibility level immediately after SQL Server is upgraded, only to find that some part of the workload has regressed and there's no baseline that would enable Query Store and Automatic plan correction to help.

Therefore, QTA was created to provide a wizard-like experience to guide us through the recommended process from a single entry-point.

Understanding QTA fundamentals

While guiding us through the recommended process, QTA doesn't follow it exactly. The very last *step 5* will not have the same outcome as we saw in the previous section: instead of providing options to revert to a last known good plan, QTA helps to find a new state that is not the pre-CE upgrade or post-CE upgrade plan, but a new plan that will hopefully outperform both of the previous plans.

The following diagram summarizes the recommended steps to minimize risk with CE upgrades using QTA, which replaces the very last step of the process described in the *Understanding where QTA is needed* section:

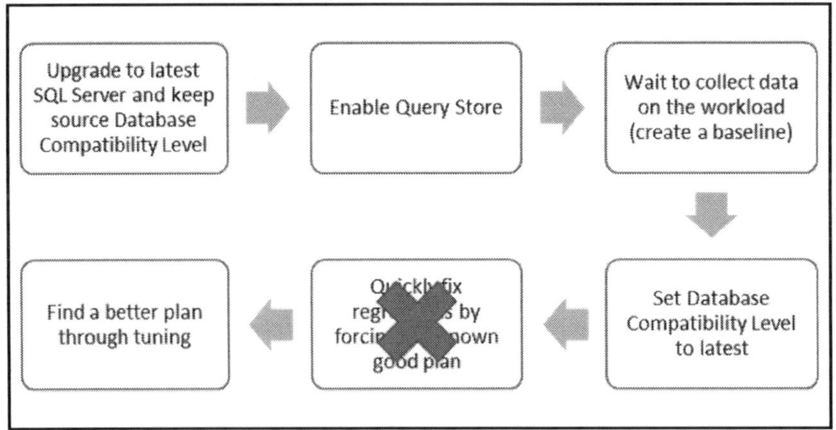

How does QTA find a better query plan for regressed queries? Starting with the same data that's available in Query Store's **Regressed Queries** report, QTA will look for query patterns that may be affected by changes in CE, specifically from CE 70 to CE 120 and higher.

At this time, QTA only handles both ad hoc and parameterized **SELECT** queries. For parameterized queries, QTA can only experiment on those for which the compiled parameter is available in the The **Parameter List** property of the query plan. We discussed this query plan property in `Chapter 4`, *Exploring Query Execution Plans* in the *Query plan properties of interest* section.

QTA will then experiment with those queries, executing them with query hints that adjust several CE model choices, and those that result in better query plans will be added to the list of proposed alternatives to the current query plan. What defines what plans are better and should be used? As we reach the end of the process, we will be able to see what alternatives exist for each plan and easily pick the one that's either faster or uses less CPU, for example. We will describe the workflow in the next section, as we upgrade our **AdventureWorksDW2012** database to SQL Server 2017's native database compatibility level 140.

In its current release, QTA can handle the following CE model changes:

- **Predicate Independence versus Correlation**: We have discussed this CE assumption in the *Introducing the cardinality estimator* section of `Chapter 4`, *Mechanics of the Query Optimizer*. If the experiments indicate that using CE 70's Independence assumption yields better estimations than the default Correlation assumption, then the resulting query plan is added to the list of recommendations. Under the covers, QTA was able to switch the default CE assumption for the specific query being experimented on by applying the following query hint:

```
USE HINT ('ASSUME_MIN_SELECTIVITY_FOR_FILTER_ESTIMATES')
```

  This hint causes SQL Server to create a query plan that accounts for the cardinality of each column in an **AND** filter predicate rather than the cardinality of all columns combined by the **AND** predicate.

- **Simple Join Containment versus Base Join Containment**: We have also discussed this CE assumption in the *Introducing the Cardinality Estimator* section of `Chapter 4`, *Mechanics of the Query Optimizer*. If the experiments indicate that using CE 70's Simple Containment assumption yields better estimations than the default Base Containment assumption, the resulting query plan is added to the list of recommendations. Under the covers, QTA was able to switch the default CE assumption for the specific query being experimented on by applying the following query hint:

```
USE HINT ('ASSUME_JOIN_PREDICATE_DEPENDS_ON_FILTERS')
```

This hint causes SQL Server to create a query plan that assumes the estimated cardinality needs to be calculated by accounting for filter predicates applicable to tables, rather than calculating only by using the base tables (without any filters).

- **Multi-statement Table-valued Functions (MSTVF) fixed estimations**: As we discussed in the *How table-valued functions function* section of `Chapter 6`, *Easily Identified T-SQL Anti-Patterns*, the Query Optimizer uses a default estimation of 100 rows for MSTVFs, since the row count is not available at compile time—this is a runtime structure. This has always been the case in SQL Server, but whereas in older version, the default estimation was just 1 row, starting with SQL Server 2014, this assumption was increased to 100 rows. It may not look like much on its own, but this estimation is used throughout the query optimization process and drives other optimizations on top of this assumption. The change back in CE 120 can be enough to impact query plans that heavily depended on the previous version's combination of optimizations based on 1 row. Under the covers, QTA was able to switch the default CE assumption of 100 rows back to 1 row for the specific query being experimented on, by applying the following query hint: `QUERYTRACEON 9488`.
- If all the listed scenarios fail to improve the query plan, then as a last resort, QTA will consider turning back to CE 70 in full, by applying the following query hint: `USE HINT ('FORCE_LEGACY_CARDINALITY_ESTIMATION')`

Exploring the QTA workflow

We've briefly described what QTA does, and in greater depth how QTA works internally. But now it's time to actually run through the recommended database compatibility upgrade we discussed in the *Understanding QTA fundamentals* section.

QTA is a session-based tool, which means we can open and close at will while the database compatibility upgrade process progresses. This is useful given that the recommended database compatibility upgrade process can run for days, depending on the business cycle that our workload serves.

QTA doesn't need to run from an SSMS installed on the server. It can execute the workflow against the server from our laptop, desktop, or whatever other designated management machine we have available.

The way QTA stores our session's state and analysis data is by creating a few tables in the targeted user database under the **msqta** schema, as seen in the following screenshot:

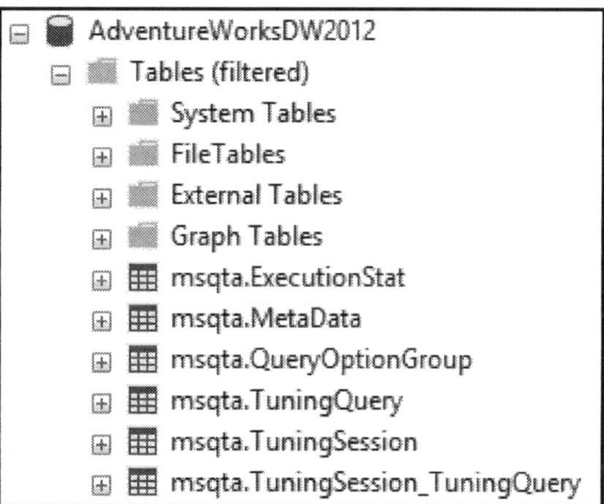

Multiple tuning sessions can be created on a single database over time, but only one active session can exist for any given database.

Before we start a database compatibility upgrade process, some housekeeping tasks are needed, such as configuring Query Store, if not already running in the database. QTA can do this for us as part of the **Create Session** wizard.

For this example, we installed SQL Server 2017, where we restored our **AdventureWorksDW2012** database. Given this database was restored, it keeps the same database compatibility level it had in the source SQL Server 2012 instance.

To start a new session, we go to SSMS and connect to our new SQL Server 2017, right-click the database name (**AdventureWorksDW2012**), select **Tasks**, select **Database Upgrade**, and click on **New Database Upgrade Session**, as shown in the following screenshot:

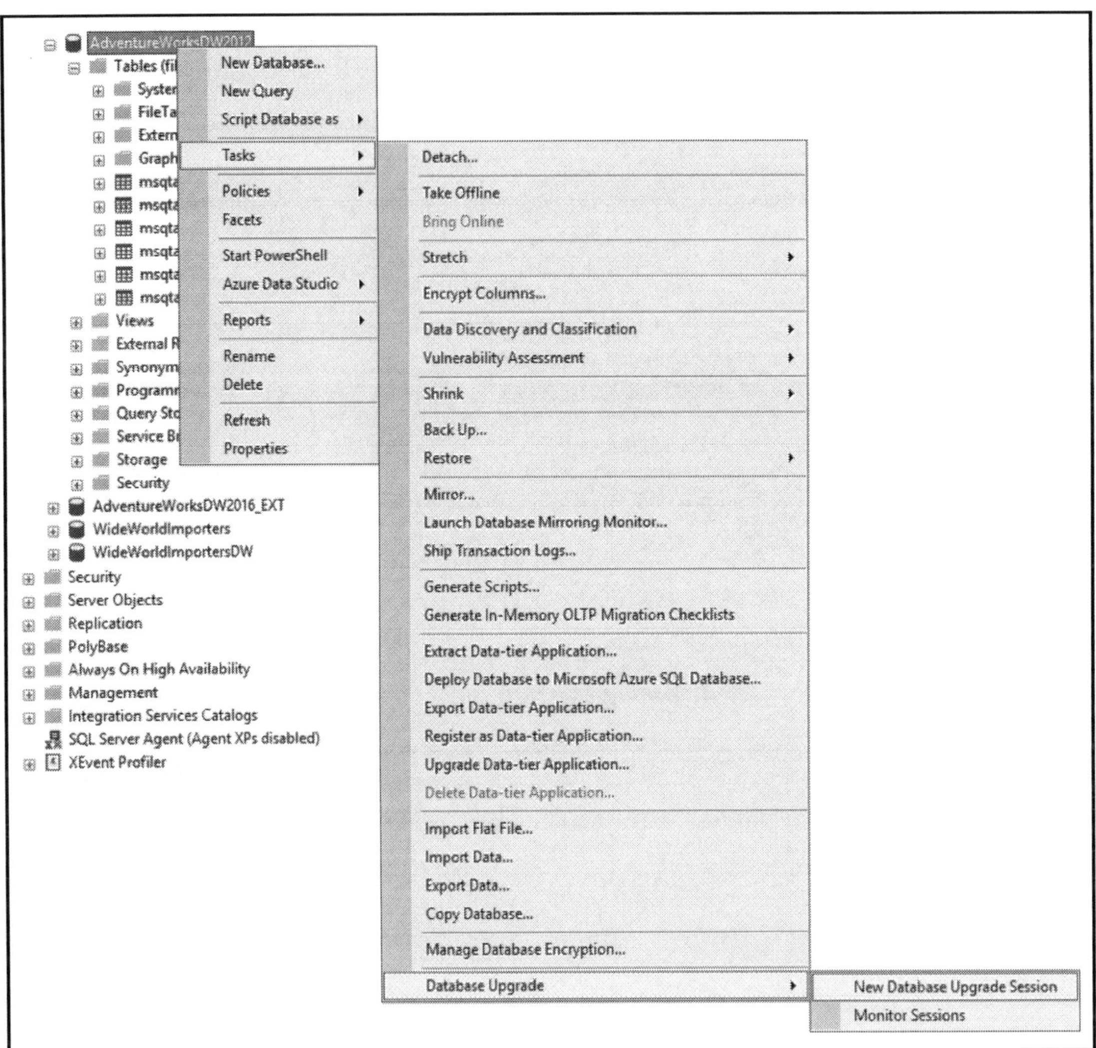

This action opens the session configuration window where the first step is to enter some information that will drive the upgrade process:

- The expected **workload duration** in days (the minimum is 1 day), which is used to configure Query Store in the next step. For our example, the business cycle we've identified is five days—meaning it can take up to five days for Query Store to capture all the application workload and some ETL processes we execute every night. We need to ensure we capture a representative baseline, so that after we conclude the database compatibility upgrade, any regressed queries can be found and analyzed by QTA.
- The intended **target database compatibility level** that the database should be set to after the QTA workflow completes. Given the database is now at database compatibility level 120 and we are working in SQL Server 2017, all higher compatibility levels are available in the drop-down. For this example, we'll select **140**.

The following screenshot displays the QTA window where we configured the session:

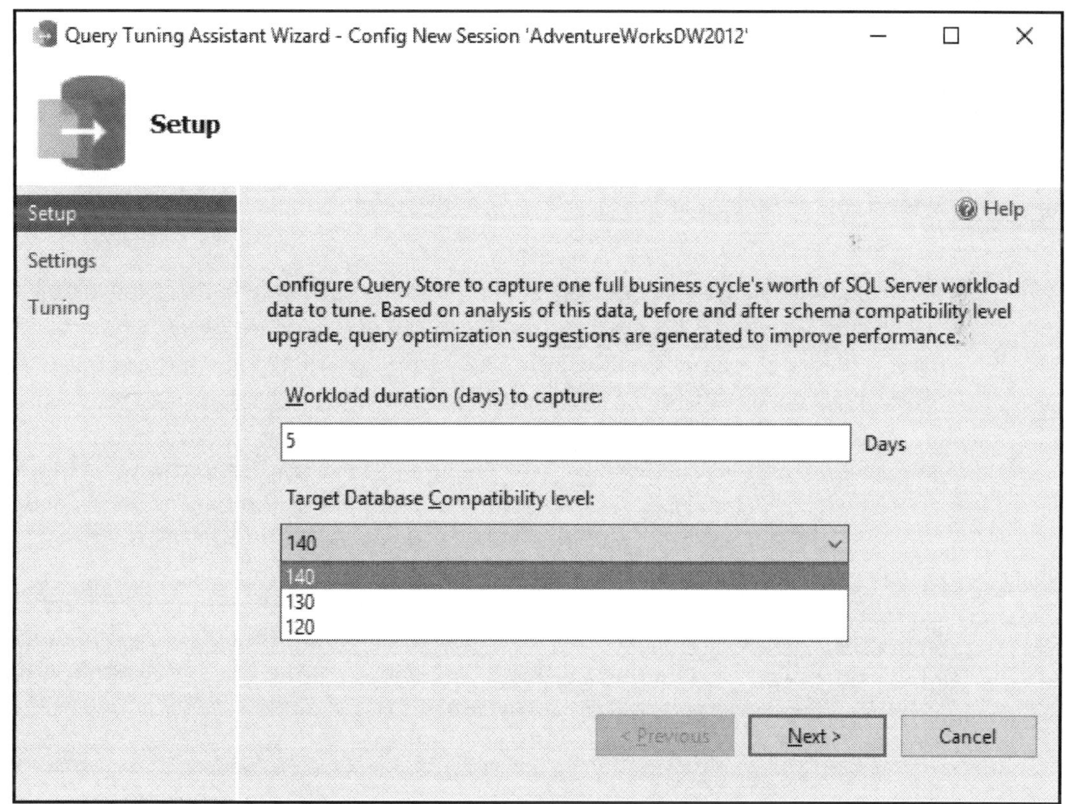

While QTA is guiding us through the recommended upgrade process, let's keep in mind that Query Store is storing all the information. This is especially relevant for the point in time after we upgrade the database compatibility. For any query that may not be eligible for QTA to deal with, we are free to use Query Store's **Regressed Queries** report to find other ways of handling other regressed queries, such as forcing a previously known good plan, while we fix the query to work natively in the new CE—in this case, 140. The following screenshot shows the **Regressed Queries** report under the Query Store in SSMS:

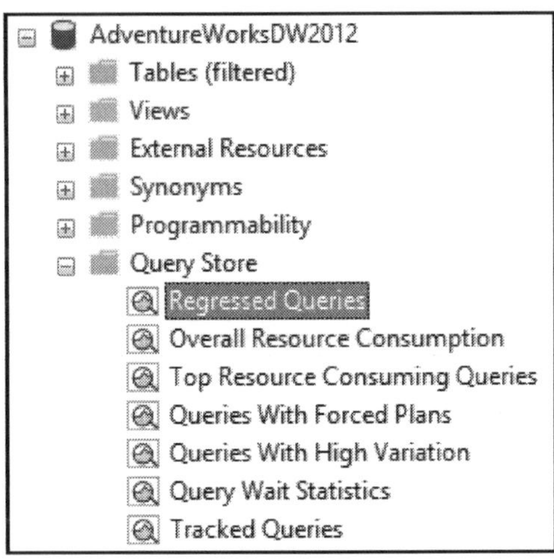

The next step is to configure Query Store. In the **Settings** window, we see the following two columns:

- **The Current state of the Query Store for our database**: notice its **Operation Mode** is Off because we have not enabled Query Store manually. If we had enabled Query Store previously, here we would be able to change its settings, editing any configuration if the **Current** radio button is selected.
- **The Recommended settings for Query Store**: Notice the proposed **Stale Query Threshold** setting is twice the number we entered for **workload duration** in the previous screen. This is because we had selected 5 days, and Query Store needs to be able to collect our five days baseline, and five additional days' worth of workload after we change to compatibility level 140. Only then are we comparing the same business cycle across CE 70 and CE 140, allowing Query Store to identify regressed queries that span the relevant time window. We can opt to accept the recommended settings by clicking on the **Recommended** radio-button.

The following screenshot displays the QTA window where we configured the Query Store:

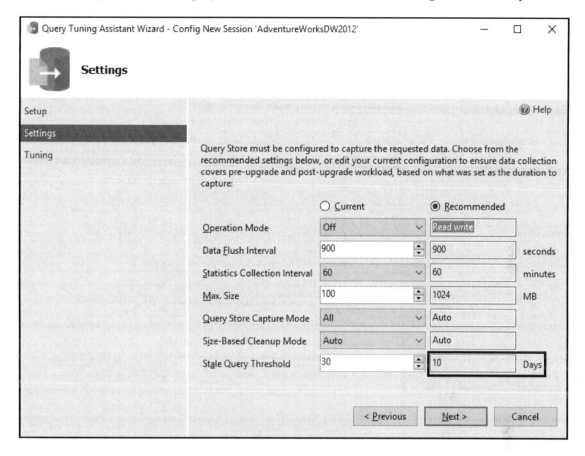

After clicking on **Next,** we get a new screen with some information on how we've configured the session, and instructing us to start running our workload—QTA does not generate any workload for us. If we're running QTA in a test server, we are then responsible for generating our test workload.

Alternatively, consider the scenario where we have gone through the recommended upgrade process in production manually, as discussed in the *Understanding where QTA is needed* section. Then we could restore the production database backup to a test server and the Query Store for that database would allow us to jump to the analysis and experimentation step later in the QTA workflow.

In our example, we're running this process in production, which means we can just let our normal business cycle happen normally as application workloads are executing. On this new screen, click on **Finish** to exit the session setup—this completes step 1 of the QTA workflow.

To start running through the upgrade process itself, we return to SSMS, right-click the database name (**AdventureWorksDW2012**), select **Tasks**, select **Database Upgrade**, and click on **Monitor Sessions,** as shown in the following screenshot:

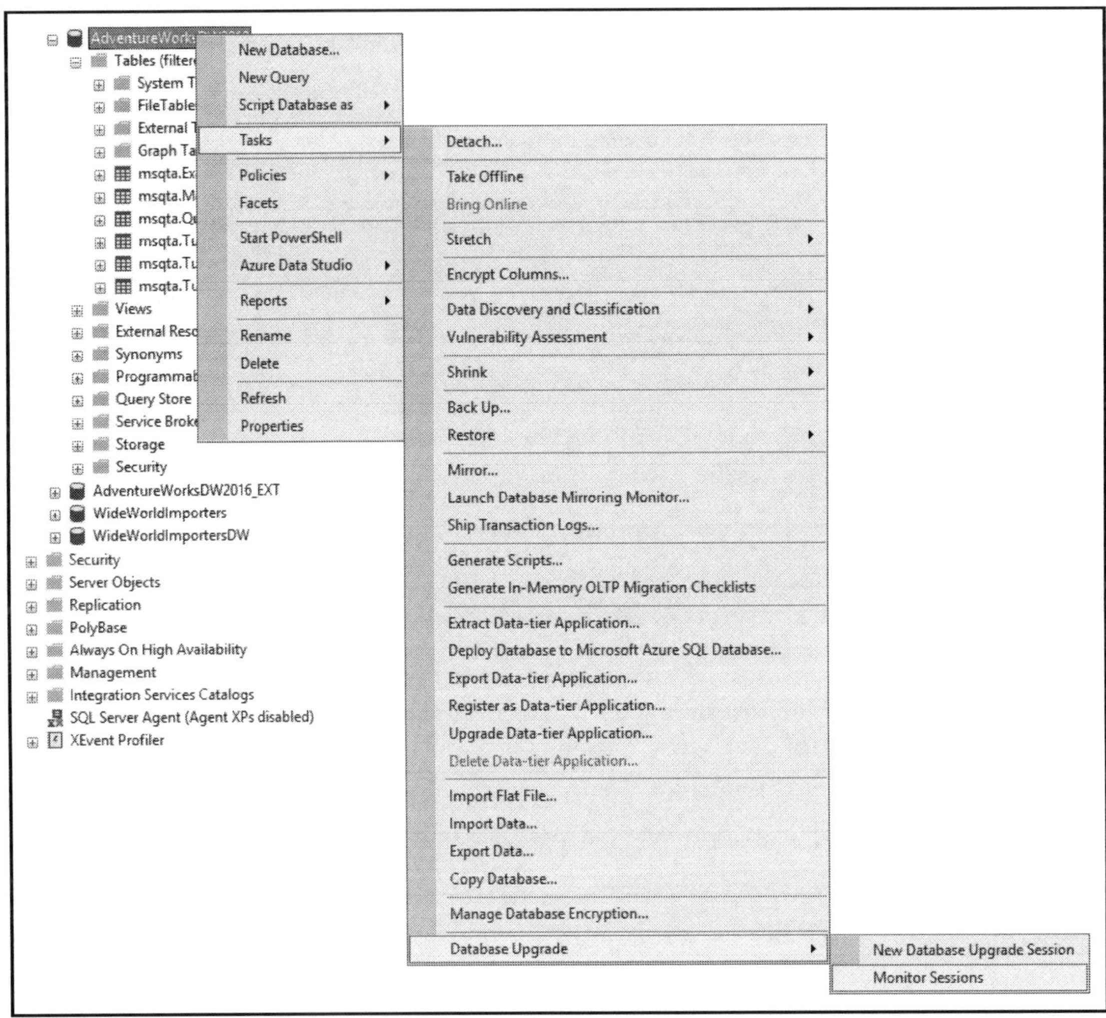

A new window tab opens in SSMS, in the scope of QTA's session management page. In the following screenshot, we can see our current session. Click on the session name and click on **Details** to open it:

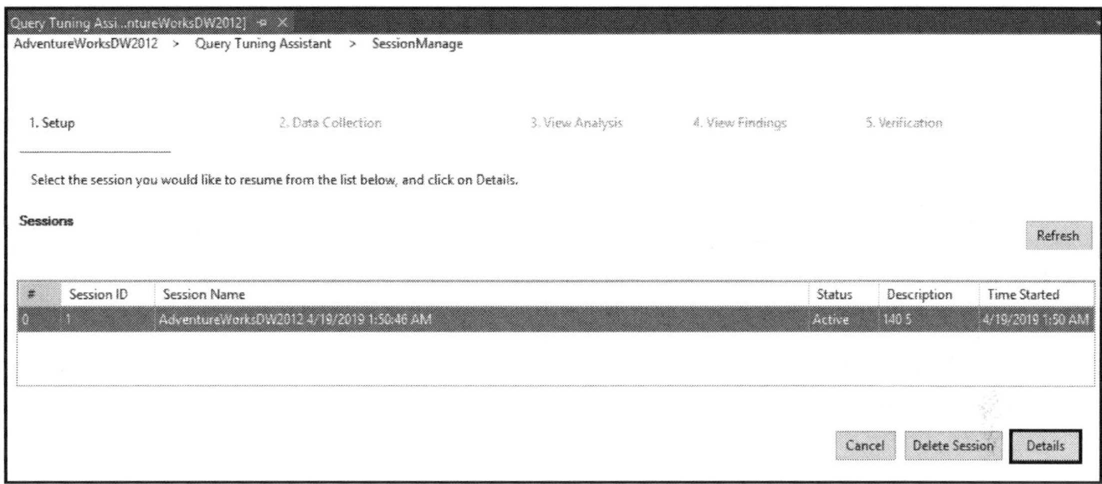

Notice in the previous screenshot that we were in step 1 of 5 of the upgrade process—**Setup**. When we opened the session, we enter step 2, **Data Collection** in **Substep 1 of 3, Baseline Data Collection,** as shown in the following screenshot:

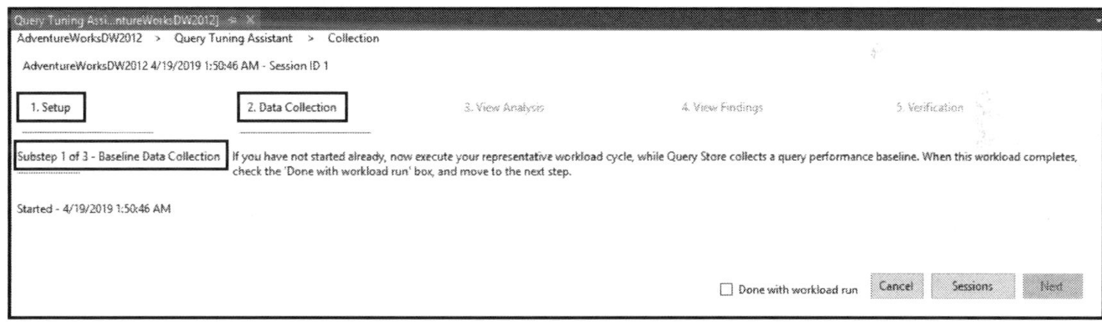

As we can read in the QTA screen, it asks us to start our workload if not already started. We're running our upgrade process in a production server, so the workload is already executing. We can close this screen and go away for 5 days while our baseline is populated. But, for example, if we decide that after just 3 days, we have enough data collected and didn't need the full 5 days, we can come back to QTA through the **Monitor Sessions** task, and we'll be right where we left off.

After our baseline is complete, we return to QTA on step 2, and check the box **Done with workload run,** as shown in the following screenshot:

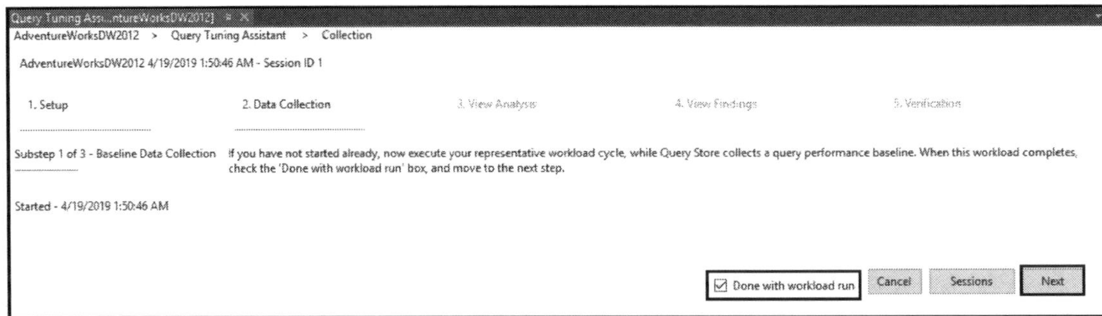

This signals QTA that it's time to move forward with the upgrade process, and when we click on **Next**, the following prompt appears, asking us to upgrade the database compatibility level to our chosen target, 140:

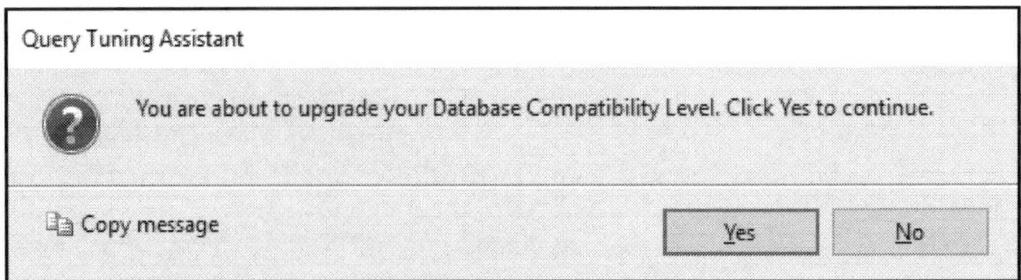

When we click on **Yes**, QTA enters **Substep 2 of 3-Upgrade Database** and upgrades the database compatibility level, as seen as in the following screenshot. Then we click on **Next** to move to the last step of data collection:

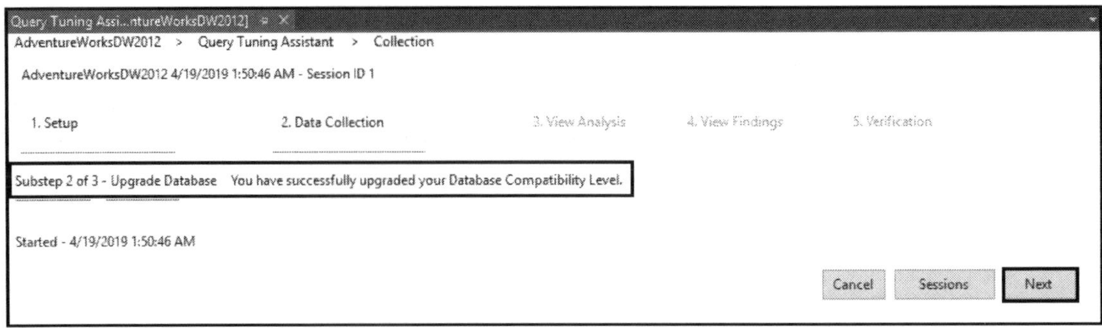

Substep 3 of 3 is **Observed Data Collection** and it's similar to **Substep 1 of 3**: we are asked to run the same workload that constitutes the baseline so it can compare the proverbial apples to apples, and through Query Store, find all regressed queries. Again, we can close the QTA window and go away for the next five days until we have a full comparison available.

As seen in the next screenshot, we have a **Refresh** button that we can use during those 5 days to keep track of what's been found so far. Clicking on it refreshes the list of top regressed queries—notice that some queries already executed over 400 times in mere seconds:

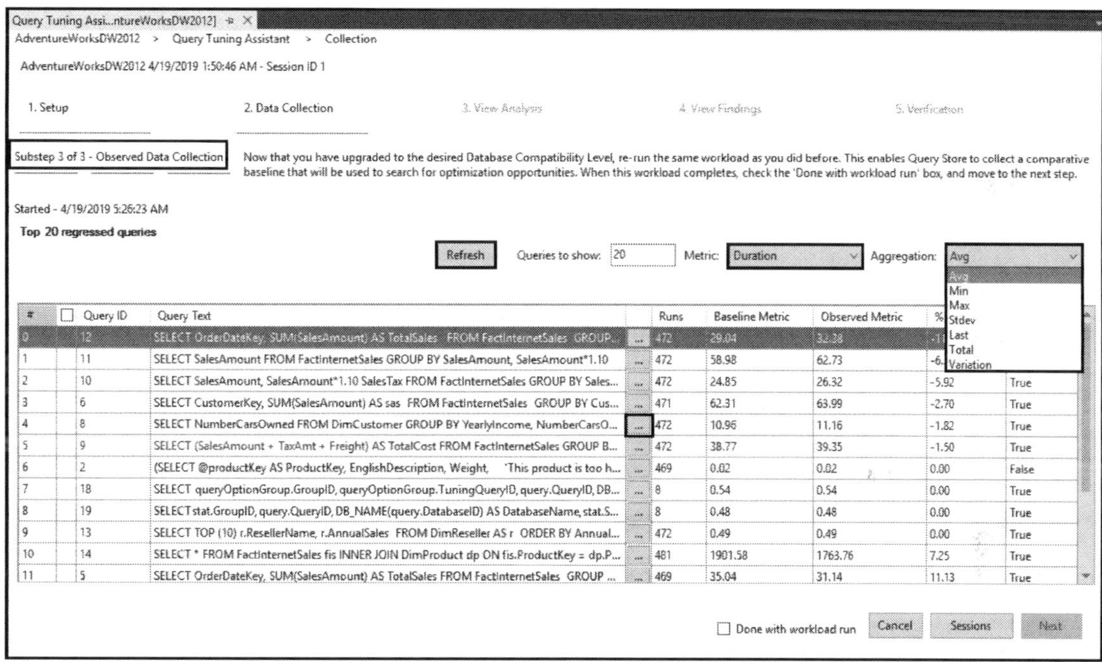

As we see in the preceding screenshot, the default settings list the **Top 20 regressed queries**, but we can change the number of **Queries to show**: from 20 to whatever number is relevant to us. The list is built on the default **Metric**, which is the overall query **Duration**, but can be changed to **CpuTime** as well. The default **Aggregation** for the chosen metric is an average (**Avg**), but others are available, as seen in the preceding screenshot. If we change any of these settings, we need to click on **Refresh**.

In the query table, we see the **Query Text** column limited to the first 100 characters, but still enough for us to recognize the query. If we don't, we can click the **ellipsis button** (**...**) and the query text will be shown in a different tab, as seen in the following screenshot:

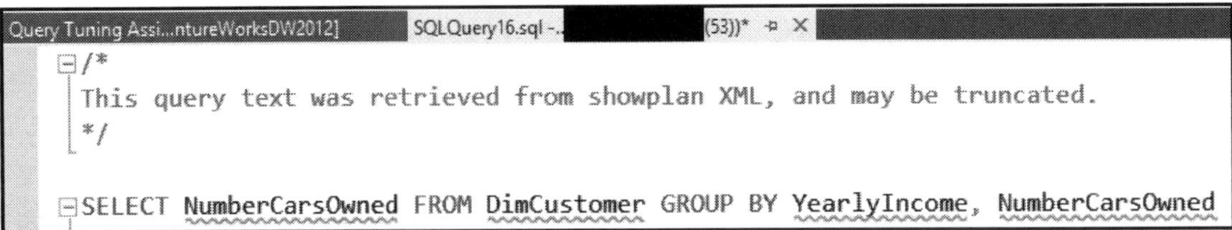

We also see the number of executions or **Runs**, the **Baseline Metric**, and the **Observed Metric**—in this case the duration in milliseconds for both the pre-upgrade and post-upgrade collections, as well as the percent **Change**, and whether the query is **Tunable**—meaning whether QTA can experiment on the query. Notice that **Query ID 2** is not tunable. It is a parameterized query and the compile time parameters are not available.

After our post-upgrade data collection is complete, we return to QTA still on step 2, and check the box **Done with workload run**, as seen in the following screenshot:

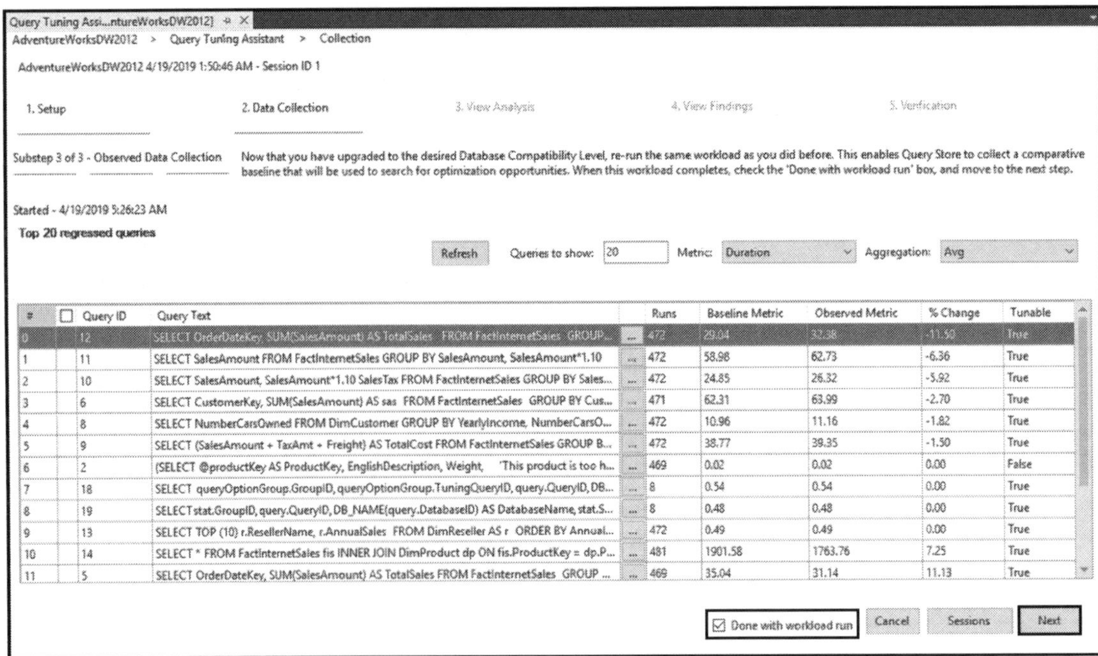

This signals QTA to move forward to the **Analysis** phase. When we click on **Next**, QTA enters step 3—**View Analysis**. Here, we look at what queries we want to submit for analysis. We looked at the queries using different metrics and aggregations, and see a few queries that got slower or had no change after the upgrade, as shown in the following screenshot:

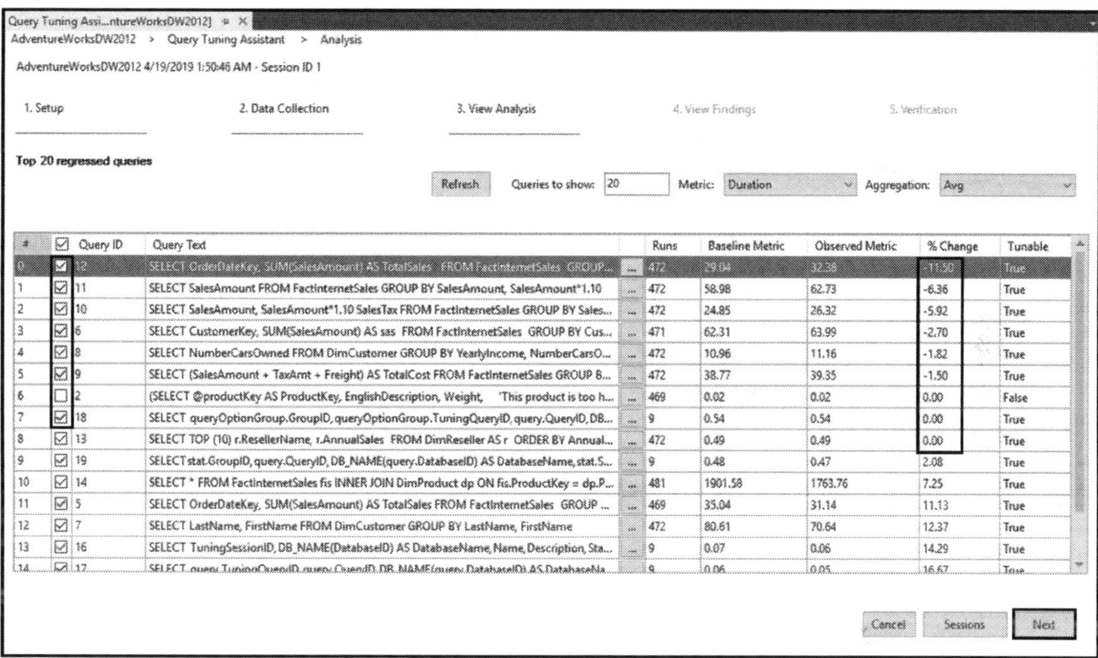

This is a one-time selection process and, for the sake of this exercise, I selected all queries to be analyzed. By clicking on **Next**, we enter the analysis process, which we must agree to, as seen in the following screenshot:

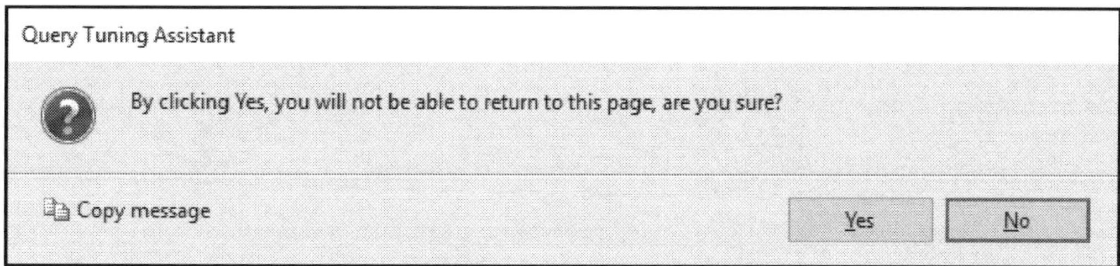

In the next screen, we can see the analysis process is ongoing—the **Status** column displays **Initial** for all queries in the following screenshot, which leads to step 4—**View Findings**:

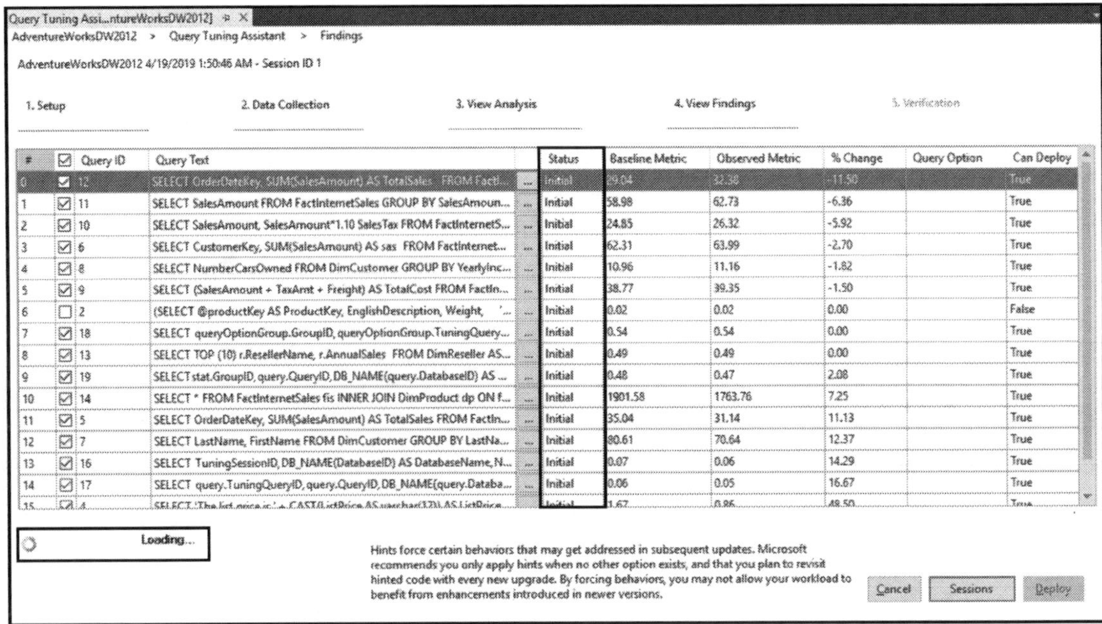

After a few minutes, the status updates to **Test complete,** as seen in the following screenshot, and we can see what improvements were found:

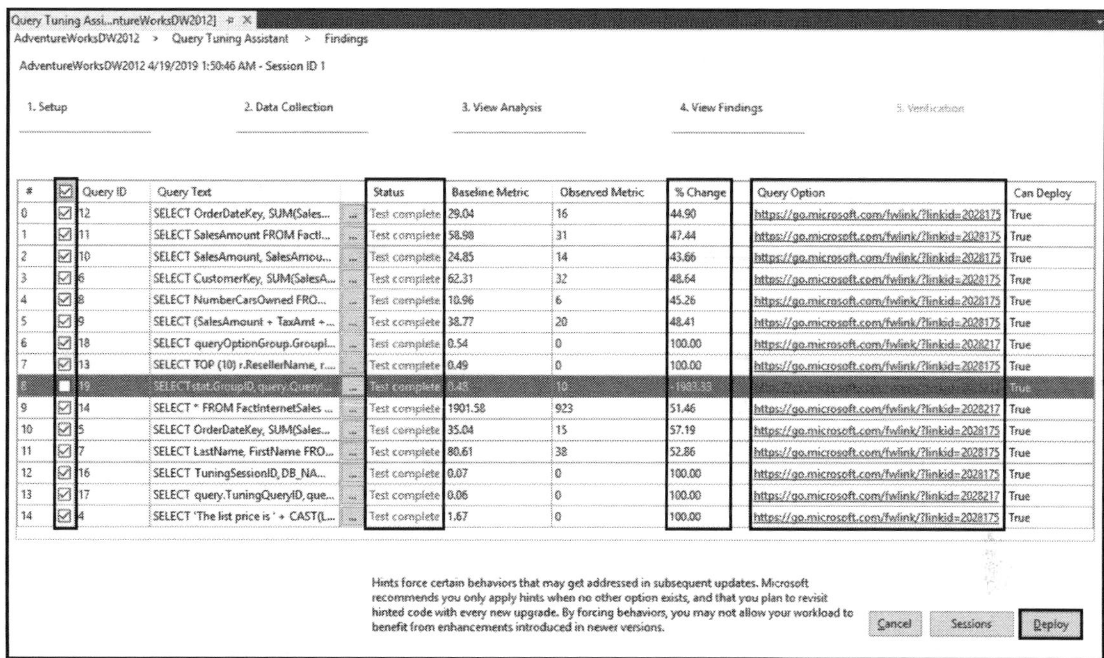

#	Query ID	Query Text	Status	Baseline Metric	Observed Metric	% Change	Query Option	Can Deploy
0	12	SELECT OrderDateKey, SUM(Sales...	Test complete	29.04	16	44.90	https://go.microsoft.com/fwlink/?linkid=2028175	True
1	11	SELECT SalesAmount FROM Fact...	Test complete	58.98	31	47.44	https://go.microsoft.com/fwlink/?linkid=2028175	True
2	10	SELECT SalesAmount, SalesAmou...	Test complete	24.85	14	43.66	https://go.microsoft.com/fwlink/?linkid=2028175	True
3	6	SELECT CustomerKey, SUM(SalesA...	Test complete	62.31	32	48.64	https://go.microsoft.com/fwlink/?linkid=2028175	True
4	8	SELECT NumberCarsOwned FRO...	Test complete	10.96	6	45.26	https://go.microsoft.com/fwlink/?linkid=2028175	True
5	9	SELECT (SalesAmount + TaxAmt +...	Test complete	38.77	20	48.41	https://go.microsoft.com/fwlink/?linkid=2028175	True
6	18	SELECT queryOptionGroup.Groupl...	Test complete	0.54	0	100.00	https://go.microsoft.com/fwlink/?linkid=2028217	True
7	13	SELECT TOP (10) r.ResellerName, r....	Test complete	0.49	0	100.00	https://go.microsoft.com/fwlink/?linkid=2028175	True
8	19	SELECT stat.GroupID, query.Query...	Test complete	0.49	10	-1983.33	[illegible]	True
9	14	SELECT * FROM FactInternetSales ...	Test complete	1901.58	923	51.46	https://go.microsoft.com/fwlink/?linkid=2028217	True
10	5	SELECT OrderDateKey, SUM(Sales...	Test complete	35.04	15	57.19	https://go.microsoft.com/fwlink/?linkid=2028175	True
11	7	SELECT LastName, FirstName FRO...	Test complete	80.61	38	52.86	https://go.microsoft.com/fwlink/?linkid=2028175	True
12	16	SELECT TuningSessionID, DB_NA...	Test complete	0.07	0	100.00	https://go.microsoft.com/fwlink/?linkid=2028175	True
13	17	SELECT query.TuningQueryID, que...	Test complete	0.06	0	100.00	https://go.microsoft.com/fwlink/?linkid=2028217	True
14	4	SELECT 'The list price is ' + CAST(L...	Test complete	1.67	0	100.00	https://go.microsoft.com/fwlink/?linkid=2028175	True

We can see the **Baseline Metric**—the workload as it executed before the database compatibility upgrade and the new **Observed Metric**, which is the result of the analysis process. The **% Change** shows all queries with the exception of query 19 improved by up to 100 percent. If we click on one of the links in the **Query Option** column (for example, query 14), it will open `docs.microsoft.com` in the scope of the proposed hint, as seen in the following screenshot:

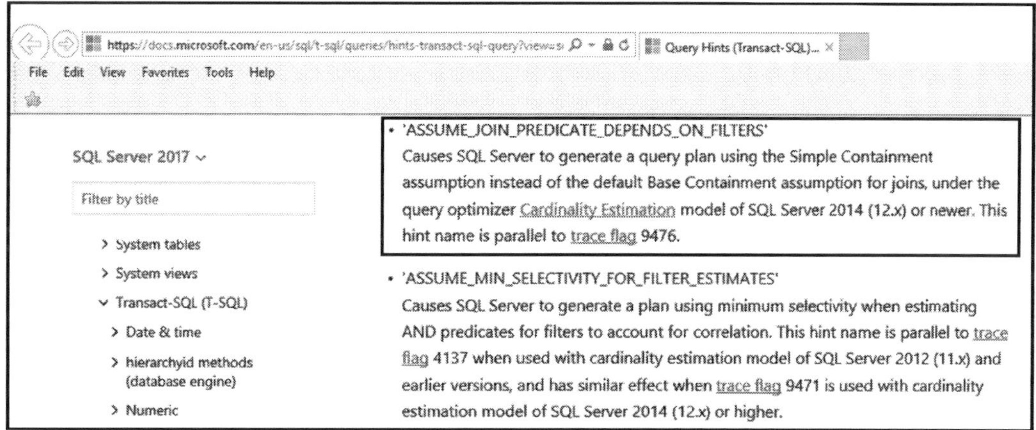

After we select which queries we want to deploy the recommendations for, based on the improvement percentage (we selected all but one), we click the **Deploy** button. This creates a plan guide with the required query hint that will improve the query performance, based on the analysis that was done which consisted of actually executing the queries and collecting runtime metrics. After deployment of the plan guides, all queries will show a status **Deployed**, and we reach step 5—**Verification**, as shown in the following screenshot:

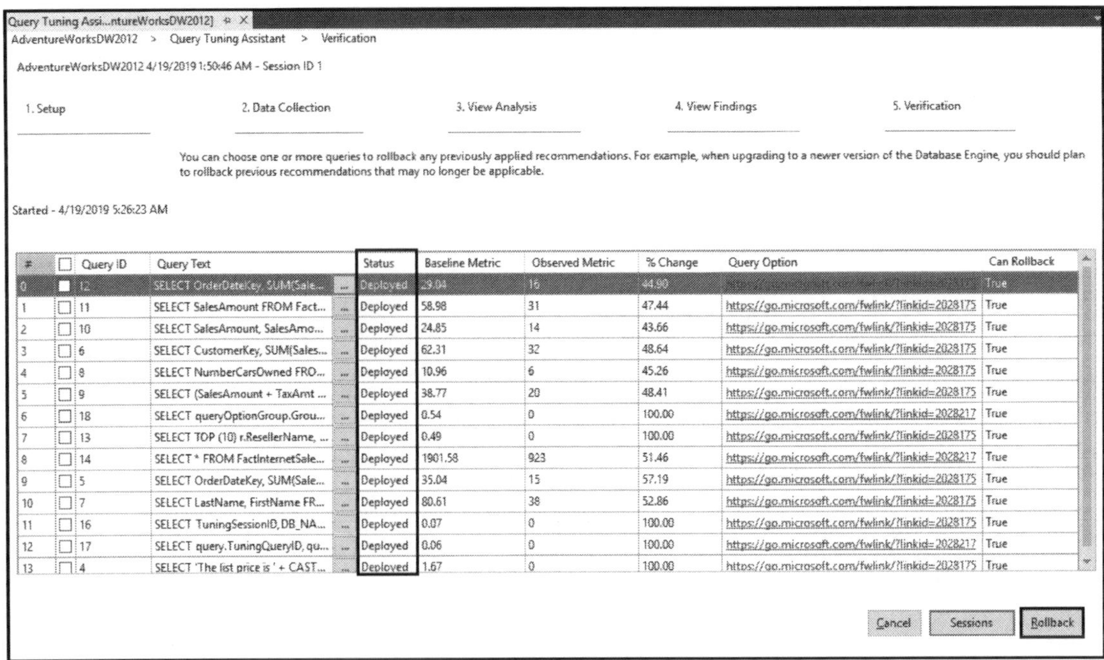

The upgrade is successfully completed, and we managed to improve the regressed queries and restore good performance to the part of our workload that had regressed after upgrading form CE 70 to CE 140.

If in the next few days, we notice that the improvement for one or more tuned queries is not as beneficial as the analysis showed, we can resume the session in the **Verification** step, select a query, and click the **Rollback** button to remove the respective plan guide.

Summary

This chapter covered the important topic of upgrading the database compatibility to leverage the latest CE while minimizing the inherent risks that are commonly associated with this upgrade.

From the set of regressed workloads the SQL Server team has handled over the years, the initial scenarios covered by QTA are some of the most common after a database compatibility level upgrade (and, therefore, a CE upgrade) that can make users question whether to upgrade. But that is just because when upgrading from an old version, such as SQL Server 2005 or 2008, our T-SQL queries were fully tuned to the only CE model set that existed at the time. When some aspects of CE changed, there was a possibility that some queries would have to be tuned for the new models. Fortunately, the SQL Server team believes that backward compatibility is an asset in the database engine and included these hints that allow selective tuning opportunities for the scenarios covered by QTA, and others less common and not covered by QTA.

Either using QTA or not, following the recommended CE upgrade process we detailed in this chapter is the only way we can ensure control over our workloads as they naturally evolve and progress throughout the years of use and database engine versions. Even when not using QTA but running through the CE upgrade process by interacting directly with Query Store and automatic tuning is a strong step toward ensuring our T-SQL queries remain scalable and deliver the level of performance that's expected for the applications they serve.

If you have gotten this far, congratulations, you are now an expert T-SQL developer! We hope that this book has helped unlock some of the mysteries of T-SQL query performance in SQL Server and illustrate that how a query is written can and does impact how that query will perform.

In this book, we learned:

- How SQL Server processes queries and the various building blocks of a T-SQL query
- How the Query Optimizer estimates the cost of a query and identifies the cheapest query plan
- How plans are cached and reused to save time and resources
- How to analyze a query plan to identify areas that may be causing the query to perform poorly

- Some best practices for writing efficient T-SQL queries that can use indexes effectively
- Several anti-patterns that can cause the Query Optimizer to choose an inefficient query plan or otherwise make the query perform poorly
- Some of the free tools available from Microsoft to help you identify and troubleshoot poor-performing queries in your environment

The knowledge gained from reading this book will help identify and troubleshoot existing query performance issues, as well as avoid anti-patterns when writing T-SQL code in the future. Most importantly, you should now have the skills to write efficient and elegant T-SQL code for all your SQL Server querying needs.

Other Books You May Enjoy

If you enjoyed this book, you may be interested in these other books by Packt:

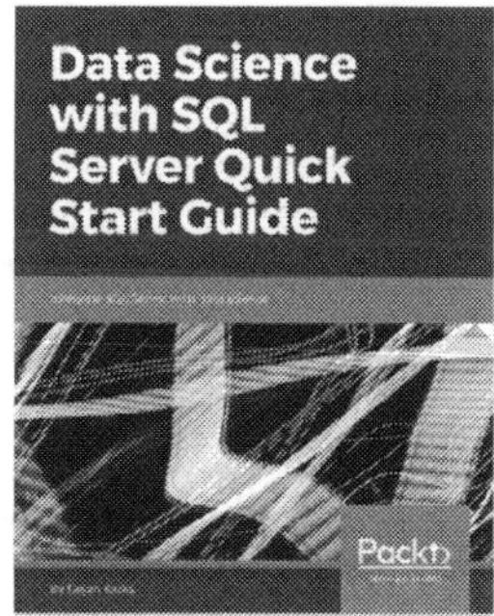

Data Science with SQL Server Quick Start Guide
Dejan Sarka

ISBN: 978-1-78953-712-3

- Use the popular programming languages,T-SQL, R, and Python, for data science
- Understand your data with queries and introductory statistics
- Create and enhance the datasets for ML
- Visualize and analyze data using basic and advanced graphs
- Explore ML using unsupervised and supervised models
- Deploy models in SQL Server and perform predictions

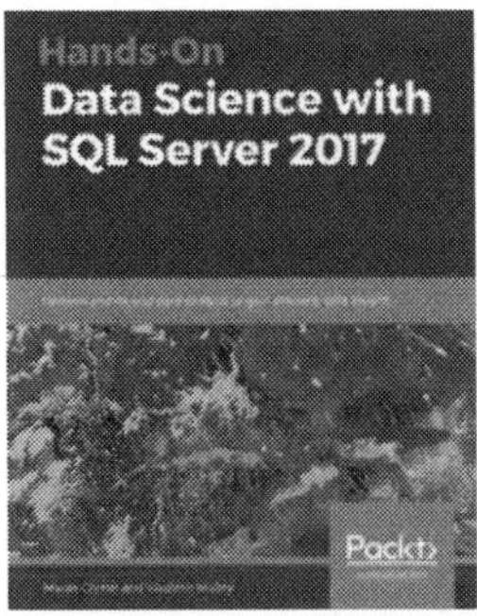

Hands-On Data Science with SQL Server 2017
Marek Chmel, Vladimír Mužný, Vladimír Mužný, Recommended for You , Vladimír Mužný, Recommended for You , Learning

ISBN: 978-1-78899-634-1

- Understand what data science is and how SQL Server is used for big data processing
- Analyze incoming data with SQL queries and visualizations
- Create, train, and evaluate predictive models
- Make predictions using trained models and establish regular retraining courses
- Incorporate data source querying into SQL Server
- Enhance built-in T-SQL capabilities using SQLCLR
- Visualize data with Reporting Services, Power View, and Power BI
- Transform data with R, Python, and Azure

Leave a review - let other readers know what you think

Please share your thoughts on this book with others by leaving a review on the site that you bought it from. If you purchased the book from Amazon, please leave us an honest review on this book's Amazon page. This is vital so that other potential readers can see and use your unbiased opinion to make purchasing decisions, we can understand what our customers think about our products, and our authors can see your feedback on the title that they have worked with Packt to create. It will only take a few minutes of your time, but is valuable to other potential customers, our authors, and Packt. Thank you!

Index

E

F

G

H

I

J

K

L

R

S

T

U

V

W